# Mastering SolidWorks®
## The Design Approach

Ibrahim Zeid

*Northeastern University*

**Prentice Hall**

Boston   Columbus   Indianapolis   New York   San Francisco   Upper Saddle River
Amsterdam   Cape Town   Dubai   London   Madrid   Milan   Munich   Paris   Montreal   Toronto
Delhi   Mexico City   Sao Paulo   Sydney   Hong Kong   Seoul   Singapore   Taipei   Tokyo

| | |
|---|---|
| **Editorial Director:** Vernon R. Anthony | **Operations Specialist:** Deidra Skahill |
| **Acquisitions Editor:** Sara Eilert | **Senior Art Director:** Diane Y. Ernsberger |
| **Editorial Assistant:** Doug Greive | **Text and Cover Designer:** Jason Moore |
| **Director of Marketing:** David Gesell | **Cover Image:** Fotolia |
| **Marketing Manager:** Kara Clark | **AV Project Manager:** Janet Portisch |
| **Senior Marketing Coordinator:** Alicia Wozniak | **Full-Service Project Management:** Lisa S. Garboski, bookworks publishing services |
| **Marketing Assistant:** Les Roberts | **Composition:** Aptara®, Inc. |
| **Project Manager:** Maren L. Miller | **Printer/Binder:** Edwards Brothers |
| **Senior Managing Editor:** JoEllen Gohr | **Cover Printer:** Lehigh-Phoenix Color/Hagerstown |
| **Associate Managing Editor:** Alexandrina Benedicto Wolf | **Text Font:** Berkeley Book |
| **Senior Operations Supervisor:** Pat Tonneman | |

Credits and acknowledgments borrowed from other sources and reproduced, with permission, in this textbook appear on the appropriate page within the text.

SolidWorks® is a registered trademark of DS SolidWorks Corp.

**Disclaimer:**

The publication is designed to provide tutorial information about the SolidWorks computer program. Every effort has been made to make this publication complete and as accurate as possible. The reader is expressly cautioned to use any and all precautions necessary, and to take appropriate steps to avoid hazards, when engaging in the activities described herein.

Neither the author nor the publisher makes any representations or warranties of any kind, with respect to the materials set forth in this publication, express or implied, including without limitation any warranties of fitness for a particular purpose or merchantability. Nor shall the author or the publisher be liable for any special, consequential or exemplary damages resulting, in whole or in part, directly or indirectly, from the reader's use of, or reliance upon, this material or subsequent revisions of this material.

Many of the designations by manufacturers and seller to distinguish their products are claimed as trademarks. Where those designations appear in this book, and the publisher was aware of a trademark claim, the designations have been printed in initial caps or all caps. AutoCAD is a registered trademark of Autodesk, Inc. Pro/Engineer is a registered trademark of Parametric Technology Corporation (PTC). CATIA is a registered trademark of Dassault Systèmes SA.

**Library of Congress Control Number: 2010925394**

**Prentice Hall**
is an imprint of

www.pearsonhighered.com

10 9 8 7 6 5 4 3 2 1
ISBN 10:      0-13-504609-2
ISBN 13: 978-0-13-504609-8

# eatures of *Mastering SolidWorks*®:
# he Design Approach

**Tutorials**

**rial 1–1:** Create the Flap

Modeling synthesis

This part is an extrusion or a revolve. A **revolve** is a symmetric part that has a constant cross section that can be revolved around an axis of revolution a given angle to create the part. A cylinder is a revolve. We can think of at least two plans to create it. As an extrusion, we create a circle with diameter of 0.125 in and extrude it a length of 1 in. When you have completed Tutorial 10–1, your drawing will similar to Figure 10–1.

1. Create Feature 1(extrusion) shown in Figure 1.11
2. Create Feature 2 (extrusion) shown in Figure 1.11
3. Create Feature 3 (fillet) shown in Figure 1.11

Within the second modeling plan, we can think cross section or features to create

**Step-by-Step Instructions**

**Step 1:** Create Feature 1 (extrusion) shown in Figure 1.11 and Figure 1.12

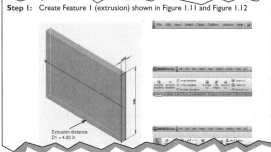

Extrusion distance
D1 = 4.00 in

**Hands-on for Tutorials**

***HANDS-ON FOR TUTORIAL 1.1.*** Create two additional cutouts, one each side of the flap. Each cutout starts from the top edge of the side with a size of 0.02 ×1.0 in, similar to Figure 1.16.

Unlike science where the goal is to understand physical phenomena, engineering is all about making products that work even at the expense of doing elaborate complex theoretical investigations.

There are good reasons for that. Engineered products and systems are too complex

**Examples and Solutions**

**Example 2.1** What is the best modeling plan to create the CAD model shown in Figure 2.2? Why?

If we realize that the cross section is the one in the top view then it is a simple extrusion, but if we create a rectangle in the front view and extrude it, then a cut is also required for the tapered face making the model creation more complex.

Thus, it is important to visualize/interpret if a model can be created as an extrusion/revolve because this affects the ease with which the model can be created, i.e. use of simpler/lesser commands versus advanced/complex commands.

**Solution** If we realize that the cross section is the one in the top view then it is a simple extrusion, but if we create a rectangle in the front view and extrude it.

Thus, it is important to visualize/interpret if a model can be created as an extrusion/revolve because this affects the ease with which the model can be created.

**Industry Chat**

**INDUSTRY CHAT**

This section provides practical insight into how the chapter material is used in industry in the real world and practice. We chat with Mr. Joseph (Joe) Fitzpatrick, the lead CAD designer and engineer of VIC.

**Chapter Section1.2:** The Engineering Design Process shown in Figure 1.1

ABE: Describe the EDP for your product

JOE: The EDP in VIC begins with a conceptual idea from the Chief Scientist who is a physicist, mathematician, and an engineer. He is responsible for steps 1-3 of the EDP shown in Figure 1.1.

The mechanical decision takes into consideration the manufacturability, cost, and production time of the machine vacuum chamber.

**Problems**

## problems

1. Using the EDP process shown in Figure 1.1, reverse engineer your iPod. Apply each step of the EDP to the iPod. For example, in applying Step 1, you ask yourself: what was the market need that led to the conception of the iPod? In applying Step 2, find the market need and why existing products were not good enough. Reverse engineering helps you discover what the iPod design team was thinking. Reverse engineering is a good first step to learn good design methodologies.
2. Same as Problem 1, but for your cell phone.
3. Same as Problem 1, but for a TV/DVD remote control.

Apply the EDP steps

# Instructor Resources

The **Online Instructor's Manual** provides answers to chapter exercises and tests a
solutions to end-of-chapter problems; drawing files to get users started; and lectu
supported PowerPoint slides.

To access supplementary materials online, instructors need to request an instruc
access code. Go to **www.pearsonhigherred.com/irc,** where you can register for an
structor access code. Within 48 hours after registering you will receive a confirm
email including an instructor access code. Once you have received your code, go to
site and log on for full instructions on downloading the materials you wish to use.

# Preface

The target audience for this book is college students in courses that use SolidWorks to learn and master CAD/CAM for design, visualization, prototyping, and manufacturing. The book's primary market is four-year colleges and two-year community colleges. Freshman Engineering Design courses should find this book useful, refreshing, and interesting. Other important markets include high schools, professionals, and training courses. We have written the book with the target audience in mind. Page iii highlights some of the book's features.

The book includes just the right amount of math in Chapter 8 (Curves), Chapter 9 (Surfaces), and Chapter 13 (Analysis Tools). The math is concentrated in one or two sections in each of these three chapters. We include the math for two reasons. First, it shows students who are curious how CAD/CAM systems work "under the hood." Second, it broadens the book appeal to many students, professors, and readers. This math may be ignored without affecting the continuity of the coverage of the material in any of these three chapters.

The philosophy behind the book is original, unique, and effective. We cover and present SolidWorks as a design system rather than a software program. Thus, instead of focusing on describing SolidWorks menus and syntax, we describe design approaches, methodologies, and techniques to help CAD designers/engineers and draftspersons achieve their engineering tasks in the fastest, easiest, and most effective way.

Based on this philosophy, the book approach uses design, modeling, and drafting concepts as the building blocks, instead of menus and commands. Thus, we develop command sequences to achieve CAD and modeling tasks. Of course, we provide SolidWorks syntax and details, but do so in keeping with the proposed philosophy of the book. We start with a CAD task to accomplish (what to do) and then go about accomplishing it (showing how to use SolidWorks to do it). This philosophy is more motivating to student learning than simply going through layers of menus and commands.

The book approach is designed to bring the real power of SolidWorks as a powerful modeling and design system instead of only a software program. We include challenging modeling and design examples and problems in the book. As part of the book's unique approach, we cover the theoretical concepts behind the various functions of SolidWorks. This should provide information to the curious minds about why things work the way they do, as well as explain their limitations and use.

The book provides plenty of illustrations, step-by-step instructions, and rich and challenging end-of-chapter problems. The book is suitable for use at various levels, from freshman to senior to graduate courses. Instructors can choose the chapters and topics that suit their teaching needs and courses. They can also choose the level of depth. The book includes both examples and tutorials. An example covers one concept whereas a tutorial is more comprehensive by covering a full design task. Each example and tutorial has a hands-on exercise at the end that serves two purposes. First, it ensures that the student has gone through the example or tutorial, because it builds on it. Second, it both challenges the student's understanding and extends it.

Another unique aspect of the book is the Industry Chat section at the end of each chapter. We select an industry sponsor for each chapter. The sponsor may have donated CAD parts or provided insight to the chapter by answering questions, or both. This section is designed to provide a sneak preview of how the chapter material is used in real life by professional CAD designers. Such industry insight helps instructors to fine-tune their teaching and helps students to know what skills they need to master before going on interviews for jobs. The author has made every effort to select a diversified set of domestic and international companies that represent the CAD field. We have companies representing different industries including medical, military, consulting, machinery, and hospitality to name a few.

Although the book is written for SolidWorks 2010, it is generic enough that the materials apply to previous versions. The book comes with the SolidWorks student version that is valid for one semester, so users of the book can install SolidWorks at home for learning purposes.

The book is organized into parts and chapters. Instructors may cover the chapters in any order and select as they need to fit their course and student needs. However, we recommend covering Chapters 1 and 2 first to build a sound background in 3D CAD/CAM modeling concepts. Chapter 1 is designed to provide a quick grasp of basic functionalities: create parts, create assemblies, and create drawings. These three functionalities correspond to the three modes of SolidWorks: part, assembly, and drawing. The idea here is that students can start designing basic and simple products after using only one chapter of the book; they do not have to wait until later chapters to learn how to design and document simple parts and assemblies. Then they can dig deeper in the latter chapters to learn more. Thus, Chapter 1 provides breadth and the remainder of the book provides depth. As for why we need Chapter 2, it covers all the essential concepts required for a sound understanding of the 3D modeling concepts and efficient use of today's parametric features-based solid modeling CAD/CAM systems such as SolidWorks.

I would like to thank many people who contributed to this book including my former students, designers who have contributed to the industry chats, the book reviewers, the Prentice Hall team, and my family. Many of my students have shaped how I should present and teach concepts to help them understand better. This book is the outcome of such valuable teaching experience.

I would like to thank the following CAD/CAM designers and their companies for sponsoring the book chapters, and for generously giving their time during the Industry Chats out of their belief that they are helping educate current students who are our future CAD/CAM designers:

Chapter 1: Joe Fitzpatrick, VIC Inc., Boston, Massachusetts
Chapter 2: Ricky Jordan, Dynetics Inc. and NASWUG, Huntsville, Alabama

Chapter 3: Keith Kneidel and Richard Wand, MJ Engineering & Consulting Inc., Westerville, Ohio
Chapter 4: Lee Bazalgette, Factorydesign Limited, London, England
Chapter 5: Jeff Hamilton, Bristol Compressors International, Inc., Bristol, Virginia
Chapter 6: Mattias Holmquist, Timelox, ASSA ABLOY AB, Stockholm, Sweden
Chapter 7: David Dunston, Zygote Media Group, American Fork, Utah
Chapter 8: Doug Webber, MSD Ignition, El Paso, Texas
Chapter 9: John Whiteside, Garmin International, Olathe, Kansas
Chapter 10: Kurt Larson, Commercial Sheetmetal Co. Inc., Canton, Massachusetts
Chapter 11: Gabe Wing, Herman Miller Inc., Zeeland, Michigan
Chapter 12: Richard Fleischner, MDA ISI, Pasadena, CA
Chapter 13: Ray Minato, Inertia Engineering + Design Inc., Toronto, Ontario, Canada
Chapter 14: Patrick Hunter, Quickparts, Atlanta, Georgia
Chapter 15: Marc Meeuwsen and Charlie Weaver, Extol Inc., Zeeland, Michigan
Chapter 16: Nishit Shah, NyproMold Inc., Clinton, Massachusetts

I would also like to thank Susan Fredholm Murphy of PE International, Boston, Massachusetts, for editing Chapter 11 and providing valuable feedback. Thanks are also due Boston Gear for granting permission to download and use some of their gears in the book tutorials. I thank Jake Hustad for providing the Universal Joint assembly. I also thank Ivette Rodriguez of ASME for granting permission to use ASME Y14.5M-1994 (R2004) material.

Many thanks are due DS SolidWorks Corporation for its technical support throughout the writing process and using SolidWorks. My sincere thanks go to my friends Marie Planchard, Jeremy Harrington, and Ilan Singer for answering all my questions and lending their unconditional support.

I owe thanks to the many reviewers who helped to shape this book. They are:

Charles Coleman, Argosy University
Paige Davis, Louisiana State University
Joe Fitzpatrick, VIC Inc., Boston, Massachusetts
Max. P. Gassman; Iowa State University
Julia Jones, University of Washington
Dean Kerste, Monroe County Community College

Julie Korfhage, formerly of Clackamas Community College

Paul Lienard, Northeastern University College of Professional Studies

Payam H. Matin, University of Maryland Eastern Shore

Jianbiao (John) Pan, California Polytechnic State University

Lisa Richter, Macomb Community College

Nishit Shah, NyproMold Inc., Massachusetts

David W. Ward, Clackamas Community College

Special thanks are due Lisa Garboski and Karen Fortgang of bookworks publishing services for their help and support in handling all the book logistics including reviewing, handling communication with Prentice Hall and the copy editor, and securing copyright permissions. They also kept me on schedule to meet a tight publishing deadline.

I thank the copy editor, Nancy Marcello, for taking the book draft and converting it to a publishable product. Nancy has done a superb job catching many subtle issues. Her hard work is definitely beneficial to all of us.

The Prentice Hall team has been very wonderful throughout the entire project from the start. I offer my sincere thanks to Sara Eilert, Doug Greive, Christine Buckendahl, Maren Miller, and Vernon Anthony for their support and making the project a more pleasant experience.

Last, but not least, my family and friends deserve many thanks for their support, and apologies to them for hiding out to finish the project. Their love and unconditional support is priceless.

The author always looks forward to and values feedback. Please contact him at zeid@coe.neu.edu with any ideas, corrections, typos, or parts/assemblies that you may want to donate. Full credit will be given to you.

Abe Zeid
Boston, MA

# Contents

# Part II    Basic Part Modeling    145

## 4    Features and Macros    147

## 5    Drawings    197

## 6    Assemblies    231

Contents

## Part V    Part Manufacturing    641

# Computer Aided Design (CAD) Basics

The primary goal of Part I is to learn how to use SolidWorks fairly quickly to create parts, assemble them, document them, and visualize them. The core use of SolidWorks in industry is to create CAD parts (SolidWorks Part mode), assemble the parts to create products (SolidWorks Assembly mode), and create drawings of the parts and assemblies for production and manufacturing (SolidWorks Drawing mode). The jump-start offered in this part should help you appreciate the power of CAD and get a glimpse of what to expect from the rest of the book. We will revisit the concepts covered here in greater depth later in the book.

Chapter 1 (Getting Started) is an overview of SolidWorks, its philosophy, how to configure it, and how to administer it. Chapter 2 (Construction Management) is about learning design shortcuts to enable the completion of design tasks in the shortest time possible. Chapter 3 (Design Intent) covers both how to embed design intelligence into CAD design and how the way you create a CAD part influences its future edits and manufacturing.

Now that we are ready to start, note that this book advocates an active learning style. This means you learn as you use SolidWorks to do the book tutorials. Although we cover CAD concepts independent of the SolidWorks syntax, we do so briefly and leave the nuts and bolts (details) of using the concepts for the tutorials. Thus, the tutorials introduce substantial new material (about both the concepts and SolidWorks) in a hands-on format.

# Getting Started

## 1.1 Book Overview

The main idea of this book, and the focus of Parts I and II, is to show how to use SolidWorks to create parts, assemblies, and drawings and how to visualize CAD models. The book's organization and the flow of the chapters accomplish this fairly quickly. Parts III, IV, and V cover advanced topics to provide more modeling techniques, analysis/development tools, and basic manufacturing.

The book's flow mimics SolidWorks main modes: Part, Assembly, and Drawing. We teach you these three basic modes using prismatic and axisymmetric parts. Once learned, we show more advanced modeling techniques to create more complex (free-form) parts. However, the chapters may be used in a different order to suit individual teaching and learning needs and philosophies.

This book is written with one goal in mind: to help you become a better CAD designer by (1) understanding the intricacy of three-dimensional (3D) modeling and (2) mastering SolidWorks. By understanding 3D modeling concepts, you become more efficient, achieve CAD tasks quicker, and eliminate the time-consuming and frustrating trial-and-error approach. By mastering SolidWorks, you gain skills required by commercial CAD/CAM systems. These skills are transferable from one CAD/CAM system to another because all the systems are built on the same theory and concepts. Even though the syntax (user interface) of these systems is different, their semantics (concepts) are the same.

The book uses the tutorial approach for learning, supported by explaining the concepts behind the tutorials. We cover the concepts of each chapter independent of Solid-Works and use the majority of the chapter to cover tutorials related to the concepts. We follow a meaningful numbering system for the tutorials and examples. Tutorials are numbered as Tutorial x–y, where x is the chapter number and y is the tutorial number within the chapter. For example, Tutorials 1–2 and Tutorial 1–3 are, respectively, Tutorial 2 and Tutorial 3 in Chapter 1. Table 1.1 lists all the book tutorials, so you can use the table for planning purposes.

You will discover that the parts and products that the book tutorials use are not the typical mechanical ones. Instead, we use parts and products that best illustrate the concepts and demonstrate the intricate 3D modeling concepts.

## 1.2 Engineering Design Process

Unlike science, in which the goal is to understand physical phenomena, engineering is all about making products that work even though it involves doing elaborate, complex theoretical investigations. There are good reasons for that. Engineered products and systems are too complex to fit closed-form solutions. Thus, engineers and designers resort to computational methods and techniques, and design tools (such as CAD) to achieve their part and product design. Designers typically begin with a rough part design of the problem to solve and then continue to refine and test it until the part design meets all the design requirements.

The well-known engineering design process (EDP) reflects this very nature of engineering design. Figure 1.1 shows the steps of the EDP. The input to EDP is an idea or a problem to solve. The output is a design to implement the idea or solve the problem.

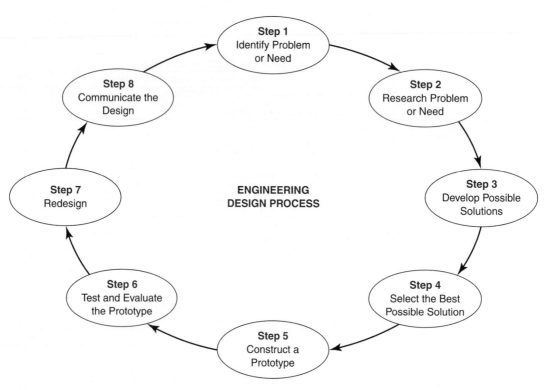

**FIGURE 1.1**
Engineering design process (EDP)

Let us apply the EDP to creating a bookshelf for your room, a simple engineering project. You may have already done this project with your parents when you were a child. We encourage you to apply the steps of the EDP shown in Figure 1.1 to this project.

## 1.3 CAD Process

The CAD process is a subset of the EDP. We use it to implement Steps 5 through 8 of the EDP shown in Figure 1.1. The CAD process is carried out on a CAD/CAM system. In a general sense, use the CAD software to create 3D models of the part design, conduct analysis on the models, redesign the part, if needed, and document the final design. Figure 1.2 shows the CAD process.

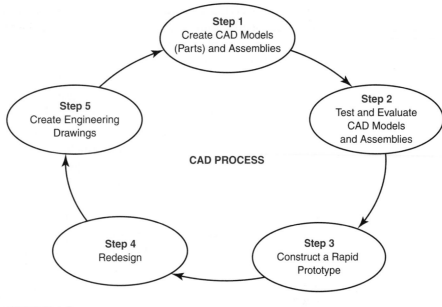

**FIGURE 1.2**
CAD process

## 1.4 Manufacturing Process

With the design complete, we manufacture it to produce the part or product (a product is an assembly of individual parts or components). The input to the manufacturing process is a design, and the output is the actual part or product that the design represents. Figure 1.3 shows the manufacturing process. It picks up where the design process

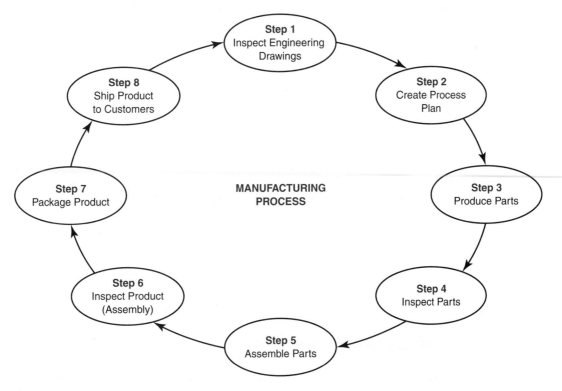

**FIGURE 1.3**
Manufacturing process

left off: engineering drawings. A manufacturing engineer inspects the engineering drawings (Step 1 in Figure 1.3) for manufacturing purposes to ensure that all dimensions make sense, are not contradictory, and that all specified tolerances are producible in a cost-effective way. In Step 2, the manufacturing engineer creates the process plan to produce the part. This plan includes and coordinates all the details of production that the factory (shop floor) supervisors, foremen, and workers need to make the parts and the products. The output from the process plan includes lists of NC programs, production machines, tools, materials, routing sheets (that specify manufacturing sequences), cost estimate sheets, time estimates, and production floor schedule.

The other manufacturing steps in Figure 1.3 are self-explanatory, and we can all relate to them. Let us apply the manufacturing process to creating your bookshelf. Once you have the design, you check it one last time (Step 1). Then, you decide on the shelf material, how much material you need to buy, the tools to use, a rough cost estimate, and how long it will take to make the bookshelf (Step 2). You can now easily apply the remaining steps to your bookshelf product.

## 1.5 CAM Process

The CAM (computer aided manufacturing) process is a subset of the manufacturing process. Like the CAD process, the CAM process is carried out on a CAD/CAM system. In a general sense, use the CAM software to create process plans, NC programs, and part inspection. Other manufacturing software exists, but it may not be part of the CAM software of a typical CAD/CAM system. Figure 1.4 shows the CAM process.

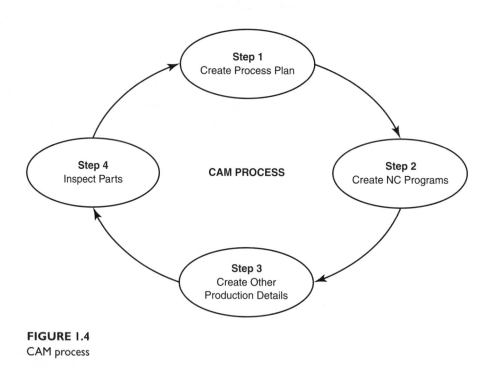

**FIGURE 1.4**
CAM process

## 1.6 SolidWorks Installation and Resources

This book comes with SolidWorks 2010 Student version (150 day access kit). The kit is good for 150 days (one semester). When you install SolidWorks, it creates shortcuts on your desktop. The ones we are interested in are SolidWorks (starts the program), eDrawings (starts eDrawings), and SolidWorks Explorer (similar to Windows Explorer; it helps you navigate folders and files). If you do not install SolidWorks yourself, ask your SolidWorks manager where to find these shortcuts.

If you were to use a nonstudent version of SolidWorks, you would face the decision of whether to install the 32-bit or 64-bit version. The 64-bit version runs faster and is better optimized than the 32-bit version. Also, the 64-bit version is very good to use for large parts and assemblies. However, for student use, the 32-bit version of SolidWorks is adequate as we create small parts and assemblies. Using the 64-bit version would require the 64-bit version of Windows OS (operating system).

SolidWorks comes with many resources to help you get started, troubleshoot, and learn as you move along. The **Help**\* menu (Figure 1.5) of SolidWorks is excellent and provides a wealth of information. To access this menu, click **Help** on the menu bar after you start SolidWorks. Figure 1.5 shows what the top menu item of **Help** leads to. The **API Help** of the **Help** menu is for advanced users who would like to program SolidWorks by using its API (application programmed interface). Become familiar with the **Help** menu as you begin to use SolidWorks.

[a]

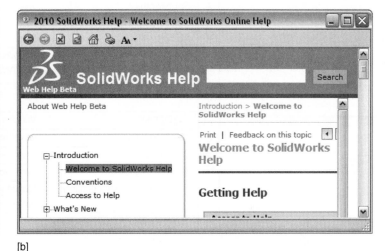
[b]

**FIGURE 1.5**
SolidWorks **Help** menu

Other resources are available on SolidWorks website, www.solidworks.com. Visit this website frequently to find the latest news. Also, visit https://forum.solidworks.com to find answers to your questions. If you are interested in SolidWorks certifications, visit www.solidworks.com/cswa.

SolidWorks has useful software that is free. The two products of interest to us are eDrawings and SolidWorks Viewer. The eDrawings is an e-mail tool that allows you communicate SolidWorks designs to anyone without his or her having to install SolidWorks software. It also allows you to mark up drawings you have been sent and then send them back. This feature is covered in more detail in Chapter 2. The SolidWorks Viewer allows you to view part and assembly files without having to install SolidWorks. It also allows

---

\*Names of SolidWorks menus, menu items, FeatureManager design tree nodes, tabs, toolbars, windows, and click sequences are shown in bold with first letter in cap. File names are shown in italic.

you to pan (move), zoom in/out, and rotate the parts and assembly models for better visualization. Download both eDrawings and SolidWorks Viewer software from www.solidworks.com/sw/support/downloads.htm.

SolidWorks also publishes a one-page *Curriculum and Community Resources for Educators and Students*. We list these resources here.

| | Resource | Description and URL |
|---|---|---|
| **Curriculum** | SolidWorks Teacher Guides | Tutorials and projects: www.solidworks.com/curriculum |
| | SolidWorks Student Guides | Various resources: www.solidworks.com/curriculum |
| | Teacher Blog | Lessons developed by teachers for teachers: http://blogs.solidworks.com/teacher |
| | SolidProfessor | Videos and CDs of how to use SolidWorks: www.solidprofessor.com |
| | | |
| **Community** | 3D ContentCentral | Library of parts, assemblies, block, and macros: www.3dcontentcentral.com |
| | SolidWorks User Group Network | SolidWorks users groups and blogs: www.swugn.org |
| | SolidWorks Contests and Sponsorships | Various student competitions: www.solidworks.com/sponsoreddesigncontest |
| | SolidWorks Discussion Forum | Resource on specific product areas: http://forum.solidworks.com |
| | SolidWorks Blog Community | Network of SolidWorks users with their own blogs about SolidWorks: www.swugn.org/pages/resources/SolidWorksBlogs.html |
| | | |
| **Others** | CADJunkie | Various tutorials and blogs: www.cadjunkie.com |
| | YouTube Video | www.youtube.com/results?search_query=solidworks |
| | CB Model Pro | Free-form surface modeling tool: www.cbmodelpro.com |
| | SolidWorks Labs | Labs: http://labs.solidworks.com |
| | SolidWorks Design Gallery | Model gallery: www.solidworks.com/pages/successes/gallery/model_gallery.html |
| | SolidWorks White Papers | Papers: www.solidworks.com/pages/services/WhitePaper.html |

## 1.7 SolidWorks Overview

SolidWorks is a Windows native application, meaning it is well integrated with Microsoft Windows operating system. We CAD/CAM users may think of SolidWorks in a similar way to familiar Windows applications such Microsoft Office. Actually SolidWorks mimics Office in its name (SolidWorks Office module) and simplicity. We also may equate SolidWorks simplicity to that of Microsoft Word, at least in accomplishing simple modeling tasks. Also, think of a SolidWorks document (part, assembly, drawing, etc.) as a Word document. This should help in using SolidWorks. For example, now you know what you need to do to create a new or open an existing SolidWorks document (file); simply click **File => New** or **File => Open**, respectively.

Next, we run SolidWorks and open a new document to provide an overview of SolidWorks. To start SolidWorks, double-click its shortcut icon (or follow your CAD lab instruction). Starting with the main menu, click **File => New => Part => OK** to open a new document. Figure 1.6 shows the three types of SolidWorks documents. Figure 1.7 shows SolidWorks interface (main window) after you open a new part document. The interface, like modern interfaces, has menus and toolbars and exhibits general behaviors. Hover over any part of the interface with the mouse, and a tooltip with information will pop up. If you want to see the hover effect on the menu bar,

Part I  Computer Aided Design (CAD) Basics

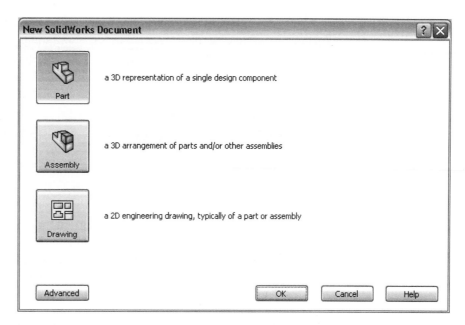

**FIGURE 1.6**
SolidWorks document types

click anywhere on the bar first to add the focus there. The main window has three panes (areas), as shown in Figure 1.7. Familiarize yourself with the window and the panes. Although most of the information in Figure 1.7 is self-explanatory, the status bar at the bottom of the window displays messages related to your current activity. Make a habit of watching this bar.

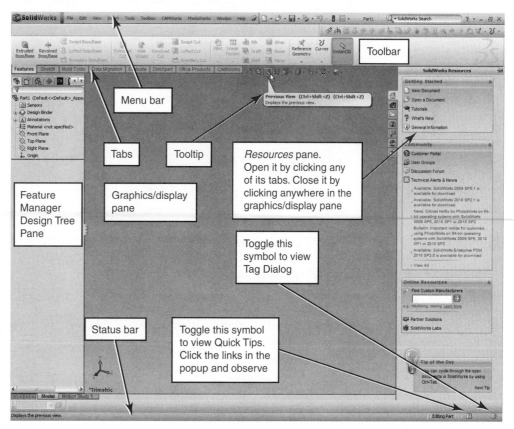

**FIGURE 1.7**
SolidWorks main window

SolidWorks offers multiple modes, depending on what you would like to do. The three basic modes are Part (create parts or components), Assembly (create assemblies), and Drawing (create drawings). Figure 1.6 shows these modes. Other modes include Simulation, Animation, Analysis, and Machining. SolidWorks displays the commands for each mode when you activate it.

## 1.8 Customize SolidWorks

SolidWorks can be customized in many ways, but the basic customization needs are the system options and document properties. Click **Tools => Options** to access both settings (see Figure 1.8). Customizing at the system level affects current and future documents (i.e., global effect). Customizing at the document level affects the current document only (i.e., local effect). Familiarize yourself with the choices available for each setting. Chapter 2 covers more advanced customizations of SolidWorks.

[a]                    [b]

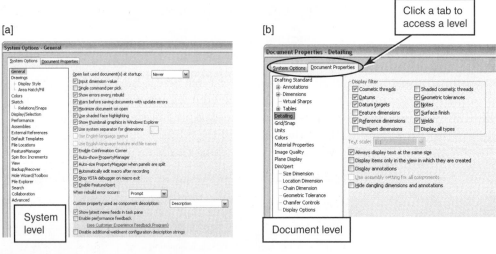

**FIGURE 1.8**
Customizing SolidWorks

## 1.9 Tutorial Template

We use one tutorial template throughout the book for consistency. If one of the template items is not needed, we ignore it. The template sections are:

Modeling task:   describe the modeling/design problem; for example, create, modify, etc.
Modeling synthesis:   discuss the various modeling plans to achieve the modeling task and select the best plan
Modeling plan:   provide a list of the steps to achieve the modeling task. These steps are elaborated in CAD steps that follow
CAD steps:   show step-by-step sequence of how to accomplish the design task
Hands-on practice:   modify or extend the tutorial to gain more competency

## 1.10 Tutorials Overview

Each chapter has a tutorial section overview that describes the CAD concepts that the chapter tutorials cover and how the tutorials are connected and related to each other (the theme they cover and how they build on each other).

The theme for the tutorials in this chapter is to get you up to speed quickly in learning the basics of the three SolidWorks modes: Part, Drawing, and Assembly. We sacrifice depth now for breadth. There will be many chances throughout the book for you to dig deeper into each mode. A quick start is provided here for those who would like to learn everything first and master the concepts later. In this spirit, first there are five tutorials: three are on the Part mode, one on the Drawing mode, and one on the Assembly mode. A sixth one covers the basics of visualization. After doing these six tutorials, you should be able to design a part or two, assemble them, create drawings to document the design, and render the parts and assemblies to add some realism in visualizing your design.

The parts we create are simple and use lines and circles. We use the four basic features of SolidWorks: extrude, extrude cut, revolve, and revolve cut. Although we provide all the dimensions required for sketching and construction, keep in mind that you can sketch freely and design with partial dimensions. Once you are satisfied with the sketch proportions, SolidWorks has the dimensions already stored. You can then just show them on the sketch.

The tutorials in this chapter use a machine donated by VIC, a company in the Boston area specialized in designing Time of Flight Mass Spectrometers (see Figure 1.9). These machines are used to analyze biological samples to aid largely in the fields of

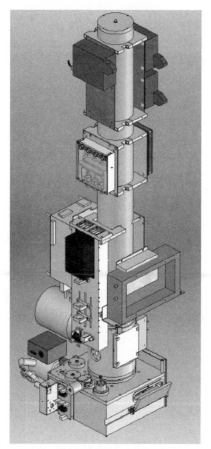

Machine [a]

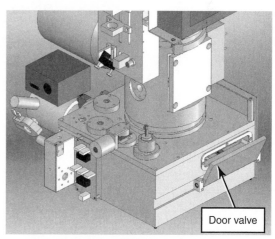

Close-up of the door valve [b]

Door valve

The Door Valve assembly
(door shown in open position) [c]

**FIGURE 1.9**
Time of Flight Mass Spectrometer (Courtesy of VIC)

drug discovery and cancer research. Samples are loaded through the door valve, a spring-loaded self-closing flap that is forced open from the inside and forced closed by the coil springs shown in Figure 1.10. Once closed, the door will rest against a rubber O-ring to create a vacuum-tight seal. Figure 1.9 shows the assembly of the door valve. You will hear from the company's lead CAD designer and engineer, Mr. Joseph Fitzpatrick, in the Industry Chat.

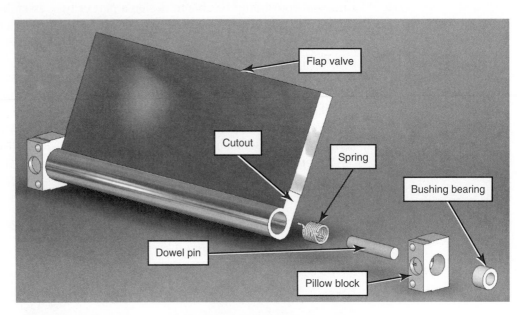

**FIGURE 1.10**
Exploded view of Door Valve assembly (Courtesy of VIC)

Figure 1.10 shows an exploded view of the Door Valve assembly. The cutout in the flap valve is to prevent the valve from catching onto the pillow block to ensure that the flap shuts firmly. The top and bottom steps (cutouts) in the pillow block align the block in the slot shown in Figure 1.9. The blind hole on the left side of the block houses a conical spring (not shown) that helps the block to move horizontally (prevent pivoting) to adjust in making contact with the machine body.

We simplify and adapt the Door Valve assembly for the purpose of this chapter as follows. We ignore the springs and related geometric details in the assembly as well as some other geometric details. We create and assemble three parts: the flap, the dowel pin, and the pillow block. The chapter has six tutorials with focused activities:

☐ **Create the parts:** Tutorials 1–1, 1–2, and 1–3 create the flap, the dowel pin, and the pillow block, respectively.
☐ **Create engineering drawings:** Tutorial 1–4 creates the engineering drawings of the three parts.
☐ **Create the assembly:** Tutorial 1–5 assembles the three parts to create the Door Valve assembly.
☐ **Render the assembly:** Tutorial 1–6 renders an image of the assembly using Aluminum 6061 Alloy as material.

You may use these tutorials with your students in the CAD lab in multiple ways, depending on your teaching philosophy, class activities, and class time. You may do one

Part I Computer Aided Design (CAD) Basics

or more tutorials per class, and require the students to do and submit the tutorial hands-on exercises at the end of the class. You may assign some tutorials as out-of-class-activities, etc. (The author would appreciate an e-mail from you to zeid@coe.neu.edu describing your experience and use of the book to include in the future editions with due credit.)

We use the following in describing and presenting all the book tutorials:

- ☐ *Click* means click the mouse left button.
- ☐ We use *select* and *click* interchangeably.
- ☐ We use the verbose approach to describe a SolidWorks procedure or skill when it is introduced. After that, we simply use it assuming you know how to do it. For example, "To finish the extrusion, right-click anywhere on the screen and select **OK** (green check mark) from the pop-up" is the verbose description, whereas "Finish the extrusion" is the non-verbose description.
- ☐ We use two pedagogical tools in the book to maximize learning: **Help** and **Why**. **Help** introduces material related to what we are describing, how to get out of a jam or a problem, etc. **Why** explains different ways of doing the same thing and why we did it the way we did.

## Tutorial 1–1: Create the Flap

### Modeling task

Create the flap valve shown in Figure 1.10.

### Modeling synthesis

This part is an extrusion with two cutouts, one on each side. An **extrusion** is a prismatic part that has a constant cross section and a uniform thickness perpendicular to the cross-section plane. A block is an example of an extrusion. There are at least two modeling plans to create the flap. We can use either two extrusions that meet at the step line or one with two cutouts. In the first plan, we create the lower extrusion followed by the top one. In the second plan, we create one extrusion, ignoring the two cutouts first. Then, we use two extruded cut features to create the two cutouts. A **feature** is a simple part that we create in one operation, for example, a block. The first plan uses two operations, whereas the second plan uses three operations. We use the second plan because it lends itself to how we will manufacture the flap.

Within the second modeling plan, we can use a cross section or features to create the flap, as shown in Figure 1.11. Sketching the cross section is harder than sketching features because you have to calculate more points. Also, it would be harder to edit the cross section in the future if the flap design were to change. Thus, it is better to think features—that is, create simple features and combine them to create the part. As shown in Figure 1.11, we need three features to create the flap: extrusion (rectangle), extrusion (circle), and a fillet. SolidWorks will take care of the coordinates where the features intersect and overlap, thus saving us time.

### Modeling plan

Each feature shown in Figure 1.11 requires two steps to create: create the feature cross section in a sketch, and then use a 3D operation (e.g., extrusion, revolve, etc.) to create the feature. A sketch requires a sketch plane.

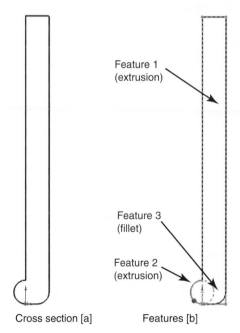

Feature 1
(extrusion)

Feature 3
(fillet)

Feature 2
(extrusion)

Cross section [a]        Features [b]

**FIGURE 1.11**
Two ways to create the flap

A **sketch plane** is a plane that you select or define to draw the geometry of the cross section. We use the right sketch plane here because of the way the flap is oriented in space, as shown in Figure 1.10.

## CAD steps

We create the flap model in five steps:

1. Create Feature 1 (extrusion) shown in Figure 1.11.
2. Create Feature 2 (extrusion) shown in Figure 1.11.
3. Create Feature 3 (fillet) shown in Figure 1.11.
4. Create the dowel pin hole shown in Figure 1.10.
5. Create the cutouts shown in Figure 1.10.

The details of these steps are shown below.

## Step 1:  Create Feature 1 (extrusion) shown in Figure 1.11 and Figure 1.12

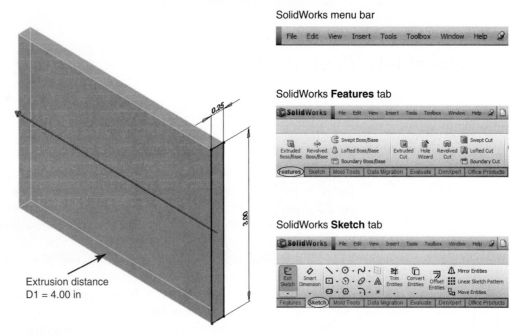

SolidWorks menu bar

SolidWorks **Features** tab

SolidWorks **Sketch** tab

Extrusion distance
D1 = 4.00 in

**FIGURE 1.12**
Feature 1 (extrusion)

| Task | Command Sequence to Click |
|---|---|
| A. Open a new part (SolidWorks **Part** mode). | **File => New => Part => OK** |
| B. Change background color of viewport. | **Tools => Options => System Options** tab **=> Colors => Viewport Background => Edit =>** Select the color you like **=> Plain (Viewport background color above) => OK** |
| C. Change part units from millimeters (default) to inches. | **Tools => Options => Document Properties** tab **=> Units => IPS (inch, pound, second) => OK** |

| Task | Command Sequence to Click |
|---|---|

**Task**

**D.** Save the part file as *flap*.

**E.** Select the right plane as the sketch plane.

**F.** Select extrusion as the feature type to create.

**G.** Sketch the cross section shown in Figure 1.12.

**H.** Dimension the rectangle.

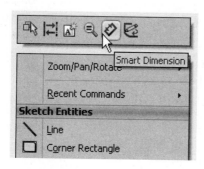

**I.** Release the tool (mouse).

**Command Sequence to Click**

**File => Save As =>** *flap* **=> Save**
**Help:** Save the file in the correct folder you want. Also, remember to save frequently to minimize losing your work in the event of crashes, or you risk ruining or corrupting the part file.
**Right Plane** from features manager tree on left of screen.
**Extruded Boss/Base** from the **Features** tab to start sketching.
**Help:** Alternatively, you start sketching after Task E and then create the feature from the sketch by selecting the sketch in features tree on left => **Features** tab => **Extruded Boss/Base**. The former way is more efficient.
Click the rectangle symbol on the **Sketch** tab => Move the mouse to the origin of the sketch (a circle appears at the origin) => Click the origin and drag to sketch (draw) a rectangle.
Right-click anywhere on the screen => Select **Smart Dimension** icon from the context toolbar that pops up and is

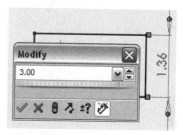

shown to the left => Click vertical line of rectangle => Move tool (mouse) to right to place dimension => Click to release tool => Input 3.00 in the **Modify** box shown above => Click green check mark to finish. Repeat for the 0.25 in.
**Help:** To modify an existing dimension, double-click it. To delete a sketch entity, right-click it => **Delete**. You can delete only entities that are not part of existing features. To delete them, you must delete the features first.
**Help:** You can move, by dragging, sketch entities that are shown in blue. Right-click anywhere on the screen and click **Select**. You may also hit **Esc** or **Enter**.

| Task | Command Sequence to Click |
|---|---|

**Task**

**J.** Hide sketch relations to make the sketch look less cluttered.

**K.** Exit the sketch.

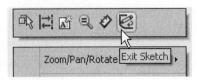

**L.** Create the extrusion.

**Command Sequence to Click**

**View => Sketch Relations**
This is a toggle.
**Exit Sketch** icon on **Sketch** toolbar. Alternatively, click the **Exit Sketch** symbol on the top right corner of the viewport. Or, right-click anywhere on the viewport and click **Exit Sketch** (shows when you hover on the last icon of the pop-up as shown to the left). When you exit the sketch, the **Extrusion** menu shows on the left pane of the screen. Change the extrusion direction to the opposite direction by dragging the extrusion arrow that shows on the viewport. Drag it to the other side of the cross section. Input 4 (extrusion depth shown in Figure 1.12) for the **D1** distance shown to the left. To finish the extrusion, right-click anywhere on the screen and select **OK** (green check mark) from the pop-up. **Help:** If the **Extrusion** menu does not show on the left pane after you exit the sketch for one reason or another, click the **Features** tab to force it to show.

**Step 2:** Create Feature 2 (extrusion) shown in Figure 1.11 and Figure 1.13

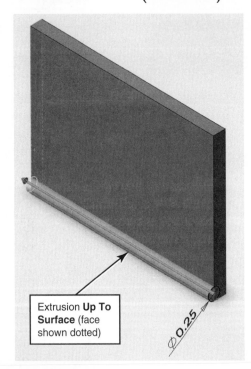

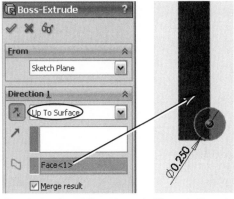

*Face* is the dotted face shown in Figure 1.13, and the pointed-to surface shown here.

**FIGURE 1.13**
Feature 2 (extrusion)

| Task | Command Sequence to Click |
|---|---|
| **A.** Select the feature sketch plane. | Click the right face of Feature 1 (cross section shown in Figure 1.12). |
| **B.** Select the feature type to create. | **Extruded Boss/Base** from the **Features** tab |
| **C.** Sketch cross section shown in Figure 1.13. | **Circle** from **Sketch** toolbar => Move mouse near left edge of right face until it changes to dotted (indicating circle center is located there) => Click mouse => Draw a circle by dragging the mouse toward the origin until a point shows on the origin, indicating that the circle is tangent to the bottom edge of the rectangle => Right-click and select **Smart Dimension** => Click the circle and move the tool away from it => Place the dimension where you want it, then click to release the tool => Input 0.25 in the **Modify** box that pops up => Click the green check mark to finish. |

 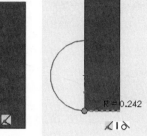 

| Task | Command Sequence to Click |
|---|---|
| **D.** Release the tool (mouse). | Right-click anywhere on the screen and click **Select**. You may also hit **Esc** or **Enter** on the keyboard. |
| **E.** Create the extrusion. | Exit the sketch => Select **Up To Surface** from the drop-down under **Direction 1** (left pane on screen) => Select the dotted face shown in Figure 1.13 (click **View Orientation** icon at top of viewport; hover over until you read it as shown to the left) => Select the **Left** view shown to the left; hover over it until you read it and click it => Click the face you now see on the screen => Display the **Isometric** view (reorient the view as you just did). By now you should see Figure 1.13 on the screen => Finish the extrusion. |

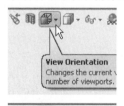

**Why:** We could have used depth of 4 in. for this extrusion instead of **Up To Surface** option. However, if you change the depth of Feature 1, you have to edit Feature 2 manually. **Up To Surface** makes the depths of both features equal and makes the depth of Feature 1 the driver; that is, changing it changes the depth of Feature 2. **Up To Surface** is a geometric constraint. We will cover constraints in detail later.

## Step 3: Create Feature 3 (fillet) shown in Figure 1.11 and Figure 1.14

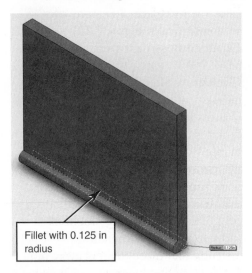

Fillet with 0.125 in radius

**FIGURE 1.14**
Feature 3 (fillet)

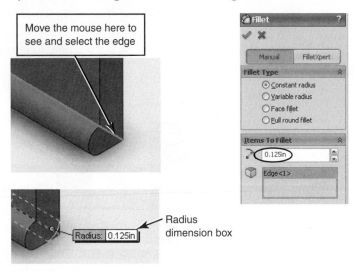

Move the mouse here to see and select the edge

Radius dimension box

| Task | Command Sequence to Click |
|------|---------------------------|
| **A.** Select the feature type to create. | **Fillet** from the **Features** tab |
| **B.** Select the edge to fillet, and create the fillet. | Click the back bottom edge (see Figure 1.14) => Input 0.125 (fillet radius) in the left pane on screen. Alternatively, you can click the **Radius** dimension box that appears and type 0.125 => Right-click on screen => **OK**. **Help:** Click where shown in Figure 1.14 to select the back edge. When you move the mouse over the edge, SolidWorks will highlight it. Alternatively, select the **Back** view to access the edge, and then select it. |

## Step 4: Create the dowel pin hole shown in Figure 1.10 and Figure 1.15

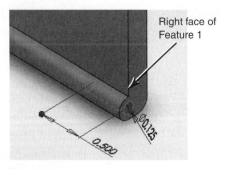

Right face of Feature 1

**FIGURE 1.15**
Dowel pin hole

Create the hole for the dowel pin. The hole size shown in Figure 1.10 accommodates the spring. We ignore this size because we ignore the spring to simplify modeling. We create a hole of the same size as that of the dowel pin, i.e., with a diameter of 0.125 in. The hole length is 0.5 in. (see Figure 1.15).

| Task | Command Sequence to Click |
|---|---|
| A. Change dimension precision to three decimal places. | **Tools => Options => Document Properties** tab **=> Dimensions => Precision** =>. Select **.123** from the drop-down under **Primary dimension => OK**.<br>**Why:** We change to three decimals from the default two decimals because we need to show 0.125, as shown in Figure 1.15; otherwise SolidWorks displays 0.13 for the diameter. |
| B. Select the feature sketch plane. | Click the right face of Feature 1 (block); see Figure 1.15. |
| C. Orient the sketch plane to align with the screen. | **Right** from the **View Orientation** drop-down |
| D. Select the feature type to create. | **Extruded Cut** from the **Features** tab |
| E. Sketch the cross section shown in Figure 1.15.<br> 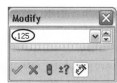 | **Circle** from **Sketch** toolbar => **Quick Snaps** from **Sketch** toolbar => **Center Point Snap** from drop-down => Click Feature 2 circle (shown dotted to the left) => Drag the mouse to draw a circle => Right-click anywhere => **Smart Dimension** => Click the circle you just drew => Drag the mouse to place the dimension => Click to release the tool => Input 0.125 in **Modify** box (shown to the left) => Right-click anywhere => **Select** to release the tool. |
| F. Create the feature. | Exit the sketch => Click **Isometric** from the **View Orientation** drop-down => Input .5 for the **D1** => Click the green check mark to finish. |
| G. Repeat the steps above to create the hole on the left side of the flap. | |

## Step 5: Create the cutouts shown in Figure 1.10 and Figure 1.16

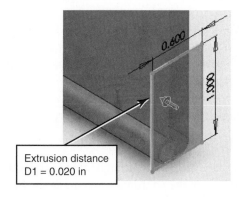

Extrusion distance
D1 = 0.020 in

**FIGURE 1.16**
Flap cutouts

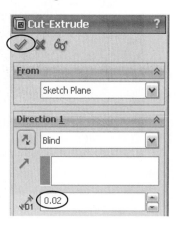

| Task | Command Sequence to Click |
|---|---|
| A. Select the feature sketch plane. | Click right face of Feature 1 (block). |
| B. Select the feature type to create. | **Extruded Cut** from the **Features** tab |
| C. Sketch the cross section shown in Figure 1.16. | **Rectangle** from **Sketch** toolbar => Drag the mouse and sketch a rectangle. Make sure that the bottom side of the rectangle snaps to the origin of the coordinate system, and that the rectangle size exceeds the size of the right face, as shown in Figure 1.16 => Right-click and select **Smart Dimension** => Add the dimensions shown in Figure 1.16. **Why:** The rectangle height must be 1 in. measured from the bottom of the flap. The rectangle width could be any large enough value. |
| D. Release the tool (mouse). | Right-click anywhere on the screen and click **Select**. You may also hit **Esc** or **Enter** on the keyboard. |
| E. Create the extruded cut. | Exit the sketch => Input 0.02 for **D1** under **Direction 1** (shown above) => Click the green check mark (shown above) to finish. |
| F. Repeat Tasks A – E to create the cutout on the left side of the flap. | In this case, click **View Orientation** (drop-down) => **Left** (view) to access the left view to sketch the cutout. |

---

***HANDS-ON FOR TUTORIAL 1–1.*** Create two additional cutouts, one on each side of the flap. Each cutout starts from the top edge of the side with a size of 0.02 × 1.0 in., similar to Figure 1.16.

---

## Tutorial 1–2: Create the Dowel Pin

### Modeling task

Create the dowel pin shown in Figure 1.10.

### Modeling synthesis

This part is an extrusion or a revolve. A **revolve** is a symmetric part that has a constant cross section that can be revolved around an axis of revolution a given angle to create the part. A cylinder is a revolve. We can think of at least two plans to create it. As an extrusion, we create a circle with diameter of 0.125 in. and extrude it a length of 1 in. As a revolve, we create a rectangle (cross section) and revolve it 360 degrees. The two plans are similar. We use the second plan to practice the creation of revolves.

### Modeling plan

Select the front sketch plane. Sketch a rectangle that is 0.9800 × 0.0625 in. with its bottom left corner at the origin of the coordinate system as shown in Figure 1.17. Also, draw a horizontal axis passing through the origin. Use the revolve operation to create the feature by revolving the cross section (rectangle) about the axis of revolution 360 degrees.

CAD steps

We create the dowel pin model in one step:

  **1.** Create the dowel pin shown in Figure 1.17.

The details of this step are shown below.

**Step 1:** **Create the dowel pin shown in Figure 1.10 and Figure 1.17**

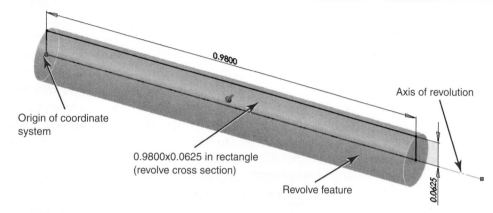

**FIGURE 1.17**
Dowel pin (revolve feature)

| Task | Command Sequence to Click |
|---|---|
| A. Open a new part (SolidWorks **Part** mode). | **File => New => Part => OK** |
| B. Change the background color of viewport, if needed. | **Tools => Options => System Options** tab => **Colors => Viewport Background => Edit =>** Select the color you like => **Plain (Viewport background color above) => OK** |
| C. Change the part units to inches from millimeters. | **Tools => Options => Document Properties** tab => **Units => IPS (inch, pound, second) => OK** |
| D. Change dimension precision to three decimal places. | **Tools => Options => Document Properties** tab => **Dimensions => Precision =>** Select **123** from the drop-down under **Primary dimension => OK.** |
| E. Save the part file as *dowelPin*. | **File => Save As =>** *dowelPin* **=> Save** |
| F. Select the front plane as the sketch plane. | **Front Plane** from features manager tree on left of screen |
| G. Select revolve as the feature type to create. | **Revolved Boss/Base** from the **Features** tab to start sketching |
| H. Sketch the cross section shown in Figure 1.17. | Click the rectangle symbol on the **Sketch** tab => Move the mouse to the origin of the sketch (a circle appears at the origin) => Click the origin and drag to sketch (draw) a rectangle. |

| Task | Command Sequence to Click |
|---|---|

**I.** Dimension the rectangle.

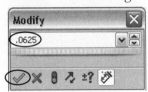

Right-click anywhere on the screen => Select **Smart Dimension** icon from the context toolbar that pops up => Click vertical line of rectangle => Move tool (mouse) to right to place dimension => Click to release tool => Input 0.0625 in the **Modify** box (shown to the left) => Click green check mark (on the bottom left of the box) to finish (shown to the left). While **Smart Dimension** is still active, repeat to input 0.980 in.

**J.** Release the tool (mouse).

Right-click anywhere on the screen and click **Select**. You may also hit **Esc** or **Enter**.

**K.** Hide sketch relations to make the sketch look less cluttered.

**View => Sketch Relations**
This is a toggle.

**L.** Exit the sketch.

**Exit Sketch** icon on **Sketch** toolbar. Alternatively click the **Exit Sketch** symbol on the top right corner of the viewport. Or, right-click anywhere on the viewport and click **Exit Sketch** (shows when you hover on the last icon of the pop-up as shown to the left).

**M.** Create the revolve.

When you exit the sketch, the **Revolve** menu shows on the left pane on screen. The values shown to the left are fine. To finish the revolve, right-click anywhere on the screen and select **OK** (green check mark) from the pop-up. Alternatively, you can click the green check mark shown to the left.

---

***HANDS-ON FOR TUTORIAL 1–2.*** Chamfer both ends of the dowel pin. Use chamfer distances **D** of 0.01, 0.02, 0.05, 0.1 in. What happens to the chamfer feature? Repeat, but for a fillet feature. What happens? What is you conclusion? **Help:** To create a fillet or a chamfer feature, click this sequence: **Features** tab => **Fillet** drop-down => **Fillet** or **Chamfer**.

---

## Tutorial 1–3:  Create the Pillow Block

### Modeling task

Create the pillow block shown in Figure 1.10.

### Modeling synthesis

This part consists of a few extrusions. Figures 1.9, 1.10, and 1.18 show the features that make up the block. The block consists of an extrusion with two cutouts and four holes.

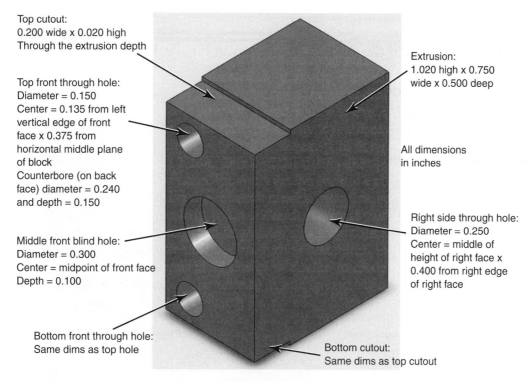

Top cutout:
0.200 wide x 0.020 high
Through the extrusion depth

Top front through hole:
Diameter = 0.150
Center = 0.135 from left
vertical edge of front
face x 0.375 from
horizontal middle plane
of block
Counterbore (on back
face) diameter = 0.240
and depth = 0.150

Middle front blind hole:
Diameter = 0.300
Center = midpoint of front face
Depth = 0.100

Bottom front through hole:
Same dims as top hole

Extrusion:
1.020 high x 0.750
wide x 0.500 deep

All dimensions
in inches

Right side through hole:
Diameter = 0.250
Center = middle of
height of right face x
0.400 from right edge
of right face

Bottom cutout:
Same dims as top cutout

**FIGURE 1.18**
Pillow block

The two cutouts (top and bottom) are used to assemble the block in the slot of the machine base, as shown in Figure 1.9. The right side through hole is to assemble the bushing bearing in which the dowel pin is, in turn, assembled. The top and bottom front through holes (with counterbores) are used to assemble the entire door valve into the machine base via screws. The middle front blind hole holds a conical spring to push the door outward when it is shut. This is needed when the machine generates vacuum pressure during its use.

### Modeling plan

Follow these steps: (1) Create the block using extruded feature; (2) create the two cutouts using extruded cut feature; (3) create the right side hole using extruded cut feature; (4) create the top and bottom holes using extruded cut feature; and (5) create the blind hole using extruded cut feature.

### CAD steps

We create the pillow block model in five steps:

1. Create the extrusion shown in Figure 1.18.
2. Create the top and bottom cutouts shown in Figure 1.18.
3. Create the right side through hole (to house the bushing bearing) shown in Figure 1.18.
4. Create the middle front blind hole (to house the conical spring) shown in Figure 1.18.
5. Create the top and bottom front through holes shown in Figure 1.18.

The details of these steps are shown below.

## Step 1:  Create the extrusion shown in Figure 1.18

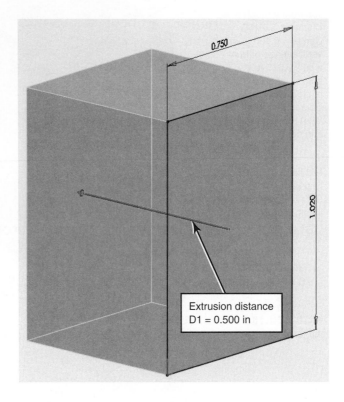

**FIGURE 1.19**
Block feature

Extrusion distance
D1 = 0.500 in

| Task | Command Sequence to Click |
|---|---|
| A. Open a new part in SolidWorks and set it up. | Follow Tasks A – D of Step 1 of creating the dowel pin. |
| B. Save the part file as *pillowBlock*. | **File => Save As =>** *pillowBlock* **=> Save** |
| C. Select the right plane as the sketch plane. | **Front Plane** from features manager tree on left of screen |
| D. Select extrusion as the feature type to create. | **Extruded Boss/Base** from the **Features** tab to start sketching |
| E. Sketch the cross section shown in Figure 1.19. | Click the rectangle symbol on the **Sketch** tab => Move the mouse to the origin of the sketch (a circle appears at the origin) => Click the origin and drag to sketch (draw) a rectangle. |
| F. Dimension the rectangle. | Right-click anywhere on the screen => Select **Smart Dimension** icon from the context toolbar that pops up => Click vertical line of rectangle => Move tool (mouse) to right to place dimension => Click to release tool => Input 1.020 in the **Modify** box (shown to the left) => Click green check mark to finish (shown to the left). While **Smart Dimension** still active, repeat to input 0.750 in. |

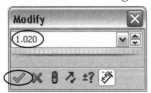

| Task | Command Sequence to Click |
|---|---|
| G. Release the tool (mouse). | Right-click anywhere on the screen and click **Select**. You may also hit Esc or **Enter**. |
| H. Hide sketch relations to make the sketch look less cluttered. | **View => Sketch Relations** This is a toggle. |
| I. Exit the sketch. | Click **Exit Sketch** icon on **Sketch** toolbar. |
| J. Create the extrusion. | When you exit the sketch, the **Extrude** menu shows on the left pane on screen. Enter 0.500 in. for **D1**. To finish the extrusion, right-click anywhere on the screen and select **OK** (green check mark) from the pop-up. |

## Step 2: Create the top and bottom cutouts shown in Figure 1.18

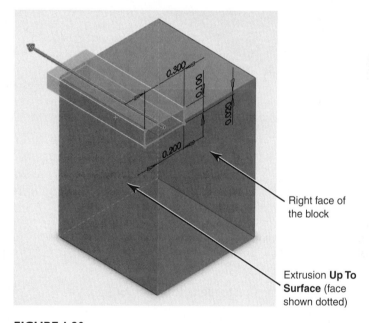

Right face of the block

Extrusion **Up To Surface** (face shown dotted)

**FIGURE 1.20**
Pillow block cutouts

| Task | Command Sequence to Click |
|---|---|
| A. Select the right face as the sketch plane. | Click the right face (see Figure 1.20) of the block. |
| B. Select extrusion as the feature type to create. | **Extruded Boss/Base** from the **Features** tab to start sketching |
| C. Sketch the cross section shown in Figure 1.20. | Click the rectangle symbol on the **Sketch** tab => Draw the rectangle and make sure its size exceeds the size of the right face as shown in Figure 1.20. |

| Task | Command Sequence to Click |
|---|---|
| D. Dimension the rectangle. | Right-click and select **Smart Dimension** => Add the dimensions shown in Figure 1.20 => Click the green check mark (on the left pane on screen) to finish. **Why:** The rectangle size ($0.300 \times 0.100$) could be anything as long as its edges exceed the face edges. The rectangle location ($0.200, 0.020$) must be as shown. |
| E. Release the tool (mouse). | Right-click anywhere on the screen and click **Select**. You may also hit **Esc** or **Enter**. |
| F. Exit the sketch. | Click **Exit Sketch** icon on **Sketch** toolbar. |
| G. Create the cutout. | Select **Up To Surface** from the drop-down under **Direction 1** (see left pane on screen) => Select the dotted face (use left view to access it) shown in Figure 1.20 => Display the **Isometric** view (reorient the view). By now you should see Figure 1.20 on the screen => Finish the extrusion. **Why:** We could have used depth of 0.50 in. for this extrusion instead of **Up To Surface** option. The use of the option is better because it ties the cutout depth to the block depth, thus making it a through cutout regardless of any future changes in the block depth. We could have used **Through All** also. It is very similar to **Up To Surface**. |
| H. Create the bottom cutout. | Repeat the tasks to create the cutout on the bottom of the block. **Why:** We could have used a mirror operation to create the bottom cutout. In this case, the bottom cutout becomes dependent on (child of) the top cutout; that is, **Extruded Boss/Base** the bottom cutout will inherit any future changes you make to the top cutout. |

**Step 3:** Create the right side through hole (to house the bushing bearing) shown in Figure 1.18

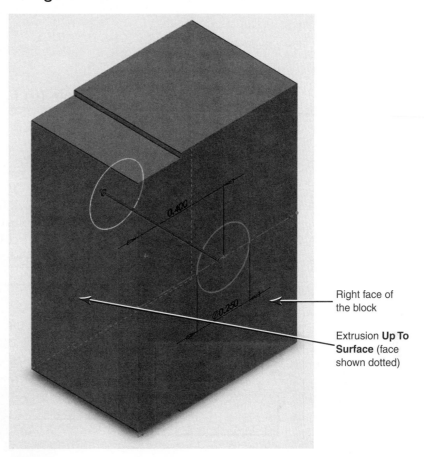

Right face of the block

Extrusion **Up To Surface** (face shown dotted)

**FIGURE 1.21**
Pillow block cutouts

| Task | Command Sequence to Click |
|---|---|
| | |

Task

A. Select the right face as the sketch plane.
B. Select extrusion cut as the feature type to create.
C. Sketch the cross section shown in Figure 1.21.

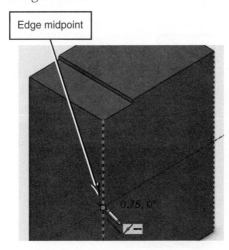

Edge midpoint

Command Sequence to Click

Click the right face (see Figure 1.21) of the block.
**Extruded Cut** from the **Features** tab to start sketching
Click **Centerline** from **Sketch** toolbar => Draw a centerline that connects the midpoints of the block's two edges (hover the mouse over the edge until you see a square indicating the midpoint of the edge) as shown in Figure 1.21 and to the left => Draw a circle with a center on the centerline (hover the mouse over the centerline until it changes color indicating the circle center will snap there) => Dimension the sketch as shown in Figure 1.21.
**Why:** We use the midpoints of the two edges to ensure that the hole center is always centered in the vertical direction of the block's right face.

| Task | Command Sequence to Click |
|---|---|
| D. Release the tool (mouse). | Right-click anywhere on the screen and click **Select**. |
| E. Exit the sketch. | Click **Exit Sketch** icon on **Sketch** toolbar. |
| F. Create the through hole. | Extrude up to the left face of the block (see Figure 1.21). |

**Step 4:** Create the middle front blind hole (to house the conical spring) shown in Figure 1.18

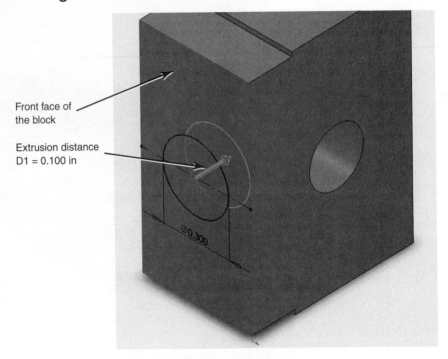

Front face of the block

Extrusion distance
D1 = 0.100 in

⌀0.300

**FIGURE 1.22**
Pillow block blind hole

| Task | Command Sequence to Click |
|---|---|
| A. Select the front face as the sketch plane. | Click the front face (see Figure 1.22) of the block. |
| B. Select extrusion cut as the feature type to create. | **Extruded Cut** from the **Features** tab to start sketching |
| C. Sketch the cross section shown in Figure 1.22. | Click **Centerline** from **Sketch** toolbar => Draw a centerline that connects the midpoints of the block's two edges (hover the mouse over the edge until you see a square indicating the midpoint of the edge), as shown in Figure 1.22 => Draw a circle with a center at the midpoint of the centerline (hover the mouse over the centerline until you see a square indicating the circle center will snap there; shown to the left) => Dimension the sketch as shown in Figure 1.22. |

Edge midpoint

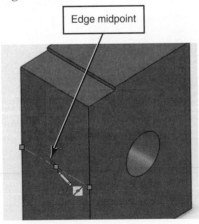

| Task | Command Sequence to Click |
|---|---|
| | **Why:** We use the midpoint of the centerline to ensure that the blind hole center is always centered in the block front face. Right-click anywhere on the screen and click **Select.** |
| **D.** Release the tool (mouse). | |
| **E.** Exit the sketch. | Click **Exit Sketch** icon on **Sketch** toolbar. |
| **F.** Create the blind hole. | Extrude a distance of 0.100 in. (see Figure 1.22). |

## Step 5: Create the top and bottom front through holes shown in Figure 1.18

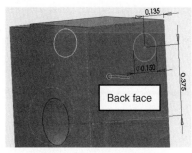

(A) Create top through hole

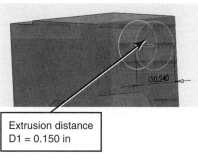

(B) Create counterbore

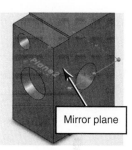

(C) Mirror plane

**FIGURE 1.23**
Pillow block front through holes

### Step 5.1: Create the top through hole shown in Figure 1.23A

| Task | Command Sequence to Click |
|---|---|
| **A.** Select the back face (Figure 1.23A) as the sketch plane. Reorient the view to access the back face. | **View Orientation** icon on top of graphics pane => **Back** view (shown to the left) |

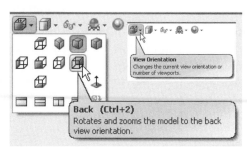

| Task | Command Sequence to Click |
|---|---|
| **B.** Select extrusion cut as the feature type to create. | **Extruded Cut** from the **Features** tab to start sketching |
| **C.** Sketch the cross section shown in Figure 1.23 A. | **Centerline** from **Sketch** toolbar => Draw a centerline that connects the midpoints of the block's two edges (hover the mouse over the edge until you see a square indicating the midpoint of the edge) as shown to the left => Click **Circle** from **Sketch** toolbar => Draw a circle and dimension it (diameter and center), as shown in Figure 1.23A. |

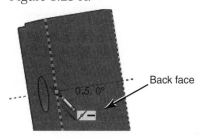

| Task | Command Sequence to Click |
|------|---------------------------|
| D. Release the tool (mouse). | Right-click anywhere on the screen and click **Select**. |
| E. Exit the sketch. | Click **Exit Sketch** icon on **Sketch** toolbar. |
| F. Create the through hole. | Extrude up to the front face of the block (shown dotted in Figure 1.23A). |

**Step 5.2:** Create the counterbore of top through hole shown in Figure 1.23B

| Task | Command Sequence to Click |
|------|---------------------------|
| A. Select the back face as the sketch plane. | Click the back face (see Figure 1.23A) of the block. |
| B. Select extrusion cut as the feature type to create. | **Extruded Cut** from the **Features** tab to start sketching |
| C. Sketch the cross section shown in Figure 1.23B. | **Circle** from **Sketch** toolbar => Draw a circle with a center coincident with the center of the hole shown in Figure 1.23A (hover over the hole center and then click it) => Drag the mouse to draw the circle => Dimension the sketch, as shown in Figure 1.28B. |
| D. Exit the sketch. | Click **Exit Sketch** icon on **Sketch** toolbar. |
| E. Create the counterbore (hole). | Extrude a distance of 0.150 in. (see Figure 1.23B). |

**Step 5.3:** Mirror the top hole with respect to the plane shown in Figure 1.23C to create the bottom hole

| Task | Command Sequence to Click |
|------|---------------------------|
| A. Create a mirror plane (see Figure 1.23C). The plane is horizontal and passes through the midpoint of any vertical edge of the pillow block (Figure 1.23A); i.e., the plane is located at a distance of 0.51 in. from the block bottom. | Click the bottom face (reorient the view to access the bottom face) of the block (see Figure 1.23A) => **Features** tab => **Reference Geometry** => **Plane** => **Offset Distance** (hover over the items of the **Selections** sheet that opens up in the left pane on screen and shown to the left) => Type 0.51 in the box (shown to the left) => **Flip** (check box under **Offset** Distance as shown to the left) => **OK** (or click the green check mark shown to the left to finish). The plane shows up on the screen with a name; *Plane2* in our case. **Why:** We use reference geometry to create the mirror plane because it is not part of the model geometry; similar to centerlines. |

| Task | Command Sequence to Click |
|---|---|

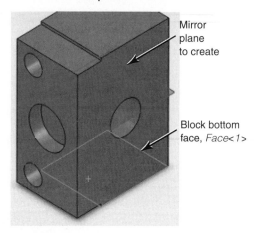

B. Create the bottom hole and its counterbore. We create a mirror feature by mirroring two features (the top hole and its counterbore).

**Mirror** from the **Features** tab (pane shown to the left shows *Plane2* already selected; if not, click it) => Select both the top hole and the counterbore hole (rotate the ISO view to see the holes, then hover/click the hole, then hold the **Shift** (or **CTRL**) key down for multiple selections and hover/click the counterbore hole) => **OK** (or click the green check mark to finish).

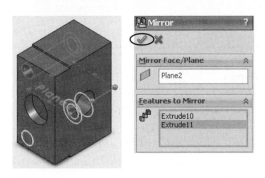

**Why:** The mirror feature is just that, one feature (both the hole and the counterbore) unlike the top hole and the counterbore that are two separate features. Also, the geometry of the mirror feature (child) depends on the geometry of its parent; when you change the diameter or the depth of holes of the parent features, the child inherits them. If we need this design intent all the time, then the mirror is a good strategy; otherwise you need to repeat the construction Steps 5.1 and 5.2.

C. Hide the mirror plane.

Click *Plane2* (or the name shown on your screen) from the features manager tree => **Hide** (the eyeglasses symbol shown in the context menu that pops up and shown to the left). This symbol is a toggle; if you click it again, you display *Plane2* again. (Notice the different colors of the mirror plane in

| Task | Command Sequence to Click |
|------|---------------------------|

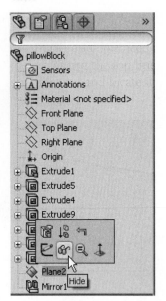

the features manager tree depending on its state.)

**Why:** We hide the mirror plane because it is not part of the model geometry. Also, had we anticipated the mirror need at the beginning of constructing this model, we could have created the cross section (rectangle) so that the coordinate system shown in Figure 1.19 was located at the center of the rectangle instead of its bottom corner. We then could have used the **Top Plane** as the mirror plane and saved creating a mirror plane. This observation illustrates the need to devise an efficient modeling plan before beginning construction. However, keep in mind that developing good modeling skills takes time and experience. As a general rule, though, use the sketch planes of cross sections you create as mid-planes to extrude on both sides of.

---

**HANDS-ON FOR TUTORIAL 1–3.** Create the bushing bearing shown in Figure 1.10. The bushing has an outer diameter of 0.250 in., an inner diameter of 0.125 in., and a length of 0.500 in.

---

## Tutorial 1–4: Create Drawings

In this tutorial, we create three engineering drawings of the three parts (flap, dowel pin, and pillow block) of the Door Valve assembly that we have created in Tutorial 1–1. We insert the three typical views (front, top, and right) into each drawing and dimension each view. We also insert an isometric view in each drawing. In practice, some companies use the ISO view, whereas others do not.

There is a two-way associativity between parts and their drawings. Changing a part model is reflected in its drawing views automatically, and, vice versa, changing the part (model) items in a drawing is reflected automatically in the part model.

Open SolidWorks in the Drawing mode to create a drawing: Click **Open => New => Drawing => OK => OK** (accept the default standard sheet size). SolidWorks drawings use the concept of sheets. You can create multiple sheets within a drawing. We use only one sheet per drawing in this chapter. Once the drawing is open, SolidWorks offers three methods to dimension a drawing: individual, auto, and model items. The first two methods are available under the **Smart Dimension** icon in the **Annotation** tab. When you click **Smart Dimension**, two tabs show in the left pane on the left: **DimExpert** and **Autodimension**. Use **DimExpert** to insert individual dimensions, and use **Autodimension** to dimension an entire view at once. Although the **Autodimension** method seems attractive, we do not recommend using it because the dimensions appear cluttered and would require manual editing to remove some and/or change the replacements of others on the screen.

The model items method is available as the **Model Items** icon in the **Annotation** tab. We recommend using this method. It works best if you create your models properly with the intent to draw; that is, use features to create the models (not cross sections), and dimension each sketch with the intent to generate drawings. We have followed these two observations in Tutorial 1–1.

SolidWorks requires an active part to feed into the drawing you are creating. You may open the part before or after you open a new drawing. With this quick overview of drawings, we create three drawings, one for each of the three parts of the Door Valve assembly.

Follow these thoughts to create the three drawings.

### Drawing task

Create the drawings of the flap, dowel pin, and the pillow block.

### Drawing synthesis

We create a drawing with four views, the three typical (front, top, and right) and the ISO. SolidWorks enforces the orthogonal projection rules; that is, it locks the three typical views together when you move them relative to each other; you can move the ISO freely though.

### Drawing plan

We open a drawing, insert its views, change line fonts (e.g., dashed for hidden lines), and insert dimensions. We insert a front view first, followed by inserting the other views. We will not fill the title block at this time.

### Drawing steps

We create the drawings of the door valve parts in three steps:

1. Create the engineering drawing for the flap.
2. Create the engineering drawing for the dowel pin.
3. Create the engineering drawing for the pillow block.

The details of these steps are shown below.

## Step 1: Create the engineering drawing for the flap

| Task | Command Sequence to Click |
|---|---|
| A. Open a new drawing (SolidWorks **Drawing** mode): You may open a new drawing first and then open the flap model, or open the flap model first and then open a new drawing. | **File => New => Drawing => OK => OK** (select drawing default size) **=> Browse** (from **Model View** pane on left of screen, and shown to the left) **=>** Select flap part from the window that pops up **=> Open**. **Help:** If you close the **Model View** pane or it does not show before selecting a model, follow this sequence to display it: Right-click anywhere on the drawing **=> Drawing Views => Model**. |

 Or

**OR**

You may open the flap part first before opening a new drawing: Click **File => Open =>** Select flap part from the window that pops up **=> Open**. Now open a new drawing: Click **File =>**

| Task | Command Sequence to Click |
|------|---------------------------|

**New => Drawing => OK => OK**
(to select drawing default size) =>
Click the right arrow (circled as shown
to the left) in **Model View** pane (to
begin inserting views).

**B.** Save the drawing.

**File => Save As =>** *flap*.
**Help:** If you open a new drawing and
do not see the **Model View** pane to
select the **Browse** button from, click:
**View Layout** tab => **Model** View (this
is a toggle) to display the pane.

**C.** Insert views.

The **Orientation** section (shown to the
left) of the **Model View** pane shows the
**Standard views** (typical). Hover over
the icons to reveal their names. The
section also shows the front view as the
default. When you move the mouse in
the drawing area, you see the view move
with the mouse ready to be inserted.
Click somewhere in the bottom left
corner of the drawing. Move the mouse
horizontally to the right of the front
view, and click somewhere to place the
right view. Move the mouse again above
the front view, and click to place the top
view. Move the mouse again diagonally
to the right and click the mouse to place
the ISO. Right-click the mouse (or hit
**Esc** on keyboard) to end view insertion.
The right view serves as the parent view
to the other three views.

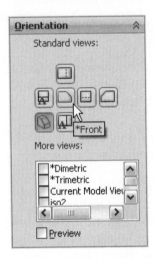

**D.** Scale the views, if needed, to fit within
the drawing sheet.

Click any view border (hover over the
view until you see its dashed border) =>
**Use custom scale** (from **Scale** section
shown to the left) => Select the scale
from the drop-down. If you click the
right view, SolidWorks applies the scale
to all its children views. Click any other
view to scale it individually. For this
tutorial we scale the ISO down using a 1:2
scale, and leave the three typical at 1:1
scale. Move the ISO after you scale it to
fit within the border of the drawing sheet.

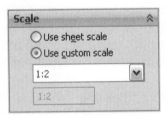

**E.** Move a view, if needed, to control its
placement on the drawing sheet.

Hover over the view border until you
see the **Pan** symbol (two orthogonal
bidirectional arrows shown to the left)
and move. The border of the currently
selected (active) view is shown in
dashed blue.

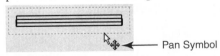

— Pan Symbol

**F.** Delete a view, if needed.

Select the view (click its border) =>
Hit the **Delete** key on the keyboard.

Figure 1.24 shows the drawing thus far.

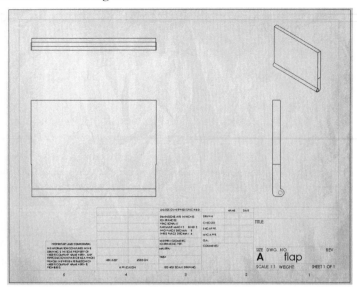

**FIGURE 1.24**
Un-dimensioned drawing of the flap

**Task**

**G.** Change angle of projection, if needed.

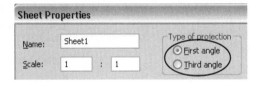

**H.** Change line font. The flap views shown in Figure 1.24 do not show the hidden lines as dashed. We need to change this default setting.

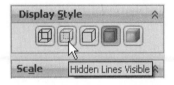

**I.** Change drawing units from mm to inches, if needed.

**J.** Insert dimensions.

**Command Sequence to Click**

Figure 1.24 shows that the top and the right views are incorrect; they are the bottom and the left views, respectively. To correct, right-click anywhere on the drawing sheet => **Properties** => **Third angle** => **OK** as shown to the left. We cover the angle of projection in detail in the drawing chapter of the book. Click the front view => Select **Hidden Lines Visible** (hover over the icons of the **Display Style** section shown to the left). **Help:** If you select a parent view (front view here), SolidWorks applies the selected style to all its children views; otherwise, it applies it only to the selected view. Reset the ISO view back by clicking it => Select **Hidden Lines Removed** (hover over the icons of the **Display Style** section on left of screen). **Tools => Options => Document Properties** tab **=> Units => IPS (inch, pound, second) => OK** **Annotation** tab => **Model Items** => Front view (or any view); make sure the **Source** (in the **Source/Destination** section of the pane shown to the left) is set to **Entire model** and the **Import items into all views** check box is checked. The resulting dimensions seem cluttered (see Figure 1.25); we need to

| Task | Command Sequence to Click |
|---|---|

**K.** Delete a dimension, if needed.

**L.** Insert individual dimension, if needed.

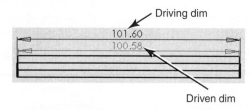

delete some and reposition others. Figure 1.26 shows the final drawing. Select it => Hit the **Delete** key on the keyboard. To reposition it, drag it. When you finish editing the dimensions, click the green check mark (on left of screen).

**Smart Dimension** from **Annotation** tab => Select the entity to dimension => Drag the mouse to place the dimension => Repeat, if needed, for another dimension. When done, click the green check mark. Notice that any dimension you insert is displayed in gray color, unlike the **Model Items** dimension that is displayed in black. The black dimensions are driving dimensions whereas the gray ones are driven (derived). All dimensions print in black, though. Figure 1.26 shows the 3.96 and 0.480 driven dimensions as an example (also, shown to the left).

**Why:** The **Model Items** method of inserting dimensions in drawing views is important in two ways. First, it is fast because it dimensions all the views at once. Second, and more importantly, it derives the dimensions from the model sketches and puts them in the views that correspond to the sketch planes of these model sketches. For example, the

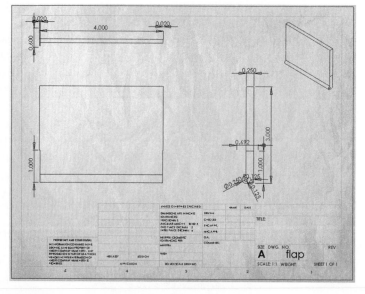

**FIGURE 1.25**
Cluttered drawing of the flap

dimensions on the right view of Figure 1.26 correspond to the dimensions of the sketches (all on the right sketch plane) shown in Figures 1.12 to 1.15. The dimensions 4.000 and 0.020 are shown on the top view of Figure 1.26 because they represent the depths of the extrusions shown in Figures 1.12 and 1.16; these depths are best viewed in the top view. The 1.000 dimension is on both the right and the front view (Figure 1.25). We opted to delete it from the right view and leave it on the front view to reduce the clutter on the former. The dimension 0.480 is derived (by SolidWorks) as the difference between the depth (0.500) of the hole extrusion (Figure 1.15) and the depth (0.020) of the cutout (Figure 1.16). As a general rule, the **Model Items** method will not show these types of derived dimensions; the user must insert them individually using the **Smart Dimension** method as shown here. In conclusion, your sketches and the way you dimension them can save you much time when it comes to **generating** the drawings of your design and models. Thus, using the **Smart Dimension** method is inefficient to use.

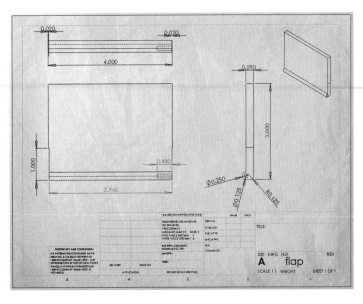

**FIGURE 1.26**
Final drawing of the flap

## Step 2: Create the engineering drawing for the dowel pin

Repeat the above instructions of Step 1 to generate the drawing for the dowel pin shown in Figure 1.27.

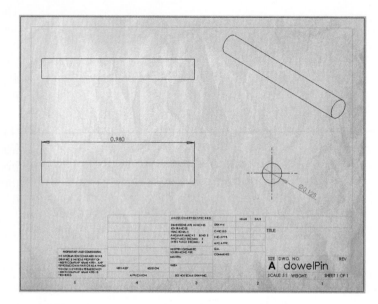

**FIGURE 1.27**
Drawing of the dowel pin

## Step 3: Create the engineering drawing for the pillow block

Repeat the above instructions of Step 1 to generate the drawing for the pillow block shown in Figure 1.28.

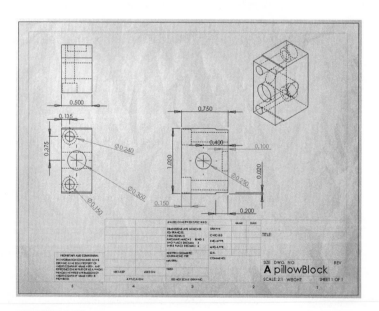

**FIGURE 1.28**
Drawing of the pillow block

## Tutorial 1–5:  Create Assembly

In this tutorial, we create the Door Valve assembly and the assembly drawing. We assemble the three parts (flap, dowel pin, and the pillow block) that we have created in Tutorials 1–1 through 1–3. You create an assembly by inserting the individual components of the assembly into the assembly model. When you insert a component, Solid-Works actually makes a copy of the component (part) geometry from its part file and inserts it. This copy is known as an instance. Thus, you can insert as many instances of a component as the assembly needs. We cover assemblies in more detail in the assemblies chapter of the book.

After you insert the components, you assemble them to create the assembly. Assembling a component in an assembly entails applying mating conditions (mates) to constrain it in the assembly. A mate positions two components relative to one another. Conceptually, the mates resemble assembling parts of a product in real life. A mate applies to two items of the components being mated, be it a face, edge, point (vertex), or axis. For example, a mate may require two faces to be coincident, two cylindrical faces to be concentric, or two edges to be parallel.

The outcome of mating two components is to prevent them from moving relative to each other in space, thus mimicking real life. An assembled component must be fixed (anchored) in space unless it is free to move for functional requirements; for example, a motor shaft must rotate. In general, a component needs three mates to lock it in space. There is a total six degrees of freedom (DOF) in the assembly modeling space: three translations along the three axes ($X$, $Y$, and $Z$) and three rotations around these axes. Three mates are what it takes to constrain the six DOF because locking one locks another.

There is a two-way associativity between parts and their assemblies. Changing a part model is reflected in all its instances automatically, and vice versa, changing the instance (model) items in an assembly is reflected automatically in the part model.

Open SolidWorks in the Assembly mode to create an assembly: Click **File => New => Assembly => OK**. At this point, SolidWorks asks you to select a component to insert. The first component you insert serves as the base part for the assembly; you assemble all the other components onto it, thus mimicking real life. Click **Browse** (from the left pane on screen) **=>** Select the flap part file from the window that opens **=> Open**. We use the flap as the base for the Door Valve assembly. The flap instance moves freely on the screen; it moves with the mouse when you move it. You can place (anchor) it in space by either clicking anywhere on the screen or by clicking the green check mark on the left pane. We recommend using the green check mark over the mouse click because it lets SolidWorks align the origin and sketch planes of the flap with those of the assembly. (We do it for the first part [base part] only.) This goes back to how we created the flap. SolidWorks uses the origin and sketch planes shown in Figure 1.12. Solid-Works uses the first sketch planes created for the flap. Thus, the way we create parts affects their use in other activities such as creating assembly and drawings (inserting dimensions as described in Tutorial 1–4).

After the first (base) component is inserted and placed in the assembly, insert all the other components of the assembly, one at a time. Use mating conditions to place and orient each component correctly in the assembly. Should we insert one component at a time, assemble it, and repeat for other components; or insert all the components first, then assemble them? The former approach is better for two reasons: (1) Inserting all, then assembling all is not scalable for large assemblies that have many components because you clutter the assembly; and (2) inserting and assembling one component at a time resembles real life.

Follow these thoughts to create the assembly.

### Assembly task

Create the assembly of the door valve.

### Assembly synthesis

We use the flap as the base part and assemble the dowel pin and the pillow block onto it. We need two instances of each. Each of the four instances requires three mating conditions: coincident, concentric, and parallel.

### Assembly plan

We open an assembly, insert the flap first, and then the dowel pin followed by the pillow block.

### Assembly steps

We create the assembly of the door valve parts in four steps:

1. Create the Door Valve assembly.
2. Create the assembly drawing.
3. Create the exploded assembly view.
4. Animate the exploded view.

The details of these steps are shown below.

## Step 1:   Create the Door Valve assembly

### Task

A. Open a new assembly (**Assembly** mode).
B. Insert and place the flap (base part).

### Command Sequence to Click

**File => New => Assembly => OK**
**Browse** (from **Part/Assembly to Insert** pane shown to the left) **=>** Select flap part from the window that pops up **=>** **Open =>** Green check mark shown on left of screen.

**Help:** If you do not see or lose the **Browse** button for any reason, click **Assembly** tab **=> Insert Components** to get it back.

**Why:** If you click the mouse anywhere on the screen to place the flap instead of clicking the green check mark, SolidWorks does not align the assembly origin and sketch planes with those of the flap. Hover over the **Front Plane, Top Plane, Right Plane**, and **Origin** of the assembly tree (left pane on screen) to see where they are relative to the flap.

| Task | Command Sequence to Click |
|---|---|

C.  Save the assembly file as *doorValve*.

**File** => **Save As** => *doorValve* => **Save**

D.  Insert the dowel pin. We need two instances of the dowel pin, as shown in Figure 1.10.

**Assembly** tab => **Insert Components** => **Browse** (from **Insert Component** pane on left of screen) => Select dowel pin part from the window that pops up => **Open** => Green check mark shown on left of screen. To insert the second instance, hold **CTRL** (on keyboard) down, and click the dowel pin first instance and drag it away. **Help:** To delete a instance of a component, right-click it => **Delete** => **Yes**.

E.  Assemble (mate) the right instance of the dowel pin into the flap (see Figure 1.29A). We apply three mating conditions; coincidence between the back face of the pin (F1) and the face of the blind hole (F2) in the flap, concentric between the cylindrical faces of the pin (F3) and the hole (F4), and make the front plane FP (sketch plane shown in Figure 1.17) of the pin parallel to one of the flap big faces F5 (parallel mate). The SolidWorks sequences to create these mating conditions are shown in subtasks E1 – E3 below.

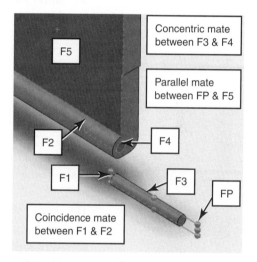

**FIGURE 1.29A**
Dowel pin mates

E1.  Mate F1 and F2 via "coincidence" condition.

**Mate** (on **Assembly** tab) => **Coincident** (from **Mate** pane on left of screen) => One end face (F1) of the pin (orient view to pick end near flap) => Face (F2) of blind hole (orient view to right to pick it) => Green check mark on screen (hover on it to see **Add/Finish Mate**, shown to the left) => Green check mark on left pane (hover on it to see **OK**, shown to the left).

E2.  Mate F3 and F4 via "concentric" condition.

**Concentric** (from **Mate** pane on left of screen) => Cylindrical face (F3) of the pin => Cylindrical face (F4) of blind hole => Green check mark on screen (hover on it to see **Add/Finish Mate**) => Green check mark on left pane (hover on it to see **OK**).

| Task | Command Sequence to Click |
|---|---|

**E3.** Make the front plane (sketch plane shown in Figure 1.17) of the pin parallel to the flap big face F5 (parallel mate).

**F.** Assemble (mate) the left instance of the dowel pin into the flap.

**G.** Insert the pillow block. We need two instances of the pillow block, as shown in Figure 1.10.

**H.** Assemble (mate) the right instance of the pillow block into the flap and dowel pin (see Figure 1.29B): We apply three mating conditions: coincidence between the left face of the pillow block (F6) and the right face of the flap (F7), concentric between the cylindrical faces of the pillow block (F8) and the dowel pin (F9), and parallel between the edges of the pillow block (E1) and the flap (E2). The SolidWorks sequences to create these mating conditions are shown in subtasks H1 – H3 below.

**H1.** Mate F6 and F7 via "coincidence" condition.

---

**Mate => Parallel =>** Expand the assembly tree => Expand the dowel pin subtree => Click **Front Plane** (FP) from the subtree (shown to the left) => Click the front face (F5) of the flap => Green check mark on screen => Green check mark on left pane.
**Why:** Although it may seem unimportant, we need the parallel condition to fully constrain the dowel pin in space. Without it, the pin can freely rotate in place in the blind hole.
Follow the above subtasks E1 – E3.

**Assembly** tab **=> Insert Components => Browse** (from **Insert Component** pane on left of screen) => Select pillow block part from the window that pops up => **Open =>** Green check mark on left of screen. To insert the second instance, hold **CTRL** (on keyboard) down, and click the pillow block first instance and drag it away.
**Help:** To delete an instance of a component, right-click it => **Delete => Yes**.

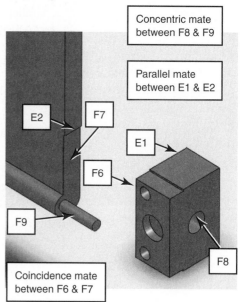

Concentric mate between F8 & F9

Parallel mate between E1 & E2

Coincidence mate between F6 & F7

**FIGURE I.29B**
Pillow block mates

**Mate** (on **Assembly** tab) **=> Coincident** (from **Mate** pane on left of screen) => Back face (F6) of the pillow block (orient view to pick face near flap) => Face (F7) of blind flap => Green check mark on screen (hover on it to see

---

| Task | Command Sequence to Click |
|---|---|

Add/Finish Mate, shown to the left) => Green check mark on left pane (hover on it to see OK, shown to the left).

H2. Mate F8 and F9 via "concentric" condition.

**Concentric** (from **Mate** pane shown on left of screen) => Cylindrical face (F8) of the pillow block hole => Cylindrical face (F9) of the dowel pin => Green check mark on screen (hover on it to see **Add/Finish Mate**) => Green check mark on left pane (hover on it to see **OK**).

H3. Make the edge E1 of the pillow block parallel to the edge E2 of the flap (parallel mate).

**Mate** => **Parallel** => Edge E1 of the pillow block => Edge E2 of the flap => Green check mark on screen => Green check mark on left pane

I. Assemble (mate) the left instance of the pillow block into the flap and the dowel pin.

Follow the above subtasks H1 – H3.

## Step 2: Create the assembly drawing

Follow Tutorial 1–5 to create the assembly drawing of the door valve shown in Figure 1.30. Save the drawing as *doorValve*. In using **Model Items** to insert dimensions, select **Selected feature** for **Source** under **Source/Destination** on left of screen. This allows you to control how many dimensions to display on the assembly drawing. There is no need to clutter the drawing. The purpose of dimensioning an assembly drawing is to show the overall dimensions of the assembly to know its size in space.

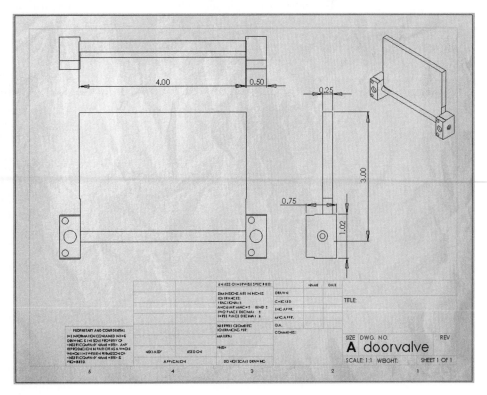

**FIGURE 1.30**
Assembly drawing of the door valve

## Step 3: Create the exploded view

An exploded view of an assembly is a view where the components of the assembly are moved along the axes of the assembly modeling space. We usually explode the ISO view. If you have ever assembled a do-it-yourself product such as a bookcase, you must have looked at the 3D view in the assembly instructions pamphlet; this 3D view is an exploded view of the bookcase assembly.

SolidWorks creates display states for the assembly. You can show the assembly ISO view in a collapsed state, as shown in Figure 1.30 where all the components are shown in assembled positions, or in an exploded state where components are shown in moved positions. SolidWorks shows the exploded view in its **ConfigurationManager** (the most right tab in the left pane; hover over it to display its name, **ConfigurationManager**).

| Task | Command Sequence to Click |
|---|---|
| A. Create a new assembly state to hold the exploded view. 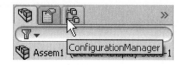 | **Configuration Manager** tab shown to the left (from the left pane where the features manager tree is) => Right-click anywhere in the **Configuration** pane that shows on left of screen => **Add Configuration** => Type *Exploded* as the **Configuration name** on the corresponding text box => Green check mark. **Help:** The active (current) state is shown in normal color (black) in the **Configurations** tree (list). Inactive states appear grayed as the **Default** state shows. |
| B. Create the exploded view (see Figure 1.31). 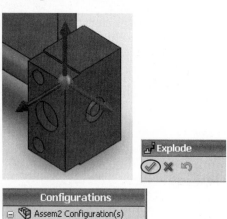 | **Exploded View** (from the **Assembly** tab) => Left pillow block instance (to select it) => Drag the red axis that shows up a reasonable distance to the left => Green check mark (to finish exploding this instance, shown to the left). Repeat for the other four instances in this order: left dowel, right pillow, right dowel, flap. Move the flap along the *Z*-axis (blue axis), not the *X*-axis (red axis). This sequence creates an exploded state (see Figure 1.31) called **ExplView1** under the **Default** state. If you expand this state (double-click it or click its "+" symbol), you should see the five explosion steps in the order you created them. This order is used later to create animation in Step 4 of this tutorial. If you click any step, SolidWorks highlights the corresponding instance. **Help:** If you want to reposition an exploded instance, expand the **Configurations** tree shown to the left => Expand **ExplView1** => Click |

| Task | Command Sequence to Click |
|---|---|
| | any step of the five (e.g., **Explode Step 1** (this highlights the corresponding instance in the display area of the screen) => Drag the arrow that shows the instance to move it.<br><br>**Help:** The three axes (red, green, and blue) are known as the triad. A triad appears in part and assembly documents to help orient viewing models. The triad is for reference only. You can hide the triad but you cannot select it or use it. |
| C. Toggle between the display states. | Double-click the **ExplView1** once to display the collapsed state. Double-click it again to display the exploded state. |

**FIGURE 1.31**
Exploded view of the Door Valve assembly

## Step 4: Animate the exploded view

A good use of an assembly exploded view is to animate it to gain an understanding of how the product (assembly) can be assembled in real life. The animation can also serve the purpose of training individuals and demonstrating the product functionality. We animate the **ExplView1** view that we created in Step 3 as follows.

| Task | Command Sequence to Click |
|---|---|
| A. Start animation.<br> | Right-click on **ExplView1**, then click **Animate collapse** from the pop-up shown to the left to open the **Animation Controller** window. The controller is similar to typical video players. Investigate its functions. |

| Task | Command Sequence to Click |
|---|---|

B. Playback (watch) animation.

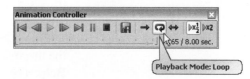

Click the **Playback Mode: Loop** arrow shown to the left, and watch the animation play. The animation is displayed in the reverse order of the five steps under **ExplView1**. If you would like to change the animation sequence, you need to delete the steps and re-create them in the desired order. The controller shown to the left is a standard VCR-like control.

C. Delete an animation step, if needed.

Right-click the step => **Delete** from the pop-up.

---

**HANDS-ON FOR TUTORIAL 1–5.** Assemble the bushing bearing shown in Figure 1.10; create an assembly drawing, an exploded view, and animate the assembly.

---

## Tutorial 1–6: Render Models

In this tutorial, we create realistic images of the Door Valve assembly for visualization purposes. Realism is a good tool to use at the conceptual design phase of a product. Rendering and visualization tools include creating elaborate shaded images using material, light sources, shadowing, and texture to mimic material looks. SolidWorks has a library of commonly used materials. Material selection fills physical properties such as density and surface finish. Visit www.matweb.com to find more materials than what SolidWorks offers. You can download new materials from its searchable materials database and add them to SolidWorks materials library.

SolidWorks offers PhotoWorks Studio to create visual realism. To access it, click **Office Products** tab => **SolidWorks Office** => **PhotoWorks**. PhotoWorks allows you to add **Appearance**, **Scene**, and **New Decal**. We cover visual realism in more detail in the rendering chapter. We add visual realism to the assembly in one step:

1. Create realistic rendering of the Door Valve assembly.

The details of this step are shown below.

## Step 1: Create realistic rendering of the Door Valve assembly

| Task | Command Sequence to Click |
|---|---|

A. Start Photo Works to render the assembly shown in Figure 1.31.

**Office Products** tab => **SolidWorks Office** => **Photo Works**

B. Save the assembly file as *doorValveShaded*.

**File** => **Save As** => *doorValveShaded* => **Save**

C. Assign material to the assembly components. We use Aluminum 6061 Alloy for the components. We can assign the material to the parts at either the assembly or the part level because of the associativity between the two.

Right-click any component in the assembly tree (on left pane on screen) => **Material** => **Edit Material** => **Aluminum Alloys** => **6061 Alloy** => **Apply** => **Close**

| Task | Command Sequence to Click |
|------|---------------------------|

**D.** Replace current material of a component, if needed.

**E.** Remove current material of a component, if needed.

Repeat the sequence and select it. The new selection overrides the old one. Right-click any component in the assembly tree (shown on left pane on screen) => **Material** => **Remove Material**

**F.** Render the assembly.

**Office Products tab** => **SolidWorks Office** => **Photo Works** => **Render**. Photo Works renders the assembly using the default settings for **Appearance**, Scene, and **New Decal**. Figure 1.32 shows the result. This photo is not permanent. To remove it, right-click anywhere on the graphics pane on the screen => **Pan**. As soon as you move the photo, it disappears. Click the **Render** icon to get it back. You may use this idea to try different rendering settings. We revisit rendering in its chapter later.

**FIGURE 1.32**
PhotoWorks rendered photo of the Door Valve assembly

**Help:** If you change the default settings of the assembly during rendering and you need them back, PhotoWorks does not offer an undo command. You need to know these settings and manually regenerate them.

**Why:** Any property changes you make to assembly components while rendering the assembly are reflected in the component (part) files because of the part/assembly associativity. If you plan to experiment with rendering, we recommend that you back up your part files in case you need them back with their default settings.

---

***HANDS-ON FOR TUTORIAL 1–6.*** Change the assembly material to Teak Wood and render again.

---

## INDUSTRY CHAT

This section provides practical insight into how the chapter material is used in industry in the real world and practice. We chat with Mr. Joseph (Joe) Fitzpatrick, the lead CAD designer and engineer of VIC.

**Chapter Section 1.2:** The Engineering Design Process shown in Figure 1.1

ABE: Describe the EDP for your product.

JOE: The EDP in VIC begins with a conceptual idea from the chief scientist who is a physicist, mathematician, and engineer. He identifies the problem and conceives a solution. He is responsible for steps 1–3 of the EDP shown in Figure 1.1. The selection of the best solution in step 4 involves the combination of mechanical, electrical, and software decision making. The mechanical decision takes into consideration the manufacturability, cost, and production time of the machine vacuum chamber. Electrical and software groups make similar decisions. In step 4, we create multiple CAD models/designs of the different machines. Some of them may never make it to step 5.

At this point, we construct a real physical prototype (step 5) of the machine electromechanical components that we make in-house. Other components are outsourced to specialized machine shops. The constructed prototype machine is sent to the chief scientist and other in-house experts for testing and evaluation (step 6). We may redesign the machine based on the feedback we receive (step 7). Once the design is finalized in SolidWorks, we create a book that has parts' drawings, parts list, assembly drawing, bill of materials (BOM), and production cost analysis of the machine.

**Chapter Section 1.3:** The CAD Process shown in Figure 1.2

ABE: Describe the CAD process for your product.

JOE: Initial concepts and designs come in as 2D sketches from the chief scientist. It is my responsibility to take these concepts and turn them to real, producible, and manufacturable components at reasonable cost (step 1). Oftentimes, I convert my CAD files to STL files, then use Ion flying simulation software to help us evaluate our assembly and component behaviors (steps 2 and 3). We may redesign, if needed, based on the simulation results (step 4). At last, we produce drawings of the final design (step 5). We send these drawings off for production.

**Chapter Section 1.4:**   The Manufacturing Process shown in Figure 1.3

ABE:   Describe the manufacturing process for your product.

JOE:   I just want to mention that I am not a manufacturing engineer, but our manufacturing engineer Roger will cover this topic.

ROGER:   Each design goes through a design review process (steps 1 and 2) before releasing the design for production. If tolerances do not fit, the project manager marks them in red and the design is revised. Once the design/engineering department releases the drawings of the design, Joe puts them on the network. I go to the network and pull the drawings out and save the SolidWorks files of the drawings in Mastercam, our CNC machining software. I manipulate the part as I need to create the toolpaths and save them in files that I send to the CNC machine tool to cut the part. An example of manipulation is changing the origin of the geometry. Joe creates the parts, in SolidWorks, from the center. So, I orient the part the way I will hold it in the machine, that is, set the origin (0, 0) point, to the upper left corner of the part, which matches the machine. Also, I use multiple levels (layers) in Mastercam to separate the toolpaths; that is, level 1 holds the toolpath to drill holes, level 2 holds the toolpath to mill the part, etc.

I use the toolpaths to make the parts using our machine shop (step 3). After making the parts I bag them by part number and assembly number, so we know which parts belong to which assembly. We inspect parts as we go along (step 4). We use inspection tools such as dial and test indicators to make sure I hit all the dimensions and tolerances. After we assemble the parts (step 5), sometimes we may inspect the assembly (step 6) to make final adjustments. Sometimes we do not know whether we need a fixture to assemble. Other times, the part may too flimsy to hold, so we design and produce a fixture to hold it during assembly.

We package our products in-house (step 7). We make our own crate out of wood and strap it all together to create a palette. We deliver the palette in our company truck (step 8). You could also use FedEx or UPS for ground shipping.

**Chapter Section 1.5:**   The CAM Process shown in Figure 1.4

ABE:   Describe the CAM process for your product.

ROGER:   Our CAM process includes producing CNC toolpaths as described above. I just want to add a few more thoughts. I make sure that we are able to hold the part all the time during machining. Sometimes we change the tolerances, if needed. During machining, I try to hit the middle of the tolerance range. Other times, we may request design changes. However, our rework is little because we can manipulate the part on the screen in SolidWorks in real-time on the fly and catch any problems on paper before we go to production. We also inspect surface finish of some parts such as seals and bearings. We finish the outside-looking surfaces to make them appeal to customers by sanding them or using a chromatic coating. For the toolpaths, I save them on the network for reuse in the future. I can access and edit/modify old programs to cut new parts. I download the toolpaths from Smartcam to the machine tools via RS232 cables.

*(continue)*

**Chapter Section 1.6:** SolidWorks Installation and Resources

**ABE:** How do you install SolidWorks?

**JOE:** We install SolidWorks on our server to make it accessible throughout the company.

**Chapter Section 1.8:** Customize SolidWorks

**ABE:** How do you customize SolidWorks?

**JOE:** Big companies customize CAD processes and settings at the company level so that different CAD designers in different departments use the same templates and standards for compatibility purposes. Small companies give more freedom to their designers to create their personal preferences such as using ANSI Standards of 1982 Y14.5, personalizing settings for parts and drawings templates. Companies use SolidWorks **System Options** tab and **Document Properties** tab accessible from **Tools** menu => **Options** to customize.

**Chapter Section 1.9:** Tutorial Template

**ABE:** What productivity tools do you use?

**JOE:** I use two essentials: templates and a programmable mouse. I set part, drawing, and assembly templates. For the part template, I select units, material (to auto populate properties), decimals, and other document settings. I save all settings to a template for future use. For the drawing template, I save drawing view placement and dimension input. My assembly template is similar to my part template.

The programmable mouse is a big productivity area. Check www.logitech.com for an example. Logitech offers a 13 programmable button mouse or a keyboard/mouse combo. Any of SolidWorks hot keys can be programmed into the mouse, in addition to storing macros on it.

**Extras**

**ABE:** Is there any other experience you would like to share with our readers?

**JOE:** The use of the standard, off-the-shelf mechanical components offers many benefits such as reducing design cost and shortening the design cycle. I usually try to create my CAD designs so that I can use as many off-the-shelf components as possible and avoid using custom parts. Typical components are springs, screws, bearings, gears, etc. Let us select the spring shown in Figure 1.10. In general you can use McMaster-Carr (www.mcmaster.com) or 3D ContentCentral from SolidWorks (www.3dcontentcentral.com). I use McMaster-Carr parts library. To use McMaster-Carr, go to its website and click this sequence: Type "spring" in the search field => Select **Torsion Springs** (for spring type) from search results => **Clockwise (Left Hand) Wound** (for Wind Direction) => **404″** (for Spring Outer Diameter) => **Steel Music Wire** (for Material). This is McMaster part # 9271K182. This is the spring we use in Figure 1.10 for our machine. I downloaded the McMaster 3D model and saved it locally. Now, you drop the part into the assembly, or open as a part in SolidWorks to modify/customize it as needed. For our machine, we turn the ends 90°and trim the ends in-house.

1. Using the EDP process shown in Figure 1.1, reverse engineer your iPod. Apply each step of the EDP to the iPod. For example, in applying Step 1, you ask yourself: what was the market need that led to the conception of the iPod? In applying Step 2, find the market need and why existing products were not good enough. Reverse engineering helps you discover what the iPod design team was thinking. Reverse engineering is a good first step to learn good design methodologies.

2. Same as Problem 1, but for your cell phone.

3. Same as Problem 1, but for a TV/DVD remote control.

4. Apply the EDP steps to design the bookshelf discussed in Section 1.2. Assume the bookshelf consists of a wooden board and two brackets that you nail to the wall to hold the board.

5. Apply the steps of the CAD process (Figure 1.2) to the bookshelf design of Problem 4.

6. Section 1.4 briefly applies the manufacturing process (Figure 1.3) to produce the bookshelf. Elaborate the process by resolving all details and find specific material and cost.

7. The following two designs, shown in Figure 1.33, of a block meet the design functional requirements. Which design you think is better and why?

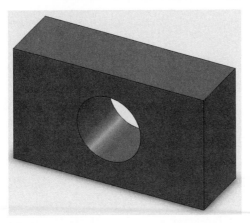 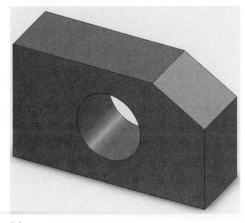

[a]                                    [b]

**FIGURE 1.33**
Two designs of a block

8. Customize your SolidWorks as follows. Under the **System Options** tab, customize the **Drawings**, **Colors**, **Sketch**, **Assemblies**, and **File Locations** to fit your needs. Under the **Document Properties** tab, customize the **Detailing** and **Units**. Change the dimension precision to three decimal places. Save the customization under a new part template, calling it *master*. Submit screenshots of the customization screens.

9. When you open SolidWorks, the default background color of the graphics display area (viewport) is gradient dark gray color. Open the *master.prtdot* template from Problem 8 and customize it further to change the **Viewport Background** color to use these three signals: 244 for Red, 250 for Green, and 255 for Blue. Submit screenshots of the customization screens.

10. Create the SolidWorks part of the chamfered block model shown in Figure 1.34. Also, create the drawing of the part. All dimensions are in mm.

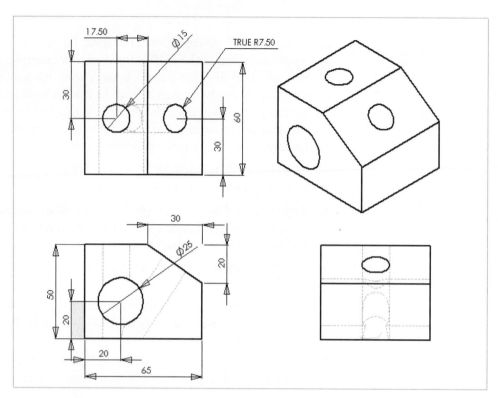

**FIGURE 1.34**
A chamfered block model

11. Create the SolidWorks part of the slotted block model shown in Figure 1.35. Also, create the drawing of the part. All dimensions are in inches.

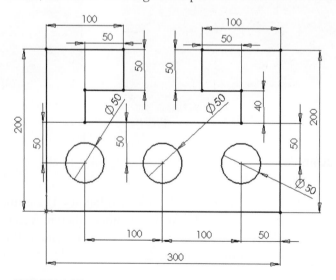

**FIGURE 1.35**
A slotted block model

12. Create the SolidWorks part of the slotted block model shown in Figure 1.36. Use an extrusion depth of 100 mm. All dimensions are in mm. Also, create the drawing of the part.

Part I Computer Aided Design (CAD) Basics

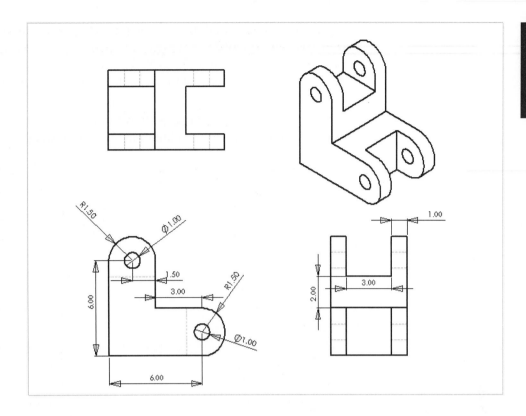

**FIGURE 1.36**
A slotted block model

13. The three parts shown in Figure 1.37 make an assembly. The pin holds the plate and the base together. All dimensions are in inches. Perform the following modeling tasks:
   **A.** Create the three individual SolidWorks parts.
   **B.** Create the assembly model.

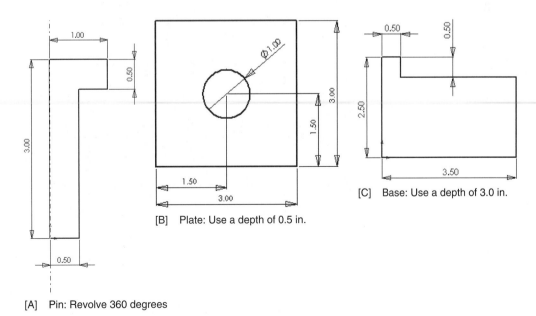

[B]  Plate: Use a depth of 0.5 in.

[C]  Base: Use a depth of 3.0 in.

[A]  Pin: Revolve 360 degrees

**FIGURE 1.37**
Three-parts assembly

C. Create an assembly drawing.

D. Create an exploded view.

E. Create an animation of the exploded view.

F. Create a visual realism of the exploded view. Use Aluminum Alloy 6061 as material.

14. Create realistic rendering of parts shown in Figures 1.34 to 1.37. Use a material of your choice, for example, aluminum alloy, steel, wood, plastic, etc.

# Construction Management

## 2.1 Overview

We provided an overview of SolidWorks in Chapter 1 as well as some tutorials that cover the essential tasks of SolidWorks: CAD modeling, engineering drawings, assembly modeling, and model rendering and visualization. The goal was to get you to practice CAD tasks firsthand rather than talk about them. Chapter 2 covers the concepts of CAD modeling and explains the basics of each.

CAD modeling is an extensive activity that requires forward thinking and planning ahead. The way the CAD model (part) is created affects its downstream activities and applications such as generating NC toolpaths. These applications usually follow the hierarchy of the part features tree to perform their tasks. Chapter 1 showed how part construction affects the ways we dimension it and create the assembly.

Managing the construction of a CAD model in SolidWorks has many facets, from selecting construction planes to using geometric constraints. This chapter covers these facets. Its goal is twofold: to enable you to (1) understand and control part construction and modeling, and (2) understand and explain SolidWorks modeling activities, menus, and actions.

## 2.2 Types of CAD Models

CAD models can be classified into four types from a construction point of view:

□ **Extrusion:** This is a part with a fixed cross section along a given axis, with a given thickness along this axis.
□ **Revolve:** This is an axisymmetric part with a fixed cross section through an angle of revolution about a given axis of revolution.
□ **Composite:** This combines both extrusions and revolves. One or more of its sub-parts may be extrusions or revolves.
□ **Free form:** This has a shape that does not exhibit any uniform shape. An auto body or a computer mouse is an example. Modeling of this class of parts requires surfaces and other techniques as we discuss later in the book.

Figure 2.1 shows the different types of CAD models. The extrusions and revolve require one sketch in one sketching plane to sketch the cross section. For example, the Figure 2.1A extrusion requires the top sketch plane to sketch the cross section, followed by extruding it in the perpendicular direction. For the Figure 2.1B extrusion, we create

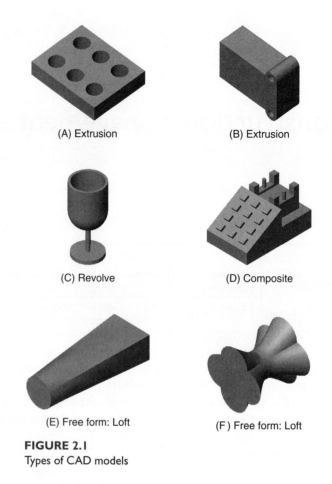

(A) Extrusion            (B) Extrusion

(C) Revolve            (D) Composite

(E) Free form: Loft            (F) Free form: Loft

**FIGURE 2.1**
Types of CAD models

the cross section in the front sketch plane. For the revolve of Figure 2.1C, we create the glass cross section and the axis of revolution in the front sketch plane. The phone model shown in Figure 2.1D is a composite part. It consists of two extrusions (the base and the receiver holder). The two cylinders can be created as additional extrusions. Finally, we can add the phone buttons as a pattern.

The two models shown in Figures 2.1E and 2.1F are free-form requiring more than one sketch in different sketch planes. We use advanced operations such as loft and sweeps to create them.

## 2.3 Planning Part Construction

Planning the construction of a part model can be simple or complex. In either case, some planning is required to make modeling efficient. No planning at all is not a good practice, and overplanning is not either. Somewhere between these two extremes is desirable. Planning usually comes with experience; the more you know about what a CAD/CAM system can do, the faster and more efficiently you can create models. The way you construct a model may be viewed as a personal preference and is also tied to the nature of the part design at hand. CAD managers in companies typically develop best practice guidelines for their CAD designers to follow.

When it comes to planning part construction on a CAD system, the best approach is to examine the part for geometric clues that may lead you to the easiest and fastest steps to create the CAD model. Table 2.1 shows some of these clues.

| TABLE 2.1 | Planning Part Construction on a CAD/CAM System |
|---|---|
| **Part Clue** | **How to Use in Part Construction on CAD System** |
| Part type | • Extrusion: create a sketch and extrude it<br>• Revolve: create a sketch and revolve it<br>• Composite: use a combination of extrusions and/or revolves<br>• Free form: use lofts, sweeps, surfaces, etc. |
| Part symmetry | • Split the part into two halves at the symmetry plane<br>• Construct one half and mirror it about the symmetry plane to finish the creation of the CAD model |
| Part patterns | If they exist (e.g., holes in a flange or phone buttons), use CAD patterns to create them (see this chapter) |
| Designated points | Make use of end-, mid-, and/or intersection points of entities during construction to avoid unnecessary calculations. SolidWorks snaps to these points when you move the mouse close to them, or hover the mouse over them, during construction |
| Geometric constraints | These include parallelism, concentricity, etc. SolidWorks has a library of them |
| Relations | These include proportions such as $D_1 = 2D_2$. SolidWorks allows you to create your own relations |
| Center planes for features | When you break the part into features to begin construction, always build features off center, i.e., use mid-planes. When you extrude a sketch, extrude it on both sides of the sketch plane. This strategy is good for mirror; use the sketch plane to mirror (see Chapter 1 tutorials). It also makes changes and part evolution easy |
| Miscellaneous | • Avoid measuring from corners; measure from mid-planes<br>• If you do not have dimensions, sketch freely<br>• Trim entities to clean up construction and avoid calculations<br>• Use transformations (move, rotate, copy, scale, offset) to speed up construction |

**Example 2.1**    What is the best modeling plan to use to create the CAD model shown in Figure 2.2? Why?

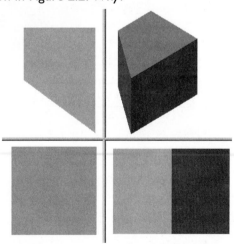

**FIGURE 2.2**
A sliced block

**Solution**    If we realize that the cross section is the one in the top view, then it is a simple extrusion; but if we create a rectangle in the front view and extrude it, then a cut is also required for the tapered face, making the model creation more complex.

     Thus, it is important to visualize/interpret whether a model can be created as an extrusion/revolve because this affects the ease of its creation; that is, the use of simpler/lesser commands versus advanced/complex commands.

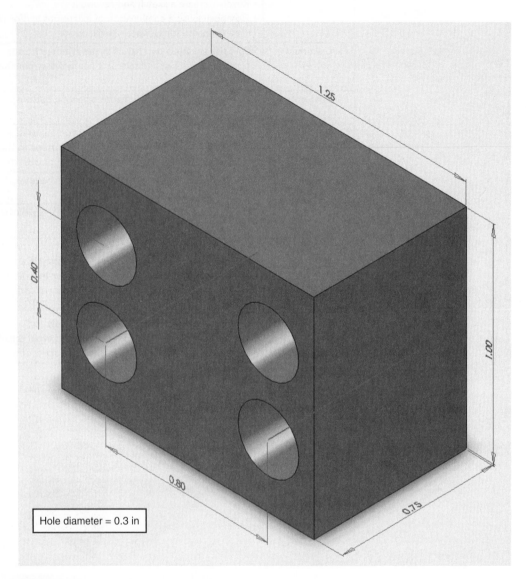

Hole diameter = 0.3 in

**FIGURE 2.3**
A block with four holes

**Solution**   The key modeling concept here is how to create the four holes in the block so that they are always equally placed from the four corners of the front face of the block, as shown in Figure 2.3; that is, the holes are always equally placed diagonally from the center of the front face. Such placement should hold even after you change the size of the block (dimensions 1.25 and 1.00) or the spacing (dimensions 0.80 and 0.40) between the holes.

The modeling plan has two steps: create the block feature and then create the four holes.

**Step 1:** Create the block feature shown in Figure 2.4

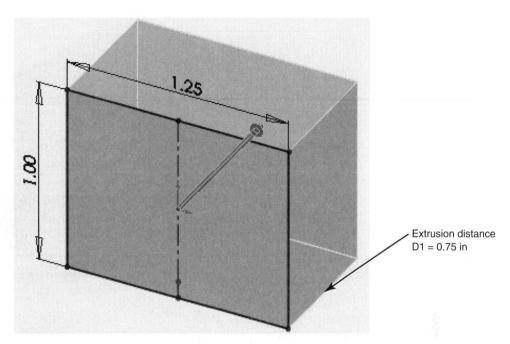

Extrusion distance
D1 = 0.75 in

**FIGURE 2.4**
Create the solid block

| Task | Command Sequence to Click |
|---|---|
| A. Start SolidWorks and open a new part file. Change the part units to inches. Save the file as *example 2.2*. | **File => New => Part => OK** <br> **File => Save As** *=> example 2.2 =>* **Save** |
| B. Select the front plane as the sketch plane. | **Front Plane** from features manager tree on left of screen |
| C. Select extrusion as the feature type to create. | **Extruded Boss/Base** from the **Features** tab to start sketching |
| D. Sketch the cross section shown in Figure 2.4. | Click the rectangle symbol on the **Sketch** tab => Sketch and dimension the rectangle shown in Figure 2.4. |
| E. Anchor the rectangle to the origin of the sketch. <br> 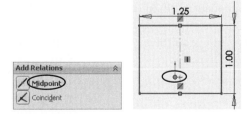 | Create the vertical centerline that passes through the midpoints of the two horizontal sides of the rectangle (shown to the left) => Select the origin of the coordinate system (simply click it) => Hold down the **CTRL** key and select the centerline => Select the **Midpoint** option under **Add Relations** section in the **Properties** window that opens as shown to the left. |
| F. Exit the sketch. | **Exit Sketch** icon on **Sketch** toolbar |
| G. Create the extrusion. | Input 0.75 in. for **D1** => Green check mark to finish. |

## Step 2: Create the four holes shown in Figure 2.5

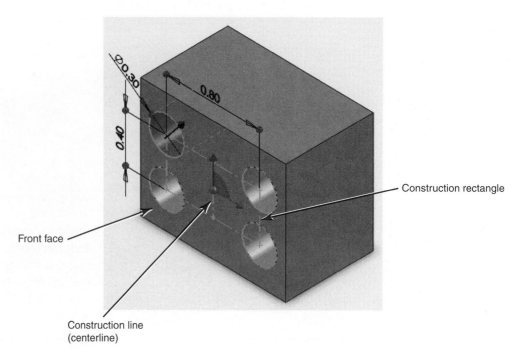

Construction rectangle

Front face

Construction line
(centerline)

**FIGURE 2.5**
Create the four holes

| Task | Command Sequence to Click |
|---|---|
| A. Select the sketch plane. | Front face of the block |
| B. Select the feature type to create. | **Extruded Cut** from the **Features** tab |
| C. Sketch a construction rectangle to position the holes. 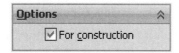 | **Rectangle** from **Sketch** toolbar => Drag the mouse and sketch a rectangle => Select **For construction** check box under **Options** in the left pane on screen (shown to the left) => Right-click and select **Smart Dimension** => Add the dimensions shown in Figure 2.5. **Why:** We use a construction rectangle, and not a rectangle, because the rectangle is not part of the block geometry. |
| D. Create vertical construction line (centerline) to anchor the construction rectangle to the origin. | Repeat Task E of Step 1. **Why:** We anchor both rectangles of Steps 1 and 2 to the origin so they both stay in same position relative to each other. If you edit either and change its dimensions, the holes will stay equally placed from the corners of the outer rectangle of Step 1. |
| E. Create four circles, one at each corner of the construction rectangle. Note, you can create a Center | **Circle** from **Sketch** toolbar => Move mouse near a corner until it is highlighted (indicating circle center is |

| Task | Command Sequence to Click |
|---|---|
| Rectangle (shown below) to replace Tasks C and D. | located there) => Click mouse => Draw a circle by dragging the mouse => Click mouse to release the tool => Input 0.15 in. for radius under **Parameters** in the left pane on screen => Green check mark to finish. Repeat to create the other three circles. |

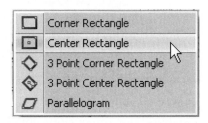

| | |
|---|---|
| | **Why:** Although we could have used a linear pattern to create the four holes, we did not. Our rule of thumb is that creating four or fewer holes is not worth using linear patterns. We would use a linear pattern to create the six holes of the block shown in Figure 2.1A. |
| F. Exit sketch. | **Exit Sketch** icon on **Sketch** toolbar |
| G. Create the holes. | Select **Up To Surface** option under **Direction 1** (shown to the left) => Orient view to pick back face of block => Green check mark. |

## 2.4 Part Construction

Creating a CAD model (part) is the first task we accomplish on a CAD system. The models we create using CAD/CAM systems are solid models; this is where Solid-Works got its name. A **solid model** is a geometric model of a part and represents the most complete definition of the part. A solid model is also known as a body (B). A solid model consists of faces (F), edges (E), vertices (V), loops (L), and genus (G). A **face** is a surface and may be planar or nonplanar. An **edge** is a curve that may be a line. A **vertex** is a point (corner). Faces meet (intersect) at edges and edges meet (intersect) at vertices. Figure 2.6 shows the solid model of a block. A **loop** is a set of contiguous edges in a face. A loop is viewed as a hole in a face. For example, the left face shown in Figure 2.6 has five loops: the four holes and the bounding rectangle of the face. A **genus** is a through hole in a solid. A genus is viewed as a 3D hole. For example, the solid model shown in Figure 2.6 has four genus.

The above model description is known as the model topology. The topology of a valid (correct) solid model must satisfy Euler equation given by:

$$F - E + V - L = 2(B - G) \qquad (2.1)$$

The solid model shown in Figure 2.6 has the following topology: $F = 6$, $E = 12$, $V = 8$, $L = 8$, $B = 1$, and $G = 4$. This topology satisfies Eq. (2.1). Therefore the model is a valid model. Obviously, CAD/CAM systems create only valid solid models.

CAD modeling utilizes both three-dimensional (3D) modeling and 3D viewing concepts. Understanding how to use the 3D modeling space effectively is crucial to mastering CAD/CAM systems and using them to their fullest potential. The remainder of the chapter covers these concepts in detail and shows how SolidWorks implements them.

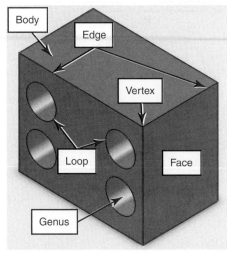

**FIGURE 2.6**
Solid model of a block

## 2.5 Parametric Modeling

CAD modeling is based on the concept of parametric modeling (parametrics). Solid-Works, like other contemporary CAD/CAM systems, uses parameters to define the model, instead of specific explicit dimensions. When we assign values to the parameters of a model, these values define the specific size of the model and become the model dimensions that a CAD system uses to generate the model drawings. You may change the values of the parameters later, and the CAD system will update the model to reflect the modifications.

The great virtue of parametric modeling is the ease of editing. Figure 2.7 shows the difference between parameters and dimensions for a simple rectangle sketch. A **parameter** is a variable that can assume any value. A **dimension** is a specific numerical value for a parameter. Parametric modeling offers three benefits. First, you sketch freely in a sketch plane. As you sketch, the CAD system creates parameters and assigns them values (dimensions). When done sketching, you may edit the dimensions as needed. You can display the names of the parameters and edit their names. The CAD system stores and manages the parameters and their values. Second, as Figure 2.7 shows, parametric modeling provides the ability to create a family of parts in which all the parts have identical shapes with different dimensions. Third, you can create relations between parameters to control the geometry of the sketch. These relations add design intent or intelligence to the model design.

The concept of parametric modeling is liberating during conceptual design; it gives you, the designer, incredible flexibility and power. All you need to do is sketch the model without worrying about dimensions. Once you like a sketch, you assign dimensions to the sketch entities and update (regenerate) the sketch. If you do not like the way the sketch looks, you change the dimensions and update the sketch again. Thus, we can start sketching and modeling without a need for dimensions, or with just minimal dimensions up front. You can actually use the sketch to define the appropriate values for the missing dimensions.

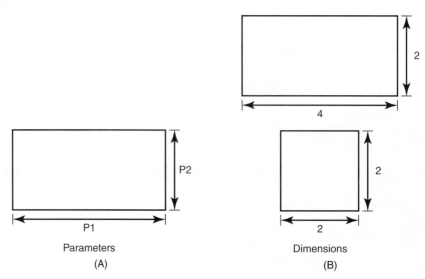

**FIGURE 2.7**
Parameters and dimensions for a rectangle sketch

**Example 2.3** Use parametric modeling. Figure 2.8 shows a sketch.

1. Create the sketch in SolidWorks.
2. Modify the dimensions of the sketch.
3. Change the dimension names.

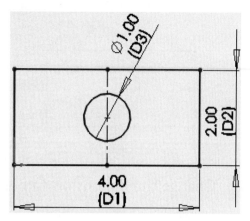

**FIGURE 2.8**
A sketch

**Solution** This example illustrates how to use SolidWorks to apply the parametric concepts. For (A), we sketch freely and then dimension the sketch. We also display the parameters. SolidWorks calls the parameters **dimension names**. For (B), Solid-Works regenerates each dimension we modify immediately after we input a new value. The idea behind (C) is to change the dimension names to something more meaningful to the design. We may use the names to create relations and constraints. Here are the modeling steps.

## Step 1: Create the sketch shown in Figure 2.8

| Task | Command Sequence to Click |
|---|---|
| A. Start SolidWorks and open a new part file. Change the part units to inches. Save the file as *example 2.3*. | **File => New => Part => OK** **File => Save As** => *example 2.3* => **Save** |
| B. Select the front plane as the sketch plane. | **Front Plane** from features manager tree on left of screen |
| C. Start sketching. | **Features** tab |
| D. Sketch the rectangle shown in Figure 2.8. Anchor the rectangle at the origin as shown in Figure 2.8, or create a Center Rectangle at the origin. | Rectangle symbol on the **Sketch** tab => Hover the mouse over the origin until you snap there => Sketch and dimension the rectangle shown in Figure 2.8. Create the vertical centerline that passes through the midpoints of the two horizontal sides of the rectangle (Figure 2.8) => Click the circle symbol on the **Sketch** tab => Hover the mouse over the centerline until you snap to its midpoint => Sketch and dimension the circle shown in Figure 2.8. |
| E. Sketch the circle shown in Figure 2.8. Anchor the circle at the center of the rectangle. Note, if you created a Center Rectangle, you would not need the vertical centerline of this step. | |
| F. Show dimension names. | **View** menu => **Dimension Names**. **Help: Dimension Names** is a toggle; click again to see. |

## Step 2: Modify the dimensions of the sketch

| Task | Command Sequence to Click |
|---|---|
| A. Edit the sketch dimensions to double its size. | Double-click any dimension => Input a new dimension value (shown to the left) => Green check mark. **Why:** The center of the hole remains at the rectangle center because the centerline always passes by the midpoints of the rectangle sides. |

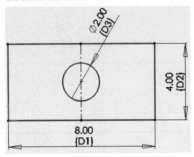

## Step 3: Change the dimension names

| Task | Command Sequence to Click |
|---|---|
| A. Change SolidWorks default dimension names. | Click any dimension => Replace the default name under **Primary Value** shown to the left with a name of your choice => Green check mark to finish. Replace **D1@Sketch1**, **D2@Sketch1**, and **D3@Sketch1**, respectively, with **width**, **height**, and **diameter**. **Why:** If you click a dimension again, you see SolidWorks has added the **@Sketch1** to each name you input. SolidWorks does that to associate a dimension to a sketch. |

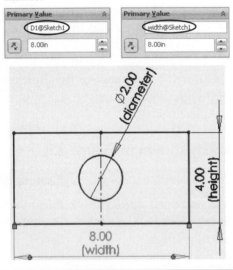

## 2.6 Customizing SolidWorks

SolidWorks allows you to customize just about anything of its main window shown in Figure 1.7. Click **Tools => Customize** to open SolidWorks **Customize** window in Figure 2.9. We encourage you to explore the many options and tabs that the annotations of Figure 2.9 suggest. You can figure out all the options shown in Figure 2.9 on your own by trying them. Here we explain the context toolbar, which appears when you select an entity, multiple entities via the **CTRL** key, or a group of entities via a window selection (click mouse and drag to define a window). The context toolbar also pops up when you right-click the entity. It is context sensitive in that the toolbar shows only the options that are applicable to the entity you select. For example, if you click a line, the line context toolbar pops up next to the line. Hover over its icons to read them, for example, **Make Horizontal**, **Make Vertical**, etc. Think of the context toolbar as a menu on the go, available to you near where you are sketching. The context toolbar disappears when you move the mouse too far away from the selected entity. Click the entity again to bring it back.

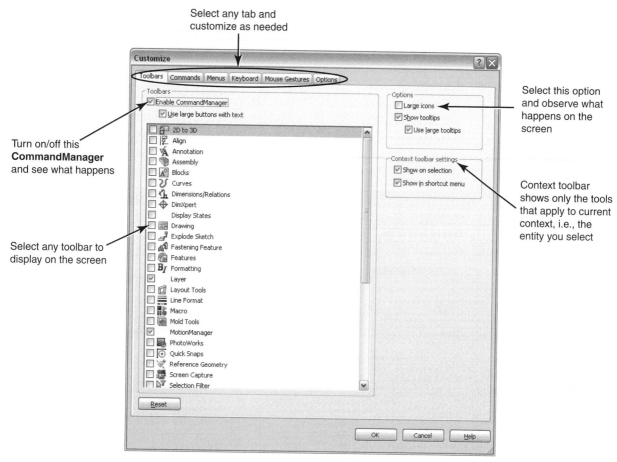

Select any tab and customize as needed

Turn on/off this **CommandManager** and see what happens

Select any toolbar to display on the screen

Select this option and observe what happens on the screen

Context toolbar shows only the tools that apply to current context, i.e., the entity you select

**FIGURE 2.9**
SolidWorks **Customize** window

**Help:** Microsoft Office 2007 uses context toolbars also. Select some text and watch a context toolbar pop up. Also, click a table or text box and observe a context tab shown at the top of the Word window. When you click the tab, a context toolbar opens up.

In addition to covering the context toolbar, we discuss menu customization. You can customize any SolidWorks menu in two ways:

1. **Quick customize:** Here, you turn on/off item(s) of a menu. SolidWorks has multiple menus, as shown in Figure 2.10. The last menu item on each menu is

**FIGURE 2.10**
SolidWorks **Customize** menus: Quick customize

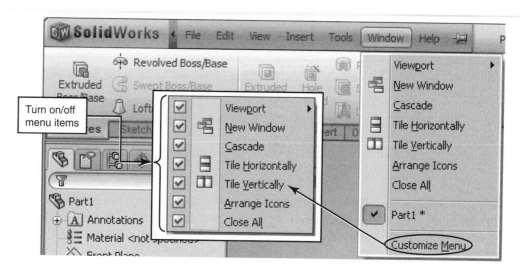

Turn on/off menu items

**Customize Menu**. When you click this item, the menu items of the menu you are in appear again, as shown in Figure 2.10, this time with the ability to turn them on/off. Now, turn on/off any menu items. When done, click anywhere on the screen to exit. Now, click on the menu again to see the results of the changes you just made.

2. **Detailed customize:** Here, you can rename menu items, change their order on the menu, or remove them from the menu, as shown in Figure 2.11. Click **Tools => Customize** => select the **Menus** tab (from the window that pops up), as shown in Figure 2.11, to customize menus in detail.

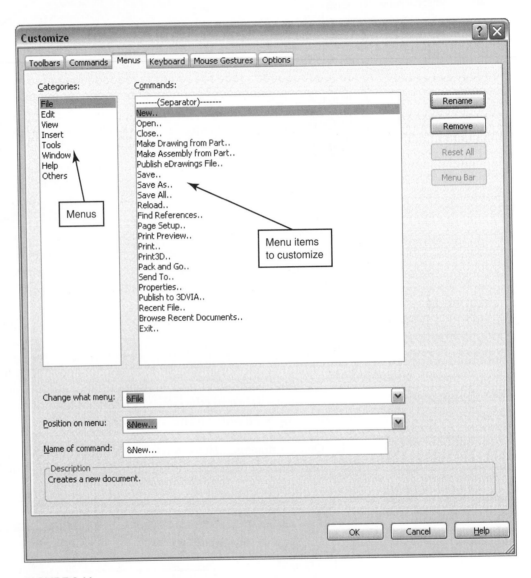

**FIGURE 2.11**
SolidWorks **Customize** menus: Detailed customize

## 2.7 Productivity Tools

We define a productivity tool as an operation or function that speeds accomplishing your design and other tasks in SolidWorks. These diverse tools include customizing SolidWorks, hot keys, programmable mouse, templates, layers, visualization, macros, family of parts, and libraries. The **hot keys** are the keystrokes that correspond to commands. For example, like Word, **CTRL+S** saves the document and **CTRL+P** prints the document. You see these hot keys next to the commands of any menu. As you learn the commands, you learn the hot keys. A **programmable mouse** is a mouse with multiple buttons whereby a CAD designer may program each button to do a CAD task. A button may perform one command or a sequence of commands. Clicking a mouse button may be faster for some people than using the hot keys on a keyboard or clicking items from menus or icons on toolbars. We cover the remaining productivity tools (templates, etc.) throughout the book as we need them.

## 2.8 Coordinate Systems

CAD systems use two coordinate systems to make part modeling easy and convenient for CAD designers. The first system is the model coordinate system (MCS). The **MCS** is the reference system that the CAD system uses to store the model geometry in the part file. The MCS is defined by the CAD system, and its location and orientation in space cannot be changed by the user (CAD designer). A CAD system uses its MCS to define its default (predefined) sketch planes (top, front, and right) and its default (predefined) views (top, front, right, etc.). The MCS is an orthogonal coordinate system defined by three orthogonal planes that intersect at the system axes: X, Y, and Z. An MCS assumes one of two orientations in a CAD system. In one, the XY plane of the MCS defines the horizontal plane (top sketch plane) and the top view; in the other, the XY plane defines the vertical plane (front sketch plane) and the front view. SolidWorks uses the latter orientation for its MCS, as shown in Figure 2.12.

The second system is the working coordinate system (WCS). The **WCS** is a coordinate system that facilitates model construction and creation. It is a user-defined system. The user may define a WCS anytime during model construction. However, only one WCS is active at any one time. The sketch plane is the XY plane of the current WCS. As the user sketches on the sketch plane, the CAD system keeps track of the transformation back and forth between the WCS and MCS coordinates. It converts the WCS coordinates into MCS coordinates and stores them in the part file. The WCS is related to the

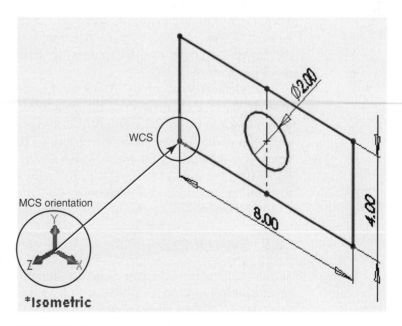

**FIGURE 2.12**
Relating WCS to MCS in SolidWorks

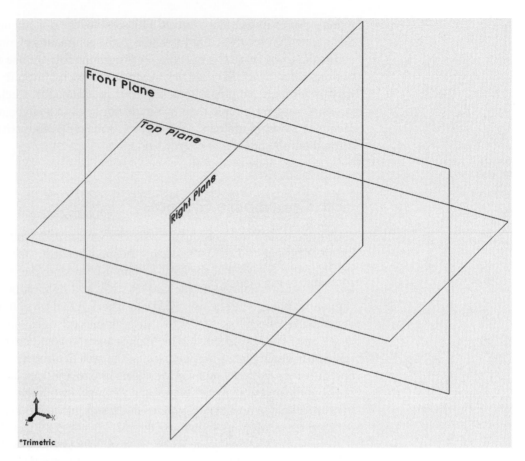

**FIGURE 2.13**
Default sketch planes of SolidWorks

MCS via the location of its origin and its orientation, as shown in Figure 2.12. Note that the origins of the MCS and WCS shown in Figure 2.12 are actually coincident and are located at the origin of the WCS. We use the shown MCS for illustrative purposes only. The CAD system displays the *X*- and *Y*-axes of the WCS only. The *Z*-axis is perpendicular to the XY plane with a positive direction defined by the right-hand rule. In terms of the day-to-day jargon of CAD systems, we hardly use the word *WCS*. We always use *sketch plane* instead.

The **default WCS** of a CAD system has the same orientation and location as its MCS. In the case of SolidWorks, the default WCS is the one that uses the front sketch plane shown in Figure 2.13. SolidWorks also offers the top and the right sketch planes as default sketch planes. Each one defines its corresponding WCS that has a different orientation than that of the MCS. Sketch the *X*-, *Y*-, and *Z*-axes for each of these three WCSs (that correspond to front, top, and right sketch planes of SolidWorks) to ensure that you understand these orientations.

## 2.9 Sketch Planes

Sketch planes control the part construction in the CAD 3D modeling space. You always begin by selecting a sketch plane, as we have done in Chapter 1, to create the cross section (sketch) of the feature you wish to create. The sketch is the basis for 3D modeling. If you need multiple sketch planes to create a 3D model, you select one at a time, create the sketch, and finish the feature before selecting another sketch plane to create another

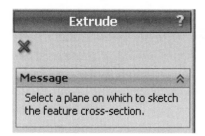

**FIGURE 2.14**
An error message

feature. If you try to create a feature without selecting a sketch plane, Solid-Works will display the error message shown in Figure 2.14. The three default sketch planes are **Front Plane, Top Plane**, and **Right Plane** (see Figure 2.13). If you need a sketch plane in a different orientation, you must create it (see Section 2.13). You can also select any face of any feature as a sketch plane. Simply click the face to begin creating a sketch.

The very first sketch plane that you use to create a feature determines its orientation in the 3D modeling space. This, in turn, affects the views of the model that you insert in engineering drawings. You need to align the orientation, in the 3D modeling space, of the 3D model of a part with the physical or perceived orientation of the actual part. You simply use the corresponding sketch plane to create the cross section of the part; that is, use the front sketch plane to create the part front cross section, the top sketch plane to create the top cross section, etc. If you use the front sketch plane to create the top cross section, you effectively have rotated the model 90 degrees in the 3D modeling space. Thus, the top view of the physical part becomes the front view of the model. Figure 2.15 shows an example.

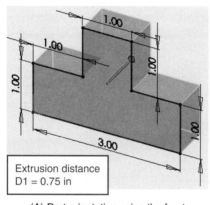

(A) Part orientation using the front sketch plane

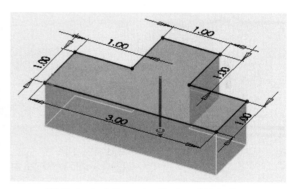

(B) Part orientation using the top sketch plane

**FIGURE 2.15**
Effect of first sketch plane on part orientation in 3D modeling space

There are ways to get around this misorientation of the model in the 3D modeling space due to starting with the incorrect sketch plane. One inefficient way is to delete the model and re-create it using the correct sketch plane. A better way is to reorient the model in the space. Click this sequence: Right-click the sketch in the features tree => **Edit Sketch Plane** from the context menu that pops up (hover over the second symbol from the left on the top row) => Expand the features tree => Select the plane you want (e.g., **Top Plane**) => Green check mark to finish. The model view(s) on the screen confirm the results. Drawing views also confirm the results.

When you sketch, you want the sketch plane to be perpendicular to the line of sight; that is, the sketch plane aligns with the screen of your computer monitor to be able to see the sketch entities you create. This would require you to align the view with the sketch plane. For example, if you want to sketch on the front sketch plane, select (click) it from the features tree => Click the **Normal To** icon (hover until you read it) from the context toolbar that pops up shown in Figure 2.16.

**FIGURE 2.16**
Orient sketch plane

A sketch plane could be an imaginary plane, like the ones SolidWorks provides (Front, Top, or Right), or it could be an actual face of a feature. In either case, select and orient it to begin sketching on it. If the sketch plane is not directly accessible to select it, change the view orientation, as we have done in Chapter 1 tutorials.

## 2.10 Sketch Status

A **sketch status** is defined as the geometric state of a sketch. After you create a sketch, you add dimensions to its parameters before you create the feature that uses the sketch. The sketch status assumes one of three states. A **fully defined** sketch means the sketch is dimensioned and constrained correctly. This is the ideal status. An **under-defined** sketch lacks necessary dimensions and/or geometric constraints. An **over-defined** sketch has more dimensions/constraints than what it needs. You should not create a feature without a fully defined sketch. SolidWorks uses color and text clues and text to convey the sketch status to the designer. Figure 2.17 shows the three SolidWorks sketch statuses. It uses a black color for a fully defined sketch. It uses a blue color to display the entities that are not properly defined in an under-defined sketch. It uses a combination of red/yellow colors and a warning to convey an over-defined sketch. In the case of Figure 2.17B, the blue entity is under defined because its location is vague. We need to dimension the far leftmost edge, as shown in Figure 2.17A.

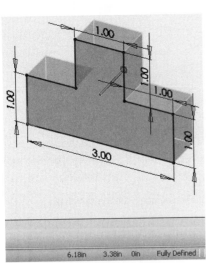

(A) Fully defined sketch

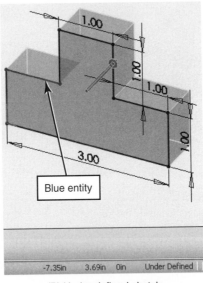

(B) Under-defined sketch

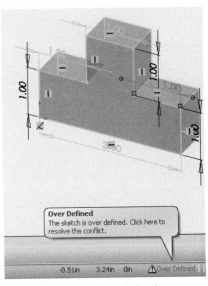

(C) Over-defined sketch

**FIGURE 2.17**
Sketch status

## 2.11 Three-Dimensional Sketching

The majority of the sketching we do is known as 2D sketching; you define a planar (2D) sketch plane and you sketch. That is what we have done in Chapter 1 tutorials and in this chapter so far. Another sketching concept is 3D sketching whereby you sketch in 3D space, not on a sketch plane. 3D sketching is uncommon and hard to use. 3D sketching cannot be used to create features. Actually, the 3D sketching option disappears from the SolidWorks menu when you begin to create a feature. It is mainly used to sketch 3D curves that are used as guide curves for sweep or loft operations, or for creating routing systems. We use the composite curve concept instead of 3D sketching here and cover 3D curves later in the book. If you are interested in trying out 3D sketching, open a new part and click this sequence: **Sketch** tab => **Sketch** drop-down => **3D sketch**. Once the 3D sketch opens, you select an entity (e.g., a line) and start sketching it along the coordinate axes. Pressing the **TAB** key allows the user to toggle between model planes, that is, XY, XZ, and YZ.

Part I Computer Aided Design (CAD) Basics

# 2.12 Construction Geometry

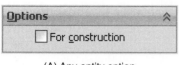

(A) Any entity option

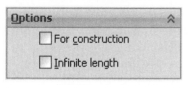

(B) Line option

**FIGURE 2.18**
Construction geometry option

When you create a sketch, you may need auxiliary geometry to assist in creating the sketch entities. Such geometry is known as *construction* geometry. Sketch entities only become part of the feature under construction. Construction geometry is ignored when the sketch is used to create a feature. Any entity you sketch can become construction geometry if you check off the **For construction** option in the left pane (**PropertyManager**) of SolidWorks window and shown here in Figure 2.18A. Check off the option after you create the entity. If you check the option again, the entity reverts back to a sketch entity. When you sketch a line, you have the option to create a centerline under the line icon on the **Sketch** tab; alternatively, you may sketch a line and then check off its option (Figure 2.18B).

Points and centerlines are always construction entities. Construction geometry uses the same line style as centerlines. Examples of using construction geometry include an axis of revolution to create a revolve feature, a circular axis to place holes (circular pattern) in a flange, etc. Figure 2.5 shows a construction rectangle and a construction line to place the four holes of the CAD part.

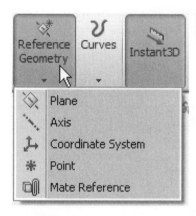

**FIGURE 2.19**
Reference geometry

## 2.13 Reference Geometry

Reference geometry, as construction geometry, is part of a feature definition, but not part of the feature geometry. Reference geometry is used to define construction geometry. Whereas construction geometry belongs to sketch creation, reference geometry belongs to feature creation. As such, construction geometry (e.g., centerline) is available on the **Sketch** tab of SolidWorks, whereas reference geometry is available on the **Features** tab under **Reference Geometry** drop-down shown in Figure 2.19. The figure shows the reference geometry that you can create and use. The various methods of creating any of these reference geometry entities are shown in Figure 2.20.

We cover each of the **Reference Geometry** entities shown in Figure 2.19. You create a plane (Figure 2.20A) in any location at any orientation to use as a

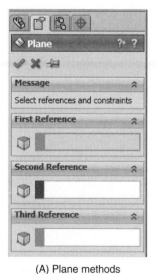

(A) Plane methods

(B) Axis methods

(C) Coordinate system methods

(D) Point methods

**FIGURE 2.20**
Methods to create reference geometry

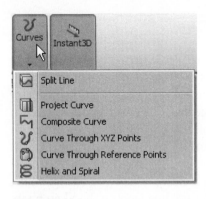

**FIGURE 2.21**
Curves through points

sketch plane if one of SolidWorks default sketch planes (Front, Top, or Right) is not adequate. You can also use a plane to create a sectional view of a model in a drawing, or for mirroring (see Step 5.3 of Tutorial 1–3 in Chapter 1). You can create an axis using the methods shown in Figure 2.20B. You can define a coordinate system (Figure 2.20C) to use to measure from, to calculate mass properties, or to export SolidWorks documents to graphics standards such as IGES, STL, STEP, etc. Reference points are useful to use to create a curve. Mate reference allows you to assemble standard parts such as nuts and bolts into an assembly by dragging and dropping the part from a features palette onto the assembly. We cover mate reference in more detail in the assemblies chapter of the book.

Figure 2.20D shows that reference points can only be created using already existing entities of a part. There is also a point option on the **Sketch** tab. That is a point you can create without a need for existing entities. You need a sketch plane to create a sketch point. Reference or sketch points can be used to create an open or closed curve passing through them via using the **Curves** drop-down on the **Features** tab shown in Figure 2.21. Use the **Curve Through Reference Points** option. The curve may be planar (2D curve) or nonplanar (3D curve) depending on whether the reference points are planar or not. You must exit the sketch to create a curve passing through sketch points. A curve passing through sketch points is inherently a 2D curve because all the sketch points defining it are planar, belonging to their sketch plane.

---

**Example 2.4** Create the part shown in Figure 2.22.

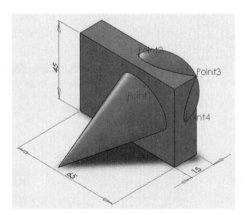

**FIGURE 2.22**
Two-feature part

**Solution** This example illustrates the use of both reference and sketch points in creating parts. The part consists of two features: a block and cone-like feature. **Point1** through **Point4** are reference points and the tip of the cone-like feature is a sketch point. **Point1**, **Point2**, and **Point4** are the center points of their respective faces. **Point3** is a corner point. The modeling plan has two steps:

1. Create the block feature.
2. Create the cone-like feature.

The details of these steps are shown below.

## Step 1:  Create the block feature shown in Figure 2.22

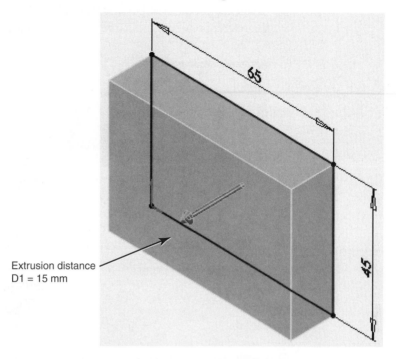

Extrusion distance
D1 = 15 mm

| Task | Command Sequence to Click |
|---|---|
| A. Start SolidWorks and open a new part file. Change the part units to inches. Save the file as *example 2.4*. | **File => New => Part => OK**<br>**File => Save As** *=> example 2.4 =>* **Save** |
| B. Select the front plane as the sketch plane. | **Front Plane** from features manager tree on left of screen |
| C. Select extrusion as the feature type to create. | **Extruded Boss/Base** from the **Features** tab to start sketching |
| D. Sketch the cross section shown. | Rectangle symbol on the **Sketch** tab => Sketch and dimension the rectangle shown. |
| E. Exit the sketch. | **Exit Sketch** icon on **Sketch** toolbar |
| F. Create the extrusion. | Input 15 mm for **D1** => Green check mark to finish. |

## Step 2:  Create the cone-like feature shown in Figure 2.22

| Task | Command Sequence to Click |
|---|---|
| A. Create the four reference points. | **Reference Geometry** drop-down on **Features** tab => **Point** => **Center of Face** option (see Figure 2.20D) => Front face of block => Green check mark. This creates **Point1**. Repeat to create **Point2** (center of block top face) and **Point4** (center of block right face). Use this sequence to create **Point3**: **Intersection** option (see Figure 2.20D) |

| Task | Command Sequence to Click |
|---|---|
| | => Any edge passing through **Point3** => Another edge. |
| B. Create a closed curve passing through the reference points. | **Curves** drop-down (see Figure 2.21) => **Curve Through Reference Points** => Select the four points => Check off the **Closed curve** option (shown to the left) = Green check mark. |
| 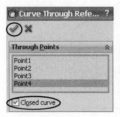 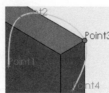 | **Help:** It turns out that the curve is planar. You can prove this claim (not covered here) using the coordinates of the four points and the parametric equation of a plane. Using the coordinate system at the back bottom left corner of the block of Step 1, the $(x, y, z)$ coordinates are **Point1** (32.5, 22.5, 15), **Point2** (32.5, 45, 7.5), **Point3** (65, 45, 0), and **Point4** (65, 22.5, 7.5). |
| C. Create the sketch point. | Select front face of block of Step 1 => **Point** from **Sketch** toolbar => Click the mouse somewhere on the screen in a location similar to that shown in Figure 2.22 => Exit the sketch. |
| D. Create a loft connecting the curve and the sketch point. A **loft** is a feature that blends two or more curves. | **Lofted Boss/Base** from **Features** tab => The curve => The sketch point => Green check mark. |
| 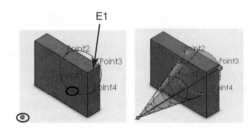 | **Why:** Create a reference point at the middle of edge E1 shown to the left. Using the **Distance** option (last option shown in Figure 2.20D), input 7.5 and select **E1**. Create a curve connecting the reference points **Point1**, **Point2**, the new midpoint, and **Point4** (in this order). The new curve is not planar. You can prove this claim (not covered here) using the coordinates of the four points and the parametric equation of a plane. If you use the curve with the sketch point to create a loft, the operation fails because the loft requires planar curves. |

## 2.14 Sketch Entities

SolidWorks **Sketch** tab provides all the entities you can use to create parts. Figure 2.23 shows the entities. Hover over any entity or click the drop-down list to investigate further. Most of the entities are self-explanatory. We just offer a few remarks. The **Ellipse** menu has a **Parabola** entity that you can use to create parabolas. Use the **Spline** menu to create a spline. A **spline** curve is defined as a general-shaped curve that provides free-hand sketching ability. To create a spline, click the **Spline** icon, and then click on the screen at multiple locations. When done, hit **Esc** on the keyboard. Use the **Text** icon to create text on faces, curves, edges, and sketch entities. This text is treated as modeling entities and can be, for example, extruded. It is unlike text you create in drawings.

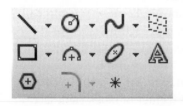

**FIGURE 2.23**
Sketch entities

Part I Computer Aided Design (CAD) Basics

## 2.15 Relations

SolidWorks refers to geometric constraints as relations. A **relation** is a geometric condition between two sketch entities such as lines or arcs. There two methods to create relations during sketching. With the first method, while sketching entities in a sketch, SolidWorks displays the possible relations that you can use. These relations include horizontal, vertical, perpendicular, coincident, midpoint (of a line), etc., as shown in Figure 2.24A. As you sketch, SolidWorks guides you by showing a symbol for the most logical relation you can use. It also shows light yellow lines to indicate the perpendicular directions at the current construction point. It shows dashed horizontal and vertical blue lines to help during construction, as shown in Figure 2.24A. If you hover over a relation symbol after sketching, SolidWorks displays its name. You can turn on/off the relation symbols, as we did in Chapter 1, by clicking this sequence: **View** => **Sketch Relations**. It is a toggle.

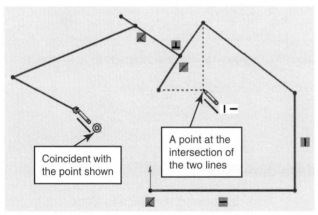

(A) Use relations during sketching      (B) Create relations after sketching

**FIGURE 2.24**
Using relations (geometric constraints)

The other method is to add relations after creating the entities, as shown in Figure 2.24B. In this case, click the **Display/Delete Relations** drop-down on the **Sketch** tab. As Figure 2.24B shows, you can display or delete existing relations, add new ones, or ask SolidWorks to fully define the sketch for you. Figure 2.24B shows the names of the six relations shown in Figure 2.24A. SolidWorks appends a numeric character (starting at 0) at the end of each relation name to distinguish between multiple relations of the same type (e.g., **Vertical1** and **Midpoint2**). A nonzero start value (e.g., **Perpendicular3**) or a gap in the numbering (e.g., **Coincident0** and **Coincident5**) indicates that the user has previously deleted entities that used the same relation type.

## 2.16 Equations

SolidWorks refers to relations as equations. An **equation** is a mathematical relationship between sketch entities, feature dimensions (e.g., extrusion depth), or other model properties. Parameters form the basis for creating equations. Section 2.5 covers parameters. An equation could relate two or more parameters. For example, we can write an equation to relate the two parameters *P1* and *P2* (e.g., *P1* = 2*P2*). For an equation to evaluate correctly, the values for all the parameters on the right side of the equation must be known (i.e., *P2* in this case). *P1* is the evaluated parameter. *P1* is also known as the dependent or driven parameter (dimension), and *P2* is the independent or driving parameter (dimension).

---

**Example 2.5**  Use equations to control modeling. This example builds on Example 2.3. We modify the sketch shown in Figure 2.8 by not anchoring the hole center at the rectangle center. Now, we need to control the sketch shape so that *D1* is always twice that of *D2* and the hole center is always coincident with the rectangle center. Create the equations to implement these relations. Prove that the equations work by changing the dimensions.

**Solution**  The coincidence of the hole and the rectangle centers can be forced by dimensioning the hole center ($x_{hole}$, $y_{hole}$) from the rectangle's two edges. The equations we need can be written as follows:

$$D1 = 2D2$$
$$x_{hole} = 0.5D1$$
$$y_{hole} = 0.5D2$$

The steps to solve this problem are:

1. Create the sketch and change dimension names (see Example 2.3).
2. Create the equations.
3. Test the equations.

## Step 1:  Create the sketch and change dimension names

| Task | Command Sequence to Click |
|---|---|
| A. Start SolidWorks and open a new part file. Change the part units to inches. Save the file as *example 2.5*. | **File => New => Part => OK**<br>**File => Save As** => *example 2.5* => **Save** |
| B. Select the front plane as the sketch plane. | **Front Plane** from features manager tree on left of screen |
| C. Start sketching. | **Features** tab |
| D. Sketch the rectangle. | Rectangle symbol on the **Sketch** tab => Hover the mouse over the origin until you snap there => Sketch and dimension the rectangle shown in Figure 2.8. |
| E. Sketch the circle. | Circle symbol on the **Sketch** tab => Sketch and dimension the circle shown in Figure 2.8. |
| F. Show dimension names. | **View => Dimension Names**.<br>**Help: Dimension Names** is a toggle; click again to see. |

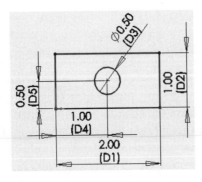

## Step 2:   Create the equations

| Task | Command Sequence to Click |
|------|---------------------------|
| **A.** Open the **Equations** dialog box shown below in Task B. | **Tools => Equations** |
| **B.** Enter equations. | Click the **Add** button shown below to |

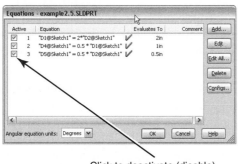

Click to deactivate (disable) the equation effect. Click again to activate

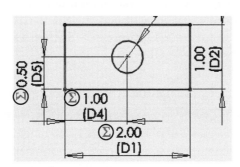

Use button to add a comment to equation

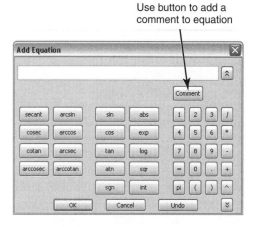

open the **Add Equation** (calculator) box. To compose an equation, click a dimension from the sketch and use the above buttons or the keyboard keys in the desired sequence (e.g., for first equation click *D1*, type = 2*, click *D2*). **Help:** SolidWorks adds an **Equations** node to the part features tree. Right-click it to manage the part equations. Also, SolidWorks adds a red equation symbol on the sketch dimensions that have equations associated with them (shown to the left). Moreover, SolidWorks does not allow changing driven dimensions (*D1*, *D4*, and *D5*), except through the driving dimension, *D2* for *D1*, *D1* for *D4*, and *D2* for *D5*. Double-click any dimension to investigate.

## Step 3:   Test the equations

| Task | Command Sequence to Click |
|------|---------------------------|
| **A.** Edit the driving dimension *D1* to change its value. | Double-click *D1* on the sketch => Enter 1.5 => Green check mark. Repeat and use 2.0 and observe. |

---

> **HANDS-ON FOR EXAMPLE 2.5.** The sketch of this example has a problem. A user can make the hole diameter, *D3*, larger than the rectangle height, *D2*. Add this equation to the sketch to solve this problem: $D3 = 0.5D2$.

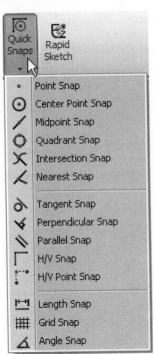

## 2.17 Geometric Modifiers

A **geometric modifier** is a qualifier to select designated points, such as end- or midpoints, on an existing (already created) sketch entity. The benefit of using these modifiers is to speed up construction by accessing these points without having to calculate their coordinates explicitly by hand. Geometric modifiers are part of what SolidWorks calls quick snaps. Geometric modifiers are **end**, **center**, and **intersection**. The **end** modifier identifies the endpoints of an entity. If the entity is an open curve, like a line, it has two endpoints. If the entity is closed, like a circle, it has two coincident endpoints. The **center** modifier identifies the center or midpoint of an entity. For a line, it is the midpoint, and for a circle it is its center. The **intersection** modifier identifies where two entities intersect. If more than one intersection point exists, the CAD software picks up the one closest to the user selection.

As you sketch, SolidWorks automatically anticipates your next move and provides the expected intent (modifier) by displaying the symbol of the expected modifier, as shown in Figure 2.24A. For example, if you sketch a line and move the mouse close to the endpoints or the midpoint of an existing line, SolidWorks shows the corresponding symbol in the right location and waits for you to select it. Figure 2.25 shows SolidWorks **Quick Snap** menu. It is available on the **Sketch** tab. We seldom use it for geometric modifiers because most of them are activated by default. Click this sequence to see these sketch default snaps: **Tools => Options => System Options** tab => **Relations/Snaps** (under **Sketch** item) => **OK**.

**FIGURE 2.25**
Quick snaps

## 2.18 Grids

A **grid** is an equally spaced set of points in either a rectangular or radial pattern. Rectangular grids are more commonly used. A grid has four parameters: spacing along two axes (*X* and *Y*), an origin, and an orientation. Grids are used to speed up construction. Grids are useful in creating shapes with repetitive shapes. They may be more useful for art construction than for engineering design. Click this sequence to display grids in SolidWorks: **Tools => Options => Document Properties** tab => **Grid/Snap** => Check (turn on or off) **Display grid** and set the other properties shown in Figure 2.26A => **OK**. Figure 2.26B shows an example grid. Displaying a grid does not mean that you

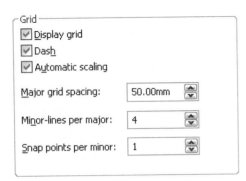

According to these specs, each major grid spacing is divided into four minor spaces, as shown in Figure 2.26B. Alternatively, you can set the minor lines to 1 and the major spacing to 12.5 mm and still achieve the same result.

(A) Grid setup

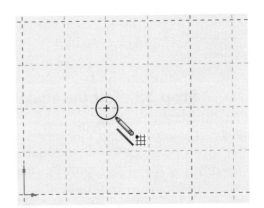

Major grid lines are shown darker than minor grid lines. The "+" symbol shows a grid point.

(B) Grid lines

**FIGURE 2.26**
Displaying a grid

Part I  Computer Aided Design (CAD) Basics

can snap to its points during construction. To turn on the snap, click **Tools =>**
**Options => System Properties** tab => **Relations/Snaps** (under **Sketch** item) =>
Check (turn on or off) **Grid => OK**. You know the snap is on when the mouse sketching moves in a snappy, unexpected way and a "+" symbol shows up when the mouse
move closer to a grid point.

---

**Example 2.6**   Change the origin location and orientation of a grid.

**Solution**   SolidWorks uses the concept of block to change the origin location and
orientation of a grid. This concept is nonintuitive and seems cumbersome. Nonetheless,
we explain it in this example. You need two steps to locate and orient a grid. First you
need to create a block by selecting one or a group of sketch entities. We use one entity
here. Select the entity that you would like to orient the grid with respect to. Second, you
locate and orient the grid. Keep in mind that you must be in a sketch to see the grid that
you set up and display. Here are the details of the two steps.

## Step 1:   Create a block

| Task | Command Sequence to Click |
|---|---|
| A. Start SolidWorks and open a new part file. Change the part units to inches. Save the file as *example 2.6.* | **File => New => Part => OK**<br>**File => Save As** => *example 2.6* => **Save** |
| B. Select the front plane as the sketch plane. | **Front Plane** from features manager tree on left of screen |
| C. Set grid spacing and display it. | **Tools => Options => Document Properties** tab => **Grid/Snap** => Check (turn on or off) **Display grid** => Use the grid setup shown in Figure 2.26A => **OK**. Now you should see the grid in the sketch as shown in Figure 2.26B. Do not turn the snap on. |
| D. Start sketching. | **Features** tab |
| E. Sketch any shape; we create a quadrilateral. | Line symbol on the **Sketch** tab => Sketch the shape shown to the left. |

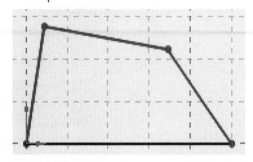

| | |
|---|---|
| F. Create a block. | **Tools => Block => Make** => Top line => Green check mark.<br>**Help:** Now, you should see a **Block1-1** node in the features tree in left pane on screen. |

## Step 2: Locate and orient the grid

**Task**

A. Orient the grid. We need to orient the grid along the top line of the quadrilateral and locate it along its midpoint.

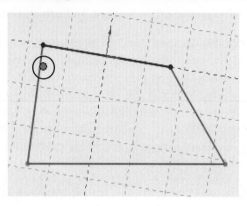

**Command Sequence to Click**

Right-click on the **Block1-1** node => **Edit Block**.

**Help:** Now, you should see the new grid and a dot indicating the existence of the block shown to the left. Also, the sketch shows a block symbol on the top right corner instead of the usual exit sketch symbol. If you click it, you exit the **Block** mode and go to the **Sketch** mode. While in **Block** mode, you can sketch entities. When you exit **Block** mode, the new grid orientation disappears and is replaced by the old orientation shown in Step 1 above. To get the new orientation back, edit the block again. If you delete the block, it deletes the sketch entity used to define it. You can use the new grid to sketch entities in the desired orientation.

## 2.19 Patterns

Patterns (as SolidWorks call them) are also known as geometric arrays. A **pattern** is a uniform layout of a sketch entity or a feature in specific directions. Examples include the keys of a phone keypad and the holes in a flange. You may pattern an entity along a curve (known as a curve-driven pattern). Two types of patterns exist: rectangular (Cartesian) and circular (angular). A rectangular pattern in one direction only is known as a linear pattern. The instances of a rectangular pattern are separated by increments in the X and Y directions. The instances of a circular pattern are by increments in the angular and radial directions.

You may pattern sketch entities or features. You need to be in a sketch to pattern sketch entities and out of sketch to pattern features. Figure 2.27 shows the patterning features for each type of patterning.

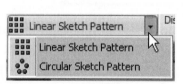

(A) Sketch patterns

(B) Feature patterns

**FIGURE 2.27**
Patterns

**Example 2.7** Create rectangular and circular patterns.

**Solution** We show how to create linear and circular sketch patterns. The tutorials demonstrate how to create feature patterns. Here are the details.

## Step I:  Create a rectangular (linear) pattern

| Task | Command Sequence to Click |
|---|---|
| A. Start SolidWorks and open a new part file. Change the part units to inches. Save the file as *example 2.7*. | **File => New => Part => OK**<br>**File => Save As** *=> example 2.7 =>* **Save** |
| B. Select the front plane as the sketch plane. | **Front Plane** from features manager tree on left of screen |
| C. Sketch these two circles. | Select circle symbol on the **Sketch** tab => Sketch and dimension the big circle at the origin => Sketch a vertical construction line shown to the left => Sketch and dimension the small circle shown to the left. |

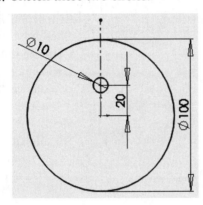

**Why:** We need the vertical construction line to help locate the center of the small circle. Without it, the sketch is undefined. Also, notice that either of the two circles is not fully defined unless you dimension its center and diameter (or radius) explicitly as shown to the left. Inputting the same values in the left pane on the screen during circle construction does not fully define it, which is a confusing observation. You can see that by observing the sketch status displayed in the status bar at the bottom of the screen. SolidWorks creates the model parameters (dimension names) only when you create the dimensions, not when you input values for the geometry during creating it. It would be ideal for SolidWorks to do so, but it does not.

D. Create the linear pattern.

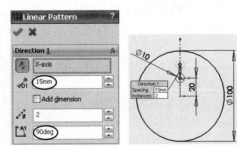

**Linear Sketch Pattern** on **Sketch** tab => Select small circle => Input 15 for **D1** and 90 for angle under **Direction1** as shown here on left => Green check mark.

**Why:** There are two directions under the **Linear Pattern** pane on the screen (only one direction shown to the left). **Direction 1** is for patterning along the *X*-axis and **Direction 2** is for patterning along the *Y*-axis. In our example, we want to pattern only in the Y direction. It would seem logical to ignore **Direction 1** and input values for **Direction 2**.

| Task | Command Sequence to Click |
|------|---------------------------|

SolidWorks will not allow you to do so. You must pattern along **Direction 1** (*X*-axis), but use a 90-degree angle instead of the default zero. Conclusion: If you want to create a rectangular pattern, use both **Direction 1** and **Direction 2**. To create a linear pattern, use **Direction 1** and use the angle to control the direction of the pattern line.

## Step 2: Create a circular pattern

Task

A. Create the circular pattern.

 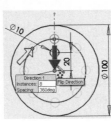

Command Sequence to Click

**Linear Sketch Pattern** drop-down on **Sketch** tab => **Circular Sketch Pattern** from the drop-down => Select the outer small circle => Input 8 for the number of instances to create (shown to the left) => Green check mark.

**Help:** The **Flip Direction** shown to the left allows you to change the placements of the instances of the circular pattern. The flip does not make a difference in our example because the pattern spans the entire 360 degrees. As an example, to show the effect of the flip, change the number of instances to 5 from 8, and the angle of the pattern from 360 to 250 degrees.

**Help:** The **Circular Pattern** pane (shown to the left) provides additional control to create the pattern. You can specify the center of rotation to create the pattern (**X** and **Y** shown to the left), the radius of the circle that houses the pattern instances (not shown here), and the angle of the pattern (not shown here).

---

***HANDS-ON FOR EXAMPLE 2.7.*** Use the inner small circle to create a circular pattern that has 8 instances. Skip instances 3 and 6 in the pattern. Help: Pattern instances are numbered starting at 1 for the original entity that you pattern. Help: While you still creating the pattern, click **Instances to Skip** on left pane on screen => Select the instances => Green check mark.

## 2.20 Selecting, Editing, and Measuring Entities

There are multiple reasons why you would want to select existing entities (e.g., to edit them, use them for new construction, delete them, etc.). You may select entities in a sketch or in a feature. The available selection methods are the common ones you always use and include the following:

☐ Click an entity to select it.
☐ To select multiple entities at the same time, press the **CTRL** or **Shift** key on the keyboard followed by clicking the entities.
☐ To select many entities, define a select window around them by dragging the mouse from left to right or right to left to enclose the entities.
☐ To select entities in a chain (e.g., a rectangle or polygon), right-click any entity in the chain and choose **Select Chain** from the menu that pops up. You must have a chain, otherwise you will not see the **Select Chain** option.
☐ To select entities in a loop, follow the same sequence for chains. Loops and chains are similar; we use loops when we select from feature faces and chains when we select from sketches.
☐ You can select any nodes (features, components, planes, drawing views, etc.) from the features tree on a part.
☐ As you move the mouse over entities to select them, SolidWorks attaches a symbol to the mouse indicating the entity type it senses. Figure 2.28 shows the symbols.
☐ If multiple entities overlap where the mouse is, you can right-click any entity and choose **Select Other** from the context menu that pops up to step through all the entities under the mouse. When you select a face, the face is hidden so you can see inside the model.

After we select an entity, we may want to edit it. Editing an entity includes offsetting, trimming, and transforming. Offsetting an entity means copying in a new location defined by an offset distance as shown in Figure 2.29A. Click **Offset Entities** on the **Sketch** tab to offset. Set and/or select the offset parameters shown in Figure 2.29A.

**FIGURE 2.28**
Select symbols

Face    Edge

Vertex    Select Other

Click to select    Click to hide

**FIGURE 2.29**
Offsetting and trimming entities

(A) Offset an entity

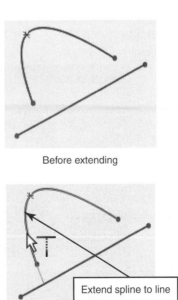

Before extending

Extend spline to line

After extending

(B) Trim an entity by extending it

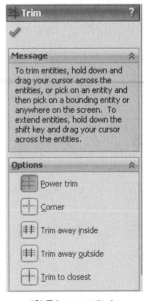

(C) Trim an entity by shortening it

Trimming an entity entails shortening or extending it. SolidWorks extends the entity to the closest entity, as shown in Figure 2.29B. SolidWorks offers different options to shorten an entity via trimming, as shown in Figure 2.29C. One of the very interesting and powerful trimming options is the **Power trim**. If you select this option and move the mouse over an entity, SolidWorks removes it. Try all the trimming options on your SolidWorks to understand how they work.

Transforming an entity includes translating (moving), rotating, scaling, mirroring, or stretching it. You can transform sketch entities or features. Figure 2.30 shows the transformation options for sketch entities. A translation requires a translation vector (i.e., a distance and direction). A rotation requires a center of rotation and an angle. Scaling requires a scale factor and a point to scale about. Mirroring requires a mirror axis. Stretching requires a point to stretch with respect to. Get acquainted with SolidWorks transformation menu (**Move Entities**) shown in Figure 2.30. You can access it from the **Sketch** tab. Mirroring has its own icon on the **Sketch** tab and shown here in Figure 2.30. Observe that you can drag the entity to transform it once you are in the transformation mode (e.g., translation, rotation, etc.).

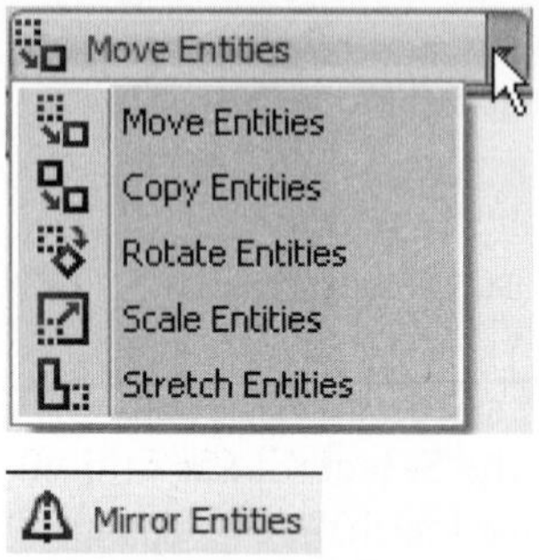

Transforming features occurs in the 3D space unlike transforming sketch entities that occurs in 2D (the sketch plane). Thus, a translation vector is defined by three components: $\Delta x$, $\Delta y$, and $\Delta z$; or it may be defined by an edge (to define direction) and a distance. A rotation requires a rotation axis and an angle. You can only translate, rotate, scale, or mirror features. The translation and rotation parameters are given with respect to the WCS of the model (i.e., the origin and the first sketch plane you used to create the model). You can also make a copy of the feature you want to transform and keep the original feature in its place. Click this sequence to access SolidWorks translate/rotate functions: **Insert** (**Features** tab) => **Features** => **Move/Copy** => **Translate/Rotate** (button at the bottom of left pane on screen). Figure 2.31 shows the pane that appears on the screen at the end of this sequence. Use this sequence to transform an entity: Select the feature to transform => Check **Copy** if needed => Select **Translate** or **Rotate** => Input parameters => Green check mark.

The scale and mirror functions have their own menus. To scale, click **Insert** (**Features** tab) => **Features** => **Scale**. You can perform uniform or nonuniform scaling. Uniform scaling preserves the feature aspect ratio (i.e., it does not distort its look). Uniform scaling uses the same scale factor for the three axes. Nonuniform scaling uses different scale factors. Figure 2.32 shows the **Scale** pane. For mirroring, you can mirror

**FIGURE 2.30**
Transforming sketch entities

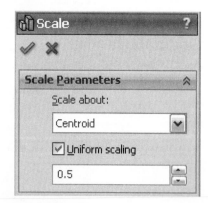

**FIGURE 2.31**
Translate/rotate features

**FIGURE 2.32**
Scale features

an entity via the **Mirror** icon on SolidWorks **Features** tab. To mirror, you need a mirror face or plane and the features to mirror. We have mirrored features in Chapter 1.

After editing or transforming entities, we may need to measure their geometric properties. We can measure sketch entities or features. We can measure coordinates of a point or length of an entity if we are in a sketch. For a feature, we can measure the coordinates of a vertex, the length of an edge, or the area and the perimeter of a face. Click this sequence to measure: **Tools => Measure** => Select any entity to measure. SolidWorks attaches the result to the entity and displays it on the screen. Measurements could be useful during design activities.

## 2.21 Construction Tree

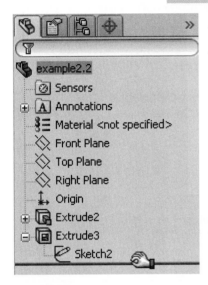

**FIGURE 2.33**
Management pane

SolidWorks provides a management pane on the left of the screen, shown in Figure 2.33. The pane has multiple tabs to help you manage part, drawing, or assembly creation. Each tab is a manager. The names of the tabs from left to right are, respectively, **FeatureManager design tree**, **PropertyManager**, **Configuration Manager**, and **DimXpertmanager**. The **FeatureManager design tree** (or the features tree as we call it in the book) is the one most commonly used. The features tree shows the design history of the part and how it is created. You can step through the tree to reverse engineer the design. The tree has nodes that you may expand or collapse. A node that is collapsible has a "+" (collapsed state) or "−" (expanded state) symbol, as shown in Figure 2.33. An expandable/collapsible node indicates a subtree. You can roll back the tree by dragging the rollback bar (shown at the bottom of the tree) to investigate the design. Place the mouse over the rollback bar (Figure 2.33) and drag it up or down. When you roll the tree up, you suppress the features from the bottom of the tree up to the suppression position. This is beneficial because it allows you to insert features at any location in the tree. When done with the insertion, roll back the tree to unsuppress it. By now, you have interacted with the features tree many times through the examples and the tutorials.

The **FeatureManager design tree** and the graphics area (pane) are dynamically linked. You can select features, sketches, drawing views, and construction geometry in either pane. You can use the features tree in many useful ways. If you right-click any node, you can perform useful functions. You get different pop-up functions depending on the type of node you click (e.g. **Front Plane**, feature, sketch, etc.). Double-click any feature to display its dimensions. You can rename a feature by slowly clicking it twice to replace its name. View the parent/child relationships by right-clicking a feature => **Parent/Child** from the pop-up. You can delete a sketch or feature by right-clicking its node in the tree => **Delete** from the pop-up. Investigate the many possibilities of using the features tree when you need them.

The **PropertyManager** opens when you create/edit sketches or features or perform any geometric operations. This where you input the values of the required parameters for an operation. The **Configuration Manager** allows you to create families of parts as we discuss in Section 2.22. The **DimXpertmanager** lists tolerance features and is not covered here.

## 2.22 Templates

Templates are also known as start or master parts. You customize the template to include your preferred settings in tools, options, and document properties. You may also include your favorite base stock (geometry and features), dimensions (preferred units, decimals, tolerances), annotations favorites, commonly used reference geometry, preset drawing views, drawing notes, layers, materials, etc. You can create different templates: one for parts, one for assemblies, one for drawings, etc. You create any template as you would create any file and save as template, as you do in Word. For example, to save a part document (file) as a template, click **File => Save As =>** Select **Part Templates (*.prtdot)** as the **Save as type** => Type file name => **Save**. The document is saved in SolidWorks **Templates** folder (see Figure 2.34) and will become available when you start a new part, as shown in Figure 2.34. SolidWorks templates are saved in this folder: *C:\Documents and Settings\All Users\Application Data\SolidWorks\SolidWorks 2010\templates*. Click this sequence to use the template: **File => New** => Select the template from the **Templates** tab shown in Figure 2.34 => **OK**. You can create multiple templates of the same type (part, assembly, assembly) for multiple designs or applications. If you do not see the **Templates** tab (Figure 2.34), click the **Advanced** button on the screen to access it.

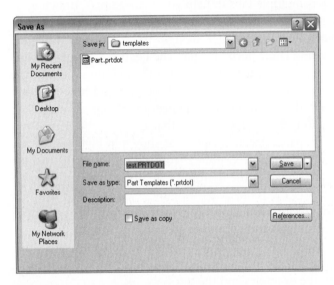
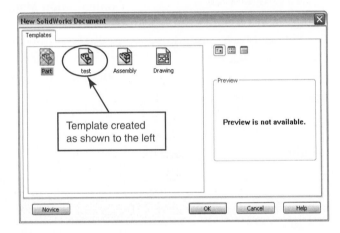

**FIGURE 2.34**
Saving and using SolidWorks part template

## 2.23 Viewing

You can view a model from different angles during construction. The typical standard views are the front, top, right, and isometric views. Other views exist (e.g. back, bottom, left, etc.). CAD/CAM systems use a viewing eye that goes around the model in the 3D modeling space to allow you to see the model from different viewing angles (i.e., change view orientation). In this scenario, an observer moves in the 3D modeling space while the CAD model is fixed in the space. This concept mimics the notion that you hold and rotate the physical (actual) model in your hand to look at it. CAD/CAM systems provide different options of model viewing: zoom in and out of a model, section a model, select a viewing orientation, select a display style, etc. Figure 2.35 shows SolidWorks **View** menu.

Viewing and constructing a model are two different activities. Viewing is controlled by the view orientation you select while construction is controlled by the active sketch plane (i.e., the WCS). While we can view the model from any angle during construction, we usually view the model perpendicular to the active sketch plane to get the best view to see the results of our construction steps.

Part I Computer Aided Design (CAD) Basics

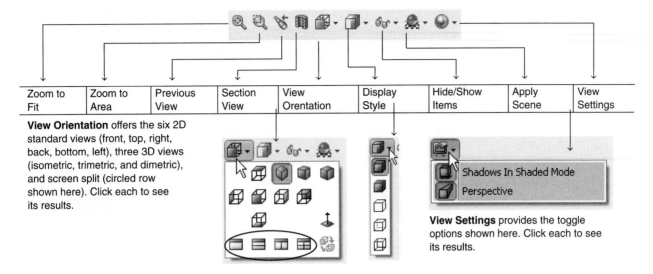

| Zoom to Fit | Zoom to Area | Previous View | Section View | View Orientation | Display Style | Hide/Show Items | Apply Scene | View Settings |

**View Orientation** offers the six 2D standard views (front, top, right, back, bottom, left), three 3D views (isometric, trimetric, and dimetric), and screen split (circled row shown here). Click each to see its results.

**View Settings** provides the toggle options shown here. Click each to see its results.

**FIGURE 2.35**
SolidWorks **View** menu

## 2.24 Model Communication

CAD models are communicated and shared by two distinct groups of people: technical and professional. Technical people include CAD designers, design engineers, and manufacturing engineers. Professional people include marketing, sales, and other personnel. Although engineering drawings are the formal method of documenting and communicating a design among technical people, professional people have other communication needs, such as generating screenshots of the model for inclusion in reports, proposals to customers, presentations, e-mail messages, etc. These needs do not require SolidWorks software, unlike engineering drawings that do require access to SolidWorks software to view them. Also, technical people know how to use SolidWorks whereas professional people do not.

Recognizing these needs and the inability or disinterest of professional people in learning how to use SolidWorks, SolidWorks offers some effective communication tools. Designers use these tools and generate files for use by professional people. The designers themselves can use these files also to liberate themselves from needing SolidWorks wherever they go. For example, they can use them to communicate with customers during the design phase, subcontractors, suppliers, and others. To generate screenshots of SolidWorks graphics/geometry pane, click this sequence: **View** menu on menu bar => **Screen Capture** => **Image Capture**. SolidWorks stores the screen capture in Windows buffer, waiting for you to use it. Simply open the application such as Word or PowerPoint and paste the capture (use **CTRL+V** combination on the keyboard). Figure 2.36 shows an example.

When you save a part, assembly, or a drawing, you can save it as an image. Click this sequence: **File** menu on menu bar => **Save As** => Select **JPEG** (*.jpg) or **Tif** (*.tif) from the **Save as type** drop-down shown in Figure 2.37. This method is effectively the same as the screen capture method; the only difference is the file format. The screen capture method saves the image in bitmap (*.bmp) format whereas here you can save it in JPEG or Tif. The BMP format produces the largest file size.

SolidWorks offers two methods to view SolidWorks files (parts, drawings, assemblies, etc.) without having SolidWorks software. VRML (Virtual Reality Modeling Language) file format enables you to view CAD models in a Web browser. In addition to displaying, we can also manipulate the models on the screen via pan,

**FIGURE 2.36**
SolidWorks screen capture

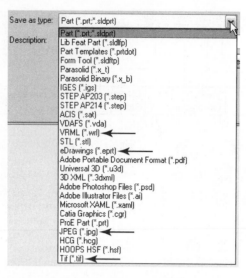

**FIGURE 2.37**
SolidWorks file formats

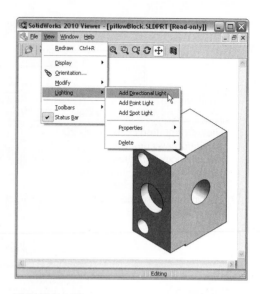

**FIGURE 2.38**
SolidWorks Viewer

rotate, and scale (zoom) functions. We need to download and install a browser VRML plug-in. Visit http://cic.nist.gov/vrml/cosmoplayer.html to download and install the Cosmo Player VRML plug-in. VRML plug-ins also require installing OpenGL or Direct3D graphics library. The VRML plug-in will not work if either graphics library is not installed or, if it is installed, it is incompatible with the version that the plug-in uses.

A better option over VRML is to use SolidWorks Viewer. You can download and install the viewer for free. Visit www.solidworks.com/sw/downloads.htm. Follow the instructions to download and install the viewer version you need (we download the 2010 version). The version must be compatible with the SolidWorks files you intend to open. The viewer is backward compatible but not forward compatible (i.e., 2009 version can open 2009 and prior files, but not 2010 files). Figure 2.38 shows the viewer. We encourage you to investigate its menus and options, especially the **Lighting** menu shown in the figure. You can use it to transform (translate, rotate, or scale) or add lighting to the model.

The best of all options is the eDrawings tool. eDrawings as a free application from SolidWorks allows you to view SolidWorks part, drawing, and assembly files. You can save any SolidWorks CAD model as an eDrawings file (**\*.eprt**), as shown in Figure 2.37. You can open the file in a Web browser. Simply drag the eDrawings file and drop it onto a Web browser window. You can rotate the CAD model in the browser. Click the mouse and rotate the model to view. The benefit of using eDrawings over VRML or SolidWorks Viewer is that you do not need to install any additional software; just use your Web browser. Another advantage is that the size of an eDrawings file is very small, so you can send it as an e-mail attachment.

In addition to opening an eDrawings file in a Web browser, SolidWorks offers eDrawings software, a very interesting free tool to open and manipulate eDrawings files. eDrawings is installed automatically with SolidWorks Professional or Premium edition. For student edition of SolidWorks, you may need to download (from www.solidworks.com/sw/downloads.htm) and install it. You can animate and view models and drawings and create documents to send to people. An interesting feature is stamping a model or a drawing. Figure 2.39, a stamped model, shows eDrawings. We encourage you to explore its capabilities.

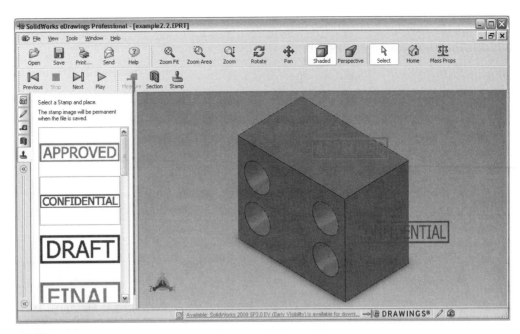

**FIGURE 2.39**
SolidWorks eDrawings

## 2.25 Tutorials Overview

The theme for the tutorials in this chapter is to get you to practice the 3D construction, modeling, and viewing concepts. The tutorials are a mix of individual parts and assemblies. This chapter is cosponsored by the North Alabama SolidWorks Users Group (NASWUG), www.naswug.com, and Dynetics, a company with headquarters in Huntsville, Alabama (www.dynetics.com). We chat with Mr. Ricky Jordan, the President of NASWUG. Mr. Jordan is also a Lead Mechanical Engineer at Dynetics. His website is www.rickyjordan.com.

## Tutorial 2–1:  Create a Coil Spring

**FIGURE 2.40**
Coil spring

### Modeling task

Create the coil spring shown in Figure 2.40. This tutorial mimics what sometimes happens in industry practice: buy off-the-shelf components and modify them in-house. For example, a company may buy a spring from McMaster-Carr (e.g., part #9271K182), use a pliers and bend the end 90 degrees, then trim the leads (cut them off with a wire cutter), and then smooth the ends on a grinding wheel.

### Modeling synthesis

We create the spring shown in Figure 2.40 to simulate actual modifications one might make to an existing product.

### Modeling plan

We create the spring as a sweep feature. The spring is a wire that is twisted into a helix shape. The wire has a circular cross section, and the helix is defined by a circle, number of coils, and a pitch (see Figure 2.40 and the tutorial steps). The planes of the wire cross section (we use the front plane) and the helix (we use the top plane) must be perpendicular.

### Design intent

Ignore for this chapter.

### CAD steps

We create the coil spring as follows:

1. Create the wire cross section.
2. Create the wire helix.
3. Create the coil spring.
4. Create the spring end.

The details of these steps are shown below.

## Step 1: Create the wire cross section

**Task**

**A.** Start SolidWorks, open a new part, change model units to inches, and save it as *tutorial 2.1*

**B.** Select the front plane to sketch the wire cross section.

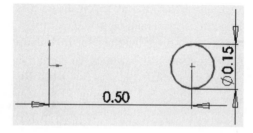

**Command Sequence to Click**

**File => New = Part => OK => Tools => Options => Document Properties** tab **=> Units => IPS (inch, pound, second) => OK => File => Save As** *=> tutorial 2.1* **=> Save**

**Front Plane** (from the features tree) **=> Sketch** (hover over the icons of the context menu until you find it) => Sketch the circle shown to the left.

## Step 2: Create the wire helix

**Task**

**A.** Select the top plane and sketch the helix circle.

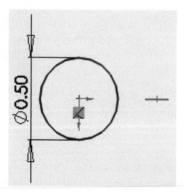

**Command Sequence to Click**

**Top Plane** from the features tree **=> Sketch** (hover over the icons of the context menu until you find it) => Sketch the circle shown to the left => Exit the sketch.

**Help:** The circle center is anchored at the origin, as shown to the left.

| Task | Command Sequence to Click |
|---|---|

**B. Create the helix.**

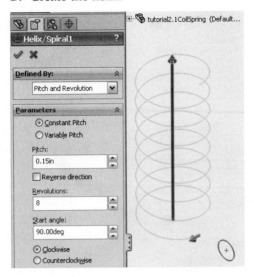

Select the above sketch in the features tree => **Insert** menu => **Curve =>** **Helix/Spiral** => Input the helix parameters shown to the left => Green check mark to finish.

**Why:** The helix has a pitch of 0.15 in., 8 revolutions (coils), and a start angle of 90 degrees. Although the number of revolutions and the start angles may be any values, the pitch value is selected for a reason. The pitch and the diameter of the wire circle are equal (0.15 in.). This causes the spring coils to touch each other, as shown in Figure 2.40. If the pitch is greater, the coils do not touch. Edit helix and try a value of 0.25 in. for the pitch.

## Step 3: Create the coil spring

| Task | Command Sequence to Click |
|---|---|

**A. Use a sweep feature to create the spring.**

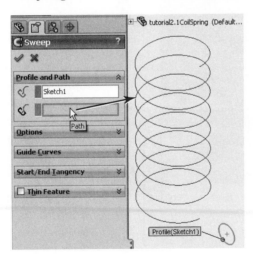

**Sweep Boss/Base** from the **Features** tab => Select the wire circle as the profile and the helix as the path (shown to the left) => Green check mark to finish.

**Why:** The screenshot to the left is not showing the helix selected yet to provide you with better visualization of what is happening. When you select it, you should see the spring shown below.

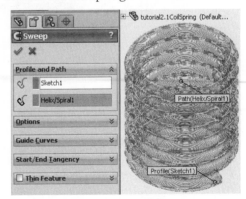

## Step 4:  Create the spring end

**Task**

**A.** Create a sketch plane.

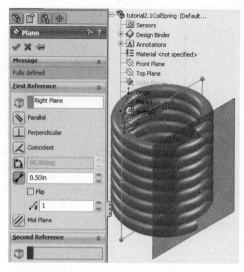

**B.** Sketch the spring end.

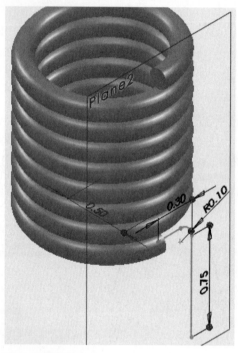

**C.** Create the cross section of the spring end.

**Command Sequence to Click**

**Right Plane** from the features tree =>
**Insert** menu => **Reference Geometry**
=> **Plane** => Select **Right Plane** from
the features tree => Input 0.5 in. for the
distance (shown to the left) => Green
check mark to finish.

**Why:** We offset the right plane by ½ inch
because the spring end comes out of the
center of the wire circle. You can see that
the new plane slices through the middle
of the circle shown to the left.

**Help:** You may need to check off the **Flip**
check box shown to the left to locate the
new plane on the correct side of the
**Right Plane.**

Select the plane defined in Task A above
from the features tree => **Sketch** (hover
over the icons of the context menu
until you find it) => Sketch two
perpendicular lines and a fillet between
them (shown to the left) => Exit the
sketch.

**Help:** Make sure that the two lines are
perpendicular and the short line is also
perpendicular to the circle at its center.
All these relations are automatic in
SolidWorks as you sketch.

**Help:** The sketch shown to the left
is used to create the spring end in
Figure 2.40.

**Front Plane** from the features tree =>
**Sketch** (hover over the icons of the
context menu until you find it) =>
**Convert Entities** from the **Sketch** tab
=> Select (from the features tree) the
sketch of the spring wire cross section
(the .15 in. circle) => Green check
mark to accept selected circle => Green
check mark to exit **Convert Entities**
mode => Exit the sketch.

| Task | Command Sequence to Click |
|---|---|

**D.** Use a sweep feature to create the spring end.

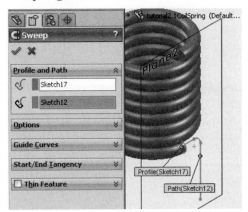

Select Task C sketch from the features tree => **Sweep Boss/Base** from the **Features** tab => Select the sketch (from Task C above) from the features tree as the profile and the sketch (from Task B above) from the features tree as the path as shown here on the left => Green check mark to finish.

**Help:** The final result should look identical to Figure 2.40.

---

**HANDS-ON FOR TUTORIAL 2–1.** Create the other end of the spring identically to the one created here.

---

## Tutorial 2–2: Create Caster Assembly

### Modeling task

Create all of the necessary parts and then assemble the caster as shown in Figure 2.41.

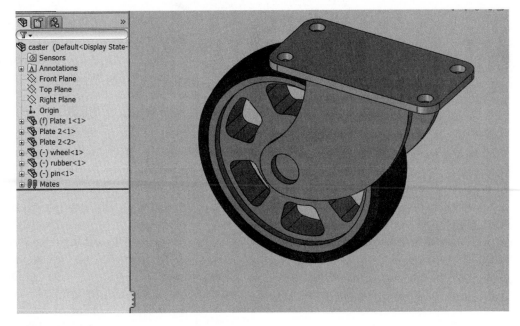

**FIGURE 2.41**
Caster assembly

### Modeling synthesis

The assembly consists of one mount plate, two side plates, one wheel, a rubber tire, and an axle pin.

### Modeling plan

We shall design and create the parts mentioned above, and then assemble the caster as shown in Figure 2.41. We must use the correct mates such that the wheel is free to rotate without moving the mount plate.

### Design intent

Ignore for this chapter.

### CAD steps

Create the Caster assembly in Figure 2.41:

1. Create the mount plate.
2. Create the side plate.
3. Create the wheel.
4. Create the rubber tire.
5. Create the axle pin.
6. Insert the mount plate first and allow it to snap to the origin.
7. Insert the side plates and locate them as shown using one coincident mate along with two concentric mates.
8. Insert the axle pin and locate using a concentric mate, a width mate, and a coincident mate.
9. Insert the wheel using a width mate and a concentric mate.
10. Finally insert the rubber tire using a width mate, a concentric mate, and a coincident mate.

The details of these steps are shown below.

## Step 1:   Create the mount plate

| Task | Command Sequence to Click |
|---|---|
| A. Create the mount plate shown below. 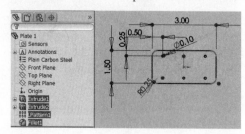 | **Sketch => Center Rectangle** then dimension as shown to the left. **Features => Extrude** and input 0.125″ for extrude depth. **Sketch => Circle** dimension as shown on the left. **Features => Extruded Cut** and select **Through All** from drop-down menu. Select **Extrude2 => Features => Linear Pattern**. Input 1″ in **Direction 1** and **Direction 2**. Input 2 for number of instances for **Direction 1** and 3 for number of instances for **Direction 2**. **Features => Fillet** and select the four outside edges. Input 0.25″ for fillet radius. |

## Step 2: Create the side plate

| Task | Command Sequence to Click |
|---|---|
| A. Create the side plate in Figure 2.41. | **Sketch => Circle** => Sketch circles C1 through C4 shown to the left. **Help:** The centers of C3 and C4 are horizontal to the origin. Circles C1 and C2 are concentric. C1 is tangent to both C3 and C4. These conditions will automatically determine the radius of C1 to be 0.45″. **Why:** Dimensioning the radius of C1 over defines the sketch as shown below. |

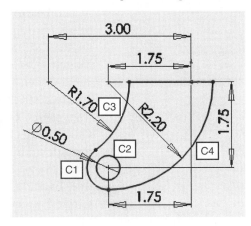

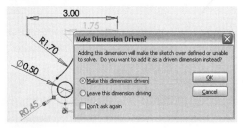

| Task | Command Sequence to Click |
|---|---|
| B. Cut the two holes. | Select the top face of the side plate as sketch plane => **Sketch => Circle** => Sketch and dimension the two circles shown to the left. |

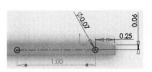

## Step 3: Create the wheel

| Task | Command Sequence to Click |
|---|---|

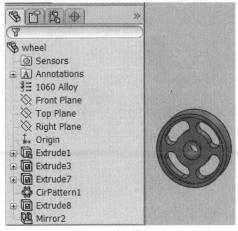

Wheel

| Task | Command Sequence to Click |
|---|---|
| A. First create the disc shown below. | Select the **Front Plane** and the **Sketch => Circle** dimension shown to the left. Now **Features => Extrude Boss/Base => Mid Plane** and input as shown. |

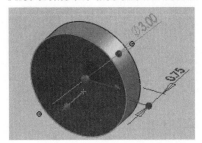

| Task | Command Sequence to Click |
|---|---|

**B.** Next we will make the following cuts as shown.

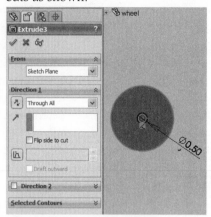

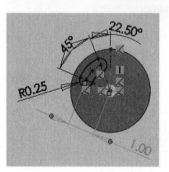

Select the surface at the front of the disc. Select **Sketch => Circle** and sketch and dimension the circle at the center of the wheel. **Features => Extruded Cut** and select **Through All** from the drop-down menu.

**Sketch =>Centerpoint Arc Slot**

Input dimensions shown to the left. Use construction lines to locate the points from center. **Features => Extruded Cut** and select **Through All** from the drop-down menu.

Select the arc slot feature from the design tree, **Extrude2**. Then immediately select **Circle Pattern**. Input 4 as the number of instances and check off **Equal Spacing.**

**C.** Finally we will make the cut shown below at a depth of 0.125″. And then mirror the cut about the front plane to make the wheel symmetrical.

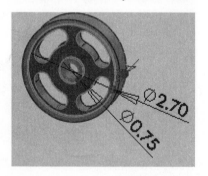

**Features => Extruded Cut**. Then select one of the two sides of the disc. **Sketch => Circle** and sketch and dimension the larger two circles shown to the left. Next select the edge of the center circle and select **Sketch => Convert Entities**. Exit the sketch and input the extrude depth as 0.125″.

**Why:** In Task B we first selected the plane to sketch on and then selected the **Extruded Cut** button. However, in D we selected the **Extruded Cut** button first and then the plane to sketch on. This was done to show the user that the order of selecting the feature type or the plane/surface to perform that feature typically does not matter.

## Step 4:  Create the tire

### Task

A.  Create the tire.

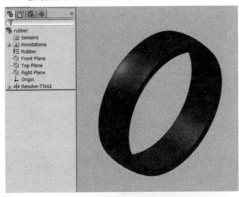

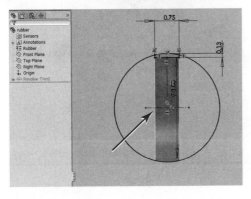

### Command Sequence to Click

Select **Front Plane => Sketch**. Now, sketch and dimension the profile shown to the left.

Select **Features => Revolve Boss/Base** and input the construction line at the center as the line to revolve about as shown to the left.

## Step 5:  Create the axle pin

### Task

A.  Create the axle pin.

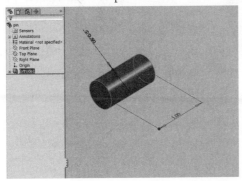

### Command Sequence to Click

Select **Front Plane => Extrude Boss/Base**. **Sketch => Circle**. Dimensions as shown to the left.
**Help:** This pin could also be created as a revolve.

## Step 6:  Insert the mount plate

Task

A.  Import the mount plate.

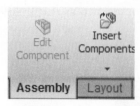

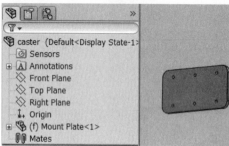

Command Sequence to Click

**File => New => Assembly**
**File => Save => Save as**
**Caster.SLDASM**
**Assembly => Insert Components.** Hit
the **Browse** key and find the **Mount
Plate** that was created in Step 1. Next
you will see that the mount plate will
follow your cursor around the graphics
pane. If you click anywhere in the
window this is where the plate will be
temporarily located. A trick for the first
part of an assembly is not to click in the
graphics window, but instead click the
green check mark immediately. This will
align the **Origin** of the part with the
**Origin** of the assembly. If done correctly
you will see an **(f)** next to the model
name in the **Feature Tree** (see **Mount
Plate** shown to the left).

## Step 7:  Insert and mate the side plates

Task

A.  Import the two side plates.

B.  Mate the side plate.

Command Sequence to Click

**Assembly => Insert Components =>
Browse**
Find the **Side Plate** that was created in
Step 2. This time drop the plate
somewhere in the graphics pane by
clicking someplace that is not another
part, as shown in Figure 2.41. To create a
second side plate, hold the **CTRL** key,
and then click any part of the side plate
and drag away. You will see a second
instance of this part appear (shown to
the left). It is important to drag far
enough away to clear the original part;
otherwise, SolidWorks will try to create a
mate between the two parts. (This feature
will be explained later).
**Assembly => Mate**
Select the two faces highlighted using a
**Coincident Mate**.
Next mate one of the side plates to the
bottom of the mount plate as shown to
the left.

| Task | Command Sequence to Click |
|---|---|

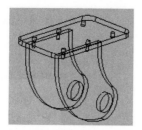

Use a **Concentric Mate** to locate each of the holes in the side plates to the holes in the mount plate as shown to the left. **Why:** The figure is shown in wire frame to help illustrate the fact that the four holes line up as they should.

## Step 8: Insert and mate the axle pin

| Task | Command Sequence to Click |
|---|---|

A. Import the axle pin.

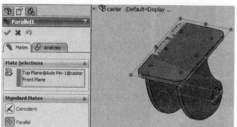

**Assembly => Insert Components => Browse**

Find the **Axle Pin** that was created in Step 5. Drop the pin somewhere in the graphics pane by clicking someplace that is not another part.

Mate the pin using a **Concentric Mate** to the lower hole in either of the side plates as well as a **coincident mate**.

Also mate the **Top Plane** of the pin parallel to the **Front Plane** of the mount plate (shown to the left).

## Step 9: Insert and mate the wheel

| Task | Command Sequence to Click |
|---|---|

A. Import the wheel.

 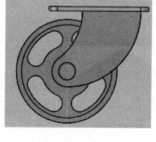

**Assembly => Insert Components => Browse**

Find the **Axle Pin** that was created in Step 3. Drop the wheel somewhere in the graphics window by clicking someplace that is not another part.

Mate the pin using a **Concentric Mate** to the axle pin. Also use a width mate by selecting both outer sides of the side plates as well as both sides of the wheel. Now while all four faces are highlighted, select **Assembly => Mate => Advanced => Width**. SolidWorks will automatically align the wheel exactly between the side plate faces. Screenshot to the left shows the result.

## Step 10: Insert and mate the tire

**Task**

A. Import the tire.

**Command Sequence to Click**

**Assembly => Insert Components => Browse**

Find the **Tire** that was created in Step 4. Drop the tire somewhere in the graphics window by clicking someplace that is not another part.

Mate the tire concentric to the wheel and also use the width mate as shown in Step 9.

Next mate the **Front Plane** of the tire to the **Top Plane** of the wheel.

When finished, the tire and wheel should rotate together when dragged by the mouse. Try this for yourself!

**Help:** If assembled correctly, the wheel should rotate along with the tire as in real life. The coincident mate used one the axle pin is to simulate the friction hold when the pin is pressed into place in real life.

---

### INDUSTRY CHAT

This section provides practical insight into how the chapter material is used in industry in real-world practice. We chat with Mr. Ricky Jordan, Lead Mechanical Engineer at Dynetics Inc. and President of NASWUG. Visit his website at www .rickyjordan.com to learn more about his SolidWorks activities and expertise. This section summarizes the chat with Ricky. The structure of the chat follows the chapter sections.

**Chapter Section 2.1:** Overview

ABE: Provide an overview of CAD construction management at Dynetics.

RICKY: We rely heavily on document templates, product data management (PDM), and common network locations specialized for data reuse to manage our CAD activities. We provide company standard templates for drawing border formats along with part and assembly templates that are already set up with our standard document meta-data. We use a common fastener library that is utilized across multiple users. The use of a common PDM system allows us to share files across multiple users without the risk of overwriting the latest design, which is a common problem when you try to manage the files using network folders. Network folders are still used to store document templates and a Design Library, which allows users to store common modeling features and annotations. Common model construction practices are taught individually to each user but will soon be detailed in documents that formally define the standards.

## Chapter Section 2.2: Types of CAD Models

**ABE:** Based on Dynetics CAD models, rank the types of CAD models shown in Figure 2.1.

**RICKY:** We use all these types. The types of features we use often depend on the project we are working on. Most of the government or military projects end up containing lots of extrusions, cuts, and holes (using the Hole Wizard) since a majority of them contain machined and fabricated metal parts. Consumer product development projects often contain injection-molded plastic parts, which lead us to rely heavily on the use of complex surface geometry. This type of work usually results in lofts, boundary surfaces, sweeps, draft, and filled surface features.

## Chapter Section 2.3: Planning Part Construction

**ABE:** How much planning and what type of planning do you typically do?

**RICKY:** We try to utilize SolidWorks right away in the process as quickly as possible. If it is a product that contains multiple machined parts, we design our features based on the solidarity of the geometry. We try to look at the model with as much design intent as possible up front. If we know that there are certain features that may change in size or configuration, we try to think ahead and design the part features so that the geometry can easily be changed downstream. As the design matures, more features are added to the part to finish out all the necessary details, and in most cases, the part is integrated into the assembly to verify fit/form/function. Some of our industrial design projects involve concept sketches initially, but we still try to create solid or surface models as early as possible since having that model is an efficient way to communicate the design. Particularly we try to plan the use of Hole Wizard holes in groups that follow the assembly of a product. If we need to design a four-hole pattern to hold down a particular component in an assembly, the four holes are most of the time contained within a single Hole Wizard feature (even if there are other holes of similar size on the panel). This allows us to utilize feature driven component patterns for fasteners at the assembly level.

## Chapter Section 2.4: Part Construction

**ABE:** What advice would you provide to our book readers about constructing CAD models?

**RICKY:** Build as much symmetry into the model as possible. Keep your feature counts as low as possible, but not so low that you lose configurability of features. For example, adding all of your fillet features in sketches takes away your ability to easily suppress or turn off fillet features in the model. Put as many of your fillet features at the bottom of the **FeatureManager Design tree** as possible. Use the Hole Wizard for ALL holes in parts. The advantage of doing this is in those cases where you may need to change a fastener clearance hole to a countersink or counterbore hole. If the Hole Wizard was utilized, a few simple clicks in the **PropertyManager** is all that is needed. If you used **Extrude-Cut** to model the holes, then you have quite a bit more work to do in comparison.

*(continue)*

**Chapter Section 2.5:**   Parametric Modeling

ABE:   How do you take advantage of parametric modeling in your CAD design?

RICKY:   One of the key things to keep in mind with parametric modeling is your design intent. If you have a series of holes that no matter what is always going to be a certain distance from a particular edge of a part, then you use the parametric dimensions to define the part in this way. If the hole locations were defined differently (for example, located symmetrically about the centerline of the part), then changing the overall size of the part might violate your design intent.

**Chapter Section 2.6:**   Customizing SolidWorks

ABE:   What are the best ways to customize SolidWorks?

RICKY:   Being able to customize the user interface is one of the most powerful features inside of SolidWorks. This is often looked at differently by each individual user. I have seen users who use the **CommandManager** and no additional toolbars. I have seen users who utilize both. I have also seen users who use nothing but toolbars and no **CommandManager**. I have found that for most users, the **CommandManager** is the most popular option. Since you can add any feature to any tab and create custom tabs, you can group features pretty much any way you like. See the Productivity Tools section below for some other options in customizing SolidWorks.

**Chapter Section 2.7:**   Productivity Tools

ABE:   What productivity tools do you use? Do you recommend beginners to use them?

RICKY:   My two favorite productivity tools in SolidWorks are the **S-Key** toolbar and keyboard shortcuts. The **S-Key** toolbar is a customizable toolbar that is called up simply by pressing the **S** key on your keyboard (this is a default keyboard shortcut with every SolidWorks install). The **S-Key** toolbar is context sensitive so you have different versions of it for the sketch, part, assembly, and drawing environments. To learn more about the **S-Key** toolbar, visit my blog at www.rickyjordan.com where you can find a series of videos titled "The S-Key Experiment." In these videos I show how you can use a customized **S-Key** toolbar with NO other toolbars or **CommandManager** active! Keyboard shortcuts are still probably the fastest way to call up features. I have also written about this on my site. For beginners, I recommend you learn the software using the **CommandManager**. After you have mastered the basic functionality of the majority of your commonly used features, then move to the two productivity enhancements I have mentioned above.

**Chapter Section 2.8:**   Coordinate Systems

ABE:   Provide some scenarios where you prefer to use a model MCS over WCS.

RICKY:   In SolidWorks, your MCS is called the origin in the **FeatureManager design tree**. This is the (0, 0, 0) location of your model. The default reference planes are centered about the origin. I use this coordinate system 99% of the time in parts and assemblies since you want to build symmetry around these default planes and in many cases dimension directly to them. I utilize these planes in parts and assemblies. The WCS (reference coordinate system) comes in handy with cases where you need to calculate moments of inertia at a given location as opposed to the origin.

**Chapter Section 2.9:** Sketch Planes

ABE: How and why would you edit sketch planes? How often do you edit any plane?

RICKY: Sometimes the need arises to edit a sketch plane. Most of the cases for us has been in the design of injection-molded parts. If we are adding a rib or boss feature on the internals of a plastic part, the geometry used to define that feature sometimes needs to be changed due to molding (draft) requirements. I would say that only 2% of our features require sketch plane edits. If your design intent is not established well up front, this percentage could be higher.

**Chapter Section 2.10:** Sketch Status

ABE: What are the reasons a sketch would be over or under defined? How do you correct this?

RICKY: Over-defined sketches can occur when you have too many parametric dimensions and/or relations in a given sketch. Simply put, usually two or more dimensions/relations are in direct conflict. You can often resolve these issues through the use of relation symbols if you have the view setting turned on (pay attention to the colors) or through the user of the **Display/Delete** relation feature, which can be found on the **Sketch** toolbar or tab. Under-defined sketches occur when you do not have enough dimensions or relations to fully define the geometry in a sketch. The best way to troubleshoot a sketch that is under-defined is to locate the line, arc, or vertex in the sketch that is colored blue (which indicates an under-defined entity). Move this entity and see which direction it can still move. That will show you which degree(s) of freedom are left. I try to always fully define sketches. The only exception to this is when I am utilizing splines in a sketch. In most cases, I leave the spline points under defined unless there is a specific design intent needed. This allows you to easily modify the spline downstream, which is important in consumer product/industrial design projects.

**Chapter Section 2.11:** Three-Dimensional Sketching

ABE: How often do you use 3D sketching? Provide some examples.

RICKY: We use 3D Sketches on occasion. Most of our use is with SolidWorks Electrical Routing. We do use them on occasion when it makes sense and can save time versus creating multiple 2D Sketches. 3D Sketching is becoming more powerful with each release of SolidWorks and I predict will be used more by users in the future. 2D Sketching is still a bit more stable, capable, and predictable when directly compared to 3D Sketching, but the gap between the two is closing.

**Chapter Sections 2.12 and 2.13:** Construction and Reference Geometry

ABE: Provide some examples of using each type of geometry.

RICKY: We use construction geometry in sketches to show design intent or to set up the driven geometry of the sketch. The most common use of

*(continue)*

construction geometry in sketches for us is sketch centerlines used for symmetry. Our most common reference geometry feature is the plane feature. We use this often on both simple and complex parts when we need a sketch to be based on a plane other than the three default planes of the model. It can be used in assembly models as well as an aide in mating components. The necessity of using reference geometry planes has been diminished with the addition of the **From** option in the **Extrude** command. This allows the user to begin the extrude feature at an offset distance from the sketch plane, or through the use of vertices, or other parallel surfaces, planes, or faces, in the model. We also utilize the reference axis command to establish circular pattern axis or linear patter directions in cases where an edge establishing the correct direction might not exist in the model.

**Chapter Section 2.14:**   Sketch Entities

ABE:   How often do you use splines in CAD modeling? Provide some examples.

RICKY:   Splines are used primarily in complex surface models, which you commonly find in consumer product design and industrial design. On these types of projects, we rely heavily on splines and use them along with other functions them to properly designate surface/curvature continuity.

**Chapter Section 2.15:**   Relations

ABE:   Provide some examples of using relations to facilitate construction.

RICKY:   Relations should ALWAYS be used in sketches. The use of relations can reduce the required dimensions to fully define the sketch. Our most common relations used are horizontal, vertical, coincident, concentric, tangent, symmetric, and equal.

**Chapter Section 2.16:**   Equations

ABE:   Provide some examples of using equations to control construction.

RICKY:   We use equations on occasion; for example, one dimension is half another one. We may use equations in instances where variables need to be calculated based on multiple dimensions in a part. These variables can then be used in other equations downstream.

**Chapter Section 2.17:**   Geometric Modifiers

ABE:   How important would you say geometric modifiers are for constructing CAD parts?

RICKY:   We do not use the Quick Snaps at all since most of the snap points that are needed are commonly available in the sketch user interface.

**Chapter Section 2.18:**   Grids

ABE:   When and how would you use grids during construction of CAD parts?

RICKY:   In general we do not use grids. There is an occasional conceptual layout where it might be beneficial to use them, but I haven't even turned that option on in MANY years.

**Chapter Section 2.19:**   Patterns

ABE:   Provide some examples of CAD parts that use patterns.

RICKY:   Common examples include flanges (circular pattern for holes) and bolt patterns for enclosures, which often result in linear patterns. We do occasionally use sketch-driven patterns and sketch-based linear/circular patterns. As mentioned in Section 2.1, we try to think of the assembly when we create patterns when the feature being patterned is a design feature for component population.

**Chapter Section 2.20:**   Selecting, Editing, and Measuring Entities

ABE:   How do you deal with existing entities effectively?

RICKY:   We utilize the **Measure** tool quite often. It is used primarily in assemblies. It is used in parts also when we need to measure between entities that do not have direct parametric relations.

**Chapter Section 2.21:**   Construction Tree

ABE:   How do you use the features manager tree effectively during CAD modeling?

RICKY:   We rely HEAVILY on the **FeatureManager Design tree**. We commonly use it to edit and suppress features. It is the primary interface in many instances to locate features for edit. The fact that it is tied to actions in the geometry area is one of the unique features in SolidWorks. When you click on a face in a model, the corresponding feature in the tree is highlighted. We use the tree to roll back in the geometry creation steps for adding features and retracing the application of features to best understand the makeup of a part. The features tree can be heavily customized in the assembly environment so that your components are better organized through the use of folders. Also note that you can move component orders around in an assembly without affecting any of the mates within that assembly. To me, the features tree is the "epicenter" of the model.

**Chapter Section 2.22:**   Templates

ABE:   Do you use templates at Dynetics? Which ones?

RICKY:   We use various templates. Please refer to Section 2.1 chat.

**Chapter Section 2.23:**   Viewing

ABE:   How do you effectively use viewing to speed up part construction?

RICKY:   Being able to efficiently view your 3D model is very important. The most efficient way of rotation viewing of the model is by utilizing the middle mouse button (or wheel) to rotate the model. I also have a keyboard shortcut for the **Normal To** view command. Utilizing the middle mouse scroll wheel will easily allow you to zoom in and out without having to go to a command in the menus or toolbars. We also use the combination of the **CTRL** key plus the middle mouse button to pan the model. An efficient user does not use toolbars or menus to manipulate the view of the model often.

**Chapter Section 2.24:**   Model Communication

ABE:   How do you communicate CAD models to Dynetics clients and suppliers?

RICKY:   We use eDrawings for models and PDF files for drawings.

*(continue)*

**Others**

ABE: Do you have any other modeling advice you would like to share with our readers?

RICKY: Do your best to be efficient in using SolidWorks. Always strive to learn more about the program with the end goal of becoming a more efficient user. Store common features and annotations in a company-wide shared Design Library so that you can cut down on creating the same feature time and time again. Leverage data reuse as much as possible. If you follow these general guidelines, you will see your design time shrink, which will result in completing your projects and tasks faster. I invite you to visit my blog at www.rickyjordan.com frequently to stay informed of all the latest SolidWorks related tips, tricks, and news.

1. What are the types of CAD models? What are the differences between them? Sketch an example part for each type. (For Solution manual: Use Section 2.2.)

2. Create the part shown in Figure 2.1A. Create its engineering drawing. *Hint:* Use a linear pattern to create the holes.

3. Same as Problem 2, but for Figure 2.1B.

4. Same as Problem 2, but for Figure 2.1C.

5. Same as Problem 2, but for Figure 2.1D. *Hint:* Use a linear pattern to create the keypad.

6. Same as Problem 2, but for Figure 2.1E. *Note:* To create a loft, follow Example 2.4. Here, you need two cross sections: front and back.

7. Write briefly the modeling planning you used to create the part shown in Figure 2.1A. Which part clues did you use from Table 2.1?

8. Same as Problem 7, but for Figure 2.1B.

9. Same as Problem 7, but for Figure 2.1C.

10. Same as Problem 7, but for Figure 2.1D.

11. Same as Problem 7, but for Figure 2.1E.

12. How many faces, edges, vertices, loops, and genus does each part in Figure 2.1 have? Verify Euler equation for each part.

13. Edit the sketch for the part shown in Figure 2.1A (created in Problem 2) to double the size of the part.

14. Same as Problem 13, but for the part shown in Figure 2.1B.

15. Same as Problem 13, but for the part shown in Figure 2.1C.

16. Use the Keyboard tab in the **Customize Menu** shown in Figure 2.11 to create your own customized keyboard shortcuts.

17. Edit the sketch plane of the part shown in Figure 2.1A so that the top view becomes the front view.

18. Same as Problem 17, but for the part shown in Figure 2.1B.

19. The sketches you used to create parts of Figures 2.1A, 2.1B, and 2.1C are fully defined. Change them to make them under-defined or over-defined. Find at least two ways to achieve the under or over status. Explain the reason(s) for each sketch status.

20. Create the nonplanar curve in Task D in Step 2 of Example 2.4, and show that the loft fails to create. Submit a screenshot of SolidWorks error message.

21. Create an equation so that the depth of the extrusion shown in Figure 2.1B (created in Problem 3) is equal to twice the depth of the extrusion.

22. Create a 60 × 60 × 60 mm cube. Create one of its diagonals as **Axis** from the **Reference Geometry** menu. Figure 2.42 shows the cube and the axis. Rotate copy the cube 30 degrees around the axis to get the result shown.

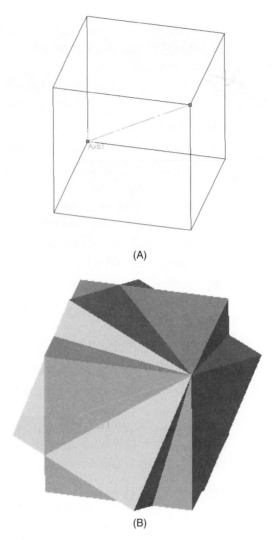

(A)

(B)

**FIGURE 2.42**
Rotating a model

23. You need to verify and get the geometric information of the vertices, edges, and faces of the cube shown in Figure 2.42. *Hint:* Use **Tools => Measure**. When you select an entity, SolidWorks displays its geometric information.

24. Translate copy the cube shown in Figure 2.42 along the following vector: $d_x = -50$, $d_y = 50$, and $d_z = 100$.

25. Scale the cube shown in Figure 2.42 uniformly by a scale of 2, and nonuniformly by scales of 1, 2, and 3 in the X, Y, and Z directions respectively.

26. Create your favorite master part template. Set sketch planes, views, units, colors, decimals, font size, etc. Use the template throughout the book to create your parts.

27. Create eDrawings of the parts of Problems 2, 3, 4, and 5. Apply some of the interesting tools that eDrawings offers such as stamping. E-mail the eDrawings file to one of your friends and ask him or her to open it in a Web browser to view your CAD work.

28. Create the SolidWorks part of the AMP connector model shown in Figure 2.43. Also, create the drawing of the part. All dimensions are in inches.

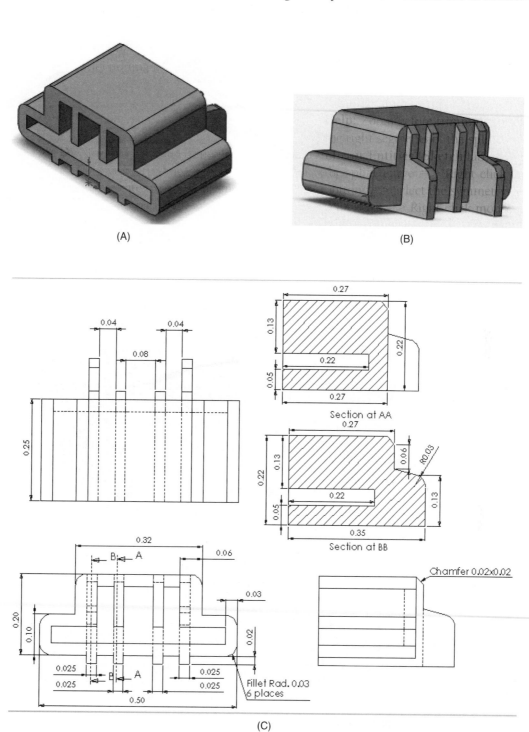

(A)

(B)

(C)

**FIGURE 2.43**
AMP connector

**29.** Create the SolidWorks part of the air cylinder model shown in Figure 2.44. Also, create the drawing of the part. All dimensions are in inches.

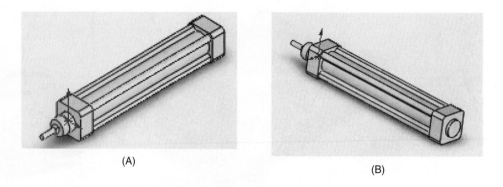

(A)

(B)

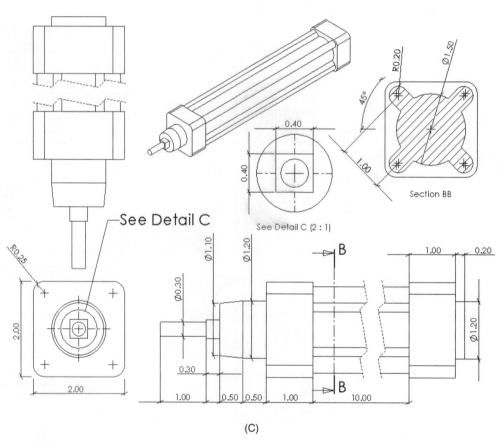

(C)

**FIGURE 2.44**
Air cylinder

30. Create the SolidWorks part of the flange model shown in Figure 2.45. Also, create the drawing of the part. All dimensions are in inches.

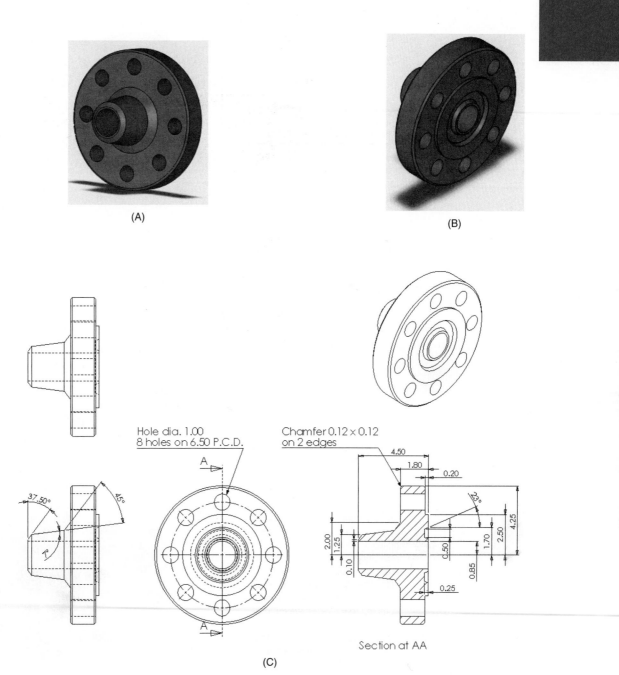

(A)

(B)

Hole dia. 1.00
8 holes on 6.50 P.C.D.

Chamfer 0.12 × 0.12
on 2 edges

37.50°

4.5°

7°

4.50

1.80

0.20

2.00

1.25

0.10

0.50

0.85

0.25

1.70

2.50

4.25

A

A

Section at AA

(C)

**FIGURE 2.45**
Flange

**31.** Create the SolidWorks part of the laser reflector model shown in Figure 2.46. Also, create the drawing of the part. All dimensions are in inches.

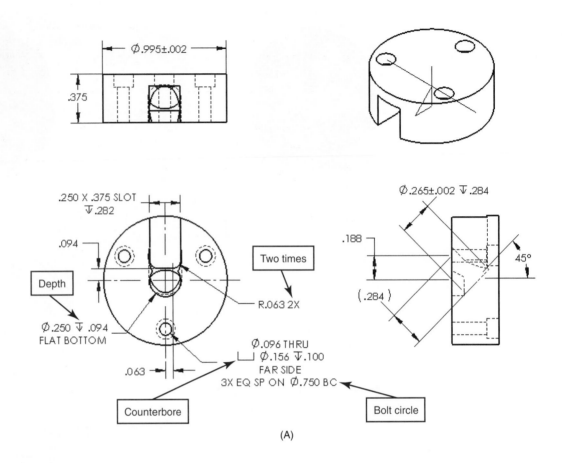

(A)

Shown to the right is a transparent ISO view of the laser mount to show its inside. It has a hole drilled at 45 degrees, another hole drilled from the bottom, and a pocket milled from the right side. The three features intersect as shown, making the geometry complex to follow. However, machining this part is simple. After cutting these three features, the machinist drills the three counterbores to finish machining the part.

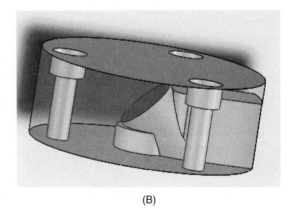

(B)

**FIGURE 2.46**
Laser reflector (Courtesy of VIC)

**32.** Create the SolidWorks part of the laser mount model shown in Figure 2.47. Also, create the drawing of the part. All dimensions are in inches.

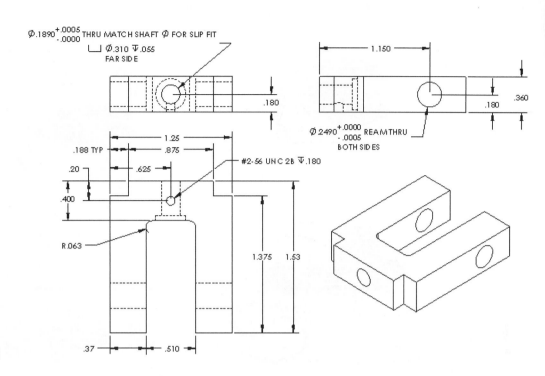

**FIGURE 2.47**
Laser mount
(Courtesy of VIC)

**33.** Create the SolidWorks part of the switch activator lever model shown in Figure 2.48. Also, create the drawing of the part. All dimensions are in inches.

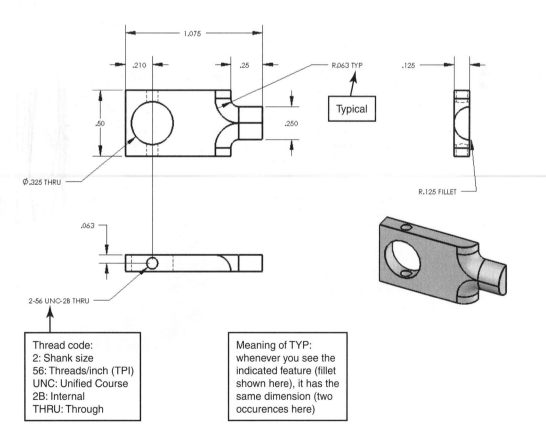

**FIGURE 2.48**
Switch activator lever
(Courtesy of VIC)

Thread code:
2: Shank size
56: Threads/inch (TPI)
UNC: Unified Course
2B: Internal
THRU: Through

Meaning of TYP:
whenever you see the
indicated feature (fillet
shown here), it has the
same dimension (two
occurences here)

**34.** Create the SolidWorks part of the floor lamp model shown in Figure 2.49. Also, create the drawing of the part. Make up your dimensions as you sketch freely. *Note:* Create as one part, not as an assembly.

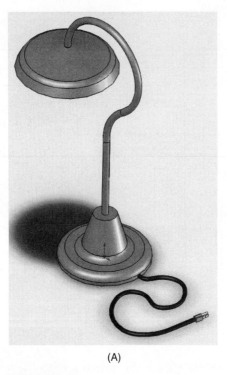

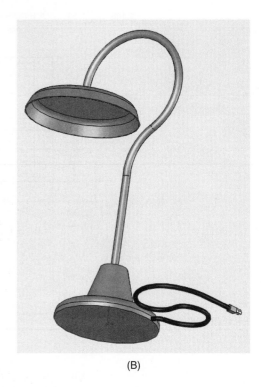

(A)                                                    (B)

**FIGURE 2.49**
Floor lamp model

**35.** Create the L bracket shown in Figure 2.50. Also, create the drawing of the part. The typical L bracket is a six-sided feature. Instead of sketching and dimensioning the L cross section (six lines), we extrude a block dimensioned to the overall size (2 × 2) and then extrude cut a smaller block (1.75 × 1.75) to produce the final L shape. Thus, you need two steps to create the L shape. *Note:* The L bracket shape is a very important one for engineers. Stock aluminum, plastic, and steel are sold in these shapes. It is important to work from stock shapes to reduce cost and increase manufacturability and availability of designs.

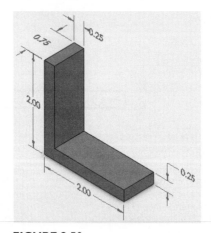

**FIGURE 2.50**
L bracket (all dims in inches)

*Note:* To create the extrude cut, select the front face of the block, sketch the two lines that form the L, and exit the sketch. There is no need to create a closed rectangle in the sketch. SolidWorks understands the context, closes the sketch with the face edges, and creates the cut. Using this idea, you can create extrude cuts with elaborate profiles in the block.

36. Create the pattern block shown in Figure 2.51. Block depth (thickness) is 0.500 in. Also, create the drawing of the part.

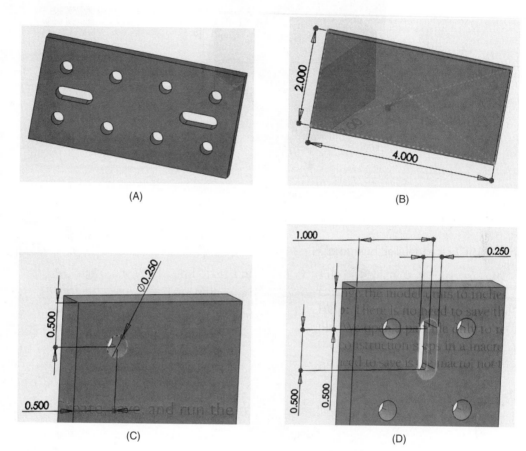

(A)

(B)

(C)

(D)

**FIGURE 2.51**
Pattern block (all dims in inches)

37. Create the pattern wheel shown in Figure 2.52. Wheel depth (thickness) is 5 mm. The hub depth is 15 mm (extending 5 mm from each face of the wheel). Also, create the drawing of the part.

**FIGURE 2.52**
Pattern wheel
(all dims in mm)

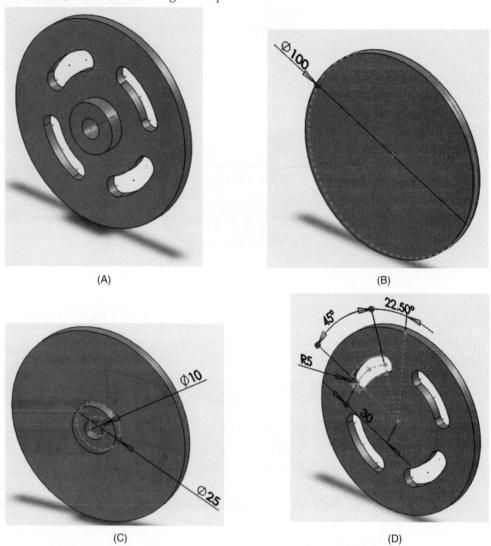

(A)

(B)

(C)

(D)

38. Create the following gasket sketch in Figure 2.53. Grid spacing is 0.5 in. Use the sketch to create an extrusion with thickness of 0.75 in. Also, create the drawing of the part.

**FIGURE 2.53**
Gasket (all dims in inches)

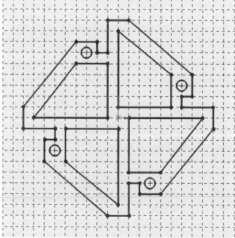

Part I Computer Aided Design (CAD) Basics

# Design Intent

## 3.1 Introduction

Design intent is important in CAD/CAM design. It influences the way we think about creating CAD models. Generally, we define **design intent** as the rationale behind the decision-making process during design. There is a difference between design intent and design functionality. Intent justifies the design whereas functionality describes what the design does. The effect of design intent is observed in design and manufacturing tasks, for example, editing/modifying the design or manufacturing the part. Design intent is not a well-defined topic; it is open for different interpretations and may take various forms. Some view design intent as relations, geometric constraints, mating conditions in assemblies, the sequence of creating a part, etc. Others believe design intent is to create the CAD part in the same way it will be manufactured (machined). Some even talk about manufacturing intent.

Although it is universally acknowledged that knowing and using design intent are important, there is a lack of both support for framework for design intent and widespread use in engineering. Yet, interest in design intent systems has grown. We define a **design intent system** as a tool for capturing design intent and making it easily accessible. These systems are important tools because they include not only the reasons behind a design decision but also the justification for it, the other alternatives considered, the trade-offs evaluated, and the arguments that led to the decision. Design intent systems improve dependency management, collaboration, reuse, maintenance, learning, and documentation.

As the design and manufacturing processes evolve around the geometric shape of the product, the current CAD/CAM systems are based on geometric modeling techniques. Although these techniques are powerful modeling tools, they are deficient in recording the embodiment details of the product such as design intent, manufacturing specifications, and other constraints. CAD/CAM systems cannot easily answer design-related questions such as, How is it supposed to work? Why is it done this way? What alternatives were considered? What can be changed? and What will be affected?

## 3.2 Capturing Design Intent

In terms of geometric modeling, we define design intent as the rationale behind selecting a particular modeling plan (strategy) to create a part. The modeling synthesis we describe in the book represents a form of design intent. We also follow the notion to "design the part as you would manufacture it." Tutorial 3–1 shows an example. We can capture design intent in various ways during geometric modeling:

1. **Modeling plan:** A plan involves careful selection of a modeling sequence and evaluating how it affects future editing, modifications, and changes. A general rule for selecting a plan is how the part is manufactured. Consider an extrusion with four holes. One plan is to create a sketch with a rectangle and four circles and extrude the sketch. Another plan is to create a sketch with a rectangle, extrude it, and then create four extrude cuts features; each feature has its own sketch. The question now is which plan is more efficient, and which is better? The first plan is more efficient, but the second plan is better. The second plan follows the manufacturing principles. We start with a block stock, machine it, and drill four holes, one at a time.

2. **Relations:** Specify relations among sketch entities to capture the design intent among them. For example, two entities may be parallel or perpendicular to each other.

3. **Equations:** Define equations to define design intent. For example, write equations to force the center of a hole always to be at the center point of a rectangle (see Example 2.5).

4. **Assembly mating conditions:** These conditions specify how components of an assembly are connected to each other.

Keep in mind that with good design intent, CAD models can be updated almost effortlessly. Changes made to one aspect of a model propagate appropriately through the model, assembly, and drawing. With poor design intent, features may update inappropriately or fail. When selecting references, construction sequence, or other modeling activities, always ask yourself how the model might change. Should a hole stay centered on the part? Should it remain a fixed distance from some face or edge? Should it move with an associated feature, such as a boss? Considering the full range of possible changes, will a drastic change in a dimension make a sketch impossible to resolve, for example, turning it inside out?

The CAD designer should carefully consider the consequences of his or her design methodology. The following is a list of typical questions that the designer may address to facilitate capturing the design intent without violating the design concepts:

☐ Which feature to create first, that is, what is the base feature (e.g., rectangle with a round post)

☐ In what order should other features follow (holes, cutouts, chamfer, fillets)

☐ What tool to use to create a feature (some geometries such as holes can be created using many different tools/commands)

☐ What sketching plane to use (the datum plane or the feature surface)

☐ What to reference the feature sketch to (datum for dimensioning, etc.)

☐ How to dimension the feature sketch (should an arc use a radius or diameter?)

☐ What constraints to use to lock the sketch shape (horizontal, vertical, parallel, etc.)

☐ What relations/dimensions to use that ensure valid sketch updates (length = 2*width)

☐ How the feature will be dimensioned in the drawing

☐ Can the component be assembled in reality?

☐ What is the ease of assembly?

☐ What assembly constraints to use (screw in a hole)

☐ Do these constraints reflect/mimic reality?

☐ What entities to select to apply assembly constraints (shaft in bearing using inner surface)

☐ Can the feature be machined/produced?

☐ How easily the feature will be machined

How much planning and consideration should a designer give to design intent? The answer is difficult. We are certain that paying too much attention to design intent prohibits creativity and innovation in design, and slows finishing modeling tasks considerably. Our advice is that design intent and intuition come with experience. Sometimes it is hard to foresee all possible cases down the design road. Thus, start with the obvious design intent in your part, and discover other design intent during modeling.

## 3.3 Documenting Design Intent

Documenting and capturing design intent make your design more reusable and easier to modify in the future. Documenting design intent facilitates communicating and enforcing any agreed-upon design principles and rules. The key to effective use of design intent is to be sure all members of the design team consistently document it all the time. The design intent can be shared via HTML or Word documents, as shown in this chapter. SolidWorks provides multiple methods to document design intent: comments, design binder, equations, design tables, configurations, dimension names, feature names, and organizing the features tree into folders. These methods are discussed in the sections to follow.

## 3.4 Comments

A designer may add comments to features. The designer documents the decisions made during the design process to enable other design team members to understand the design intent of the features design, thus enabling them to modify the design more easily. Click this sequence to add a comment to a feature: Right-click a feature from the features tree = > **Comment** (from the windows that pops up) = > **Add Comment** = > Type your comments in the window that opens up = > **Save** and **Close**. This sequence opens the sticky note shown in Figure 3.1A. We recommend that your note begin with a date/time stamp and your name followed by your comment. Your comments should be succinct, short, and explain your decisions. When you hover over the feature, your note appears in a balloon, as shown in Figure 3.1B. The features tree has a folder

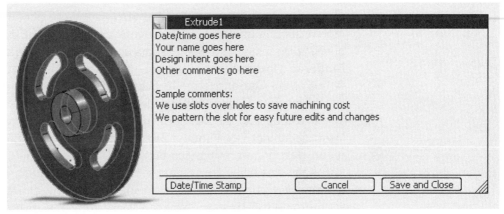

(A) Add comments

**FIGURE 3.1**
Comments

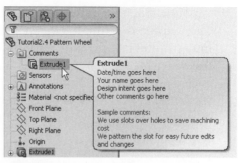
(B) View comments

(C) Edit/delete comments

**FIGURE 3.1**
(*Continued*)

(branch) called **Comments** that appears in the tree only when you add comments to features. Features that have comments appear in the **Comments** folder. To edit or delete comments of a feature, right-click it in the **Comments** folder, and select from the menu that pops up shown in Figure 3.1C.

## 3.5 Design Binder

The design binder is an embedded Microsoft Word document that allows you to add more elaborate information about your design than the comments you add in sticky notes. You can add text, screenshots, etc. Follow this sequence to display the **Design Binder** in a features tree: Open the part $=>$ **Tools** (SolidWorks menu) $=>$ **Options** $=>$ **System Options** tab $=>$ **FeatureManager design tree** (pane on left) $=>$ Select **Show** (for **Design Binder**) from drop-down list $=>$ **OK** (see Figure 3.2A). When you expand the **Design Binder** on the features tree, you see a Design Journal Word document (see Figure 3.2B). It is an empty document. Double-click it to open it and start documenting (see Figure 3.2C). The document has three lines; the first one is the part name (see Figure 3.2C). You can include screenshots of the design in addition to writing. When you edit and save the journal, it is saved with the part; you would not see it. However, you can save a copy of it if you click Word **File = > Save Copy As**. Right-click the **Design Journal** item in the features tree to delete it (see Figure 3.2B). If you delete it, an empty document replaces it. You always have a Design Journal document in the features tree.

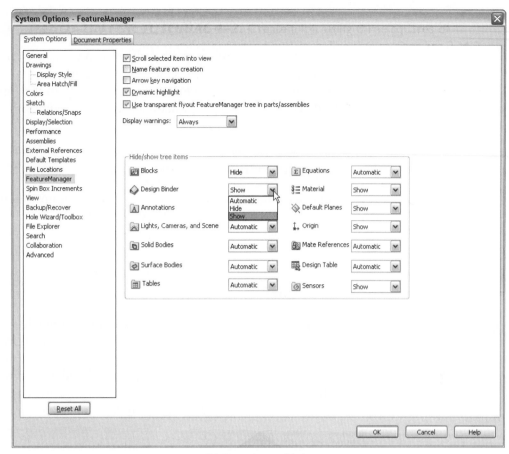

(A) Show Design Binder

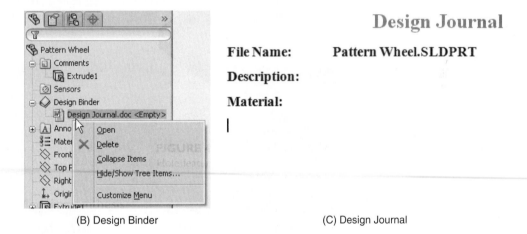

(B) Design Binder

**Design Journal**

**File Name:**     **Pattern Wheel.SLDPRT**

**Description:**

**Material:**

(C) Design Journal

**FIGURE 3.2**
Design Binder

## 3.6 Equations

Section 2.16 in Chapter 2 covers how to create and use equations. In the context of design intent, you can add a comment to the equation (see screenshot in Step 2 of Example 2.5). When you use equations, make sure you use meaningful names for the dimensions (variables) used in the equation for better readability of the equation.

## 3.7  Design Tables and Configurations

Design tables are a design tool that allows you to change dimensions and create a new instance of the part. These instances form a family of parts (configurations). We cover design tables and configurations later in the book. In the context of design intent, you can add comments in each by adding text in the Comment field.

## 3.8  Dimension Names

Changing the default dimension names to more meaningful names enhances design intent. Example 2.3 in Chapter 2 shows how to change dimension names. These names make equations or design tables more readable.

## 3.9  Feature Names

Changing the default names of features to more meaningful names makes it much easier to follow the features tree and makes the design intent clearer for someone who wants to reverse engineer the part creation steps. The default names are usually the feature type followed by a number (e.g., **Extrude1**, **Extrude2**, **Revolve1**, **Cut-Extrude1**, etc.). To change a feature's name, click the name twice slowly (do not double-click) in the features tree and type the new name. A properly named features tree of a part is much easier to read and modify. You do not need to change the name of every node on the features tree, only the important ones. For example, there is no need to rename fillets, chamfers, etc. Figure 3.3 shows the same features tree with default names and better names. The value of better naming is clearly delineated. To make naming features easier, you can enable the **Name** option (check box) by clicking this sequence: **Tools = >**

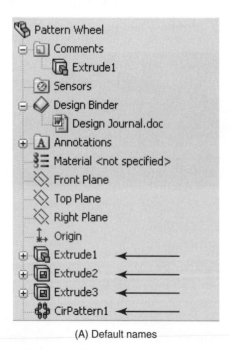

(A) Default names

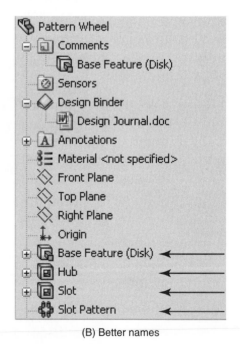

(B) Better names

**FIGURE 3.3**
Naming features

**Options = > FeatureManager = > Name feature on creation**. When you click the green check mark to finish the feature creation, SolidWorks highlights the feature name and allows you to input a new name. Turning on (enabling) this option saves you the two slow clicks to rename a feature.

## 3.10 Folders

You can organize the features tree into groups to help force the user to think of the design in terms of groups. You can use folders to create these groups. When you create features that should belong to one group, roll back the feature to the appropriate group. You can create folders in a part or assembly tree. You can rename new folders and drag features into them, thus reducing the length of the tree. When you select a folder in the features tree, all the parts of the folder are highlighted in the graphics pane on the screen. Conversely, when you select a feature in the graphics pane, its corresponding folder is highlighted and expanded in the features tree. SolidWorks imposes two rules on the folder to maintain the parent–child relationships (integrity) of the features tree. First, you can place only a set of continuous features into a folder; you cannot use the **CTRL** key to select noncontinuous features. Second, you cannot create folders (subfolders) inside folders.

To create a new folder, right-click any feature on the features tree, and select **Add to New Folder** or **Create New Folder** from the pop-up, as shown in Figure 3.4A. Rename the new folder and drag and drop any features to it. If you try to drag and drop features into a folder in such a way to alter the creation order, you get an error message to that effect, as shown in Figure 3.4B. For example, you cannot move **Extrude2** feature to the **Block** folder. You must move **Extrude1** feature first to maintain the features tree hierarchical structure.

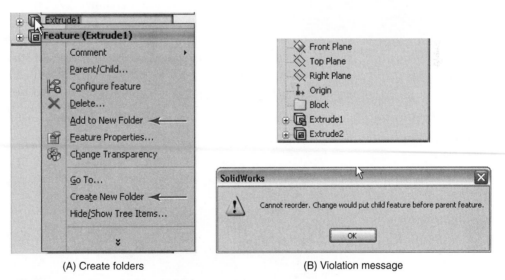

(A) Create folders                    (B) Violation message

**FIGURE 3.4**
Folders

To delete a folder, right-click it and select **Delete** from the pop-up. Deleting a folder does not delete its content (features inside it). It only removes the folder from the features tree and leaves its features in their respective locations in the tree.

## 3.11 Tutorials Overview

The theme for the tutorials in this chapter is to get you to practice creating and documenting design intent. MJ Engineering & Consulting Inc. (www.mjengineering.com) has sponsored this chapter. MJ Engineering is a full-service machine and system design consulting firm applying state-of-the-art technology to industrial operations. It specializes in the analysis and design of mechanical, structural, hydraulic, pneumatic, and electrical systems. MJ Engineering has a proven track record of designing cost-effective and efficient machinery on time and under budget. Its engineers and designers are competent in all phases of the manufacturing and design processes and have special experience with finite element analysis, robotics, automation, control systems integration, fabrication, machining, forging, casting, and metal formation.

## Tutorial 3–1: Design Intent via Two Modeling Plans

### Modeling task

Create the slider block shown in Figure 3.5 by using a good modeling plan.

### Design intent

The 1.00″ hole should cut through the block and be located horizontally from the midpoint of the square cut. The hole on the chamfer face should cut through to the 1.00″ hole.

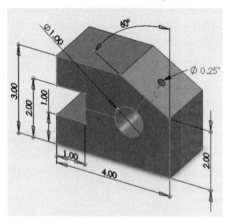

Part thickness = 2 in.

**FIGURE 3.5**
A slider block

### Modeling synthesis

This tutorial applies the concept that design intent is to create the CAD part such that it will lend itself to quick and painless modification in the future. It also applies the concept that a part should be designed the same way it will be manufactured (machined). This part is an extrusion with two holes, a slot, and a chamfer. We can think of at least two modeling plans to create the block. In Plan A, we call it cross-section based, we create the front face and extrude it. In Plan B, we break down the part into basic features and create each feature individually. Figure 3.6 shows the two plans. The first plan uses a total of two operations, whereas the second plan uses five operations. Both result in the same part; however, later you will see why Plan B ends up with a part that is easier to work with and to modify.

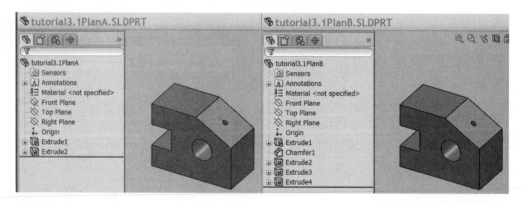

**FIGURE 3.6**
Plan A and Plan B

## Modeling Plan A

We are going to attempt to include as much geometry in one sketch as possible, therefore ending up with minimal features in the design tree.

### CAD steps

We create the slider block in one step:

1. Create the part.

The details of this step are shown below.

## Step I: Create the part shown in Figure 3.7

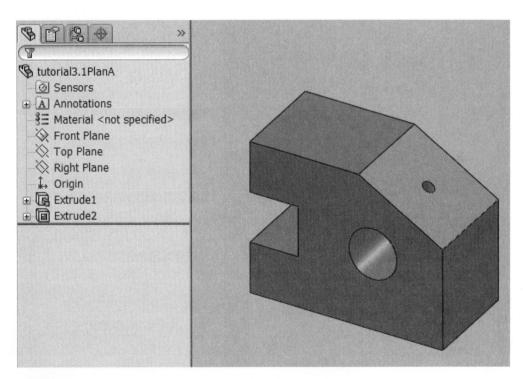

**FIGURE 3.7**
Part to create

| Task | Command Sequence to Click |
|---|---|
| A. Create the main feature. 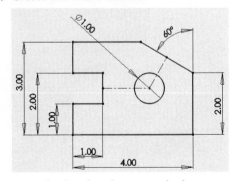 | **Sketch = > Front Plane** and sketch and dimension as shown to the left. *Help*: Use construction lines to locate the 1.00″ circle. |
| B. Extrude the sketch as a mid-plane extrusion. | **Features = > Extrude = > Mid Plane = > 2.00″** |

| Task | Command Sequence to Click |
|------|---------------------------|
| C. Cut the hole on the chamfer face. 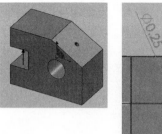 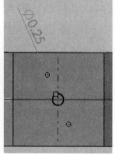 | Select the chamfer face = > **Sketch Use** geometric constraints to locate the center of the circle on the **Front Plane** and the axis of the hole from Step A. **Extrude = > Up To Surface** = > Select the face of the hole from Step B. **Why?** This hole will now cut through to the first hole even if the location of the first hole of the part changes in the future. |

## Modeling Plan B

For this plan we will use five features.

## CAD steps

We create the slider block in five steps:

1. Create the main extrusion.
2. Create the chamfer.
3. Create the square cut.
4. Create the 1.00″ circle cut.
5. Create the hole on the chamfer face.

The details of these steps are shown below.

## Step 1: Create the main extrusion shown in Figure 3.8

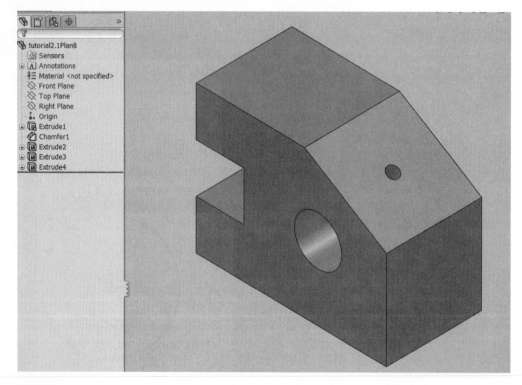

**FIGURE 3.8**
Part to create

| Task | Command Sequence to Click |
|---|---|
| A. Select the front plane as the sketch plane.<br>B. Create the box.<br>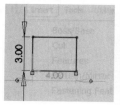 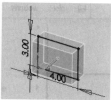 | **Sketch = > Front Plane** from features manager tree on left of screen<br>Sketch and extrude the rectangle as shown to the left. **Features = > Extrude = > Mid Plane = > 2.00″** |

## Step 2: Create the chamfer

| Task | Command Sequence to Click |
|---|---|
| A. Create the chamfer.<br>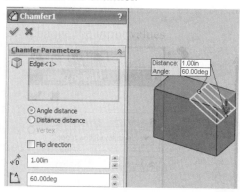 | Select the appropriate edge and then **Features = > Chamfer**. Fill in the boxes as shown to the left = > Click green check mark to accept. |

## Step 3: Create the square cut

| Task | Command Sequence to Click |
|---|---|
| A. Create the square cut.<br>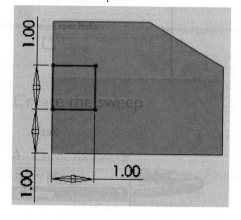 | Select the face = > **Features = > Extrude Cut**. Sketch the rectangle and dimension as shown to the left. Click green check mark in top right-hand corner = > Select **Through All** from drop-down and accept. |

**Step 4:** Create the 1.00″ circle cut

Task

A. Create the hole.

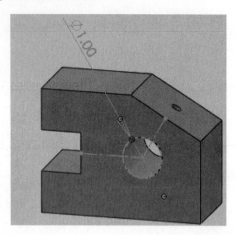

Command Sequence to Click

**Features = > Extrude Cut.** Sketch the circle and dimension as shown to the left. Use the construction lines as in Task A in Step 1 from Plan A to locate the center of the circle. Click green check mark in top right-hand corner = > Select **Through All** from drop-down and accept.

**Step 5:** Create the hole on the chamfer face shown in Figure 3.8

Task

A. Create the hole on the chamfer face.

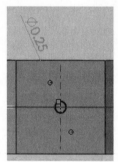

Command Sequence to Click

**Features = > Extrude Cut.** Sketch the circle and dimension as shown to the left. Use the axis from the first hole and the **Front Plane** as in Task A in Step 2 from Plan A to locate the center of the circle. Click Green check mark in the top right-hand corner = > Select **Up To Surface** from drop-down = > Select the face of the first hole and accept.

**Why:** Modeling Plan B lends itself more to how the part would be manufactured in real life; therefore, it is better than Plan A.

---

***HANDS-ON FOR TUTORIAL 3–1.*** Modify the block from each plan. Notice that it is easier to modify geometry if it is broken into individual features. For example, if a second revision of the design calls for the hole in the front face to be a blind depth of 0.5″, then Plan B is far easier to modify than Plan A.

---

Part I Computer Aided Design (CAD) Basics

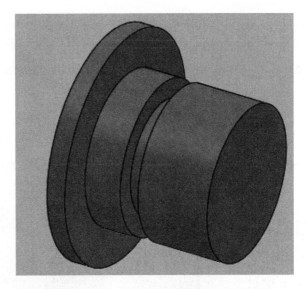

**FIGURE 3.9**
Drain plug

## Tutorial 3–2:  Design Intent via Three Modeling Plans

### Modeling task

Create the drain plug in Figure 3.9.

### Design intent

The overall length of the part shall remain 1.00″ regardless of changes to other features.

### Modeling synthesis

This tutorial applies the concept that design intent is to create the CAD part in the same way it will be manufactured (machined). We can think of at least three modeling plans to create the plug. In the first plan, called Addition method, we will continuously add features to previous features. For the second plan, Cross-section method, we will revolve the entire part in one feature. Finally in the third plan, Manufacturing method, we will create the part using both revolves and cuts to mimic how the part would be manufactured on a lathe.

### Modeling plan

The three plans are Plan A: Addition; Plan B: Cross Section; and Plan C: Manufacturing.

### CAD steps

Create the part three times using the plans and save in three separate files.

1. Create the plug using Plan A: Addition method.
2. Create the plug using Plan B: Cross-section method.
3. Create the plug using Plan C: Manufacturing method.

The details are shown below.

## Step 1: Drain plug: Plan A Addition method

Task

A. Create each disc extruded from the face of the previous feature.

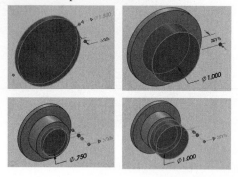

Command Sequence to Click

**Sketch** = > **Circle** = > Dimension as shown to the left.
**Features** = > **Extrude** = > Dimension as shown to the left.
**Why?** Changing any one extrusion value will have a chaining effect on the subsequent extrusions. This can cause problems.

## Step 2: Drain plug: Plan B Cross-Sectioned method

Task

A. Create the plug using one revolve feature.

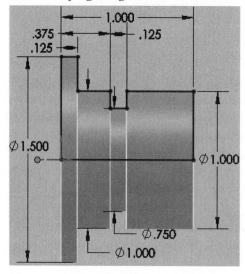

Command Sequence to Click

**Front Plane** = > **Sketch** = > **Line** = > Start by drawing the outline to roughly about the size of the desired dimensions shown to the left. Second, add the correct dimensions using the **Smart Dimension** tool.
**Help:** Draw a construction line of any length at the center of the sketch. This can be used to dimension from to create "Diameter" dimensions as opposed to "Radius" dimensions. Also, this line will be used to revolve the sketch about to create the feature.

## Step 3: Drain plug: Plan C Manufacturing method

Task

A. Start modeling by using the stock shape (round bar) that the machinist would start from.

Command Sequence to Click

**Sketch** = > **Right Plane** = > **Circle** = > Sketch and dimension as shown to the left.
**Extrude** = > **Blind** = > 1.00″

| Task | Command Sequence to Click |
|---|---|

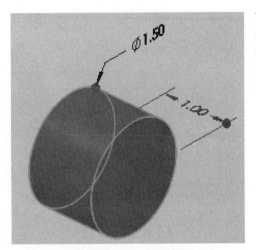

**Why:** This part lends itself to a lathe manufacturing process. Most likely the machinist will start from a piece of round bar stock material and cut away the desired geometry.

B. Make the first cut.

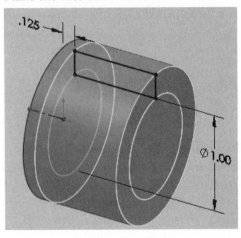

**Sketch = >** Front Plane = >
**Rectangle** = > Sketch and dimension as shown to the left.
**Revolve Cut** = > Select the construction line at the center of the sketch to revolve about.

C. Create the groove.

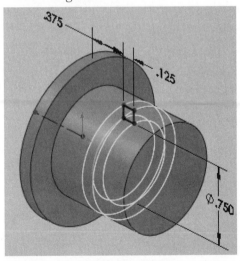

**Sketch = >** Front Plane = >
**Rectangle** = > Sketch and dimension as shown to the left.
**Revolve Cut** = > Select the construction line at the center of the sketch to revolve about.

---

***HANDS-ON FOR TUTORIAL 3–2.*** Use each of the three plans to modify the part by deleting the groove while maintaining the design intent. Notice how easy it is to work with Plan C. What are the difficulties you encountered during modifying Plan A and Plan B?

---

## Tutorial 3–3: Design Intent via Design Specifications

### Modeling task

Create the hand wheel part shown in Figure 3.10.

**FIGURE 3.10**
Hand wheel

### Design intent

The hub shall remain at the center of the wheel. The spokes will connect the wheel to the hub. The part shall be designed such that we can easily modify the wheel and hub diameter.

### Modeling synthesis

There are multiple ways to create the hand wheel. We can think of two ways: as one part or as one assembly. We use the former way in this tutorial.

### Modeling plan

We create the hand wheel using three features: the wheel, the hub, and the spokes as a pattern.

### CAD steps

We create the hand wheel in six steps:

1. Create the hub revolve.
2. Create the wheel revolve.
3. Create the sweep profile.
4. Create the sweep path.
5. Create the spoke sweep.
6. Pattern the spoke.

The details are shown below.

## Step 1: Create the hub revolve

Task

A. Create the hub.

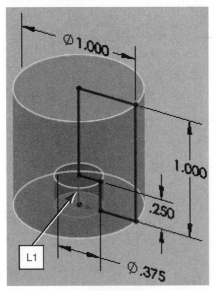

Command Sequence to Click

**Front Plane** = > **Sketch** = >
**Rectangle** = > Sketch and
dimension the circle as shown to
the left.
**Revolve Boss/Base** = > Revolve
about a central, vertical
construction line L1.
**Help:** Note the .375″ × .250″ hole
at the center of the hub.

## Step 2: Create the wheel revolve

Task

A. Create the wheel.

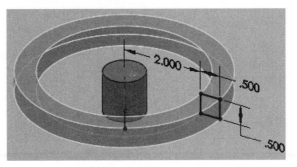

Command Sequence to Click

**Front Plane** = > **Sketch** = >
**Rectangle** = > Sketch and
dimension the circle as shown to
the left.
**Revolve Boss/Base** = > Revolve
about the axis of the hub.

## Step 3: Create the sweep profile

Task

A. Create the sweep profile.

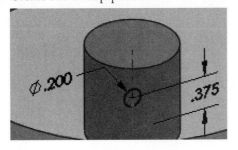

Command Sequence to Click

**Right Plane** = > **Sketch** = >
**Circle** = > Sketch and dimension
the circle as shown to the left.
**Help:** The circle is vertically .375″
from the origin.

## Step 4: Create the sweep path

| Task | Command Sequence to Click |
|---|---|
| A. Create the sweep path. | **Front Plane = > Sketch** use **lines** and **3 point arcs** to create the sketch shown to the left. **Help:** Use **Tangent** relations at both ends of each arc. The path is coincident to the center axis to the left and coincident to the inner edge of the wheel to the right. |

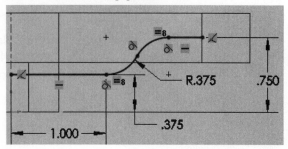

## Step 5: Create the spoke sweep

| Task | Command Sequence to Click |
|---|---|
| A. Create the spoke sweep. | **Features = > Swept Boss/Base** = > Select the circle from Task A of Step 3 as the profile and the sketch from Task A of Step 4 as the path. |

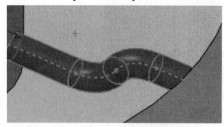

## Step 6: Pattern the spoke

| Task | Command Sequence to Click |
|---|---|
| A. Pattern the spoke. | **Features = > Circular Pattern** = > Select the axis of the hub to revolve about and the spoke as the feature to pattern. |

---

***HANDS-ON FOR TUTORIAL 3–3.*** We enforce the design intent in our modeling plan via using the following relation: **Coincident** relation between the right end of the sweep path and the inner edge of the wheel. Remove this relation and modify the wheel radius to 1.00″. What happens to the spokes?

---

## Tutorial 3–4: Design Intent via Mating Conditions

### Modeling task

Create the Pin Block assembly in Figure 3.11 by using assembly mating conditions.

**FIGURE 3.11**
Pin Block assembly

**Design Intent**

The pin shall remain centered on the block regardless of changes.

**Modeling synthesis**

This tutorial applies the concept that design intent is to create the CAD part in the same way it will be used in an assembly.

**Modeling plan**

We will create the pin and the block about a center plane. We will then use this center plane to mate the two parts.

**CAD steps:**

We create the Pin Block assembly in three steps:

1. Create the pin.
2. Create the block.
3. Create the Pin Block assembly.

The details are shown below.

## Step 1: Create the pin

| Task | Command Sequence to Click |
|---|---|
| A. Create the pin.<br>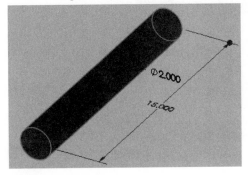 | **Front Plane = > Sketch = > Circle** = > Sketch and dimension the circle as shown to the left.<br>**Features = > Extrude = > Mid Plane = > 15.0″** |

## Step 2: Create the block

| Task | Command Sequence to Click |
|---|---|
| A. Create the block.<br>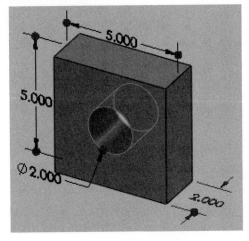 | **Front Plane = > Sketch = > Rectangle** = > Sketch and dimension the block as shown to the left.<br>**Features = > Extrude = > Mid Plane = > 2.0″**<br>Help: This part is made using a 2.0″ extrusion and a circle through cut located using a **Coincident** relation to the origin. This uses fewer dimensions to fully define the part. |

## Step 3:   Create the Pin Block assembly

| Task | Command Sequence to Click |
|---|---|
| A. Create the Pin Block assembly shown in Figure 3.11. | **Insert Components** = > Select the block from Step 2. Without clicking in the graphics pane, just hit the green check mark to accept. **Why?** This will fix the origin of the part to the origin of the assembly. This is a good practice to use when inserting the first part of an assembly. **Insert Components** = > Select the pin from Step 1. Mate the pin to the block using a **Concentric Mate** with the circular face from each part. Also mate using a **Coincident Mate** between the **Front Plane** of each part. |
| B. Now we will change the size of the block along with the length of the pin. | Notice that, with the changes shown to the left, the design intent is withheld. |

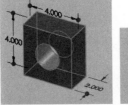
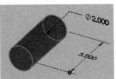
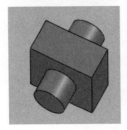

> ***HANDS-ON FOR TUTORIAL 3–4.*** Currently, the hole and the shaft diameters are not related. Add a new design intent in the form of an equation that forces the two diameters to be equal. Change the value from 2.000″ to 3.000″.

## Tutorial 3–5:   Poor Design Intent

### Modeling task

Re-create the Pin Block assembly shown in Figure 3.11 by using different mating conditions.

### Design intent

As mentioned above, the pin should remain centered on the block regardless of changes.

### Modeling synthesis

This tutorial applies the concept that design intent is to create the CAD part in the same way it will be used in an assembly.

### Modeling plan

We will create the pin and the block about a center plane. We will then use this center plane to mate the two parts.

### CAD steps

We create the Pin Block assembly in four steps:

1. Re-create the pin.
2. Re-create the block.
3. Re-create the Pin Block assembly.
4. Modify the pin and block.

The details are shown below.

## Step 1: Re-create the pin

#### Task

A. Create the pin.

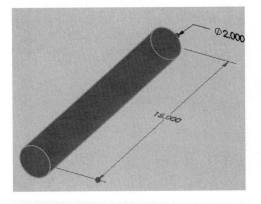

#### Command Sequence to Click

**Front Plane = > Sketch = > Circle = >** Sketch and dimension the circle as shown to the left.
**Features = > Extrude = > Blind = > 15.0"**
**Why?** We use a **Blind** extrusion from the **Front Plane** this time instead of **Mid Plane** as in Tutorial 3–4.

## Step 2: Re-create the block

#### Task

A. Create the block.

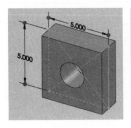 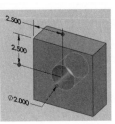

#### Command Sequence to Click

**Front Plane = > Sketch = > Rectangle = >** Sketch and dimension the block as shown to the left.
**Features = > Extrude = > Mid Plane = > 2.0"**
**Why?** This time we dimension the circle from the edges, as opposed to Tutorial 3–4 where we located the center using a **Coincident** relation to the **Origin**.

## Step 3: Re-create the Pin Block assembly

### Task

A. Create the Pin Block assembly shown in Figure 3.11.

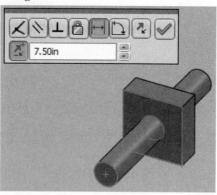

### Command Sequence to Click

**Insert Components** = > Select the block from Step 2. Without clicking in the graphics pane, just hit the green check mark shown to the left to accept. **Insert Components** = > Select the pin from Step 1.
Mate the pin to the block using a **Concentric Mate** with the circular face from each part. Also mate using a **Distance Mate** between the two faces shown to the left.

## Step 4: Modify the pin and block

### Task

A. Now we will change the size of the block along with the length of the pin.

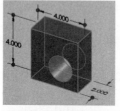 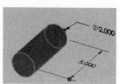

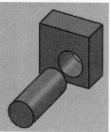

### Command Sequence to Click

Using the new dimensions shown to the left, note how the assembly has not kept the design intent.

---

**HANDS-ON FOR TUTORIAL 3–5.** Currently, the hole and the shaft diameters are not related. Add a new design intent in the form of an equation that forces the two diameters to be equal. Change the value from 2.000″ to 3.000″.

---

Part I Computer Aided Design (CAD) Basics

## INDUSTRY CHAT

This section provides practical insight into how the chapter material is used in industry in the real world and practice. We chat with Mr. Keith Kneidel (Engineer) and Mr. Richard Wand (President) of MJ Engineering & Consulting Inc. (www.mjengineering.com), the sponsor of this chapter.

**Chapter Section 3.1:**   Introduction

ABE:   How do you define design intent?

KEITH AND RICHARD:   From the outset, design intent is hard to define. It changes from project to project: large assemblies, small assemblies, FEM/FEA, weldments; each project has its own design intent. Having said that, design intent to MJ Engineering is how you want a CAD model to grow and change as you modify its design and dimensions. It has a lot to do with how you want to use the part. You need to spend time to plan part construction before you start using your CAD system. However, do not spend too much time; otherwise, design intent becomes counterproductive. Remember, you can always go back and modify the construction.

**Chapter Section 3.1:**   Introduction

ABE:   How important is design intent to your CAD designs?

KEITH AND RICHARD:   Design intent is very important to us. Good design intent allows easy communication among engineering and design team members. We emphasize the use of good design intent at MJ Engineering. Therefore, any of our engineers and designers may pick up anyone's design. If a draftsperson cannot change a designer's work, then design intent is poor. Poor design intent wastes valuable time and resources, and reduces or eliminates the productivity gains from using CAD systems.

**Chapter Section 3.1:**   Introduction

ABE:   What do you consider poor design intent?

KEITH AND RICHARD:   Quite frankly, it is difficult to get someone to fully understand design intent. Design intent is much of an art. It has a lot to do with personal CAD experience, knowledge, and habits. Also, good design intent for one company may not be good for another company. It all depends on the company design, process, and activities. In most cases if you cannot quickly figure out how a design is made, then it has poor design intent. One example we have run into is with a simple pneumatic cylinder and piston rod assembly downloaded from the Internet. This particular assembly uses in-context relationships to define the piston rod based on the cylinder body. In addition to being a little confusing to new users, the result is that if you move

*(continue)*

the piston rod in the assembly, as you would in real life, it moves to the correct position. However, as soon as you rebuild the model, the piston rod snaps back to the original position because that is how the model is defined. In most cases a designer wants to have a cylinder in an assembly that can be shown in different stages of its stroke.

**Chapter Section 3.2:**   Capturing Design Intent

ABE:   Section 3.2 lists four ways of capturing design intent. Which ones do you use in your company design activities, and why?

KEITH AND RICHARD:   We frequently use all of them except equations. We do not typically use equations primarily because they can make design modifications difficult. If you change one parameter, the designer may not notice other changes that happen automatically.  Also we find that there isn't much that you can do with an equation that can't be done with a design table or sketch relations. We recognize that there are places to use equations and that they are an important functionality to have, but in most of our day-to-day modeling we capture design intent via other methods.

**Chapter Sections 3.3–3.10:**   Documenting Design Intent

ABE:   How do you document design intent?

KEITH AND RICHARD:   We use design tables, dimension schemes (names), feature names, and folders. We do not use comments, equations, or design binders. Folders are very important. We use them to organize models (e.g., put all fillets in one folder or group features in one reference folder). Using folders we can suppress and unsuppress features quickly. One example is an assembly we are currently working on. The main assembly contains several large models merely as reference. We need to know where the reference models are located in the assembly space, but we often suppress them to increase modeling speed. Using folders allows quick selection of these components and also documents that the components in the folder are simply a reference and are not to be included in the drawings. Design tables are more powerful than equations. We can put equations in design tables. Design tables are Excel spreadsheets and most engineers know how to use Excel. [For our book readers, we cover design tables in Chapter 6.] We do not use design binders because they may increase the part/assembly file size. It also depends on the size of a company. A small company might not have a need to use binders as a communication tool among team members. A large company that has offices in different locations might find the use of design binders more important. Instead of using design binders, we use Windows file folders. We have a design folder for each design project. It has catalogs, photos, etc.

We also use templates (start model or part) for parts, assemblies, and drawings to help with design intent. For example, our typical start part starts with two configurations (default and simplified). We use this for models that we know are going to be part of a large assembly. During the design of the part, the designer can use the simplified configuration to create a version of the part that has many features suppressed and is suitable for a large assembly.

**Others**

**ABE:** Any other experience you would like to share with our book readers?

**KEITH AND RICHARD:** We are surprised that you cover design intent in Chapter 3 and not later in the book because it is an advanced topic that requires extensive CAD knowledge. The coverage in this chapter is appropriate because it is at a basic introductory level. You may need more detailed coverage later in the book using design tables and assemblies. Design intent is a complex topic. It is good to have a basic coverage here so the book readers think of it throughout the book.

Finally, from an industry standpoint, we would expect a drawing standards document from a company using SolidWorks. As we are a consulting firm serving many companies across many industries, this document serves us as the company design intent right from the start. We define two types of design intents: intra- and inter-design intents. Intra-design intent occurs within the same company. Inter-design intent occurs among companies, for example, between a company and its suppliers or subcontractors.

# problems

1. Why is design intent important in CAD/CAM design?
2. List and discuss briefly the different methods to capture design intent.
3. List and discuss briefly the different methods to document design intent.
4. Use the **Comment** method to document the design intent for any of Problems 28–37 of Chapter 2.
5. Use the **Design Binder** method to document the design intent for any of Problems 28–37 of Chapter 2.
6. Use the **Folder** method to document the design intent for any of Problems 28–37 of Chapter 2.

# Basic Part Modeling

The primary goal of this part is to explore and cover engineering drawings, assemblies, and rendering in detail. There is a chapter on each of these topics in Part II to understand it in depth. Part II also covers the full set of features that can be used in CAD modeling. We have covered these topics briefly in Part I but purposely limited our models there to the basic features of extrusions and revolves.

Chapter 4 (Features and Macros) is all about learning when and how to use the full set of features available to enable you to design any parts and the complex geometry you may run into. Chapter 5 (Drawings) covers the details of drawings including the creation and control of the title block. Chapter 6 (Assemblies) covers assembly details including the bottom-up and top-down approaches. Chapter 7 (Visualization) closes Part II by showing how to create realistic renderings of parts and assemblies including showing material and texture. CAD visualization is important to convey and present designs efficiently.

# Features and Macros

## 4.1 Introduction

We have used a limited set of features thus far in the book: extrusions and revolves. In terms of SolidWorks, we have used **Extruded Boss/Base** and **Revolved Boss/Base**, and their subtracting counterparts: **Extruded Cut** and **Revolved Cut**. Figure 4.1 shows the full **Features** menu, including these four. Amazingly, these four features can create about 80% or more of the mechanical parts. Other important and useful features are also shown in Figure 4.1.

**FIGURE 4.1**
Available features

The four features used thus far create one class of parts: the ones with uniform thickness or axisymmetric. We use **Extruded Boss** or **Cut** to create uniform thickness parts. These parts have the same cross section along one direction. We create the cross section as a sketch and extrude in a direction perpendicular to the sketch. We use the **Revolved Boss** or **Cut** to create axisymmetric parts. These parts have the same cross section through an angle. Like extrusions, we create the sketch, but we also create an axis of revolution and revolve the sketch around it.

Other classes of parts exist that the four features cannot create. These are the parts whose cross sections are variable or the parts that have nonplanar faces or other geometric shapes that require special features to create. The features that allow us to create these types of parts are sweep, loft, the Hole Wizard, rib, draft, and shell, as shown in Figure 4.1. Other features include hole, smart fasteners, etc. All these features are discussed in this chapter and its tutorials. You can also access more features by clicking this sequence: **Insert** menu => **Features**.

A **feature** is defined as a solid that when combined with other features (solids) creates parts or assemblies. Some features, such as a bosses and cuts, originate as sketches whereas others, such as shells and fillets, modify other features. Features are always listed in the features tree (**FeatureManager design tree**).

Today's modeling is referred to as feature-based modeling and the resulting models are known as feature-based models. The first feature you create in a part is known as the base. You use the base feature as the basis to create other features. The base feature could be an extrusion, a revolve, a loft, or a sweep. A base feature obviously cannot be negative (i.e., a cut). SolidWorks would not allow you to do that. When you begin feature creation, **Extruded Boss/Base** and **Revolved Boss/Base** are the only selectable feature types. You might also expect **Swept Boss/Base** and **Lofted Boss/Base** to be selectable when you begin feature creation, but they are not. The **Lofted Boss/Base** becomes selectable only after you create a cross section, and the **Swept Boss/Base** becomes selectable after you create a cross section and a path (sweep direction). See Table 4.1.

**TABLE 4.1    Available Features**

| No. | Feature | Input (Sketch) | Resulting Feature | When to Use in Modeling? |
|---|---|---|---|---|
| 1 | Extrusion | Cross section and a thickness 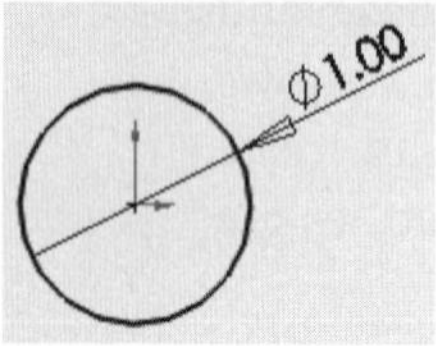 | 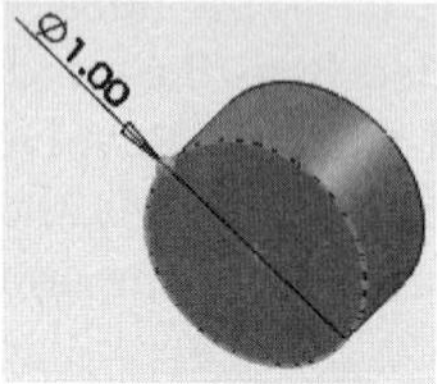 | • Use for parts with constant cross section (CS) and uniform thickness (UT)<br>• If needed, break part into subparts, each with a constant CS and UT |
| 2 | Revolve | Cross section, an axis of revolution, and an angle of revolution 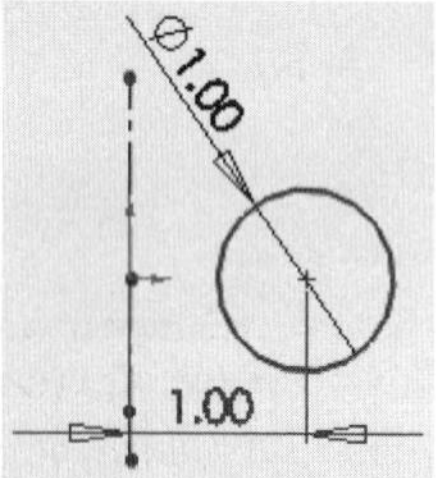 | 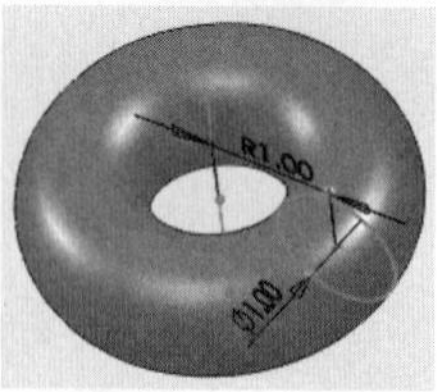 | • Use for parts that are axisymmetric<br>• If needed, break part into subparts, each is axisymmetric |
| 3 | Sweep | Linear sweep: Cross section and a line as a path 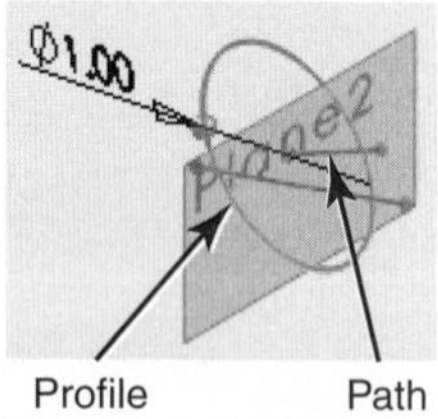 <br>Profile        Path | 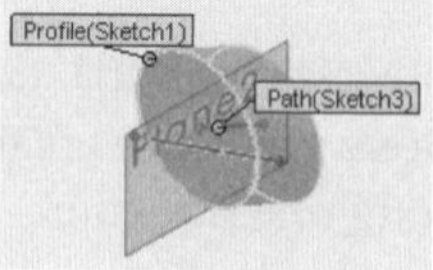 | • Use for parts with constant cross section (CS) along a linear direction (path shown to the left) that may or may not be perpendicular to the cross section<br>• If the path is perpendicular to the cross section, the linear sweep becomes an extrusion |
|  |  | Nonlinear sweep: Cross section and a curve as a path 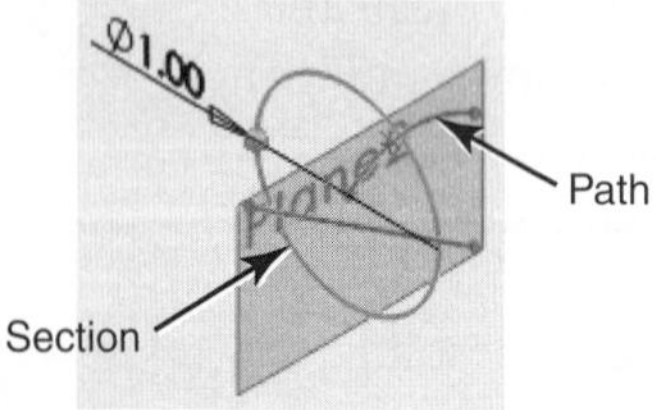 <br>Section                Path | 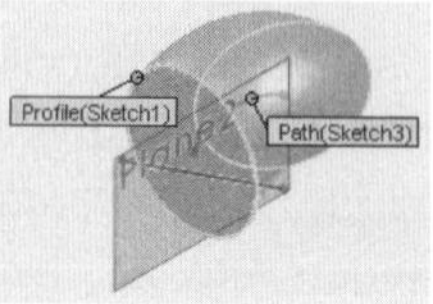 | • Use for parts with constant cross section (CS) along a nonlinear direction (path shown to the left) that may or may not be perpendicular to the cross section |

TABLE 4.1 (Continued)

| No. | Feature | Input (Sketch) | Resulting Feature | When to Use in Modeling? |
|-----|---------|----------------|-------------------|--------------------------|
| 4 | Loft | Linear loft: At least two cross sections (profiles) | | • Use for parts with variable cross section along a given direction<br>• The cross sections are blended linearly from one end to the other |
| | | Nonlinear loft: At least two cross sections (profiles) and a curve as a guide curve (path) | | • Use for parts with variable cross section along a given direction<br>• The cross sections are blended nonlinearly from one end to the other along the guide curve |
| 5 | Rib | Rib profile, e.g., line or step-wise line | | • Use when a stiffener between angled walls (faces) of a part is required to increase part structural strength |
| 6 | Shell | Shell face and shell wall thickness | | • Use when you need to remove material from an existing part<br>• The material removal (shelling) occurs in a direction perpendicular to the selected shelling face<br>• Although you can achieve same result using an extrude cut for simple shells, a shell operation is faster to use |
| 7 | Draft | Direction of pull, parting line, and a draft angle. The direction of pull must be perpendicular to the parting lines | | • Use when you need to draft faces at an angle; usually used for injection molding, to allow pulling the molded part from the mold cavity |

## 4.2 Features

If we would like to master feature-based modeling, we should be able to answer three fundamental questions:

1. What are the available features that a CAD/CAM system offers for modeling parts?
2. What is the input required to create each feature?
3. Which feature should we use for a given modeling problem?

Section 4.1 provides the answer to the first question. Table 4.1 answers the other two questions, and it shows a simple, basic example of each feature. Keep in mind that the third question may have multiple answers; one of them is always the best answer. For example, we may use a loft or a sweep. However, if the part has a constant cross section along a curve, sweep is better to use because it requires fewer steps to create the part. If the part has a variable cross section, a loft is better to use. The tutorials in this chapter provide some modeling examples.

The other features shown in Figure 4.1 and not covered in Table 4.1 are dealt with in the tutorials of the chapter.

---

**Example 4.1**   Create the free-form torus shown in Figure 4.2.

**Solution**   The torus shown in Figure 4.2 is a variation of the torus (donut shape) feature (No. 2) shown in Table 4.1. Although that feature in Table 4.1 is a revolve, the free-form torus shown in Figure 4.2A can be created only as a sweep. The key modeling concept here is to use pierce relations to force the torus cross section (a circle) to conform to the sweep path and the guide curve, as shown in Figure 4.2B.

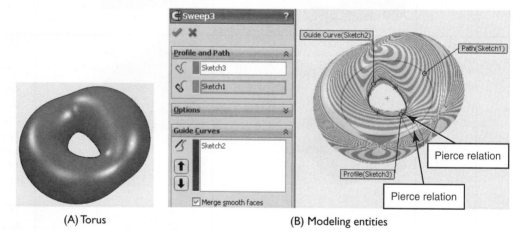

(A) Torus                         (B) Modeling entities

**FIGURE 4.2**
Free-from torus

The modeling plan has the following steps:

1. Create the sweep path (Sketch1 shown in Figure 4.2B).
2. Create the guide curve (Sketch2 shown in Figure 4.2B).
3. Create the profile (Sketch3 shown in Figure 4.2B).
4. Create two pierce relations: one between the profile and the sweep path, and one between the profile and the guide curve (see Figure 4.2B).
5. Create the sweep (see Figure 4.2A).

Keep in mind that the profile sketch plane must be perpendicular to the sketch planes of the sweep path and the guide curve. Thus, Sketch1 and Sketch2 are created in the front plane and Sketch3 is created in the top plane. We could have used the right plane instead of the top plane to sketch the profile. The details of the steps are shown as follows.

### Step 1: Create the sweep path (Sketch1 shown in Figure 4.2B)

| Task | Command Sequence to Click |
|---|---|
| A. Start SolidWorks and open a new part file. Change the part units to inches. Save the file as *example4.1*. | **File => New => Part => OK**<br>**File => Save As** => *example4.1*<br>**=> Save** |
| B. Select the top plane as the sketch plane. | **Top Plane** from features manager tree on left of screen |
| C. Sketch the sweep path. | **Sketch** tab => **Circle** (symbol on **Sketch** tab) => Sketch a circle anchored in the origin and dimensioned as shown to the left. |

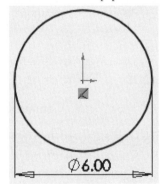

Ø6.00

| Task | Command Sequence to Click |
|---|---|
| D. Exit the sketch. | **Exit Sketch** icon on **Sketch** toolbar |

### Step 2: Create the guide curve (Sketch2 shown in Figure 4.2B)

| Task | Command Sequence to Click |
|---|---|
| A. Select the top plane as the sketch plane. | **Top Plane** from features manager tree on left of screen |
| B. Sketch the guide curve. | **Sketch** tab => **Spline** (symbol on **Sketch** tab) => Sketch a free spline as shown to the left.<br>**Why:** Both Sketch1 (sweep path) and Sketch2 (guide curve) are created on the top plane. Why not create them in one sketch instead of two? If you do that, SolidWorks uses the guide curve in a way that we do not want. Go ahead—try it and discover the result you get. |

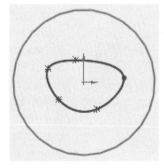

| Task | Command Sequence to Click |
|---|---|
| C. Exit the sketch. | **Exit Sketch** icon on **Sketch** toolbar |

## Step 3: Create the profile (Sketch3 shown in Figure 4.2B)

| Task | Command Sequence to Click |
|---|---|
| **A.** Select the front plane as the sketch plane. | **Front Plane** from features manager tree on left of screen |
| **B.** Sketch the profile. 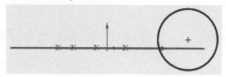 | **Sketch** tab => **Circle** (symbol on **Sketch** tab) => Sketch a circle anywhere as shown to the left.<br>**Why:** Do not dimension the diameter of the circle because it over-constrains it when we apply the pierce relations later. |
| **C.** Create a point on the circle circumference.  | **Point** (symbol on **Sketch** tab) => Click anywhere on the circle as shown to the left => **Esc** to release the pointer.<br>**Help:** Click **View** menu => **Sketch Relations** to view the relations that we create. |

## Step 4: Create two pierce relations

| Task | Command Sequence to Click |
|---|---|
| **A.** Create a pierce relation between the profile and the sweep path. 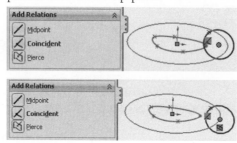 | Click the circle center point => Hold the **CTRL** key on the keyboard, and select the sweep path circle => This opens the **Add Relations** pane shown to the left => Select **Pierce** relation as shown to the left.<br>**Help:** When you select **Pierce**, the center of the profile circle moves to the circumference of the sweep profile as shown to the left. You also see the **Pierce** relation symbol as shown to the left. |
| **B.** Create a pierce relation between the profile and the guide curve. 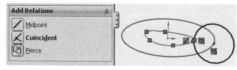 | Click the point we created on the circle => Hold the **CTRL** key on the keyboard, and select the guide curve spline => This opens the **Add Relations** pane shown to the left => Select **Pierce** relation as shown to the left.<br>**Help:** The **Pierce** relation forces the point to lie on the spline, forcing the circle to stretch along with it as shown to the left. You also see the **Pierce** relation symbol as shown to the left. |

## Step 5: Create the sweep (see Figure 4.2A)

| Task | Command Sequence to Click |
|---|---|
| A. Exit the sketch. | **Exit Sketch** icon on **Sketch** toolbar |
| B. Create the sweep. | **Features** tab => **Swept Boss/Base** |

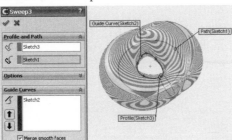

=> Small circle (Sketch3) as the profile
=> Big circle (Sketch1) as the path =>
Expand the **Guide Curves** pane shown
to the left => Spline (Sketch2) as the
guide curve => Green check mark to
finish (see sweep to the left).

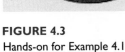

**FIGURE 4.3**
Hands-on for Example 4.1

---

**HANDS-ON FOR EXAMPLE 4.1.** Re-create the free-form torus by
replacing the spline by a circle that is not centric with the big circle. The
new torus is shown in Figure 4.3.

## 4.3 Spur Gears

Gears are an important and essential element in mechanical design because a
wide range of products and applications uses gears. There are various types of
gears (e.g., spur, helical, bevel, spiral, worm, planetary, and
rack and pinion, to name a few). The spur gear, which we
cover here, is the simplest type of gear. Typical mechanical
design courses in college cover the principles and design of
gears. In this section, we cover spur gears from a CAD
point of view, that is, how we construct a gear once it is designed. Although gears are standard elements that can be
purchased off the shelf, it is important to learn how to create a gear feature in a CAD system.

A gear tooth is the intricate part of a gear. Figure 4.4
shows two meshing gears. Figure 4.5A shows the conjugate
line and the pressure angle. Figure 4.5B shows the involute
profile. Gearing and gear meshing ensure that two disks
(the two gears) in contact roll against one another without
slipping. Moreover, the gear teeth should not interfere with
the uniform rotation that one gear would induce in the
other, a requirement known as the conjugate action. The
conjugate action also ensures that the perpendicular line to
a tooth profile at its point of contact with a tooth from the
other gear always passes through a fixed point on the centerline connecting the centers of the two meshing gears.
The conjugate line, shown in Figure 4.5A, is also known as
the line of force because the driving force from the driving

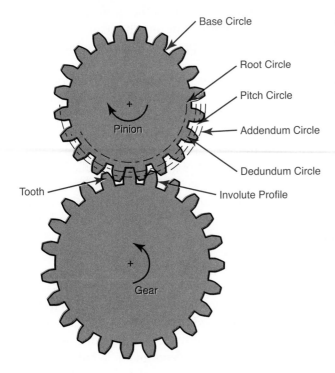

**FIGURE 4.4**
Meshing gears

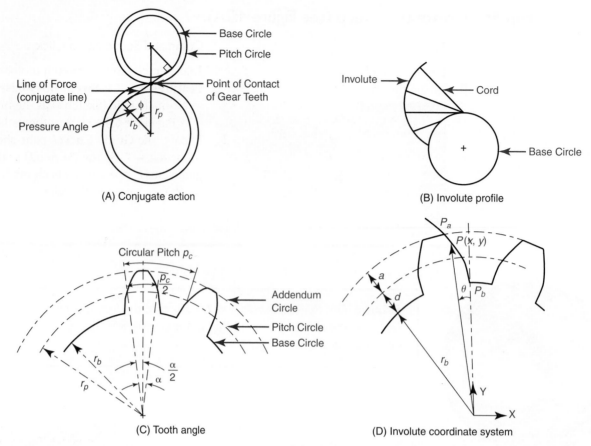

**FIGURE 4.5**
Details of a gear tooth

gear (driver) is transmitted in the direction of this line to the other gear (driven). The angle between the perpendicular radius to the conjugate line and the centerline is constant for two meshing gears. This angle, known as the pressure angle, is shown as the angle Ø in Figure 4.5A.

The key to successful functional gears is the conjugate action. Although various profiles can produce conjugate action, the involute profile is the best because it allows for imperfections in gear manufacturing and yet maintains the conjugate action. The imperfection may produce a slightly different distance between the two shafts of the gears from the designed value. Figure 4.5B shows how the shape of the involute profile is generated. An **involute** is defined as the path of the endpoint of a cord as it is pulled straight (held taut) and unwrapped from a circular disk, as shown in Figure 4.5B. The involute geometry ensures that a constant rotational speed of the driving gear produces a constant rotational speed in the driven gear. For spur gears, the teeth are cut perpendicular to the plane of the gear, where the involute profile resides.

The creation of a gear CAD model requires two basic concepts: knowledge of the gear geometry and the involute equation. The geometry is shown in Figure 4.4. The **base circle** is the circle where the involute profile begins. The **pitch circle** defines the contact (pitch) point between the two gears (see Figure 4.5A). The **dedendum circle** is usually the same as the base circle, as can be concluded from Figure 4.5A (dedendum $d = r_p - r_b$). The **addendum circle** is the circle defined at the top of the tooth, as shown in Figure 4.5C (addendum $a = r_a - r_b$, where $r_a$ is the addendum circle radius). Typically, the addendum and the dedendum are equal. In such case, the pitch and base circles' sizes determine the values for both. The **root circle** is smaller than the base circle to allow cutting the tooth during manufacturing. The tooth profile between the base and root circles is not an involute. It could be any geometry such as a line.

The creation of a gear CAD model requires two steps: calculate the tooth angle $\alpha$ and the tooth involute profile. Although many books on mechanical engineering design offer extensive, in-depth coverage of gear analysis, we offer a simplified, but accurate, version to create a CAD model of the gear. We begin with the definition of circular pitch. As shown in Figure 4.5C, the **circular pitch**, $p_c$, is defined as the distance along the pitch circle between corresponding points on adjacent teeth. As shown in Figure 4.5C, we use $p_c$ as the circular pitch of the gear, $r_p$ as the pitch circle radius, and $\alpha$ as the tooth angle. Using these variables, we can write:

$$p_c = \frac{\pi d_p}{N} \qquad (4.1)$$

where $d_p = 2r_p$ is the pitch circle diameter, and $N$ is the number of gear teeth. From the tooth geometry shown in Figure 4.5C, we can write:

$$\frac{p_c}{2} = r_p \alpha \qquad (4.2)$$

Substituting $p_c$ from Eq. (4.2) into Eq. (4.1) and reducing gives:

$$\alpha = \frac{\pi}{N} \text{ radians or } \alpha = \frac{180}{N} \text{ degrees} \qquad (4.3)$$

The derivation of the involute equation is more complex and is not covered here. We align the involute of one tooth with the XY coordinate system, as shown in Figure 4.5D, where the lowest point on the involute, $P_b$, lies on the Y-axis. This orientation does not represent a limitation, but rather simplifies the form of the involute equation, which is therefore given by:

$$\begin{aligned} x &= -r_b(\sin\theta - \theta\cos\theta) \\ y &= r_b(\cos\theta + \theta\sin\theta) \end{aligned} \qquad 0 \le \theta \le \theta_{max} \qquad (4.4)$$

where $r_b$ is the base circle radius (see Figure 4.5A):

$$r_b = r_p \cos\phi \qquad (4.5)$$

and $(x, y)$ are the coordinates of any point $P$ on the involute at an angle $\theta$ as shown in Figure 4.5D. The lowest point $P_b$ on the involute corresponds to the value of $\theta = 0$ and lies on the base circle. Point $P_a$ lies on the addendum circle and does not necessarily correspond to the value of $\theta = \theta_{max}$. We can arbitrarily select a large enough value for $\theta_{max}$ so that the involute crosses the addendum circle and then trims it to that circle. Therefore, we create the involute profile by generating points on it using Eq. (4.4) and connecting them with a spline curve.

The root circle is always less than the base circle. For simplicity, we use the root circle radius, $r_r$, to be 0.98 of the base circle radius (there are formulas that do not give consistent results). Thus, we write:

$$r_r = 0.98r_b \qquad (4.6)$$

The following steps summarize the calculations needed to create a gear CAD model:

1. The input parameters needed are the pitch circle radius $r_p$, the pressure angle $\varnothing$, and the gear number of teeth $N$.

2. Calculate $r_b$ using Eq. (4.5).
3. Calculate $r_r$ using Eq. (4.6).
4. Calculate the gear dedendum $d = r_p - r_b$.
5. Assuming that the addendum and dedendum are equal, calculate the addendum circle radius as $r_a = r_p + a$ (see Figures 4.5C and 4.5D).
6. Use Eq. (4.3) to calculate the tooth angle $\alpha$.
7. Start with $\theta = 0$ and use $\Delta\theta = 5°$, calculate $\theta_{i+1} = \theta_i + \Delta\theta$ for any point on the involute, where $i + 1$ and $i$ are the indices for the current and previous points, respectively.
8. Use Eq. (4.4) to calculate coordinates of the involute points.

---

**Example 4.2** Create the CAD model of a spur gear that $r_p = 60$ mm, $\varnothing = 20°$, and $N = 20$.

**Solution** Using the preceding calculation steps, we get $r_b = 54.382$ mm, $d = a = 3.618$ mm, $r_a = 63.618$ mm, $r_r = 55.254$ mm, and $\alpha = 9°$. Using Eq. (4.4) with $\Delta\theta = 5°$, we generate 11 points on the involute, for a $\theta_{max} = 50°$. We generate the points on the involute profile as shown in Table 4.2. It is beneficial to write a computer program to generate these points. You may use JavaScript (HTML Web page), C, C++, or Matlab to write the program. We use JavaScript here. The advantage of using JavaScript is that we do not need to install anything; we just need a text editor (Notepad) to write the program and a Web browser to run it. Use Firefox to run the program because it has a JavaScript debugger (click **Tools** [Firefox menu] => **Error Console**). JavaScript syntax is very similar to C or C++. You embed JavaScript in HTML tags, and you save the file with *.html* extension (e.g., *involute.html*). To run the program, drag and drop *involute.html* (program file) onto Firefox browser window, or use **File** (Firefox menu) => **Open File**. Here is the program (save as *involute.html*):

```
<html>
<script language = "javascript">
rb = 54.382;
delta = 5*Math.PI/180.0;
document.write("The result shows theta (degrees), x, y:
<br>");
for (i = 0; i<11; i++)
{
```

| TABLE 4.2 | Coordinates of Involute Points | |
|---|---|---|
| $\theta$ | x | y |
| 0 | 0 | 54.382 |
| 5 | −0.01245 | 54.59628 |
| 10 | −0.09961 | 57.23422 |
| 15 | −0.33492 | 58.28120 |
| 20 | −0.78966 | 59.71306 |
| 25 | −1.53172 | 61.49640 |
| 30 | −2.62459 | 63.58902 |
| 35 | −4.12631 | 65.94044 |
| 40 | −4.08856 | 68.49256 |
| 45 | −8.55577 | 71.18042 |
| 50 | −11.56431 | 73.9330 |

```
theta = i*delta;
x = rb*(Math.sin(theta) - theta*Math.cos(theta));
y = rb*(Math.cos(theta) + theta*Math.sin(theta));
document.write(theta*180/Math.PI + " " + x + " " + y
+"<br>");
}
</script>
</html>
```

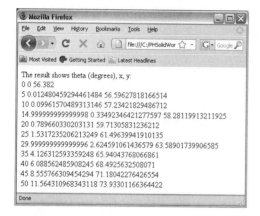

**FIGURE 4.6**
Involute coordinates

**FIGURE 4.7**
Spur gear

The output of the program is shown in Figure 4.6.

We use these points to create a spline in SolidWorks. SolidWorks can read a text file with these coordinates to create the spline. The file format must be one point per line, where the $(x, y, z)$ coordinates of each point are separated by a space or tab. We use a $z$-coordinate of zero for all points. The text file *involute.txt* that corresponds to Table 4.2 is as follows:

| | | |
|---|---|---|
| 0 | 54.382 | 0 |
| −0.01245 | 54.59628 | 0 |
| −0.09961 | 57.23422 | 0 |
| −0.33492 | 58.28120 | 0 |
| −0.78966 | 59.71306 | 0 |
| −1.53172 | 61.49640 | 0 |
| −2.62459 | 63.58902 | 0 |
| −4.12631 | 65.94044 | 0 |
| −4.08856 | 68.49256 | 0 |
| −8.55577 | 71.18042 | 0 |
| −11.56431 | 73.93301 | 0 |

Using a text file is very efficient for many reasons. It eliminates typing the points in SolidWorks, thus reducing entry errors. We can use the file as many times as we need instead of typing and retyping the coordinates.

The general steps to create the spur gear (see Figure 4.7) are:

1. Create the involute profile using points stored in *involute.txt* file.
2. Create the base, pitch, root, and addendum circles.
3. Create the tooth.
4. Create all the teeth.
5. Finish the gear model.

The details of each step are shown below.

## Step 1:  Create the involute profile

### Task

A. Open a new part.
B. Use a spline to connect the involute points.

### Command Sequence to Click

**File = New => Part => OK**
**Insert => Curve => Curve Through <u>X</u>YZ Points... => Browse** (button in the **Curve File** window that opens) => Find and select the *involute.txt* file => **Open => OK**.
**Help:** You must not select any sketch plane before you create the curve; otherwise, the menu selection is grayed

| Task | Command Sequence to Click |
|------|---------------------------|

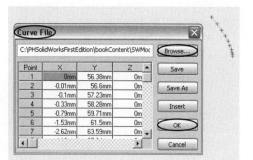

out. The screenshot to the left shows the curve points. Move the **Curve File** window with the mouse to see them because they disappear after you click **OK**.

## Step 2: Create the base, pitch, root, and addendum circles

| Task | Command Sequence to Click |
|------|---------------------------|

**A.** Create base, pitch, root, and addendum circles.

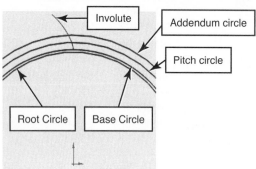

Select **Front** sketch plane and orient it => **Circle** on **Sketch** tab => Create the circles with centers at the origin (0, 0) as shown to the left.

**Why:** As shown to the left, the involute shoots up and crosses the addendum circle. We trim it later to the addendum circle.

## Step 3: Create the tooth

| Task | Command Sequence to Click |
|------|---------------------------|

**A.** Convert the involute profile curve into a sketch entity.

Click the spline => **Convert Entities** (**Sketch** tab).

**Why:** The involute spline is not part of the sketch. We must convert to a sketch entity to use it to create the tooth.

**B.** Create the tooth symmetry line, shown in Figure 4.5C.

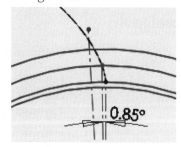

**Centerline** (**Sketch** tab) => Construct a centerline passing through origin at angle = 93.35° as shown to the left.

**Why:** SolidWorks has a limitation. You can create a radial line only with an angle measured counterclockwise from the horizontal. Thus, we have to construct a vertical centerline (shown in Figure 4.5D) and the centerline to the right of the symmetry line (shown in Figure 4.5C). We measure the angle between these two additional centerlines (insert a dimension using the two lines). This angle comes out to be 0.58°. Add it

| Task | Command Sequence to Click |
|---|---|
| | to ½ the tooth angle (9/2) to get 5.35°, and add the result to 90° to get 93.35°. |
| C. Trim the involute spline to the addendum circle. | **Trim Entities** (**Sketch** tab) => **Trim to closest** (on left pane of screen) => Segments of the spline that are outside the addendum circle. **Help:** Zoom before trimming to select the right segments of the spline. |
| D. Mirror the trimmed involute curve about the symmetry line created in Task B. Also create two straight lines to form the tooth parts below the base circle. 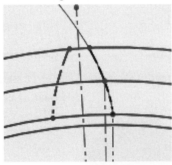 | **Mirror Entities** (**Sketch** tab) => Select the spline curve => Right-click mouse button => Select the symmetry centerline => Right-click mouse button to finish. Now create the two lines: **Line** => Origin => Endpoint of right involute shown to the left, then **Line** => Origin => Endpoint of left involute shown to the left. **Why:** We assume that the tooth profile between the base and root circles is linear because it is very small. |
| E. Trim all the circles and the two lines. Also fillet the corners of the tooth with a 1 mm radius fillet. 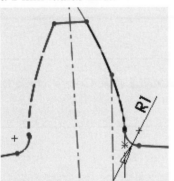 | **Trim Entities** (**Sketch** tab) => **Trim to closest** (on left pane of screen) => Do for all to get the result shown to the left. To fillet, use **Sketch Fillet** (**Sketch** tab) => Type 1 mm for fillet radius => One line and root circle => One line and root circle. **Help:** Zoom before trimming to select the right segments of the spline. |

## Step 4:  Create all the teeth

| Task | Command Sequence to Click |
|---|---|
| A. Use a circular pattern to create the 20 teeth. Trim the root circle to create the final teeth sketch shown below. | **Circular Sketch Pattern** (**Sketch** tab) => 20 for the number of teeth => Select the tooth profile (root fillet, spline, top arc, spline, root fillet) => Green check mark to finish. **Help:** You must select seven entities for the tooth profile: fillet, line, spline, arc, spline, line, and fillet. If you do not, the extrusion of Step 5 will fail because the |

| Task | Command Sequence to Click |
|---|---|
| 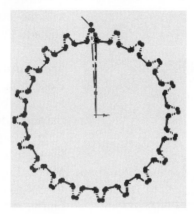 | sketch is open. Zoom close enough to the tooth profile to pick up the seven entities.<br>Use **Trim Entities** (**Sketch** tab) => **Trim to closest** to remove the root circle segments enclosed by the teeth (shown to the left)<br>**Why:** We had to wait to trim the root circle after creating the teeth because we have no way of knowing the tooth pitch at the root circle. We know only the circular pitch. |

**Step 5:** Finish the gear model

| Task | Command Sequence to Click |
|---|---|
| A. Extrude the sketch to create the spur gear shown below.<br>  | Select sketch => **Extruded Boss/ Base** (**Features** tab) => Use 25 mm for **D1**. |

---

> **HANDS-ON FOR EXAMPLE 4.2.** Create a hole for the gear shaft. Use a diameter of 50 mm.

## 4.4 Design Library and Library Features

Design reuse and using off-the-shelf standard components are important concepts that speed up design and thus make it less expensive. The field of mechanical design has many standard parts that designers use every day in their designs, for example, fasteners (nuts and bolts), gears, bearings, etc. Although these parts are universally standard, a company may have some parts that are unique to it and are reusable only in its own designs. SolidWorks provides the concepts of a design library and library features.

A **library feature** is a part that you create once, like any part, and save in a library, known as the design library, for reuse in the future. You may save a library feature with the *.sldprt* or. *sldlfp* extension. A library feature may or may not have a base feature. If it has a base, you cannot insert it into a part that already has a base because you cannot have two base features in a single part. However, you can insert a library feature that has a base feature in an empty part. Most of the time library features are inserted into assemblies as components or inserted into new, empty (blank) parts to adapt to new designs.

Commonly used library features include holes, slots, and many others. You can use several library features to construct a single part. Not only does this save time, but it also ensures consistency in your CAD models.

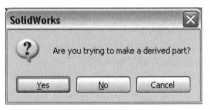

**FIGURE 4.8**
Using a library feature

Using library features is easy; you drag a library feature from the design library and drop it onto the open part or assembly. If you try to insert a library feature with a base in a part that already has a base, SolidWorks displays the message shown in Figure 4.8. If you select **Yes**, it inserts the feature in the open part. If you answer **No**, it opens a blank part and inserts it there.

You save library features in a design library, which can be organized into folders. SolidWorks comes with a Design Library. The path to this library folder is *install_directory\Documents and Settings\All Users\Application Data\SolidWorks\SolidWorks 2010\design library*. The install directory may be *C* and *2010* is the year of your SolidWorks version. Click the **Design Library** tab in SolidWorks task pane (on the right of the screen), as shown in Figure 4.9A, to open the Design Library, which is organized into folders, as shown in Figure 4.9B. You can also add you new custom folders to the library. Save your library features into this SolidWorks **Design Library** to have them accessible, as shown in Figure 4.9B. If you do not, then you have to navigate to the folder where you saved them.

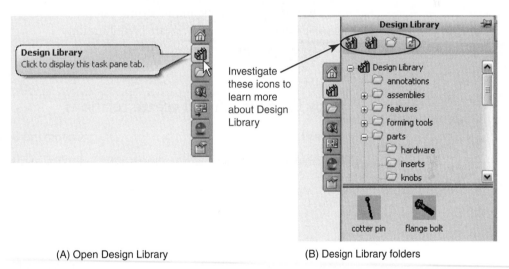

(A) Open Design Library      (B) Design Library folders

**FIGURE 4.9**
SolidWorks Design Library

## 4.5 Configurations and Design Tables

Family of parts is a natural outcome of the parametrics concept of solid modeling. Defining a solid (part) in a sketch by parameters (dimensions are values for the parameters) enables us to modify the dimensions and create different-size clones of the part with a click of a button. These clones are what we refer to as *family of parts*. SolidWorks calls them *configurations*. We can also create clones of assemblies by changing the dimensions of some key parameters of the part or assembly. The clones have the same topology as the parent, but different geometry. For example, consider a two-feature part:

**FIGURE 4.10**
Design Table

a base block and a shaft boss. You clone the part into a square block and a skinny long boss, a rectangle block and short fat boss, etc.

We use design tables to specify sets of different values for the parameters. When we execute the design table, each set becomes a part (clone) in the family. SolidWorks uses a Microsoft Excel sheet as its design table. You can insert a design table into an open part or assembly by clicking this sequence: **Insert** menu => **Tables** => **Design Table**. This opens **Design Table** pane under the **PropertyManager** tab on the left pane of SolidWorks screen, as shown in Figure 4.10. You can specify one of the three sources shown to create the design table. When you click the green check mark to finish, SolidWorks acts accordingly. For example, if you select **Auto-create** (default option), SolidWorks displays a list of the open part dimensions and asks you to select some to include in the design table. The table is created with the current values of the part dimensions as the default set (configuration). The set shows as a row in the table. You can add other rows with different values for dimensions. Each row is a configuration.

---

**Example 4.3**   Link dimensions and create configurations.

**Solution**   This example builds on Example 2.5. We link two dimensions via a common variable name. When we change one dimension, the other changes. The general steps are:

1. Copy Example 2.5 and create relations.
2. Create corner block and link dimensions.
3. Change dimensions to create configurations.

The details of each step are shown below.

**Step I:**   Copy Example 2.5 and create relations

| Task | Command Sequence to Click |
|---|---|
| **A.** Rename features and display dimensions. Also, define relations. Copy part file of *example 2.5* and save as *example 4.2*. | Follow steps of Example 2.5. In addition to the names and relations of Example 2.5, we rename **Extrude1** as **Block**.<br>**Help:** To rename it, click its name in the features tree once to select it and again to rename it. |
| **B.** Display feature dimensions and names.<br> | Right-click the **Annotations** node in the features tree => **Show Feature Dimensions** (this is a toggle) shown to the left.<br>**Help:** Click **Tools => Options => Show dimension names** (Systems **Options** tab) to show names in addition to dimensions. All the dimensions for the part appear. Notice that the dimensions that are part of a feature's definition (such as the depth of an extruded feature) are shown in blue. |

## Step 2: Create corner block and link dimensions

| Task | Command Sequence to Click |
|---|---|
| **A.** Add a corner block to the block (we need it to illustrate this step). 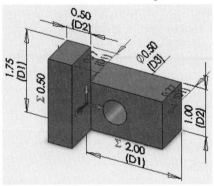 | Block front face => **Extruded Boss/Base** (**Features** tab) => **Sketch** tab => **Rectangle** => Sketch a rectangle at the bottom left corner of the front face and dimension it (1.75 × 0.5) as shown to the left => **Exit Sketch** => Input 0.75 for extrusion **D1** => Green check mark. |
| **B.** Link both depths (*D1*) of block and corner. | Right-click the block depth **D1** => **Link Values** (from the **Shared Values** window that pops up) => Type Depth (for **Name**) in the **Shared Values** pop-up => **OK** => Right-click the corner block depth **D1** => **Link Values** (from **Shared Values** pop-up) => Select **Depth** from the **Name** drop-down => **OK** <br> **Why:** This sequence creates a variable called **Depth** that links the depths of both blocks. Both depths assume the new name, **Depth**. Changing one depth changes the other. <br> **Help:** To delete the linking for either or both depths, right-click the depth => **Unlink Value**. |

## Step 3: Change dimensions to create configurations

| Task | Command Sequence to Click |
|---|---|
| **A.** Change linked dimensions. | Click one of the linked dimensions => Change its value to a new one => Hit **Enter** on keyboard => Observe the change of the two blocks. |

---

**HANDS-ON FOR EXAMPLE 4.3.** Use the design table instead of using the manual method described in the example to create the configurations.

## 4.6 Macros

Design automation offers two benefits: (1) it enhances productivity, and (2) it helps with repetitive, mundane tasks. For example, if we were to follow the same design process over and over, automating it would be the logical thing to do.

Macros aid in design automation. Macros are also viewed as a way to customize your CAD/CAM system. A **macro** is a short computer program that is used to repeat commonly performed operations. We use them to automate design tasks. Follow these steps to create macros:

1. Look for highly repeatable processes.
2. Preselect all of the input variables.
3. No user input is required during creating macro geometry.
4. Record the macro with macro recorder.
5. Edit/tweak the macro.

**FIGURE 4.11**
**Macro** menu

After you create a macro, you can use it for recording, edit it, run it, pause it, stop it, and assign it to a shortcut key or to a menu item. When you assign a macro to a shortcut key or to a menu item, you can specify which method (function) of the macro to run. Figure 4.11 shows the **Macro** menu. Click **Tools** to access this menu.

A higher level of automation than using macros is to use Visual Basic (VB) or another programming language to perform full automation and have better control of the automation. As a matter of fact, VB is the programming engine behind macros. Instead of you writing the macro VB code, SolidWorks macro interface enables you to generate the code automatically while you perform the design tasks as usual. It is this VB code that you save in a file when you save the macro. You can use the VB editor to write VB code.

If you take a closer look at the macro VB code, it uses what we call SolidWorks API (application programming interface). The code makes "calls" to API functions. Think of API as the gateway between the application you want to write and the SolidWorks code that has been already written and you want to use. In other words, the API provides you with access to SolidWorks geometric engines.

You can learn VB programming by creating multiple macros, studying their generated VB code, and expanding on it. That is what we call the "brute force" approach. Just keep in mind that VB is an object-oriented programming (OOP) language that requires knowledge and understanding of the object-oriented design and how objects are defined and implemented.

The programming approach could be useful to create an entire assembly from a few parameters. We can write a program to define some variables and store them in a row in a design table. Each row represents a new version of the assembly. We then delete all rows from the table and keep the last row, which is the new assembly.

---

**Example 4.4**  Develop a macro to create an extrusion.

**Solution**  This is a simple macro to illustrate macros. The general steps are:

1. Start a new model.
2. Create, save, and run the macro.
3. Run the macro in a new part.

The details of each step are shown below.

## Step 1:   Start a new model

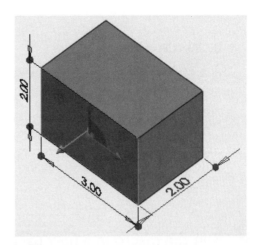

**FIGURE 4.12**
Extrusion to create with a macro

| Task | Command Sequence to Click |
|---|---|
| A. Start SolidWorks and open a new part file. Change the part units to inches. | **File => New => Part => OK.** Change the model units to inches. **Help:** There is no need to save the part file. We open a part file only to record the construction steps in a macro. What we need to save is the macro, not the part. |

## Step 2:   Create, save, and run the macro

| Task | Command Sequence to Click |
|---|---|
| A. Start recording the macro.<br> | **Tools => Macro => Record.** This sequence opens the **Macro** toolbar shown to the left. **Help:** Hover over the icons of the toolbar to know what each one does. The leftmost icon (green arrow) runs the macro. The next icon (black square) stops the macro running or recording. The next icon (red circle) starts and pauses recording. |
| B. Create the extrusion shown in Figure 4.12. | Create the rectangle on the front plane with the dimensions shown in Figure 4.12 and extrusion distance of 2 in. **Help:** As you construct, the macro is recording your steps in the background. |
| C. Stop and save the macro. | Click the stop (black square) icon on the **Macro** toolbar. |

| Task | Command Sequence to Click |
|---|---|
| | **Help:** When you stop the macro, the system asks you to save the macro. It asks you for a macro file name and a directory to save it at. Use *Macro1* as a name. A macro file uses the *.swp* extension. |
| **D.** Run the macro. | Click the run (green arrow) icon on the **Macro** toolbar => Select *Macro1* (from the window that opens) as the macro to run. |
| | **Help:** The macro runs and creates a new extrusion as shown on the features manager tree. Each time you run the macro, it creates a new extrusion. You may also open a new part and run the macro there. |

## Step 3: Run the macro in a new part

| Task | Command Sequence to Click |
|---|---|
| **A.** Open a new part. Change the part units to inches. | **File => New => Part => OK.** Change the model units to inches. |
| **B.** Run the macro. | **Tools => Macro => Run =>** *Macro1* from the window that opens |

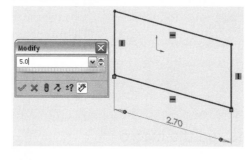

**Why:** The macro acts as though it is asking you to input new width and height for the extrusion being created, as shown to the left, but it ignores these inputs. This is because the macro is a VB (Visual Basic) code that runs with the old values of 3 and 2 shown in Figure 4.12. If you want a macro with a user input, you need to create a VB form to receive user input. The input from the form needs to be fed to the macro VB code by modifying the code. See the Hands-on for this example. You obviously need to learn VB programming.

---

**HANDS-ON FOR EXAMPLE 4.4.** Edit the macro to accept the width, height, and depth of the extrusion as user input. Submit screenshots of the form that accepts the input and three extrusions with different depths.

---

## 4.7 Tutorials Overview

The theme for the tutorials in this chapter is to practice creating and using features, gears, configurations and design tables, and macros. The tutorials show how to use the Hole Wizard, smart fasteners, slots, and much more. Factorydesign Limited, a company with headquarters in London, England (www.factorydesign.co.uk), has sponsored this chapter. Factorydesign specializes in designing consumer products, commercial goods, packaging, transportation, and spaces. It uses the best state-of-the-art practices for sustainable design throughout the entire engineering design process (EDP). We chat with Mr. Lee Bazalgette, a Design Engineer at Factorydesign and a Certified SolidWorks Professional, in the Industry Chat.

## Tutorial 4–1: Create Sweep Features

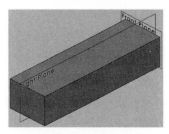

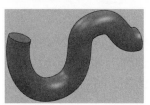

**FIGURE 4.13**
Sweep features

### Modeling task

Create both linear and nonlinear sweep features.

### Modeling synthesis

Here, we create linear and nonlinear sweeps. Sweeps use a constant cross section. A linear sweep is along a straight line. A nonlinear sweep is along a curve (spline).

### Modeling plan

Sketch the cross section of each sweep feature shown in Figure 4.13, and sweep along a path.

### Design intent

Ignore for this chapter.

### CAD steps

We create each part in step one:

1. Create a linear sweep.
2. Create a nonlinear sweep.

The details of these steps are shown below.

## Step 1: Create a linear sweep

| Task | Command Sequence to Click |
|---|---|
| A. Sketch the sweep profile. | **File => New => Part =>** Create a sketch on the front plane as shown to the left. |

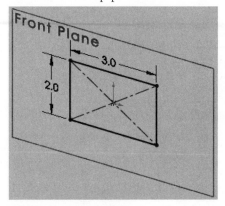

| Task | Command Sequence to Click |
|---|---|
| B. Create the sweep path. | Create a sketch on the right plane as shown to the left. **Help:** Use the Origin to start the line. |

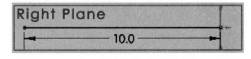

| Task | Command Sequence to Click |
|---|---|
| C. Create the sweep. | **Features => Swept Boss/Base** (shown to the left) => Select Sketch1 as the sweep profile and Sketch2 as the sweep path. The part should look like Figure 4.13A. |

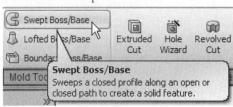

## Step 2: Create a nonlinear sweep

| Task | Command Sequence to Click |
|---|---|
| A. Sketch the sweep profile. | **File => New => Part =>** Create a sketch on the front plane as shown to the left. |

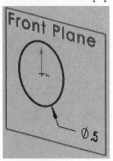

| | |
|---|---|
| B. Sketch the points that define the sweep path. | Sketch the points on the right plane approximately as shown to the left. |

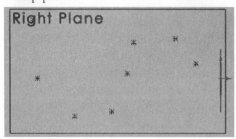

| | |
|---|---|
| C. Sketch the path. | **Sketch => Spline** => Use the **Spline** tool to connect the points as shown to the left. |

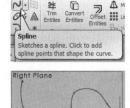

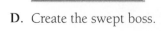

| | |
|---|---|
| D. Create the swept boss. | **Features => Swept Boss/Base =>** Create the swept boss shown in Figure 4.13B. |

Part II  Basic Part Modeling

## Tutorial 4–2: Create Loft Features

### Modeling task

Create the wine glass shown in Figure 4.14 by using a loft feature.

### Modeling synthesis

Here, we use multiple cross section profiles to create a loft feature to model a wine glass.

### Modeling plan

First we loft the base solid and then loft the cup as a thin feature loft.

### Design intent

Ignore for this chapter.

### CAD steps

We create the wine glass in two steps:

1. Loft the base.
2. Loft the cup.

The details of these steps are shown below.

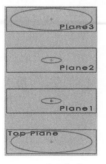

**FIGURE 4.14**
Loft feature

### Step 1: Loft the base

| Task | Command Sequence to Click |
|---|---|
| A. Sketch the four loft profiles. | Create the four sketches as shown to the left. The first and the last sketch are 2.0″ in diameter and the second and third sketches are 0.5″ in diameter.<br>**Help:** The first circle is sketched on the **Top Plane**. The succeeding three circles should be sketched on reference planes each spaced 1.0″ apart. |
| B. Create the loft. | **Features => Lofted Boss/Base =>** Select the sketches in order from the first through the fourth.<br>**Help:** Select the sketch from the **FeatureManager design tree** as shown to the left instead of from the graphics |

| Task | Command Sequence to Click |
|------|---------------------------|

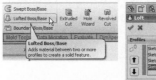 

pane. When selecting from the graphics pane, the system interpolates the sketches using these points. If the points do not line up correctly, the resulting loft will be twisted. This will be explored in the Hands-on for this tutorial.

C. Create the loft.

Hit **Enter** to create the loft as shown to the left.

# Step 2:  Loft the cup

| Task | Command Sequence to Click |
|------|---------------------------|

A. Sketch the loft profiles.

Create three more reference planes and four more sketch profiles as shown to the left.

**Help:** Plane4 is 1.0″ away from Plane3. Plane5 and Plane6 are also spaced 1.0″ away from each other. The circles on Plane4 and Plane5 are 3.0″ in diameter, and the circle on Plane6 is 2.0″ in diameter.

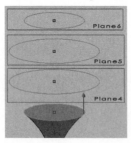

B. Create the loft.

Select the sketches as performed in Task B of Step 1. This time, however, select the **Thin Feature** option and input the values as shown to the left. This will create a cup to contain liquid.

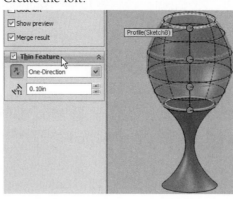

C. Accept and save the part.

Hit **Enter** to accept and **Save** the part as *Wineglass.sldprt*.

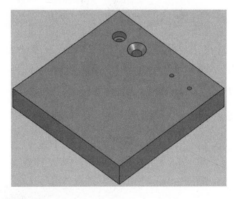

**HANDS-ON FOR TUTORIAL 4–2.** Create a loft using three squares of different sizes as cross sections separated by 1 inch. The square sizes are 2 × 2, 1 × 1, and 2 × 2, respectively. Create the loft connecting the three sections such that the loft is twisted incorrectly as shown below.

## Tutorial 4–3:  Use the Hole Wizard

### Modeling task

Use the Hole Wizard to create the holes shown in Figure 4.15.

**FIGURE 4.15**
Hole features

### Modeling synthesis

The Hole Wizard is used to create special holes such as counterbores, countersinks, or tapped holes in a part in one step, as opposed to manually creating these features using many steps.

### Modeling plan

Here we create a block to showcase many of the Hole Wizard options.

### Design intent

Ignore for this chapter.

CAD steps

We create the holes in four steps:

1. Create the block.
2. Create a counterbore hole.
3. Create a countersink hole.
4. Create a tapped hole.

The details of these steps are shown below.

## Step 1: Create the block

| Task | Command Sequence to Click |
|---|---|
| **A.** Create a block. | Create the block as shown to the left. |

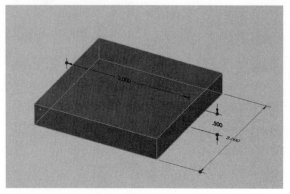

## Step 2: Create a counterbore hole

Task

**A.** Preselect the face.

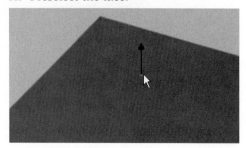

**Command Sequence to Click**

When using the Hole Wizard, it is important to preselect the face where you would like to insert the hole, as shown to the left.

**Why:** If you select the **Hole Wizard** tool first, then you will be forced to create the location of the holes using a 3D Sketch operation. This is possible but much more complicated.

| Task | Command Sequence to Click |
|---|---|

**B.** Create an ANSI Inch counterbore through hole for a #6 socket head cap screw.

Make the selections as shown to the left.

**C.** Position the hole.

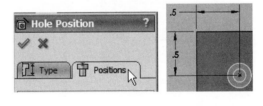

Select the **Positions** tab. The center of the hole feature is located exactly where the point(s) are located in the sketch. Locate this hole 0.5″ from the edges as shown to the left. Accept to exit the wizard.

**D.** Locate the feature in the **Feature Manager design tree**.

Notice that the feature is labeled in the features tree shown to the left.

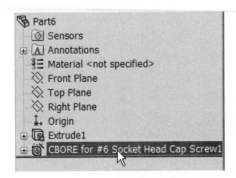

## Step 3: Create a countersink hole

| Task | Command Sequence to Click |
|---|---|
| **A.** Create a countersink hole .375″ deep for a #10 82 degree flat head screw. | Preselect the face and create the hole as shown to the left. |

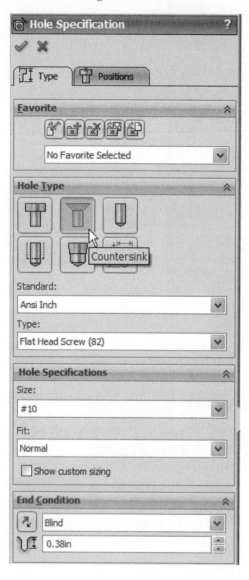

| | |
|---|---|
| **B.** Locate the countersink hole. | Locate this hole 0.5″ from the top edge and 1.0″ from the left edge as shown to the left. |

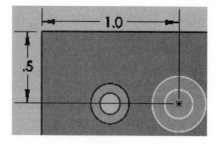

## Step 4: Create a tapped hole

| Task | Command Sequence to Click |
|---|---|
| **A.** Create two #2–56 tapped holes using the default blind depth value. | Preselect the face and create the hole as shown to the left. |

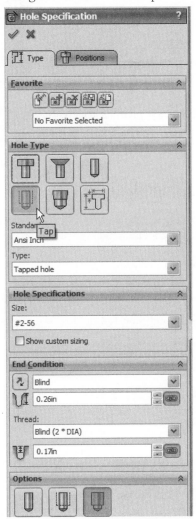

| Task | Command Sequence to Click |
|---|---|
| **B.** Locate the tapped holes. | Locate the holes 0.5″ from the top edge and 2.0″ and 2.50″ from the left edge, respectively, as shown to the left.<br>**Help:** To create a second hole, use the **Point** tool from the **Sketch** menu. |

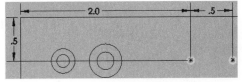

---

**HANDS-ON FOR TUTORIAL 4–3.** Create a 1/16 tapered pipe tap through all located 0.5 from the top edge and 1.5 from the left edge. Then create a linear pattern of the counterbore hole, the 2–56 tapped holes, and the 1/16 pipe tap.

---

## Tutorial 4–4:  Create Compression Spring

### Modeling task

Create the constant length compression spring shown in Figure 4.16.

### Modeling synthesis

The spring can be created using a helix sketch along with a profile sketch to create a swept boss.

### Modeling plan

First we sketch the necessary profiles to create the helix sketch and then the swept boss.

### Design intent

Ignore for this chapter.

### CAD steps

We create the spring in three steps:

1. Sketch the profiles.
2. Create the helix.
3. Create the sweep.

The details of these steps are shown below.

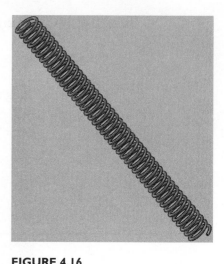

**FIGURE 4.16**
Compression spring

## Step 1:  Sketch the profiles

| Task | Command Sequence to Click |
|---|---|
| **A.** Sketch the profile. | Open a new part and sketch the circle shown to the left on the **Front Plane**. |

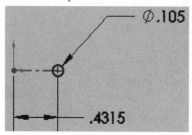

| Task | Command Sequence to Click |
|---|---|
| **B.** Sketch the second profile. | Sketch the profile shown to the left on the **Top Plane**. |

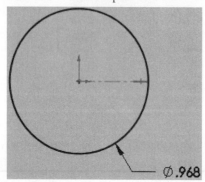

## Step 2:   Create the helix

Task

**A.** Create the helix.

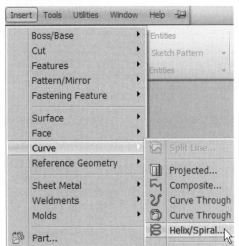

Command Sequence to Click

Select the second **profile =>
Insert => Curve => Helix/
Spiral** shown to the left.

**B.** Change the input values.

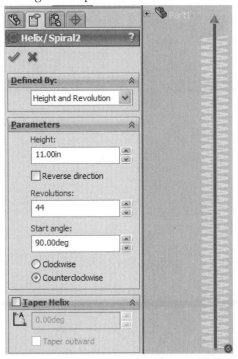

Set the values shown to the left.

## Step 3:   Create the sweep

Task

**A.** Create the sweep.

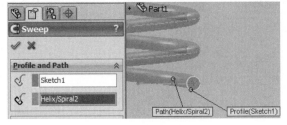

Command Sequence to Click

**Features => Swept Boss/Base
=>** Select the first sketch as the
profile and the helix as the path as
shown to the left.

## Tutorial 4–5: Create Spiral

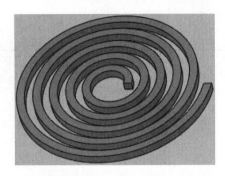

**FIGURE 4.17**
Spiral spring

**Modeling task**

Create the spiral as shown in Figure 4.17.

**Modeling synthesis**

We create a spiral similar to that of a stovetop range used for cooking.

**Modeling plan**

First we will sketch the necessary profiles to create the helix sketch and then the swept boss.

**Design intent**

Ignore for this chapter.

**CAD steps**

We create the spiral in three steps:

1. Sketch the profiles.
2. Create the helix.
3. Create the sweep.

The details of these steps are shown below.

### Step 1: Sketch the profiles

| Task | Command Sequence to Click |
|---|---|
| A. Sketch the profile. | Open a new part and sketch the circle as shown to the left on the **Front Plane**. |

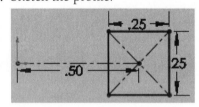

| | |
|---|---|
| B. Sketch the second profile. | Sketch the profile as shown to the left on the **Top Plane**. |

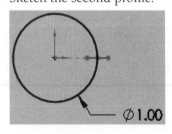

## Step 2: Create the helix

**Task**

A. Create the helix.

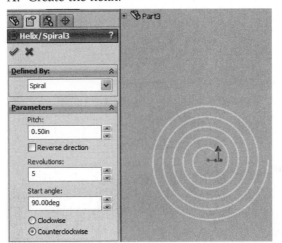

**Command Sequence to Click**

Select the second **profile => Insert => Curve => Helix/Spiral**. Use the **Spiral** option from the first drop-down and set the parameters as shown to the left.

## Step 3: Create the sweep

**Task**

A. Create the sweep.

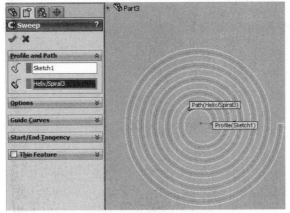

**Command Sequence to Click**

**Features => Swept Boss/Base** => Select the first sketch as the profile and the helix as the path as shown to the left.

> ***HANDS-ON FOR TUTORIAL 4–5.*** Change the spiral cross section to a circle with a 2.0" diameter. Can you generate the spiral? Why or why not? Explain.

## Tutorial 4–6: Create Features

### Modeling task

This tutorial covers some of the most useful modeling features that have not yet been touched upon.

### Modeling synthesis

This tutorial starts with the same block as used in Tutorial 4–3. We will then use that geometry to show features such as fillets, slots, chamfers, ribs, and shelling and draft techniques.

### Modeling plan

First we suppress the holes (Click a feature in features tree) => **Suppress** from the context menu that pops up (hover over icons until you read it) in the block that was created in Tutorial 4–3. Upon completion of each step, we save the part as a new name and return to the original geometry for the next step.

### Design intent

Ignore for this chapter.

### CAD steps

We create each feature in one step:

1. Create a chamfer.
2. Create a fillet.
3. Create different kinds of slots.
4. Use the shell feature.
5. Add draft to the part.
6. Add a rib to the part.

The details of these steps are shown below.

## Step I: Create a chamfer

Task

A. Use an **Angle distance** chamfer.

Command Sequence to Click

**Features => Chamfer** as shown to the left.

B. Select two edges.

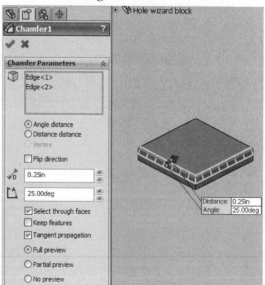

Select the two edges, and set the parameters as shown to the left.
**Help:** Using the **Flip direction** option will change which direction is the angle and which direction is the distance.

| Task | Command Sequence to Click |
|---|---|

C. Use two edges to create a **Distance distance** chamfer.

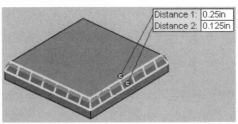

Turn the part around, and use the other two edges to create a **Distance distance** chamfer as shown to the left.

D. Create a **Vertex** chamfer.

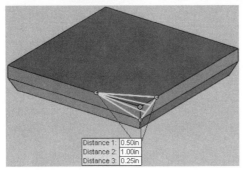

Turn the part over to use one of the vertexes to create a **Vertex** chamfer. Set the values as shown to the left.

E. Save the part as *Chamferblock.sldprt*.

## Step 2:   Create a fillet

| Task | Command Sequence to Click |
|---|---|

A. Select the **Fillet** tool.

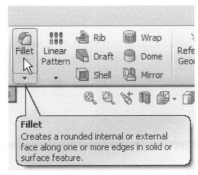

**Features => Fillet** as shown to the left.

B. Create a **Constant radius** fillet.

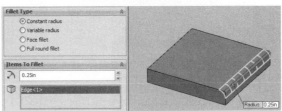

Select the edge, and set the parameters as shown to the left.

C. Create a **Variable radius** fillet.

Select the edge, and set the parameters as shown to the left. To set the **V1** value, the user must select it in the box and then input the value as shown to the left.

| Task | Command Sequence to Click |
|---|---|
| 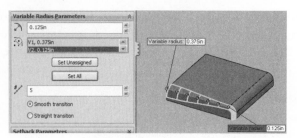 | Repeat this for the **V2** value also. Input 5 for the number of instances. |
| **D.** Create a **Face** fillet. | Select the side and top face to create the **Face** fillet as shown to the left. |
| 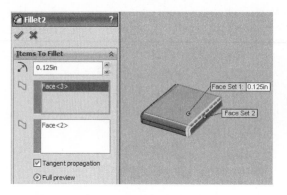 | |

E. Save the part as *Filletblock.sldprt*.

## Step 3: Create different kinds of slots

| Task | Command Sequence to Click |
|---|---|
| **A.** Create a straight slot. | **Features => Extruded Cut =>** Sketch the straight slot as shown to the left => Accept => **Through All.** |
| 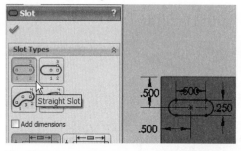 | |
| **B.** Create a centerpoint straight slot. | **Features => Extruded Cut =>** Sketch the centerpoint straight slot as shown to the left => Accept => **Through All.** |
| 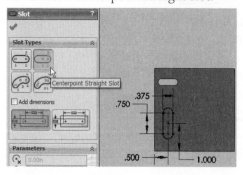 | |

| Task | Command Sequence to Click |
|---|---|

C. Create a 3 point arc slot.

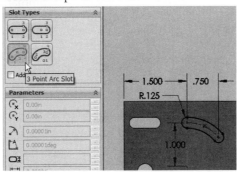

**Features => Extruded Cut =>**
Sketch the 3 point arc slot as
shown to the left => Accept =>
**Through All.**

D. Create a centerpoint arc slot.

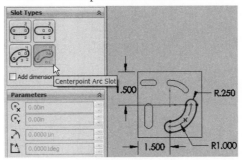

**Features => Extruded Cut =>**
Sketch the centerpoint arc slot as
shown to the left => Accept =>
**Through All.**

E. Save the part as *SlotBlock.sldprt*.


## Step 4: Use the shell feature

| Task | Command Sequence to Click |
|---|---|

A. Select the **Shell** tool.

**Features => Shell** as shown to
the left

B. Select the face.

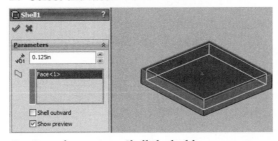

Select the face and input the thickness
value as shown to the left.

C. Save the part as *ShellBlock.sldprt*.

## Step 5:   Add draft to the part

Task

Command Sequence to Click

A. Select the **Draft** tool.

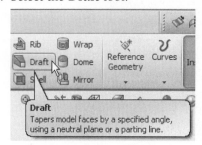

**Features => Draft** as shown to the left

B. Select the faces.

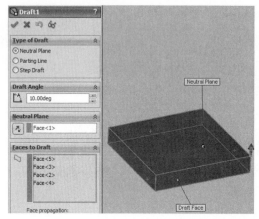

Select the large face as the **Neutral Plane**, and select the four side faces as the **Faces to Draft** as shown to the left. Input 10 degrees as the **Draft Angle**.

C. Save the part as *DraftBlock.sldprt*.

## Step 6:   Add a rib to the part

Task

Command Sequence to Click

A. Modify the block.

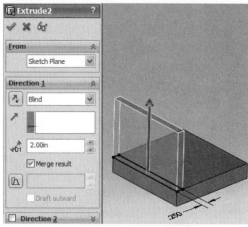

**Features => Extrude Boss/Base =>** Add the extrusion as shown to the left.

B. Select the **Rib** tool.

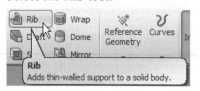

**Features => Rib** as shown to the left

| Task | Command Sequence to Click |
|---|---|

C. Sketch the rib.

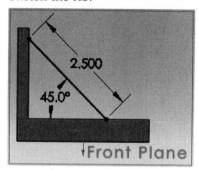

A rib can be created from an open sketch. Sketch on the **Front Plane** as shown to the left and **Exit** the sketch.

D. Create the rib.

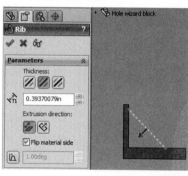
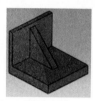

Make the selections as shown to the left to create the rib.

**FIGURE 4.18**
Stepped rib

---

**HANDS-ON FOR TUTORIAL 4–6.**

Modify the rib feature to create a stepped rib, as shown in Figure 4.18.

---

## Tutorial 4–7:   Use the Smart Fasteners Wizard

### Modeling task

Use the Smart Fasteners Wizard at the assembly level to add a fastener to a hole in a part.

### Modeling synthesis

The Smart Fasteners wizard can be used to insert the correct fastener through a hole created using either the Hole Wizard or a cylindrical cut, created at the part level.

### Modeling plan

Using the block and shaft assembly from Tutorial 6–10 to create a hole in the bracket part and then use the Smart Fasteners Wizard to insert a screw at the assembly level.

### Design intent

Ignore for this chapter.

## CAD steps

We add a fastener to a hole in three steps:

1. Open the block and shaft assembly.
2. Modify two of the parts.
3. Use the Smart Fasteners Wizard.

The details of these steps are shown below.

## Step 1:   Open the block and shaft assembly

**Task**

A. Open the block and shaft assembly from Tutorial 6.10.

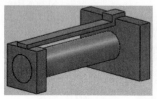

**Command Sequence to Click**

**File => Open** => Open the file of the assembly shown to the left.

## Step 2:   Modify two of the parts

**Task**

A. Open the bracket.

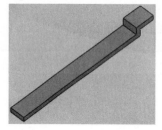

**Command Sequence to Click**

Open the piece shown to the left in a new window.

B. Insert a counterbore through hole for a #2 socket head cap screw.

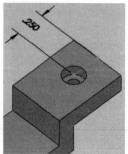

Insert a counterbore through hole for a **#2 Socket Head CapScrew** as shown to the left. **Save** and **Close** the part to return to the assembly.

**Help:** Use the skills acquired in Tutorial 4–3 to insert the correct hole type.

| Task | Command Sequence to Click |
|---|---|

**C.** Modify the big block.

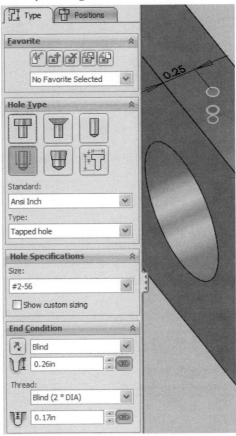

Insert a **2–56 Tapped hole** to the big block part as shown to the left. **Save** and **Close** the part to return to the assembly.

## Step 3: Use the Smart Fasteners Wizard

| Task | Command Sequence to Click |
|---|---|

**A.** Initiate the **Smart Fasteners Wizard**.

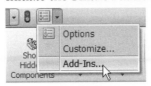

Use the **Add-Ins** menu under the **Options** tab as shown to the left to initiate the **Smart Fasteners Wizard** components.

**B.** Select the following **Add-Ins**.

Make the selections as shown to the left.

| Task | Command Sequence to Click |
|------|---------------------------|

**C.** Preselect the features.

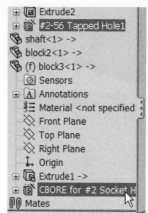

Preselect the features in the **FeatureManager design tree as** shown to the left.

**D.** Start the **Smart Fasteners Wizard**.

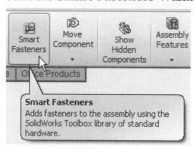

**Smart Fasteners**
Adds fasteners to the assembly using the SolidWorks Toolbox library of standard hardware.

**Assembly** tab **=> Smart Fasteners** as shown to the left

**E.** Accept the default setting.

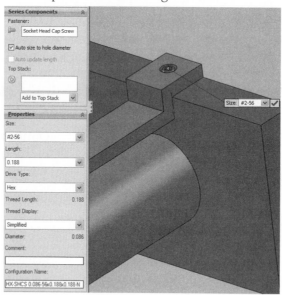

SolidWorks will automatically insert the correct fastener and length based on the selection of features as shown to the left.

---

**HANDS-ON FOR TUTORIAL 4–7.** Using the Hole Wizard at the part level, cut a #4 countersink hole through the bracket at the other end. Also cut a through hole through the smaller block and tap the shaft to line up with the countersink hole.

---

Part II Basic Part Modeling

## INDUSTRY CHAT

This section provides practical insight into how the chapter material is used in industry in the real world and practice. We chat with Mr. Lee Bazalgette, Design Engineer at Factorydesign Limited. Figure 4.19 shows two products that Factorydesign has designed. The aircraft seat (Figure 4.19A) is a lightweight short haul seat, currently being flown by www.jet2.com; and the hair dryer (Figure 4.19B) is for Remington. Both products have been modeled in SolidWorks and rendered in 3D Studio Max. Visit www.factorydesign.co.uk to learn more about Factorydesign product innovations.

(A) Aircraft seat

(B) Hair dryer

**FIGURE 4.19**
Sample products (Courtesy of Factorydesign)

### Chapter Section 4.1:   Introduction

**ABE:**   What features does Factorydesign use the most from those shown in Figure 4.1? Give some typical parts that you design.

**LEE:**   We mostly use extrusion, revolve, shell, and pattern. We use a lot of surface modeling as opposed to features. For example, we use loft, boundary, and fill surfaces. We work on different arrays of products such as consumer products (hair dryers), airplane parts (passenger seats, washroom design), packaging, home ware, and public amenities, to name a few.

### Chapter Section 4.2:   Features

**ABE:**   How do you decide what the best feature for a given design is? Or, does it matter? Provide some examples.

**LEE:**   We tend to lay out a design in 2D within a base part, and then we can see the various shapes and based on that we select the features. As the design changes, we change the features and rebuild the model. We try to minimize the number of features needed for a design as much as possible; the fewer features the shorter the rebuild times. If we have more than one feature that we can use for the same modeling problem, we rely on our prior experience. For example, if you know something is symmetrical, you need to build only half of it and then use mirror. The mirror body feature is very robust and can be placed at the bottom of the features tree to quickly see the whole part. In this way there are fewer features, faces, etc. in the rebuild above the mirror feature, so it will be quicker.

*(continue)*

Similarly, a pattern of bodies along a curve is less complex than a pattern of features. So, for example, if you wanted to make a load of dimples on a complex face, you could try to pattern the dimple feature itself, or you could revolve a sphere as a separate body, pattern the body and then use the combine feature to subtract the spheres away from your main part. The result would be similar, but the rebuild time might be less with the body pattern, especially if you want the pattern to be parametric and update with model changes.

**Chapter Section 4.3:** Spur Gears

ABE: Do you use gears? How do you design them? Do you use off-the-shelf models or build them from the involute equation? If you design them, which equations do you use?

LEE: We do not use gears. Generally we do not use libraries. Most of our designs are one of a kind.

**Chapter Section 4.4:** Design Library and Library Features

ABE: How much do you use library features? How do you organize Factory-design Limited's design library? Give an example of a library feature that does not use a base feature.

LEE: We very rarely use library features.

**Chapter Section 4.5:** Configurations and Design Tables

ABE: How much do you use configurations and design tables? Provide some examples.

LEE: We use configurations quite often when we have one design that has sizes or slight different patterns or details. For example, a modular design may have identical components of different lengths, such as an extrusion. We do not use design tables very often.

**Chapter Section 4.6:** Macros

ABE: Do you use macros in your CAD designs? Do you use VB programming to develop macros? Provide some macro examples.

LEE: We very rarely use macros. If we need them, we download them from the Web. For example, visit www.lennyworks.com and click this sequence to access its macros: **SolidWorks** (link on the left) => **Macro Downloads** => Browse the macros to select and download.

**Others**

ABE: Any other experience you would like to share with our book readers?

LEE: We offer two recommendations:

- In our designs, we avoid creating references between parts. Instead, we create a flat assembly where you have one master part and you reference all parts back to it. We do that to avoid losing references to edges and other entities (www.robrodriguezblog.com).
- Remember to use **CTRL+Q** in a part or assembly to force a thorough high-quality rebuild of your part. This sequence shows errors that SolidWorks does not normally detect because these errors are within the modeling tolerances of the software. This sequence is useful if you have complex geometry such as surfaces and edges that may shift during modeling, thus causing accidental model regeneration failure.

1.  What is a feature? Give two examples of features.

2.  Why cannot an extruded cut or a revolved cut be a base feature?

3.  Give an example part for which you must use linear sweep to model. Sketch the part. What is the input (sketch) needed to create the CAD model? Can you use extrusion to create the model? Why or why not?

4.  Give an example part for which you must use nonlinear sweep to model. Sketch the part. What is the input (sketch) needed to create the CAD model? Can you use extrusion to create the model? Why or why not?

5.  Give an example part for which you must use linear loft to model. Sketch the part. What is the input (sketch) needed to create the CAD model? Can you use extrusion to create the model? Why or why not?

6.  Give an example part for which you must use nonlinear loft to model. Sketch the part. What is the input (sketch) needed to create the CAD model? Can you use extrusion to create the model? Why or why not?

7.  Table 4.1 shows a rib feature. Which is better way to create it: using a rib or an extrusion? Explain your answer.

8.  Table 4.1 shows a block that is shelled. Which is a better way to create it: shelling or extrusion? Explain your answer.

9.  A spur gear has a pitch circle radius of 3 in., a pressure angle of 14.5°, and a number of teeth of 20. Calculate all the parameters required to create the gear CAD model. Also, calculate the coordinates of 10 points on the involute profile. Create the CAD model. Submit a screenshot of the spur gear 3D CAD model.

10. Same as Problem 9, but for a pitch circle radius of 100 mm, a pressure angle of 14.5°, and a number of teeth of 30.

11. Reverse engineer the gear in SolidWorks Design Library. Open a new part and click this sequence to access the gear: Click the **Design Library** tab in SolidWorks task pane **=> Design Library => Parts => Hardware**. Drag the gear icon and drop onto the graphics pane. Study the features tree. Find how the involute profile is created. Compare with the method covered in Section 4.3 of this chapter. Submit the steps of constructing the gear and the involute.

12. Create a macro to automate the gear creation method covered in Section 4.3.

13. Same as Problem 12, but for the gear from SolidWorks Design Library.

14. Create the CAD model of the brace drill handle shown in Figure 4.20. Also, create an engineering drawing. All dims are in mm.

15. Create the hollow loft feature shown in Figure 4.21. All dims are in inches.

**FIGURE 4.20**
Brace drill handle

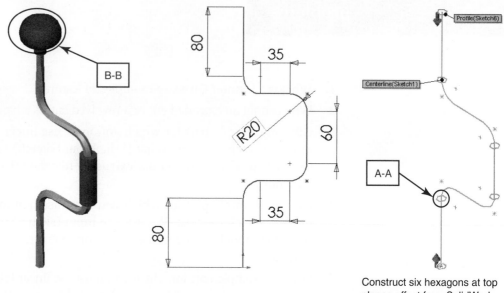

Construct six hexagons at top planes offset from SolidWorks **Top Plane** by 80, 120, 180, 220, 300

| x | y | z |
|---|---|---|
| 7 | 290 | 0 |
| 21 | 292 | 0 |
| 20 | 310 | 0 |
| 0 | 315 | 0 |

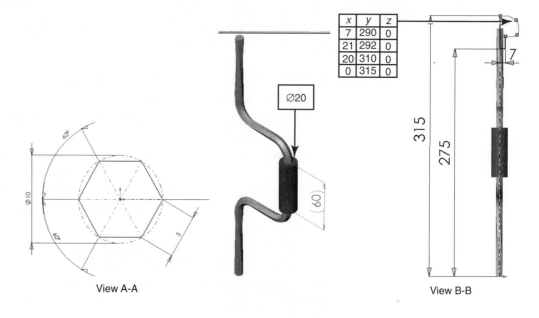

View A-A

View B-B

**FIGURE 4.21**
A horn feature

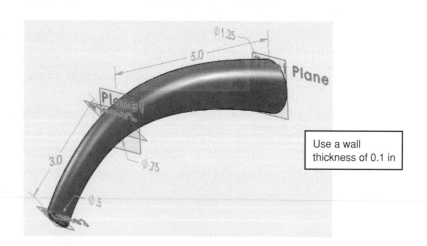

Use a wall thickness of 0.1 in

16. Create the loft feature shown in Figure 4.22. Assume dimensions. *Hint:* This loft shows you the local and global influence of the guide curve. *Hint:* Use **Guide Curve Influence** of SolidWorks menu.

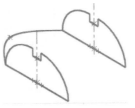

Two profiles and guide curve   Local influence of guide curve   Global influence of guide curve

**FIGURE 4.22**
Influence of guide curve

17. Use a variable pitch helix and sweep to create the worm gear model shown in Figure 4.23. Assume all dimensions.

Variable pitch helix          Worm gear

**FIGURE 4.23**
Worm gear

18. Create the CAD model of the helical spring shown in Figure 4.24. All dims are in cm.

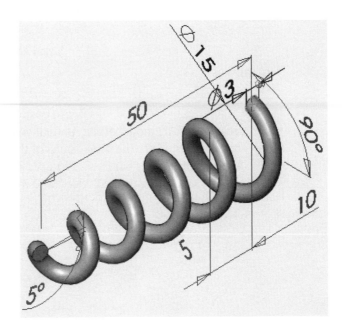

**FIGURE 4.24**
Helical spring

**19.** Create the CAD model of the 3D probe shown in Figure 4.25. All dims are in mm.

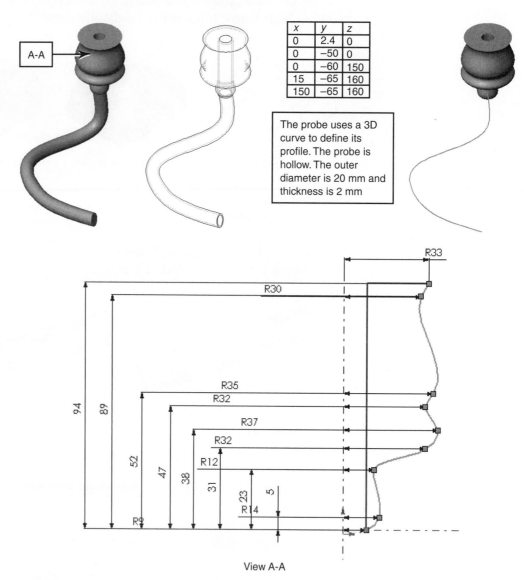

| x | y | z |
|---|---|---|
| 0 | 2.4 | 0 |
| 0 | −50 | 0 |
| 0 | −60 | 150 |
| 15 | −65 | 160 |
| 150 | −65 | 160 |

The probe uses a 3D curve to define its profile. The probe is hollow. The outer diameter is 20 mm and thickness is 2 mm

View A-A

**FIGURE 4.25**
3D probe

**20.** Create the CAD model of the football goalpost shown in Figure 4.26. All dims are in inches. *Hint:* The dimensions of the post are per NFL specs: post is 10 feet (120 in.) high, crossbar is 18.5 feet (222 in.) wide from the inner edges of the uprights, and uprights are 20 feet (240 in.) high. Check out www.sportsknowhow. com/pops/football-field-pro.html. The diameter of the post tubes is arbitrary and we use 8 in here.

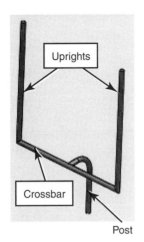

Football goalpost

**FIGURE 4.26**
Football goalpost

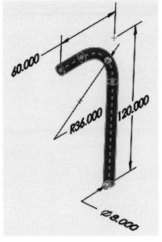

Post dimensions

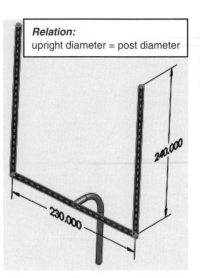

Dimensions of crossbar and uprights

CHAPTER

5

# Drawings

## 5.1 Introduction

Engineering drawings are important in engineering for two reasons. First, designers use them to document their designs. Second, they are the defacto standard in design communications among the various groups and departments that are involved in the product life cycle (e.g., manufacturing, tooling, production, inspection, assembly, etc.). The typical (standard) sizes of engineering drawings are A, B, C, D, and E.

Generating engineering drawings requires knowledge of drafting and communication rules. In general, it is not a good idea to over-dimension or under-dimension views, just as it is not a good idea to over-define or under-define sketches. The drawing should be fully defined, just like a sketch. Figure 5.1 shows the three possible scenarios of dimensioning a drawing. If you over-dimension in SolidWorks, the extra dimensions are

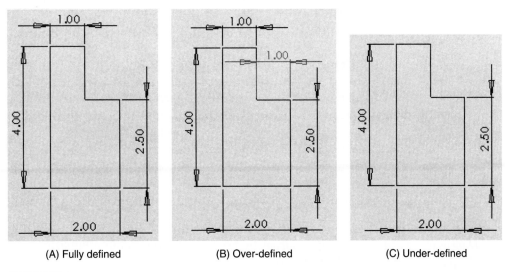

(A) Fully defined  (B) Over-defined  (C) Under-defined

**FIGURE 5.1**
Dimensioning a drawing

shown gray (Figure 5.1B). If you must show a redundant dimension, use the text "REF" next to it or include it in parentheses. So you would display the extra dimension shown gray in Figure 5.1B as 1.00REF or (1.00).

Why is dimensioning a drawing so important? The way you display dimensions on the views implies how to manufacture the part. Let us limit our discussion to machining

197

a part, that is, milling and/or drilling it. Dimensioning drawings requires manufacturing knowledge. The CAD designer needs to know the common manufacturing processes and how they work. The designer also must be familiar with the common stock shapes available off the shelf. We cover some basics later in the book. The way you dimension the drawing tells the machinist the way you want to produce the part even if you do not mean it. More importantly, the dimensioning scheme you use will influence the machining cost significantly.

The dimensioning scheme shown in Figure 5.1A is ideal from a machining point of view. The scheme tells the machinist to use the left and bottom faces as references (datums) to measure from. The machinist begins with a rectangular block as a stock, cuts the left and bottom faces, and squares them, that is, makes them perpendicular to each other. Next, the machinist measures and cuts the two horizontal dimensions (2.00 and 1.00) using the left face. Finally, the machinist measures and cuts the two vertical dimensions (4.00 and 2.50) using the bottom face to finish the part machining. Note: One problem with the part dimensions as shown here is that the machinist cannot produce them because they require zero tolerances. We must specify tolerances. This is the topic of a later chapter. Without tolerances, the machining cost is prohibitively expensive.

The dimensioning scheme also conveys which are the most important dimensions to the part functional requirements. In other words, you are telling the machinist that the 1.00 and 2.00 horizontal dimensions are more important than any other combination (e.g., 1.00 and 1.00) or the other 1.00 and 2.00. Similarly, the 4.00 and 2.50 vertical dimensions are more important than the 4.00 and 1.50 or the 2.50 and 1.50 combinations. The horizontal 1.00 and 1.00 combination and the 2.50 and 1.50 combination are the worst dimensioning scheme because they make the machining cost expensive for this part. This scheme forces the machinist to machine the step faces (horizontal and vertical) very accurately to make them datums to measure from.

The best way to dimension a drawing in SolidWorks is to use the concept of model items we covered in Tutorial 1–4 in Chapter 1. Review the tutorial as it covers the basic important concepts in creating drawings.

## 5.2 Engineering Drafting and Graphics Communication

Section 5.1 provides a glimpse of how important dimensioning and tolerancing a part are. Some CAD designers, especially beginners or those without manufacturing experience or knowledge, do not see the value of dimensioning for manufacturing, but it is crucial. If the machinist cannot read the design intent embedded in your dimensioning scheme, the machinist will use his or her own interpretations to machine the part, resulting in a high rejection (scarp) rate during inspection and making the production very inefficient and expensive. You may want to consult the following books for more details on dimensioning and tolerancing:

☐ *Dimensioning and Tolerancing Handbook* by Bruce A. Wilson, Genium Publishing Corporation (ISBN 0-931690-80-3)
☐ *Technical Drawing* by Frederick E. Giesecke et al., Pearson Publishing Company (ISBN 0-13-008183-3).

The guidelines to follow for engineering drafting and graphics communication are standard. The American National Standards Institute (ANSI) and the International Organization for Standardization (ISO) committees maintain these standards in coordination and consultation with companies. There are abbreviation rules for use on drawings and in text, dimensioning rules, and tolerancing rules. The American Society of Mechanical Engineers (ASME) publishes two documents on these subjects. The ASME Y1.1-1989,

"Abbreviations for Use on Drawings and in Text," covers the abbreviation rules. The ASME Y14.5M-1994, "Dimensioning and Tolerancing," covers the rules on how to display dimensions and tolerances on a drawing. ASME has published a revision of its well-known ASME Y14.5M-1994; the new revision is ASME Y14.5-2009.

## 5.3 ASME Abbreviation Rules

ASME indicates where and how abbreviations should be used as well as some basic rules. ASME publishes the above mentioned book (the ASME Y1.1-1989) that lists the abbreviations in alphabetical order. Here are some rules:

1. **Minimize using abbreviations:** Using abbreviations on drawings should be minimized for clarity purposes. ASME's book begins by stating, "the purpose is to establish standard abbreviations rather than to promote the use of abbreviations." The reason being is that abbreviations are language-dependent.
2. **Pay attention to foreign use:** Abbreviations are conventional representations of words or names and may differ from one language to another. Thus companies that are multinational should not use abbreviations.
3. **Pay attention to clarity:** Abbreviations should be used only where necessary to save space and time. Also, use only the obvious interpretations that are easy to understand; otherwise, spell out the word.
4. **Be aware of duplicates:** Duplicate abbreviations exist for some words because of the established practice. Thus, be careful.
5. **Define when extensively used:** Books and large publications that use abbreviations should define them in one convenient place for readers to find.
6. **Take advantage of single use:** Single organizations may use abbreviations more freely than others because it is easier to set communication standards within one company.
7. **Avoid using nonstandard abbreviations:** Refrain from making up and using your own abbreviations. Nobody will understand them.
8. **Follow military rules:** Military agencies set and publish their own abbreviations for contractors to use.
9. **Use all capital letters:** All abbreviations should be shown in capital letters on drawings and in lowercase in text.
10. **Avoid using subscripts:** Subscripts should not be used in abbreviations.

Figure 5.2 shows sample abbreviations.

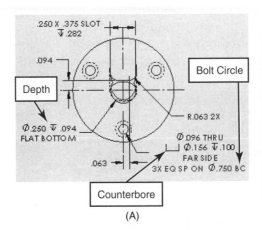

(A)

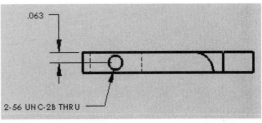

This is a thread code:
2: shank size; 56: threads/inch (TPI); UNC: Unified Course; 2B: Internal; THRU: Through

(B)

**FIGURE 5.2**
Sample abbreviations

## 5.4 ASME Drafting Rules

Some of the ASME drafting rules are:

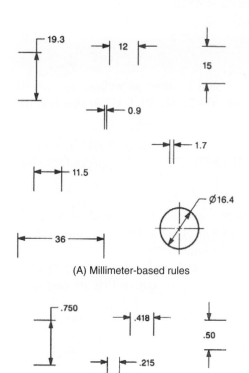

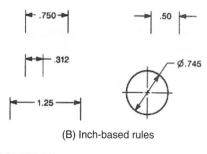

(A) Millimeter-based rules

(B) Inch-based rules

**FIGURE 5.3**

Sample drafting rules
(Reprinted from ASME Y14.5M-1994 [R2004], by permission of The American Society of Mechanical Engineers. All rights reserved.)

1. **Use tolerances:**   Each dimension should have a tolerance except those dimensions that are labeled as reference, as discussed in Section 5.1.
2. **Provide full feature definition:**   Each feature should be fully dimensioned so it is fully understood.
3. **Show only what is needed:**   Show necessary dimensions for a complete definition of the part. Do not give more dimensions than necessary. Minimize the use of reference dimensions.
4. **Follow functional requirements:**   Select and arrange dimensions to meet the functional and mating requirements of a part. See Section 5.1, for example, on whether to use a 4.00 and 2.50 or 2.50 and 1.50 combination. Also, there should be one and only one way to interpret the dimensions.
5. **Do not specify manufacturing methods:**   Define the drawing without specifying manufacturing methods. For example, show a hole diameter on the drawing without indicating whether it is to be drilled, milled, punched, reamed, etc.
6. **Show processing dimensions:**   If needed, you may show processing dimensions to indicate, for example, finish or shrink allowance. In such a case, label the dimension as NON MANDATORY (MFG DATA), all in caps as shown here.
7. **Show dimensions clearly:**   Arrange dimensions so that they are easy to read, provide required information, are shown in true profile, and refer to visible outlines.
8. **Use linear dimensions for specific parts:**   Use linear dimensions for wires, cables, sheets, and rods that are produced according to gage or code numbers. These dimensions usually show the diameter or the thickness.
9. **You may not specify 90° angle:**   If you have a pattern in which the centerlines are shown at right angles on the drawing, there is no need to show the angle; a 90° angle applies.
10. **Keep temperature in mind:**   All dimensions shown on a drawing are assumed to be measured at room temperature (20°C or 68°F). If measurements are made at other temperatures, provide appropriate compensation.
11. **Understand geometric tolerances:**   When you apply geometric tolerances, they apply to the full depth, length, and width of the feature. We cover geometric tolerances later in the book.

Figure 5.3 shows the millimeter and inch rules. These rules are explained further in Section 5.6.

## 5.5 ASME Dimensioning Rules

We need to be familiar with the types of dimensions in order to understand their rules. These types are Cartesian, radial, angular, true length, and ordinate or baseline. Cartesian dimensions are specified along the horizontal and vertical directions of the drawing views as we have done in Chapter 1's tutorials. Radial dimensions specify a circle or arc's radius or diameter. Angular dimensions specify an angle. True length dimensions specify a dimension along a line that is not horizontal or vertical. Ordinate or baseline dimensions specify all dimensions in one direction from a reference face or datum.

As a general rule for using ordinate (baseline) dimensions, using fewer datums reduces the machining cost of the part because it requires fewer part surfaces (faces) that must be machined with high accuracy to measure other dimensions from. Figure 5.1A shows the Cartesian and ordinate dimensioning types. The other dimensioning types are more obvious. The horizontal and vertical dimensions shown are for both the Cartesian and ordinate types. The horizontal dimensions (2.00 and 1.00) use the left face of the part as the datum. The vertical dimensions (4.00 and 2.50) use the bottom face of the part as the datum. The optimum ordinate dimensioning strategy (scheme) is to use only one datum per direction. This strategy guarantees the least machining cost to manufacture the part.

Some of the ASME dimensioning rules are:

1. **Be careful when to use a zero before the decimal point:** If the dimension is in millimeters and less than 1, use a zero before the decimal point; for example, use 0.5, not .5. If the dimension is in inches, do not use a zero; for example, use .5, not 0.5. See Figure 5.3.

2. **Do not use a zero or the decimal point for a whole number millimeter dimension:** For example, use 35, not 35.0.

3. **Do not add a zero to a decimal millimeter dimension:** For example, use 35.6, not 35.60.

4. **Use the same number of decimal places as its tolerance for an inch dimension:** For example, use 4.500, not 4.5 if the dimension tolerance requires three decimal places.

5. **Show decimal points clearly:** The decimal points must be uniform, dense, and large enough to be clearly visible.

6. **Use dimension lines correctly:** ASME rules prefer that dimension lines be broken for the insertion of the dimension value (number). You may use unbroken dimension lines, as shown in Figure 5.1. In such a case, the dimension value should be shown above the dimension line for horizontal lines. Figure 5.1 follows this rule because the CAD/CAM system uses and enforces ASME rules.

7. **Group dimension lines:** If possible, have all related dimension lines shown next to each other in one group to make easier to for users to read the engineering drawing. In Figure 5.1, we could move the 4.00 dimension line to the right next to the 2.50 dimension line to make them as one group.

8. **Space dimension lines:** The space between the first dimension line and the part outline should not be less than 10 mm; and the space between succeeding parallel dimension lines should not be less than 6 mm.

9. **Do not cross dimension lines:** Avoid crossing dimension lines. When unavoidable, the dimension lines are unbroken. Figures 5.1 and 5.4 follow this rule where all dimension lines (lines with arrows) are not crossing.

10. **Do not cross extension (projection) lines:** An **extension line** is a line that is perpendicular to the part outline to allow placing the dimension line. For example, in Figure 5.1A, the two vertical lines extending down to place the 2.00 dimension line are extension lines. There is always a gap between the extension line and the part outline as shown. Extension lines should neither cross each other nor cross dimension lines. Where unavoidable, break the extension line.

11. **Use leaders (leader lines) if needed:** A **leader** is a line used to place a dimension (e.g., a circle radius), a note (text on a drawing), or a symbol (special character) on a drawing. A leader terminates in an arrowhead if it ends on a part outline. If it ends inside the part outline, terminate it with a dot. Also, a leader should be an inclined straight line with a short horizontal portion extending to the first or last letter of the note, or the first or last digit of the dimension. Also, make adjacent leaders parallel to each other for ease of display.

**12. Use reference dimensions if needed.** When an overall dimension is specified, one intermediate dimension is omitted or identified as a reference dimension.

Figure 5.4 shows sample dimensioning (we refer to the rule numbers listed above).

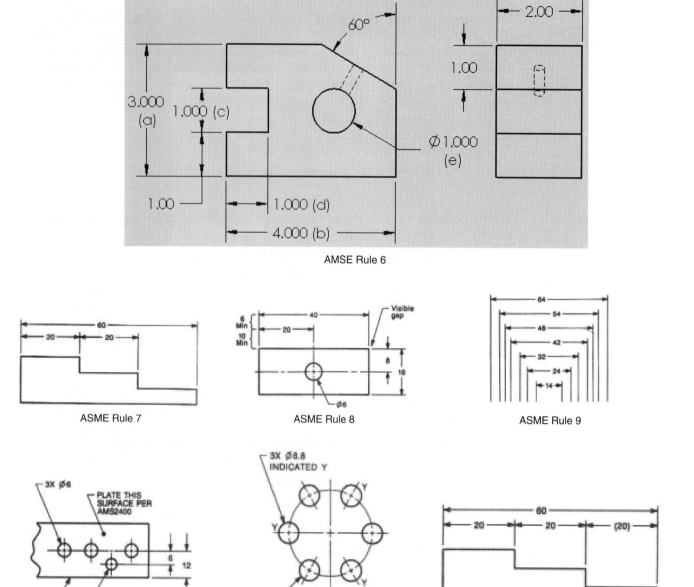

**FIGURE 5.4**
Sample dimensioning rules (inches)
(Reprinted from ASME Y14.5M-1994 [R2004], by permission of The American Society of Mechanical Engineers. All rights reserved.)

The drawing illustrating ASME Rule 6 and shown in Figure 5.4 displays a combination of baseline and chain dimensioning. This drawing will communicate the importance (accuracy) of dimensions (a), (b), (c), (d), and (e). Although the dimensions with the lesser decimal places are less important to the functionality of the part, not enough accuracy will create a nonfunctional part; too much accuracy will be complicated and too expensive to manufacture. The outer shape of this part is fully defined. However, the two hole features have not been identified or located.

**FIGURE 5.5**

Sample dimensioning rules
(millimeters)

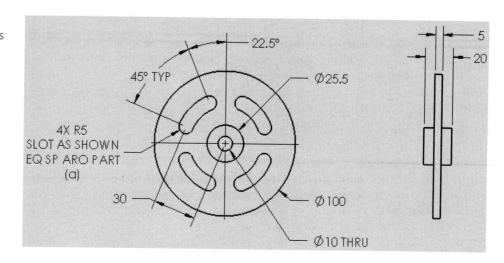

The drawing shown in Figure 5.5 is dimensioned in metric units of millimeters. Dimension (a) reads as follows: Four times, radius 5 mm. Slots are spaced equally around the part. As in ASME dimensioning rule 2 above, there are no trailing zeros to designate accuracy or tolerance when dimensioning in metric units.

## 5.6 Dimensions

This section briefly describes the types of dimensions and the ASME dimensioning rules that you need to follow. We extend the discussion here by showing how SolidWorks implements these rules, thus helping you to follow them. Figure 5.6 shows SolidWorks

**FIGURE 5.6**

Types of dimensions

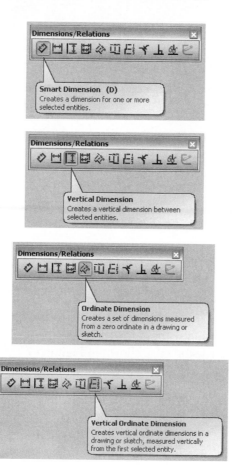

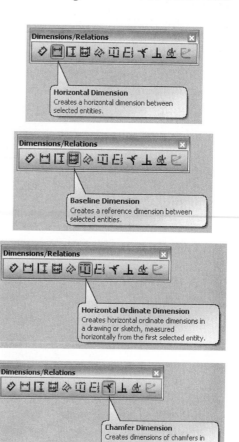

Dimensions/Relations toolbar. Click this sequence to show/hide (toggle) the toolbar: **View => Toolbars => Dimensions/Relations**. You can insert a dimension type by clicking: Select icon from **Dimensions/Relations** toolbar => Select entity to dimension => Place dimension => Green check mark to finish. See Example 5.1.

When you insert a dimension, SolidWorks allows you to add symbols (abbreviations) to it. While the dimension mode is active, you see the **Dimension Text** block on the bottom left of the screen. See Tutorial 5–3.

---

**Example 5.1** Create the model shown in Figure 5.7, and use it to show baseline, ordinate, and chamfer dimensions in a drawing.

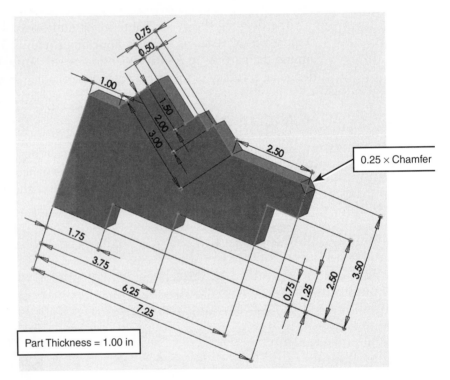

**FIGURE 5.7**
A stepped block

**Solution** The block shown in Figure 5.7 is an extrusion. The dimensions shown are designed to illustrate the use of baseline and ordinate dimension types in a drawing. The modeling plan has three steps:

1. Create the extrusion without the chamfer.
2. Chamfer the extrusion edge shown in Figure 5.7.
3. Create a drawing and insert views and dimensions.

# Step 1: Create the extrusion without the chamfer shown in Figure 5.8

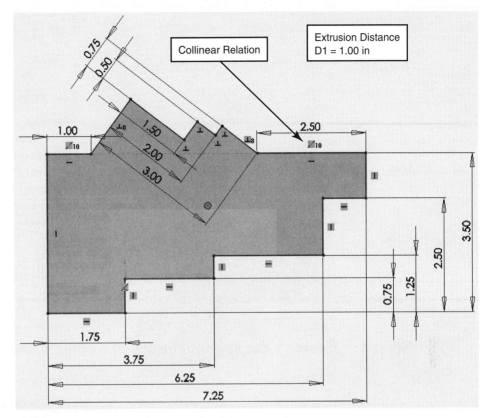

**FIGURE 5.8**
Create the stepped block

**Help:** The cross section shown in Figure 5.8 is anchored at the origin at one of its corner points. It also uses three types of relations: horizontal, vertical, and collinear. SolidWorks creates the horizontal and vertical lines implicitly by predicting your intention as you sketch. The dimensioning scheme of the cross section is selected to minimize the number of reference faces (datums) and to lend itself to the baseline and ordinate dimension schemes we use in the drawing.

| Task | Command Sequence to Click |
|---|---|
| A. Start SolidWorks and open a new part file. Change the part units to inches. Save the file as *example 5.1*. | **File => New => Part => OK** <br> **File => Save As** *=> example 5.1* **=> Save** |
| B. Select the front plane as the sketch plane. | **Front Plane** from features manager tree on left of screen |
| C. Select extrusion as the feature type to create. | **Extruded Boss/Base** from the **Features** tab to start sketching |
| D. Sketch the cross section shown in Figure 5.8. | Click the line symbol on the **Sketch** tab => Sketch and dimension the cross section shown in Figure 5.8. <br> **Help:** To create the collinear relation, select a line, press/hold **CTRL**, select the other line, and select the collinear relation from the pane that opens on left of screen. |
| E. Exit the sketch. | **Exit Sketch** icon on **Sketch** toolbar |

| Task | Command Sequence to Click |
|---|---|
| F. Create the extrusion. | Input 1.00 in. for **D1** => Green check mark to finish. |

## Step 2: Chamfer the extrusion edge

| Task | Command Sequence to Click |
|---|---|
| A. Select the chamfer feature. | **Features** tab => **Fillet** drop-down => **Chamfer** |
| B. Select the feature type to create. | **Extruded Cut** from the **Features** tab |
| C. Select edge to fillet. | Select the edge shown to the left => Input 0.25 for the distance as shown to the left, and use the default 45° => Green check mark to finish. |

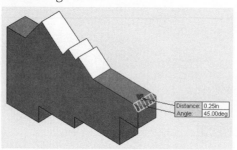

## Step 3: Create a drawing and insert views and dimensions

| Task | Command Sequence to Click |
|---|---|
| A. Open a new drawing and insert a front view. Save it as *example 5.1.2*. | **File => New => Drawing => OK** **File => Save As** => *example 5.1.2* **=> Save** |
| B. Insert baseline dimensions. | **Insert => Model Items** => Green check mark to finish. Delete the chamfer dimensions, and then click this sequence to re-create them: **Chamfer Dimension** icon on **Dimensions/Relations** toolbar => Chamfer => One of its adjacent edges => Position the chamfer dimension => Green check mark to finish. See result shown to the left. **Help:** The baseline dimensions inserted (shown to the left) are identical to those shown in Figure 5.7 because we use the **Model Items**. Thus the baseline dimensions are identical to those shown in Figure 5.8. |

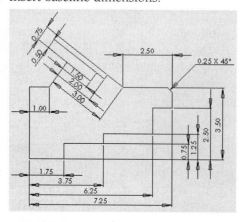

| | |
|---|---|
| C. Insert ordinate dimensions. | Delete all the dimensions created in Task B above except the chamfer. Then click **Ordinate Dimension** icon on the **Dimensions/Relations** toolbar => The inclined edge (see edge with 0 dimension on left) => An edge parallel to it (to insert the 0.5 dimension) => The other edge (to insert the 0.75 dimension). Click the **Horizontal Ordinate Dimension** icon => The far left vertical edge |

| Task | Command Sequence to Click |
|---|---|

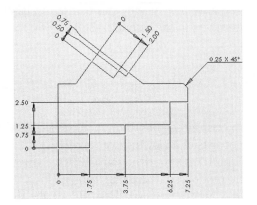

(to establish the vertical zero line) => The vertical edges one after the other. Then click **Vertical Ordinate Dimension** => The bottommost edge (to establish the horizontal zero line) => The horizontal edges one after the other. See the result shown to the left. **Help:** You notice that the ordinate dimensions you insert are shown in gray color because they are not **Model Items**. Click this sequence to change them to black color: **Tools Options => System Options** tab **=> Colors => Dimensions, Non Imported (Driven)** from the drop-down list **=> Edit =>** Black color box **=> OK => OK**. Then in a separate paragraph, show the other dim options. Then do the Hands-on for this example.

**Why:** Both baseline and ordinate dimensions are acceptable for machining purposes. They both define the same number of datums. Use either of them.

---

**HANDS-ON FOR EXAMPLE 5.1.** Create two 1-inch diameter through holes in the front face of the block. The centers of the two holes are (1.5, 2) and (3.5, 2) from the left bottom corner of the block. Use both baseline and ordinate dimensioning schemes to dimension them in a drawing.

## 5.7 Drawing Content and Layout

As we covered in Chapter 1, you can create a part or an assembly drawing. Figures 1.26 through 1.28 show part drawings, and Figure 1.30 shows an assembly drawing. As demonstrated in these figures, drawing content includes the views, dimensions, bill of materials, and a title block. Typically, a drawing includes three views: front, top, and right. You may include the isometric view as a fourth view, as shown in Figures 1.26 through 1.28 and 1.30. Other views, such as sectioned views, may be added if they are needed to clarify the drawing.

In addition, a drawing may include tolerances, notes, balloons, hole callouts, weld symbols, surface finish symbols, surface roughness values, and a bill of materials (BOM). A BOM is usually used in assembly drawings. It typically shows the part number, how many instances of it are used in the assembly, and what its material is. If a BOM is used in a part drawing, it shows the same information as the assembly BOM except for the number of instances. Companies may create special BOMs to fit their needs.

SolidWorks groups most of the drawing content under the **Annotations** menu. While in a drawing, click **Insert** (SolidWorks menu) **=> Annotations** to access all possible annotations (see Figure 5.9) you can add to a drawing. Figure 5.9 also shows a note (the text that

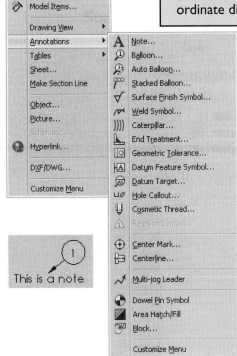

**FIGURE 5.9**
SolidWorks annotations

reads as such) and a balloon (the circle that points to the note). Balloons can be added to notes, as shown in Figure 5.9, or they can be used to label parts of an assembly and relate them to item numbers in the assembly BOM.

## 5.8 Types of Projection

A CAD/CAM system uses projection to generate views (2D) from a model (3D). The system does this by projecting the model onto the projection plane. The system uses a viewing model that consists of a viewing eye (observer), a CAD model, and a projection plane, as shown in Figure 5.10. In orthographic views, the observer is placed at an infinite distance from the model and the plane, thus making the line of sight parallel perpendicular to both the model face we are viewing and the plane. Also, the plane is parallel to the model face we are viewing.

The CAD/CAM system generates a drawing view by converting the 3D coordinates of the model geometry into 2D view coordinates, determines the visible and invisible geometry, and renders the resulting view onto the projection plane (the computer screen). The system displays the view based on the location of the projection plane. If the location of Figure 5.10A (known as first-angle projection) is used, the system displays the left view of the model. If the location of Figure 5.10B (known as third-angle projection) is used, the system displays the right view. Effectively, the views of the third-angle projection are opposite to those of the first-angle projection. For example, the third-angle projection produces the front, top, and right views of the model, whereas the first-angle projection produces the back, bottom, and left views. You may ask why there are two different sets of views. The United States and Canada use the third-angle projection whereas Europe and other countries use the first-angle projection.

SolidWorks offers both types of projections. To set the angle of projection, right-click anywhere on the drawing sheet => **Properties** => Select **Third angle** (or **First angle**) => **OK**. Refer to Tutorial 1–4 in Chapter 1 for more details.

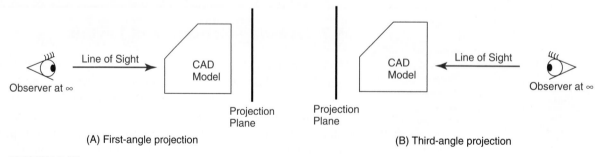

**FIGURE 5.10**
Projection of a CAD model

## 5.9 Views

CAD/CAM systems offer different types of views to convey a model design. SolidWorks offers the following types (see Figure 5.11):

1. **Named (orthographic) views:** These are the standard orthographic views: front, top, right, back, bottom, and left. These are the views we have created so far in the book.

2. **Section view:** This view type allows you to look at the inside of the model by cutting a section in it. The cut could be straight (use one section line) or stepped

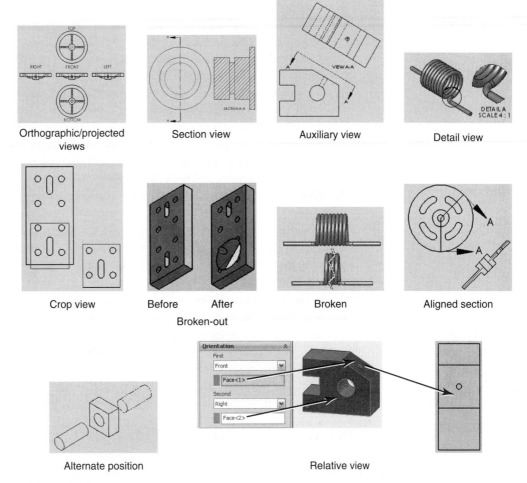

| | |
|---|---|
| Orthographic/projected views | Section view |
| Auxiliary view | Detail view |

| | | | |
|---|---|---|---|
| Crop view | Before    After<br>Broken-out | Broken | Aligned section |

Alternate position

Relative view

**FIGURE 5.11**
Types of views

(use stepped section line). The CAD/CAM system requires you to define a direction (section line) for the sectional view. To create a section view, click **Insert => Drawing view => Section** => Sketch a line => Move (do not drag) the mouse to where to place the section view and click there.

3. **Projected view:** You may project an existing view in a given direction. This speeds up and standardizes view creation. For example, you may select a front view and click to the right or left of it to create a right or left view, respectively. Click **Insert => Drawing view => Projected** => Select a view => Move the mouse in any direction (left, right, top, bottom) of the selected view to insert the new view.

4. **Auxiliary view:** This view is similar to the projected view, but it is unfolded normal to a selected edge in an existing view. To create an auxiliary view, select an edge, then click **Insert => Drawing view => Auxiliary** => Click in the graphics pane on the screen to place the view.

5. **Detail view:** A CAD designer uses this view to zoom in to a portion of a view (orthographic, ISO, sectional, assembly, or another detail view) to show more details, usually at an enlarged scale. To create a detail view, click **Insert => Drawing view => Detail** => Circle the desired portion of the drawing with the mouse => Move (do not drag) the mouse to where to place the detail view and click there.

6. **Crop view:** You can crop any drawing view except a detail view. A crop view allows you to cut a piece of an existing view. The crop view deletes the view you crop. The creation of a crop view is a two-step process. First, you need to define a closed crop profile such as a circle. Second, create the crop view by clicking **Insert => Drawing view => Crop**.

7. **Broken-out section:** Using a broken-out section, you can carve/remove material from a region of an existing view for a given depth to show inner details. A closed profile, usually a spline, defines the region (broken-out section). Follow this sequence to create a broken-out section: **Insert => Drawing view => Broken-out Section** => Sketch a closed spline => Green check mark to finish. The section will be removed from the drawing view.

8. **Broken view:** A broken view makes it possible to display a drawing view in a large scale on a smaller size drawing sheet. The view still shows the actual dimension values. We usually break the view in areas where view details are not important to that view. To create a broken view, click **Insert => Drawing view => Break** => Select a drawing to break => Select the broken view settings (vertical or horizontal break line, gap size, and break line style) from the **Broken View** panel that shows on the left => Green check mark to finish.

9. **Aligned section view:** This view is similar to a section view, but the section line comprises two or more lines connected at an angle. To create an aligned section view, click **Insert => Drawing view => Aligned Section** => Sketch a line on through the desired view to create the view => Move (do not drag) the mouse to place the new view => Click there. To create an aligned section view with more than one line, you must create the (connected) lines and select them first (use **CTRL** for multiple selection) before you click the sequence to create the view.

10. **Alternate position view:** This view is used in an assembly drawing to show the assembly in different positions to demonstrate its range of motion. You can superimpose one drawing view precisely on another. The alternate view (position) is shown with phantom lines. Use this sequence to create a position view: **Insert => Drawing view => Alternate Position** => Select the view to create the alternate view in => Move the desired components to the desired locations => Green check mark to finish.

11. **Relative view:** This view allows you to create a true view of angled faces in a model. Consider a block with a chamfered corner that has a hole in its center. If you need to create a true view of the chamfer (where the observer is looking perpendicular at the chamfer plane), you need to create a relative view. The relative view requires two orthogonal faces or planes: the chamfer face and the front face of the block. SolidWorks creates a view of the chamfer face perpendicular to the front face of the block. Click this sequence: **Insert => Drawing view => Relative To Model** => Switch to the model that is open or right-click in the graphics pane and open the model => Select the chamfer face => Select the front face => Green check mark to finish => Click mouse to place the view in desired location.

## 5.10 Sheets and Title Blocks

SolidWorks uses the concept of sheets in a drawing. A drawing may consist of one or more sheets. The use of multiple sheets allows you to include more views in a drawing than what one sheet can hold, instead of creating a whole new file. For example, you may use one sheet to show the three standard orthographic and the ISO views. Then use another sheet to show a detail view and a section view. In the case of an assembly, you may use one sheet to show the standard views and one sheet to show an exploded view.

To create a new drawing, click **File => New => Drawing => OK =>** Select the sheet (drawing) size and format from the window that pops up **=> OK**. This opens what is called a drawing template. The template consists of both the sheet itself and the sheet format. At the sheet level of the template, the user will find the views and all associated information. Once the drawing template is open, the system will prompt you to insert views. After you insert the views, you see a tab called **Sheet 1** in the features tree shown in the left pane of the screen. You can rename the sheet. To insert another sheet, right-click in the graphics pane **=> Add Sheet** from the menu that pops up (Figure 5.12). This adds Sheet 2 and displays it on the screen, waiting for you to insert views. The first sheet disappears. SolidWorks creates tabs, one per sheet at the bottom of the screen. You can toggle the sheets by selecting a tab. As shown in Figure 5.12, you can manipulate sheets in various ways. For example, you can copy and paste an existing sheet as follows: Right-click the sheet you want to copy **=> Copy =>** Right-click in the graphics pane **=> Paste =>**. The menu in Figure 5.12 will appear asking you in which order the tabs will appear, and select **=> OK**. A very useful feature at the sheet level is to lay out predefined views. Predefined views will automatically determine the orientation, display style, location, and scale of a view in which a part/assembly reference will be added later. This method will be explained in further detail in Tutorial 5–1.

The second part of the drawing template is called the sheet format. Sheet format determines the size of the drawing, the borders and title block, the default sheet scale, the type of view projection (**First** or **Third Angle**), and the next letter of the alphabet to be used in view datum labels. These can be changed by right-clicking anywhere on the sheet in the graphics pane and selecting **Properties**. The dialog box opens, as shown in Figure 5.13.

**FIGURE 5.12**
Sheet menu

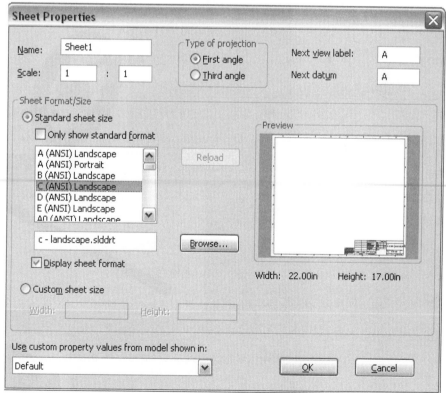

**FIGURE 5.13**
Sheet properties

**FIGURE 5.14**
Save Sheet Format

Changes to any of the fields in Figure 5.13 along with changes to the title block will be saved with this sheet format. SolidWorks provides sheet formats that can be customized and saved to replace any of these formats or saved as new formats.

Each of the SolidWorks formats has a generic title block that can also be customized in many ways. Typically the title block will contain **Notes** that are linked to **Custom Properties**. Custom Properties can be linked from the part/assembly level, the sheet format level, or in the case of special properties, the sheet itself. You can edit the title block and customize it to your needs. To edit the title block, right-click a sheet in the features tree => **Edit Sheet Format** => When done editing, right-click the sheet again in the features tree => **Edit Sheet** to return to the content of the sheet. The method to edit a title block is covered in Tutorial 5–2.

Sheet formats have a file extension of *.slddrt* and can be saved as shown in Figure 5.14. Any custom properties in the title block or changes in the sheet properties will be saved at this level. Sheet formats do not save views. Formats are automatically saved to *SolidWorks install directory\data*, but can be saved anywhere. If the default location is chosen, the new format will appear in the list shown in Figure 5.13; otherwise, the user can browse to find a format.

Drawing templates allow you to save both the sheet and the sheet format for reuse in the future, thus saving you the time of creating them whenever you need them. Drawing templates are saved with *.drwdot* file extension and can be saved in any location. If they are saved in SolidWorks default location (*templates*, as shown in Figure 5.15A), they will appear in the **Templates** tab that shows up when you click **File => New**, as shown in Figure 5.15B.

(A)

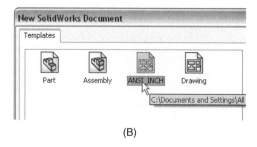

(B)

**FIGURE 5.15**
Save Sheet Format

## 5.11  Layers

Think of layers as a management concept offered by CAD/CAM systems. Conceptually, a **layer** is sheet of transparency whereby you can assign geometric content to it (e.g., geometric entities, dimensions, etc.). You can assign colors, styles, and thickness to layers. Any entities that you construct on a layer inherit its attributes. Essentially, use layers to format entities conveniently in groups, instead of formatting one entity at a time.

You can move entities between layers, and you can turn layers on and off. SolidWorks provides layers only in the Drawing mode, that is, when you open a drawing. It does not provide layers in the Model mode (part construction) like other CAD/CAM systems do. Layers are less important and less used in SolidWorks than in AutoCAD.

SolidWorks replaces layers with the drawing sheets covered in Section 5.10. You can use drawing sheets to hide and show drawing views, assembly components, lines, and various other items without using layers.

SolidWorks displays the **Layer** toolbar on the bottom left corner of a drawing sheet on the screen, as shown in Figure 5.16A. The toolbar is active only in the Drawing mode. Select a layer name from the drop-down list to make it active, and click the layer icon next to the name to open the **Layers** window, shown in Figure 5.16B. As shown, you can create a new layer and give it a new name, or delete an existing layer. Use the **Move** button to move entities from one layer to another; select the entities to move from the drawing and click **Move**. As shown also, the layer properties (attributes) from left to right are Name, Description, on/off, color, Style, and Thickness. Double-click the name or description field to edit. Click the on/off icon (lightbulb) to turn a layer on or off; it is a toggle. Click the color, **Style**, or **Thickness** icon to edit and change the corresponding property. Figure 5.16B shows the line thickness options. The arrow shown on the left indicates the current selected (active) layer where construction takes place; that is, the newly added content belongs to the current layer. To activate a layer, click to the left before its name.

**FIGURE 5.16**
Layers

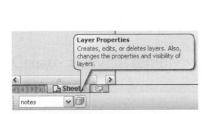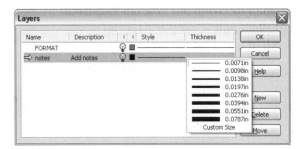

(A) Layer toolbar                                      (B) Layers properties (attributes)

## 5.12 Hatching and Dimension Control

SolidWorks offers many other menus and options for drawings and drafting. We list them here:

1. **Control display styles and hatch:** Click this sequence: **Tools => Options => System Options** tab **=> Display Style** or **Area Hatch/Fill** to explore them. Figure 5.17 shows both options

**FIGURE 5.17**
Drawing options

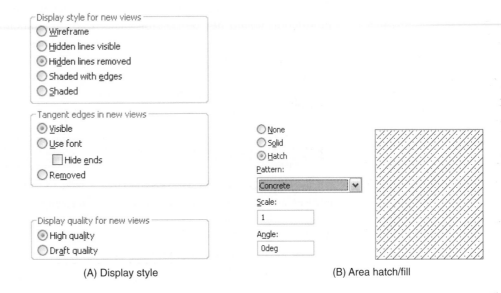

(A) Display style                                      (B) Area hatch/fill

2. **Control dimensions display:** Click this sequence: **Tools => Options => Document Properties** tab => **Dimensions** => Select any option to investigate/set. Figure 5.18 shows the options.

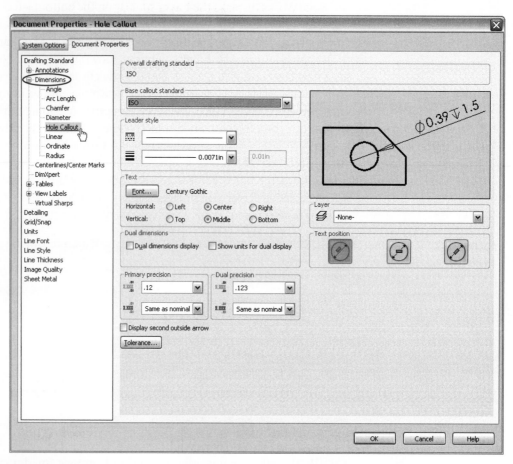

**FIGURE 5.18**
Dimensions options

## 5.13  ASME Tolerancing Rules

Tolerancing is an important concept to manufacturing. Without tolerances, modern production would not be possible. The ASME tolerancing rules and concepts set the standards for the engineering practice. CAD/CAM systems use these rules and concepts in their tolerancing software modules, and your CAD/CAM system should help you to follow the ASME dimensions and tolerancing rules. We cover tolerances and their rules in a separate chapter but see Section 5.14.

## 5.14  Tolerances

Although we cover tolerances in full details later in the book, here are some basics. Tolerances are our way of dealing with manufacturing imperfections. We cannot produce what is known as a perfect form of a part. For example, we cannot create a box of size $3 \times 2 \times 4$ inches. Manufacturing imperfections are due to many reasons, such as the skill level of the machinist, accuracy and age of the machine tool, environmental conditions, cutting conditions, etc.

Designers assign tolerances to dimensions based on the functional requirements of the part and its assembly. A designer does not need to assign tolerances to each dimension in a drawing, but only to the important ones. Typically, the designer may designate a general tolerance in the drawing (as a note) to indicate the value of the tolerance that should be applied to any dimension on the drawing that does not have a tolerance. Or, the designer may leave out the general tolerance altogether, and the machinist uses his or her experience.

## 5.15 Bill of Materials

**FIGURE 5.19**
Create a BOM

The bill of materials is typically displayed as a table. This can be imported from an Excel file or created at the drawing level by SolidWorks. SolidWorks will automatically create and populate the cells of the table with all of the information relating to a specific assembly. To create a BOM, click this sequence: **Insert** (menu) => **Tables** => **Bill of Materials**, as shown in Figure 5.19. The default BOM has three columns, **ITEM NO.**, **PART NUMBER**, and **QTY.**, that are each linked to properties found in the assembly itself. Any changes at the assembly level will affect the BOM. The user can add more columns with other linked properties or replace any of the default columns with different information. The order of item numbers reflects the order of appearance in the **FeatureManager design tree** (Figure 5.20). Figure 5.21 shows the types of BOM that you can create.

| ITEM NO. | PART NUMBER | QTY. |
|----------|-------------|------|
| 1 | Plate 1 | 1 |
| 2 | Plate 2 | 2 |
| 3 | pin | 1 |
| 4 | wheel | 1 |
| 5 | rubber | 1 |

**FIGURE 5.20**
Relationship of BOM to **FeatureManager**

- ◇ Right Plane
- ↳ Origin
- ⊞ 🏷 (f) Plate 1<1> (Default<<Default:
- ⊞ 🏷 Plate 2<1> (Default<<Default>_[
- ⊞ 🏷 Plate 2<2> (Default<<Default>_[
- ⊞ 🏷 pin<1> (Default<<Default>_Displ
- ⊞ 🏷 (-) wheel<1> (Default<<Default>
- ⊞ 🏷 (-) rubber<1> (Default<<Default>

**BOM Type** ≫
- ○ Top-level only
- ◉ Parts only
- ○ Indented

There are three types of BOM that can be created as shown to the left. These types show up when you insert a BOM in a drawing.

| 8 | Imported |
|---|----------|
| 9 | Imported1 |
| 10 | STP-MTR-17048 |

**Parts only** selected will show every part from all levels of assemblies.

| 8 | LWL12B |
|---|--------|
|  | Imported |
|  | Imported1 |
| 9 | STP-MTR-17048 |
| 10 | S-00009 |

**Indented** selected will show the parts at the top level as well as the parts of the subassemblies indented as shown to the left.

| 8 | LWL12B |
|---|--------|
| 9 | STP-MTR-17048 |
| 10 | S-00009 |

**Top-level only** selected will show the parts and subassemblies without listing the parts of the subassemblies.

**FIGURE 5.21**
Types of BOM

**FIGURE 5.22**
BOM settings

The BOM settings shown in Figure 5.22 determine what information is displayed on the drawing.

☐ **Table Position** will allow the user to locate the table by hand using any of the corners of the table. The table will automatically snap to various points throughout the drawing. Also, when creating the sheet format, an anchor point can be established such that the BOM will automatically be located at this point.

☐ **BOM Type** There are three different types of BOM tables. They are described in more detail in Figure 5.21.

☐ **Configurations** will allow the user to set which configuration of the assembly will be referenced in the table.

☐ **Part Configuration Grouping** is used to determine how parts with multiple configurations will be displayed in the table.

☐ **Item Numbers** typically start at 1 but can be changed according to design choices.

☐ **Border** section will be used to change the weight of the lines surrounding the table as well as the lines used to separate cells.

☐ **Layer** can be used to associate the BOM with a layer of the drawing.

The BOM behaves much like a sheet in an Excel file. The right-click is a very powerful option to find many of the typical table functions such as delete column, insert row, etc. Also, there is an option to split the table in order to fit it according to other items on the drawing. The BOM created can also be saved as an Excel file and then modified using the Excel program.

## 5.16 Model and Drawing Associativity

The associativity between a model and its drawing links the changes (edits) between the two. If you modify the model (part), its views in a drawing are updated automatically and vice versa; if you change the model item in a drawing, the part is updated automatically. Tutorial 5–3 shows an example.

SolidWorks allows you to control this associativity. When you right-click a dimension in a sketch, you can select **Mark For Drawing** to turn on/off this property. This property is on by default. If you turn it off for a dimension, the dimension will not show as a model item in the drawing.

## 5.17 Design Checker

In design and drafting practice, some companies designate a special person to check engineering drawings; this person is known as a design checker. Think of the checker as an intermediary between the design/engineering department and the manufacturing department. The checker typically has both design and manufacturing experience. The checker's tasks are to (1) ensure that the design as documented in the drawing can be produced with the least manufacturing cost, (2) look for inconsistencies in the part dimensioning, (3) check the tolerances and make sure that manufacturing processes can produce them, (4) check the dimensioning scheme according to the concepts and principles covered in this chapter, and (5) ensure that materials are specified. After the design checker reviews the drawing, the checker may either send it back to the design department for correction, or sign off on it and send it to the manufacturing department for processing.

SolidWorks provides an "electronic" design checker for design standards compliance checking. For this to work, you need to capture all the tasks of the "human" checker and codify them in an electronic document as rules that SolidWorks can use to check; effectively you create a checking template with predefined design checks (standards) that

**FIGURE 5.23**
Design Checker

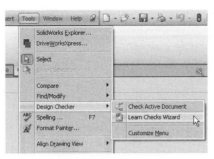

(A) Design Checker menu

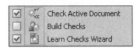

(B) Customize Design Checker menu

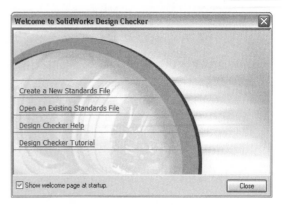

(C) Standards file

SolidWorks uses to assess the drawing. SolidWorks Design Checker is an add-in. Follow this sequence to enable it: **Tools => Design Checker**. The menu has the default items shown in Figure 5.23A. If you select a menu item, a **Design Checker** tab opens in the task pane to the right of the graphics pane on the screen.

Click this sequence to customize the menu: **Tools => Design Checker => Customize Menu** to open the menu shown in Figure 5.23B. Check off the **Build Checks** item. When you access the Design Checker again, you should see the newly added item. If you select **Build Checks**, a window (Figure 5.23C) opens to allow you to create a standards file. Go ahead and experiment with it to create your own file, and use it to check one of your existing drawings using the **Check Active Document** option shown in Figure 5.23A. In the file, you can specify the dimensioning standard to use (e.g., ISO), units (e.g., mm), and sheet format (specify the format).

## 5.18 Tutorials Overview

The theme for the tutorials in this chapter is to get you to practice creating engineering drawings. Bristol Compressors International Inc., a company with headquarters in Bristol, Virginia, USA (www.bristolcompressors.com), has sponsored this chapter. Bristol Compressors manufactures a full line of hermetic compressors that are used in domestic and commercial air conditioning and heat pump applications. It has large-product engineering, manufacturing, and warehouse facilitates in Bristol. We chat with Mr. Jeff Hamilton, a Senior Product Engineer at Bristol Compressors, in the Industry Chat.

## Tutorial 5–1:   Create Standard Sheet Template

### Modeling task

Create a customized drawing template.

### Modeling synthesis

Creating a custom drawing template is important to a designer to standardize and save time when creating a drawing for a certain project or for a company. A drawing template can be created from scratch. However, below we start from SolidWorks **B-Landscape** drawing template, customize it, and save it as a new drawing template.

### Modeling plan

We will first open the B-Landscape drawing template, customize it, and save it as a new template to be used again later. Figure 5.24 shows the drawing template.

CAD steps

We create and customize a drawing template in one step:

1. Create the drawing template shown in Figure 5.24.

The details of this step are shown below.

## Step 1: Create the drawing template shown in Figure 5.24

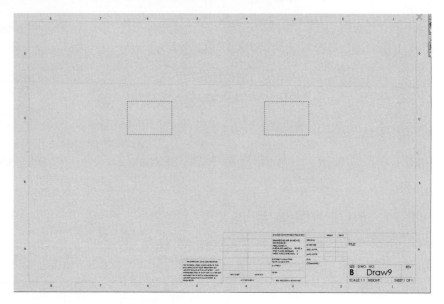

**FIGURE 5.24**
Drawing template

| Task | Command Sequence to Click |
|---|---|
| A. Open **B-Landscape** drawing template. 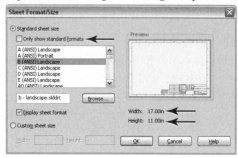 | **File => New => Drawing** => Select the **B-Landscape** as shown to the left. **Help:** Make sure you check off the **Only show standard formats** check box shown to the left to get ANSI formats (otherwise, you see ISO formats). **Why:** If you see the **Width** and **Height** of the sheet in mm, it means that the drawing template uses the mm dimensions. You need to edit the template and select inches for Units. Open the template file and click this sequence to change units: **Tools** menu **=> Options => Document Properties** tab **=> Units => IPS (inch, pound, second) => OK => File => Save** (to save the template changes you just did). **Help:** The drawing template file is located in this folder: *C:\Documents and Settings\All Users\Application Data\ SolidWorks\SolidWorks 2010\templates.* The template file name is *Drawing.drwdot.* |

| Task | Command Sequence to Click |
|------|---------------------------|

**Help:** Now when you open a new drawing, you should see the inches shown to the left.

B. Insert predefined view.

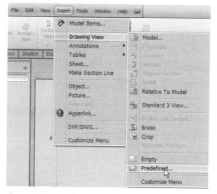

**Insert => Drawing View => Predefined** as shown to the left => Move the mouse away without clicking. The drawing view will follow. Drop the view by clicking somewhere on the left of the sheet.

C. Customize the view.

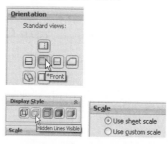

Customize the view using the menu that pops up at left of the screen. Customize as shown to the left: Use the **Front** view for **Orientation, Hidden Lines Visible** for **Display Style**, and **Use sheet scale** for **Scale**.

**Why:** Up until now we have been sketching our parts on the front plane. This will work well if we use a predefined front plane view.

D. Insert projected view.

**View Layout** tab **=> Projected View** => Drag and drop the second view as shown in Figure 5.24. Define this view as **Right**. Typically a projected view will use the same setting as its parent view.

E. Customize the document properties.

| Type | Unit | Decimals | Fractions | More |
|------|------|----------|-----------|------|
| **Basic Units** | | | | |
| Length | inches | .123 | | |
| Dual Dimension Length | millimeters | .12 | | |
| Angle | degrees | .1 | | |
| **Mass/Section Properties** | | | | |
| Length | inches | .12 | | |
| Mass | pounds | | | |
| Per Unit Volume | inches^3 | | | |
| **Motion Analysis** | | | | |
| Time | second | .12 | | |
| Force | pound-force | .12 | | |
| Power | watt | .12 | | |
| Energy | BTU | .12 | | |

**Tools => Options => Document Properties => Units**

Change the **Length Decimals** to .123 unit and the **Angle Decimals** to .1 unit as shown to the left.

F. Save the drawing template as *ANSI_INCH.DRWDOT*.

**File => Save As** => *ANSI_INCH _DRWDOT* as shown to the left

**Help:** Save the template file in a folder of your choice.

**Why:** This file will be used as a drawing template for further tutorials.

---

**HANDS-ON FOR TUTORIAL 5-1.** Modify the template to add two additional views: the top and the ISO. The top view should be above the front view, and the ISO view should be in the top right corner.

---

## Tutorial 5–2:  Create Custom Title Block

### Modeling task

Create and save a custom title block (sheet format).

### Modeling synthesis

Creating a custom sheet format is important to a designer to standardize and save time when creating a drawing on a certain project or for a company. A format can be created from scratch. However, below we will start from the B-Landscape format shown in Figure 5.25, which a part of the *ANSI_INCH* drawing template created in Tutorial 5–1.

### Modeling plan

We will first open the **B-Landscape** drawing template of Tutorial 5–1, customize its title block, and save it to be used again later.

### CAD steps

We create the custom title block in one step:

1. Create the custom block shown in Figure 5.25.

## Step 1:  Create the custom block shown in Figure 5.25

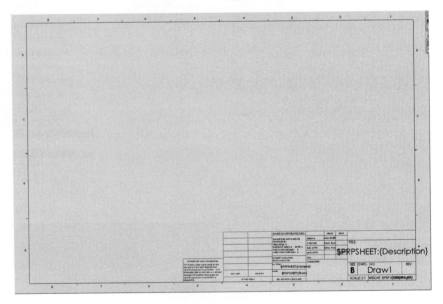

**FIGURE 5.25**
Title block

| Task | Command Sequence to Click |
|---|---|
| A. Open *ANSI_INCH* drawing template. | **File => New => Drawing** => Select *ANSI_INCH* as shown to the left. |

| Task | Command Sequence to Click |
|---|---|

**B.** Change the sheet scale.

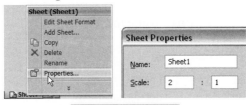

SCALE: 2:1

On the sheet name in the lower left hand corner, right-click => **Properties.** Change the sheet scale from 1:1 to 2:1 as shown to the left.

Notice that the **SCALE** note in the title block has automatically updated to show the new sheet Scale as shown to the left.

**C.** Populate the title block.

**File => Properties => Custom** tab as shown to the left. Use the selections in the drop-down menu to modify certain properties.

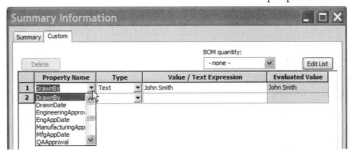

**D.** Input the title block other information.

Populate the fields as shown below with your own personal information.

**Help:** Notice that the sheet format has been updated with this new information.

| | Property Name | Type | Value / Text Expression | Evaluated Value |
|---|---|---|---|---|
| 1 | DrawnBy | Text | John Smith | John Smith |
| 2 | CheckedBy | Text | Jane Doe | Jane Doe |
| 3 | EngineeringApprov | Text | Jane Doe | Jane Doe |
| 4 | MfgAppDate | Text | 5/21/09 | 5/21/09 |
| 5 | | | | |

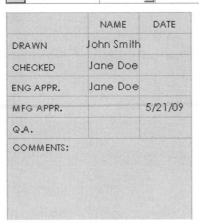

**E.** Save the drawing template.

**File => Save As** => *ANSI_INCH*

---

**HANDS-ON FOR TUTORIAL 5–2.** Modify the sheet format to add the name of your organization in the cell above the title cell of the title block.

## Tutorial 5–3: Use Model-Drawing Associativity

### Modeling task

Create a detail drawing of a part using model items.

### Modeling synthesis

In SolidWorks there are two main types of dimensions: model items and reference dimensions. Model items are those that were used in the part modeling process to create and define the geometry. This type of dimension can modify the geometry at the part level and also at the drawing level. Reference dimensions, however, are typically inserted at the drawing level and have no power to modify the model geometry in any way.

### Modeling plan

For this tutorial we insert a part into the *ANSI_INCH* template created and customized in Tutorials 5–1 and 5–2.

### CAD steps

We create the detailed drawing in one step:

1.  Create the detailed drawing shown in Figure 5.26.

## Step 1:  Create the detailed drawing shown in Figure 5.26

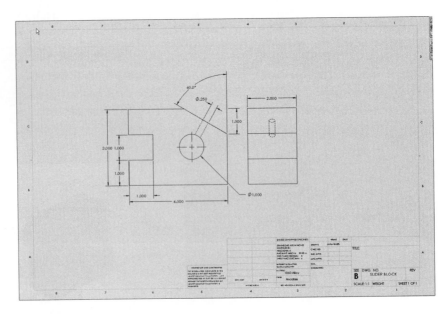

**FIGURE 5.26**
An engineering drawing

| Task | Command Sequence to Click |
|---|---|
| A.  Open *ANSI_INCH* drawing template. | **File => New => Drawing** => Select the *ANSI_INCH* template. |

| Task | Command Sequence to Click |
|---|---|

**B.** Insert the slider block from Tutorial 3–1 Plan B.

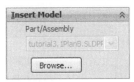

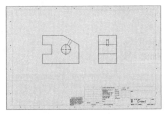

Click once on the left predefined view. **Browse** and find the slider block created in Tutorial 3–1 Plan B => Green check mark to finish. The **Front** and **Right** views automatically populate the sheet as shown to the left.

**C.** Insert the model items.

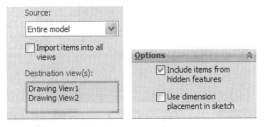

Use the **CTRL** key to select both views. **Annotations => Model Items => Entire model** as shown to the left
Also, it is a good idea to check the **Include items from hidden features** and accept as shown to the left.

**D.** Clean up the drawing.

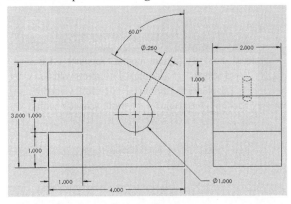

It is important to clean up the drawing by moving the dimensions around (as shown to the left) to abide by the rules discussed earlier in this chapter.

**E.** Detail the two hole callouts.

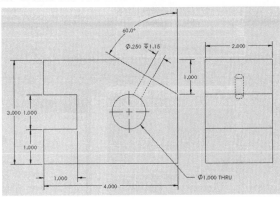

Detail the two hole callouts as shown to the left. The 1.0″ hole should tell the machinist to cut the hole through the entire part. The .250 hole should be cut to a depth of 1.15″.
**Why:** We modeled the .250 hole to cut only as far as the 1.0″ hole. However, because the cut is from an angled face, the depth of the cut isn't immediately obvious; therefore, we will provide this information.
**Help:** This can be accomplished by clicking once on the dimension you wish to edit. You may enter information using the buttons

shown to the left and using the keyboard in accordance with the drafting rules set forth in Section 5.4. Notice that when a symbol is used to detail a diameter, a depth, and other symbols, the text is written in between carets. The user can also type out these codes in notes, callouts, balloons, etc.

F. Save the drawing as *sliderBlock.slddrw*.

**File => Save As** => *sliderBlock*
**Why:** Make sure to save the file as a drawing, not as a template, to avoid overwriting *ANSI_INCH* template.

G. Change properties at the part level to investigate model-drawing associativity.

Right-click on one of the drawing views. Select the option to open the part. In the design tree right-click on the **Material**. Select **1060 Alloy** as shown to the left.
**File => Properties** => Populate the list using the drop-down menu as shown.
**Help:** The Anodize is typed manually in the column labeled **Evaluated Value** as shown to the left. **File => Save**.
**Help:** The title will update as shown to the left.

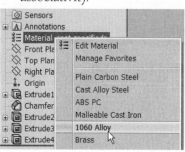

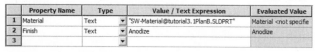

|   | Property Name | Type | Value / Text Expression | Evaluated Value |
|---|---------------|------|-------------------------|-----------------|
| 1 | Material | Text | "SW-Material@tutorial3.1PlanB.SLDPRT" | Material <not specifie |
| 2 | Finish | Text | Anodize | Anodize |
| 3 |  |  |  |  |

---

**HANDS-ON FOR TUTORIAL 5–3.** Follow Task G to add weight property to the title block.

---

## Tutorial 5–4: Create Assembly Drawing with Bill of Materials

### Modeling task

Create an assembly drawing.

### Modeling synthesis

Assembly drawings, like part drawings, are very important in conveying the information necessary to create the assembly. For this tutorial, we use the Caster assembly created in Tutorial 2–2 in Chapter 2. Many assemblies are very large and complicated; therefore, a proper display of the information is key to creating the product correctly.

### Modeling plan

We will insert the Caster assembly into our *ANSI_INCH* template.

### CAD steps

We create the assembly drawing in one step:

1. Create assembly drawing with bill of materials shown in Figure 5.27.

## Step I: Create assembly drawing with bill of materials shown in Figure 5.27

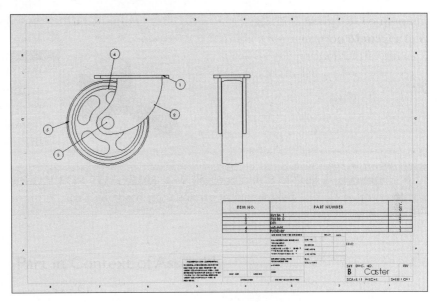

**FIGURE 5.27**
Caster assembly

| Task | Command Sequence to Click |
|---|---|
| **A.** Open *ANSI_INCH* drawing template created in Tutorial 5–2. | **File => New => Drawing** => Select the *ANSI_INCH* template. |
| **B.** Change the template front view to top view. | Click once on the **Front** predefined view of the template => **Top** view from the **Orientation** section of left pane of screen => **Yes** (as shown to the left). |

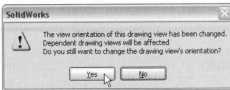

**Why:** We modify the template to replace the front view with the top view for this tutorial due to the orientation of the Caster assembly in the assembly file. Continuing from the previous step, browse and find the Caster assembly created in Tutorial 2–2 => Green check mark to finish. The **Top** and **Right** views automatically populate the sheet as shown to the left.

**C.** Create the assembly views of the Caster assembly created in Tutorial 2–2.

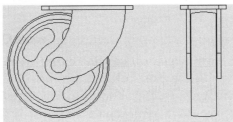

| Task | Command Sequence to Click |
|---|---|

**D.** Insert a BOM.

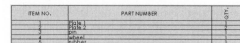

Click one of the **Top** views => **Insert => Tables => Bill of Materials** as shown to the left. Locate the BOM in the bottom right of the drawing directly above the title block and adjacent to the right edge of the drawing border.

**E.** Create balloons to label parts.

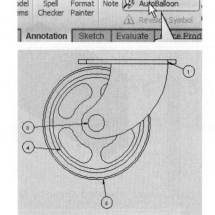

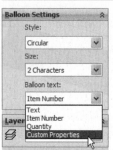

**Annotations => AutoBalloon** as shown to the left. This will automatically label each item as it appears in the BOM as shown to the left.

**Help:** The default setting is to read the item number in the balloon. However, this property can be changed by clicking on any one balloon or by highlighting multiple balloons at once and selecting from the property menu shown to the left.

---

***HANDS-ON FOR TUTORIAL 5.4.*** Change the property of the balloon to read file name of the part instead of the item number.

---

## INDUSTRY CHAT

This section provides practical insight into how the chapter material is used in industry in the real world and practice. This section summarizes the chat with Mr. Jeff Hamilton (Senior Product Engineer) of Bristol Compressors, the sponsor of this chapter. The structure of the chat follows the chapter sections.

**Chapter Section 5.1:** Introduction

ABE: What are the drawing practices at Bristol Compressors?

JEFF: Like most industries, we require easily read, fully defined part drawings that show the most cost-efficient means of manufacture. Typically, all dimensions on design drawings show specific tolerances. Reference dimensions are used when a dimension is repeated for clarity. Most dimensions are shown in decimal inch value, with some customer drawings dual dimensioned with metric as the secondary dimension. In addition to finished part design drawings, in-plant production drawings are created detailing each step in the manufacturing process. In some cases, design prints may be changed in response to change in the manufacturing process.

**Chapter Section 5.2:**  Engineering Drafting and Graphics Communication

ABE:   How do you train your designers in drafting and graphics communication?

JEFF:   We typically follow ASME standard Y14.5M-1994 for all production drawings. Much of the instruction process is done on the job in conjunction with document control and the checking processes.

**Chapter Section 5.3:**  ASME Abbreviation Rules

ABE:   Do you use abbreviations in drawings? Provide examples.

JEFF:   We do use ASME abbreviations in our dimensioning and annotations. Many times annotations can be quite complex and abbreviating saves time and precious drawing space. All annotations, not just abbreviations, are shown in capital letters.

**Chapter Section 5.4:**  ASME Drafting Rules

ABE:   Describe the practices of using ASME drafting rules at Bristol Compressors.

JEFF:   Again, we follow the typical ASME standard drafting rules. All parts are dimensioned clearly and fully. We do not require a specific distance between dimensions and the model geometry, but all dimensions must be clearly legible, even if the drawing is reduced in size for printing.

**Chapter Section 5.5:**  ASME Dimensioning Rules

ABE:   Describe the practices of using ASME dimensioning rules at Bristol Compressors.

JEFF:   Typically, all linear and radial dimensions follow ASME standards and are shown in three place decimal values for inches. Angular dimensions are typically shown in degrees and minutes. Specific spacing of dimensions is not controlled as long as the dimensions are clearly legible and convey the design and manufacturing intent. Extension lines that cross dimensions are shown as broken. Leaders are used for radial dimensions and some geometric tolerancing. Where possible, the arrow is shown from the inside of the arc. We do not use ordinate dimensioning.

**Chapter Section 5.6:**  Dimensions

ABE:   Describe the dimensioning practices at Bristol Compressors.

JEFF:   In many cases we insert dimensions directly from the model. However, we also use smart dimension and the chamfer dimension function to create most of our drawing inserted dimensions. We do not use baseline or ordinate dimensioning. Dimensions are normally placed outside the part geometry. Both annotated hole dimensions and hole callouts are utilized.

*(continue)*

**Chapter Section 5.7:** Drawing Content and Layout

ABE: Describe the drawing content/layout of a typical drawing at Bristol Compressors.

JEFF: All drawings include at least two views, clearly defining the part or assembly, along with any additional views or sections. Drawing views include dimensions, notes, tolerances, surface finishes and balloons. On a single part drawing, a bill of material is not required as all material specifications are defined in the drawing notes. Standard item number balloons are used for assembly drawings with bills of material. Typically, drawing views are scaled at 1:1 or 1:2 with enlarged details at 2:1 or 4:1.

**Chapter Sections 5.9:** Views

ABE: Describe the typical views you use at Bristol Compressors.

JEFF: We typically show at minimum a front and side, or top view, shown in third-angle projection. Due to the complexity of parts, hidden lines are typically not shown in drawing views. Tangent lines are displayed, but at a thinner line weight for clarity. Auxiliary, detail and section views are used as necessary to fully define the part. Contrary to the ASME standard, most detail views are shown connected to the parent view rather than using an identifying leader. If drawing space allows, a solid, isometric view is shown to clearly show the finished part.

**Chapter Section 5.10:** Sheets and Title Blocks

ABE: Describe the Bristol Compressors drawing template and how it is used.

JEFF: We rely quite heavily on the drawing template. All company standards, from dimensional units to font and arrow size are incorporated into the template. Location points for general and revision tables are also located in the drawing template. The details of the template were defined before anyone began the first drawing in SolidWorks, in order to reduce work and maintain a consistency to drawing standards and practices. Templates and title blocks are occasionally updated as the need arises.

**Chapter Section 5.11:** Layers

ABE: Do you use layers? If yes, how?

JEFF: Typically, only two layers are used on drawings unless a special need arises. One layer is used for dimensioning and the other for turning the production approval notation on and off. The dimension layer, along with the document template information, maintains the color and line-type consistencies between all views and drawings. This is primarily for printing purposes.

**Chapter Section 5.13:** ASME Tolerancing Rules

ABE: Describe the practices of using ASME tolerancing rules at Bristol Compressors.

JEFF: We follow ASME rules for all dimensional and geometric tolerancing. This is already programmed into SolidWorks.

### Chapter Section 5.14: Tolerances

**ABE:** Describe the tolerances practices at Bristol Compressors.

**JEFF:** Industry convention is now to use a standardized tolerance block on all drawings. However, tolerance of all dimensions continues to be the legacy practice at our location.

### Chapter Section 5.15: Bill of Materials

**ABE:** Describe the BOM of Bristol Compressors. What BOM types do you use?

**JEFF:** Part drawings typically do not use a bill of material. Because our assembly bills of material are configured differently (horizontally) and many times contain more information than would be available in a part model, we use a general table to construct our bills of material. I have used the SolidWorks bill of material and found it very powerful and flexible for most applications.

### Chapter Section 5.16: Model and Drawing Associativity

**ABE:** How do you use this functionality?

**JEFF:** We maintain the drawing and model associativity, so we want this functionality left "on."

### Chapter Section 5.17: Design Checker

**ABE:** Do you use SolidWorks Design Checker? If yes, how?

**JEFF:** As most all of our standard drawing information and practices are incorporated into the drawing template, this function is not required.

### Others

**ABE:** Any other experience you would like to share with our book readers?

**JEFF:** The drawing template is the key to maintaining your company's drawing standards and practices. It is a very powerful tool. Take time to set this up and utilize it correctly, as it will greatly reduce the amount of individual customization and rework.

1.  What are the dimensions of the different drawing sizes (A–E)? You may use SolidWorks to answer this question; open a new drawing to find out.

2.  Why is dimensioning a drawing important?

3.  Are abbreviations good to use in drawings? Why or why not?

4.  Select a drawing from Chapter 2 Problems section, and investigate it to see whether it follows the ASME drafting rules covered in Section 5.4.

5.  Select a drawing from Chapter 2 Problems section, and investigate it to see whether it follows the ASME dimensioning rules covered in Section 5.5.

6.  What content does a drawing typically hold?

7.  What is the problem when your CAD/CAM system gives the opposite view in a drawing than what you expected (e.g., you get the back view instead of the front view)? How do you fix this problem?

8.  List the types of views.

9.  Why does SolidWorks provide sheets to use in a drawing? List the sheet properties.

10. What are the benefits of creating a drawing template?

11. Select a drawing from Chapter 2 Problems section, and investigate what dimension type (as discussed in Section 5.6) it follows, if any. If the dimensioning scheme is not good to manufacture the part, suggest a new one.

12. When do you use a BOM? What does a typical BOM show?

13. How useful is the associativity between a model and its drawings?

14. Select a drawing from Chapter 2 Problems section, and add some abbreviations to it.

15. Select a drawing from Chapter 2 Problems section, and add some notes and balloons to it.

16. Select a drawing from Chapter 2 Problems section, and change the type of angle of projection from third to first. What happens to the drawing views?

17. Select a drawing from Chapter 2 Problems section, and insert two additional views: an auxiliary view and a detail view.

18. Select a drawing from Chapter 2 Problems section, and add your custom title block.

19. Select a drawing from Chapter 2 Problems section, and change its dimensioning to baseline dimension type.

20. Select a drawing from Chapter 2 Problems section, and change its dimensioning to ordinate dimension type.

21. Add a bill of materials to the Door Valve assembly of Tutorial 1–5 in Chapter 1.

22. Select a drawing from Chapter 2 Problems section, and change its dimensioning to ordinate dimension type.

23. Select a drawing from Chapter 2 Problems section, and add some symbols (abbreviations) to it.

24. Select a drawing from Chapter 2 Problems section, and use SolidWorks Design Checker to check it. Create your own standards document.

# Assemblies

## 6.1 Introduction

Products are made up of components (parts) that are assembled together. We manufacture the parts first, and then we assemble them. Similarly, in CAD, we create the parts individually and assemble them to create an assembly model. An **assembly** is a collection of parts positioned and oriented correctly relative to each other. Assemblies can be created by assembling parts, subassemblies, or both. For example, a universal joint has four parts: center block, yoke, pin, and bushing. A car has many parts (such as tires and rims) and subassemblies (such as steering system and engine).

Assembly modeling is different from part modeling in multiple ways. The most distinctive difference is creating mates. A **mate** is a geometric condition between faces of different parts that allows you to position or orient a part correctly in the assembly model. A part features tree lists the features of the part. An assembly features tree lists the parts and the mates of the assembly. If you expand the **Mates** node of the tree, you see all the mating conditions. Unlike parts, you can also create assembly drawings, create exploded views, check for interference between parts, and create animation (motion study) of the assembly. We cover all these topics in this chapter.

When you create an assembly model, you need to have an assembly plan, similar to having a modeling plan to create a part model. Think of a CAD assembly plan along the lines of a real-life assembly plan. Let us consider again the assembly of a bookcase. A bookcase consists of the base panel, the side panels, the back panel, the top panel, the shelves, and the screws. You start with the base panel, attach the side panels to it, attach the top panel to the side panels, attach the back panel to the side and the base panels, and finally insert the shelves into their slots in the side panels. Use the screws to attach all the panels together. As you use the panels, you position and orient them correctly. If we create the same assembly in CAD, we first create all the part files, that is, the base panel, the side panel, the back panel, the top panel, the shelf, and the screw. We then create a new assembly part and insert the components (parts) one at a time. We follow the same manual sequence (order) of inserting the components as just discussed.

As done with manual assembly, the first part we insert is usually the base component onto which we assemble other components. For example, in a car assembly the base part is the chassis. Note, we use the terms *part* and *component* interchangeably in this chapter. We also use *assembly file* and *assembly model* interchangeably.

Inserting parts into an assembly model uses the concept of instance. An **instance** is a copy of the part that is linked to the part. This linkage allows the CAD/CAM system to maintain the associativity between the instance and its parent part, much like the associativity between a model and its drawing, which we discussed in Chapter 5.

If you change the part, its instance is updated automatically in each assembly that uses it, and vice versa; if you edit or modify the instance, its part is updated automatically.

You can use one or more instances of the same part in the same assembly. In the case of the bookcase assembly, you would use one instance each of the base panel, the back panel, and the top panel. You would use two instances of the side panel. You would use four instances of the shelf, assuming that the bookcase has four shelves. You would use multiple instances of the screw, depending on how many screws you need. Each instance is assembled correctly using the correct mating conditions.

You may create assembly templates similar to part and drawing templates. You set up the assembly units (dimension units), the structure and layout of the assembly BOM, and all other preferences. Assembly templates help promote company standards and increase productivity. You open assembly templates and use them as you do with part and drawing templates.

## 6.2 Assembly Mates

Tutorial 1–5 in Chapter 1 covers the basics of creating an assembly, an assembly drawing, an exploded view, and an animation of the assembly. We extend the coverage here. After you insert a component in the assembly model, you assemble it. Assembling a component in an assembly entails applying mating conditions (mates) to constrain it in the assembly. A mate positions two components relative to one another. A mate applies to two entities of the components being mated, be it a face, an edge, a point (vertex), or an axis. For example, a mate may require two faces to be coincident, two cylindrical faces to be concentric, or two edges to be parallel.

The outcome of mating two components is to prevent them from moving relative to each other in space, thus mimicking real life. An assembled component must be fixed (anchored) in space unless it is free to move for functional requirements (e.g., a motor shaft must rotate). In general, a component needs three mates to lock it in space. There is a total of six degrees of freedom (DOF) in the assembly modeling space: three translations along the three axes ($X$, $Y$, and $Z$) and three rotations around these axes. Three mates are what it takes to constrain the six DOF because locking one locks another.

SolidWorks offers three groups of mates: standard, advanced, and mechanical as shown in Figure 6.1. We cover the standard mates in this section and the mechanical mates in the tutorials. The important concepts about mates are:

☐ **Why to mate:** We mate components to position and orient them correctly relative to each other in their assembly. This is how CAD/CAM systems mimic the physical assembly process in real life, whether we do it manually or using assembly lines.

☐ **What to mate:** As any component (part) is a feature, it consists of faces, edges, and vertices. Thus, when you mate, you mate these elements of the two components you want to assemble. In addition, you can mate centerlines of revolve features such as holes and shafts.

☐ **How to mate:** Mating is about restricting motions of components relative to each other. A component has six degrees of freedom (DOF) in the assembly modeling space: three translations (along the $X$-, $Y$-, and $Z$-axes) and three rotations (about the $X$-, $Y$-, and $Z$-axes) as shown in Figure 6.2A. When you add mates, you remove DOF, thus constraining motion between the two components. How many mates do you need to assemble two components? It depends on the relative motion between them; usually you use three DOF to fully constrain a component motion. For example, consider the assembly of the pendulum shown in Figure 6.2B. You need

**FIGURE 6.1**
Types of assembly mates

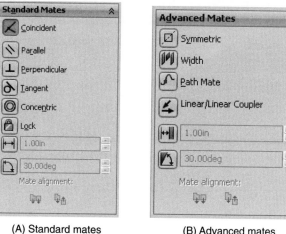

(A) Standard mates

(B) Advanced mates

(C) Mechanical mates

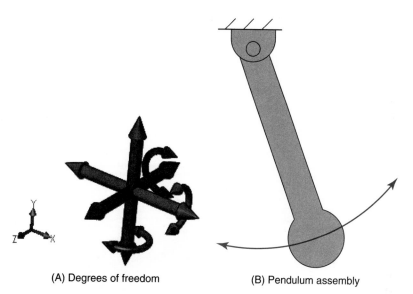

(A) Degrees of freedom

(B) Pendulum assembly

**FIGURE 6.2**
Motion of a component in 3D assembly modeling space

two mates for it. A concentric mate between the pendulum and its shaft of rotation eliminates two translational DOF and two rotational DOF. A coincident DOF between the faces of the pendulum and the shaft side (end) face eliminates the last remaining translational DOF.

The mates shown in Figure 6.1A are the most frequently used mates. To master them, create the three simple parts (two blocks and a shaft) shown in Figure 6.3 and assemble them. Investigate mating faces to faces, edges to edges, vertices to vertices, and any other combination (e.g., edge to face, etc.). You need to investigate two issues: (1) what mates and what does not and (2) how mates are executed by the CAD/CAM system, that is, which DOF a mate eliminates. For example, when you mate two faces via a coincident mate, the two parts move perpendicular to the faces to mate. Also, a coincident mate makes faces butt each other, or become coplanar. If you mate the top two faces of the two blocks shown in Figure 6.3, the two faces become coplanar. If you mate the front face of one block with the back face of another block, they butt each other. These are the issues you need to investigate. As you try the same mate with different faces, edges, and vertices, observe how SolidWorks executes them.

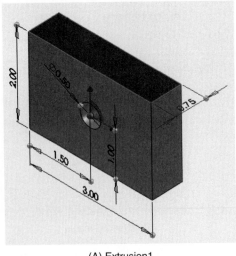

(A) Extrusion1

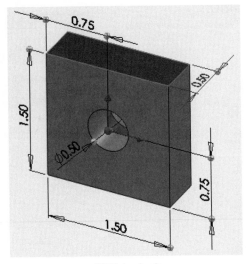

(B) Extrusion2

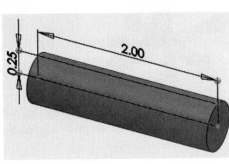

(C) Shaft

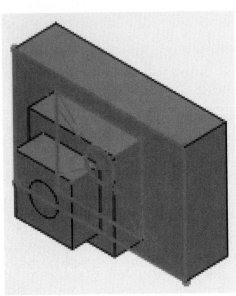

(D) Assembly

**FIGURE 6.3**
Three-part assembly

What are the best practices to set up mates to create an assembly? When you assemble, keep the following rules in mind:

1. Always have a base part onto which you assemble other components to increase the robustness and performance of the assembly.
2. Use face-to-face mates as much as possible because they tend to be more robust and predictable.
3. Use subassemblies to limit the number of top-level mates. SolidWorks solves all top-level mates whenever it rebuilds an assembly.
4. Use smart mates. Instead of using the **Mate** menu, you can drag the face of one component onto the face of another in the assembly. SolidWorks can read our intention and assemble the two closest faces. Similarly, you can drag one part from one window onto another part of the assembly in another window.

Part II Basic Part Modeling

After you assemble components, you need to test them to see whether they are fully constrained in the 3D assembly space. Although you could use the **Move Component** menu, you can simply drag a component with the mouse and try to move or rotate it. If there is a permissible DOF, the component moves or rotates. If the component is fully fixed, it will not move. You may ask, What happens if the component is not constrained properly in the assembly space? The exploded view may have been generated incorrectly. The assembly line will not know how to assemble the components correctly. Also, users will misunderstand how the assembly (product) is supposed to function.

## 6.3 Bottom-Up Assembly Modeling

Two approaches exist to create assemblies: bottom-up or top-down. You may also combine the two approaches. The bottom-up approach is more intuitive and therefore more commonly used. This is the traditional approach we used in Chapter 1, and we use it in the tutorials in this chapter.

You follow three steps to create assemblies using the bottom-up approach: (1) create the parts, (2) insert them into an assembly model, and (3) use mates to position and orient the parts. There is a bidirectional associative relationship between the parts and their assembly. **Bidirectional associativity** means that changes in one file affect the other file automatically. If you change a part in its part file, the changes are reflected in its instance(s) in the assembly file; conversely, if you edit the instance in the assembly, the part is updated.

The bottom-up approach is the preferred approach to use if the parts have already been designed or created, such as off-the-shelf and standard components (e.g., hardware, pulleys, motors, gears, etc.).

## 6.4 Top-Down Assembly Modeling

The top-down approach is also known as *in-context approach*. It is preferred for conceptual design when a design team is trying to conceive a new product and the layout of its components relative to each other in the assembly. It is a first step to define the design intent of the product (assembly) being designed. The top-down approach is also more efficient to use than the bottom-up for large and complicated assemblies because it reduces errors within the assembly. The top-down approach uses a layout sketch (also known as a skeleton or napkin sketch) to relate the assembly parts together. Some view the layout sketch as a way to claim space for the components in the assembly because it shows how the components are laid relative to each other. Others view it as a block diagram or reference sketch of the assembly, establishing relationships and parameters for the parts of the assembly and their dimensions to facilitate their automatic placement and assembly in the assembly.

The top-down approach begins with a layout sketch where the designer sketches the skeleton of the parts. The main goal of the layout sketch is just that: a sketch to show both the assembly layout and the main dimensions of the assembly. Use the layout sketch to define the component size, shape, and location within the assembly; make sure that each component references the geometry in the layout sketch. You cannot create more than one layout sketch in the assembly. The plane of the layout sketch is the front plane by default, and you cannot change it. If you select another sketch plane (e.g., right

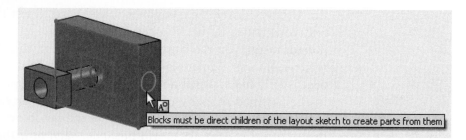

**FIGURE 6.4**
Error message due to violation of layout sketch plane

plane) while in the layout sketch, SolidWorks will not permit you to create parts from the geometry you created on this sketch plane. You get the error message shown in Figure 6.4. See Example 6.1 about how to use the layout sketch.

You can create and modify the assembly before and after you create components. In addition, you can use the layout sketch to make changes in the assembly at any time. The major advantage of designing an assembly using a layout sketch is that if you change the layout sketch (especially changing locations of components), the assembly and its parts are automatically updated. You can make changes quickly and in just one place. Another advantage to using the layout sketch is that it reduces the parent–child relationships; thus parts are more robust and easier to change and edit.

Creating assemblies using the top-down approach requires the use of the concept of blocks. After you create the sketch entities in the layout sketch, you group them into blocks. Each block defines the sketch entities of a component (part) of the assembly. A block behaves as a single entity. The layout sketch must be active in order to create and edit blocks. After defining a block, use it to make a part. You can save the part either within the assembly file or in its own external file. If you save it within the assembly file, it is referred to as a virtual component (part). Later, you can save virtual components in external files or delete them. The name of a virtual component is the name of its block shown inside square brackets (indicating that it is a virtual component). You may edit the component name to rename it. See Example 6.1 for details.

When you are at the early stages of design and still experimenting with it, we recommend using virtual components because of the advantages they offer. You can easily rename a virtual component by changing its name in the assembly features tree (no need to change name of external file). Also, you do not clutter the assembly folder with many unused components. Finally, you can make an instance of a virtual component in one step.

How can we use the top-down assembly approach to manage design teams, so that all team members can work concurrently on their parts of the project? You can make parts from the blocks of the layout assembly and save these parts externally. Each team member works on his or her respective part. When team members open the assembly at any time, they see all the latest work.

The layout sketch method described above is used to create entire assemblies via the top-down approach. Another method is the in-context method. Sometimes, you may create new parts/features (know as in-context features) in an existing assembly. In this case, the part (component) you create is mated to another existing component in the assembly, and the geometry for the component you build is based upon the existing component. Creating features in context is useful for parts whose geometry depends completely on other parts, for example, brackets and fixtures. Tutorial 6–10 shows how to use this method.

**Example 6.1** Create the three-part assembly shown in Figure 6.3 using the top-down assembly approach.

**Solution** We have used the bottom-up assembly approach to create the three-part assembly shown in Figure 6.3. As such, we create each of the three parts in their file, open a new assembly file, insert an instance of each part, and create mates to assemble the instances. This example shows how to create the same assembly using the top-down assembly approach. This gives us the opportunity to contrast the two approaches for better understanding. We create the assembly in three steps: (1) create a layout sketch, and make blocks from the sketch, (2) make parts from the blocks, and (3) create the parts. The details of these steps are shown below.

You need to use the following strategy when you create the layout sketch. Create the cross section of each component of the assembly as you would if you were to create it individually as a part. That sketch would be the front cross section of the part. If the component has features that require other sketch planes, you would create them in the component's individual external part file as we show in the example. If you attempt to create them while the layout sketch is active, you get the error message shown in Figure 6.4. For this example, we require three cross sections: one for each block and one for the shaft as shown in Figure 6.3. We use the two cross sections shown in Figure 6.3 as they are. However, we use the circular cross section of the shaft instead of the rectangle shown in Figure 6.3. We use extrusions to create the three components. The entities of each cross section are later grouped into one group. Each group is then used to create a component.

## Step 1: Create the layout sketch shown in Figure 6.5 and make blocks

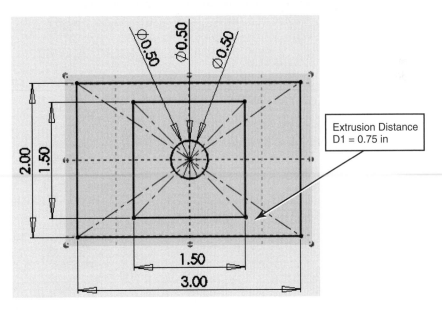

**FIGURE 6.5**
Create the layout sketch

| Task | Command Sequence to Click |
|---|---|
| A. Start SolidWorks and open a new assembly file. | **File => New => Assembly => OK** |

| Task | Command Sequence to Click |
|---|---|

**B.** Open a layout sketch; change the assembly units to inches.

**Create Layout** from the **Begin Assembly** panel on left of screen and shown to the left.

**Tools => Options => Document Properties** tab => **Units** (on the left pane) => **IPS (inch, pound, second)**

**Help:** A **Layout** node (shown to the left) is added to the features tree and the layout sketch itself is displayed in the graphics pane ready to be used. The node is designated by a symbol that looks like a four-bar mechanism as shown to the left. Note that the orientation of the layout sketch plane is identical to that of the front plane sketch. The layout sketch is displayed in the ISO view. Reorient to the front plane orientation before sketching (Right-click it and select the **Normal To** icon from the context menu that pops up).

**C.** Save the assembly file.

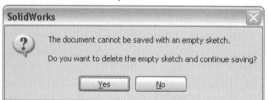

**File => Save As =>** *example6.1* **=> Save**

**Why:** You cannot save the assembly with an empty sketch. You get the error shown to the left. Create a sketch (see next step), then **Save**.

**D.** Create the layout sketch entities for *Extrusion1*.

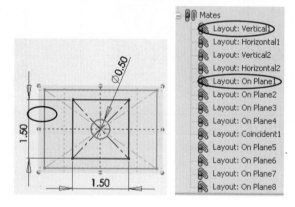

**Layout** tab **=> Center Rectangle** => Sketch and dimension the rectangle for *Extrusion1* as shown in Figure 6.3.

**Circle** => Sketch and dimension the circle as shown in Figure 6.3. The final sketch is shown to the left.

**Help:** As you sketch entities in the layout sketch, the relations are added under the **Mates** node of the features tree as shown to the left. If you hover over a mate in the tree, the corresponding entity is highlighted in the graphics pane. For example, the circled left line has the circled relations in the **Mates** node.

**E.** Make a block of the sketch entities created in Task D. This block represents the cross section of *Extrusion1* shown in Figure 6.3.

**Make Block** (**Layout** tab) => Select the four sides of the rectangle, the two diagonal lines, and the circle => Green check mark to finish.

Part II Basic Part Modeling

| Task | Command Sequence to Click |
|------|---------------------------|

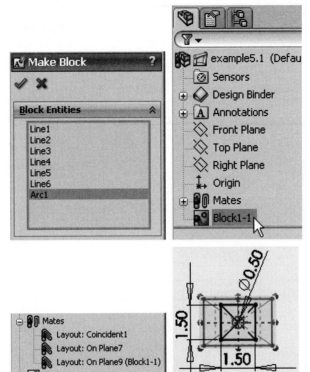

The screenshots shown to the left show the **Block Entities** and the resulting block.

**Why:** You must select the two diagonal lines because they are part of the center rectangle definition. If you do not select them, the layout sketch becomes over-defined and SolidWorks cannot interpret it. Line1 (rectangle top horizontal line) – Line4 (rectangle right vertical line) are the rectangle sides in counterclockwise direction. Line5 (Line6) is the diagonal line connecting the top (bottom) left corner to the bottom (top) right corner. Arc1 is the circle.

**Help:** After you make the block, two changes happen. First, the dimensions disappear from the sketch because they are now part of the block definition. To see and/or edit them, you must edit the block. Second, the mates change from the above 13 to only 3 (as shown to the left): **Layout: Coincident1** (see above **Mates**), **Layout: On Plane7** (see above **Mates**), and a new **Layout: On Plane9 (Block1-1)**.

**Help:** When you edit the block, you are in the block mode. You must exit this mode (as you exit the sketch) to delete the block (Right-click it => **Delete** from the pop-up menu). If you delete the block, the block together with all its entities are deleted. Use **Explode Block** to release its entities, yet delete it.

**Help:** When you make a block, its entities are displayed faded in a gray color (as shown to the left) to help separate them from entities that do not belong to a block yet.

F.  Save the assembly.

**File => Save As => Yes** (to rebuild the assembly) => *example6.1* => **Save**

**Help:** Click the **Layout** icon on the **Layout** tab if you want to open or close the layout sketch.

| Task | Command Sequence to Click |
|------|---------------------------|

**G.** Create the layout sketch entities for *Extrusion2*.

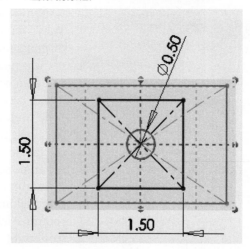

**Layout** tab **=> Center Rectangle =>** Sketch and dimension the rectangle for *Extrusion2* as shown in Figure 6.3. **Circle =>** Sketch and dimension the circle as shown in Figure 6.3. The final sketch is shown to the left.

**H.** Make a block of the sketch entities created in Task G. This block represents the cross section of *Extrusion2* shown in Figure 6.3.

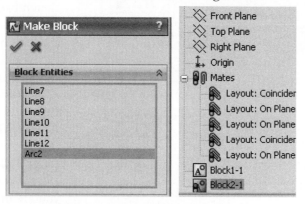

**Make Block** (**Layout** tab) **=>** Select the four sides of the rectangle, the two diagonal lines, and the circle **=>** Green check mark to finish. The screenshots shown to the left show the block entities and the resulting block.

**I.** Create the layout sketch entities for *Shaft*.

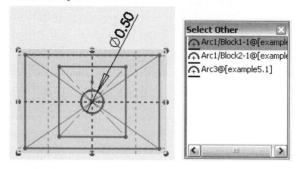

**Layout** tab **=> Circle =>** Sketch and dimension the circle of *Shaft* shown in Figure 6.3. **Circle =>** Sketch and dimension the circle as shown in Figure 6.3. The final sketch is shown to the left. **Why:** The sketch shown to the left has three coincident circles: one for *Extrusion1*, one for *Extrusion2*, and one for *Shaft*. If you create a block right after you create a sketch, the circle is not selectable to create the next block. If you do not create the block immediately, click this sequence to select any circle you want: **Make Block =>** Right-click circle = **Select Other** shown to the left **=>** Select the circle you need from the pop-up menu.

| Task | Command Sequence to Click |
|------|---------------------------|

**Command Sequence to Click**

**Help:** You must be in the layout sketch to make a block. Click the **Layout** icon (**Layout** tab) to enter/exit the layout sketch.

J. Make a block of the sketch circle created in Task I. This block represents the cross section of *Shaft* shown in Figure 6.3.

**Make Block** (**Layout** tab) => Select the circle => Green check mark to finish. This task creates Block3-1 for *Shaft*.

K. Exit layout sketch.

Click **Exit Sketch** symbol on top right corner of graphics pane.

## Step 2: Make parts from the blocks

**Task**

**Command Sequence to Click**

A. Make *Extrusion1* part from Block1-1.

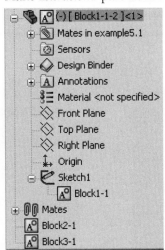

**Make Part from Block** (**Layout** tab) => Select the block (**Block1-1**) you created in Task D of Step 1 => Green check mark to finish. **Block1-1** disappears from the features tree and a virtual component appears in the tree. If you expand the **Component** node, you see **Block1-1** as a child of Sketch1 of the component as shown to the left.

**Help:** **Block1-1** defines the component (part) sketch. Note the part name resembles the block name and is shown inside square brackets to indicate that it is a virtual part. At this point, you do not see any difference in the visual appearance of the assembly on the screen.

**Help:** Click the virtual **Part** node in the features tree to invoke its context menu shown to the left. Hover over each item of the menu and investigate it to learn more. The first icon (**Open Part**) of the menu enables you to open the part and create it. When you open the part, you see its sketch that you use to create the part (feature).

**Help:** Right-click the **Part** node in the features tree and investigate the items of the pop-up menu. The **Save Part (in External File)** does just that. It converts the virtual part into a real part.

B. Make *Extrusion2* part from Block2-1.

Repeat Task A and use Block2-1.

C. Make *Shaft* part from Block3-1.

Repeat Task A and use Block3-1.

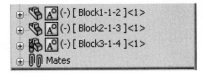

**Help:** Make sure you select Block3-1. If you click the shaft circle, you may pick up Block1-1. If you do, right-click it

| Task | Command Sequence to Click |
|------|---------------------------|

(from the **Selected Blocks** box in left pane of screen) and delete it. Then click this sequence to create the *Shaft* part: The red X mark to exit the **Make Part From Block** => Select **Block3-1** node from the features tree => **Make Part From Block** (**Layout** tab) => Green check mark to finish. The final assembly tree is shown to the left with the three virtual parts.

## Step 3: Create the parts shown in Figure 6.6

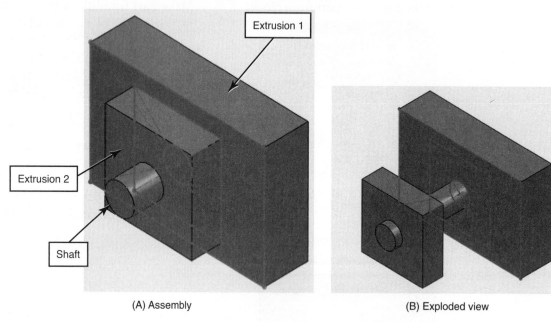

(A) Assembly  (B) Exploded view

**FIGURE 6.6**
Three-part assembly

| Task | Command Sequence to Click |
|------|---------------------------|

**A.** Create *Extrusion1* part.

Virtual part **Block1-1 node** from the assembly features tree => **Open Part** (from context menu that pops up) => Select Sketch1 from part features tree => **Extruded Boss/Base** (**Features** tab) => Reverse the extrusion arrow direction (drag it to the other direction) => Input 0.75 for distance **D1** => Green check mark => **File** => **Save**. Exit the file (**File** => **Close**) and select **Yes** to update the assembly.

| Task | Command Sequence to Click |
|---|---|
| | **Why:** You have created the *Extrusion1* virtual part. When you save it, you save it inside the assembly file. You do not see a file name unless you save it externally as discussed in Task A of Step 2. |
| | **Help:** When you return to the assembly file (still open), you see the newly created *Extrusion1* part. Change the view to ISO for a better view (shown to the left). The other blocks are visible and will be used to create the other parts. |
| B. Create *Extrusion2* part. | Repeat Task A and use Block2-1. Use 0.5 for D1. Keep default extrusion direction indicated by the extrusion arrow. |
| C. Create *Shaft* part. | Repeat Task A and use Block3-1. Use 2.0 for D1. Use **Mid Plane** for Direction 1. **Why:** We select the extrusion directions in Tasks A (extrude to right of layout sketch) and B (extrude to left of layout sketch) so as to push the extrusions away (in both sides) from the layout sketch plane. For this Task C, we use the **Mid Plane** so that the shaft looks assembled in the two extrusions. The final three-part assembly is shown in Figure 6.6. |

**FIGURE 6.7**
Four-part assembly

**HANDS-ON FOR EXAMPLE 6.1.** Add a 1.0 × 1.0 × 0.5 inch extrusion with 0.5 inch thick and a 0.5 inch hole to the assembly. Figure 6.7 shows the assembly with the new extrusion.
**Hint:** Can you create the part in the layout sketch? If you cannot, create the part separately, and then use the bottom-up approach to assemble it as shown in Figure 6.6.

## 6.5 Assembly Drawing

Assembly drawings are similar to part drawings in content; you use views, dimensions, notes, etc. However, there are some differences. Assembly drawings use BOMs and balloons to fully document the assembly. When you dimension a drawing, you show the overall dimensions instead of every dimension (which you can access from a part drawing). Consult Chapters 1 and 4 on creating assembly drawings.

## 6.6 Assembly Exploded View and Animation

An exploded view of an assembly is a view in which the components of the assembly are moved along the axes of the assembly modeling space. We usually explode the ISO view. If you have ever assembled a do-it-yourself product such as a bookcase, you must have looked at the 3D view in the assembly instructions pamphlet; this 3D view is an exploded view of the bookcase assembly.

SolidWorks creates display states for the assembly. You can show the assembly ISO view in a collapsed state where all the components are in assembled positions, as shown in Figure 6.6A, or in an exploded state where components are shown in moved positions, as shown in Figure 6.6B. SolidWorks shows the exploded view in its **Configuration Manager** (the rightmost tab in the left pane; hover over it to display its name, **Configuration Manager**).

After you create the exploded view, you can animate it as shown in Chapter 1 tutorials. The animation basically displays the creation steps of the exploded view in a continuous (animation) fashion on the screen. SolidWorks provides the **Animation Controller** window to help you control the animation while it is running. Check Chapter 1 tutorials.

Chapter 1 tutorials cover the basics of creating an assembly exploded view, and we extend this coverage here by discussing more on assembly configurations. An assembly configuration holds an assembly state. For example, you can define different settings (such as hide/show, display mode, color, texture, transparency, etc.) for assembly components and save them in different display states (configurations). An assembly state may also hold an exploded view. You create multiple states of the assembly to show the progression of the movements of its components.

You can create new configurations or edit existing ones. Click this sequence to create one: **Configuration Manager** => Right-click and select **Add Derived Configuration**. To edit an existing configuration, edit its components one at a time. Click this sequence to edit a component: Right-click the component from the **Configuration Manager** => **Edit Feature**.

## 6.7 Assembly Motion Study

Assembly motion enables you to check the assembly motion. SolidWorks provides two types of motion for an assembly: animation and basic motion. Animation is a motion driven by key points and constrained by assembly mates. Basic motion is a more realistic simulation using assembly mates, springs, gravity, and motors. We cover the animation method in this chapter.

When you open an assembly drawing file, there is a default **Motion Study 1** tab shown in the bottom left corner of the screen, as in Figure 6.8. The tab shows the two types of motion. If you need more motion studies, click the **New Motion Study** icon on the **Assembly** tab to open a new motion tab. You can delete the motion tabs you create (Right-click any tab => Delete from the pop-up menu), but you cannot delete the default motion tab (although you can rename it).

You create motion study–specific mates to perform a motion study. The motion study–specific mates are different from and independent of the assembly model mates that you use to assemble components in the assembly. You can easily see that the motion study–specific mates are different from the assembly mates by viewing the **Mates** node in the features tree in the assembly model. Using motion study specific–mates allows you to create multiple motion studies to analyze the assembly motion with different mates without changing the assembly model.

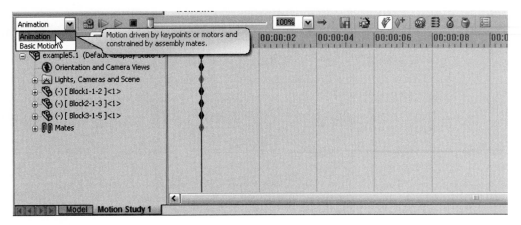

**FIGURE 6.8**
Assembly motion study

The motion study–specific mates allow you to restrict motion between components for motion studies. For example, you can create distance and angle mates, and change their values in an animation. The chapter tutorials show how to create a motion study based on the animation method.

## 6.8 Interference and Collision Detection

Interference and collision detections help check whether assemblies are created correctly and whether the dimensions of their parts are correct relative to each other. Interference checks whether the parts overlap each other, whereas collision checks whether parts collide while they move. Thus, interference analyzes static (still) parts, whereas collision analyzes dynamic (moving) parts.

We use interference detection to find clashes between assembly components. This detection option takes a list of components and finds interferences between them. It shows graphically the paired components with their interference (overlapping) regions shaded in a designated color, usually red. You may also change the display settings of interfering and noninterfering components to see the interference better. You may also select to ignore intentional interferences such as press fits, threads, etc. You can choose to distinguish between coincidence (from coincidence mate) and true interferences. Correcting interferences could be achieved by changing the dimensions of the interfering components or by filleting or chamfering some of their edges.

We use collision detection to check when faces of components clash or collide during motion. If they do, you hear an audible sound, and the components stop moving, thus preventing parts from penetrating each other. You move the parts with a mouse by dragging them. You have the options of stopping the motion upon collision, highlighting the colliding faces, and generating a system sound. The chapter tutorials show the details.

## 6.9 Assembly Design Tables

Design tables are used in assemblies in a similar fashion to their use in parts. A **design table** is an Excel spreadsheet that is used to create multiple configurations in a part or assembly document. You can use design tables to control configurations of parts, mates, as well as distance and angle relationship between parts. Follow these steps to deal with design tables: create them, modify them, and test them. The chapter tutorials show the details.

## 6.10 Tutorials Overview

The theme for the tutorials in this chapter is to get you to practice creating and using assemblies. We focus on mechanical mates; that is, we work with assemblies that use the mates shown in Figure 6.1C. In order to focus our efforts on assembly modeling, we use off-the-shelf components to save the time of creating them. We use Web resources to download the parts we need for each tutorial. If we use our own parts, we do not cover how to create them; instead, we show the part with its geometry. You can create them yourself and use them. In addition to using the mechanical mates, the tutorials show how to use and analyze assemblies.

Timelox, a division of ASSA ABLOY AB (www.timelox.com), has sponsored this chapter. The Timelox R&D CAD group is located in Sweden. Timelox is a leading-edge developer and manufacturer of electronic locking systems for the international hotel and hospitality industry. Timelox provides customized, integrated card locking systems. Timelox systems are user-friendly and meet the security and operational requirements of both large and small hotels and resorts. Timelox uses the latest technology including RF communication, RFID tags, integrated surveillance cameras, wireless check-in systems, and smart cards. We chat with Mr. Mattias Holmquist, a Lead CAD Designer at Timelox, in the Industry Chat.

**Tutorial 6–1:** ## Create Cam and Follower Assembly

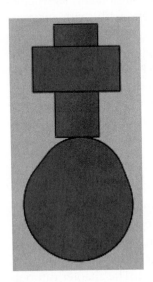

**FIGURE 6.9**
Cam follower assembly

### Modeling task

Create an assembly that will use the Pin Block assembly from Tutorial 3–4 in Chapter 3 to follow a cam created in this tutorial. Figure 6.9 shows the assembly.

### Modeling synthesis

The cam must be extruded from a fully closed loop consisting of tangent arcs (or splines).

### Modeling plan

The cam is sketched, then extruded. Next the cam, along with the pin block, will be brought into a new assembly and arranged to create a cam following system.

### Design intent

Ignore for this tutorial.

### CAD steps

We create the cam and follower assembly in five steps:

1. Create the cam.
2. Insert the cam and Pin Block subassembly into the Cam assembly.
3. Locate the cam.
4. Locate the Pin Block subassembly.
5. Create the cam mate.

Part II Basic Part Modeling

The details of these steps are shown below.

## Step 1:   Create the cam

### Task

A. Create the cam.

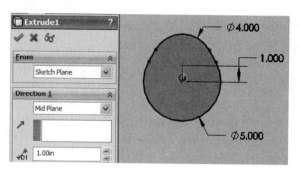

### Command Sequence to Click

Open a new part and save it as *Cam.sldprt*. Sketch on the front plane and extrude as shown to the left.

## Step 2:   Insert the cam and Pin Block subassembly

### Task

A. Insert the cam and Pin Block subassembly into the assembly.

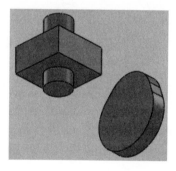

### Command Sequence to Click

Insert the two items into free space as shown to the left. The user may need to right-click on the name of the part/assembly and select **Float** to allow all necessary degrees of freedom.

## Step 3:   Locate the cam

### Task

A. Locate the cam.

### Command Sequence to Click

Locate the cam as follows: Use a coincident mate with the cam front plane and the assembly front plane as shown to the left. **View =>
Temporary Axis** to turn the axis on in the graphics pane. Use a coincident between the assembly origin and the axis of the larger end of the cam.

## Step 4: Locate the Pin Block subassembly

### Task

**A.** Locate the Pin Block subassembly.

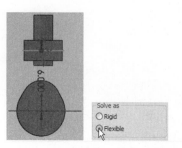

### Command Sequence to Click

Locate the Pin Block as follows: Use a coincident mate with the top plane of the Pin Block assembly and the front plane of the cam part as shown to the left. Use a coincident mate between the axis of the hole in the block and the origin of the assembly. Use a distance mate between the front plane of the Block assembly and the top plane of the Cam assembly. Finally, right-click on the name of the Pin Block assembly in the **FeatureManager design tree** and select the **Properties** menu. Select **Flexible** in the bottom right corner as shown to the left.

**Why:** This will allow the pin to slide independently of the block.

## Step 5: Create the cam mate

### Task

**A.** Create the cam mate.

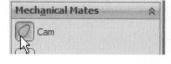

### Command Sequence to Click

**Assembly => Mate => Mechanical Mates => Cam**

**B.** Select the cam faces.

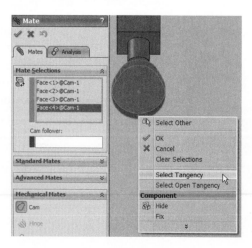

Right-click => **Select Tangency** on any one of the side faces of the cam. This will automatically select and fill in the menu as shown to the left.

| Task | Command Sequence to Click |
|---|---|
| C. Select the follower. | Select the bottom of the pin as shown to the left. |

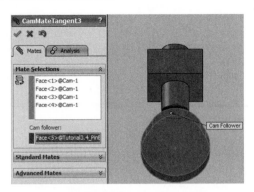

| Task | Command Sequence to Click |
|---|---|
| D. Test the cam follower. | Use the mouse to rotate the cam. Notice that the pin will oscillate as the cam rotates. |

---

**HANDS-ON FOR TUTORIAL 6–1.** Create a second configuration of the cam that has two lobes that are 180° out of phase from each other. Test this cam in the assembly.

---

## Tutorial 6–2: Create Working Hinge Assembly

### Modeling task

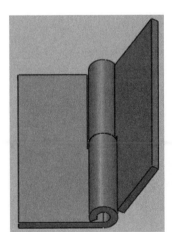

**FIGURE 6.10**
Hinge assembly

Create a working hinge that opens and closes with limits to simulate real life. Figure 6.10 shows the assembly.

### Modeling synthesis

The hinge mate we use in this tutorial is similar to using a concentric mate and a co-incident mate. The advantage, however, of using this advanced mate is to attach limits to the travel of the hinge as well as using only one mate as opposed to two.

### Modeling plan

First, we create the assembly. Second, we add the necessary assembly mates to create a working hinge with maximum and minimum conditions.

### Design intent

The hinge must operate correctly from max open to max close.

### CAD steps

We create a functional hinge assembly in three steps:

1. Create the Hinge assembly.
2. Create the hinge mate.
3. Test the hinge mate.

The details of these steps are shown below.

## Step 1:  Create the Hinge assembly

**Task**

**A.**  Create the hinge plate.

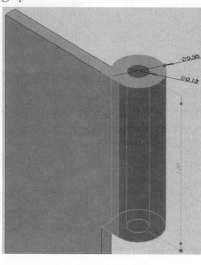

**Command Sequence to Click**

Create the hinge plate using two extrusions as shown to the left.

## Step 2:  Create the hinge mate

**Task**

**A.**  Create a Hinge assembly.

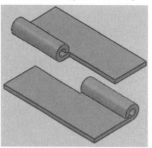

**Command Sequence to Click**

Import two instances of the hinge part into a new assembly as shown to the left.

**B.**  Create the hinge mate.

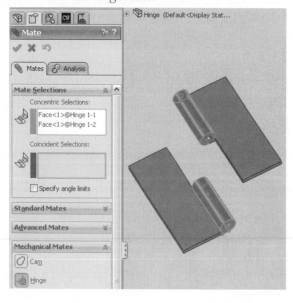

**Assembly** tab => **Mate** => **Mechanical Mates** => **Hinge** => Select the two outer cylindrical faces shown to the left for the concentric mate.

| Task | Command Sequence to Click |
|---|---|
| C. Select the coincident pair of faces. | Select the two planar faces that are butting each other as shown to the left for the coincident mate. |

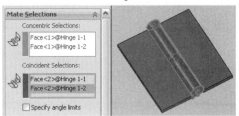

| Task | Command Sequence to Click |
|---|---|
| D. Set the limits of the hinge mate. | Check off **Specify angle limits** => Select the two flat faces of the two hinge instances => Input 180° as the limits as shown to the left. |

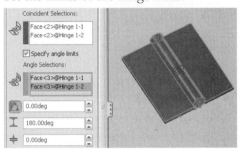

## Step 3: Test the hinge mate

| Task | Command Sequence to Click |
|---|---|
| A. Anchor one of the hinge plates. | One of the hinge plates will have to be fixed to operate the rotation of the hinge. One way to do this is to right-click => **Fix** as shown to the left. This anchors the item in space. |

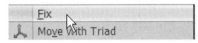

| Task | Command Sequence to Click |
|---|---|
| B. Rotate the hinge. | Use the mouse to rotate the hinge through the entire range of motion as shown to the left. |

---

**HANDS-ON FOR TUTORIAL 6–2.** Create and assemble the hinge pin, and change the limits of the hinge to allow a range of motion of zero to 270°.

---

## Tutorial 6–3: Mate Two Gears with Gear Mate

**FIGURE 6.11**
Gear train assembly

### Modeling task

Use a gear mate to relate the rotational ratio of two downloaded gears. Figure 6.11 shows the assembly.

### Modeling synthesis

The gear mate can be used to mate any circular shapes such that they will rotate relative to one another. For this tutorial, a gear is downloaded from the Boston Gear website and used in an assembly. However, the gear mate does not require teeth to use it.

### Modeling plan

The necessary parts for this tutorial will be downloaded from the Boston Gear website (Courtesy of Boston Gear LLC, a subsidiary of Altra Industrial Motion, Inc.). The necessary mates will be added to the assembly to create a functional relationship between the gears.

### Design intent

The gears must spin in the correct direction and with the correct ratio as to simulate real life.

### CAD steps

We create the gear train in three steps:

1. Create a sketch to locate the gears.
2. Download and locate the gears.
3. Create the gear mate.

The details of these steps are shown below.

## Step 1: Create a sketch to locate the gears

| Task | Command Sequence to Click |
|---|---|
| A. Sketch the anchor points for the gears.<br> | **Sketch => Front Plane**. Sketch a one-inch centerline as shown to the left. **Why:** For simplicity, we will place the gears at the endpoints of the line, thus avoiding creating shafts to mount the gears on. |

## Step 2: Download and locate the gears

| Task | Command Sequence to Click |
|---|---|
| A. Download the gear.<br> | Visit www.bostongear.com/ to register for free and download part# na20b from the 3D CAD library as shown to the left. |
| B. Locate the gears.<br> | Two instances of the downloaded gear will be used. Mate the front face of the gears to the front plane of the assembly. Use a concentric mate between one gear and one endpoint of the centerline. Repeat for the second gear as shown to the left. |

| Task | Command Sequence to Click |
|---|---|
|  | **Help:** Note that SolidWorks does not use the teeth to mesh the gears. Thus you need to align the teeth manually before creating the gear mate to properly visualize the gear meshing. |

## Step 3: Create the gear mate

| Task | Command Sequence to Click |
|---|---|
| **A.** Create the gear mate. | **Assembly => Mates => Mechanical Mates => Gear** as shown to the left. SolidWorks will automatically create the ratio based on the dimensions of the model. The user can change the ratio, and it will be displayed in a yellow box instead of a white one. |

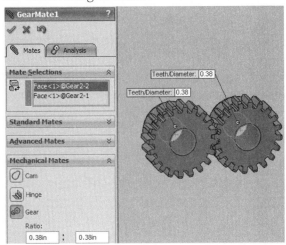

---

> **HANDS-ON FOR TUTORIAL 6–3.** Change the gear ratio from 0.38:0.38 to 1.00:0.38. Do the teeth mesh correctly when you rotate the gears with the mouse?

---

## Tutorial 6–4: Create Functional Rack and Pinion

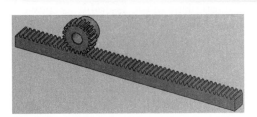

**FIGURE 6.12**
Rack and pinion assembly

### Modeling task

Use a rack and pinion mate to relate the rotation of a spur gear to the travel of a linear gear rack. Figure 6.12 shows the assembly.

### Modeling synthesis

The gear rack mate can be used to mate any circular shape to any linear shape such that they will move relative to one another. They do not need teeth for a gear mate. For this tutorial a gear is downloaded from the Boston Gear website and used in an assembly.

### Modeling plan

The necessary parts for this tutorial will be downloaded from the Boston Gear website (Courtesy of Boston Gear LLC, a subsidiary of Altra Industrial Motion, Inc.). The necessary mates will be added to the assembly to create a functional relationship between the gears.

### Design intent

The spur gear must spin in the correct direction to relate to the travel of the rack gear as to simulate real life.

### CAD steps

We create the gear train in four steps:

1. Download the rack.
2. Insert and position the rack and the spur gear.
3. Create the rack and pinion mate.
4. Create an assembly drawing with BOM.

The details of these steps are shown below.

## Step 1: Download the rack

| Task | Command Sequence to Click |
|---|---|
| A. Download the rack. | Visit www.bostongear.com/ and download part# L2020–4 from the 3D CAD library. |

## Step 2: Insert and position the rack and the spur gear

**Task**

A. Insert the gear.

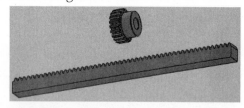

**Command Sequence to Click**

Insert the L2020–4 gear rack along with the na20b spur gear from Tutorial 6–3 into a new assembly as shown to the left.

B. Locate the rack.

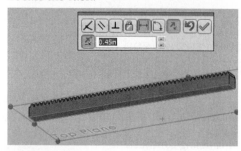

Use a coincident mate between the front plane of the rack and the front plane of the assembly. Use a distance mate between the bottom face of the rack and the top plane of the assembly as shown to the left.

C. Locate the spur gear.

Locate the spur gear with a coincident mate between the two faces shown to the left. Also use a concentric mate between the bore of the spur gear and the origin of the assembly.

## Step 3: Create the rack and pinion mate

### Task

**A.** Set the gears for correct visualization.

**B.** Create the rack and pinion gear mate.

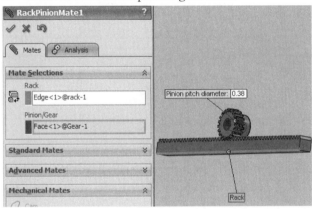

### Command Sequence to Click

Rotate the spur gear until it looks like the teeth are correctly meshed as shown to the left.

**Why:** The teeth of the gear have no impact on how the parts will behave relative to each other in the model. Therefore, we manually set the gears for visual demonstration only.

**Assembly => Mates => Mechanical Mates => Rack pinion => Select the rack and pinion** as shown to the left => Green check mark to finish. SolidWorks will automatically create the ratio based on the dimensions of the model. The user can change the ratio.

## Step 4: Create an assembly drawing with BOM

### Task

**A.** Create a new drawing.

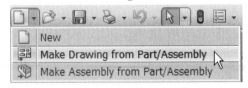

**B.** Insert a BOM.

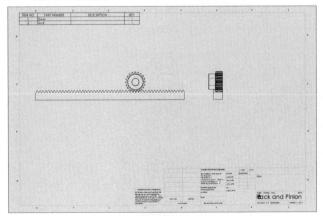

### Command Sequence to Click

**New => Make Drawing from Part/Assembly** as shown to the left

Select the **Front** view => **Insert => Tables => Bill of Materials.** Position the BOM at the top left corner of the drawing as shown to the left.

| Task | Command Sequence to Click |
|---|---|
| C. Add balloons. | Select the **Front** view again =>**Annotation => AutoBalloon => Accept** as shown to the left. |

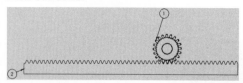

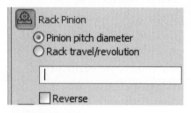

**FIGURE 6.13**
Menu to correct pinion pitch diameter

> **HANDS-ON FOR TUTORIAL 6–4.** If you observe this rack and pinion system, you will notice that the teeth do not mesh correctly while moving the parts with the mouse. Why do they not mesh correctly? Correct the pinion pitch diameter (shown in Figure 6.13) such that the teeth mesh correctly. *Hint:* Visit the website to find the correct pitch diameter value.

## Tutorial 6–5: Create a Functional Ball Screw

### Modeling task

Use a screw mate to relate a rotating shaft to the transverse travel of a bearing.

### Modeling synthesis

The screw mate can be used to relate the linear travel of a bearing or a nut to the rotation of a ball screw. This tutorial shows one way to use the screw mate.

### Modeling plan

First, we create the parts. Second, we add the necessary assembly mates to create a functional relationship between the ball screw and the nut. Figure 6.14 shows the assembly.

### Design intent

The bearing must travel away from the handle as it is rotated counterclockwise.

### CAD steps

We create the Ball Screw assembly in five steps:

1. Create the screw and the nut.
2. Create the Ball Screw assembly.
3. Create the screw mate.
4. Create an exploded view.
5. Animate the exploded view.

**FIGURE 6.14**
Ball Screw assembly

The details of these steps are shown below.

## Step 1:   Create the screw and the nut

Task

Command Sequence to Click

**A.** Create the screw.

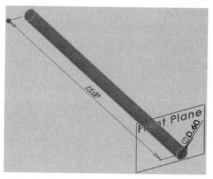

Sketch the screw cross section on the front plane and extrude as shown to the left.

**B.** Create the nut.

Sketch the nut cross section on the front plane and revolve as shown to the left.

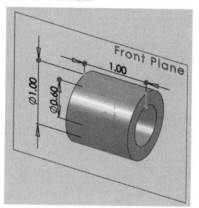

## Step 2:   Create the Ball Screw assembly

Task

Command Sequence to Click

**A.** Insert the screw into a new assembly.

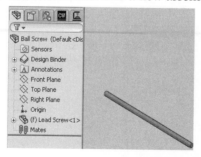

Insert the screw from Step 1 into a new assembly as shown to the left, and allow the screw to be fixed in space automatically.

| Task | Command Sequence to Click |
|---|---|

**B.** Insert the nut and the hand wheel.

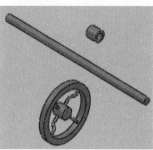

Insert the nut from Step 1. Insert the hand wheel from Tutorial 3–3 as shown to the left.

**C.** Locate the hand wheel.

Align the axis of the hand wheel to the axis of the lead screw. Mate one end of the lead screw to the bottom face of the hand wheel as shown to the left.

## Step 3: Create the screw mate

| Task | Command Sequence to Click |
|---|---|

**A.** Align the bearing.

Slide the bearing toward the end near the hand wheel as shown to the left.

**B** Create the screw mate.

**Assembly => Mates => Mechanical Mates => Screw**. Select the faces and settings as shown to the left.

| Task | Command Sequence to Click |
|---|---|
| C. Test the ball screw. | Rotate the hand wheel counterclockwise. The nut will travel away from the wheel end. |

## Step 4: Create an exploded view

| Task | Command Sequence to Click |
|---|---|
| A. Create an exploded view. | **Insert => Exploded View** as shown to the left |

| | |
|---|---|
| B. Select and move components. | SolidWorks prompts you to select a component.<br>**Help:** The order in which you select and move components will be the order that SolidWorks will use to animate the exploded view. |
| C. Move the hand wheel. | Select the hand wheel and drag it toward the positive *X*-axis as shown to the left. |

| | |
|---|---|
| D. Move the lead screw. | Select the lead screw and drag it toward the negative *X*-axis as shown to the left. |

| | |
|---|---|
| E. Move the bearing. | Select the bearing and drag it toward the positive *Y*-axis as shown to the left. |

## Step 5: Animate the exploded view

### Task

A. Collapse the assembly.

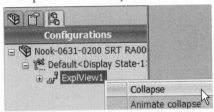

B. Explode the assembly.

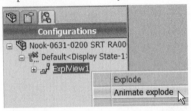

### Command Sequence to Click

Once the explode is created, you can return to the normal view by right-clicking on the exploded configuration in the **Configuration Manager** tree and selecting **Collapse** as shown to the left.

From the collapsed view, Right-click => **Animate Explode**.
**Help:** The resulting exploded view is shown to the left.

---

***HANDS-ON FOR TUTORIAL 6–5.*** Re-create the assembly such that the bearing is fixed and the lead screw and hand wheel will travel when rotated. *Hint:* Use the right-click menu to set the bearing to **Fix** and the lead screw to **Float.** Test the motion by rotating the hand wheel.

---

## Tutorial 6–6: Study Universal Joint Motion

### Modeling task

Create an assembly that will simulate a real-life interaction of a universal Joint and Spline assembly. Figure 6.15 shows the universal joint assembly.

### Modeling synthesis

A universal joint is used to transmit torque between two shafts that are not aligned. Here the universal joint is downloaded along with the spline. The universal joint and spline are inserted into an assembly and, using the correct mates and reference planes, will demonstrate a working universal joint.

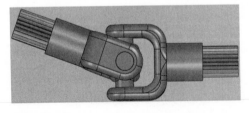

### Modeling plan

The parts are downloaded from 3D ContentCentral. The spline part and universal joint subassembly are inserted into an assembly. Using a system of reference planes and mates, the universal joint will rotate along with the splines as in real life.

### Design intent

Ignore for this tutorial.

**FIGURE 6.15**
Universal joint assembly

## CAD steps

We download and create the universal joint in five steps:

1. Download the universal joint and the spline.
2. Create a new assembly with reference planes.
3. Insert and position two spline shafts.
4. Insert and position the universal joint.
5. Test the assembly.

The details of these steps are shown below.

## Step 1: Download the universal joint and the spline

| Task | Command Sequence to Click |
|---|---|
| A. Visit 3D Content Central to download "universal joint222" and "spline shaft." | The user should visit http://www 3dcontentcentral.com/. In the search bar, type "universal joint222" to download and save the universal joint subassembly. Then type "spline shaft" to download and save the first item in the search results. |

## Step 2: Create a new assembly with reference planes

| Task | Command Sequence to Click |
|---|---|
| A. Open and save a new subassembly, "U-Joint."<br>B. Ignore the insert parts option. | **File => New => Assembly =><br>File => Save as => U-Joint**<br>SolidWorks will automatically prompt you to insert items. Here we ignore this option by selecting **Cancel** as shown to the left. |

| | |
|---|---|
| C. Create reference planes to locate the spline. | **Insert => Reference Geometry<br>=> Plane** => Then select **Right Plane** and enter 4.75 in. as the offset distance as shown to the left. |

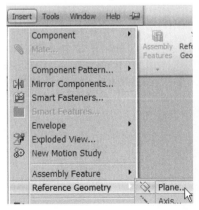 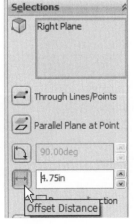

| Task | Command Sequence to Click |
|---|---|

**D.** Open a sketch on the right plane.

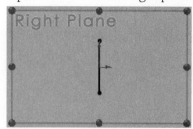

Sketch a vertical line as shown to the left. The length of the line does not matter.

**E.** Create a second reference plane.

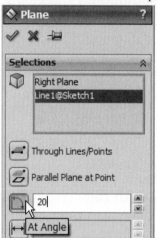

**Insert => Reference Geometry => Plane** => Then select **Right Plane.** Then select the line you drew in Task D. Input 20° as shown to the left.

**F.** Create a third reference plane.

Select **Plane2** that was created in Task E. Create a plane that is offset by 4.75 in. This time also select the **Reverse direction** option as shown to the left.

**G.** Create a sketch on **PLANE1** and **PLANE3**.

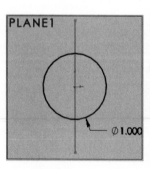 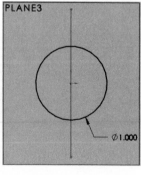

Open a sketch on **PLANE1** and sketch a 1.00 in. circle centered on the assembly origin. Repeat to create a sketch on **PLANE3** as shown to the left.

## Step 3: Insert and position two spline shafts

| Task | Command Sequence to Click |
|------|---------------------------|
| A. Insert the spline shaft. | Mate one end of the first spline coincident to **PLANE1** and concentric to the circle on **PLANE1**. Mate one end of the second spline coincident to **PLANE3** and concentric to the circle on **PLANE3**. The result should look as shown to the left looking down on the top plane. |

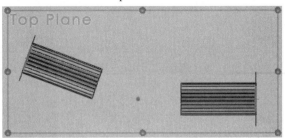

## Step 4: Insert and position the universal joint

| Task | Command Sequence to Click |
|------|---------------------------|
| A. Insert the Universal Joint222. 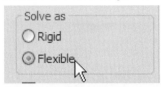 | Insert the U-joint that was downloaded in Task A of Step 1. Right-click on the **U-Joint** subassembly name in the **FeatureManager design tree** and select **Properties => Flexible** as shown to the left. |
| B. Position the Universal Joint222. 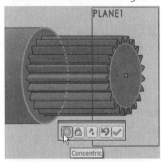  | Use a concentric mate between one of the claws' edges and the sketch as shown to the left. Repeat this for the other claw and the other sketch. Then use coincident mate between one of the spline's right plane and the corresponding claw's front plane. Repeat this for the other side. |

## Step 5: Test the assembly

| Task | Command Sequence to Click |
|------|---------------------------|
| A. Rotate the U-Joint. | Drag either of the splines to make them rotate, and watch the behavior of the u-joint as it is rotated. |

---

**HANDS-ON FOR TUTORIAL 6–6.** Create a motion study for the u-joint.
*Hint:* Follow the steps from Tutorial 6–6.

---

## Tutorial 6–7:  Create Motion Study

### Modeling task

Use the Cam assembly created in Tutorial 6–1 to create a motion study.

### Modeling synthesis

A motion study is a visual demonstration of how an assembly moves. You can use the mates of the assembly to restrict movement of parts at the assembly level. The **Motion Manager** is a timeline interface from which you can use one of three types of studies: animation, basic motion, and motion analysis. This tutorial covers the animation part of the motion study.

### Modeling plan

Use the Cam assembly from Tutorial 6–1 of this chapter to create an animation motion study. Figure 6.16 shows the motion timeline.

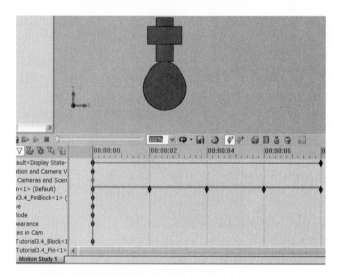

**FIGURE 6.16**
Motion timeline

### Design intent

Ignore for this tutorial.

### CAD steps

We create the motion study in three steps:

1.  Prepare the cam.
2.  Set the timeline.
3.  Review and save the motion study.

The details of these steps are shown below.

## Step 1: Prepare the cam

| Task | Command Sequence to Click |
|---|---|
| **A.** Open the Cam assembly from Tutorial 6–1.  | Open the Cam assembly, and drag the cam until it is orientated vertically as shown to the left. |
| **B.** Open the **Motion Study** tab. 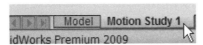 | Open the **Motion Manager** by clicking on the **Motion Study 1** tab at lower left of screen as shown to the left. |

## Step 2: Set the timeline

| Task | Command Sequence to Click |
|---|---|
| **A.** Set the timeline at the first point.  | With the cam vertical, drag the timeline to 2 seconds as shown to the left. |
| **B.** Set the cam. 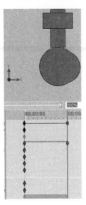 | Drag the cam in a clockwise direction until it is horizontal as shown to the left. **Help:** Notice the timeline records the motion of the cam and follower. SolidWorks will insert what is called a key after each drag motion is recorded. |

| Task | Command Sequence to Click |
|---|---|

C. Set the next point.

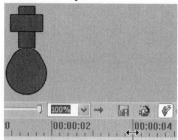

Drag the timeline to 4 seconds as shown to the left.

D. Reset the cam.

Drag the cam clockwise until it is vertical again and opposite from where it started as shown to the left.

E. Set the 6- and 8-second keys.

Repeat the previous steps for the 6- and 8-second keys, each time turning the cam 90°.

## Step 3: Review and save the motion study

| Task | Command Sequence to Click |
|---|---|

A. Calculate the motion.

Select the **Calculate** button as shown to the left.

B. Watch the playback.

Review the playback to ensure proper, smooth operation.

C. Save the motion study.

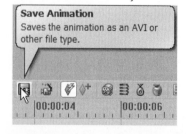

The motion study can be saved as an *.avi* file type as shown to the left.

---

**HANDS-ON FOR TUTORIAL 6–7.** Create a second motion study that will revolve in the opposite direction twice as fast as the first.

## Tutorial 6–8: Detect Collision and Interference

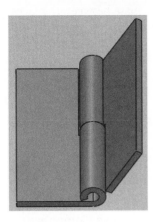

**FIGURE 6.17**
Hinge assembly to test

### Modeling task

Use the hinge from Tutorial 6–2 to study the use of the collision and interference detection tools.

### Modeling synthesis

The interference and collision tools can be very useful in analyzing an assembly. This tutorial makes use of the hinge created in Tutorial 6–2 to demonstrate these tools.

### Modeling plan

Use the Hinge assembly (see Figure 6.17) from Tutorial 6–2 of this chapter to demonstrate collision detection and interference check.

### Design intent

Ignore for this tutorial.

### CAD steps

We use three steps:

1. Rebuild the Hinge assembly.
2. Detect collision.
3. Check interference.

   The details of these steps are shown below.

## Step 1: Rebuild the Hinge assembly

### Task

A. Open the Hinge assembly from Tutorial 6–2.
B. Suppress the hinge mate.

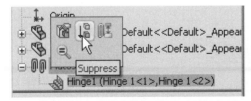

C. Remate the parts.

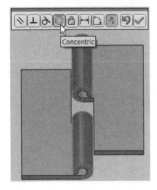

### Command Sequence to Click

**File => Open** => *hinge* => **Open**

**Hinge1** from features tree => **Suppress** from the context menu that shows up (hover over icons until you read it as shown to the left).
**Why:** The hinge mate has built-in limits of travel. For this tutorial the limits of travel will be a collision between the parts.
Use a concentric mate between the round faces of each part as shown to the left.

| Task | Command Sequence to Click |
|---|---|
| D. Use a coincident mate. | Use a coincident mate between the faces as shown to the left. |

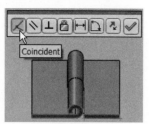

## Step 2: Detect collision

| Task | Command Sequence to Click |
|---|---|
| A. Move component.<br>B. Select **Collision Detection**. | **Assembly** tab **=> Move Component**<br>Set the options as shown to the left. |

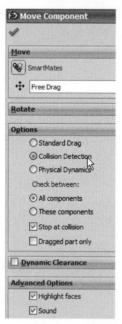

| Task | Command Sequence to Click |
|---|---|
| C. Move the hinge.<br>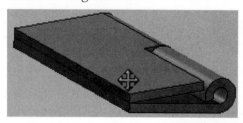 | Move the hinge until it cannot move as shown to the left. SolidWorks will detect the collision of the two hinge plates and prevent the parts from moving any farther as well as sounding a tone and highlighting the faces in collision. |

## Step 3: Check interference

| Task | Command Sequence to Click |
|---|---|

**A.** Do an interference check.

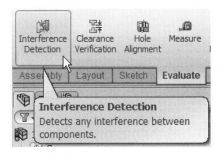

**Evaluate => Interference Detection** as shown to the left.

**B.** Select components.

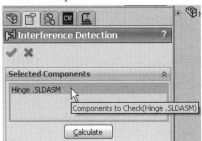

SolidWorks automatically selects the entire assembly to check as shown to the left. However, you can right-click => **Clear Selections** and input as many individual parts as needed.

**C.** Check for interferences.

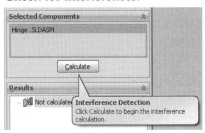

**Calculate =>** There are no interferences as shown to the left.

**D.** Rotate the hinge parts and recheck for interferences.

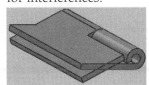

Rotate the parts such that they are meshed together as shown to the left. Recalculate.

**E.** Review the results.

The results will show the volume of interference as shown to the left.

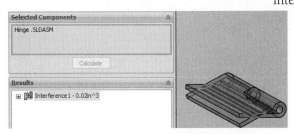

---

**HANDS-ON FOR TUTORIAL 6–8.** Increase the diameter of the hinge pin by 10%, and check the collision and the interference of the assembly.

---

## Tutorial 6–9:  Create Design Table

| Configuration | Pin Location |
|---|---|
| Default | 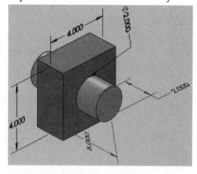 |
| 2 | |
| 3 | |

**FIGURE 6.18**
Design table

### Modeling task

Create a design table to control the position of the pin in the Pin Block assembly from Tutorial 3–4 in Chapter 3. Figure 6.18 shows the design table.

### Modeling synthesis

The design table in an assembly can be used to control the suppression or configuration of parts, mates, and assembly features and also the numeric distance or angle relationships between parts. For this tutorial we will use the design table to control the location and the suppression of the pin.

### Modeling plan

Create and set up the design table such that the configurations control the position of the pin.

### Design intent

Ignore for this tutorial.

### CAD steps

We create the design table in five steps:

1. Create a distance mate.
2. Configure the distance mate.
3. Create the design table.
4. Modify the design table.
5. Test the design table.

The details of these steps are shown below.

## Step 1:  Create a distance mate

| Task | Command Sequence to Click |
|---|---|
| **A.** Open the Pin Block assembly. | **File => Open => Browse** to find the Pin Block assembly created in Tutorial 3–4 in Chapter 3 as shown to the left. |

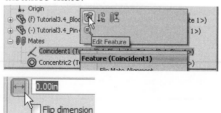

| Task | Command Sequence to Click |
|---|---|
| **B.** Convert the coincident mate to a distance mate. | Convert the **Coincident** mate between the **Front Plane** of the pin and the **Front Plane** of the assembly to a **Distance** mate by right-clicking on the mate in the features tree => **Edit Feature** as shown to the left => Select the **Distance** mate as shown to the left => Leave the value at zero, and accept. |

## Step 2:   Configure the distance mate

### Task

A.  Configure the distance mate.

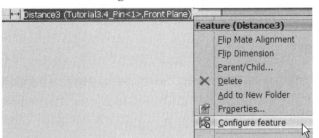

### Command Sequence to Click

Right-click on the **Distance** mate in the features tree => Select **Configure feature** as shown to the left.

B.  Add configurations.

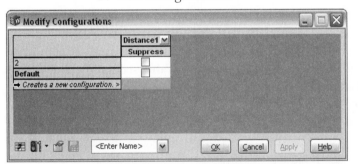

Add Configuration 2 by clicking in the box **<Creates a new configuration>** and typing 2 and then **Enter Name** as shown to the left. Repeat to create Configuration 3.
**Help:** The **Configuration Manager** has been populated by the configurations named "2" and "3" as shown to the left.

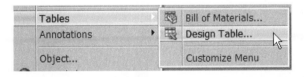

## Step 3:   Create the design table

### Task

A.  Create the design table.

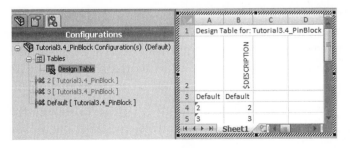

### Command Sequence to Click

**Insert => Tables => Design Table** as shown to the left => Choose **Auto-Create** => Green check mark to finish.
**Help:** SolidWorks will automatically populate the Excel worksheet with the three configurations. The first column is the name of the configurations. The second column is the description of each configuration as shown to the left.

## Step 4: Modify the design table

| Task | Command Sequence to Click |
|---|---|

**A.** Insert the name of the distance mate into the design table.

Click on the distance mate, **Distance1**, in the features tree.

**B.** Right-click on the highlighted dimension.

Right-click on the highlighted dimension in the graphics pane as shown to the left.

**C.** Copy the name of the dimension **D1@Distance1** from the PropertyManager.

**D1@Distance1** is listed under **Primary Value** section of the **Dimension** pane shown in the **PropertyManager** as shown to the left.

**D.** Open the design table.

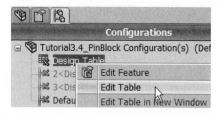

In the **Configuration Manager** tree => Right-click => **Edit Table** as shown to the left.

**E.** Paste the dimension name into the table.

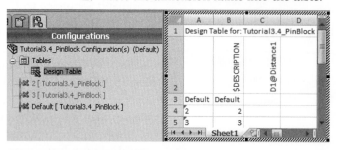

Paste the distance dimension into the second column of the design table as shown to the left.

**F.** Fill in the values.

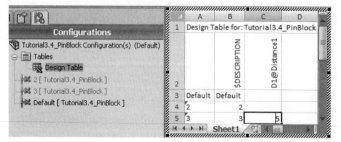

Fill in the values as shown to the left. Then click in the graphics pane but away from the table itself. SolidWorks will now update the other configurations based on the new input values.

## Step 5: Test the design table

| Task | Command Sequence to Click |
|---|---|
| A. Open the "2" Configuration. | Double-click on the "2" configuration in the **Configuration Manager** tree. Observe the position of the pin as shown to the left. |

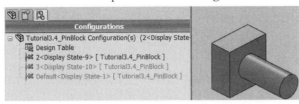

| Task | Command Sequence to Click |
|---|---|
| B. Open the "3" Configuration. | Double-click on the "3" configuration in the **Configuration Manager** tree. Observe the position of the pin as shown to the left. |

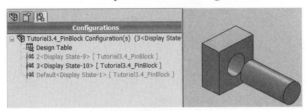

---

***HANDS-ON FOR TUTORIAL 6–9.*** Repeat Task B of Step 2 to create a "4" configuration such that the distance mate is suppressed.

---

## Tutorial 6–10: Create Part in Context of Assembly

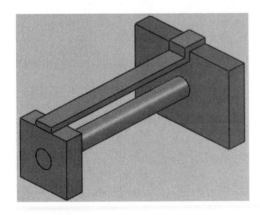

**FIGURE 6.19**
Assembly with cross bar as part in context

### Modeling task

Create a part in the context of an assembly such that the part's dimension will reference other parts and assembly features. Figure 6.19 shows the assembly with the part in context (cross bar).

### Modeling synthesis

Creating a part in the context of an assembly can be useful when the size of the part is completely dependent on other parts or assembly features. This tutorial covers the steps to create the part and use other parts to determine the size.

### Modeling plan

First, three parts are created and then inserted into an assembly. Second, a part is created in the context of the assembly that will reference the size and location of the original parts.

### Design intent

The part created in context must always contact the two larger blocks to act as a bracket.

### CAD steps

We create the cross bar in five steps:

1. Create the two blocks and the shaft.
2. Mate the parts.
3. Create the cross bar (part in context).

4. Save the part.
5. Edit the assembly.

The details of these steps are shown below.

## Step 1: Create the two blocks and the shaft

**Task**

A. Create each of the three parts.

**Command Sequence to Click**

Create the parts shown to the left. Save each one individually as a solid part.

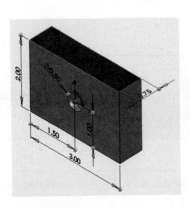
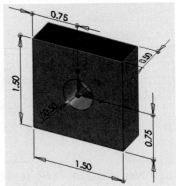

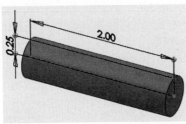

B. Insert the larger block.

Insert the 3.0″ × 2.0″ block first. Allow SolidWorks to locate this block on the origin automatically. Insert the other parts as shown to the left.

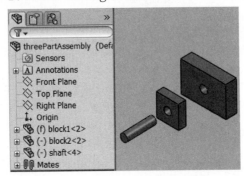

## Step 2: Mate the parts

**Task**

A. Mate the parts as shown.

**Command Sequence to Click**

Mate both blocks concentric to the shaft. Mate the top of each block parallel to the other. Mate the outside faces of each block coincident to the ends of the shaft as shown to the left. Mate the top plane of the shaft parallel to the top plane of the assembly.

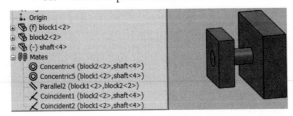

## Step 3: Create the cross bar (part in context)

| Task | Command Sequence to Click |
|---|---|
| A. Insert a new part. | **Insert => Component => New Part** as shown to the left |

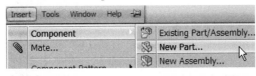

**Help:** Notice that the new part exists in the features tree. Also, the part has no geometry, but the construction planes of the part are automatically aligned with the planes of the assembly.

**B.** Edit the part.

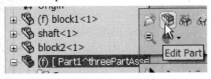

Right-click on the name of the new part in the features tree and select **Edit Part**. **Why:** This is how all parts and assemblies can be edited in the context of another assembly.

**C.** Select the sketch plane for the cross section.

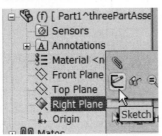

Select the **Right Plane** of the new part => **Extruded Boss/Base** as shown to the left.

**D.** Sketch the cross section of the part.

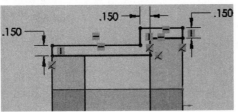

Use the **Line** tool to sketch the cross section as shown to the left. Use the geometry of the block to locate the endpoint of the lines.

**E.** Extrude the part.

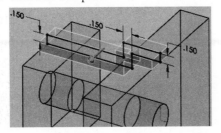

Extrude the part as a .50 in. **Mid Plane** extrusion and accept as shown to the left.

**F.** Exit the **Edit Part** mode.

Select the character in the top left of the screen to exit the **Edit part** mode as shown to the left, and return to typical assembly operations.

## Step 4: Save the part

**Task**

A. Open the part in its own window.

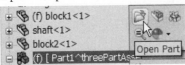

**Command Sequence to Click**

Right-click on the name of the part in the features tree as shown to the left.

B. Save the part as *block3.sldprt*.

**File => Save as** => *block3.sldprt*
**Help:** The part now exists as a typical part, and typical operations can be performed on this part as normal. However, the main extrusion will always reference the parent assembly until those references are broken. This will be covered later.

The part now exists as a typical part and typical operations can be performed on this part as normal. However, the main extrusion will always reference the parent assembly until those references are broken. The "—>" symbol that you can see next to the name of the part and **Extrude1** shown to the left let the user know that this part is referencing some other assembly or part.

C. Notice the Context Symbol "—>".

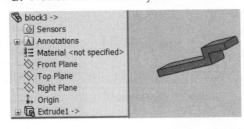

**Help:** The in-context relations can be broken by opening the part and deleting them from the **Display/Delete Relations** drop-down menu on the **Sketch** tab.

D. Close the *block3* window.

Close the *block3* window to return to the assembly.

## Step 5: Edit the assembly

**Task**

A. Edit the assembly.
B. Notice the reaction of *block3*.

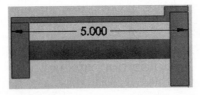

**Command Sequence to Click**

Change the length of the pin to 5.0 in. The separation between the block increases as we increase the length of the pin as shown to the left. *block3* will also increase to keep the sketch relations true.

---

***HANDS-ON FOR TUTORIAL 6–10.*** Edit the shaft diameter such that it references the diameter of the hole in the block1 part. Also edit the hole in block2 such that it references the shaft diameter. Then change the diameter of the hole in the block to 1.0 in.
**Help:** You will have to delete the 0.25 in. dimension in the cross section sketch of the shaft.

---

## INDUSTRY CHAT

This section provides practical insight into how the chapter material is used in industry in the real world and practice. This section summarizes the chat with Mr. Mattias Holmquist (Lead CAD Designer) of Timelox, the sponsor of this chapter. The CAD design of Timelox is done in Sweden where Mattias lives and works. The structure of the chat follows the chapter sections. Figure 6.20 shows a typical Timelox lock assembly for a door. The assembly has 200 parts in total, and not all of them are shown in the figure.

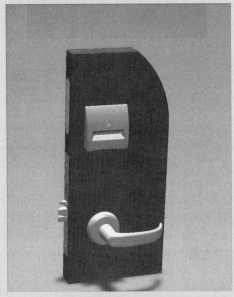

(A) Lock assembly: door front

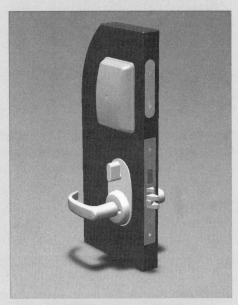

(B) Lock assembly: door back

(C) Lock exploded view: door front

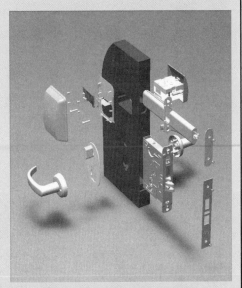

(D) Lock exploded view: door back

**FIGURE 6.20**
Lock assembly for a door (Courtesy of Timelox)

*(continue)*

**Chapter Section 6.1:** Introduction

**ABE:** What are the assembly practices at Timelox? Do you use assembly templates?

**MATTIAS:** We use SolidWorks assembly modeling for mating our assembly parts. We also use it to confirm and verify our product design. We verify measurements and functionality between parts. We also do as much simulation as possible where we actuate mechanisms and study them. Our assemblies are small to medium size as measured by the number of parts per assembly. Our largest assembly has about 200–300 unique parts. An example of our assemblies is a complete lock with electronics, lock case, handles, and communication electronics, etc.

We do use assembly templates. The setup of Timelox assembly template includes units, views, colors, annotations, dimensions, etc.

**Chapter Section 6.2:** Assembly Mates

**ABE:** What types of mates do you use the most: standard, advanced, or mechanical? Also, can you critique the best assembly practices described at the end of Section 6.2?

**MATTIAS:** We use **Standard Mates** (Figure 6.1A) the most. Sometimes we use **Symmetry** and **Width** from the **Advanced Mates** group (Figure 6.1B). We also use the **Hinge** mate from **Mechanical Mates** (Figure 6.1C). We use advanced mates more often than mechanical mates. We usually use three mates to lock a part in space. Among the **Standard Mates**, we use **Coincident** mate the most. Sometimes we use the **Lock** mate to fix components together. This can be very useful when importing assemblies from other CAD systems and all mates are lost. Also, we use the **Lock** mate during analysis of imported mechanisms, where we use a combination of **Fix** in the design tree and **Lock** for parts that move together. Using a combination of **Fix** and **Lock** you do not have to use so many mates to constrain less interesting parts, and you can focus on the mechanism you want to study. It is very handy and saves a lot of time.

As for the best assembly practices, here is how we use them:

1. **Base part:** I try to find out which part to mount on. For example, we start with a wall mount for an assembly that is to be mounted on a wall. I also use a static (fixed) part that would not move in case of moving parts; for example, a bezel (the front of the card reader) when doing a card reading mechanism, and a wall is static for wall-mounted devices.
2. **Face-to-face mates:** We use these mates frequently. They are more stable and you will constrain a rotational DOF. Often it is very useful to mate a face to a plane or a plane to a plane, especially if the geometries are complex.
3. **Use subassemblies:** I use subassemblies a lot in my design because we have many parts that are made by third-part manufacturers. I insert each of these details as a subassembly.
4. **Use of smart mates:** We do not use smart mates too much. We have not had the time or the need to investigate them.

**Chapter Section 6.3:** Bottom-Up Assembly Modeling

ABE: Describe your company's assembly modeling approach.

MATTIAS: We use the bottom-up assembly approach all the time. We also quite often change a part design in the assembly. We may modify part dimensions for better fit or move some holes around to adjust their locations. We prefer to use the bottom-up assembly approach because it allows us to use old parts to save time and money instead of designing and making new parts.

**Chapter Section 6.4:** Top-Down Assembly Modeling

ABE: Do you use the top-down assembly approach? If yes, describe how you use it.

MATTIAS: We use the top-down assembly approach also. In comparison with the bottom-up approach, we use the top-down approach about 5% to 10% of the time. We usually use the in-context method of the top-down approach by starting a new part inside an assembly. We never use the layout sketch method. The top-down assembly approach to us means in-context design. For example, if you want to design a light guide, and if the guide needs a contour to flush with a surface, I use the curve on a surface to start the guide design. Or, a quick way to do the contours for a PCB is just to offset the edges of the enclosure and the edges of the mounting holes.

**Chapter Section 6.5:** Assembly Drawing

ABE: Describe the content of your assembly drawing.

MATTIAS: Our assembly drawing typically includes collapsed views and exploded views with balloons. The collapsed view shows how the assembly would look coming out of the shipping box. We show only the overall dimensions of the assembly on the collapsed view. Sometimes, we add control or checkpoints on the assembly drawing, in addition to some manufacturing and quality control (QC) instructions. We also show labels with information such as part name, part serial number, etc. Finally, we typically do not include a BOM in the assembly drawing; instead we use a separate BOM document.

**Chapter Section 6.6:** Assembly Exploded View and Animation

ABE: How often do you use exploded views and animation? Why do you use them?

MATTIAS: We use exploded views a lot. We use them for design reviews by sending them to team members as images or as eDrawings. We also use them to provide assembly instructions. We do not use animation.

**Chapter Section 6.7:** Assembly Motion Study

ABE: Do you use assembly motion study? What type (animation or motion) do you use?

MATTIAS: We do not use motion studies at all.

*(continue)*

**Chapter Section 6.8:** Interference and Collision Detection

ABE: Do you use interference and collision detection? Describe how you use them.

MATTIAS: Sometimes we use them, not too often, however. It is easier to check manually.

**Chapter Section 6.9:** Assembly Design Tables

ABE: Do you use assembly design tables? Describe how you use them.

MATTIAS: We do not use assembly design tables. I just use ordinary configurations, but I do not put them in tables.

**Others**

ABE: Any other experience you would like to share with our book readers?

MATTIAS: Compared to other CAD systems, SolidWorks is easy to use, intuitive, and user-friendly. It has good functionality. The software has improved over the years. As for assembly modeling in particular, improvements in assembly functionality include adding the hinge mate and the ability to handle large assemblies.

1. What is the difference between part modeling and assembly modeling?

2. What is an instance? Why does a CAD system use instances in assemblies?

3. What does an assembly mate do?

4. List the part entities that you can use for mating.

5. The basic mates are coincident, parallel, perpendicular, and concentric. Give an example of each mate as applied between faces, edges, and vertices of two components. For each example, list the entities the mate uses and the results of the mate. Use SolidWorks to verify your answers.

6. What are the best practices you should follow to create assemblies?

7. What are the differences between the bottom-up and top-down assembly modeling?

8. Why is the top-down assembly approach called in-context assembly modeling?

9. What do you use the layout sketch for in the top-down assembly approach?

10. Why is the layout sketch also called the skeleton sketch?

11. What is the advantage of using the layout sketch?

12. Why do you make blocks before making parts in top-down assemblies?

13. Imagine you are a CAD manager or a lead engineer. How can you use the top-down assembly modeling to manage your design team?

14. There are two methods for top-down assembly modeling: layout sketch and in-context. Describe the in-context method.

15. When you use the top-down assembly modeling, you do not mate parts. The system creates the mates as you sketch in the layout sketch. What happens to the mates when you make a block?

16. What is the difference between the virtual and external parts in top-down assembly? Use Example 6.1 to illustrate your answer. Save the virtual parts as external parts. Edit the external parts, open the assembly, and observe the assembly updates automatically.

17. What is the difference between interference detection and collision detection between assembly components? Give an example.

18. What does an assembly design table enable you to do for an assembly?

19. Use the bottom-up approach to create the assembly model shown in Figure 6.21. Also, create an assembly drawing, exploded view, and animation (follow Tutorial 1–5 in Chapter 1). Check for interference and collision detections.

**FIGURE 6.21**
A door hinge (all dims are in inches)

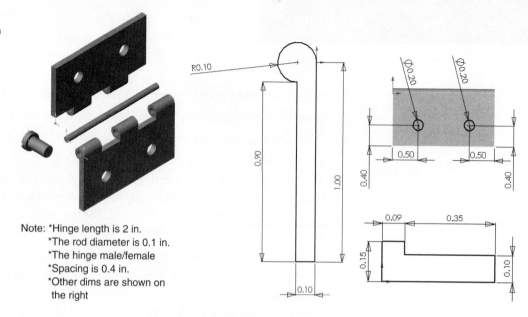

Note: *Hinge length is 2 in.
*The rod diameter is 0.1 in.
*The hinge male/female
*Spacing is 0.4 in.
*Other dims are shown on the right

20. Figure 6.22 shows a rocker arm. The arm rotates about its shaft by the cam action on one of its ends. A valve is attached to the other end and moves up and down (simulating opening and closing an engine intake or exhaust). Use the bottom-up approach to create the assembly model for the arm. Also, create an assembly drawing, exploded view, and animation (follow Tutorial 1–5 in Chapter 1). Check for interference and collision detections. Make up your dimensions as you sketch freely.

**FIGURE 6.22**
A rocker arm (make up your dimensions in inches or mm)

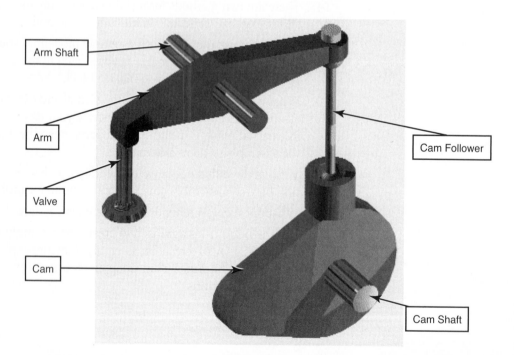

21. Use the bottom-up approach to create the Couch assembly model shown in Figure 6.23. Also, create an assembly drawing, exploded view, and animation (follow Tutorial 1–5 in Chapter 1). Check for interference and collision detections.

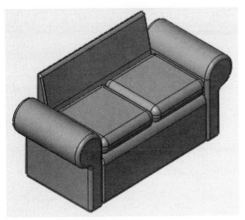

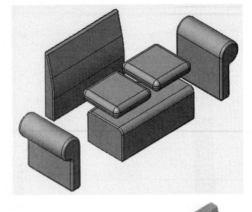

Note: All fillets have a diameter of 0.1 in., except cushion (use 0.2 in. diameter fillets)

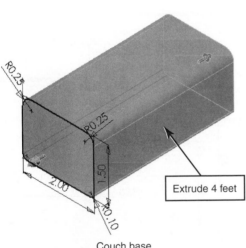

Extrude 4 feet

Couch base

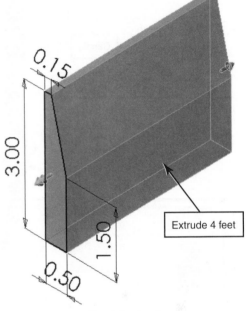

Extrude 4 feet

Couch backrest

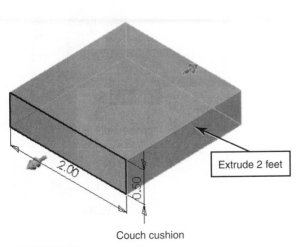

Extrude 2 feet

Couch cushion

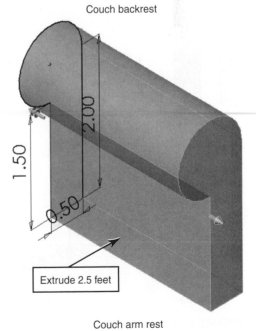

Extrude 2.5 feet

Couch arm rest

**FIGURE 6.23**
A couch

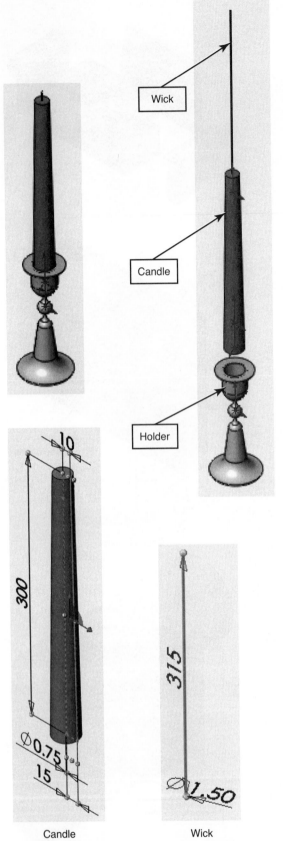

**22.** Repeat Problem 21, but use the top-down assembly approach.

**23.** Use the bottom-up approach to create the Candle Holder assembly model shown in Figure 6.24. Also, create an assembly drawing, exploded view, and animation (follow Tutorial 1–5 in Chapter 1). Check for interference and collision detections. All dims are in mm.

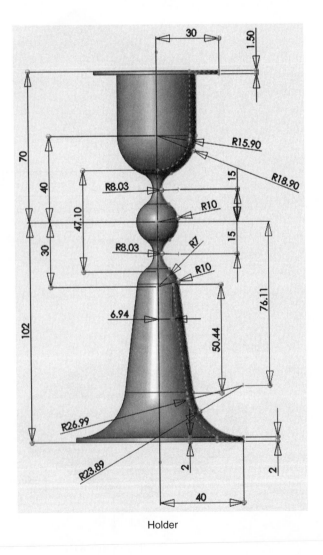

Holder

Candle

Wick

**FIGURE 6.24**
A candle holder

24. Repeat Problem 23, but use the top-down assembly approach.

25. Use the bottom-up approach to create the Ballpoint Pen assembly model shown in Figure 6.25. Also, create an assembly drawing, exploded view, and animation (follow Tutorial 1–5 in Chapter 1). Check for interference and collision detections. All dims are in mm. *Hint:* You may disassemble your own ballpoint pen to understand the pen assembly better.

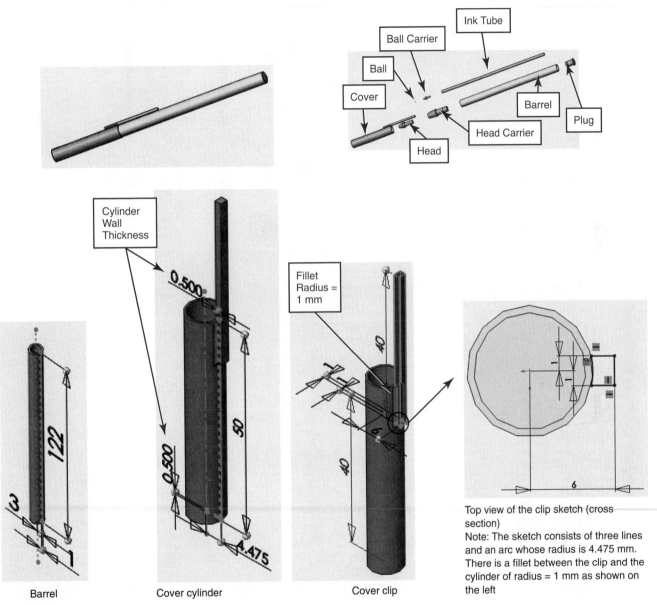

Barrel    Cover cylinder    Cover clip

Top view of the clip sketch (cross section)
Note: The sketch consists of three lines and an arc whose radius is 4.475 mm. There is a fillet between the clip and the cylinder of radius = 1 mm as shown on the left

**FIGURE 6.25**
A ballpoint pen

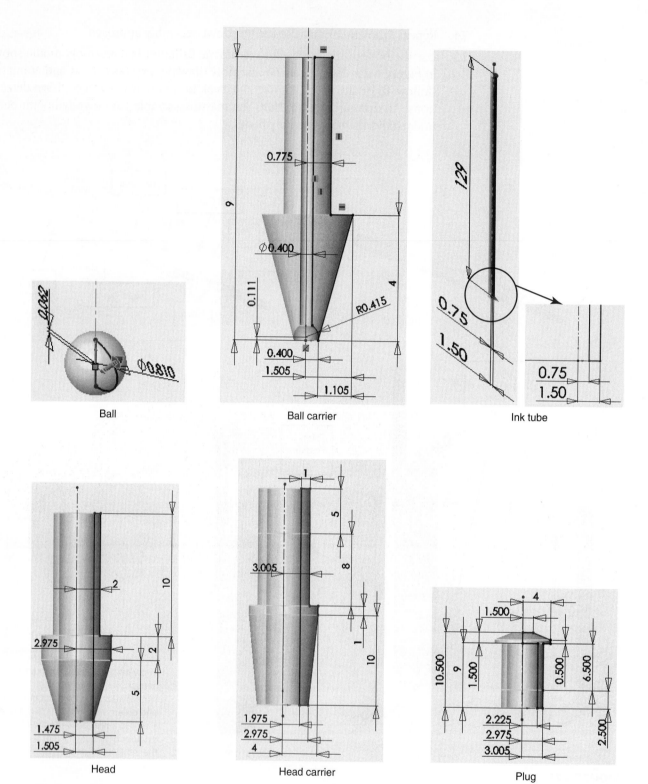

Ball

Ball carrier

Ink tube

Head

Head carrier

Plug

**FIGURE 6.25**
*(continued)*

26. Use the bottom-up approach to create the Three-Hole Paper Punch assembly model shown in Figure 6.26. Also, create an assembly drawing, exploded view, and animation (follow Tutorial 1–5 in Chapter 1). Check for interference and collision detections. All dims are in inches. *Hint:* You may disassemble your own three-hole punch to understand the punch assembly better. There are different types of paper punches. The one shown in Figure 6.26 uses a rotating shaft with a groove where the punching pins are assembled. The shaft groove rotates within a 90° range: from 45° above the horizontal plane to 45° below it. The shaft acts as a nut and the punching pins act as screws. When the handle rotates the shaft inside its housings, the pins travel vertically down because they are inside the rotating groove of the shaft. When the handle is released, the pins push the groove back up under the spring forces of their springs.

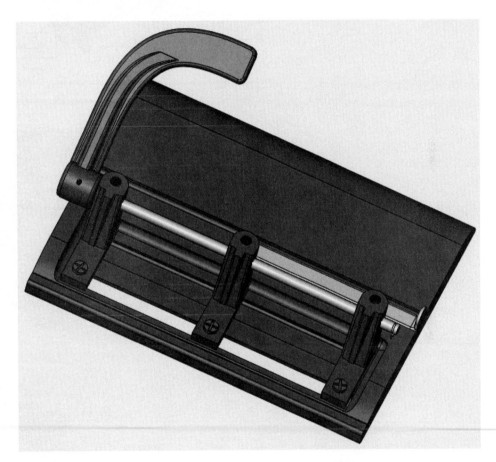

**FIGURE 6.26**
Three-hole paper punch

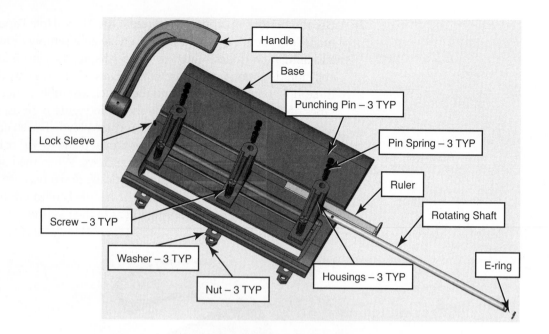

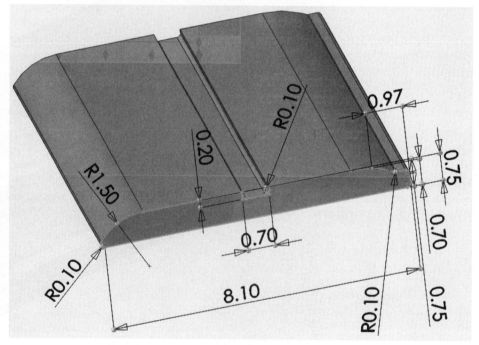

Base - step 1

**FIGURE 6.26**
*(continued)*

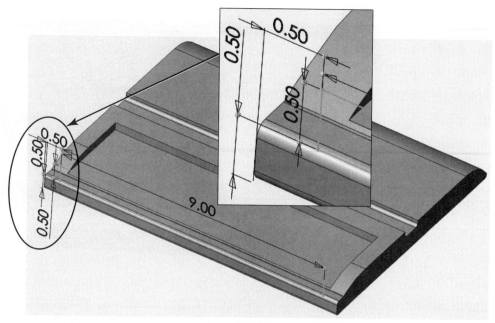

Base - step 2

Base - step 3

**FIGURE 6.26**
*(continued)*

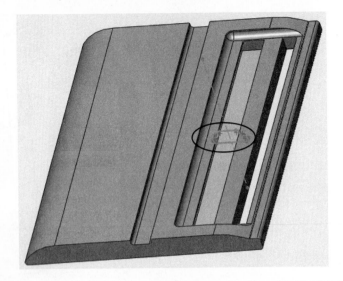

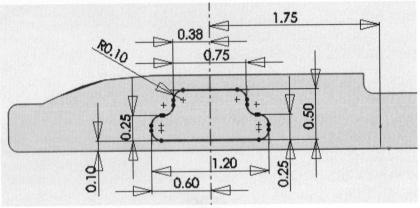

Base - step 4

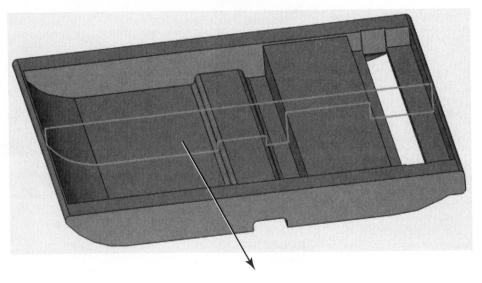

**FIGURE 6.26**
*(continued)*

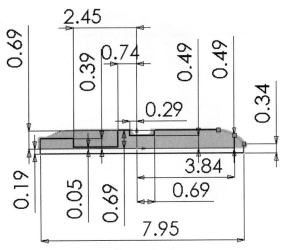

Base - step 5
Note: Fillet all edges of the base as appropriate

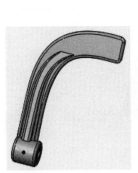

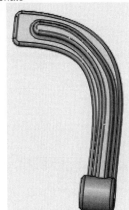

Handle

Handle - step 1

**FIGURE 6.26**
*(continued)*

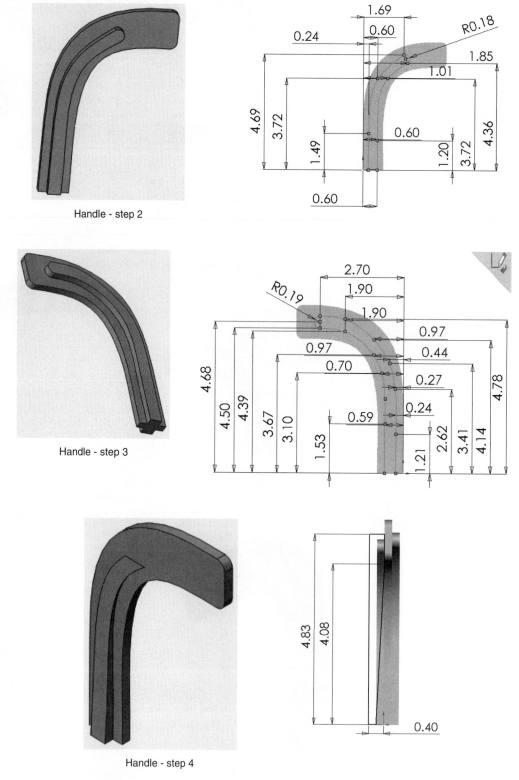

Handle - step 2

Handle - step 3

Handle - step 4

**FIGURE 6.26**
(continued)

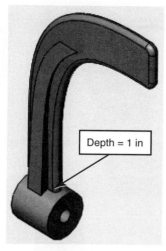

Handle - step 5

Depth = 1 in

Ø1.00

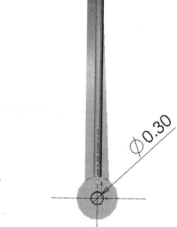

Ø0.30

Ø0.12

0.50

Handle - step 6
Note: Fillet all edges of the handle as appropriate

Ø0.12

0.50

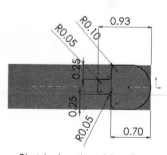

Housing

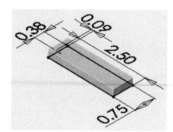

0.38  0.09  2.50

0.75

Housing - step 1 (extrude distance = 0.25 in.)

Housing - step 2 (create loft)

R0.05  R0.10  0.93

0.25

0.25

R0.05

0.70

Sketch plane is at 2 in. offset from step 1 bottom plane

**FIGURE 6.26**
(continued)

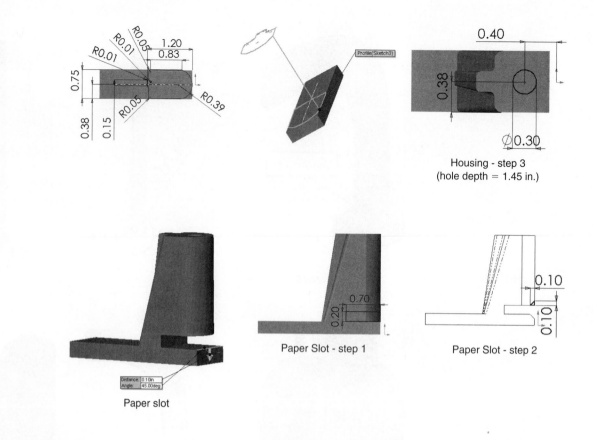

Housing - step 3
(hole depth = 1.45 in.)

Paper slot

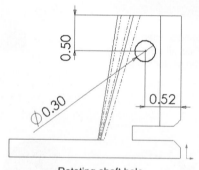

Paper Slot - step 1

Paper Slot - step 2

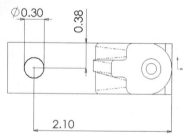

Punching pin hole

Rotating shaft hole

Hole to clamp housing to
base

**FIGURE 6.26**
*(continued)*

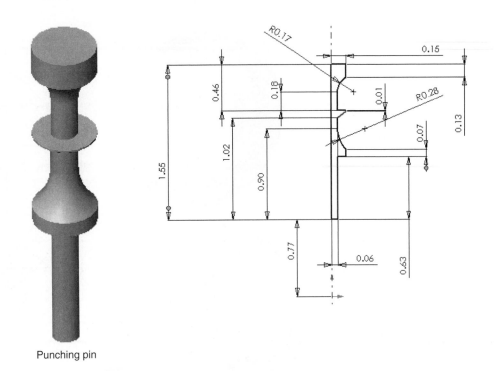

Punching pin

Pin spring

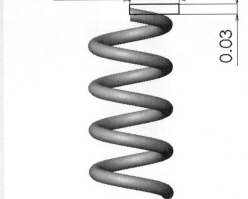

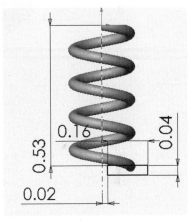

Spring specs: radius = 0.11 in., Wire radius = 0.02 in., Height = 0.53 in.,
Revolution = 4.25 in., Starting angle = 90°

**FIGURE 6.26**
*(continued)*

E-ring
Extrude ditance = 0.05 in.
Fillet radius = 0.005 in. for all

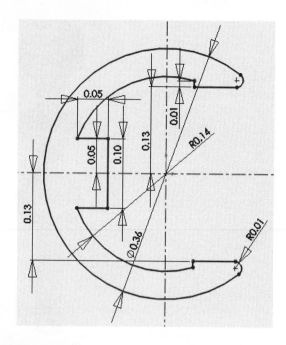

Lock sleeve
Extrude distance = 0.6 in.
Extrude taper angle = 0.5°
Fillet faces radius = 0.005 in.

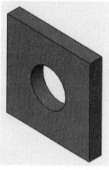

Washer
Extrude distance = 0.1 in.

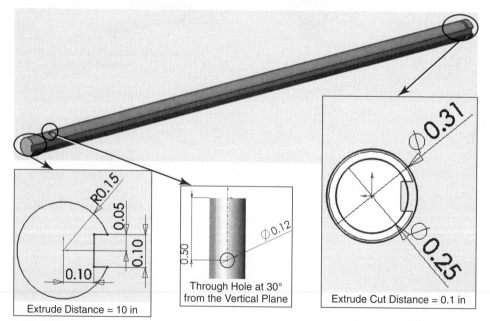

Extrude Distance = 10 in

Through Hole at 30°
from the Vertical Plane

Extrude Cut Distance = 0.1 in

**FIGURE 6.26**

(continued)

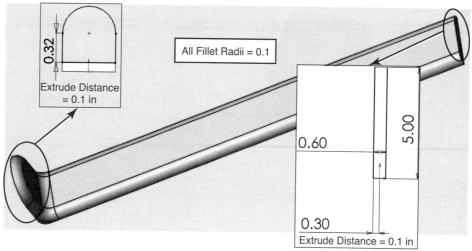

All Fillet Radii = 0.1

Extrude Distance = 0.1 in

0.32

5.00

0.60

0.30

Extrude Distance = 0.1 in

Ruler

Screw

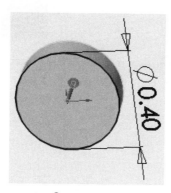

Screw - step 1
Extrude distance = 0.1 in.

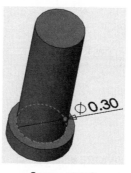

Screw - step 2
Extrude distance = 0.8 in.

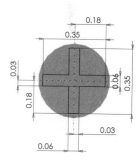

Screw - step 3
Extrude distance = 0.05 in.

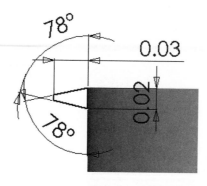

Screw - step 4
Helix data: Height = 0.1 in, Revolution = 15.25,
Starting angle = 90

**FIGURE 6.26**
*(continued)*

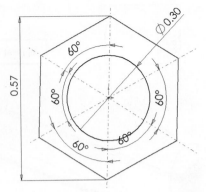

Nut - step 1
Extrude distance = 0.2 in.

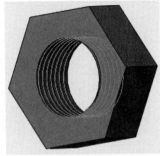

Nut - step 2
Helix data: Height = 0.18 in.,
Pitch = 0.02 in., Start angle = 90°

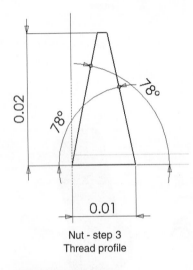

Nut - step 3
Thread profile

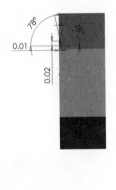

**FIGURE 6.26**
(continued)

# Rendering and Animation

## 7.1 Introduction

Visualization has long been recognized as an effective tool of communication, and more so for engineering. CAD/CAM software offers very rich menus for visualization, including 3D views, hidden line removal, wireframe, and shaded views. Click the **Display Style** icon at the top of the graphics pane on the screen to experience these styles. Engineering visualization tools include rendering, photo realism, and prototyping. We cover rendering in this chapter and prototyping later in the book. Rendered photos are used both for sales and marketing (sales brochures) and for conveying design ideas to teams.

Rendering generates realistic images, almost like photographic scenes taken with your digital camera. You can render the screen graphics back onto the graphics pane of SolidWorks, to a printer, or to a file. Using files is a good idea because rendering requires very intensive computations and may take a long time. You can schedule batch rendering into files. Each time you change a model, its rendering scene is recomputed and redisplayed. When you move the model on the screen, you notice that motion is slow because the scene rendering is happening in real time. To increase its rendering speed, CAD/CAM software uses the graphics card of your computer to support real-time rendering, so as you rotate or move a CAD model on the screen, it is rendered quickly.

Creating scenes is a trial-and-error process because you want to evaluate various effects on the scene until you find the best rendering. One major issue that is detrimental to rendering time and image size is the rendering resolution, which is much like graphics resolution. The higher the resolution, the more time it takes to render and the larger the image size is. The resolution is known as the anti-aliasing effect. Aliasing is the jaggedness (known as staircase effect) of the model edges due to the screen pixels. Higher anti-aliasing produces high-quality images, but it takes a long time to compute (render) the scene.

Rendering is a complex topic. We need to understand rendering models, how to create a scene, what texture to use, what types of lights are available and their effect, etc. Without such understanding, rendering remains a mystery and the use of rendering software becomes inefficient. SolidWorks has PhotoWorks as an Add-In. The tutorials cover how to use it effectively.

## 7.2 Scenes and Lighting

Digital rendering uses a rendering scene and a rendering model. The rendering scene describes the lighting environment including the types of lights in the scene. Figure 7.1 shows the elements of a scene, which includes the CAD model to render and the lights.

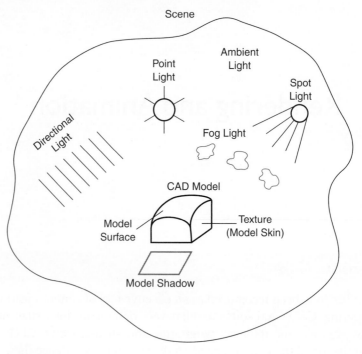

**FIGURE 7.1**
A rendering scene

SolidWorks uses a room with four walls to define the boundaries of its scene. These are the top (ceiling), bottom (floor), the left wall, and the right wall. The CAD model includes its material and texture. We can assign a texture map to a model. The scene may have one type or multiple types of lights. The outcome of the rendering process is a shaded model with shadowing.

SolidWorks offers different types of lights. You can turn any or all of the following lights on or off for a given scene:

1. **Ambient light:** It illuminates the model evenly from all directions. Ambient light has intensity and color that you can modify. You cannot delete or add additional ambient lights.

2. **Directional light:** This light is placed at infinity from the scene. Thus, it shines parallel rays from a given direction onto the CAD model. You can modify the intensity, color, and position of this light. The directional light simulates sunlight.

3. **Point light:** This is a concentrated light that comes from a source located at a specific location in the model space. This light source emits light in all directions. You can modify the intensity, color, and position of this light.

4. **Spot light:** Think of it as a beamed light source. The light comes from a restricted, focused light with a cone-shaped beam that is brightest at its center. You can shoot (aim) the spot light at a specific area of the model. You can modify the intensity, color, and position of the light source. You can also adjust the angle through which the beam spreads.

5. **Fog light:** It simulates scattering of the light by fog. It enables the effect of a fog light. You can specify fog lights in point or spot light. You can control the light intensity, which controls the brightness of the fog light effect.

## 7.3  Rendering Models

Rendering is a digital method to simulate how CAD models respond to different types of lighting around them. The response depends on the types of existing lights in the model scene (environment) and the type of the model material. The model material affects how the model reflects the lights that are shined on its surfaces. The goal of rendering is to display a CAD model on the screen as it would look in real life.

We use rendering models to render scenes after we create them. Figure 7.2 shows a typical rendering model. The light reflection occurs with respect to the surface normal vector at the point of contact between the surface and the light ray. The angles $\theta_i$ and $\theta_r$ are, respectively, the angle of incidence and the angle of reflection. A light source in the scene sends light rays to the CAD model surfaces (faces). When a light ray hits a surface, it is reflected off it. If the light is reflected evenly in one direction (Figure 7.3A, i.e., $\theta_i = \theta_r$), we have a shiny surface (known as specular surface) like a mirror. If the light is reflected unevenly in many directions (Figure 7.3B, i.e., $\theta_i \neq \theta_r$), we have a dull surface (known as diffuse surface) like wood and paper. The scene camera (viewer's eye) receives the reflected rays from any direction that is not necessarily coincident with the reflected rays. All these angles, scene lights, and variables are used to calculate the rendered image. These calculations are beyond the scope of this book and are not covered here.

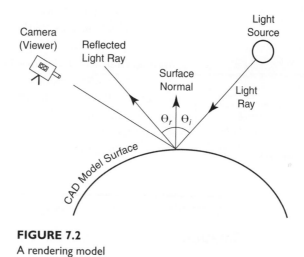

**FIGURE 7.2**
A rendering model

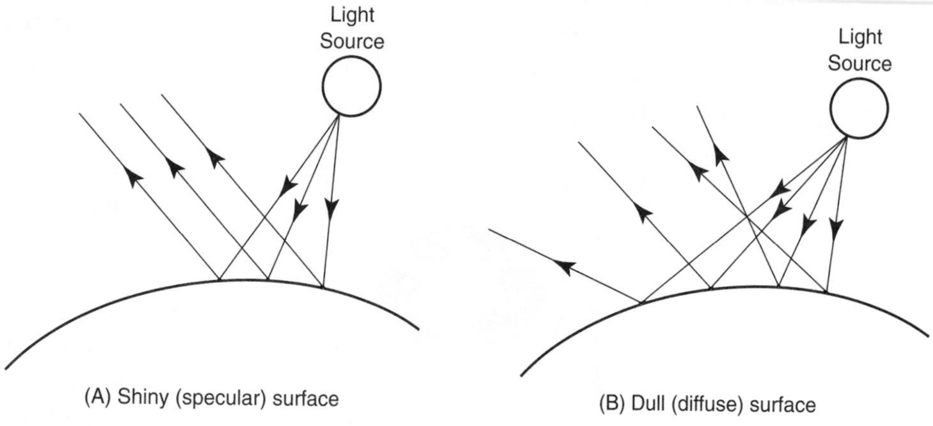

(A) Shiny (specular) surface          (B) Dull (diffuse) surface

**FIGURE 7.3**
Types of reflection

The computational algorithm that performs these calculations is known as ray tracing and is not covered here. The algorithm requires intensive memory and computations. It is even more expensive if it uses anti-aliasing techniques to increase the quality of the rendered scene.

Caustic effects are the result of combined reflective and diffuse reflections. These effects result from interactions between different objects in the scene or from cascading reflections from surfaces of one object in the scene. For example, a light emitted from a light source goes through one or more specular and/or diffuse reflections before reaching the viewer's eye. Consider the sun shining on a swimming pool. By the time sunlight reaches the bottom of the pool, it gets reflected more than once going through the water, hits the pool floor, and goes through diffuse reflection before reaching the viewer's eye. What the viewer sees are the caustic effects on the pool floor.

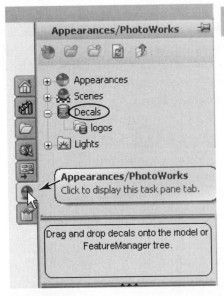

**FIGURE 7.4**
Decals library

## 7.4 Decals

A **decal** is an image that you would display on a face(s) of a CAD model. You use decals for marketing purposes. SolidWorks provides a decal library that you can use or add to it. You can drag and drop decals from the decal library onto the current CAD model displayed in the graphics pane and manipulate them. To access the library, click the **Appearances/PhotoWorks** tab in the task pane shown in Figure 7.4. The figure also shows the **Decals** library, which resides in this folder: *C:\Program Files\SolidWorks\SolidWorks (2)\data\graphics\Decals\Logos*. The left pane of the screen also has the **Render Manager** tab (the rightmost tab). The tab has the **Decals** folder that allows you to find existing decals, edit their properties, and add/save new ones.

Decals have an order that controls their visibility. If multiple decals are applied, they are rendered in the order applied. If a decal is applied on top of another, it appears on top. You can use this fact to display overlapping decals to create fancy visual effects.

---

**Example 7.1**    Create a decal on the free-form torus shown in Figure 4.2.

**Solution**    We add a decal in one step.

**Step 1:**    Add a decal

**Task**

A. Open the free-form torus part.
B. Select the face on which to attach the decal.
C. Create a new decal.

Recycling

**Command Sequence to Click**

**File => Open** *=> example 4.1 =>* **Open**
Select the torus face.

**SolidWorks Office** tab =>
**PhotoWorks => New Decal** =>
Select the Recycling decal that appears on the task pane on left of the screen and shown here to the left => Green check mark to finish.
**Help:** When you click **PhotoWorks** from SolidWorks **Office** tab, it goes to the menu bar. Click it there to display to access the **New Decal** icon.

| Task | Command Sequence to Click |
|---|---|
| **D.** Resize the decal to fit on the torus face. | Use the decal handles (corner of box shown to the left) and axes (shown to the left) to fit the decal to the surface as shown to the left. |

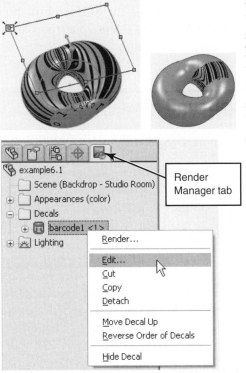

**Help:** If you need to edit the decal, click this sequence: **Render Manager** tab (where part features tree is; on left of screen) => Expand **Decals** node => Right-click the **Barcode** node => **Edit** as shown to the left.

| **E.** Save the part. | **File => Save** |

---

## 7.5 Textures

You can control the appearance of CAD models at two levels: scene lighting and material texture. The visualization effects of scene lights are limited to using different types of light and colors. Scene lighting cannot display the material look, for example, metal, plastic, brick, etc. The material appearance is controlled by its texture. You can assign a texture map to material, which gives the material its appearance. When you assign the material to a CAD model, the model assumes the material's appearance and texture.

Texture maps are based on image files; that is, a texture map is an image of the texture, stored in an image file. A texture file is shrink-wrapped around a CAD model, just like wallpaper or gift wrap. You need to select the location and orientation of the texture relative to the model before applying the texture. This is analogous to wrapping something in gift wrap. You locate and orient the gift relative to the wrap.

You access texture through PhotoWorks; click this sequence: **PhotoWorks => Appearance** to open the **Appearances Manager** shown in Figure 7.5. Under the **Basic** tab (Figure 7.5A), you can assign appearance, transparency, and color. When you select appearance, you are able to specify a material such as steel or plastic. You can save your combination of appearance, transparency, and color in a configuration (scroll all the way down on the left pane to see it; it is not shown here in Figure 7.5).

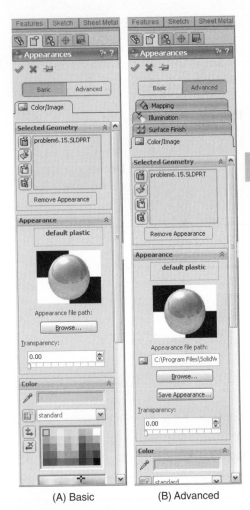

(A) Basic          (B) Advanced

**FIGURE 7.5**
Appearances

**FIGURE 7.6**
Materials library

Under the **Advanced** tab (Figure 7.5B), you have four tabs. The **Mapping** tab allows you to select and map a texture to render. The **Illumination** tab allows you to select the different types of light and set their values. Using the **Surface Finish** tab, you can select a finish. The **Color/Image** tab offers what the **Basic** tab offers (appearance, transparency, and color).

## 7.6 Materials

Materials are used in CAD/CAM for multiple purposes: CAD, CAM, and appearance. For CAD, we use them to calculate mass properties, perform finite element analysis, do dynamic analysis, etc. For CAM, we use materials to select machining parameters such as cutting speed, feed rate, cutting conditions (coolant on/off), etc. For rendering, materials affect the final look of the CAD model. Specifying texture along with material makes the rendered CAD model look almost real.

SolidWorks comes with a materials library. You can also create your own new material types or edit existing ones by clicking this sequence: Right-click **Material <not specified>** (node in features manager tree) => **Edit Material**. This sequence opens the **Material** window shown in Figure 7.6. You can assign a material to the part by selecting from the menu on the left. You can also add your own material by adding a custom material. You must create a material category before you can add a material. If you right-click **Custom Materials** (Figure 7.6), the pop-up menu only allows you to create material libraries and categories. If you right-click a category (**Steel** or **Plastic**), the pop-up menu allows you to add or remove material. Thus, the hierarchy is Library => Categories => Materials, that is, a library has categories and a category has materials. For example, **Custom Materials** shown in Figure 7.6 is a library, **Plastic** is a category of that library, and **Custom Plastic** is a material.

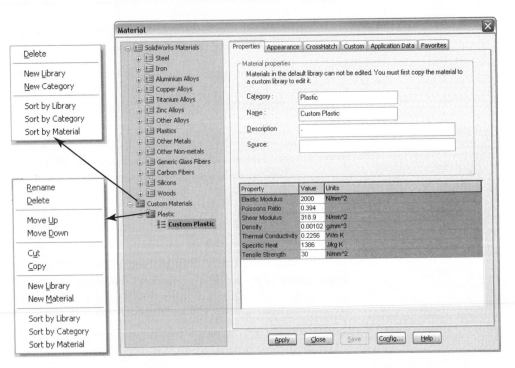

**Example 7.2**   Add texture to the free-form torus shown in Figure 4.2.

**Solution**   We add texture by assigning a material in one step.

## Step 1:   Add texture

| Task | Command Sequence to Click |
|---|---|
| A.  Open the free-form torus part. | **File => Open** => *example 4.1* **=> Open** |
| B.  Change the material.  | Right-click the **Material** node of the features tree => **Edit Material** => Select **BUYL** (under **Rubber** node in the **Material** window that opens => **Apply** **=> Close**. The screenshot to the left shows the new texture. |
| C.  Save the part. | **File => Save** |

---

> **HANDS-ON FOR EXAMPLE 7.2.** Change the torus material to ABS plastic.

## 7.7  Appearance and Transparency

Using appearance, you can add material look and feel to models without adding the physical properties of materials; that is, you add visual characteristics to the models. The **Basic** tab allows you to add material appearance to the model. As part of appearance, you can specify how transparent the model is. You can assign appearance to parts, features, faces, or surfaces. Transparency allows you to see through the model. Zero transparency means the model is like a brick wall; you cannot see through it. Full or maximum transparency (with a setting of 1) means the model is like a glass wall; you can see through it.

## 7.8  Background and Scenes

We are able to set the background as part of PhotoWorks. (We can set the background color as part of the system options by clicking **Tools => Options => System Options => Colors**.) You can drag and drop scenes from the scenes library onto the current CAD model displayed in the graphics pane. To access the library, click the **Appearances/PhotoWorks** tab in the task pane shown in Figure 7.4. The figure also shows the **Scenes** library, which resides in this folder: *C:\Program Files\SolidWorks\ SolidWorks (2)\data\graphics\scenes*. The left pane of the screen also has the **Render Manager** tab (the rightmost tab). The tab has the **Scene** folder that allows you to find existing scenes, edit their properties, and add/save new ones.

## 7.9 Cameras and Camera Sleds

Thus far, we are able to create scenes with different types of lights and backgrounds. As in Figure 7.1, we can add cameras to the scene. You add a camera in a given location in the scene. The main objects in the scene are the CAD model and the camera, which can move relative to each other. The camera can rotate around the CAD model while it is fixed in the 3D modeling space. Or, the CAD model can rotate around the camera being fixed. Obviously, moving the camera around the CAD model is beneficial because it allows you to view the model from different angles in space.

Cameras are part of motion studies in SolidWorks. You can access the motion study via the tab located at the bottom of the left pane, shown here in Figure 7.7. Click the **Motion Study 1** tab to access cameras. This tab allows you to control the camera and the lights. Right-click as shown in Figure 7.7A to add a new camera and lights. If you right-click the **Motion Study 1** tab, you can add new motion studies and do more as shown in Figure 7.7B. SolidWorks adds a new motion tab for each motion study you create. To delete a motion study, right-click its tab and select **Delete** (see Figure 7.7B).

You can create cameras that are fixed in space in targeted locations or that are floating and rotating around the CAD model. In the fixed model, the model moves and rotates relative to the camera, that is, the camera is fixed at a target point. In the floating model, the camera moves and rotates relative to the model. While the end result (viewing the model from different angles) is the same, we prefer the camera floating model because it resembles real-life photography.

The floating camera model requires guiding the camera motion in space by creating target points or paths (curves) for the camera's travel. SolidWorks calls these paths *camera sleds*. Think of it as though you mount the camera on the sled and let it ride it. As the sled moves, the camera moves with it. Sleds are usually used to create animation.

(A) Add camera and lights

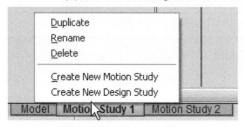

(B) Add/delete motion study

**FIGURE 7.7**
Cameras and motion studies

## 7.10 Animation

Animation is a useful visualization concept whereby we observe a continuous motion of an object in an attempt to understand its dynamic behavior with time. There are two types of animation: real time or playback. In real-time animation, we physically follow the motion of the physical object in space and record its motion. This type of animation is not useful in CAD/CAM because we do not have the part built yet; and even if we did, it would be impractical. Playback animation is what we use (Hollywood uses it also to create motions of cartoon characters and movies). In playback animation, we create key frames at key points. We assemble the key frames and display them in a continuous fashion to create the illusion of motion. We can interpolate between the key frames linearly or nonlinearly.

The camera sled moves along the defined path (linear or nonlinear) between the key frames (target points). As the camera moves, it takes shots of the model from different angles and displays them to the viewer in a continuous fashion. This is done by creating a sequence of camera views of the model from different angles (points on the sled path) and then displaying them. The camera may also move through the model to reveal its inside. A camera sled is a "dummy" component you create in the CAD model. You attach the camera to a sketch entity on the camera sled. You can hide the sled (the dummy component) from the sketch to view only the camera movement during the animation.

We refer to this type of animation as camera-based animation, as opposed to kinematics- or dynamic-based animation. You use the animation in motion studies. For example, you may use kinematics to create key frames of the model and then use the camera to combine them and show the animation.

## 7.11 PhotoWorks

PhotoWorks, as do other rendering packages, utilizes all scene and rendering concepts covered here and makes them available to the CAD designer to use. Figure 7.8 shows the tools that you can use to create camera-based animations. The tutorials in this chapter demonstrate the mechanics of how to create some animations.

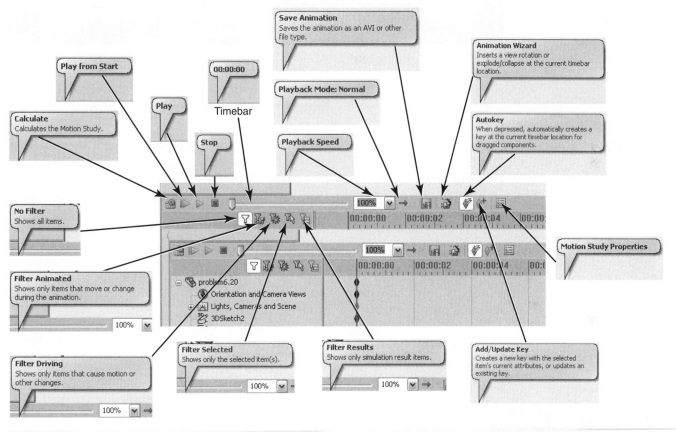

**FIGURE 7.8**
PhotoWorks animation tools

## 7.12 Tutorials Overview

The theme for the tutorials in this chapter is to get you to practice creating with and using PhotoWorks. We focus on rendering and playback animation: the use of the different types of scenes, lights, and animation tools shown in Figure 7.8. Zygote Media Group, with headquarters in American Fork, Utah, USA (www.zygote.com), has sponsored this chapter. Zygote specializes in designing and producing 3D content for the biomedical, entertainment, and professional markets. Zygote delivers high-quality 3D human anatomy for animators and engineers. Figure 7.9 shows a sample of Zygote's high-quality rendering. We chat with Mr. David Dunston, Executive Partner and Designer at Zygote, in the Industry Chat.

**FIGURE 7.9**
High-quality animation of human anatomy (Courtesy of Zygote)

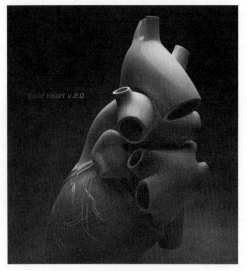

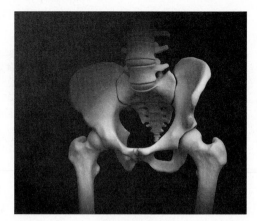

(A) Human heart                                    (B) Human hips

## Tutorial 7–1:   Create Scene

### Modeling task

Create a scene for a model downloaded from 3D ContentCentral. Figure 7.10 shows the model.

### Modeling synthesis

SolidWorks uses an Add-In software called PhotoWorks. Within PhotoWorks a number of operations enhance the appearance and realism of a model. This tutorial covers the basics of how to create a scene around an existing model.

### Modeling plan

The default model is downloaded as an assembly and then saved as a part file. From there a scene is created to enhance the presentation of the part.

### Design intent

Ignore for this chapter.

### CAD steps

We create the scene in four steps:

1. Download the Push Cart assembly.
2. Add-In the PhotoWorks Studio.
3. Create a scene.
4. Render the scene.

**FIGURE 7.10**
Tutorial 7–1 scene creation

The details of these steps are shown below.

## Step 1: Download the Push Cart assembly

**Task**

A. Download and open the tube rack from 3D ContentCentral.

**Command Sequence to Click**

Visit www.3-dcontentcentral.com. Type "push cart" into the search bar, and download and open the first item that appears as shown to the left.

B. Save the assembly as a part file.

**File => Save as.** Save the assembly as a part file.
**Why:** Rendering is very memory intensive for the computer. Rendering the assembly as a part will run much smoother and quicker.

## Step 2: Add-In PhotoWorks Studio

**Task**

A. Add-In the PhotoWorks Studio.

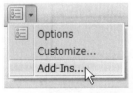

**Command Sequence to Click**

Use the **Property** tab to open the menu of **Add-Ins =>
PhotoWorks** shown to the left.

| Task | Command Sequence to Click |
|---|---|
| B. Change the PhotoWorks Studio options. | **PhotoWorks Options => System Options => Clear image before rendering**. Make sure this item is selected as shown to the left. |

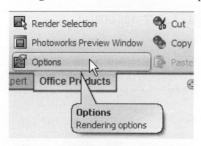

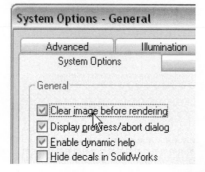

| Task | Command Sequence to Click |
|---|---|
| C. Set **Anti-Aliasing quality** to **Medium**. | **PhotoWorks Options => Document Properties => Anti-aliasing quality => Medium** as shown to the left |

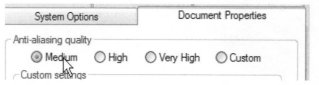

## Step 3: Create a scene

| Task | Command Sequence to Click |
|---|---|
| A. Open the **Photoworks Preview Window**. | **Office Products => Photoworks Preview Window** as shown to the left<br>This tool is used to get a quicker preview of the changes made while using PhotoWorks Studio. |

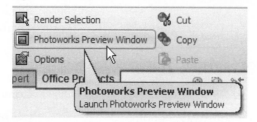

| Task | Command Sequence to Click |
|---|---|
| B. Open the **Scene Editor**. | **Office Products => Scene** as shown to the left to open the **Scene Editor** |

| Task | Command Sequence to Click |
|---|---|
| C. Select the factory backdrop. | **Manager** tab **=>** **Factory** as shown to the left |

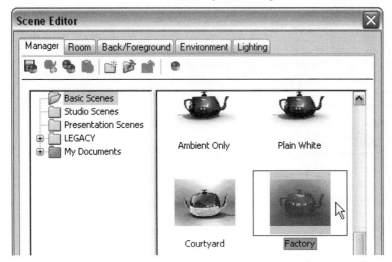

| | |
|---|---|
| D. Set the room options. | Set the **Size/Alignment** options as shown to the left. |

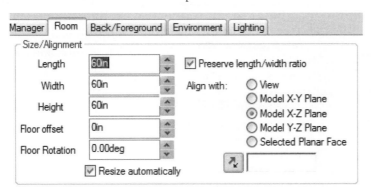

| | |
|---|---|
| E. Change the floor setting. | Under **Visibility and appearances** select the button next to the **Floor** as shown to the left. Then select the **factory floor.p2m** as shown to the left. |

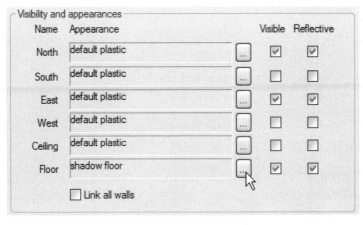

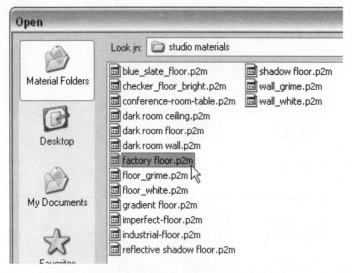

F.  Change the wall setting.

Repeat the previous step for the **North Wall** and change that to the **cream high gloss plastic.p2m** as shown to the left. Then select **Link all walls** as shown to the left, **Apply**, and then **Close** the editor.

Visibility and appearances

| Name | Appearance | | Visible | Reflective |
|------|-----------|---|---------|-----------|
| North | cream high gloss plastic (linked) | ... | ☑ | ☑ |
| South | cream high gloss plastic (linked) | ... | ☐ | ☐ |
| East | cream high gloss plastic (linked) | ... | ☑ | ☑ |
| West | cream high gloss plastic (linked) | ... | ☐ | ☐ |
| Ceiling | default plastic | ... | ☐ | ☐ |
| Floor | factory floor | ... | ☑ | ☑ |

☑ Link all walls

## Step 4: Render the scene

Task

A. Open the **Photoworks Preview Window**.

Command Sequence to Click

**Office Products => Render** as shown to the left to apply the setting to the assembly. Save the part as *Pushcart* and **Close**.

---

***HANDS-ON FOR TUTORIAL 7–1.*** Create a ceiling using the waffle pattern.p2m material located in the **pattern** folder shown in Figure 7.11. *Hint:* You will have to rotate the model and see the ceiling from below; otherwise, the ceiling is not rendered.

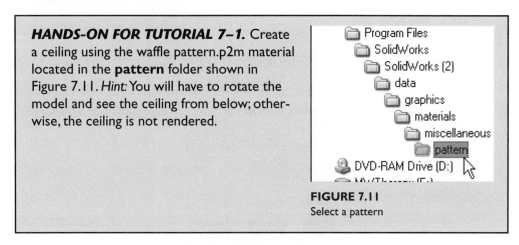

**FIGURE 7.11**
Select a pattern

---

## Tutorial 7–2: Use Ambient and Directional Lights

### Modeling task

Edit the ambient light and the directional light of a scene.

### Modeling synthesis

Within a scene there are four types of lighting: ambient, directional, spot, and point light. Each of these types of lighting serves a function to create a natural-looking scene. This tutorial will cover the basic skills to modify both the ambient and the directional light of an existing scene.

### Modeling plan

Using the scene created in Tutorial 7–1 and shown in Figure 7.12, first modify the ambient light and then the Directional1 light source, and turn off the Directional2 light source.

### Design intent

Ignore for this chapter.

### CAD steps

We use the lights in four steps:

1. Turn off the **Directional2** light.
2. Modify the ambient light.
3. Modify the **Directional1** light.
4. Render the scene.

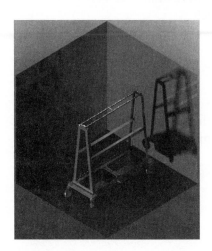

**FIGURE 7.12**
Modify lighting

The details of these steps are shown below.

## Step 1: Turn off the Directional2 light

| Task | Command Sequence to Click |
|---|---|
| A. Open the ambient properties. 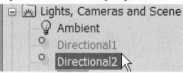 | Under the **FeatureManager design tree**, double-click on the **Lights, Cameras and Scene** folder. Then double-click the **Directional2** light shown to the left. |
| B. Access PhotoWorks properties. 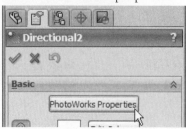 | Switch to the **PhotoWorks Properties** by selecting the button as shown to the left. |
| C. Deselect the **On** option.  | Ensure that **On in Photoworks** is deselected as shown to the left. |

## Step 2: Modify the ambient light

| Task | Command Sequence to Click |
|---|---|
| A. Open the ambient properties.  | Under the **FeatureManager design tree**, double-click on the **Lights, Cameras and Scene** folder. Then double-click the **Ambient** light as shown to the left. |
| B. Set the ambient light.  | Set the **Ambient** light as shown to the left, and select the green check mark. |

# Step 3: Modify the Directional1 light

**Task**

A. Open the Directional1 properties.

**Command Sequence to Click**

Double-click on the **Directional1** as shown to the left.

B. Set the Directional1 light.

Set **Directional1** as shown to the left, and select the green check mark.

## Step 4: Render the scene

Task

A. Open the **Photoworks Preview Window**.

Command Sequence to Click

**Office Products => Render** as shown to the left to apply the setting to the assembly. **Save** and **Close**.

---

***HANDS-ON FOR TUTORIAL 7–2.*** Edit the light such that it provides a red color glow as shown in Figure 7.13.

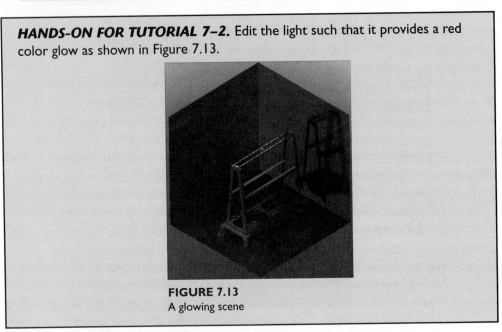

**FIGURE 7.13**
A glowing scene

---

## Tutorial 7–3: Use Point Light

**FIGURE 7.14**
Add point light to a scene

### Modeling task

Add a point light to an existing scene to brighten one side. Figure 7.14 shows the final rendered scene.

### Modeling synthesis

The point light is similar to a tiny lightbulb located at a specific point within the scene that radiates light in all directions. This tutorial will cover the ability to add a point light to a scene.

### Modeling plan

First we will add a point light and then set its location and lighting properties.

### Design intent

Ignore for this chapter.

### CAD steps

We use the point light in two steps:

1. Add the point light.
2. Render the scene.

The details of these steps are shown below.

## Step 1:  Add the point light

| Task | Command Sequence to Click |
|---|---|
| A. Add the point light.  | Under the **FeatureManager design tree**, right-click on the **Lights, Cameras and Scene** folder. Then select **Add Point Light** as shown to the left. |
| B. Bring up the point light properties. 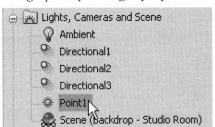 | Inside **Lights, Cameras and Scene** folder, double-click on **Point1** as shown to the left to bring up the **Properties** menu. |
| C. Set the properties. 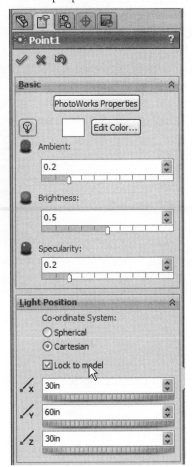 | Set each of the properties as shown to the left. |

| Task | Command Sequence to Click |
|---|---|
| **D.** Turn the light on in PhotoWorks. | Select the **PhotoWorks Properties** button as shown to the left. Then select the **On in PhotoWorks** option as shown to the left. |

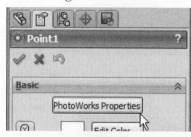

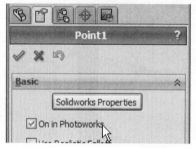

## Step 2: Render the scene

| Task | Command Sequence to Click |
|---|---|
| **A.** Render the scene. | **Office Products => Render** to apply the setting to the scene. **Save** and **Close**. |

*HANDS-ON FOR TUTORIAL 7–3.* Add a new point light such that it glows from under the end of the cart as shown in Figure 7.15. *Hint:* Turn off the **Point1** light that was created in this tutorial to truly see the effect of the location of this light.

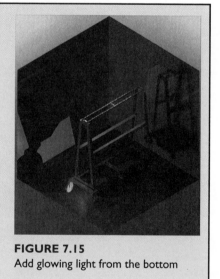

**FIGURE 7.15**
Add glowing light from the bottom

## Tutorial 7–4: Use Decals

### Modeling task

Add a decal to the surface of an existing model.

### Modeling synthesis

A decal does not change the part, but only adds the graphics to a chosen surface. This tutorial will cover the ability to add a decal to the surface of a part.

**FIGURE 7.16**
Add decal to surface

### Modeling plan

Add the selected decal to the surface as shown in Figure 7.16 and then render the model.

### Design intent

Ignore for this chapter.

### CAD steps

We add a decal in three steps:

1. Reset the lighting.
2. Add the decal.
3. Render the scene.

The details of these steps are shown below.

## Step 1:  Reset the lighting

| Task | Command Sequence to Click |
|---|---|
| A. Turn **Point1** on. | Open the **Point1** properties. Ensure that both the options are on as shown to the left. |

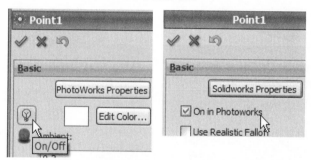

| Task | Command Sequence to Click |
|---|---|
| B. Turn **Point2** off. | Open **Point2**, created in the Hands-on for Tutorial 7–3, properties. Ensure that both options are off as shown to the left. |

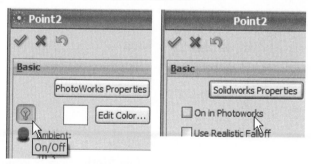

## Step 2:  Add the decal

| Task | Command Sequence to Click |
|---|---|
| A. Select the face. | Select the face and then select **Office Products => New Decal** as shown to the left. |

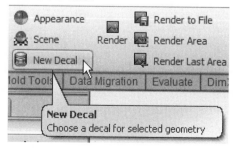

| Task | Command Sequence to Click |
|------|---------------------------|

**B.** Select the SolidWorks logo.

Select the logo as shown to the left.

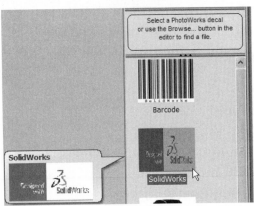

**C.** Fit the decal.

Stretch the decal from the corners such that it fills the selected surface as shown to the left.

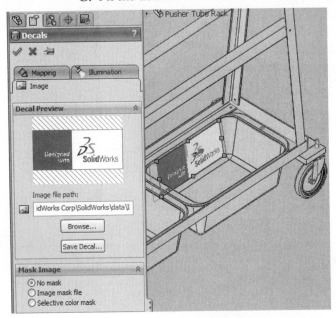

## Step 3: Render the scene

| Task | Command Sequence to Click |
|------|---------------------------|

**A.** Open the **Photoworks Preview Window.**

**Office Products => Render** as shown to the left to apply the setting to the assembly. **Save** and **Close.**

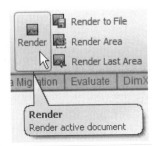

**FIGURE 7.17**
Tutorial 7–4 hands-on

## Tutorial 7–5: Use Spot Light

**FIGURE 7.18**
Add a spot light to a scene

### Modeling task

Add a spot light to an existing scene.

### Modeling synthesis

The spot light is similar to a flashlight. It is a focused light with a cone-shaped beam that can be aimed at a specific item or part of a scene. This tutorial will cover the ability to add a spot light to a scene.

### Modeling plan

First we will set the lighting so that only the ambient and Directional1 lights are being used. Then we will add a spot light and set its location and lighting properties. Finally, we will render the scene as shown in Figure 7.18.

### Design intent

Ignore for this chapter.

### CAD steps

We add the spot light in three steps:

1. Set the lighting.
2. Add a spot light.
3. Render the scene.

The details of these steps are shown below.

## Step 1: Set the lighting

**Task**

A. Set the lighting.

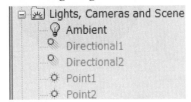

**Command Sequence to Click**

Set the lighting so that only the **Ambient** is illuminated as shown to the left.

| Task | Command Sequence to Click |
|---|---|

**B.** Preview the render.

Use the **Photoworks Preview Window** to check that the lighting is similar to that shown to the left.

## Step 2: Add a spot light

| Task | Command Sequence to Click |
|---|---|

**A.** Add a spot light.

Right-click on the folder **Lights, Cameras and Scene** and select **Add Spot Light** as shown to the left.

**B.** Set the basic properties.

Under the **SolidWorks Properties**, set the **Basic** options as shown to the left.

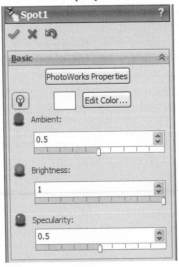

Part II Basic Part Modeling

| Task | Command Sequence to Click |
|---|---|
| C. Position the light and target. | Under the **SolidWorks Properties**, set the **Light Position** options as shown to the left. |

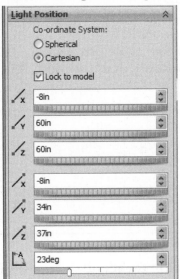

D. Set the PhotoWorks properties as shown below.

## Step 3: Render the scene

| Task | Command Sequence to Click |
|---|---|
| A. Open the **Photoworks Preview Window**. | **Office Products => Render** as shown to the left to apply the setting to the assembly. **Save** and **Close**. |

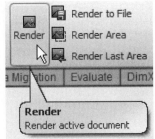

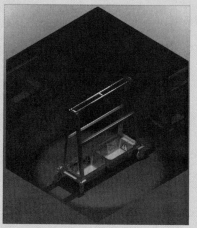

**FIGURE 7.19**
Modify spot light

## Tutorial 7–6:  Add Background Color to Scene

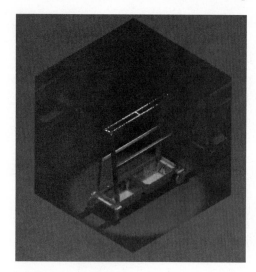

**FIGURE 7.20**
Tutorial 7–6

### Modeling task

Add a background color to an existing scene.

### Modeling synthesis

The background color is used to enhance the appearance of a scene. The colors and patterns can be either chosen from the list of options or created custom. This tutorial will cover the ability to add background color to a scene.

### Modeling plan

Using the push cart from the previous tutorial, we set the background colors and then render the scene as shown in Figure 7.20.

### Design intent

Ignore for this chapter.

### CAD steps

We add the background color in two steps:

1. Set the background color.
2. Render the scene.

The details of these steps are shown below.

### Step 1:  Set the background color

Task

A. Open the **Scene Editor.**

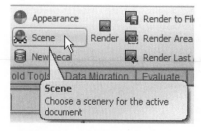

Command Sequence to Click

**Office Products => Scene** as shown to the left

| Task | Command Sequence to Click |
|---|---|
| B. Select the options as shown. | Select the **Back/Foreground** tab, and set the options as shown to the left **=>** **Apply => Close.** |

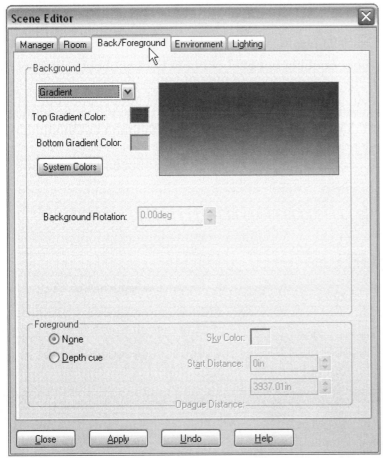

## Step 2: Render the scene

| Task | Command Sequence to Click |
|---|---|
| A. Render the scene. | **Office Products => Render** |

> **HANDS-ON FOR TUTORIAL 7–6.** Change the background to an **Image** instead of **Gradient.** Browse to find an image the library provides, or insert one of your own.

## Tutorial 7–7: Use Material and Texture

### Modeling task

Use the material properties of a part.

### Modeling synthesis

SolidWorks has built-in information about many common materials found in engineering and in nature. The software will automatically tell the user the volume and mass properties based on the model and the material chosen. This tutorial covers the basics of how to change the material as well as the texture and then record properties of the part.

**FIGURE 7.21**
Add material and texture

**Modeling plan**

Create a part and modify the material and material texture as shown in Figure 7.21.

**Design intent**

Ignore for this chapter.

**CAD steps**

We use materials and texture in three steps:

1. Create a new part.
2. Change the material texture.
3. Change the material.

The details of these steps are shown below.

## Step 1: Create a new part

| Task | Command Sequence to Click |
|---|---|
| **A.** Create this part. | Create the sphere shown to the left. **Hint:** Sketch a semicircle and revolve it 360°. |

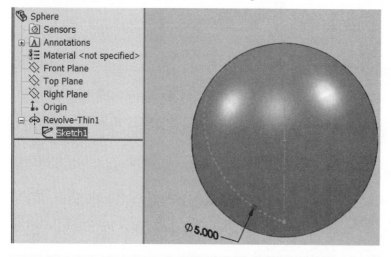

| **B.** Change the material. | Set the material to **Mahogany** as shown to the left. |

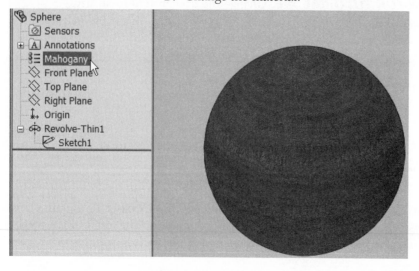

| Task | Command Sequence to Click |
|---|---|

**C.** Render the part as shown below.

**D.** Record the mass.

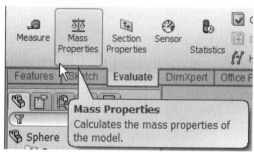

**Evaluate** tab **=> Mass Properties** as shown to the left
**Why:** SolidWorks will correctly measure the mass of the part based on the stored value of density and the volume of the part created. The mass should read 1.42 lb.

## Step 2: Change the material texture

| Task | Command Sequence to Click |
|---|---|

**A.** Select the body.

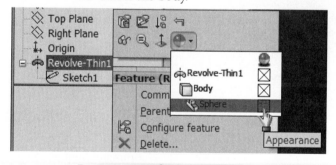

Right-click on the **Revolve** feature in the design tree. Select **Sphere** as shown to the left.

**B.** Browse to find a new texture as shown below.

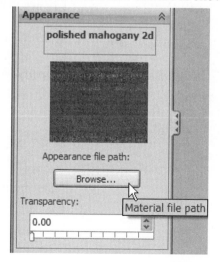

| Task | Command Sequence to Click |
|---|---|
| C. Select an engrained polished texture. | Select **polished mahogany endgrain.p2m** as shown to the left. |

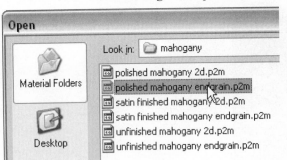

D. Render the part as shown below.

## Step 3: Change the material

| Task | Command Sequence to Click |
|---|---|
| A. Change the material to **Water**. | Change material to water as shown to the left. |

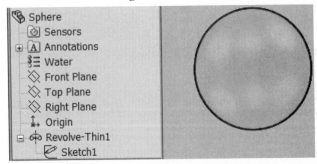

**Why:** We use a sphere, hypothetically made of water, to show the transparency property. Water material shows this property elegantly as shown in Task C.

B. Record the mass.

Mass should read 2.36 lb.

| Task | Command Sequence to Click |
|------|---------------------------|

**C.** Render the part.

**Help:** The **Water** material comes with a transparency setting of .75 as shown to the left.

---

***HANDS-ON FOR TUTORIAL 7–7.*** Change the transparency setting of water to zero and 1 and observe the difference. Submit a rendered screenshot of each setting.

---

## Tutorial 7–8: Create Camera View

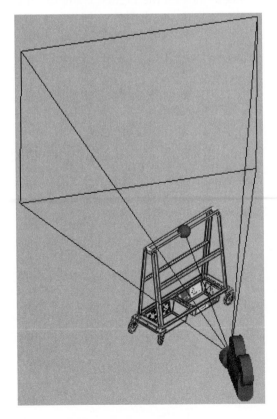

**FIGURE 7.22**
Add a camera to a scene

### Modeling task

Add a camera view to the model.

### Modeling synthesis

A camera view can be added to look at the part or assembly in a very specific way. Multiple cameras can be used as well as moved around the part to create an animation effect of the model. When using the Camera wizard, there are many position, aim, and focal options. When the camera view is created, it will be accessed through the view orientations menu such as the front, top, isometric, etc. views.

### Modeling plan

Using the push cart from the previous tutorials to add a camera that is at some distance away and is focused at the top center of the rack as shown in Figure 7.22.

### Design intent

Ignore for this chapter.

### CAD steps

We create the camera view in two steps:

1. Open the push cart.
2. Add a camera.

The details of these steps are shown below.

## Step 1: Open the push cart

**Task**

A. Open the push cart.

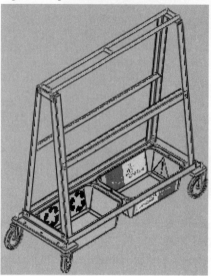

**Command Sequence to Click**

Open the push cart shown to the left that was used in previous tutorials of this chapter.

## Step 2: Add a camera

**Task**

A. Add a camera.

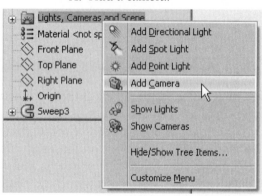

**Command Sequence to Click**

Right-click on the **Lights, Cameras and Scene** folder, and select **Add Camera** as shown to the left.

B. Select the first set of options as shown below.

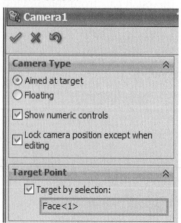

| Task | Command Sequence to Click |
|---|---|

**C.** Set **Camera Position.**

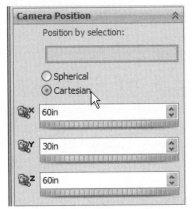

Set the position to **Cartesian** and fill in the coordinates as shown to the left. **Why:** These coordinates will position the camera at this point relative to the origin of the model.

**D.** Set the remaining options.

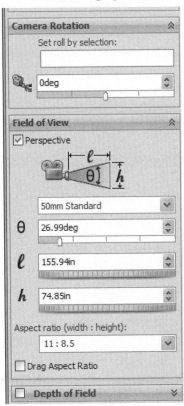

Ensure that the remaining options are as shown to the left.

**E.** Ensure that the camera is shown.

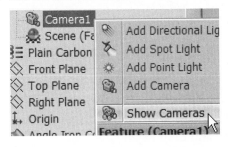

If you cannot see the camera, make sure it is shown by right-clicking on the **Camera1** in the features manager tree and selecting **Show Cameras** as shown to the left.

**F.** Accept.

Accept and return to the graphics pane. When orientated in the isometric view, the model should look the same as Figure 7.22.

## Tutorial 7–9: Create Motion Study

### Modeling task

Add a camera view motion study to the model.

### Modeling synthesis

Cameras can be used to view the model from different perspectives as opposed to just from the graphics pane. This tutorial shows the user how to view the model from the graphics pane as well as with the camera created in the previous tutorial.

### Modeling plan

Use the push cart from the previous tutorial to add a camera motion study that uses one camera that will travel between multiple points over time as shown in Figure 7.23.

**FIGURE 7.23**
Create motion study

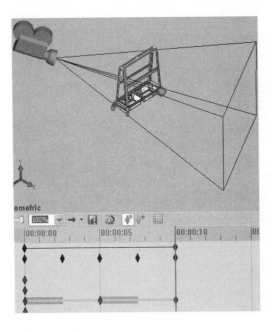

### Design intent

Ignore for this chapter.

### CAD steps

We create the motion study in six steps:

1. Create a 3D sketch.
2. Create first key point.
3. Create second and third key points.
4. View the motion study.
5. View the motion study from the camera.
6. View the motion study both isometric and from the camera.

The details of these steps are shown below.

## Step 1: Create a 3D sketch

### Task

A. Create a 3D sketch as shown.

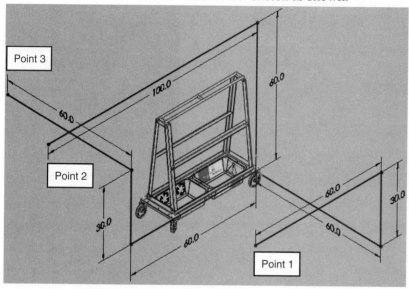

### Command Sequence to Click

Create the 3D sketch as shown to the left.

**Help:** All lines are along the *X*-, *Y*-, or *Z*-axis. Use the **Tab** key to change between sketch planes. The three endpoints will be used to locate the camera at various times of the motion study.

## Step 2: Create first key point

### Task

A. Select **Motion Study.**

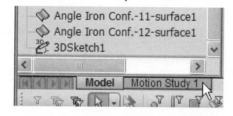

### Command Sequence to Click

At the bottom of the screen, select **Motion Study** as shown to the left.

B. Set a 10 s timeline.

C. Set the first key point.

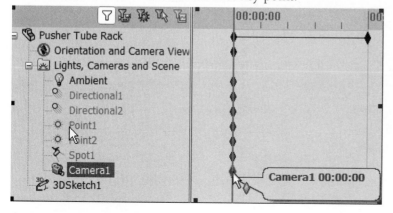

Drag the **Key** next to the part name out to 10 s on the timeline as shown to the left.
**Help:** The **Key** is the little black diamond next to each of the components such as lighting and camera properties as shown to the left. Expand the **Lights, Cameras and Scene** folder. Double-click the **Key** point to the right of **Camera1** as shown to the left.

| Task | Command Sequence to Click |
|---|---|
| **D.** Set camera position at key point 1. | Under **Camera Position** select **Position by selection** as shown to the left and select **Point 1** from the 3D sketch. Accept. |

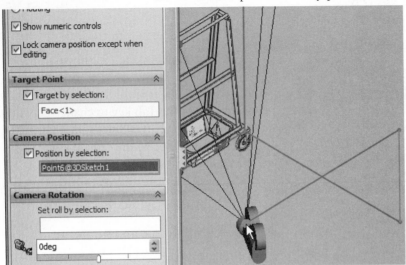

## Step 3: Create second and third key point

| Task | Command Sequence to Click |
|---|---|
| **A.** Create a second key point. | Drag a key point from the first out to a time of 5 s as shown to the left. |

| Task | Command Sequence to Click |
|---|---|
| **B.** Set the second key point camera position. | Double-click the second key point, and set the camera position to **Point 2** from the 3D sketch as shown to the left. |

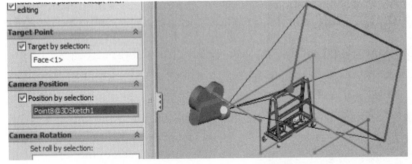

| Task | Command Sequence to Click |
|---|---|
| **C.** Repeat for a third key point. | Create a third key point at 5 s, and position the camera also at **Point 2** of the 3D sketch as shown to the left. |

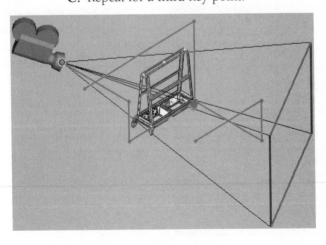

## Step 4:  View the motion study

| Task | Command Sequence to Click |
|---|---|
| **A.** Show cameras. | Right-click on **Camera1** in the features design tree, and select **Show Cameras** as shown to the left. |

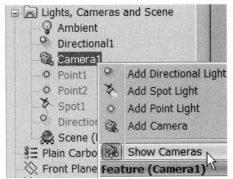

**Help:** Turn off the sketches to see a cleaner motion study.

**B.** Set the key properties.

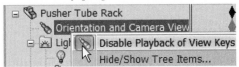

Right-click on **Orientation and Camera View**, and ensure that the first option is depressed as shown to the left.

**C.** Set the **Isometric** view.

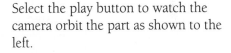

Right-click on the key to the right of the **Orientation and Camera View.** Set the orientation to **Isometric** as shown to the left.

**D.** Play the study.

Select the play button to watch the camera orbit the part as shown to the left.

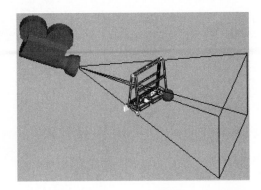

## Step 5: View the motion study from the camera

Task

A. View from the camera.

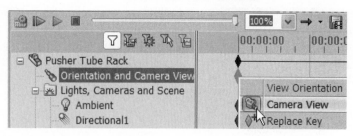

B. Play the study.

Command Sequence to Click

Right-click the **Key** to the right of the **Orientation and Camera View**. Select **Camera View** as shown to the left. **Why:** This will allow you to view the model from the camera as it orbits the part.

## Step 6: View the motion study both isometric and from the camera

Task

A. Create a view key.

B. Set the view keys.

C. Play the study.

Command Sequence to Click

Drag the **Key** to the right of the **Orientation and Camera View** out four times to create a key every 2.5 s as shown to the left.

Set the first two keys to view from the isometric position. Set the last three keys to view from the camera view. Click the **Play** icon.

---

### HANDS-ON FOR TUTORIAL 7–9.
Using the four view orientation keys created in Task A of Step 6, alternate the view between the camera and the top view as shown in Figure 7.24.

**FIGURE 7.24**
Alternate view

---

# Tutorial 7–10:   Create Camera-Based Animation

### Modeling task

Add a camera sled to the model and use it to guide the camera through a motion study.

### Modeling synthesis

The camera sled is a dummy object used to guide a camera through a model. The sled is forced to follow a path to which the camera is attached.

### Modeling plan

Use the push cart from the previous tutorial to add a camera sled and a path that the sled will follow throughout a timeline.

### Design intent

Ignore for this chapter.

### CAD steps

We create the animation in seven steps:

1. Create a new assembly.
2. Sketch the sled path.
3. Create a camera sled.
4. Insert and position the sled.
5. Create a camera.
6. Set up the motion study.
7. View the motion study from the camera.

The details of these steps are shown below.

## Step 1:   Create a new assembly

### Task

A. Start a new assembly.
B. Insert the push cart.

### Command Sequence to Click

**File => New => Assembly**
Allow the push cart to align to the origin as shown to the left.

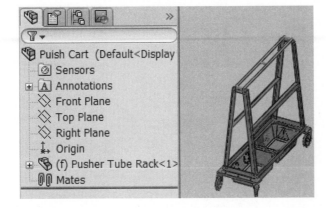

## Step 2: Sketch the sled path

| Task | Command Sequence to Click |
|---|---|
| **A.** Suppress the 3D sketch. | Right-click on the 3D sketch of the push cart model, and select **Suppress** as shown to the left. |

**B.** Open a sketch on the **Top Plane** as shown below.

| **C.** Sketch a sled path | Sketch a 250" circle on the top plane as shown to the left. |
|---|---|
| | **Why:** This circle acts as the path for the camera sled. |

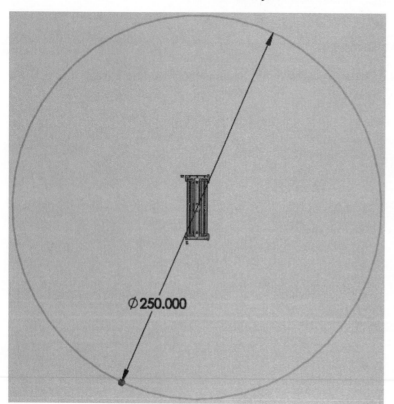

Ø250.000

## Step 3:   Create a camera sled

### Task

**A.** Create the camera sled as shown below.

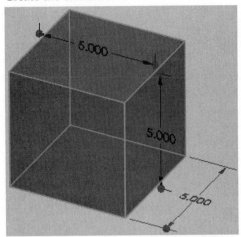

**B.** Create a sketch on the sled top plane.

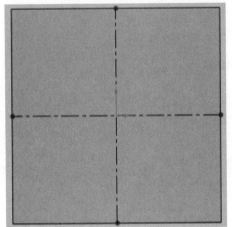

**C.** Save the part.

### Command Sequence to Click

**Why:** The size and shape of the sled is irrelevant.

Create the sketch shown to the left on the top plane of the sled.
**Why:** This sketch will be used to locate the sled and also the camera itself.

Save the part as *Camera Sled*.

## Step 4: Insert and position the sled

### Task

A. Insert the camera sled part.

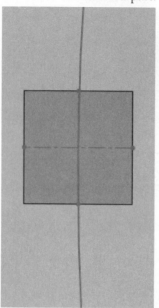

### Command Sequence to Click

Insert and locate the camera sled so that the top plane of the sled and the top plane of the assembly are coincident as shown to the left. Then mate the origin of the block to the circle that was sketched in Task C of Step 2. Finally, mate the right plane of the sled parallel to the right plane of the assembly.

## Step 5: Create a camera

### Task

A. Insert the camera sled part.

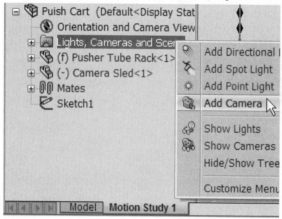

### Command Sequence to Click

Open the **Motion Study** at the bottom of the screen. Right-click on the **Lights, Cameras and Scene** folder and **Add Camera** as shown to the left.

B. Set up the options.

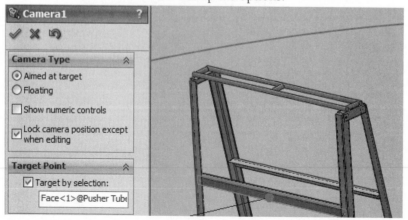

Select **Target by selection** and select the cross bar of the push cart as shown to the left.

| Task | Command Sequence to Click |
|---|---|
| C. Set the position options. | Select **Position by selection** and select the **Origin** of the camera sled as shown to the left. |

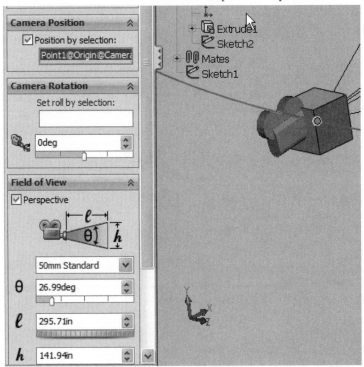

## Step 6: Set up the motion study

| Task | Command Sequence to Click |
|---|---|
| A. Drag the camera sled key. | Drag the **Camera Sled** key out to 2.5 s as shown to the left. Drag the block ¼ around the circle. Notice that the timeline automatically fills in a time. For this tutorial, we will drag it back to 2.5 s. |

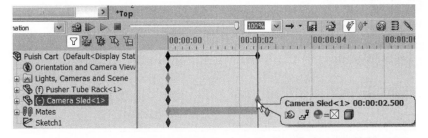

| | |
|---|---|
| B. Drag the camera sled. | Drag the block ¼ around the circle. Notice that the timeline automatically fills in with a green stripe as shown to the left. |

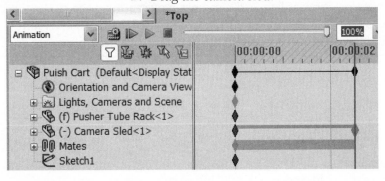

| | |
|---|---|
| C. Create a second key. | Drag another key from the camera sled out to 5 s. |

| Task | Command Sequence to Click |
|------|---------------------------|
| **D.** Drag the block. | Drag the block another ¼ around the circle as shown to the left. |

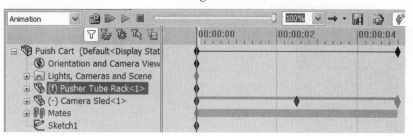

**E.** Play the motion study.

## Step 7: View the motion study from the camera

| Task | Command Sequence to Click |
|------|---------------------------|
| **A.** Select **Disable Playback of View Keys**. | Ensure that this option is depressed as shown to the left. |

| Task | Command Sequence to Click |
|------|---------------------------|
| **B.** Select **Camera View**. | Right-click the view key and select **Camera View** as shown to the left. |

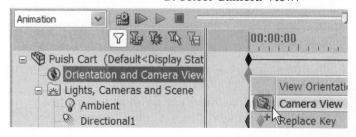

**C.** Play the motion study.

---

***HANDS-ON FOR TUTORIAL 7–10.*** Create a motion study such that the push cart moves in a straight line as the camera moves around the circle.
*Hint:* Set the part to float and then lock it to two out of the three assembly planes. Use the third degree of freedom to move the part along a straight line.

---

**INDUSTRY CHAT**

This section provides practical insight into how the chapter material is used in industry in the real world and practice. This section summarizes the chat with Mr. David Dunston (Executive Partner and Designer) of Zygote Media Group, the sponsor of this chapter. The structure of the chat follows the chapter sections.

**Chapter Section 7.1:**   Introduction

**ABE:**   How important is rendering to Zygote Media Group?

**DAVID:**   In a sense rendering is everything. Every good carpenter, author, and chef should know that no matter how good the product is, it doesn't matter if you can't sell it. Renderings sell. They sell concepts. They sell quality. They sell the product.

**Chapter Section 7.2:**   Scenes and Lighting

**ABE:**   Which of the five types of lights do you use the most?

**DAVID:**   I usually work with point lights, but directional or spot lights work just as well. Point lights are a little faster to set up but spot lights can actually save you rendering time.

I start with what I call the "primary light." The purpose of the primary light is to create depth and show detail of the model. All other lights exist to make the model look like it fits into the scene. The primary light is the light that should generate shadow. I typically don't turn shadows on with any other lights. I like to position my primary light above, on the side, and slightly in front of the model being rendered. As I build up my scene, I like to work with one light at a time. If I start from an old scene that was previously created, I will turn off all of the lights and begin again with the primary light, making sure the effect from that light is just right. If you start with more lights than one, it makes it hard to tell what is going on. As I refine each light, I will add one at a time until I reach the desired effect.

The second most important light, or the "secondary light," should generate a refracted lighting effect. This light should be positioned opposite of the primary light, but still remain in front of the model. For a nice effect you can make the secondary light a color, and the primary light's shadow slightly blue. This ties the model into the scene very well. All lights in the scene, other than the primary light, should have a brightness of about 30%. You may now add one or two more lights in order to get rid of any unnatural dark core shadows. Sometimes I will put a light directly under the model to get rid of dark spots. You could try to add a little light to your scene with an ambient light instead of all of the other lights, but this typically will make your primary light too hot.

This lighting technique is a simple way to simulate a realistic or HDRI (High Dynamic Range Image) rendering effect without the extra rendering time of such. If you prefer to use an HDRI effect, you will need to get rid of all the extra lights and add walls for the light to bounce around on.

**Chapter Section 7.3:**   Rendering Models

**ABE:**   Do you create elaborate scenes to render your CAD models?

**DAVID:**   I tend to render with simple lighting in order to build up, what looks like, a complicated scene.

**Chapter Section 7.4:**   Decals

**ABE:**   Do you use decals? If yes, for what purpose?

**DAVID:**   I use decals rarely. I basically only use decals when the client needs a logo for branding.

*(continued)*

**Chapter Section 7.5:** Textures

ABE: Do you use textures? If yes, for what purpose?

DAVID: Most of the models that Zygote creates for CAD users don't involve textures. If the model is being created is for a graphic artist, we always create textures.

**Chapter Section 7.6:** Materials

ABE: Do you assign materials to your CAD models? For what purposes: calculations, rendering, or both?

DAVID: We always assign materials to models, if nothing else than for rendering purposes.

**Chapter Section 7.7:** Appearance and Transparency

ABE: Do you use appearance and transparency in your rendering? How?

DAVID: Transparency is a powerful tool. You can communicate a lot with transparency. To be honest, though, I frequently render several images and later create transparent effects in Photoshop. The reason for this is time. It tends to take a lot of time to create the perfect transparent effect in 3D.

**Chapter Section 7.8:** Background and Scenes

ABE: Do you use background scenes in your rendering? Provide examples.

DAVID: Backgrounds are great for creating depth. You can create depth behind a model with shading or texture. I find that most artwork shines better when you add layering of some kind. Backgrounds can also give a frame of reference for size of a medical device or such.

**Chapter Section 7.9:** Cameras and Camera Sleds

ABE: Do you use cameras? Do you also use camera sleds? Provide examples.

DAVID: I use a camera when I need control over the amount of perspective within an image. Camera sleds are great if you need movement to show form of the model.

**Chapter Section 7.10:** Animation

ABE: Do you use animation? If yes, why? Provide examples.

DAVID: Yes. Animation, like a rendering, sells the concept or product. I heard someone say once that "an image is worth a thousand words and an animation is worth a thousand words at 30 frames a second."

**Others**

ABE: Any other experience you would like to share with our book readers?

DAVID: My roots in 3D began with modeling. Nothing can speak better than a well-crafted 3D model, but the image is what puts it into words. Understanding 3D CAD modeling is essential to using rendering software to bring 3D models to life and adding realism.

1. Describe the elements of a digital rendering scene.

2. List the five types of lights that SolidWorks uses. What type of light rays does each type provide?

3. Sketch a typical rendering model. What type of reflections do a shiny surface and a dull surface reflect?

4. What are caustics? Provide an example.

5. Use your organization logo and save it as a decal image in PhotoWorks Decals library. Use it to render a CAD model. Submit screenshots of the rendered CAD model with the decal.

6. Search and find a cool texture. Add the texture file to PhotoWorks textures. Use it to render a CAD model. Submit screenshots of the rendered CAD model.

7. Search and find the material properties for bronze. Add the bronze material to SolidWorks materials. Use it to render a CAD model. Submit screenshots of the material properties and the rendered CAD model.

8. Repeat Problem 7, but use transparency to see through the CAD model.

9. Search and find a cool background scene. Add the background scene to PhotoWorks. Use it to render a CAD model. Submit screenshots of the rendered CAD model.

10. Create a camera and camera sled to animate any of the CAD models shown in Chapter 6 problems.

# Advanced Part Modeling

The primary goal of Part III is to explore and cover in detail the topics of curves, surfaces, and sheet metal and weldment parts. This part shows the real power of geometric modeling as well as how to model and design complex parts such as a computer mouse, fan blades, hair dryers, etc. Two of the important modeling concepts covered here are 3D curves and surfaces. Combining these concepts will enable you to model any complex shape you come across.

Chapter 8 (Curves) covers the details of curves, their parametric representation, and their types of 2D and 3D representation. Chapter 9 (Surfaces) extends the curve theory and covers the parametric representation of surfaces, the available types of surfaces we can use in modeling, and how to use surfaces to create solid models. Chapter 10 (Sheet Metal and Weldments) shows how we can create sheet metal parts and weldments. Chapter 11 (Sustainable Design) closes Part III by covering the important topic of environmentally conscious design and lifecycle assessment (LCA) and analysis.

# Curves

## 8.1 Introduction

Curves form the backbone of geometric modeling and creating solid models. A sketch consists of multiple curves that are connected to form closed contours (loops). Loops may be nested. A sketch that consists of only one contour generates a solid without holes, whereas a sketch with multiple contours generates a solid with holes in it. Figure 8.1 shows examples. A one-contour sketch is demonstrated in Figure 8.1A. You can create a sketch with only one-level nesting; that is, an outside contour with one or more disconnected contours inside it, as in Figure 8.1B. However, if you attempt to use more than one-level nesting, the solid creation operation fails, as shown in Figures 8.1C and 8.1D.

(A) One-contour sketch

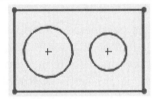

(B) One-level nesting sketch with two nested contours

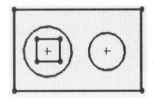

(C) Two-level nesting sketch: rectangle inside left circle

(D) Error due to sketch shown in (C)

**FIGURE 8.1**
Nesting contours to create solids

Mathematically, two families of curves exist. The first family is the analytic curves. These curves have closed-form equations defining them. Examples of analytic curves include lines, circles, ellipses, parabolas, and hyperbolas. This family is also known as conics because the curves result from intersecting a cone with a plane. For example, intersecting a cone with a plane passing through its axis produces a line. Intersecting a cone with a plane perpendicular to its axis produces a circle. And, if the plane is not perpendicular to the cone, the intersection results in an ellipse, parabola, or hyperbola.

The second family of curves is the synthetic curves. A **synthetic curve** is defined by a polynomial that uses a set of data points. These data points control the curve shape. Examples include a cubic curve and a B-spline (or a spline as SolidWorks calls it). Figure 8.2 shows sample curves with SolidWorks menus. These curves are accessible from SolidWorks **Sketch** tab. The ellipse is defined by two radii (each connecting two opposite points, as shown in Figure 8.2A), and the spline is defined by points $P_0$, $P_1, \ldots, P_n$.

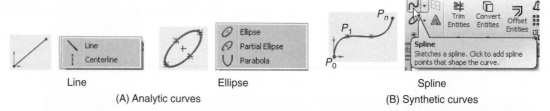

Line       Ellipse       Spline

(A) Analytic curves       (B) Synthetic curves

**FIGURE 8.2**
Families of curves

Synthetic curves offer more flexibility in modeling than do analytic curves. They are efficient to use for creating free-form shapes. All you need to do is to define the curve points (Figure 8.2B) by either clicking in the sketch area or entering $(x, y, z)$ coordinates. Once created, you can easily modify the curve shape by editing its points to change their locations.

## 8.2 Curve Representation

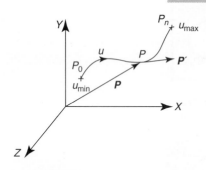

**FIGURE 8.3**
Parametric curve

CAD/CAM software uses parametric equations to represent curves. A **parametric equation** is an equation that uses a parameter (e.g., $u$) to describe the $(x, y, z)$ coordinates of a point. Figure 8.3 shows the parametric representation of a curve. The parameter $u$ starts with a minimum value, $u_{min}$, at one end of the curve and finishes with a maximum value, $u_{max}$, at the other end of the curve. The parameter increases in value from $u_{min}$ to $u_{max}$, thus defining the parameterization direction of the curve as indicated by the arrow on the curve. Any point $P$ on the curve is defined by its position vector, $P$, that is a function of $u$,

$$P = P(u) \quad u_{min} < u < u_{max} \tag{8.1}$$

Alternatively, point $P$ is defined by its $(x, y, z)$ coordinates. Thus,

$$P = \begin{bmatrix} x \\ y \\ z \end{bmatrix} = \begin{bmatrix} x(u) \\ y(u) \\ z(u) \end{bmatrix} \quad u_{min} < u < u_{max} \tag{8.2}$$

The tangent vector $P'$ at any point on the curve (Figure 8.3) is given by:

$$P' = \frac{dp}{du} = \begin{bmatrix} x' \\ y' \\ z' \end{bmatrix} \quad u_{min} < u < u_{max} \tag{8.3}$$

The tangent vector is an important concept in CAD/CAM applications such as mass property calculations and NC (numerical control) programming. For these two applications, we use the tangent vector at any point on the curve to calculate the normal vector to the curve at the same point. For mass properties, the direction of the normal vector is used to determine the inside (where material is) and the outside (where holes exist) of the solid. For NC programming, we move the cutting tool along the direction of the normal vector until it makes contact with the part surface to be machined. This minimizes the lateral forces on the cutting tool, which in turn reduces the chance of breaking the tool upon contact with the surface to be machined.

## 8.3 Line Parametric Equation

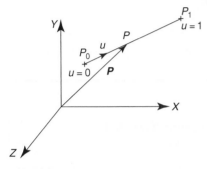

**FIGURE 8.4**
Parametric line

Figure 8.4 shows the parametric representation of a straight line defined by two endpoints, $P_0$ and $P_1$. The parameterization direction of the line shown in Figure 8.4 goes from $P_0$ to $P_1$, indicating that you start sketching the line at $P_0$ and finish at $P_1$. The parametric equation of this line is given (in vector form) by:

$$P = P(u) = P_0 + u(P_1 - P_0) \quad 0 \leq u \leq 1 \tag{8.4}$$

or (in scalar form),

$$P = P(u) = \begin{bmatrix} x(u) \\ y(u) \\ z(u) \end{bmatrix} = \begin{bmatrix} x_0 + u(x_1 - x_0) \\ y_0 + u(y_1 - y_0) \\ z_0 + u(z_1 - z_0) \end{bmatrix} \quad 0 \leq u \leq 1 \tag{8.5}$$

Using Eq. (8.3), the tangent vector of the line is given by:

$$P' = \begin{bmatrix} x' \\ y' \\ z' \end{bmatrix} = \begin{bmatrix} x_1 - x_0 \\ y_1 - y_0 \\ z_1 - z_0 \end{bmatrix} \tag{8.6}$$

Equation (8.6) shows that the tangent vector is constant (independent of $u$), as expected. You can easily derive the line slope from the tangent vector. For example, the line slope in the XY plane is given by:

$$\frac{dy}{dx} = \frac{dy/du}{dx/du} = \frac{y'}{x'} \tag{8.7}$$

The elegance of the parametric representation is that it is independent of the dimensionality of the modeling space whether it is 2D ($x$ and $y$ coordinates only) or 3D ($x$, $y$, and $z$ coordinates). In other words, use $z = 0$ in the 3D equations and you get 2D modeling. As a matter of fact, when you sketch in a sketch plane, the $z$ value is set to zero; when you are done sketching, SolidWorks transforms the sketch "2D" WCS coordinates to "3D" MCS coordinates.

---

**Example 8.1**    A designer created a line connecting point $(-3, 2, 1)$ to point $(0, -4, 2)$. Find the line parametric equation, its midpoint, its endpoints, and its tangent vector.

**Solution**    Using Eq. (8.5), the line parametric equation is

$$P(u) = \begin{bmatrix} x(u) \\ y(u) \\ z(u) \end{bmatrix} = \begin{bmatrix} -3 \\ 2 \\ 1 \end{bmatrix} + u \begin{bmatrix} 3 \\ -6 \\ 1 \end{bmatrix} = \begin{bmatrix} 3u - 3 \\ -6u + 2 \\ u + 1 \end{bmatrix} \quad 0 \leq u \leq 1 \tag{8.8}$$

Differentiating Eq. (8.8) with respect to $u$, the tangent vector is:

$$P' = \begin{bmatrix} x'(u) \\ y'(u) \\ z'(u) \end{bmatrix} = \begin{bmatrix} 3 \\ -6 \\ 1 \end{bmatrix} \qquad (8.9)$$

The midpoint of the line occurs at $u = 0.5$. Thus, it is

$$\begin{bmatrix} -1.5 \\ -1 \\ 1.5 \end{bmatrix}$$

The endpoints of the line occur at $u = 0$ and $u = 1$ and are the same as the points given in the example. Thus, you can check whether Eq. (8.8) is correct by substituting the values $u = 0$ and $u = 1$.

---

**HANDS-ON FOR EXAMPLE 8.1.** Find the line equation if the designer reverses the order of the endpoints to sketch the line.

---

## 8.4 Circle Parametric Equation

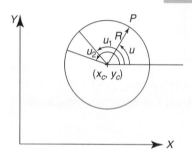

**FIGURE 8.5**
Parametric circle

We consider the case of a circle defined by a center point $(x_c, y_c)$ and a radius $R$ only to simplify the formulation. When you sketch a circle, you must define a sketch plane because a center and a radius define an infinite number of circles. Figure 8.5 shows this definition of a parametric circle. The parameter $u$ is the angle, measured in counterclockwise direction. The circle equation is given by:

$$P(u) = \begin{bmatrix} x(u) \\ y(u) \end{bmatrix} = \begin{bmatrix} x_c + R\cos u \\ y_c + R\cos u \end{bmatrix} \qquad 0 \le u \le 2\pi \qquad (8.10)$$

We can normalize the $u$ limits in Eq. (8.10) to $(0, 1)$ instead of $(0, 2\pi)$. This gives:

$$P(u) = \begin{bmatrix} x(u) \\ y(u) \end{bmatrix} = \begin{bmatrix} x_c + R\cos 2\pi u \\ y_c + R\cos 2\pi u \end{bmatrix} \qquad 0 \le u \le 1 \qquad (8.11)$$

Note that the circle, although closed, has two coincident endpoints, one for each $u$ limit.

The tangent vector of the circle is given by:

$$P'(u) = \begin{bmatrix} x'(u) \\ y'(u) \end{bmatrix} = \begin{bmatrix} -R\sin u \\ R\cos u \end{bmatrix} \qquad 0 \le u \le 2\pi \qquad (8.12)$$

Or,

$$P'(u) = \begin{bmatrix} x'(u) \\ y'(u) \end{bmatrix} = \begin{bmatrix} -2\pi R\sin u \\ 2\pi R\cos u \end{bmatrix} \qquad 0 \le u \le 1 \qquad (8.13)$$

Equations (8.10) through (8.13) can also be used to define arcs. The only difference is the $u$ limits, that is, $u_1 \le u \le u_2$. Figure 8.5 shows this arc segment.

Part III Advanced Part Modeling

**Example 8.2**  Find the equation of a circle with a radius of 2.0 in. and a center at the origin. Find the midpoint of the circle. What is the tangent vector and slope at this point?

**Solution**  Using Eq. (8.10) with the given data, we get:

$$P(u) = \begin{bmatrix} x(u) \\ y(u) \end{bmatrix} = \begin{bmatrix} 2\cos u \\ 2\cos u \end{bmatrix} \quad 0 \le u \le 2\pi \tag{8.14}$$

The midpoint of the circle occurs in the mid-range of the $u$ parameter, that is, at $u = \pi$. Equation (8.14) gives:

$$P(u) = \begin{bmatrix} x(u) \\ y(u) \end{bmatrix} = \begin{bmatrix} -2 \\ 0 \end{bmatrix} \tag{8.15}$$

These coordinates agree with the visual inspection of Figure 8.5; the point is the leftmost point on the circle perimeter. Note that the midpoint of the circle is not its center; the center does not lie on the circle perimeter. The tangent vector at the midpoint is obtained by substituting $u = \pi$ in Eq. (8.12) to get:

$$\mathbf{P}'(u) = \begin{bmatrix} x'(u) \\ y'(u) \end{bmatrix} = \begin{bmatrix} 0 \\ -2 \end{bmatrix} \tag{8.16}$$

The slope at this point is given by $\dfrac{y'}{x'} = \infty$ as expected because the tangent vector is vertical at this point; that is, it makes a 90° angle measured from the horizontal axis counterclockwise.

---

**HANDS-ON FOR EXAMPLE 8.2.** Find the parametric equation of the quarter circle in the second quadrant. What is the midpoint of this arc? What is the tangent vector at this point?

---

## 8.5  Spline Parametric Equation

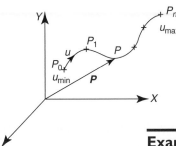

**FIGURE 8.6**
Parametric spline

Different types of splines exist. The most commonly used one by CAD/CAM systems is the cubic B-spline curve, or spline for short. Figure 8.6 shows a spline connecting $n + 1$ data points. The spline equation takes the following form:

$$P(u) = f_0(u)P_0 + f_1(u)P_1 + \cdots + f_n(u)P_n \quad u_{\min} \le u \le u_{\max} \tag{8.17}$$

where the highest degree of any of these $f(u)$ functions is cubic.

---

**Example 8.3**  A spline is given by:

$$P(u) = \begin{bmatrix} x(u) \\ y(u) \end{bmatrix} = \begin{bmatrix} 2 + 3u^2 - 2u^3 \\ 2 + 3u - 3u^2 \end{bmatrix} \quad 0 \le u \le 1 \tag{8.18}$$

Find the endpoints and the midpoint of the spline. Also, find the tangent vector and the slope at the midpoint. Using your CAD/CAM system, create the spline defined by the above equation. Submit a screenshot of the spline. *Hint:* Use enough points to create a smooth spline.

**Solution**  The endpoints occur at $u = 0$ and $u = 1$. The midpoint of the spline occurs at $u = 0.5$. Substituting these values in Eq. (8.18), we get:

$$P(0) = \begin{bmatrix} 2 \\ 2 \end{bmatrix}, \quad P(0.5) = \begin{bmatrix} 2.5 \\ 2.75 \end{bmatrix}, \quad \text{and} \quad P(1) = \begin{bmatrix} 3 \\ 2 \end{bmatrix}$$

Differentiating Eq. (8.18) gives the tangent vector to the spline at any point on it as:

$$\boldsymbol{P}'(u) = \begin{bmatrix} 6u - 6u^2 \\ 3 \quad - 6u \end{bmatrix} \quad 0 \leq u \leq 1$$

The tangent vector at the midpoint is $\boldsymbol{P}'(0.5) = \begin{bmatrix} 1.5 \\ 0 \end{bmatrix}$, and the slope is $\dfrac{y'}{x'} = \dfrac{0}{1.5} = 0$; that is, the tangent vector is horizontal at the midpoint.

To create the spline using SolidWorks, we calculate 11 points on the spline using Eq. (8.18) for $u$ values of 0, 0.1, 0.2, . . ., 1.0. We use the same idea of Example 4.2 in Chapter 4 to generate the points on the spline. Here is the JavaScript program we use:

```
<html>
<script language = "javascript">

document.write("The result shows u, x, y: <br>");
u = -0.1;
for (i = 0; i < 11; i++)
{
u = u + 0.1;
x = 2 + 3*u*u  -  2*u*u*u;
y = 2 + 3*u - 3*u*u;
document.write(u + " "+ x + " "+ y "y" + "<br>");
}
</script>
</html>
```

We store the points in a text file, named *spline.txt*, in the $x$, $y$, $z$ format shown below:

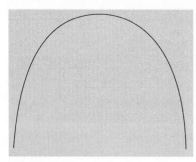

**FIGURE 8.7**
Spline

| | | |
|---|---|---|
| 2.000 | 2.000 | 0 |
| 2.028 | 2.270 | 0 |
| 2.104 | 2.480 | 0 |
| 2.216 | 2.630 | 0 |
| 2.352 | 2.720 | 0 |
| 2.500 | 2.750 | 0 |
| 2.648 | 2.720 | 0 |
| 2.784 | 2.630 | 0 |
| 2.896 | 2.480 | 0 |
| 2.972 | 2.270 | 0 |
| 3.000 | 2.000 | 0 |

We read this file in SolidWorks and create the spline shown in Figure 8.7. Review Example 4.2 in Chapter 4 should you need to refresh your memory on how to create a curve using $(x, y, z)$ coordinates.

---

**HANDS-ON FOR EXAMPLE 8.3.** Find the coordinates of the points on the spline where $u = 0.25$ and $u = 0.75$.

## 8.6 Two-Dimensional Curves

SolidWorks implements the curve parametric theory presented here and provides versatile ways for the designer to create curves. Curves may be planar (2D curves) or nonplanar (3D curves). The 2D curves are sketch entities; that is, they lie in the sketch plane regardless of how complex they may look. The use as well as creation of 2D curves in SolidWorks is simple, as illustrated in Figures 8.1 and 8.2.

SolidWorks offers an option to create curves from equations. Click this sequence to access it: **Tools** (SolidWorks menu) => **Sketch Entities => Equation Driven Curve**. You must be in a sketch to access it. Although this method of creating 2D curves may seem attractive at first glance, unfortunately it is against the parametric theory that forms the core of geometric modeling and parametric solid modeling used in all CAD/CAM systems today. It requires a curve equation in the form of $y = f(x)$, not in the parametric form of $y = f_1(u)$ and $x = f_2(u)$. Therefore, we neither cover this option nor use it in this book.

## 8.7 Three-Dimensional Curves

3D curves, unlike 2D curves, do not belong to only one sketch plane. A segment of a 3D curve may belong to one sketch plane while another segment may belong to another sketch plane. 3D curves are valuable to use in some designs, and they simplify feature creation significantly as shown in the tutorials in this chapter. The 3D curves become more powerful and elegant when we combine them with surfaces, as shown later in the book.

How can we create 3D curves? SolidWorks provides the following methods (refer to the tutorials of the chapter on how to use each method):

1.  **3D points:**  This method requires a list of $(x, y, z)$ coordinates of the 3D points as we have done in Example 8.3 and Example 4.2. The user may input the coordinates while creating the curve or store them in a text file and read it into SolidWorks.

2.  **3D sketching:**  This method allows you to sketch line and arc segments in different sketch planes. Its use is limited and it is usually used for routing.

3.  **Composite curve:**  You can create composite curves by combining curves, sketch geometry, and model edges into a single curve. The individual curves may belong to one sketch or different sketches. If they belong to the same sketch, the resulting composite curve is 2D. If they belong to multiple sketches, the resulting curve is 3D. You may use a composite curve as a guide curve when creating a loft or a sweep.

4.  **Project a curve onto a model face:**  This method takes a 2D curve created on a sketch plane and converts it into a 3D curve by projecting it onto a model face. The model face needs to be nonplanar to create a 3D curve; otherwise, the projected curve remains 2D.

5.  **Projected curve:**  This is a very powerful method to create 3D curves. You can create a 3D curve from two 2D curves. These 2D curves are two projections of the 3D curve on two intersecting sketch planes. The 3D curve represents the surface/surface intersection of two extruded surfaces generated by the two 2D curves, as shown in Figure 8.8. A common practice is to sketch the two best projections of the 3D curve on two different sketches (e.g., front and top or front and right) and then use the projected curve method to create the 3D curve. If the resulting curve needs tweaking, delete it, modify the two sketches, and then re-create it. Continue this iterative process until you are satisfied with the resulting 3D curve.

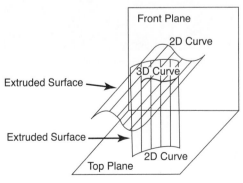

**FIGURE 8.8**
Creating a 3D projected curve

## 8.8 Curve Management

After you create curves, you can manage and manipulate them in different ways. You can modify, edit, trim, split (divide), and/or intersect them. These manipulations are easily done as an outcome of the curve parametric formulation presented in this chapter. We have already done all these manipulations except breaking a curve. Follow this sequence to split a curve: Right-click it => **Split Entities** (from the pop-up window) => Click the curve where you want to split it => Hit **Esc** key on the keyboard to finish. To verify the split, hover over the entities and observe the curve segments. You may also verify the split by right-clicking a segment => **Delete** from the pop-up menu.

## 8.9 Tutorials Overview

The theme for the tutorials in this chapter is to practice creating and using 3D curves to create complex parts. The tutorials show how to use all the methods for creating 3D curves that we have covered. A tutorial covers each method; in addition, there are tutorials that apply these methods to create some interesting parts. MSD Ignition, with headquarters in El Paso, Texas, USA (www.msdignition.com), has sponsored this chapter. MSD Ignition specializes in performance and racing ignition components including high output ignitions, spark plug wires, coils, and distributors. Its ignitions are used on professional race cars ranging from the stock cars of NASCAR to 330 mph top fuel dragsters. Many of its components are used in extreme conditions from vibration and heat to voltage and current requirements, which place extra importance on the overall design. We chat with Mr. Doug Webber, Mechanical Designer and CAD Administrator at MSD Ignition, in the Industry Chat. Figure 8.9 shows sample MSD design of a race car ignition.

(A) Race car ignition (Actual product)          (B) Race car ignition (SolidWorks model)

**FIGURE 8.9**
Race car ignition (Courtesy of MSD Ignition)

## Tutorial 8–1:  Create a 3D Curve Using 3D Points

Modeling task

Create a 3D curve through $(x, y, z)$ points.

**FIGURE 8.10**
A sweep using 3D curve

## Modeling synthesis

There are many ways to create a 3D curve in 3D space in SolidWorks. The method to input points in space and then connect them with a curve will be covered in this tutorial.

## Modeling plan

Input seven (*x, y, z*) coordinates and connect them with a curve using the **Curve Through XYZ Points** function. Then create a swept boss using the curve. Figure 8.10 shows the resulting swept feature.

## Design intent

Ignore for this chapter.

## CAD steps

We create the 3D curve and the feature in two steps:

1. Create a curve.
2. Create a swept boss/base.

The details of these steps are shown below.

## Step 1:  Create a curve

| Task | Command Sequence to Click |
|---|---|
| **A.** Open a new part. | Open a new part and set the units to millimeters as shown to the left. |

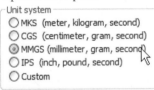

**B.** Input the coordinates.

Insert => Curve => Curve
**Through XYZ Points** to open the
**Curve File** as shown to the left.

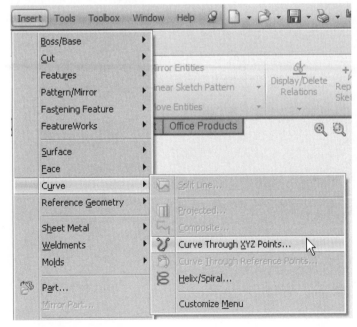

| Task | Command Sequence to Click |
|---|---|

C. Insert the coordinate values.

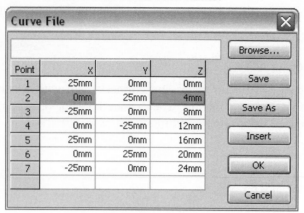

Insert the values as shown to the left.

**Help:** Double-click the cell to enter a value.

D. Accept to view the curve.

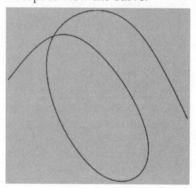

Select **OK** to view the curve shown to the left.

## Step 2: Create a swept boss/base

| Task | Command Sequence to Click |
|---|---|

A. Access the **Plane** function.

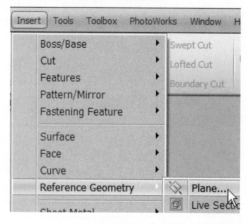

**Insert => Reference Geometry => Plane** as shown to the left

| Task | Command Sequence to Click |
|------|---------------------------|

**B.** Create a new plane.

Set the plane normal to the curve and select **Set origin on curve** as shown to the left

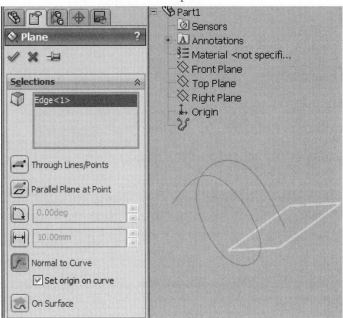

**C.** Create a sweep profile.

Sketch the 5 mm circle on Plane1 a shown to the left.

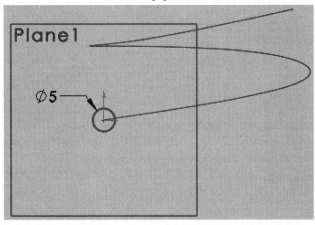

**D.** Create a swept boss/base.

**Features => Swept Boss/Base =>** Select the profile and path as shown to the left.

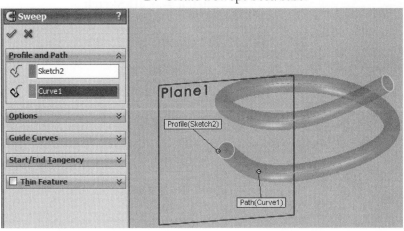

**HANDS-ON FOR TUTORIAL 8–1.** Add five more points to the existing curve and regenerate the curve. Submit screenshots of the curve.

## Tutorial 8–2: Create a 3D Curve Using 3D Sketching

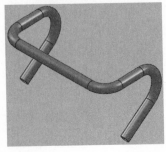

**FIGURE 8.11**
Bicycle handlebars

### Modeling task

Create a sweep using a 3D sketch as the sweep path.

### Modeling synthesis

3D curves can be created using 3D sketching. 3D sketching is similar to 2D sketching in that it uses many of the same tools and relations; but in 3D sketching the user can switch between sketching planes to create a 3D curve. This tutorial covers the ability to create a sweep using a 3D sketch as the sweep path.

### Modeling plan

Create the bicycle handlebars by sweeping a constant cross section along a 3D curve. Figure 8.11 shows the handlebars.

### Design intent

Ignore for this chapter.

### CAD steps

We create the handlebars in three steps:

1. Create the 3D sketch.
2. Create the sweep profile.
3. Create the sweep.

The details of these steps are shown below.

### Step 1: Create the 3D sketch

Task

**A.** Open a new part.

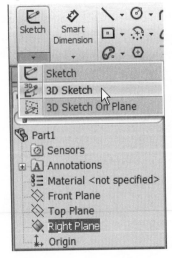

Command Sequence to Click

Open a new part and start a 3D sketch by selecting the tab as shown to the left.
**Sketch => 3D Sketch**

| Task | Command Sequence to Click |
|------|---------------------------|

**B.** Use the **Line** tool.

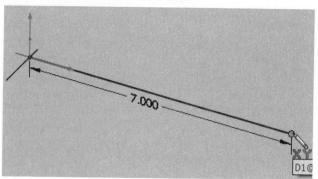

Select the **Line** tool and sketch the line as shown to the left.

**Help:** Ensure that the XY icon appears next to the cursor. This signifies what plane you are sketching in. Use the **TAB** key on the keyboard to toggle between sketch planes.

**C.** Finish the sketch.

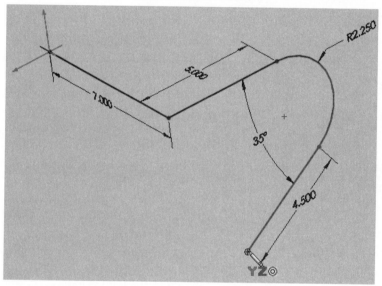

Toggle to the YZ plane and sketch the remaining lines as shown to the left.

**D.** Define the sketch.

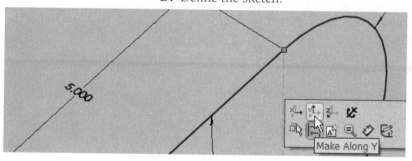

Draw a construction line from the center of the arc to the end of the 5 in. line. Right-click on the construction line and select the **Make Along Y** relation as shown to the left, and exit the sketch.

**Why:** This will fully define the sketch.

## Step 2: Create the sweep profile

| Task | Command Sequence to Click |
|------|---------------------------|

**A.** Create a sketch plane.

Select the 3D sketch and **Insert => Reference Plane => Normal to Curve.** **Help:** The plane will be located at the end of the line closest to where you select it as shown to the left.

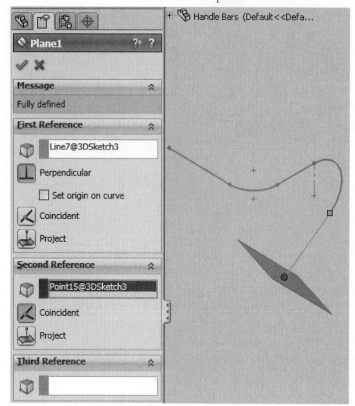

**B.** Sketch the sweep profile.

Open a sketch on the reference plane. Sketch the two concentric circles as shown to the left located on the end of the 3D sketch.

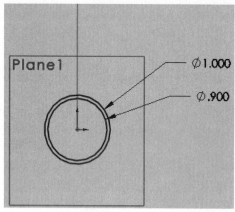

## Step 3:  Create the sweep

| Task | Command Sequence to Click |
|---|---|

**A.** Create a swept boss/base.

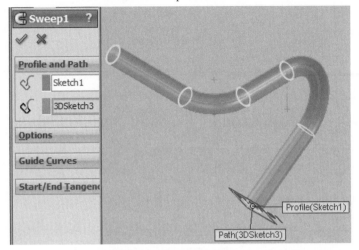

Create a swept boss/base using the circles as the sweep profile and the 3D sketch as the sweep path as shown to the left.

**B.** Mirror the sweep.

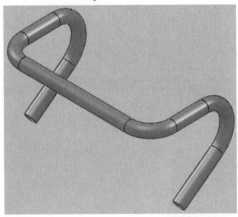

**Features => Mirror** the swept boss about the right plane to complete the handlebars as shown to the left.

> ***HANDS-ON FOR TUTORIAL 8–2.*** Create the handlebars using the composite curve method instead of the 3D sketch method.

# Tutorial 8–3:  Create a 3D Curve Using Composite Curves

### Modeling task

Create a composite curve in an existing part, and use the curve to create a swept boss.

### Modeling synthesis

Composite curves are created by combining curves, sketch geometry, and model edges into one single curve. The composite curve is often used as a guide curve in a loft or as a sweep path. This tutorial covers the steps to create a composite curve and then use the curve as a sweep path.

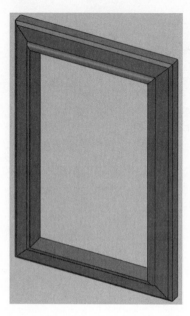

**FIGURE 8.12**
Picture frame with decorative routing

## Modeling plan

Create a picture frame. Create a composite curve by selecting all of the outside edges of the frame. Use the composite curve to create a swept boss to model the decorative routing of the frame as shown in Figure 8.12.

## Design intent

Ignore for this chapter.

## CAD steps

We create the frame in four steps:

1. Create the frame part.
2. Create the composite curve.
3. Create the routing of the frame.
4. Change frame material.

The details of these steps are shown below.

## Step 1: Create the frame part

### Task

A. Create the part shown below.

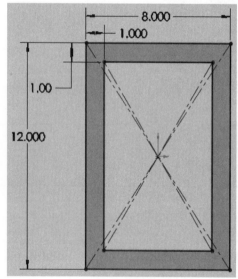

Part Thickness = 0.5 in

### Command Sequence to Click

Sketch and extrude the part from the front plane as shown to the left.
**Help:** Create a **Center Rectangle** that passes through the origin as shown to the left.

## Step 2: Create the composite curve

| Task | Command Sequence to Click |
|---|---|
| A. Select the edges. | Select the four outside edges of frame as shown to the left. |

| Task | Command Sequence to Click |
|---|---|
| B. Create the composite curve. | **Insert => Curve => Composite** as shown to the left => Green check mark to finish |

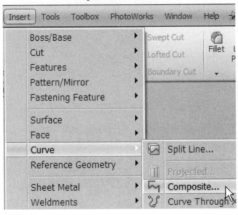

## Step 3: Create the routing of the frame

| Task | Command Sequence to Click |
|---|---|

**A.** Open a sketch on the top plane as shown below.

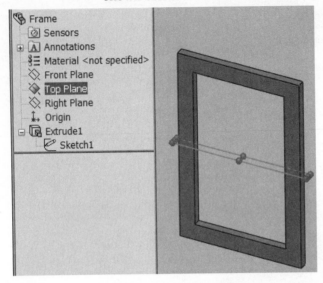

**B.** Sketch the profile.

Sketch the profile of the routing as shown to the left.

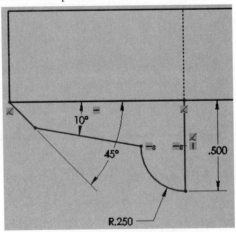

| Task | Command Sequence to Click |
|------|---------------------------|
| C. Create a swept boss/base. | Create a swept boss/base using the composite curve as the sweep path and the sketch as the sweep profile as shown to the left. |

**Step 4:** Change the frame material

| Task | Command Sequence to Click |
|------|---------------------------|
| A. Change the material to teak wood. | Right-click => **Edit Material** => **Woods** => **Teak** => **Apply** => **Close** |

---

***HANDS-ON FOR TUTORIAL 8–3.*** Instead of using a composite curve to create the sweep path for the routing, open a 2D sketch and convert the four outer edges to sketch entities and use those as the sweep path.

---

## Tutorial 8–4: Create a 3D Curve by Projecting a Sketch onto a Curved Face

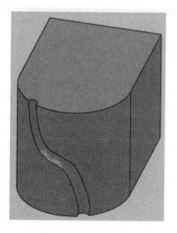

### Modeling task

Use a curve projected on a cylindrical face to cut a feature in the part.

### Modeling synthesis

This tutorial shows how to cut a feature onto a cylindrical face by sweeping a profile along a projected curve.

### Modeling plan

Create a new part. Project a curve onto a cylindrical face, and use it to cut a groove in the part as shown in Figure 8.13.

**FIGURE 8.13**
Engraving a curved face

### Design intent

Ignore for this chapter.

### CAD steps

We create the 3D curve and the face engraving in three steps:

1. Create the part.
2. Create the projected curve.
3. Create the swept cut.

The details of these steps are shown below.

## Step 1: Create the part

### Task

A. Open a new part and create the feature shown below.

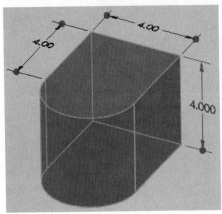

### Command Sequence to Click

Sketch the part on the top plane and extrude it as shown to the left.

## Step 2: Create the projected curve

### Task

A. Sketch a spline.

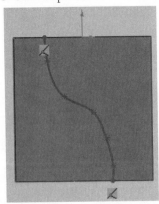

### Command sequence to click

Approximately sketch a spline on the front plane as shown to the left. Make sure the ends of the spline are coincident with the top and bottom edges of the feature. Make sure the spline is one continuous entity.

| Task | Command Sequence to Click |
|------|---------------------------|

**B.** Create a projected curve.

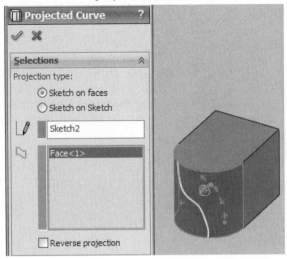

**Insert => Curve => Projected.**
Select the spline and the cylindrical face as shown to the left.
**Help:** Make sure to select the **Sketch on faces** type as shown to the left.

## Step 3: Create the swept cut

| Task | Command Sequence to Click |
|------|---------------------------|

**A.** Sketch a sweep profile.

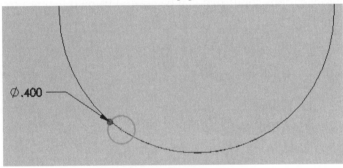

Open a sketch on the top plane, and sketch as shown to the left.
**Help:** Use a **Pierce** relation to locate the center of the circle on the end of the projected curve.

**B.** Create a swept cut.

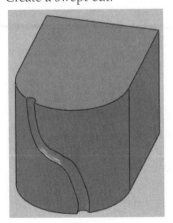

Create a swept cut using the circle as a sweep profile and the projected curve as the sweep path as shown to the left.

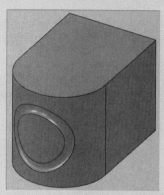

**HANDS-ON FOR TUTORIAL 8–4.** Create a swept cut of the first letter of your name using the same steps as the tutorial. If the letter of your name is self-intersecting (such as K, X, H), break the letter down into multiple sketches and sweep each independently. Submit a screenshot. Figure 8.14 shows the letter O.

**FIGURE 8.14**
Engraving with the letter O

## Tutorial 8–5: Create a 3D Curve Using Projected Curves

### Modeling task

Create a 3D curve from projected curves (2D sketches).

### Modeling synthesis

Projecting two 2D curves from multiple sketch planes creates a 3D curve. This tutorial shows examples of various solids that can be created using different projected sketches and a sweep profile.

### Modeling plan

Each step in this tutorial uses two different 2D sketches on different planes to create a projected 3D curve. After we create the 3D curve, we sweep a circular profile along the 3D curve to create a solid. Case 1 is shown in detail. The remaining cases are illustrated but are not shown in detail; the same steps can be followed as in case 1 in order to accomplish the goal.

### Design intent

Ignore for this chapter.

### CAD steps

We create 3D curves using the following 2D curves:

     Case 1: Use two lines.
     Case 2: Use two circles.
     Case 3: Use two arcs.
     Case 4: Use a line and a circle.
     Case 5: Use a line and an arc.
     Case 6: Use two ellipses.
     Case 7: Use an ellipse and a line.
     Case 8: Use an ellipse and a circle.
     Case 9: Use an ellipse and an arc.
     Case 10: Use two splines.
     Case 11: Use a spline and a line.
     Case 12: Use a spline and a circle.
     Case 13: Use a spline and an ellipse.

The details of these cases are shown below.

## Case 1: Use two lines

| Task | Command Sequence to Click |
|---|---|
| **A.** Sketch the 2D sketches. | Open a new part and set the units to millimeters. Create the sketches as shown to the left. |
| | **Help:** Use the sketch plane as shown in each sketch. |

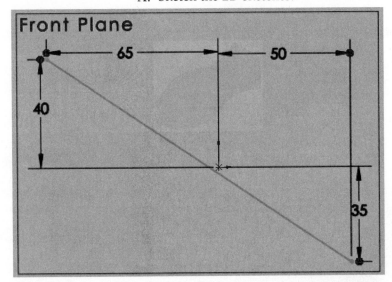

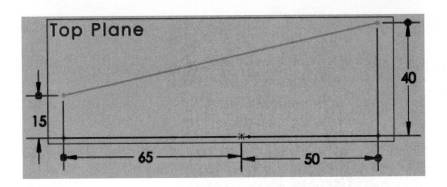

**B.** Open a projected curve.

**Insert => Curve => Projected** as shown to the left

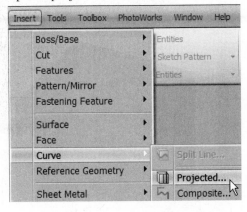

Chapter 8: Curves

371

| Task | Command Sequence to Click |
|---|---|

C. Create a projected curve as shown below.

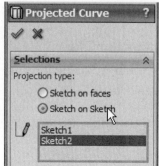 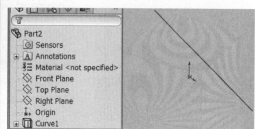

D. Create a swept boss/base.

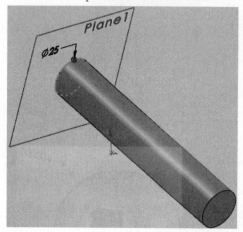

Using a plane normal to the projected curve, sketch a 25 mm circle and sweep it along the projected path as shown to the left.

## Case 2:   Use two circles

| Task | Command Sequence to Click |
|---|---|

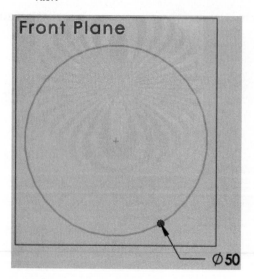

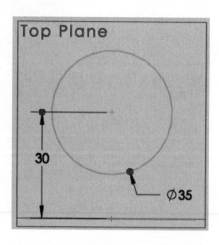

| Task | Command Sequence to Click |
|------|---------------------------|

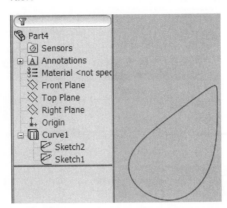 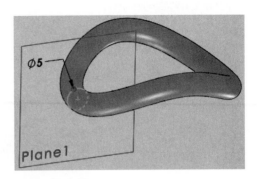

## Case 3: Use two arcs

| Task | Command Sequence to Click |
|------|---------------------------|

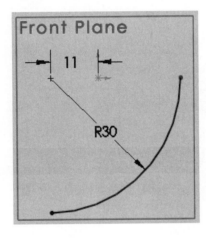 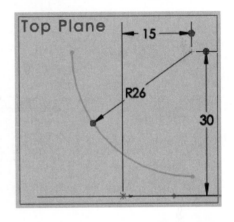

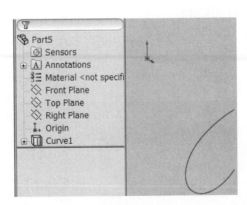 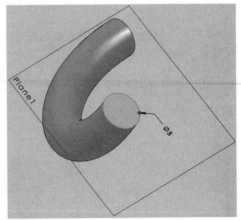

## Case 4: Use a line and a circle

Task

Command Sequence to Click

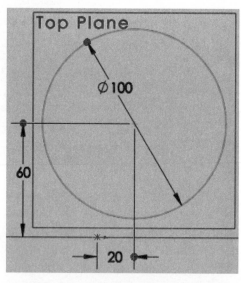

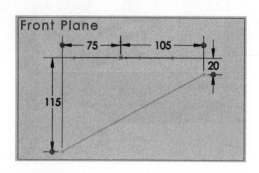

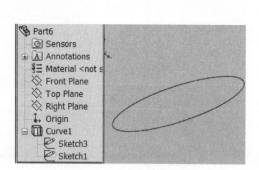

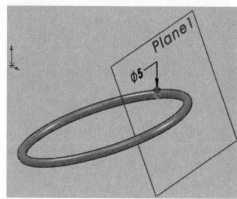

## Case 5: Use a line and an arc

Task

Command Sequence to Click

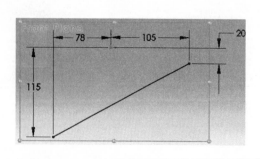

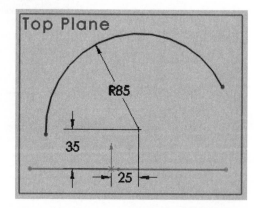

| Task | Command Sequence to Click |
|---|---|
| 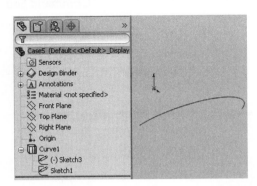 | 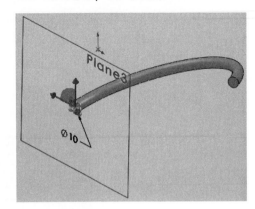 |

## Case 6: Use two ellipses

| Task | Command Sequence to Click |
|---|---|
| | 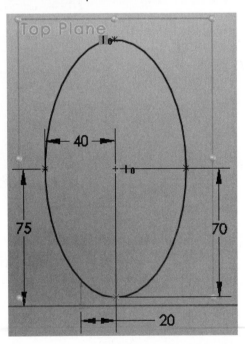 |
| 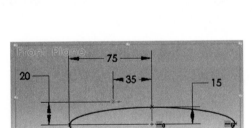 | |
| 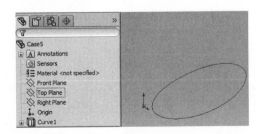 | 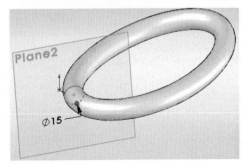 |

## Case 7: Use an ellipse and a line

Task

Command Sequence to Click

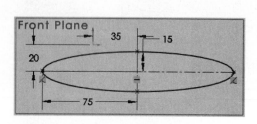

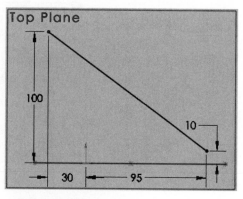

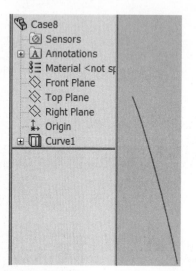

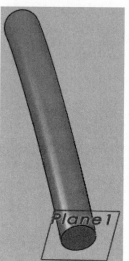

## Case 8: Use an ellipse and a circle

Task

Command Sequence to Click

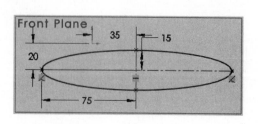

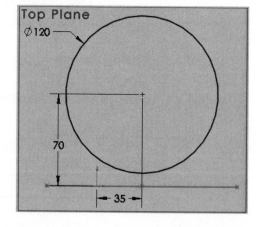

| Task | Command Sequence to Click |
|---|---|
| 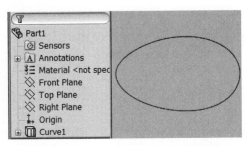 |  |

## Case 9: Use an ellipse and an arc

| Task | Command Sequence to Click |
|---|---|
| | 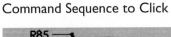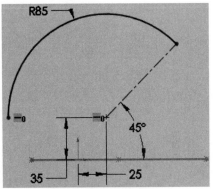 |
| 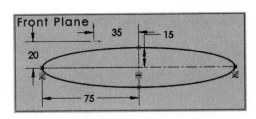 | |
| 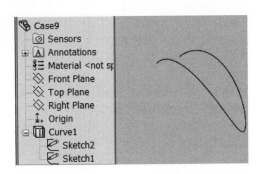 | 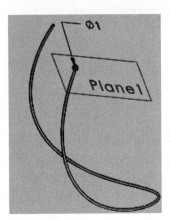 |

## Case 10: Use two splines

| Task | Command Sequence to Click |
|---|---|
| | 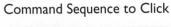 |
| 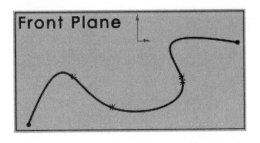 | 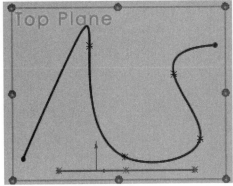 |

| Task | Command Sequence to Click |
|---|---|
| 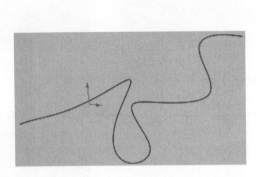 | 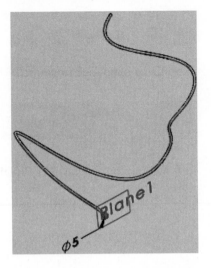 |

## Case 11: Use a spline and a line

| Task | Command Sequence to Click |
|---|---|
| 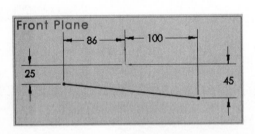 | 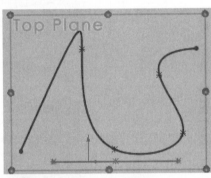 |
| 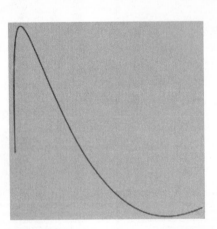 | 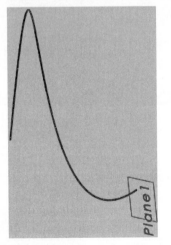 |

## Case 12: Use a spline and a circle

Task

Command Sequence to Click

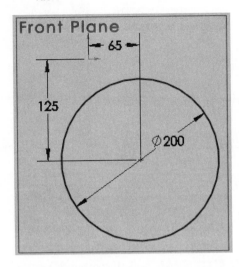

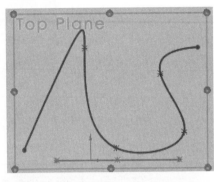

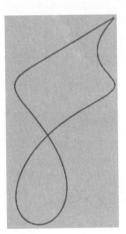

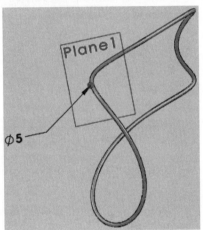

## Case 13: Use a spline and an ellipse

Task

Command Sequence to Click

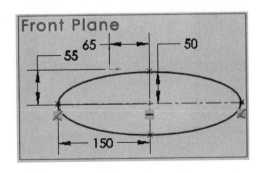

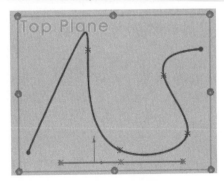

| Task | Command Sequence to Click |
|---|---|
| 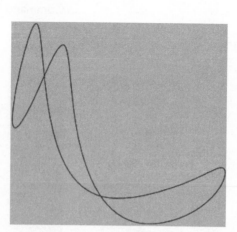 | 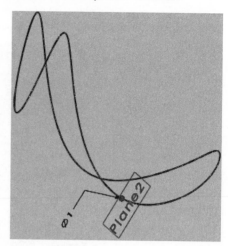 |

---

**HANDS-ON FOR TUTORIAL 8–5.** Create a 3D curve using an ellipse and a parabola. Sweep a circle along the 3D curve for better visualization. Submit screenshots of the two sketches, the 3D curve, and the sweep.

---

## Tutorial 8–6:  Create a Stethoscope Model

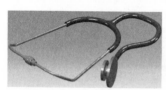

**FIGURE 8.15**
A stethoscope

### Modeling task

Use 2D and 3D curves to create a swept boss as well as revolved features to create a stethoscope model.

### Modeling synthesis

The stethoscope shown in Figure 8.15 is created using 2D and 3D curves.

### Modeling plan

We create the stethoscope using both 2D and 3D curves and swept bosses. The remaining parts are created using revolved features. The features are also mirrored to complete the model.

### Design intent

Ignore for this chapter.

### CAD steps

We create the stethoscope in four steps:

1. Use 2D curves to create the rubber tubing.
2. Use projected curves to create the 3D curve of the metal tubing.
3. Create the earplugs and mirror the features.
4. Create the diaphragm housing.

The details of these steps are shown below.

## Step 1:  Use 2D curves to create the rubber tubing

Task

**A.** Sketch a single tube.

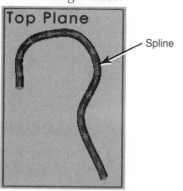

Command Sequence to Click

Approximately sketch the spline on the top plane starting from the origin and sweep a 0.25 in. circular sweep profile along it as shown to the left.
**Help:** Use the front plane to sketch the sweep profile.

**B.** Create the double tube.

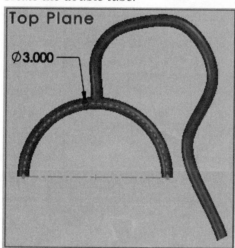

Sweep the same cross section as in Task A along the circular arc shown to the left, and then use a 0.50 in. fillet between the two sweeps as shown to the left.

## Step 2:  Use projected curves to create the 3D curve of the metal tubing

Task

**A.** Create two sketches for a 3D curve.

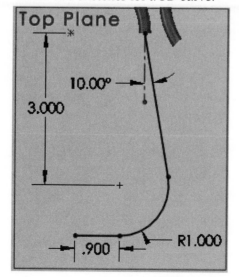

Command Sequence to Click

Sketch the two sketches as shown to the left. Use the planes that are shown for each sketch.

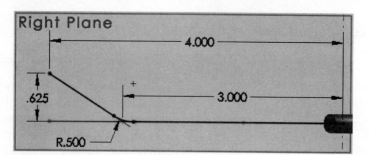

B. Create the 3D curve.

**Insert => Curve => Projected => Sketch on Sketch** as shown to the left => Green check mark to finish

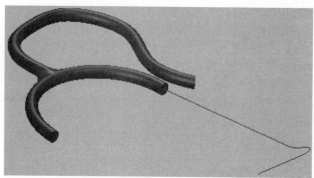

C. Create the metal tubing.

Sweep a 0.125 in. diameter profile along the projected curve as shown to the left.

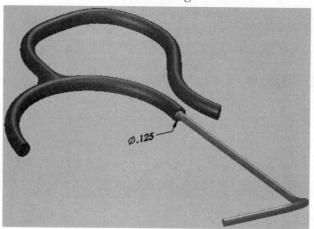

## Step 3: Create the earplugs and mirror the features

| Task | Command Sequence to Click |
|---|---|
| A. Create a reference plane (Plane2) as shown below. | **Insert => Reference Geometry => Plane** => Use the top plane to insert an offset plane 0.625 in. away. Create the sketch shown to the left on the new plane. Also sketch a horizontal centerline (coincident with the horizontal line of the sketch) to use as the revolve axis. |

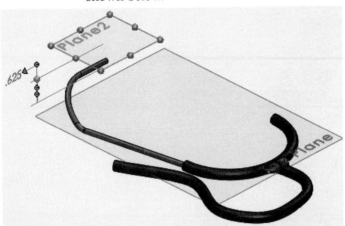

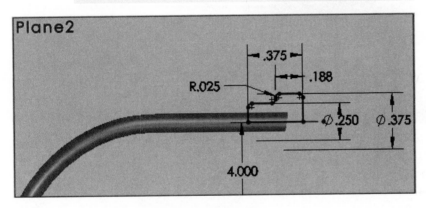

| | |
|---|---|
| B. Revolve the sketch.  | **Revolved Boss/Base** from **Features** tab => Select the axis of revolve as shown to the left => Green check mark to finish. |
| C. Mirror the features. 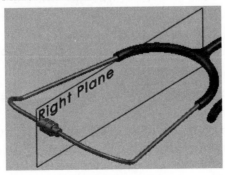 | Mirror the earplug and the metal tubing features about the right plane as shown to the left. |

## Step 4: Create the diaphragm housing

| Task | Command Sequence to Click |
|------|--------------------------|
| A. Sketch the diaphragm housing cross section and revolve it. | Use the top plane to create the sketch as shown to the left and revolve it 360° around its centerline as shown to the left. |

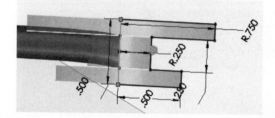

---

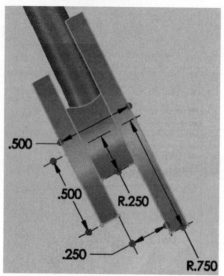

**FIGURE 8.16**
Stethoscope redesign

### *HANDS-ON FOR TUTORIAL 8–6.*
Redesign the stethoscope 3D curve shown in Tasks A and B of Step 2 to make it look more realistic, as shown in Figure 8.16.

---

### INDUSTRY CHAT

This section provides practical insight into how the chapter material is used in industry in the real world and practice. This section summarizes the chat with Mr. Doug Webber (Mechanical Designer and CAD Administrator) of MSD Ignition, the sponsor of this chapter. The structure of the chat follows the chapter sections.

**Chapter Section 8.1:** Introduction

ABE: How much analytic curves versus synthetic curves does MSD Ignition use?

DOUG: Generally, we use synthetic curves more than analytic curves. The majority of our curves create wires. These wires take complex shapes that cannot be modeled via lines and circles.

**Chapter Section 8.2:**   Curve Representation

ABE:  Describe some of the curve modeling problems that MSD Ignition encounters.

DOUG:  Mostly when it comes to curves, we create wires. Our major products are high-performance racing ignitions used in auto racing such as NASCAR and drag racing. I create enclosures for our electronic systems and need to show all major components including the wires.

When you get to the racing world, we need a lot of energy. Some cars use an alcohol nitro methane mix known in the racing world as Top Fuel. It takes a lot of energy from a spark plug to ignite this fuel. In a quarter of a mile driving distance, a top fuel car burns over 8 gallons of fuel. This is not very fuel efficient, but these engines generate in the neighborhood of 7,000 HP.

For our modeling purposes, I use surfaces with curves to make surfaces for enclosures. I use curves and fillets, and do some surfacing to get the shape we want.

**Chapter Section 8.3:**   Line Parametric Equation

ABE:  Is there a specific way of using and trimming lines in your sketches?

DOUG:  For sketching, we use some lines and arcs and use fit splines to connect them. This is an easy way of creating and routing wires. I know the starting point, routing points, and the ending point. So I create lines and/or arcs at these points, connect them with a fit spline and then use these lines and arcs. It is very easy to manipulate the spline shape to create the wire in any shape I want.

**Chapter Section 8.4:**   Circle Parametric Equation

ABE:  Is there a specific way of using and trimming circles in your sketches?

DOUG:  No. If I have to trim something in 3D space, I use a construction line as a **Trim** tool and use the basic **Trim** command.

**Chapter Section 8.5:**   Spline Parametric Equation

ABE:  Do you use splines in your designs? Provide some examples to show their benefits.

DOUG:  Yes. We use splines for surface generation, spline fits, and lofts. If I am lofting a surface between two edges of a model, I need to maintain continuity of these edges. These edges form the two end cross sections of the loft surface. So, I use SolidWorks Convert Entities and then fit a spline to each sketch on each end to create one continuous entity instead of a bunch of line segments. With the two splines, one on each end, it is easy to control the loft.

**Chapter Section 8.6:**   Two-Dimensional Curves

ABE:  Is there a specific way of using and trimming 2D curves in your sketches?

DOUG:  That can be standard. 2D curves are easy to use in sketching and drawings. We use standard trimming tools, and use the spline handles to control the shape. The handles are at every control point of a spline and allow control of both tangent magnitude (weight) and the tangent radial direction (vector) of that point.

*(continue)*

## Chapter Section 8.7:   Three-Dimensional Curves

**ABE:** Do you use 3D curves in modeling at MSD Ignition? Which methods do you use?

**DOUG:** Yes, we do. We use all the methods described in Section 8.7. It all depends on what I do. I use 3D points very little. I can create points on a graph.

3D sketching is my most used method as long as I can break the screen into four views, so I can see. Isometric view is good to grab points from. I use the orthographic views to drag a point along an axis. That makes dragging the point easy.

I have done some composite curves, mainly with wires or sleeving for wires. I may take one of the curves from one of my wires to create the sleeving. Also, if I create a complex wire, I use a composite curve on each end, and then combine and move the curves through the assembly.

I have used the projected curves method multiple times. For example, I use it to create the O-ring for some of our designs. As a matter of fact, our O-ring looks similar to case 2 of Tutorial 8–5.

Projecting a curve onto a surface is a very useful method to create 3D curves. I have used it. We have a clamp that goes over a piece of tubing in an ignition system. The clamp has to feed to the tube. It is the fuel connector. So, we need to cut the O-ring on the clamp. We project the clamp onto a surface. The O-ring runs over the cylinder head. We do custom designs, so we use this method of creating 3D curves.

## Chapter Section 8.8:   Curve Management

**ABE:** Is there a specific way of managing curves in your sketches?

**DOUG:** It is hard to say. We make sure that curves are well formed and continuous. I use primarily fit splines. They are really easy to control. I use line segments to create these splines. If you move the lines or change their lengths, the spline changes. That makes it easy to manage the splines. Fit splines are generally $C^1$ (slope) continuity. Each individual spline is $C^2$ (curvature) continuity. When making splines tangent to each other, that is $C^1$ continuity.

## Others

**ABE:** Any other experience you would like to share with our book readers?

**DOUG:** As for the book readers, the best advice is "explore everything." Lots of times, this is how I learn. Most of what I have done and learned is by exploring commands and going online for help. There is an amazing amount of power in SolidWorks that you can discover if you spend the time to find out what it is capable of doing. Provide students with the basics and let them explore. Everybody figures a different way of doing the same thing.

Another advice is certification. A CSWA (Certified SolidWorks Associate) is good to have; so encourage your students to take the certification exam. Certification most definitely helps get a job. Certified SolidWorks CAD designers give companies an edge. When we talk to engineering contractors, they say, "all of our engineers are SolidWorks certified." We usually use contractors when work gets too much, and we need outside help. For example, we outsource our FEM/FEA jobs.

1. What is the difference between analytic and synthetic curves? Which family is better? Why?

2. Provide one modeling example to illustrate the use of analytic and synthetic curves. Sketch the entities of the sketch, and write down which curves you would use to create them.

3. If a parametric curve has $u$ limits of $u_{min}$ and $u_{max}$, what is the $u$ value at its midpoint?

4. Use the tangent vector Eq. (8.3) to find the curve slopes in the XY, XZ, and YZ planes.

5. Find the parametric equation of the line connecting point $(2, 1, 0)$ to point $(-2, -5, 0)$. Find the line midpoint and its tangent vector. Sketch the line, and show the endpoints and the parameterization direction on the sketch.

6. For the line of Problem 5, find the coordinates of the points located at $u = 0.25$ from both ends of the lines.

7. Reverse the parameterization direction of the line of Problem 5, and re-solve the problem.

8. Repeat Problems 5 and 6 but for points $(1, 3, 7)$ and $(-2, -4, -6)$.

9. Find the line slopes of Problem 8 in the XY, XZ, and YZ planes.

10. Find the equation of a circle with a diameter of 3.0 in. and a center at $(1, -2)$. Find the four quarter points on the circle. Use Eq. (8.12). What are the tangent vectors and slopes at these points?

11. Repeat Problem 10 but for a circle with a radius of 1 in. and a center at the origin.

12. Use both Eqs. (8.12) and (8.13) to write the equation of an arc whose diameter is 1.5 in. and that is located in the third quadrant with a center at the origin.

13. A spline is given by:

$$P(u) = \begin{bmatrix} x(u) \\ y(u) \end{bmatrix} = \begin{bmatrix} 1 + 4u - u^2 \\ 2 - u + u^2 \end{bmatrix} \quad 0 \leq u \leq 1$$

Find the endpoints and the midpoint of the spline. Also, find the tangent vector and the slope at the midpoint. Using your CAD/CAM system, create the spline defined by the above equation. Submit a screenshot of the spline. *Hint:* Use enough points to create a smooth spline.

14. A spline is given by:

$$P(u) = \begin{bmatrix} x(u) \\ y(u) \end{bmatrix} = \begin{bmatrix} -2 - 2u^2 \\ -1 + u - 2u^2 \end{bmatrix} \quad 0 \leq u \leq 1$$

Find the endpoints and the midpoint of the spline. Also, find the tangent vector and the slope at the midpoint. Using your CAD/CAM system, create the spline defined by the above equation. Submit a screenshot of the spline.

*Hint:* Use enough points to create a smooth spline.

15. A spline is given by:

$$P(u) = \begin{bmatrix} x(u) \\ y(u) \end{bmatrix} = \begin{bmatrix} 2u \\ 2 - u \end{bmatrix} \quad 0 \le u \le 1$$

What shape is this spline? Why? Verify your answer by creating it on your CAD/CAM system. Submit a screenshot of the spline points and its shape.

16. Find a three-dimensional curve of your choice, and create it using the 3D points method. Does this method have any limitations on what kind of a 3D curve you can create? Discuss the limitations in detail, if any.

17. Find a three-dimensional curve of your choice, and create it using the 3D sketching method. Does this method have any limitations on what kind of a 3D curve you can create? Discuss the limitations in detail, if any.

18. Find a three-dimensional curve of your choice, and create it using the composite curve method. Does this method have any limitations on what kind of a 3D curve you can create? Discuss the limitations in detail, if any.

19. Find a three-dimensional curve of your choice, and create it using the projected curve method. Does this method have any limitations on what kind of a 3D curve you can create? Discuss the limitations in detail, if any.

20. Find a three-dimensional curve of your choice, and create it using the projected curve on a model face method. Does this method have any limitations on what kind of a 3D curve you can create? Discuss the limitations in detail, if any.

21. Figure 8.17 shows the $(x, y, z)$ coordinates of 3D points that define the two edges (profiles) of a laboratory chair. Create each edge. Sweep a circle with radius of ½ in. along each curve. Submit screenshots of the two 3D curves, the sweep parameters, and the final sweep result. All dims are in inches.

| −7 | 0 | 0 |
|---|---|---|
| −7 | 1 | 0.5 |
| −7 | 2 | 0.5 |
| −7 | 5 | 0 |
| −7 | 9 | 1 |
| −5.5 | 9 | 3 |
| −5.5 | 8.5 | 5 |
| −5.5 | 9 | 10 |

Curve for Edge 1

| 7 | 0 | 0 |
|---|---|---|
| 7 | 1 | 0.5 |
| 7 | 2 | 0.5 |
| 7 | 5 | 0 |
| 7 | 9 | 1 |
| 5.5 | 9 | 3 |
| 5.5 | 8.5 | 5 |
| 5.5 | 9 | 10 |

Curve for Edge 2

**FIGURE 8.17**
3D points of the edges of a laboratory chair

22. Figure 8.18 shows the front and top sketches of half the profile of a skateboard. Use your CAD/CAM system to create the 3D curve that represents the skateboard profile. Sweep a circle with radius of ½ in. along the curve. Submit screenshots of the planar curves, the 3D curve, the sweep parameters, and the final sweep result. All dims are in inches.

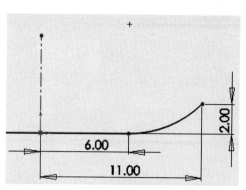

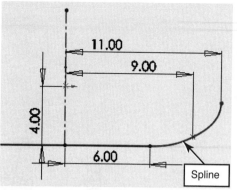

Front plane sketch (symmetric about vertical axis)　　Top plane sketch (symmetric about vertical axis)

**FIGURE 8.18**
2D projections of a skateboard profile

23. Figure 8.19 shows the front and right sketches of bicycle helmet. Use your CAD/CAM system to create the 3D curve that represents the helmet profile. Sweep a circle with radius of ½ in. along the curve. Submit screenshots of the planar curves, the 3D curve, the sweep parameters, and the final sweep result. All dims are in inches.

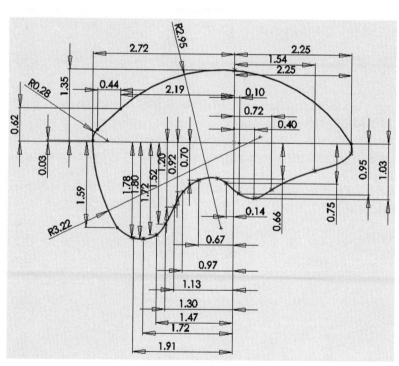

Front plane sketch

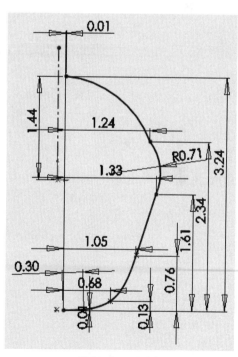

Right plane sketch

**FIGURE 8.19**
2D projections of a bicycle helmet profile

24. Figure 8.20 shows the front and right sketches of the profile of a weed whacker debris shield. Use your CAD/CAM system to create the 3D curve that represents the profile. Sweep a circle with radius of ½ in. along the curve. Submit screenshots of the planar curves, the 3D curve, the sweep parameters, and the final sweep result. All dims are in inches.

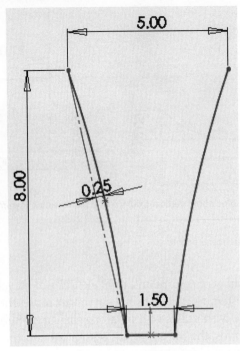

Front plane sketch

Right plane sketch
Note: This arc passes matches the two endpoints
of the front plane sketch and has the same
distance of 0.25 in. from the vertical line

**FIGURE 8.20**
2D projections of the profile of a weed whacker debris shield

25. Figure 8.21 shows the front and left sketches of the profile of an S-shaped chair. Use your CAD/CAM system to create the 3D curve that represents the profile. Sweep a circle with radius of ½ in. along the curve. Submit screenshots of the planar curves, the 3D curve, the sweep parameters, and the final sweep result. All dims are in mm.

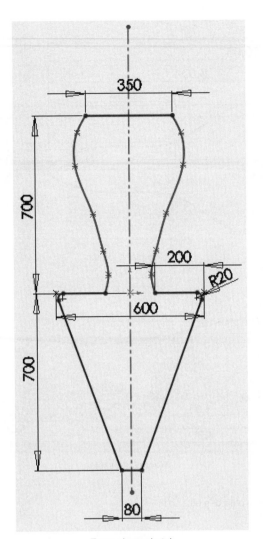

Front plane sketch

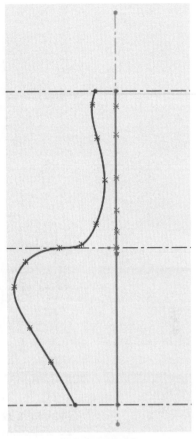

Left plane sketch
Note: Sketch this spline as closely as possible as
shown here

**FIGURE 8.21**
2D projections of the profile of an S-shaped chair

26. Figure 8.22 shows the top and front sketches of the profile of a bike seat. Use your CAD/CAM system to create the 3D curve that represents the profile. Sweep a circle with radius of ½ in. along the curve. Submit screenshots of the planar curves, the 3D curve, the sweep parameters, and the final sweep result. All dims are in inches.

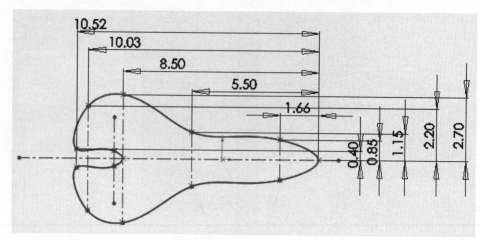

Top plane sketch

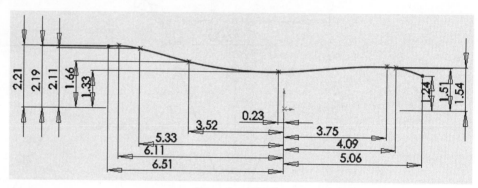

Front plane sketch

**FIGURE 8.22**
2D projections of the profile of a bike seat

# Surfaces

## 9.1 Introduction

Even with the modeling power that the features and curves provide, they are still incapable of handling all the modeling problems and scenarios we encounter. Even if they were capable, they would be very cumbersome to use. Consider, for example, modeling an intricate computer mouse, a table spoon, a hair dryer, a shoe, or a sports car body. This class of objects, called free-form parts, is characterized by having free-form surfaces of intricate shapes. Surfaces then are the best modeling technique to use to create the solid models of these parts.

Surfaces build on curves, from both the theory and the modeling aspects. Creating surfaces requires the creation of curves first, as illustrated in the tutorials of this chapter. We view surfaces as extensions of curves. Surface equations, as we cover in this chapter, extend the parametric representation of curves. Thus, surfaces are classified in the same way as are curves: analytic and synthetic. Examples of analytic surfaces are plane, ruled surface, surface of revolution, and sweep. An example of synthetic surfaces is spline surface.

Combining 3D curves and surfaces provides the most sophisticated and advanced modeling technique, which enables you to create the solid model of any part you may imagine. However, before you get carried away and let your design imagination run wild, you must always ask yourself this very basic question: Can the part be manufactured? A "yes" answer to this question is not enough. A follow-up question is, At what cost? These two questions explain why about 80% of the parts in practice can be modeled using extrusions and revolves, which we covered in Chapter 1.

## 9.2 Surfaces

Figure 9.1 shows all the surfaces you can create in SolidWorks. A **surface** is defined as a thin planar or nonplanar sheet that does not have a thickness. Creating a surface in itself is not useful. Surfaces are an intermediate step between creating curves and solids. We use them to create solids (features) that curves cannot create. Like features, surfaces are always listed in the features tree (**FeatureManager design tree**). If you were to expand a **Surface** node in the tree, you would see the sketch that defines the surface.

**FIGURE 9.1**
Available surfaces

If we would like to master surface creation, we should be able to answer three fundamental questions:

1. What are the available surfaces that a CAD/CAM system offers for modeling parts?
2. What is the input required to create each surface?
3. Which surface should we use for a given modeling problem?

Figure 9.1 provides the answer to the first question. Table 9.1 answers the other two questions, and it shows a simple, basic example of each surface. Keep in mind that the third question may have multiple answers; one of them is always the best answer. For example, we may use a loft or a sweep. However, if the surface has a constant cross

**TABLE 9.1 Available Surfaces**

| No. | Surface | Input (Sketch) | Resulting Surface | When to Use in Modeling? |
|---|---|---|---|---|
| 1 | Extrusion | Cross section and a thickness | | • Use for surfaces with constant cross section<br>• If needed, break surface into sub-surfaces, each with a constant cross section. |
| 2 | Revolve | Cross section, an axis of revolution, and an angle of revolution | | • Use for surfaces that are axisymmetric<br>• If needed, break surface into sub-surfaces, each is axisymmetric |
| 3 | Sweep | Linear sweep: Cross section and a line as a path | | • Use for surfaces with constant cross section (CS) along a linear direction (path shown to the left) that may or may not be perpendicular to the cross section<br>• If the path is perpendicular to the cross section, the linear sweep surface becomes an extrusion |
| | | Nonlinear sweep: Cross section and a curve as a path<br>Curve | | • Use for surfaces with constant cross section (CS) along a nonlinear direction (path shown to the left) that may or may not be perpendicular to the cross section |

TABLE 9.1 Continued

| 4 | Loft | Linear loft: At least two cross sections (profiles) | | • Use for surfaces with variable cross section along a given direction<br>• The cross sections are blended linearly from one end to the other |
|---|---|---|---|---|
| | | Nonlinear loft: At least two cross sections (profiles) and a curve as a guide curve (path) | | • Use for surfaces with variable cross section along a given direction<br>• The cross sections are blended nonlinearly from one end to the other along the guide curve |
| 5 | Boundary | A set of connected curves in two directions | | • Use when you need to blend a surface between connected curves. It requires curves in two directions |
| 6 | Loft (same as in No. 4, but different case) | Two or more curves, with or without guide curves | | • Use when you need to blend a surface between connected curves. It may or may not use guide curves |
| 7 | Filled | A set of planar or nonplanar curves defining a closed boundary | | • Use when you need to create a surface patch defined by a closed boundary defined by multiple curves |

**TABLE 9.1** *Continued*

| 8 | Planar | A sketch consisting of curves defining a closed boundary, i.e., the curves are planar | | • Use when you need to create planar surfaces bounded by certain boundary |
|---|---|---|---|---|
| 9 | Knit | A set of surfaces to knit (here we knot a surface fill on the top with a loft surface on the sides) | | • Use when you need to combine (knit) a set of surface patches into one surface. The resulting surface may or may not be closed<br>• Use the knit surface to cut a solid block, thus converting the knit surface to a solid with the same shape |

section along a curve, sweep is better to use because it requires fewer steps to create the surface. If the surface has a variable cross section, a loft is better to use.

To learn surfaces quickly, keep in mind that the majority of them parallel features, with the difference that they are hollow. For example, the first four surfaces shown in Figure 9.1 parallel extruded boss, revolved boss, swept boss, and lofted boss, respectively. The tutorials in this chapter provide some modeling examples.

The other surfaces shown in Figure 9.1 and not covered in Table 9.1 are dealt with in the tutorials of the chapter.

## 9.3 Using Surfaces in Solid Modeling

The goal of creating surfaces is not to create surfaces, but to use them to create complex features and solids. How can we do that? There are two methods. The first method is to thicken a surface to create a solid and is shown as the **Thicken** icon on the far right of the **Surface** menu in Figure 9.1. The user specifies a thickness. You need to be aware that, depending on the surface shape and the thickness value you specify, the thicken operation may fail and the solid may not be created. Understanding how the thicken operation works explains its potential failure. When you thicken the surface, conceptually the CAD/CAM system creates a copy of the surface and displaces it by the thickness amount. The cross sections of the thickened surface (solid) must be perpendicular to the surface profile and nonintersecting, as shown in Figure 9.2. If the thicken operation results in intersecting cross sections, the operation fails. Intersecting cross sections usually happen if the surface has abrupt sharp changes, as shown in Figure 9.2A. Figure 9.2B depicts the SolidWorks error message when the thicken operation fails.

The second method of using surfaces to create solids is to have a surface cut a solid (feature) to carve out the solid we want. If the surface is open (like a sheet), it splits the solid into two; we keep the part we want and throw away the other part. In this case, make sure that the surface extends beyond the solid faces from all directions. If the surface is

**FIGURE 9.2**
Failure of surface thicken operation

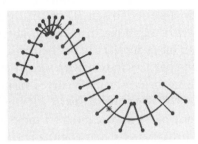

(A) A surface with sharp changes

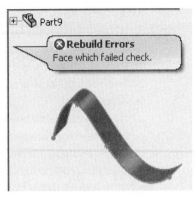

(B) Failure error message

closed (like a closed shell), it carves out part of the solid. In this case, make sure that the surface is completely enclosed within the solid we want to cut. We usually enclose the surface shell within a box. Figure 9.3 shows examples. The chapter tutorials demonstrate how to use surfaces to create solids.

**FIGURE 9.3**
Using a surface to cut a solid

Before split      After split

(A) Split a solid with a surface sheet

Before carving

(B) Cut a surface with a closed surface shell

After carving
Note: On the left is a
sphere surface shell.
Above is a sphere solid

## 9.4 Surface Visualization

If surfaces extend curves, they must use the parametric formulation, and they do. The difference is that they use two parameters $(u, v)$. Figure 9.4 shows a surface patch with the two parameters. Like curves, each parameter has its minimum and maximum

**FIGURE 9.4**
Surface visualization

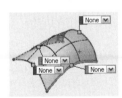
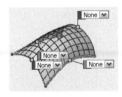
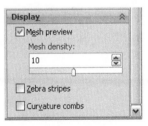

3 × 3 mesh      3 × 3 mesh      Control mesh size

(A) Surface mesh

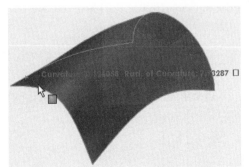

(B) Surface curvature

Click this sequence (it is a toggle) to show/hide surface curvature:

**View => Display => Curvature**

**Help:** As you move the mouse over the surface, Solid-Works displays the curvature and the radius of curvature as shown to the left. The curvature is the inverse of the radius of curvature (shown to the left), i.e.,

$$\text{Curvature} = \frac{1}{\rho}$$

values, and each parameter has a parameterization direction. Mathematically, think that the surface equation maps a rectangle defined by the parametric limits, in the *u-v* parametric space, to a surface patch in the Cartesian 3D modeling space shown in Figure 9.4.

There are two ways to visualize surfaces in 3D space: *u-v* grid and curvature. The *u-v* grid shows constant *u* and *v* curves as a mesh, as shown in the loft, boundary, and filled surfaces of Table 9.1. The *u* × *v* mesh density can be controlled as it substitutes *u* and *v* values in the surface equation and displays the constant *u* and *v* curves. Note that the surface patch boundary curves influence the nearby mesh curves the most. That influence dies out or fades away as the mesh curve gets farther away. Figure 9.4 shows sample surface meshes. You can control the size of the surface mesh for some surfaces in SolidWorks (e.g., a boundary surface). Figure 9.4A shows a coarse and a fine mesh. You control the mesh size in the **Display** section of the boundary surface pane on the left of the screen. You specify the mesh density by typing a value or using the slider shown in Figure 9.4A.

The display of a surface curvature is a topological map shown in color to help demonstrate how the surface curves and twists in space. Figure 9.4B shows an example.

## 9.5 Surface Representation

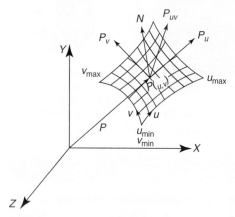

**FIGURE 9.5**
Parametric surface patch

CAD/CAM software uses parametric equations to represent surfaces. A surface equation uses two parameters (e.g., *u* and *v*) to describe the (*x*, *y*, *z*) coordinates of a point. Any point *P* on the surface is located (defined) by two values of the *u* and *v* parameters. Figure 9.5 shows the parametric representation of a surface. Each of the parameters *u* and *v* starts with a minimum value at one corner of the surface and finishes with a maximum value at the opposite corner. The parameter increases in value from the minimum value to the maximum one, thus defining the parameterization direction of the surface, in both *u* and *v* directions, as indicated by the arrows shown on the surface in Figure 9.5. The parameters have their lowest values typically at the bottom left corner of the surface patch, as shown in Figure 9.5.

Any point *P* on the surface is defined by its position vector **P** that is a function of *u* and *v*, that is,

$$P = \mathbf{P}(u, v) \qquad u_{min} < u < u_{max}, v_{min} < v < v_{max} \qquad (9.1)$$

Alternatively, point *P* is defined by its (*x*, *y*, *z*) coordinates. Thus,

$$P = \begin{bmatrix} x \\ y \\ z \end{bmatrix} = \begin{bmatrix} x(u, v) \\ y(u, v) \\ z(u, v) \end{bmatrix} \quad u_{min} < u < u_{max}, v_{min} < v < v_{max} \qquad (9.2)$$

A point on a surface has four vectors: two tangent vectors, one in each direction (**P**$_u$ and **P**$_v$), a normal vector **N**, and a twist vector **P**$_{uv}$. The tangent vector $P_u$ in the *u* direction at any point on the surface (Figure 9.5) is given by:

$$\mathbf{P}_u = \frac{\partial P}{\partial u} = \begin{bmatrix} x_u \\ y_u \\ z_u \end{bmatrix} \quad u_{min} < u < u_{max}, v_{min} < v < v_{max} \qquad (9.3)$$

Similarly, the tangent vector $P_v$ in the *v* direction is given by:

$$\mathbf{P}_v = \frac{\partial P}{\partial v} = \begin{bmatrix} x_v \\ y_v \\ z_v \end{bmatrix} \quad u_{min} < u < u_{max}, v_{min} < v < v_{max} \qquad (9.4)$$

We explain the twist vector concept as follows. A tangent vector measures how a surface changes in the $u$ or the $v$ direction, that is, if you follow the surface in one direction only. For example, $P_u$ shows how the surface $v =$ constant curves change in the $u$ direction. Similarly, $P_v$ shows how the surface $u =$ constant curves change in the $v$ direction. The twist vector measures the change of the tangent vector; that is, $P_{uv}$ measures the change of $P_u$ in the $v$ direction, and $P_{vu}$ measures the change of $P_v$ in the $u$ direction. Mathematically, we express this by this equation:

$$P_{uv} = P_{vu} = \frac{\partial^2 P}{\partial u \partial v} = \begin{bmatrix} x_{uv} \\ y_{uv} \\ z_{uv} \end{bmatrix} \quad u_{min} < u < u_{max}, v_{min} < v < v_{max} \quad (9.5)$$

The normal vector $N$ to the surface at a point is perpendicular to the plane formed by the two surface tangent vectors at the point. Thus, we can write:

$$N = P_u \times P_v \quad u_{min} < u < u_{max}, v_{min} < v < v_{max} \quad (9.6)$$

We can also use $N = P_v \times P_u$. The difference is a minus sign. CAD/CAM software uses one form consistently.

These four surface vectors provide ample insight into the surface behavior. Other surface calculations include the radius of curvature and the curvature, which we do not cover here. The relation between the curvature, $\chi$, and the radius of curvature, $\rho$, is given by:

$$\chi = \frac{1}{\rho} \quad (9.7)$$

## 9.6 Plane Parametric Equation

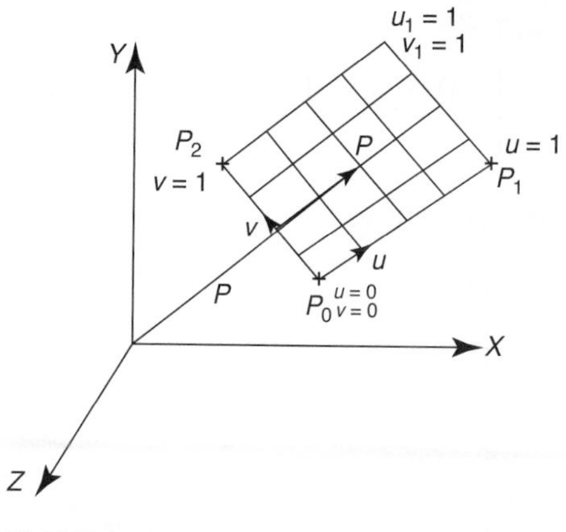

FIGURE 9.6
Parametric plane

Figure 9.6 shows the parametric representation of a plane defined by three points, $P_0$, $P_1$, and $P_2$. The parameterization directions of the plane are shown in the figure. The parametric equation of this plane is given (in vector form) by:

$$P = P(u, v) = P_0 + u(P_1 - P_0) + v(P_2 - P_0)$$
$$0 \le u \le 1, 0 \le v \le 1 \quad (9.8)$$

or (in scalar form),

$$P = P(u, v) = \begin{bmatrix} x(u, v) \\ y(u, v) \\ z(u, v) \end{bmatrix} = \begin{bmatrix} x_0 + u(x_1 - x_0) + v(x_2 - x_0) \\ y_0 + u(y_1 - y_0) + v(y_2 - y_0) \\ z_0 + u(z_1 - z_0) + v(z_2 - z_0) \end{bmatrix}$$
$$0 \le u \le 1, 0 \le v \le 1 \quad (9.9)$$

Using Eqs. (9.3) and (9.4), the tangent vectors of the plane are given by:

$$P_u = \begin{bmatrix} x_u \\ y_u \\ z_u \end{bmatrix} = \begin{bmatrix} x_1 - x_0 \\ y_1 - y_0 \\ z_1 - z_0 \end{bmatrix} \quad (9.10)$$

$$P_v = \begin{bmatrix} x_v \\ y_v \\ z_v \end{bmatrix} = \begin{bmatrix} x_2 - x_0 \\ y_2 - y_0 \\ z_2 - z_0 \end{bmatrix} \quad (9.11)$$

Equations (9.10) and (9.11) show that the tangent vectors are constant (independent of $u$ and $v$), as expected.

Using Eq. (9.5), the twist vector of the surface is zero because both tangent vectors of the plane as given by Eqs. (9.10) and (9.11) are independent of $v$. Thus,

$$P_{uv} = \begin{bmatrix} 0 \\ 0 \\ 0 \end{bmatrix} \tag{9.12}$$

Using Eq. (9.6), the normal vector to the plane is given by:

$$N = \begin{vmatrix} i & j & k \\ x_1 - x_0 & y_1 - y_0 & z_1 - z_0 \\ x_2 - x_0 & y_2 - y_0 & z_2 - z_0 \end{vmatrix} \tag{9.13}$$

The determinant shown in Eq. (9.13) is the result of the cross product shown in Eq. (9.6). You may need to consult a book on linear algebra to refresh your memory. We defer evaluating the determinant when we have a specific problem. Keep in mind that the normal to the plane at any point is the same, that is, constant. Thus, Eq. (9.13) produces a vector with a constant direction because it is independent of $u$ and $v$.

The elegance of the parametric representation is that it is independent of the dimensionality of the modeling space whether it is 2D ($x$ and $y$ coordinates only) or 3D ($x, y$, and $z$ coordinates). In other words, use $z = 0$ in the 3D equations and you get 2D modeling.

---

**Example 9.1**   Find the parametric equation of a plane passing through the three points $P_0$ (−3, 2, 1), $P_1$ (0, −4, 2), and $P_2$ (4, 0, 7). Find the plane midpoint and all its vectors.

**Solution**   Using Eq. (9.9), the plane parametric equation is:

$$P = P(u, v) = \begin{bmatrix} x(u, v) \\ y(u, v) \\ z(u, v) \end{bmatrix} = \begin{bmatrix} -3 + 3u + 7v \\ 2 - 6u - 2v \\ 1 + u + 6v \end{bmatrix} \quad 0 \le u \le 1, 0 \le v \le 1 \tag{9.14}$$

Differentiating Eq. (9.14) with respect to $u$ and $v$, the tangent vectors are:

$$P_u = \begin{bmatrix} x_u \\ y_u \\ z_u \end{bmatrix} = \begin{bmatrix} 3 \\ -6 \\ 1 \end{bmatrix} \tag{9.15}$$

$$P_v = \begin{bmatrix} x_v \\ y_v \\ z_v \end{bmatrix} = \begin{bmatrix} 7 \\ -2 \\ 6 \end{bmatrix} \tag{9.16}$$

The twist vector is given by Eq. (9.12). Using Eq. (9.13), the normal vector is:

$$N = \begin{vmatrix} i & j & k \\ 3 & -6 & 1 \\ 7 & -2 & 6 \end{vmatrix} = -34i - 11j + 36k \tag{9.17}$$

The midpoint of the line occurs at $u = 0.5$ and $v = 0.5$. Thus, substituting in Eq. (9.14), it is:

$$\begin{bmatrix} 3.5 \\ -2 \\ 4.5 \end{bmatrix}$$

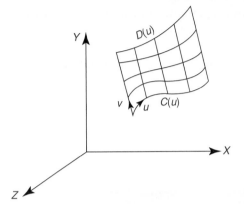

**FIGURE 9.7**
Parametric ruled surface

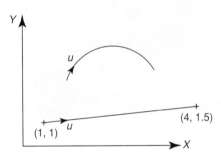

**FIGURE 9.8**
Ruled surface rails

---

> ***HANDS-ON FOR EXAMPLE 9.1.*** Find the plane equation if $P_2$ becomes $P_0$ and vice versa.

## 9.7 Ruled Surface Parametric Equation

A ruled surface interpolates two planar curves linearly in the $v$ direction, as shown in Figure 9.7. The two curves are known as the rails of the surface. The parameterization direction of the two curves should be the same. It defines the $u$ direction of the ruled surface. The $u$ limits of the two curves should be the same. The parametric equation of the ruled surface is given by:

$$P = P(u, v) = (1 - v)C(u) + vD(u)$$
$$u_{min} \leq u \leq u_{max}, 0 \leq v \leq 1 \qquad (9.18)$$

The surface vectors can easily be determined once Eq. (9.18) has a specific form.

---

**Example 9.2**   Find the equation of the ruled surface connecting a spline and a line shown in Figure 9.8. Use Eq. (9.18) as the spline equation. The line connects the two points $P_0(1, 1)$ and $P_1(4, 1.5)$. Find the midpoint of the surface.

**Solution**   Using the two points, the line equation is:

$$P(u) = \begin{bmatrix} x(u) \\ y(u) \end{bmatrix} = \begin{bmatrix} 1 + 3u \\ 1 + 0.5u \end{bmatrix} \quad 0 \leq u \leq 1 \qquad (9.19)$$

Note that both rails have the same parameterization direction and the same $u$ limits. Let us use the line as rail $C(u)$ and the spline as rail $D(u)$. Thus, Eq. (9.18) gives:

$$P(u, v) = \begin{bmatrix} x(u, v) \\ y(u, v) \end{bmatrix} = \begin{bmatrix} 1 + 3u + v - 3uv + 3u^2v - 2u^3v \\ 1 + 0.5u + v + 2.5uv - 3u^2v \end{bmatrix}$$
$$0 \leq u \leq 1, 0 \leq v \leq 1 \qquad (9.20)$$

The midpoint of the surface is located at $(0.5, 0.5)$. Substituting these $u$ and $v$ values in Eq. (9.20) gives:

$$P(0.5, 0.5) = \begin{bmatrix} x(0.5, 0.5) \\ y(0.5, 0.5) \end{bmatrix} = \begin{bmatrix} 2.5 \\ 2 \end{bmatrix}$$

---

> ***HANDS-ON FOR EXAMPLE 9.2.*** Find the surface vectors. Evaluate them at the surface midpoint.

## 9.8 Surface Management

After you create surfaces, you can manage and manipulate them in different ways. You can investigate their curvatures and change their appearances by assigning them materials. Surfaces are harder than curves to manipulate manually.

## 9.9 Tutorials Overview

The theme for the tutorials in this chapter is to get you to practice creating and using surfaces. The tutorials show how to create surfaces and how to use them to create solids. They also demonstrate how to thicken a surface to create a solid, how to split a solid with a surface, and how to carve a solid out of a block using a closed knit surface. This chapter is coauthored with the assistance of a Garmin engineer, Garmin International, with headquarters in Olathe, Kansas, USA (www.garmin.com), and other offices in Europe and Asia. Garmin is the lead manufacturer of GPS (global positioning system) products, including the navigation systems with maps used in cars. We chat with Mr. John Whiteside, CAD Manager at Garmin, in the Industry Chat. Figure 9.9 shows sample Garmin products.

(A) Garmin Dakota 10 GPS
(Actual product)

(B) Garmin Dakota 10 GPS
(SolidWorks model)

**FIGURE 9.9**
Sample products (Courtesy of Garmin International, Inc.)

## Tutorial 9–1: Learn Surface Modeling and Operations

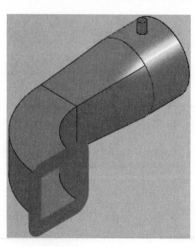

Modeling task

Use the surface commands to create the air duct surfaces shown in Figure 9.10.

Modeling synthesis

This tutorial covers the basic surface operations and types of modeling.

Modeling plan

The model is created using the basic surface commands.

Design intent

Ignore for this chapter.

**FIGURE 9.10**
Air duct surfaces

CAD steps

We create the air duct surfaces in nine steps:

1.  Initiate the **Surfaces** command tool.
2.  Create an extruded surface.
3.  Create a revolved surface.
4.  Trim surface.
5.  Thicken surface.
6.  Create a lofted surface.
7.  Create a swept surface.
8.  Create a knit surface.
9.  Create radiate surfaces.

The details of these steps are shown below.

## Step 1: Initiate the Surfaces command tool

### Task

A.  Open a new part and save it as *tutorial9.1*.

B.  Open the **Surfaces** command tool.

### Command Sequence to Click

**File => New => Part => OK**
**File => Save As** *=> tutorial9.1*
**=> Save**
Right-click the **Features** tab => Select the **Surfaces** option from the drop-down list that appears as shown to the left. The **Surfaces** tab appears in the command bar as shown to the left.

## Step 2: Create an extruded surface

### Task

A.  Sketch a circle.

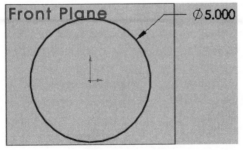

### Command Sequence to Click

**Front Plane** => **Sketch** => Sketch a 5.0″ circle centered on the origin as shown to the left.

B.  Select surface command.

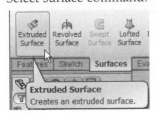

**Extruded Surface** from **Surfaces** tab as shown to the left

| Task | Command Sequence to Click |
|---|---|
| **C.** Create the extruded surface. | Using the **Mid Plane** option, extrude the circle a distance of 3.0 in. as shown to the left. |

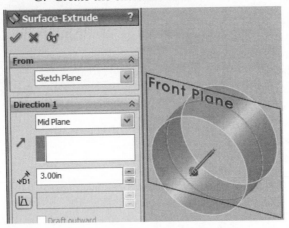

## Step 3: Create a revolved surface

| Task | Command Sequence to Slick |
|---|---|
| **A.** Create a sketch on the front plane. | Sketch a solid line and a centerline on the front plane as shown to the left. |

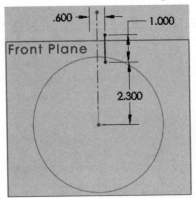

| Task | Command Sequence to Slick |
|---|---|
| **B.** Select surface command. | **Revolved Surface** from **Surfaces** tab as shown to the left |

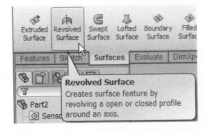

**C.** Revolve 360° about the centerline as shown below.

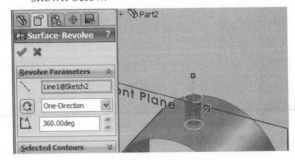

## Step 4: Trim surface

| Task | Command Sequence to Click |
|---|---|
| A. Select the **Trim Surface** tool. | **Trim Surface** from **Surfaces** tab as shown to the left |

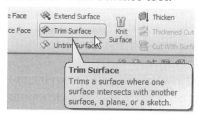

**B.** Make the following selections.

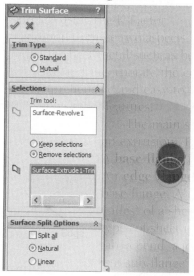

Select the revolved surface as the **Trim** tool and the extruded surface as the part to be trimmed as shown to the left. **Help:** Select the area of the extruded surface inside the revolved surface. **Why:** We need to remove the part of the extruded surface that is inside the revolved surface.

**C.** Trim the revolved surface.

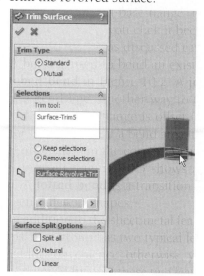

Use a second trim operation to remove the revolved surface inside of the extruded surface as shown to the left. **Why:** We need to remove the part of the revolved surface that is inside the extruded surface.

## Step 5: Thicken surface

### Task

A. Thicken the extruded surface.

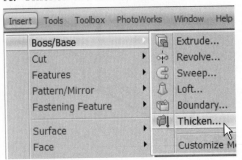

**Command Sequence to Click**

**Insert** menu => **Boss/Base** =>
**Thicken** as shown to the left

B. Create a solid feature.

Select the extruded surface and the
options as shown to the left.

C. Thicken the revolve feature.

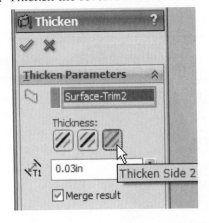

Follow the same steps as in Task B.
However, thicken the revolve feature
this time instead, as shown to the left.

## Step 6: Create a lofted surface

### Task

A. Create a reference plane.

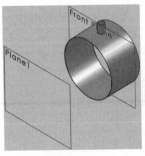 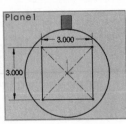

**Command Sequence to Click**

Create a reference plane parallel to the
front plane and 7″ away as shown to the
left. Create a sketch on the reference
plane as shown to the left.

| Task | Command Sequence to Click |
|---|---|
| B. Select the **Lofted Surface** command. | **Lofted Surface** from **Surfaces** tab as shown to the left |

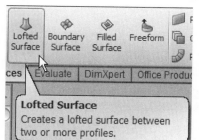

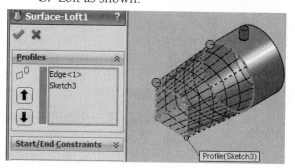

| C. Loft as shown. | Loft a surface between the two selected profiles as shown to the left. |
|---|---|

## Step 7: Create a swept surface

| Task | Command Sequence to Click |
|---|---|
| A. Create an arc as a sweep path. | Create a sketch in the top plane as shown to the left. |

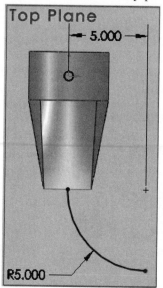

| Task | Command Sequence to Click |
|---|---|

**B.** Create a sweep cross section.

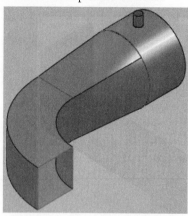

Select the square sketch that was sketched in Task A of Step 6 as the sweep profile. Select the arc as the sweep path. The resulting sweep surface is shown to the left.

## Step 8: Create a knit surface

| Task | Command Sequence to Click |
|---|---|

**A.** Create a knit surface.

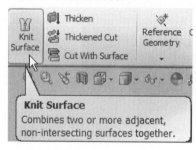

Select the **Knit Surface** command from the **Surfaces** tab as shown to the left, and select both the lofted and the swept surfaces.

**Why:** There is no visible difference when the knit is created. However, there is a knit feature in the design tree. The knit ties the two surfaces into one.

## Step 9: Create radiate surfaces

| Task | Command Sequence to Click |
|---|---|

**A.** Select **Radiate** surfaces.

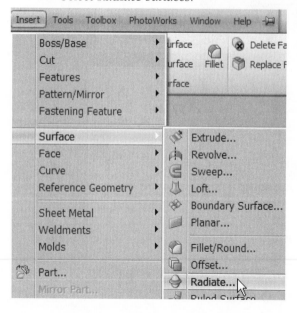

**Insert** menu => **Surface** => **Radiate** shown to the left

| Task | Command Sequence to Click |
|---|---|

**B.** Select the options as shown below.

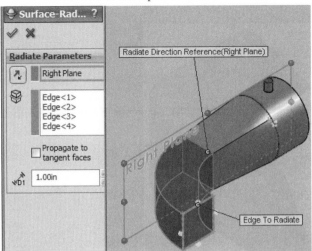

Radiate the four edges of the swept surface. Use the right plane as a directional reference, and radiate each edge 1.0 in. as shown to the left.

---

### HANDS-ON FOR TUTORIAL 9–1.

a. Create a **Radiate** surface on the opposite end of the model. Submit a screenshot in the ISO view.

b. Create the four planar curves (half a circle on the far right and three splines) as shown in Figure 9.11. The curves must form a closed boundary. Each curve is in its own plane. The half circle is in the front plane. The left spline is in a plane parallel to the front plane. The other two (side) splines are in planes parallel to the right plane. Sketch freely to create the curves shown as close as possible. Use two possible surface commands to construct the surface. Submit a screenshot and a list of the surface commands used to create the model.

**FIGURE 9.11**
Boundary curves

---

## Tutorial 9–2: Visualize Surface Curvature

**FIGURE 9.12**
Surface visualization

### Modeling task

Use the **Curvature** display tool, along with curvature combs, to visualize surface curvature.

### Modeling synthesis

This tutorial covers the ability to analyze the smoothness of a surface using curvature combs and curvature display as shown in Figure 9.12.

### Modeling plan

The curvature of the surface model created in the previous tutorial is studied using both the curvature combs of a sketch and the **Curvature** display tool.

### Design intent

Ignore for this chapter.

### CAD steps

We perform surface curvature analysis in two steps:

1. Display curvature.
2. Display curvature combs.

The details of these steps are shown below.

## Step 1: Display curvature

| Task | Command Sequence to Click |
|---|---|

A. Open the model from Tutorial 9–1.

**File => Open** => *tutorial9.1*
**=> Open**
**Help:** The model is shown to the left.

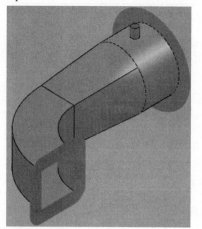

B. Initiate the curvature display.

**View => Display => Curvature** as shown to the left

| Task | Command Sequence to Click |
|---|---|
| C. View the model curvature as shown below. 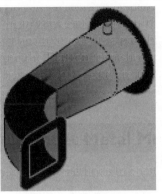 | The color of each section depends on the radius of curvature for that surface. The colors range from black (least curvature) through blue, green, and red (most curvature). |
| D. Dynamic highlight.  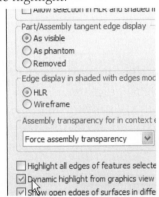 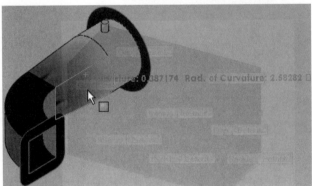 | Open the **System** options. Under the **Display/Selection**, turn on **Dynamic highlight from graphics view** as shown to the left. **Why:** This will display the value of the curvature (in degrees) and the radius of the curvature (in inches) as the cursor hovers over the part as shown to the left. |

## Step 2: Display curvature combs

| Task | Command Sequence to Click |
|---|---|
| A. Access the sweep path (arc shown below) of surface sweep. 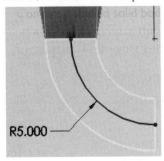 | **Surface-Sweep1** tree node of the model in the features tree => **Edit** from the context menu that pops up. |

| Task | Command Sequence to Click |
|---|---|

**B.** Display curvature combs.

Right-click on the arc => **Show Curvature Combs** from the menu that pops up as shown to the left.

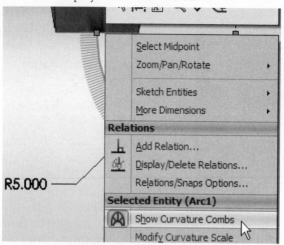

R5.000

**C.** Modify the curvature scale.

Right-click again on the curve and select **Modify Curvature Scale.** Slide the bars and notice the change in display of the combs as shown to the left.

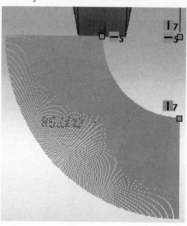

---

***HANDS-ON FOR TUTORIAL 9–2.*** Display the curvature and the curvature combs for the surface created in the hands-on for Tutorial 9–2.

---

## Tutorial 9–3: Convert a Surface to a Solid

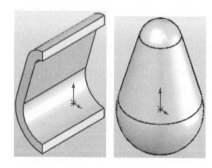

**FIGURE 9.13**
Surface-based solids

### Modeling task

Use two methods to convert a surface to a solid.

### Modeling synthesis

This tutorial covers two methods to turn a surface into a solid. The first is the use of the thicken function, and the second is to cut a solid with a surface leaving a solid behind. Figure 9.13 shows the two solids we create in this tutorial.

### Modeling plan

Create a surface and then thicken it. Then create a surface, embed it inside of a solid, and use the surface to cut away the solid, leaving a second solid behind.

### Design intent

Ignore for this chapter.

### CAD steps

We create the surface-based solids in two steps:

1. Thicken a surface to create a solid.
2. Cut a solid using a surface.

The details of these steps are shown below.

## Step 1: Thicken a surface to create a solid

| Task | Command Sequence to Click |
|---|---|
| A. Create the sketch. | Create the sketch on the front plane as shown to the left. |

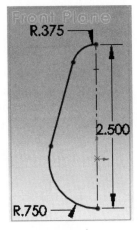

| | |
|---|---|
| B. Extrude a surface. | Extrude 2.0 in. from the mid-plane as shown to the left. |

| | |
|---|---|
| C. Thicken the surface to create a solid. | **Insert => Boss/Base => Thicken**<br>Make the part .125 in. thick from the mid-plane as shown to the left. |

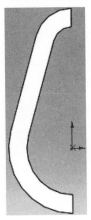

## Step 2: Cut a solid using a surface

| Task | Command Sequence to Click |
|---|---|

**A.** Save the part

Save the part from Step 1 as *Tutorial9.3_eggshell.sldprt*. Delete the **Thicken** feature as shown to the left.

**B.** Return to the original sketch.

Delete the **Surface-Extrude** feature also, leaving only the original sketch as shown to the left.

**C.** Create a revolve surface.

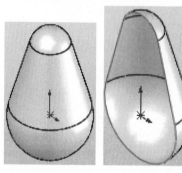

Revolve this sketch 360 degrees to create the revolve surface as shown to the left.

| Task | Command Sequence to Click |
|---|---|

**D.** Extrude a box around the eggshell.

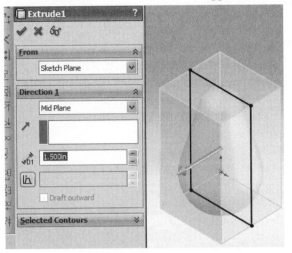

The box is sketched on the front plane and extruded 1.50″ from the mid-plane as shown to the left.

**Help:** Make the box large enough to fully enclose the shell surface as shown to the left.

**E.** Cut the solid block with the surface.

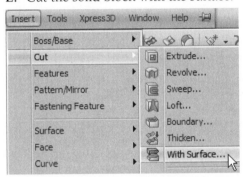

**Insert** menu => **Cut** => **With Surface** as shown to the left

**F.** Observe the remaining solid.

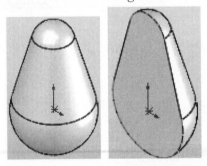

---

***HANDS-ON FOR TUTORIAL 9–3.*** Thicken the surface extrude from Step 1 until it fails. Explain why it fails, and submit a screenshot with the value of the thickest possible dimension.

---

## Tutorial 9–4: Use Surface Intersections

### Modeling task

Use surface intersection to create intricate 3D curves.

### Modeling synthesis

The idea here is to intersect two surfaces to create intricate intersection curves. If one of the intersecting surfaces is a helix surface, we generate visually pleasing and creative

**FIGURE 9.14**
Surface-intersection-based solid

intersection curves as this tutorial shows. These curves may be used to create sweeps of different shapes. You may use taper helixes to add to the visual complexity of the intersection curve.

### Modeling plan

Create a surface revolve and a surface sweep. The surface revolve uses two arcs. The surface sweep uses a line as the sweep profile and a helix as the sweep path. Intersect the two surfaces to create a 3D curve. Sweep a circle (sweep profile) along the intersection curve (sweep path) for better visualization. The resulting swept feature is shown in Figure 9.14.

### Design intent

Ignore for this chapter.

### CAD steps

We create the intersection curve and the feature in three steps:

1. Create the surface revolve.
2. Create the surface sweep.
3. Create the intersection curve and the swept feature.

The details of these steps are shown below.

## Step 1: Create the surface revolve

| Task | Command Sequence to Click |
|---|---|
| A. Create the sketch. | Create the sketch on the front plane as shown to the left. |

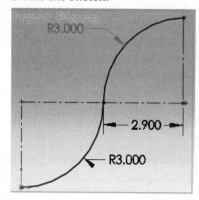

| | |
|---|---|
| B. Create a surface revolve. | Revolve the sketch 360° as shown to the left. |

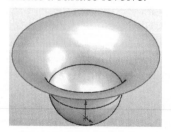

## Step 2:  Create the surface sweep

| Task | Command Sequence to Click |
|---|---|

**A.** Create the helix circle.

Create the sketch on the top plane as shown to the left.

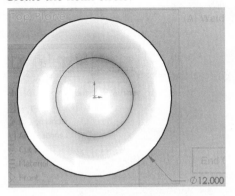

**B.** Create a helix.

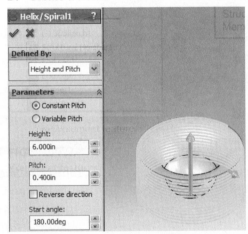

Select the sketch (circle) of Task A => **Insert** menu => **Curve** => **Helix/Spiral** => Use the helix parameters shown here to the left => Green check mark to finish.

**C.** Create the profile (line) of the swept surface.

Sketch a line in the top plane as shown to the left.

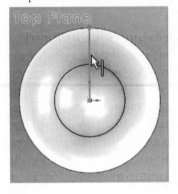

| Task | Command Sequence to Click |
|---|---|
| **D.** Create the swept surface by sweeping the line along the helix. | **Swept Surface** from **Surfaces** tab => Sketch from Task C (sweep profile) => Helix from Task B (sweep path). => Green check mark to finish as shown to the left. |

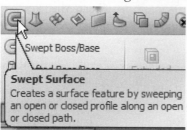

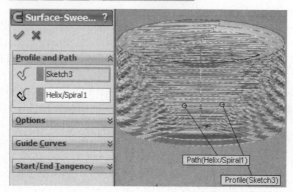

## Step 3: Create the intersection curve and the swept feature

| Task | Command Sequence to Click |
|---|---|
| **A.** Create an intersection curve. | **Tools => Sketch Tools => Intersection Curves** => Select both the surface revolve and the surface sweep => Green check mark to finish as shown to the left. |

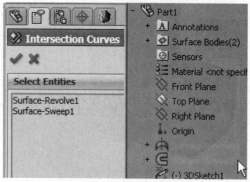

| | |
|---|---|
| **B.** Hide all other features. | Right-click each entity in the feature tree => **Hide** as shown to the left. |

| | |
|---|---|
| **C.** Create a swept boss. | Sketch a 0.25 in. diameter circle on the front plane, and sweep it along the intersection curve as shown to the left. |

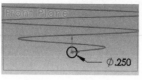

## Tutorial 9–5:  Use Zebra Stripes

**FIGURE 9.15**
Zebra stripes

### Modeling task

Use zebra stripes to visualize surfaces as shown in Figure 9.15.

### Modeling synthesis

Zebra stripes are used to see small changes in a surface that may be hard to see with a standard display. Zebra stripes stimulate the reflection of long strips of light on a very shiny surface. With zebra stripes, you can easily see wrinkles or defects in a surface, and you can verify whether two adjacent faces are in contact, are tangent, or have continuous curvature.

### Modeling plan

Use zebra stripes to observe the surface shapes of multiple different solids, both simple and complex.

### Design intent

Ignore for this chapter.

### CAD steps

We show zebra stripes for three surfaces:

1. Zebra stripes of a cube
2. Zebra stripes of a sphere
3. Zebra stripes of a loft

The details of these surfaces are shown below.

## Surface 1:  Zebra stripes of a cube

| Task | Command Sequence to Click |
|---|---|
| A. Create the cube as an extrusion. | Use the dimensions shown here to the left. |

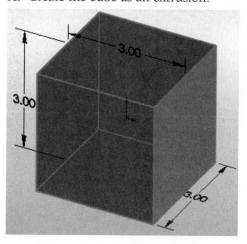

| Task | Command Sequence to Click |
|---|---|
| **B.** Observe the zebra stripes. | **View => Display => Zebra Stripes** as shown to the left |

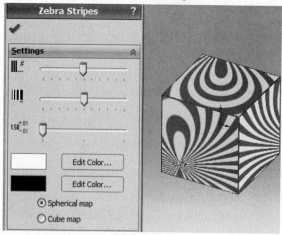

## Surface 2: Zebra stripes of a sphere

| Task | Command Sequence to Click |
|---|---|
| **A.** Create the sphere as a revolve. | Use the dimensions shown here to the left. |

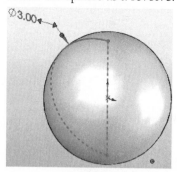

| Task | Command Sequence to Click |
|---|---|
| **B.** Turn on the zebra stripes. | **View => Display => Zebra Stripes** as shown to the left |

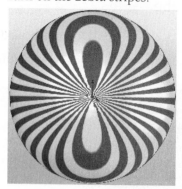

## Surface 3:  Zebra stripes of a loft

### Task

**A.** Create three reference planes to create the loft surface.

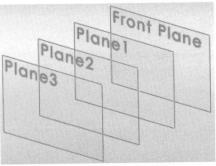

**B.** Create two squares on two sketches.

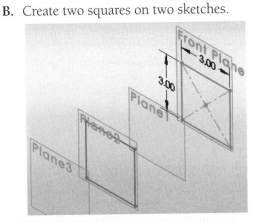

**C.** Create two circles on two sketches.

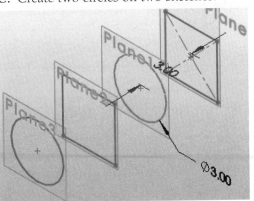

**D.** Loft a surface from the front plane to Plane3.

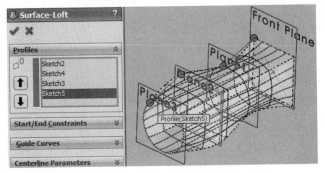

### Command Sequence to Click

Each reference plane is 3.0 in. apart and parallel to the front plane as shown to the left.

Create the sketch shown to the left on the front plane and Plane2.

Create the sketch shown to the left on Plane1 and Plane3.

**Lofted Surface** from the **Surfaces** tab => Select the four sketches as shown to the left.

**Help:** Make sure that you select the sketch as corresponding points. If you do not, you create a twisted loft.

**Why:** A lofted surface interpolates the entities of the sketches. SolidWorks uses your clicks (points) as the corresponding points on the sketches. This is particularly important when the

| Task | Command Sequence to Click |
|---|---|

| | entities being interpolated are closed continuous curves such as circles. **View => Display => Zebra Stripes** as shown to the left |

E. Turn on the zebra stripes.

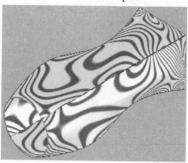

F. Edit the colors and setting of the zebra stripes.

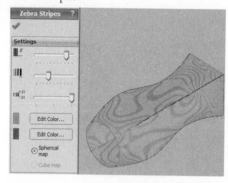

Use the slider bars to change the width and the number of zebra stripes that are displayed. Then change both the colors of the stripes and the background with the **Edit Color** options as shown to the left.

***HANDS-ON FOR TUTORIAL 9–5.*** Close both ends of the surface using two new surfaces. Display the zebra stripes for both ends and submit screenshots of the results.

## Tutorial 9–6: Create a Table Spoon

**FIGURE 9.16**
Table spoon

### Modeling task

Use 3D curves and surfaces to create a spoon model shown in Figure 9.16.

### Modeling synthesis

Use 3D projected curves and a lofted surface to create the table spoon.

### Modeling plan

Create the sketches necessary to form the 3D projected curves to outline the spoon. Use a lofted surface to create the spoon surface and then thicken it.

### Design intent

Ignore for this chapter.

## CAD steps

We create the spoon in three steps:

1. Create a projected curve of the spoon profile.
2. Create a lofted surface of the spoon.
3. Thicken the surface to create the spoon model.

The details of these steps are shown below.

## Step 1: Create a projected curve of the spoon profile

| Task | Command Sequence to Click |
|---|---|
| A. Create Sketch1 (first curve of spoon profile). | Sketch as shown to the left on the top plane. |

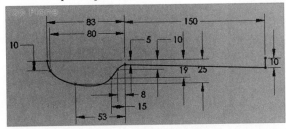

| B. Create Sketch2. | Mirror Sketch1 about the front plane to create Sketch2 as shown to the left. |
|---|---|

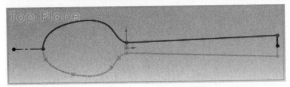

| C. Create Sketch3 (second curve of spoon profile). | Sketch as shown to the left on the front plane. |
|---|---|

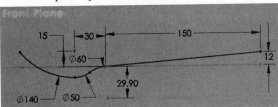

| D. Create Sketch4. | Sketch4 is created on the front plane by using the **Convert Entities** command and selecting Sketch3. |
|---|---|
| E. Create the spoon profile as two projected curves. | **Insert => Curve => Projected.** Create a projected curve using Sketch1 and Sketch3. Create a second projected curve using Sketch2 and Sketch 4 as shown to the left. |

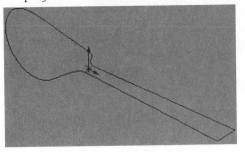

## Step 2: Create a lofted surface of the spoon

| Task | Command Sequence to Click |
|------|---------------------------|
| **A.** Create a reference plane. | Create a reference plane offset from the right plane as shown to the left. |

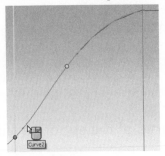

| Task | Command Sequence to Click |
|------|---------------------------|
| **B.** Create Sketch5. | Sketch as shown to the left on Plane1. |

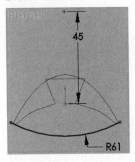

| Task | Command Sequence to Click |
|------|---------------------------|
| **C.** Create Sketch6. | Sketch as shown to the left on the right plane. |

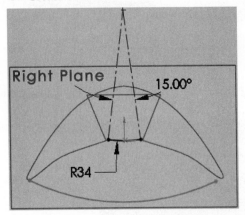

| Task | Command Sequence to Click |
|------|---------------------------|
| **D.** Create a lofted surface. | Create a lofted surface using the projected curves as profiles and Sketch5 and Sketch6 as guide curves as shown to the left. |

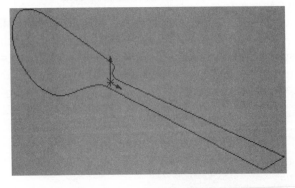

## Step 3: Thicken the surface to create the spoon model

| Task | Command Sequence to Click |
|---|---|
| A. Create the spoon model. | **Insert => Boss/Base => Thicken** => Use a thickness of 2 mm as shown to the left. |
| | Help: Use **Thicken Side 1**. |

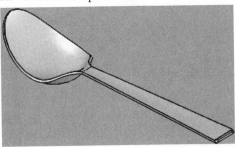

**HANDS-ON FOR TUTORIAL 9–6.** Find the threshold thickness at which the thicken function fails. Use the three thicken options: **Thicken Side 1**, **Thicken Side 2**, or **Thicken Both Sides**. Explain why the thicken operation fails. Submit screenshots.

## Tutorial 9–7: Create a Computer Mouse

(A) Mouse model

**FIGURE 9.17**
Computer mouse

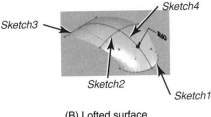

(B) Lofted surface

### Modeling task

Use surfaces to create the computer mouse shown in Figure 9.17A.

### Modeling synthesis

We create the mouse shown in Figure 9.17A using the two different methods (cut a solid with a surface and thicken a surface) discussed in Section 9.3. We create a lofted surface to use in both methods. The lofted surface is defined by four curves created on four sketches, as shown in Figure 9.17B. Sketch1 is half a circle. Sketch2 is an arc. Sketch3 is a line. Sketch4 is two arcs. The right arc is a 3-point arc such that its endpoints coincide with the midpoints of Sketch1 and Sketch2, and a radius to 60 mm. The left arc is a tangent arc such that it is tangent to the right arc and coincident with the Sketch3 midpoint.

### Modeling plan

Create the four sketches shown in Figure 9.17B. Use the sketches to create a lofted surface. Use the lofted surface to create the mouse model.

### Design intent

Ignore for this chapter.

### CAD steps

We create the computer mouse in four steps:

1. Create Sketch1 through Sketch4.
2. Create a lofted surface.
3. Create mouse by splitting a block with the lofted surface.
4. Create mouse by thickening the lofted surface.

The details of these steps are shown below.

## Step 1: Create Sketch1 through Sketch4

Task | Command Sequence to Click

A. Create Sketch1.

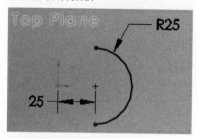

Sketch as shown to the left on the top plane.

B. Create Sketch2.

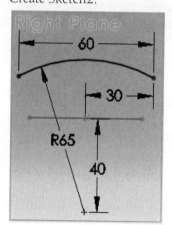

Sketch as shown to the left on the right plane.

C. Create Sketch3.

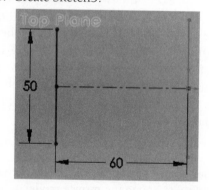

Sketch as shown to the left on the top plane.

D. Create Sketch4.

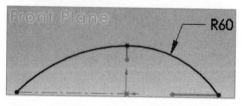

Use 3-point arc to create the right arc. It passes through the midpoints of Sketch1 and Sketch2. It has a radius of 60 mm. The left arc is tangent to the right arc and passes through the midpoint of Sketch3 (line) as shown to the left.

## Step 2:  Create a lofted surface

Task

**A.** Create a lofted surface as shown.

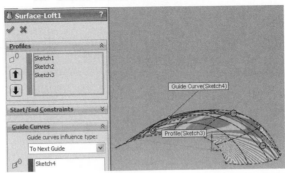

Command Sequence to Click

Loft the surface as shown to the left using all four sketches. Use Sketch1, Sketch2, and Sketch3 as the profiles and Sketch4 as the guide curve.

**B.** Create Sketch5.

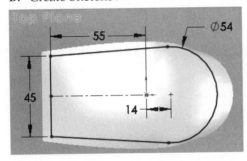

Sketch as shown to the left on the top plane.
**Why:** Sketch5 is the flat bottom of the mouse. We use it in the next two steps.

**C.** At this point save the model under two different names: *tutorial9.7_Mouse1* and *tutorial9.7_Mouse2*.

**File => Save As =>** Type a file name **=> Save**

## Step 3:  Create mouse by splitting a block with the lofted surface

Task

**A.** Begin working with *tutorial9.7_Mouse1*.

**B.** Extrude Sketch5.

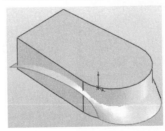

Command Sequence to Click

**File => Open =>** *tutorial9.7_Mouse1* **=> Open**
Extrude Sketch5 25 mm as shown to the left.

| Task | Command Sequence to Click |
|---|---|
| **C.** Cut the extrude with the lofted surface. | **Insert => Cut => With Surface** and then hide the loft surface as shown to the left. |

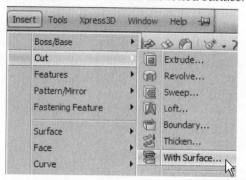

| Task | Command Sequence to Click |
|---|---|
| **D.** Fillet the edges. | Fillet the top and side edges such that the mouse is smooth as shown to the left. Use a 5 mm fillet radius. |

## Step 4: Create mouse by thickening the lofted surface

| Task | Command Sequence to Click |
|---|---|
| **A.** Begin working with *tutorial9.7_Mouse2*. | **File => Open** *=> tutorial9.7_Mouse2* **=> Open** |
| **B.** Create a surface extrude. | Extrude Sketch5 as a surface<br>**Up To Surface => Surface-Loft1** as shown to the left |

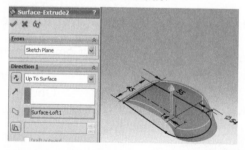

| Task | Command Sequence to Click |
|---|---|
| **C.** Trim Surface-Loft1. | **Insert => Surface => Trim**<br>**Help:** Trim as shown to the left. |

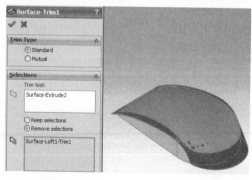

| Task | Command Sequence to Click |
|---|---|

**D.** Knit the surfaces.

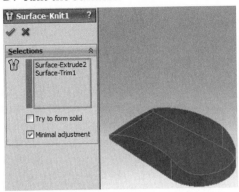

**Knit Surface** on **Surfaces** tab => Select the extruded and trimmed lofted surfaces as shown to the left => Green check mark to finish.

**E.** Fillet as shown.

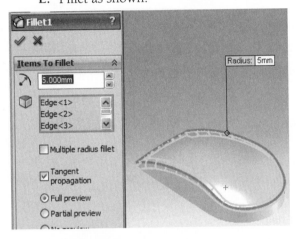

**Fillet** on **Surfaces** tab => Fillet the top and side edges such that the mouse is smooth as shown to the left. Use a 5 mm fillet radius.

**F.** Thicken the surface by 1 mm.

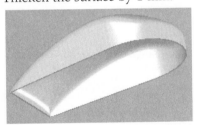

**Thicken** on **Surfaces** tab => Select the surface in the graphics pane => Input 1 mm for the thickness as shown to the left => Green check mark to finish.

---

### HANDS-ON FOR TUTORIAL 9–7.

(a) Shell *tutorial9.7_Mouse1* using a thickness of 1 mm. Cut a 20 mm hole at the bottom surface for the track ball.

**Help:** When you shell the model, you will not see any visual difference. It is only when you create the hole that you can see the hollow space inside the shell.

(b) Close the bottom of *tutorial9.7_Mouse2*. Then cut a 20 mm hole in the bottom face for the track ball.

**Help:** Before thickening the surface, insert a planar surface. Now knit the surfaces again, and use the thicken function to thicken the mouse by 1 mm. Finally create the hole of diameter 20 mm.

## Tutorial 9–8: Create a Baseball Hat

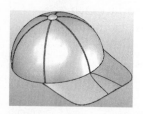

**FIGURE 9.18**
Baseball hat

### Modeling task

Use 3D curves and surfaces to create the baseball hat shown in Figure 9.18.

### Modeling synthesis

The hardest part of the baseball hat to create is the visor because it requires nonplanar (3D) curves to define. We use the projected curves modeling technique together with surfaces to create the visor. When we sketch the 2D curves to define a 3D curve, we sketch freely; that is, no prior coordinates are known. We evaluate the shape of the visor after we create it. If we do not like it, we go back and tweak the curve data. We repeat this process until we are satisfied with the visor shape and look.

### Modeling plan

The head cover and the button are created using simple revolve features. The visor is created using 3D curves and surfaces. The patches are created using swept cuts and circular patterns.

### Design intent

Ignore for this chapter.

### CAD steps

We create the baseball hat in four steps:

1. Create the head cover.
2. Create the button.
3. Create the visor.
4. Create the patches.

The details of these steps are shown below.

## Step 1: Create the head cover

**Task**

A. Create the required geometry.

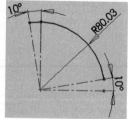

**Command Sequence to Click**

Sketch as shown to the left on the front plane.

**Help:** The arc is tilted 10° from the horizontal as shown; that is, the arc angle is 90°.

**Help:** The revolve axis is the line tilted 10° from the vertical direction as shown to the left.

| Task | Command Sequence to Click |
|---|---|
| **B.** Create the hat cover as a thin revolve, 1 mm thick. | Select sketch from Task A => **Revolved Boss/Base** from **Features** tab => **No** (to closing the sketch) => Check box (to turn on **Thin Feature**) => Use 360° and 1 mm for **T1** as shown to the left => **Centerline** (for axis of revolve; use the line that is 10° from vertical) => Green check mark to finish. |

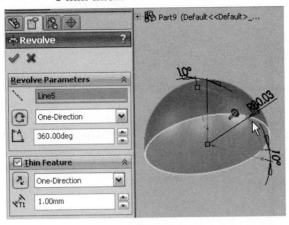

## Step 2: Create the button

| Task | Command Sequence to Click |
|---|---|
| **A.** Create the required geometry. | Sketch as shown to the left on the front plane. |
| 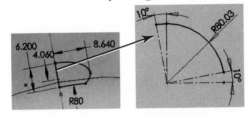 | **Help:** This sketch consists of an ellipse, a circular arc, and a line. |
| | **Help:** The **R80** arc shown to the left has a center at the origin. The line is in the same direction as the centerline of Task A of Step 1. |
| | **Help:** The screenshot to the far left shows where to create the geometry shown to the left. The centerline that the arrow head points to is coincident with the line at the arrow tail. |
| **B.** Create the button as a revolve. | Revolve the sketch from Task A 360° about the vertical axis as shown to the left. |
| 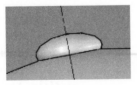 | |

## Step 3: Create the visor

| Task | Command Sequence to Click |
|---|---|
| **A.** Create the first 2D curve of the visor 3D curve. | Sketch a spline with seven points as shown to the left on the front plane. |

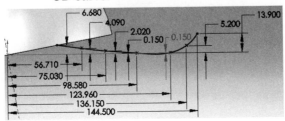

| Task | Command Sequence to Click |
|---|---|

**B.** Create a plane, Plane1, to sketch the second 2D curve of the visor 3D curve.

Create a reference plane parallel to the top plane and passing through the endpoint of the spline created in Task A as shown to the left.

**C.** Create the second 2D curve of the visor 3D curve.

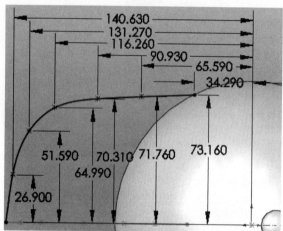

Sketch a spline with seven points as shown to the left on Plane1.

**Help:** The endpoint that shows no coordinates is coincident to the endpoint of the spline created in Task A.

**D.** Create the 3D curve of the visor.

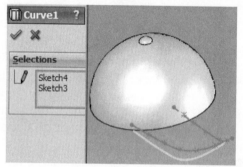

**Insert => Curve => Projected.**
Create a projected curve using the two 2D curves we just created as shown to the left.

**E.** Create the visor arc on a separate sketch.

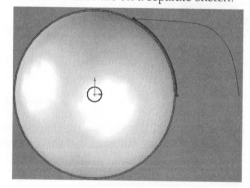

Using the bottom face of the head cover as the sketch plane, sketch the arc as shown to the left.

**Help:** Make sure that one endpoint of the arc is coincident with one endpoint of the 3D curve, and the other endpoint is horizontal to the origin.

| Task | Command Sequence to Click |
|------|---------------------------|

**F.** Create the visor line on a separate sketch.

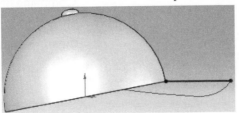

Sketch a line on the front plane as shown to the left. The line passes through the endpoints of the arc and the 3D curve.

**G.** Create the visor surface patch.

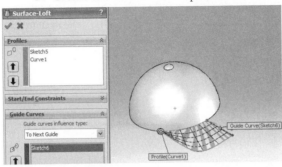

Use a surface loft to create the visor of the hat as shown to the left.

**H.** Create the other half of the visor.

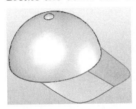

Mirror surface loft from Task E about the front plane as shown to the left.

**I.** Fillet the visor.

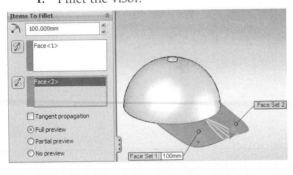

**Face** fillet the two halves of the visor using a 100 mm radius fillet as shown to the left.

**J.** Convert the visor surface to a solid.

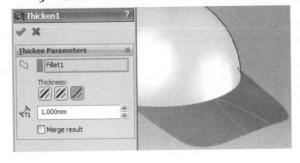

Use the **Thicken** option on **Surfaces** tab to make the visor 1.0 mm thick.

## Step 4:  Create the patches

| Task | Command Sequence to Click |
|---|---|
| **A.** Create the patch path (for sweep cut). 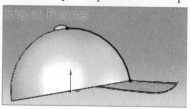 | Sketch the arc as shown to the left on the front plane. |
| **B.** Create the patch profile (for sweep cut). 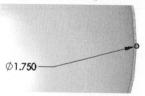 | Sketch the circle on the bottom face of the head cover as shown to the left. |
| **C.** Create the patches (grooves). 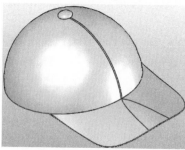 | Create a swept cut using the sweep path from Task A and the sweep profile from Task B as shown to the left. |
| **D.** Create the remaining patches. 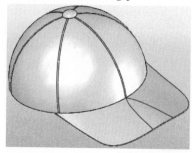 | Circular pattern the swept cut from Task C six times evenly around the central axis of the head cover as shown to the left. |

---

**_HANDS-ON FOR TUTORIAL 9–8._** Add a row of vent holes to the hat, as shown in Figure 9.19. Assume any necessary dimensions. Submit a screenshot of the final model.

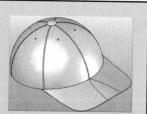

**FIGURE 9.19**
Baseball hat with vent holes

Part III  Advanced Part Modeling

# Tutorial 9–9: Create a Hair Dryer Handle

### Modeling task

Use 2D curves and surfaces to create the hair dryer handle shown in Figure 9.20A.

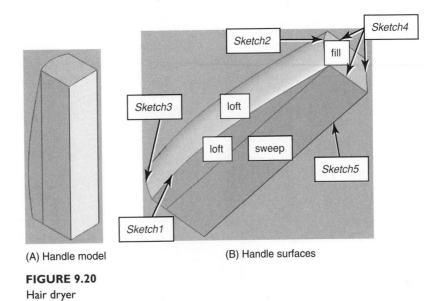

(A) Handle model                  (B) Handle surfaces

**FIGURE 9.20**
Hair dryer

### Modeling synthesis

We need six surfaces (3 lofts, 1 sweep, and 2 fills) to create the handle. Figure 9.20B shows the five sketches we need to create the surfaces. Sketch1 is a spline. Sketch2 and Sketch3 are identical arcs. Sketch4 is three lines. Sketch5 is one line. Sketch1, Sketch2, and Sketch3 are used to create a surface loft. Sketch1 is used to create another loft. Sketch4 and Sketch5 are used to create a surface sweep. Sketch4 is used to create a surface fill.

### Modeling plan

We create the sketches in the order shown in Figure 9.20B. We use the sketches to create the surfaces.

### Design intent

Ignore for this chapter.

### CAD steps

We create the hair dryer handle in one step:

1. Create the hair dryer handle.

The details of this step are shown below.

## Step 1: Create the hair dryer handle

**Task**

**Command Sequence to Click**

**A.** Create the spline sketch (Sketch1).

Sketch the spline as shown to the left on the front plane.

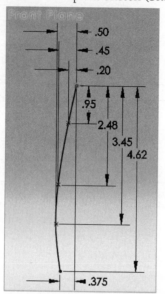

**B.** Create the top arc (Sketch2).

Sketch the arc as shown to the left on the top plane.

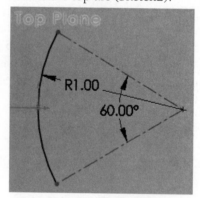

**C.** Create the bottom arc (Sketch3).

Create a reference plane that is parallel to the top plane and 4.62 in. away. Sketch the arc on Plane1 as shown to the left.

**Why:** This arc and the one of Task B are identical in orientation. They are shown here in opposite orientations because of the way SolidWorks displays them on the screen.

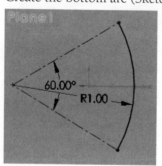

| Task | Command Sequence to Click |
|---|---|
| **D.** Create one left surface of the handle. | Create a **Lofted Surface** between Sketch2 and Sketch3 as shown to the left. Use Sketch1 as a guide curve. |

| Task | Command Sequence to Click |
|---|---|
| **E.** Create three lines (Sketch4). | Sketch the three lines as shown to the left on the top plane. |

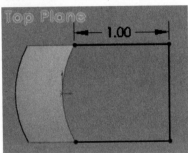

| Task | Command Sequence to Click |
|---|---|
| **F.** Create one line (Sketch5). | Sketch the line as shown to the left on the front plane. |

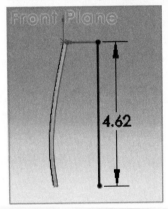

| Task | Command Sequence to Click |
|---|---|
| **G.** Create the sweep surface of the handle. | Sweep Sketch4 along the path of Sketch5 as shown to the left. |

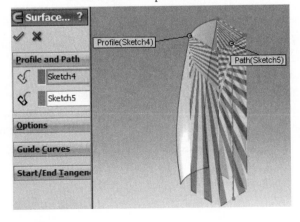

| Task | Command Sequence to Click |
|---|---|

**H.** Select the **Filled Surface** tool.

Select the **Filled Surface** tool from **Surfaces** tab to create the top of the handle as shown to the left.

**I.** Select the four edges of Sketch1 and Sketch4 to create a filled surface.

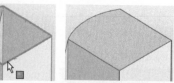

Select the top four edges as shown to the left => Green check mark to finish.

**J.** Create one loft surface of the handle.

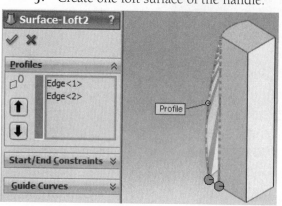

Loft a surface between the two edges shown to the left. Repeat this for both sides.

**K.** Create a filled surface on the bottom of the handle.

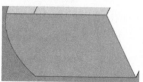

Repeat Tasks H and I as shown to the left.

---

**HANDS-ON FOR TUTORIAL 9–9.** Create a solid using the surfaces created in this tutorial. Fillet the edges of the resulting solid.
**Help:** Create a knit surface of the handle's six surfaces. Create a block large enough to enclose the knit surface. Then cut the block with the knit surface using this sequence: **Insert** (menu) => **Cut** => **With Surface**. Hide the knit surface in the features tree to ensure that the solid body is created.

# Tutorial 9–10: Create an Oil Container

### Modeling task

Use surfaces to create a model of the motor oil container shown in Figure 9.21.

### Modeling synthesis

The motor oil container is physically made out of one piece of plastic like many other containers. Figure 9.21 shows a typical oil container. This tutorial shows you how to model the container using various surfaces and then creating a solid at the end.

### Modeling plan

The plan is to create two surface extrudes and then a lofted surface between them. Close the bottom of the bottle with a filled surface. Finally knit the surfaces together and use one thicken function to create a solid container.

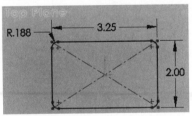

**FIGURE 9.21**
Oil container

### Design intent

Ignore for this chapter.

### CAD steps

We create the oil container in four steps:

1. Create the body and the spout of the container.
2. Create the neck of the container.
3. Create the bottom of the container.
4. Convert the surfaces to a solid.

The details of these steps are shown below.

## Step 1: Create the body and the spout of the container

| Task | Command Sequence to Click |
|---|---|
| A. Create the cross section (Sketch1). | Sketch as shown to the left on the top plane. |

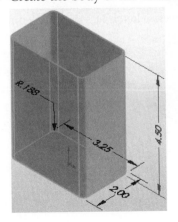

| Task | Command Sequence to Click |
|---|---|
| B. Create the body of the container. | Extrude Sketch1 4.50 in. as shown to the left. |

| Task | Command Sequence to Click |
|---|---|
| C. Create Plane1 to construct the spout. | Create a reference plane 6.625 in. away from and parallel to the top plane. |

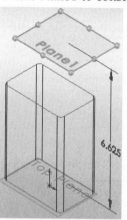

| Task | Command Sequence to Click |
|---|---|
| D. Create the spout cross section (Sketch2). | Sketch as shown to the left on Plane1. |

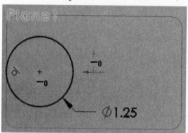

| Task | Command Sequence to Click |
|---|---|
| E. Create the spout of the container. | Extrude Sketch2 0.75 in. toward the first extrusion as shown to the left. |

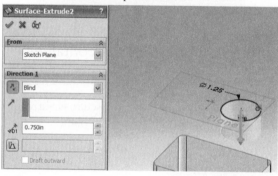

## Step 2: Create the neck of the container

| Task | Command Sequence to Click |
|---|---|
| A. Create a profile of the neck (Sketch3). | Create a reference plane (Plane2 shown here to the left) parallel to the top plane and 4.50 in. away. Convert the top edge of **Surface-Extrude1** into a sketch on this reference plane. **Why:** This will become a loft profile for the neck of the bottle. |

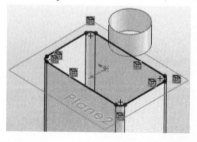

| Task | Command Sequence to Click |
|---|---|

**B.** Create the neck of the container.

Loft a surface from the sketch on Plane2 to the circular edge of the surface extrude of Task E of Step 1. Set **Start/End Constraints** as shown to the left.

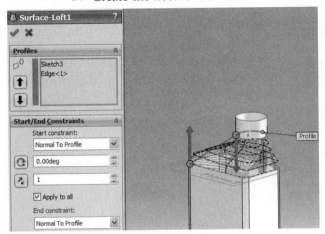

## Step 3: Create the bottom of the container

| Task | Command Sequence to Click |
|---|---|

**A.** Create the container bottom.

**Filled Surface** on **Surfaces** tab => Select the bottom edges of the first extrude as shown to the left, including the fillets => Green check mark to finish.

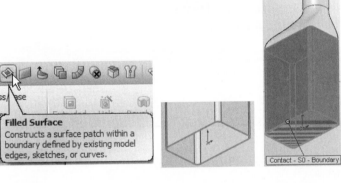

## Step 4: Convert the surfaces to a solid

| Task | Command Sequence to Click |
|---|---|

**A.** Select the **Knit Surface** tool.

**Insert** menu => **Surface** => **Knit** as shown to the left

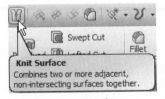

**B.** Create a knit surface.

**Insert** menu => **Surface** => **Knit** => Select all of the surfaces created in this tutorial => Green check mark to finish as shown to the left.

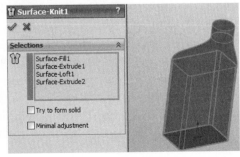

| Task | Command Sequence to Click |
|---|---|

**Task**

C. Create the solid of the container.

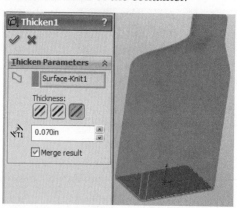

**Command Sequence to Click**

**Insert => Boss/Base => Thicken.**
Select the knit surface of Task B =>
Input .070 in. as shown to the left
=> Green check mark to finish.

---

### HANDS-ON FOR TUTORIAL 9–10.

(a) Make the necessary cuts and fillets in the bottle to make it look more realistic as shown in
Figure 9.22. Submit a screenshot.

(b) Create the threads around the spout of the
container. Assume necessary dimensions to
model the threads. Submit the model.

**FIGURE 9.22**
Tutorial 9–10 oil container

---

### INDUSTRY CHAT

This section provides practical insight into how the chapter material is used in
industry in the real world and practice. This section summarizes the chat with
Mr. John Whiteside (CAD Manager) of Garmin, the sponsor of this chapter. The
structure of the chat follows the chapter sections.

**Chapter Section 9.1:** Introduction

ABE: How much surfacing does Garmin use?

JOHN: Not many of the products we create today are modeled without the use
of surfaces. Not only can surfaces produce the free-form appearance of
modern electronics, but they can also be used to solve modeling situations
that would be otherwise difficult, e.g., when slides and undercuts in injection
mold tools must close off at a parting line with a specific amount of draft.

**Chapter Section 9.2:** Surfaces

ABE: What surfaces does Garmin use in modeling?

JOHN: Knit, extend, and offset are typical types and used in situations in which a
cut or extrusion needs to land on what would be an extension or offset
of a solid surface that doesn't actually exist in the model. We also use
surfaces to define complex sheet metal parts that defy modeling with

normal sheet metal modeling methods. Of course, we also sometimes use lofted surfaces to define the exterior of products.

**Chapter Section 9.3:**    Using Surfaces in Solid Modeling

ABE: How do you use surfaces in your solid modeling activities?

JOHN: Surface modeling can be used to solve intricate or tricky modeling situations. These situations typically come up while modeling for injection molding tooling. For example, there might be a feature that is formed by the intersection of the three sliding portions of the injection molding tool. Another example is to use a surface to cut out a portion of a solid body before shelling.

**Chapter Section 9.4:**    Surface Visualization

ABE: Do you have a need to visualize surfaces? If yes, how?

JOHN: Yes we do, but shaded display is usually enough. Occasionally it is necessary to visualize the appearance of the way surfaces meet at a tangent. For example, surfaces that meet with $C^2$ tangent continuity are more aesthetically pleasing than no continuity. Visualization tools help to find areas with undesirable curvature.

**Chapter Section 9.5:**    Surface Representation

ABE: What do you find is the practical use of surface representation?

JOHN: The parts used in our products are predominantly produced by tools created by computer numerically controlled machining centers. Without numeric surface representation, this would be impossible.

**Chapter Section 9.6:**    Plane Parametric Equation

ABE: Do you use planes in your design? If yes, how?

JOHN: There are plenty of bounded planar surfaces in the models of our products. Thankfully, we don't have to define them with quite as much detail as shown in Section 9.6.

**Chapter Section 9.7:**    Ruled Surface Parametric Equation

ABE: Do you use ruled surfaces in your designs? Provide some examples to show their benefits.

JOHN: We create surfaces as shown in Section 9.7 all the time. We use the term "lofted surface."

**Chapter Section 9.8:**    Surface Management

ABE: How do you manipulate surfaces? Provide examples.

JOHN: We often select model faces to communicate with tool makers. For example, if a surface has changed from one revision model to the next, we will color it red so that the tool maker can see the change.

Others

ABE: Any other experience you would like to share with our book readers?

JOHN: Surfaces are a great way to solve intricate or tricky modeling problems. However, don't forget that it is possible to create intricate shapes using lofted and swept solid body operations.

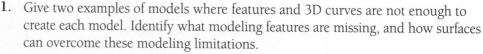

## problems

1. Give two examples of models where features and 3D curves are not enough to create each model. Identify what modeling features are missing, and how surfaces can overcome these modeling limitations.

2. Provide one model to illustrate the use of three of the surfaces shown in Table 9.1. The model should use all the three surfaces at once. Use SolidWorks to create the model.

3. If a parametric surface has $u$ limits of $u_{min}$ and $u_{max}$ and $v$ limits of $v_{min}$ and $v_{max}$, what are the $u$ and $v$ values of its midpoint?

4. Find the parametric equation of the plane connecting point $(2, 1, 0)$ to point $(-2, -5, 0)$, and point $(2, 1, 0)$ to point $(0, 3, -2)$. Find the plane midpoint and its vectors. Sketch the plane and show the data points and the parameterization direction on the sketch.

5. For the plane of Problem 4, find the coordinates of the point located at $u = 0.25$ from the $u = 1$ end and at $v = 0.25$ from the $v = 1$ end.

6. Reverse the $u$ parameterization direction of the plane of Problem 5, and re-solve the problem.

7. Repeat Problems 5 and 6 but for points $(1, 3, 7)$, $(-2, -4, -6)$, and $(5, 0, -8)$.

8. Reverse the $u$ parameterization direction of the plane of Problem 7, and re-solve the problem.

9. Two splines are given by:

$$P(u) = \begin{bmatrix} x(u) \\ y(u) \end{bmatrix} = \begin{bmatrix} 1 + 4u - u^2 \\ 2 - u + u^2 \end{bmatrix} \quad 0 \le u \le 1$$

and

$$P(u) = \begin{bmatrix} x(u) \\ y(u) \end{bmatrix} = \begin{bmatrix} -2 - 2u^2 \\ -1 + u - 2u^2 \end{bmatrix} \quad 0 \le u \le 1$$

Find the equation of the ruled surface connecting the two splines. Find the corner points and the midpoint of the surface. Also, find the surface vectors at the midpoint.

10. A spline is given by:

$$P(u) = \begin{bmatrix} x(u) \\ y(u) \end{bmatrix} = \begin{bmatrix} 2u \\ 2 - u \end{bmatrix} \quad 0 \le u \le 1 \qquad (8.18)$$

Use this spline together with a line connecting points $(2, 5)$ and $(4, 6)$, and find the equation of the ruled surface that connects the spline and the line. What is the degree of the equation of the resulting ruled surface? If it is linear in both $u$ and $v$, the surface is a plane. If this is the case, derive the equation of the plane using the input given in this problem. Compare the ruled surface and the plane equations. Are they identical? What is your conclusion?

11. Find a model of your choice that (a) requires a surface and (b) can be created by thickening the surface. The surface boundary must be defined by a 3D curve.

12. Find a model of your choice that (a) requires a surface and (b) can be created by splitting a solid with the surface to obtain the final shape of the model.

444

Part III  Advanced Part Modeling

13. Find a model of your choice that (a) requires surfaces and (b) can be created by carving a solid out of a block. You must use the surfaces to create a knit surface that is used as a tool for carving out the final solid out of the block.

14. Find a good example of creating a ruled surface that you can use to create a solid.

15. Using Problem 21 in Chapter 8, create a surface that connects the two edges of the laboratory chair defined in Figure 8.17. Thicken the surface by a value of 15 mm to create the chair solid. Submit screenshots of the two 3D curves, the surface, and the solid. All dims are in inches.

16. Using Problem 22 in Chapter 8, create the surface whose boundary is defined by the 3D curve. Thicken the surface by 0.5 in. to create the skateboard. Submit screenshots of the planar curves, the 3D curve, the surface, and the final skateboard solid. All dims are in inches.

17. Using Problem 23 in Chapter 8, create the surface whose boundary is defined by the 3D curve. Thicken the surface by 0.5 in. to create the bicycle helmet. Submit screenshots of the planar curves, the 3D curve, the surface, and the final helmet solid. All dims are in inches.

18. Using Problem 24 in Chapter 8, create the surface whose boundary is defined by the 3D curve. Thicken the surface by 0.5 in. to create the weed whacker debris shield. Submit screenshots of the planar curves, the 3D curve, the surface, and the final shield solid. All dims are in inches.

19. Using Problem 25 in Chapter 8, create the surface whose boundary is defined by the 3D curve. Thicken the surface by 0.5 in. to create the S-shaped chair. Submit screenshots of the planar curves, the 3D curve, the surface, and the final chair solid. All dims are in inches.

20. Using Problem 26 in Chapter 8, create the surface whose boundary is defined by the 3D curve. Thicken the surface by 0.5 in. to create the bike seat. Submit screenshots of the planar curves, the 3D curve, the surface, and the final seat solid. All dims are in inches.

21. Figure 9.23 shows the model of a table fork. The model requires 3D curves and surfaces. The figure shows the two projections of the 3D curve that defines the fork profile. Thicken the surface to create the fork. *Hint:* You may want to model your own fork, so you can physically look at it when you need to.

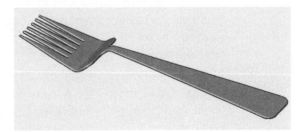

**FIGURE 9.23**
Table fork model

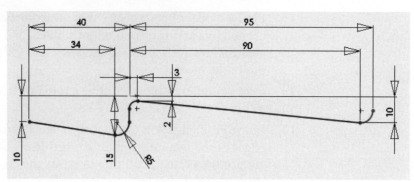

Top sketch of fork half profile

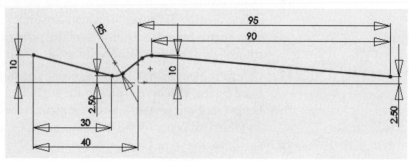

Front sketch of fork half profile

**FIGURE 9.23**
*(continued)*

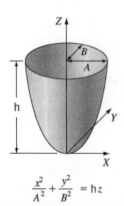

$$\frac{x^2}{A^2} + \frac{y^2}{B^2} = hz$$

**FIGURE 9.24**
Elliptic paraboloid

22. Figure 9.24 shows an elliptic paraboloid. Its equation is given by:

$$\frac{x^2}{A^2} + \frac{y^2}{B^2} = hz$$

a. Use $A = 3$, $B = 2$, and $h = 4$. There are two methods to create the surface. Use both of them to create the surface. Submit the steps (including screen-shots and dimensions) of how you created the surface for each method.

b. Generate three points on each surface and use your CAD/CAM system to verify that the surface you created implements its equation. How accurate is your CAD/CAM system for each method? Which creation method is more accurate? Submit the $(x, y, z)$ coordinates generated by the CAD/CAM system and the coordinates generated from the equation.

c. Convert one of the paraboloid surfaces into a solid. Submit the steps (including screenshots and dimensions) of how you created the solid.

*Note:* This problem introduces an important concept in CAD/CAM design. Sometimes, a designer may run an engineering analysis that produces surfaces that must be included in part design for better performances (e.g., lift and drag, or aerodynamics of car surfaces).

23. Figure 9.25 shows the model of a soda bottle. Create the model. The bottle bottom has five identical legs. A leg would require creating different splines on different sketch planes (at angles from each other) and then creating a loft surface between them. Create one and pattern it. After patterning, fill the gaps with loft surfaces. Create the other surfaces and then thicken all the surfaces to create the bottle model. *Hint:* You may want to model your own soda bottle, so you can physically look at it when you need to.

Part III  Advanced Part Modeling

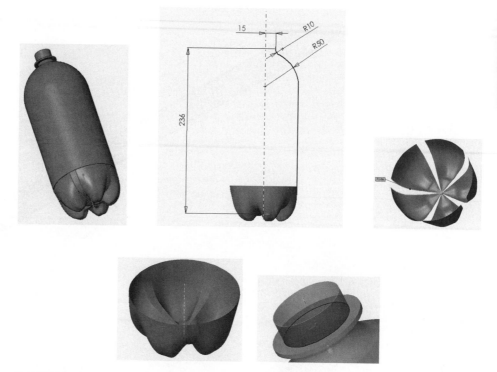

**FIGURE 9.25**
Soda bottle model

24. Create the following model of a drill bit. Sketch freely.

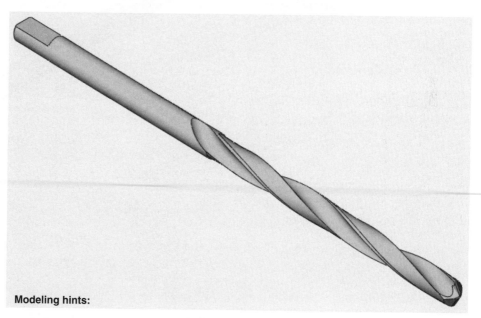

**Modeling hints:**

**FIGURE 9.26**
Model of a drill bit

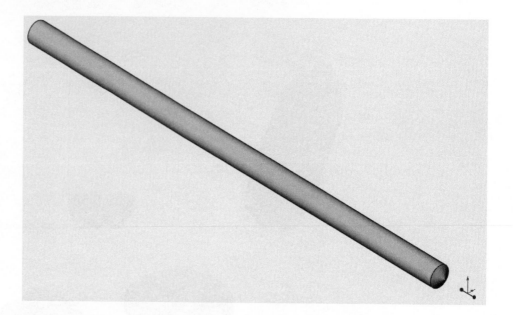

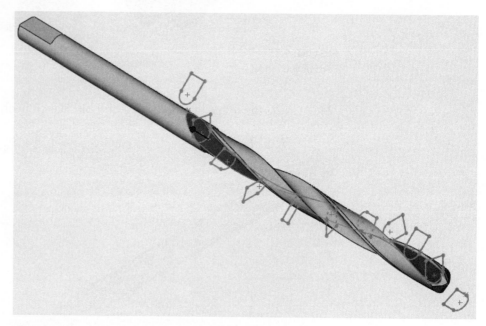

**FIGURE 9.26**
(*Continued*)

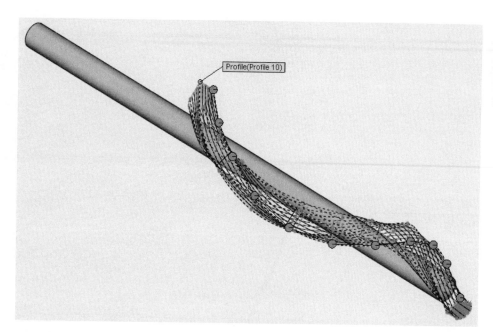

**FIGURE 9.26**
(*Continued*)

25. Create the following model. Sketch freely.

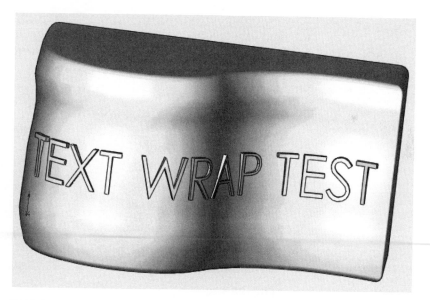

**FIGURE 9.27**
Engraved model

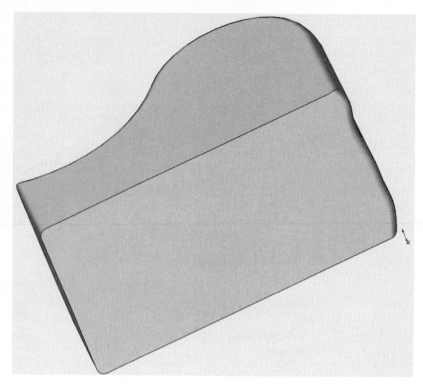

**FIGURE 9.27**
(*Continued*)

26. Find your favorite rock or other object that requires 3D curves and surfaces to model as a solid. Create the solid model of the rock or the object. Figure 9.28 shows an example.

**FIGURE 9.28**
Model of a rock

# Sheet Metal and Weldments

## 10.1 Introduction

The previous chapters have focused heavily on presenting and harnessing the power of features, curves (especially 3D curves), and surfaces to create solids. As a matter of fact, there are no parts that cannot be created using these modeling tools. However, this chapter covers the basics of one class of parts that, although it can be modeled using these tools, is created more efficiently via other specialized modeling techniques. This class is sheet metal parts and weldments (welded parts). These parts are used heavily in industry, and CAD/CAM systems provide special modeling techniques to create them efficiently. For example, a weldment is created as a steel or welded frame or structure instead of as an assembly. Even though they are not related, we cover both sheet metal and weldments in one chapter because they belong to this special class.

## 10.2 Sheet Metal

**Sheet metal** is thin, flat pieces of metal that come in different sizes that can be cut and bent into a variety of shapes. The thickness of sheet metals can vary significantly, from 1 mm to 6 mm (0.25 in.). An extremely thin piece of metal is considered a foil or leaf (e.g., kitchen aluminum foil), and pieces thicker than 6 mm are considered plates. Sheet metal is a fundamental form to metalworking. Many parts of objects around us are made from sheet metal. Examples include airplane wings, car bodies, medical tables, roofs for buildings, brackets, chases, enclosures, panels, channels, hinges, razor blades, weldments, and signage. Industries that use sheet metal include audio-video, electronics, fiber optics, medical, security, semiconductors, and telecommunications.

Sheet metal processes and equipment include punching (via punch press), rolling, embossing, stamping, breaking, notching, shearing, spot welding, insertion, and finishing. Machining tolerance could be as small as 0.0005 in. Commonly used materials include aluminum, steel, brass, copper, silver, gold, nickel, platinum, and titanium. NC (numerical control) programming may be used to program sheet metal fabrication.

Sheet metal comes as flat sheets or coiled strips. The coils are formed by running flat sheets through a roll slitter. The thickness of a sheet metal is known as its gauge. Gauges range from 30 gauge to 8 gauge. The higher the gauge, the thinner the sheet.

If you need a sheet metal part as an enclosure, you can design it in two ways: either on its own without any references to the parts it will enclose or in the context of the assembly that contains the enclosed components.

One common operation of sheet metal is bending a sheet. Sheet metal bending is also known as a brake. The machine that bends sheet metal is known as a bending brake or bending machine. The machine can create simple bends and creases, or create box and pan shapes. Bending changes the shape of the metal by plastically deforming it. When a sheet metal is bent, the inside surface of the bend is compressed, and the outer surface of the bend is stretched. Somewhere within the metal thickness lies its neutral axis (NA). An NA is a line or layer in the metal that is free from any forces; that is, it is neither compressed nor stretched. Thus, the length of the metal remains the same along the NA.

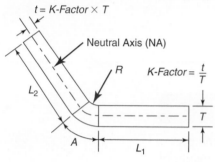

**FIGURE 10.1**
Bending a sheet metal

The location of the NA is referred to as the K-Factor of the sheet metal; that is, the K-Factor is used to calculate the location of the neutral axis. The K-Factor is important in determining the length of the sheet metal that is required to produce certain bends. Consider the example shown in Figure 10.1. We want a sheet metal workpiece with a bend angle $A°$ and a bend radius $R$, in which one leg measures $L_1$, and the other measures $L_2$. The NA is located at thickness $t$ from the inner surface, and the metal total thickness is $T$. It is obvious from Figure 10.1 that the total length of the flat piece that we should bend is not $L_1 + L_2$, as we might first assume. We need to add the bend part for the angle $A$. This part is known as the bend allowance (BA), which we must add to the leg lengths to get the final bend shape that we want.

The location of the NA (K-Factor) varies depending on the material itself, the bend radius, $R$, the ambient temperature, the direction of the material grain, the method used for bending, etc. The **K-Factor** is the ratio of the location of the NA as measured by the thickness, $t$, shown in Figure 10.1 with respect to the thickness, $T$, of the sheet metal part; that is,

$$\text{K-Factor} = \frac{t}{T} \tag{10.1}$$

The K-Factor is usually calculated by trial and error. The K-Factor is typically between 0.3 and 0.5. For most types of steel it is between 0.33 and 0.4.

The bend allowance, BA, is given by:

$$BA = \frac{\pi A(R + KT)}{180} \tag{10.2}$$

Sometimes, we let the lengths of the two legs, $L_1$ and $L_2$, meet (intersect), as shown in Figure 10.1. In this case, the total length, $L_1 + L_2$, exceeds the length of the flat sheet by an amount called the bend deduction (BD); that is,

$$BD = L_1 + L_2 - \text{flat length} \tag{10.3}$$

CAD/CAM systems provide tables for K-Factor, BA, and BD for most commonly used materials. SolidWorks has these tables in this folder: *C:\Program Files\SolidWorks\SolidWorks\lang\english\Sheetmetal Bend Tables*. It also has gauge tables in another folder: *C:\Program Files\SolidWorks\SolidWorks\lang\english\Sheet Metal Gauge Tables*.

## 10.3 Sheet Metal Features

The best way to understand sheet metal modeling and design is to ask a simple question: How different are sheet metal parts from ordinary parts? From the outset one could trivialize modeling of sheet metal parts by recognizing them as simple extrusions connected together. (This would obviously be the wrong view of modeling and designing

**FIGURE 10.2**
Sheet metal features

sheet metal parts.) We now answer the question. The modeling of sheet metal parts has two unique aspects. First, the sheet metal parameters covered in Section 10.2 must be modeled correctly to ensure the proper manufacturing (i.e., the gauge, the K-Factor, the bend angles, etc.). Second, we need to calculate the size of the flat sheet that we must use to create a final shape; we must be able to flatten the sheet metal part that we model (final model) using the K-Factor.

In addition to these two aspects, sheet metal modeling should provide features that are unique to sheet metal such as bends, flanges, corners, etc. These features must be easy to create and incorporate the concepts covered in Section 10.2. SolidWorks provides a comprehensive and easy-to-use sheet metal module with ample features. Figure 10.2 shows these features.

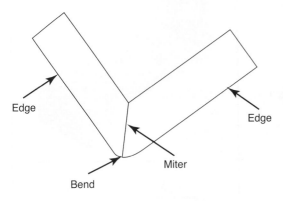

**FIGURE 10.3**
Sheet metal flanges

The main sheet metal feature is a flange. Think of a flange as an extrusion. Three types of flanges exist: base, edge, and miter. A **base flange** is the first flange you create in a sheet metal part. An **edge flange** is one that is built off of an existing edge on a base flange. A **miter flange** is a flange that connects two panels (sides) of a sheet metal cut at a 45° angle. Figure 10.3 shows the types of sheet metal flanges. Other sheet metal features include a tab, a bend, a jog, a corner, a rip, a hem, and a lofted bend. A **tab** is a sub-flange that you can bend. For example, you can use an edge flange to build a tab and then bend it. The first time you click the **Base Flange/Tab** icon shown in Figure 10.2, you create a base flange. For subsequent clicks, you create a tab each time you click it because you can have only one base feature in a part, as discussed earlier in the book.

A **bend** is used to bend an existing flange about a bend line. The bend is labeled **Sketched Bend** in Figure 10.2. A **jog** is used to add two bends to an existing flange about a bend line. Another way to think about it is that a part (defined by the bend line) of an existing flange is offset (jogged) up or down, thus creating two bends. A **corner** is used to treat a bend area, that is, weld at the bend corner to stiffen the sheet metal or break/trim the corner. A **rip** creates a gap between two edges. A **hem** curls an edge on itself. Figure 10.3 shows all these sheet metal features and how to create them. A **lofted bend** is a transition from one shape to another. Think of it as a bend between different shapes.

In addition to the sheet metal features, the interface shown in Figure 10.2 offers two groups. One group has two typical features: **Extruded Cut** and **Simple Hole**. They are offered for convenience; otherwise, you have to go to the **Features** tab (Figure 10.2) to access them. Why only these two features? Because they are the most commonly used in the context of sheet metal design. The most common tasks you do for a sheet metal is cut it, bend it, make cuts in it, and/or make holes in it. The other group has functions related to manufacturing: **Unfold**, **Fold**, and **Flatten**. Flattening is particularly useful because it allows you to know the exact dimensions of a sheet metal stock that you need to manufacture the final product. You need the flattening because of the K-Factor effect. Table 10.1 shows SolidWorks sheet metal features and how to create them.

## TABLE 10.1 Available Sheet Metal Features

| Feature | Input | Before Feature Creation | After Feature Creation |
|---------|-------|-------------------------|------------------------|
| Base flange | Flange sketch | | |
| Edge flange | Edge to flange (E), flange angle (90°), flange length (30), flange position (bend outside) | | |
| Miter flange | Flange cross section (CS) and edges to flange. CS must be perpendicular to edges | | |

| TABLE 10.1 Available Sheet Metal Features (*continued*) | | | |
|---|---|---|---|
| **Feature** | **Input** | **Before Feature Creation** | **After Feature Creation** |
| Tab | A sketch of the cross section (CS) of the tab | | |
| Bend (sketched bend) | A bend line (BL) and fixed face (FF) to bend with respect to | | |
| Jog | A bend line (BL) and fixed face (FF) to bend with respect to **Help:** The difference between bend and jog is that the latter creates two bends instead of one, thus the effect of jog | | |

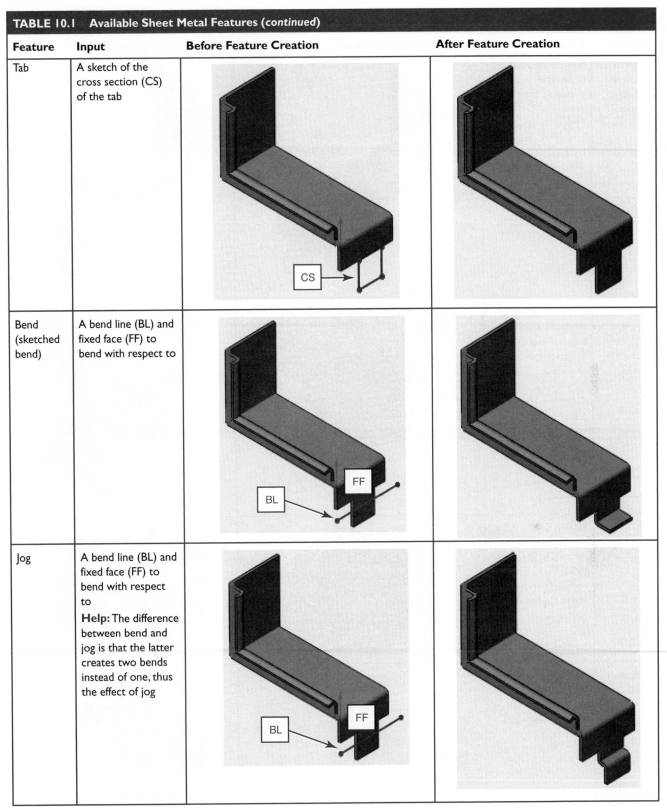

(*continued*)

**TABLE 10.1 Available Sheet Metal Features (continued)**

| Feature | Input | Before Feature Creation | After Feature Creation |
|---|---|---|---|
| Corner (we use break corner) | Corner to break, break type (use chamfer), and distance **Help:** We break (chamfer) the top right corner | | |
| Hem | Edge(s) to hem **Help:** Hemming an edge is like bending (folding) it on itself as shown | | |
| Rip | Edge(s) to rip, and a rip direction(s) (see arrows on the right) **Why:** You cannot rip edges of the above flanged model | | |
| Lofted bend | Two sketches with no sharp corners **Why:** Corners must be filleted to allow creating a bend for sheet metal | | |

TABLE 10.1   Available Sheet Metal Features (*continued*)

| Feature | Input | Before Feature Creation | After Feature Creation |
|---------|-------|-------------------------|------------------------|
| Unfold | Fixed face and bend to unfold | 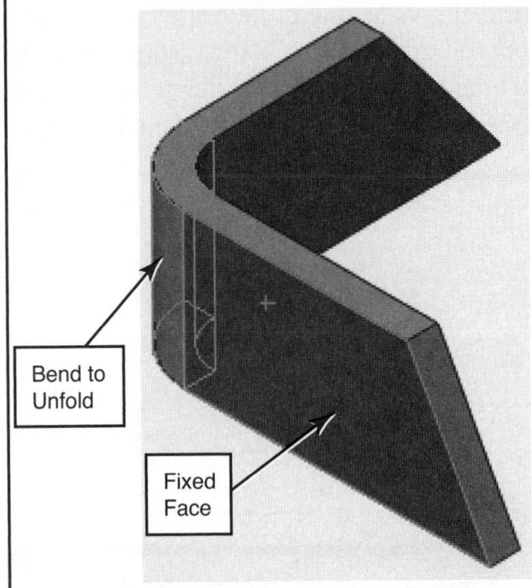 Bend to Unfold / Fixed Face | 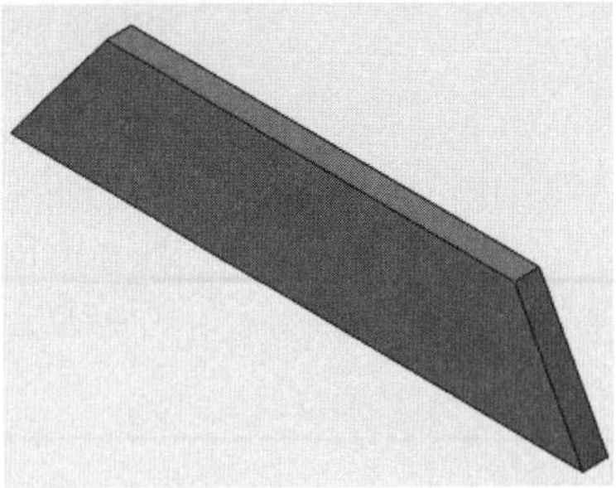 |
| Fold | Fixed face and bend to fold (of unfolded part) | 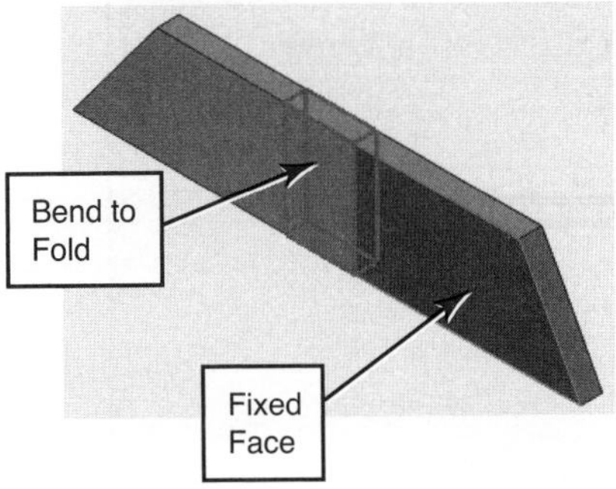 Bend to Fold / Fixed Face | 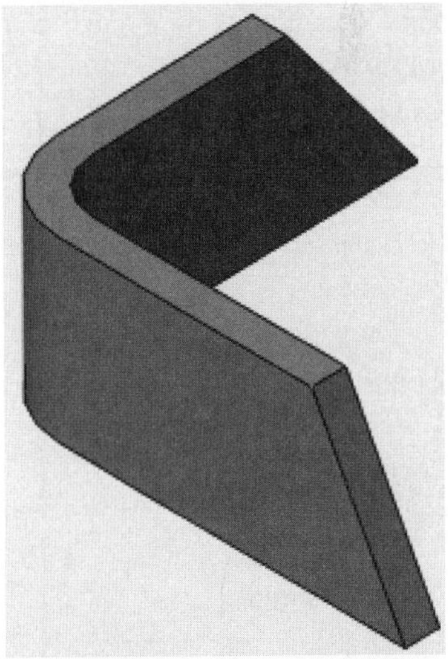 |
| Flatten | Un-flattened part.<br>**Help:** Unfolding and flattening a part are not the same as shown here | 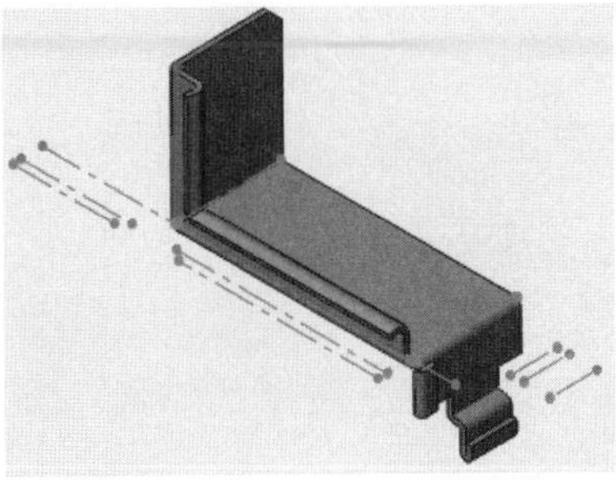 | 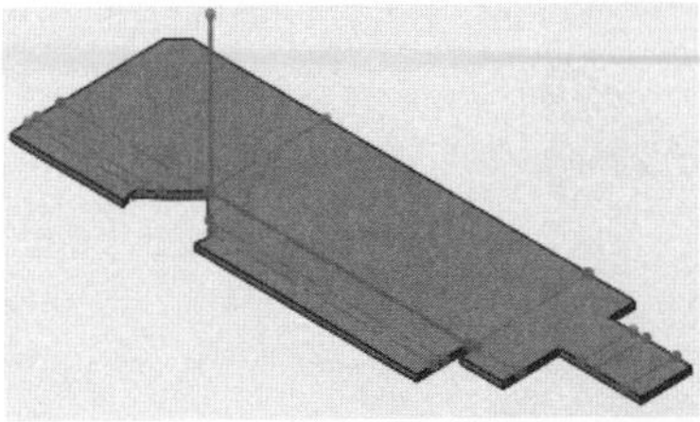 |

# 10.4 Sheet Metal FeatureManager Design Tree

Thus far in the book, when we create a base feature in a part, only the feature is created as we expect and shows as one node in the part features tree. Sheet metal modeling is different. When you create a base flange feature in a sheet metal part, SolidWorks creates a total of three features: the base flange and two supporting features, as shown in Figure 10.4. **Sheet-Metal1** contains the bend parameters including the bend radius, bend allowance, and relief type. Right-click it to edit the default values if needed. **Base-Flange1** is the base feature that represents the sheet metal part we want. This tree node

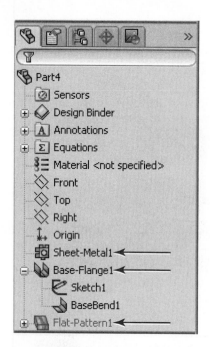

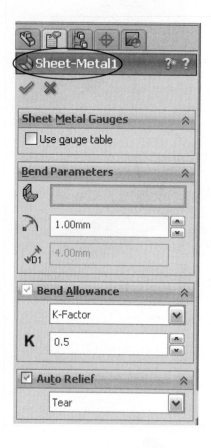

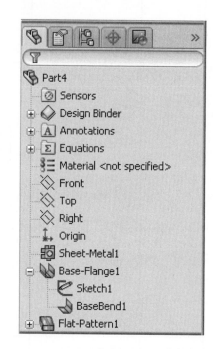

(A) **Base-Flange1:** Bent state

(B) Bend parameters

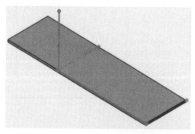

(C) **Base-Flange1:** Flatten state

**FIGURE 10.4**
Sheet metal supporting features

has two sub-nodes: the feature sketch and the bend radius. **Flat-Pattern1** enables you to flatten/unflatten the part. The flat state is suppressed by default; it shows the part in its bent state. To flatten the part, click the **Flat-Pattern1** node and select the **Unsuppress** icon from the context menu that pops up (hover on icons to read them). When you click it again, it puts the part back in its bent state. You can achieve the same result by clicking the **Flatten** icon shown in Figure 10.2. Note that when you flatten the part, the new features you create are inserted below the **Flat-Pattern1** node in the features tree; otherwise, they are inserted above it.

## 10.5 Sheet Metal Methods

There are four methods to create sheet metal parts. They are:

1. **Create a sheet metal part using the sheet metal features covered in Section 10.4 and shown in Table 10.1:** Here, you start by creating a base flange and add the needed sheet metal features until the part is complete.

2. **Create a sheet metal part by converting a solid body:** After you create a solid as usual, use **Insert** (SolidWorks menu) **=> Sheet Metal => Convert To Sheet Metal**. This requires a fixed face and edges that are planar with the fixed face. These are the bend edges that are used to create the sheet metal part. Figure 10.5 shows an example. We select the bottom face as the fixed face and its four edges as the bend edges. When you select the face and its edges, SolidWorks selects the four vertical edges as the rip edges to create the sheet metal part.

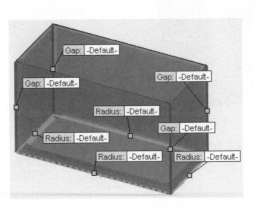

(A) Solid part and input

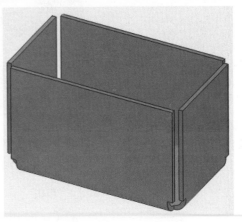

(B) Resulting sheet metal part

**FIGURE 10.5**
Converting a solid part to a sheet metal part

3. **Convert a shelled solid body to a sheet metal part:** This method requires a shelled solid. After you have the shelled solid, use **Insert Bends** to create the sheet metal part. Following is the sequence of using this method.

## Step 1: Create the solid

| Task | Command Sequence to Click |
|---|---|
| A. Create an extrusion. | Sketch the sketch shown to the left and extrude it. |

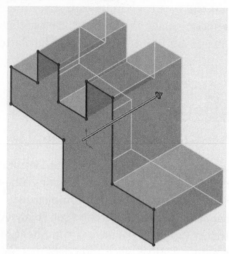

| Task | Command Sequence to Click |
|---|---|
| B. Shell the extrusion. | **Shell** (**Features** tab) => Select front and back faces of extrusion => Type 4 (mm) for shell thickness => Green check mark to finish as shown to the left. |

## Step 2: Create the sheet metal part

Task

A. Create the sheet metal part.

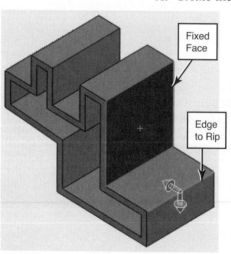

Fixed Face

Edge to Rip

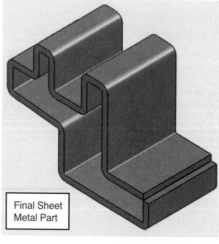

Final Sheet Metal Part

Command Sequence to Click

**Sheet Metal** tab => **Insert Bends** => Select a face as a fixed face => Select an edge to rip => Green check mark to finish.

**Why:** You can select one edge to rip. If you select more than one edge, the bend operation fails. After the operation is complete, as shown to the left, a sheet metal part is created. You can flatten it.

4. Design a sheet metal part from the flattened state: In this method, you create the sheet metal as one sketch and then create bend lines (in another sketch) where you want to bend (fold) the flat sheet (sketch) to create the part. The following sequence shows how to use this method.

## Step 1: Create the sketches

| Task | Command Sequence to Click |
|------|---------------------------|
| A. Create the sketch of the sheet metal part. | Use the front plane, and sketch the profile shown to the left. |

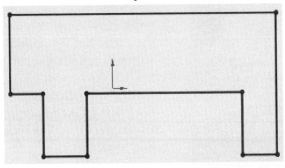

| Task | Command Sequence to Click |
|------|---------------------------|
| B. Sketch the bend lines on another sketch. | Use the front plane, and sketch the three bend lines shown to the left. |

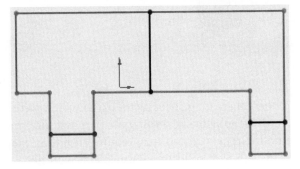

## Step 2: Create the sheet metal part

| Task | Command Sequence to Click |
|------|---------------------------|
| A. Create the sheet metal part without bends. | **Sheet Metal** tab => Select **Sketch1** (Task A of Step 1 above) => **Base Flange/Tab** => Input 4 mm for thickness => Green check mark to finish as shown to the left. |

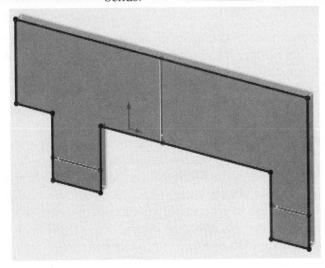

| Task | Command Sequence to Click |
|---|---|
| **B.** Create the bends.<br><br><br><br>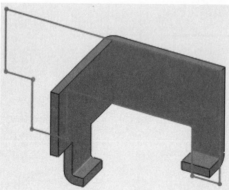 | Select **Sketch2** (Task B of Step 1 above) => **Sketched Bend** (**Sheet Metal** tab) => Green check mark to finish as shown to the left<br>**Help:** Another alternative would be to use this sequence: **Sketched Bend** => Select any bend line to identify **Sketch2** => Green check mark.<br>**Why:** Although the final sheet metal part is the same, the bent part may differ, depending on how you make your selection. For example, the bent part may be the right half instead of the left half shown to the left. The reason for this unpredictability is that we did not select a **Fixed Face** in the **Bend Parameters** box. The tutorials show how to do this. |

Out of these four methods of creating sheet metal parts, which method is the best? This is a hard question to answer. Obviously, starting the part as a sheet metal part is the most straightforward method. Other methods may require additional steps or features. For example, if you convert a shelled solid to a sheet metal, you need these features: **Base Extrude, Shell, Rip,** and **Insert Bends**. In some cases, this may be the only way; for example, conical bends are not supported by sheet metal features. Thus, you need to follow the shell method.

## 10.6 Weldments

**Welding** is a fabrication process that joins metal (steel, aluminum) or thermoplastic components together by melting the joints (workpieces) and adding a filler material to mix with the joints' materials. When the joints are cooled down, a strong joint connection is created. Example products that use welds are metal frames used in building construction, exhaust system and pipes of a car, campfire grill, trailer dolly, rainwater system (house gutters), heat exchangers, and condensers.

Welding processes include gas welding, arc welding, spot welding, resistance welding, solid state welding, and others. All these processes have one thing in common: they all require an energy source to heat up and melt the weld joints and the filler material. They all differ in the source of generating the energy (e.g., gas, electric arc, resistance, etc.). For example, gas welding burns gas to generate very hot flames to melt and fuse metal joints with the filler material. You probably have seen or used one of those small portable cylinders that burns propane and produces a flame torch that you can use for welding.

Welding equipment and supplies include welding machines, cylinders, spot welders, cutters, torches, welding hoods (to contain fumes), grinders, filler metals, air compressors, cutting guides, clamps and holders, safety equipment, etc. Gas welding uses gas cylinders that are filled with gas (propane) under high pressure. These cylinders are regulated and follow strict standards and codes.

Weld defects can occur, and they include inclusions, segregation, and porosity. **Inclusions** are impurities of foreign substances that get into the weld puddle (area of molten metal) during welding and become embedded in the weld joints after they solidify. These inclusions have the same effect as a crack because they are typically much weaker than the weld joint material. **Segregation** is a condition in which the weld puddle does not have uniform metal mix. For example, there may not be enough filler material flowing uniformly in the puddle. **Porosity** is the formation of voids or tiny pinholes that result from trapping air bubbles in the puddle.

If welding is all about connecting weld joints together, what kind of weld joints can we design and use? There are many types of weld joints, and Figure 10.6 shows the common types. The parts that are welded are shown with a number in a circle. The weld puddle (area) is shown as hatched.

Which joint type is best suited for a particular application? The answer depends on many factors. Weld joints are designed primarily to meet strength and safety requirements. Other considerations in selecting the type of weld joint design are the joint load and the ratio of the joint strength to the base metal strength. The type (tension or compression)

**FIGURE 10.6**
Types of weld joints

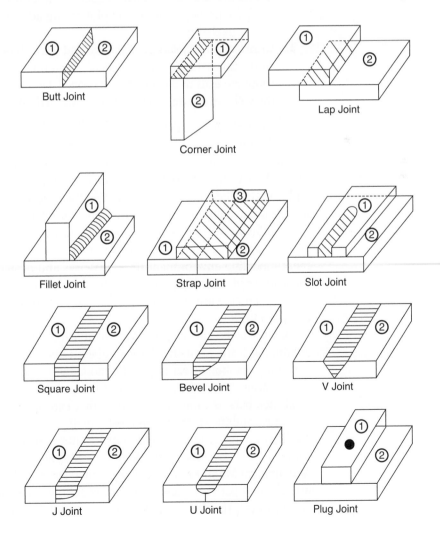

and amount of the load that the joint carries determines the joint type. For example, if we have a vertical compression load at the joint, a butt joint would be a weak joint, whereas a corner or a lap joint would be better and stronger. The strength ratio could be used to determine the safer mode of failure of the weld joint. For example, we may use a butt joint that shears off first before the welded parts themselves fail.

We refer to the welded parts as weldments. A **weldment** is a part we design using CAD/CAM systems. Weldments can take various shapes such as structural members, blocks, etc. You can use 2D and 3D sketches to define the basic framework of a weldment structure. After you define the frame, you create the structural members and add gussets, end gaps, etc.

## 10.7 Weldment Features

Welded parts are mostly structures consisting of frames or trusses, that is, skeletons. Each frame consists of members that are welded (connected) together. The frames usually form a 3D sketch. After creating the frame (skeleton), we add cross sections to it to create the structural members, followed by creating the weld joints, and closing the members' ends (if needed). Thus, the modeling steps of creating welded parts (weldments) are:

1. **Create the weld frame:** Use a 2D or 3D sketch depending on the frame design at hand.
2. **Create the structural members:** Each member uses a cross section. These members trace the frame shape. Think of it as you add meat (members) to the bones (frame skeleton).
3. **Create the weld joints:** Add the welded joints based on their types (Figure 10.6). Also, stiffen the joints (if needed) by adding ribs.
4. **Close the ends of the members if needed:** Use end caps to close the open ends of the weld structure. These ends are welded onto the open ends of the structure.

As with sheet metal modeling, modeling welded parts requires unique features such as weld joints, stiffeners, and end caps. These features must be easy to use. SolidWorks provides a comprehensive and easy-to-use **Weldments** module with ample features. Figure 10.7A shows these features. The features come in three groups: base, weld-specific, and generic. The base feature is the Weldment feature shown in Figure 10.7B. It is not a feature in the common sense that we know such as extrusion or revolve. You cannot edit the Weldment feature, but you can delete it (right-click it in a features tree to see what you can do with it). Think of the Weldment feature as a container that sets up the weldment modeling environment in SolidWorks and designates the part as a weldment. All the features of a welded part (see Figure 10.7C) you create become children of the Weldment (parent) feature in the features tree. If you delete the parent, all its children are deleted with it.

On the technical side, the Weldment feature deactivates SolidWorks default mode of combining features (using Boolean operations) as you create them, so that you always have only one body (feature) in the modeling space at any time. The Weldment feature, in the meantime, activates the multi-body mode of modeling, thus keeping the structural members as individual features that can be deleted or manipulated separately. It does not combine them as you create them.

The second group of Weldment features shown in Figure 10.7 is the weld-specific features. They are Structural Member, Trim/Extend, End Cap, Gusset, and Filled Bead. A **Structural Member** sweeps a predefined (by SolidWorks) cross section (profile) along user-defined paths created using 3D sketching. The profiles follow industry standards. SolidWorks provides drop-down lists to select from to ensure adherence to these

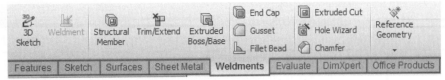

(A) **Weldments** tab

(B) Weldment feature

(C) Welded part whose tree is shown to the left

**FIGURE 10.7**
Weldment features

standards. You would need to select the type of standard (ANSI or ISO), the profile type (C channel, pipe, square tube, etc.), and the profile size. You can group structural members as you create them. When you delete one member of the group, the entire group is deleted.

A **Trim/Extend** feature closes the structural members by trimming or extending them relative to each other to create a coherent, integrated welded part. An **End Cap** feature closes the open end faces of structural members. This is useful if you want to prevent any foreign materials (water, debris, etc.) from going inside the structural members of a welded part. A **Gusset** is a rib that you add between two adjoining planar faces to stiffen a weld joint. Adding gussets between faces has strict requirements. You cannot add gussets between nonplanar faces or faces that do not share edges. We leave the details of creating gussets to the tutorials. A **Fillet Bead** creates a T (fillet) joint (see Figure 10.6) between two structural members.

The third and final group of Weldment features shown in Figure 10.7 is the generic features. These are features we have already used before in modeling any parts. They are included as part of the **Weldments** tab as a convenience to the designer to circumvent going to the **Features** tab to grab them from there. These features are the ones most commonly needed in the context of designing welded parts. As shown in Figure 10.7, they are Extruded Boss/Base, Extruded Cut, Hole Wizard, Chamfer, and Reference Geometry. Another important item of the generic group is the **3D Sketch** icon that we use to create the frame of a welded part. Table 10.2 shows SolidWorks Weldment features and how to create them.

**TABLE 10.2   Available Weldment Features**

| Feature | Input | Before Feature Creation | After Feature Creation |
|---|---|---|---|
| 3D Sketch | Sketch entities along the 3D axes | None | |
| Structural Member | Sketch (skeleton) segment(s), standard (ANSI or ISO), profile type, and profile size | Skeleton Segment | |
| Trim/Extend | Body to trim, trimming boundary, and others (see left side of Solid-Works screen for other inputs) | Body to Trim / Trimming Boundary | |
| End Cap | End face of structural member, cap thickness, thickness direction, and type of chamfer corners | End Face | |

**TABLE 10.2    Available Weldment Features (*continued*)**

| Feature | Input | Before Feature Creation | After Feature Creation |
|---------|-------|------------------------|------------------------|
| Gusset | Faces to support, gusset profile type, thickness amount and direction, and gusset location | Faces to Support | |
| Fillet Bead | Two faces to fillet, and others (see left side of SolidWorks screen for other inputs) | Faces to Fillet | 3 |

## 10.8  Weld Symbols

The last feature (Fillet Bead) in Table 10.2 shows a weld symbol with the fillet size (3 mm). We need to understand these weld symbols because we use them in welding engineering drawings to specify the weld joint type and parameters. There are ISO and ANSI weld symbols. Table 10.3 shows SolidWorks ISO weld symbols. Table 10.4 shows SolidWorks ANSI weld symbols. Note that all these symbols can also be displayed in an upside-down fashion (have identification line on top as shown for the first symbol in Table 10.3) to accommodate the other style and preference of displaying.

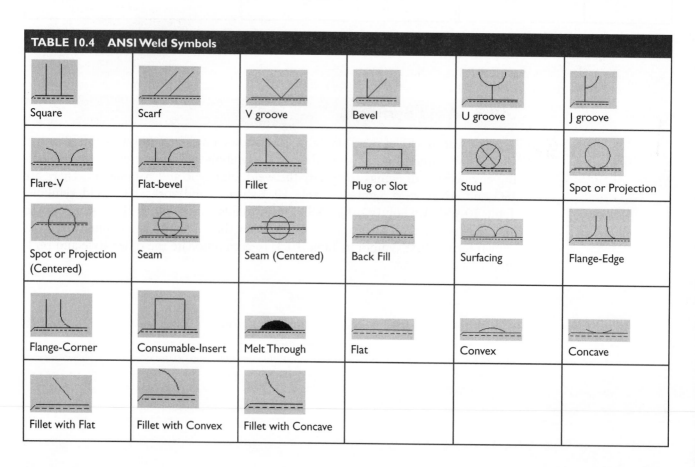

**TABLE 10.3    ISO Weld Symbols**

| | | | | | |
|---|---|---|---|---|---|
| Or / Butt | Square butt | Single V butt | Single V butt with root | Single bevel butt | Single bevel butt with root |
| Single U butt | Single J butt | Backing run | Fillet | Plug or slot | Spot |
| Spot (centered) | JIS spot | Seam | Seam (centered) | JIS seam | Flat |
| Convex | Concave | Fillet with Flat | Fillet with Convex | Fillet with Concave | |

**TABLE 10.4    ANSI Weld Symbols**

| | | | | | |
|---|---|---|---|---|---|
| Square | Scarf | V groove | Bevel | U groove | J groove |
| Flare-V | Flat-bevel | Fillet | Plug or Slot | Stud | Spot or Projection |
| Spot or Projection (Centered) | Seam | Seam (Centered) | Back Fill | Surfacing | Flange-Edge |
| Flange-Corner | Consumable-Insert | Melt Through | Flat | Convex | Concave |
| Fillet with Flat | Fillet with Convex | Fillet with Concave | | | |

## 10.9 Tutorials Overview

The theme for the tutorials in this chapter is to practice creating and using sheet metal and weldments. The tutorials show how to create sheet metal and weld parts, as well as create sheet metal and welding drawings. Commercial Sheetmetal Co. Inc., located in Canton, MA, USA (www.commercialsheetmetal.net), has sponsored this chapter. Commercial Sheetmetal specializes in the manufacturing of ROHS compliant card-guide chassis, frames, panels, brackets, and custom enclosures. Its enclosures are NEMA rated and UL/CUL approved and can be fabricated in aluminum, steel, stainless steel, and galvanized steel. It serves many industries including the biomedical, semiconductor, fire/safety sector, telecommunications, construction, and commercial and military industries. We chat with Mr. Kurt Larson, Senior Engineer at Commercial Sheetmetal, in the Industry Chat. Figure 10.8 shows sample products of Commercial Sheetmetal Co. Inc.

**FIGURE 10.8**
Sample products (Courtesy of Commercial Sheetmetal Co. Inc.)

(A) Communications chassis
(Actual sheet metal part)

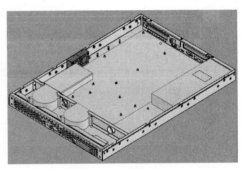

(B) Communications chassis
(SolidWorks model)

## Tutorial 10–1: Learn Sheet Metal Modeling and Operations

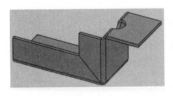

**FIGURE 10.9**
A sheet metal part

### Modeling task

Use the sheet metal commands to create the part shown in Figure 10.9.

### Modeling synthesis

This tutorial covers the basic sheet metal operations.

### Modeling plan

The model is created using the basic sheet metal commands.

### Design intent

Ignore for this chapter.

### CAD steps

We create the part in four steps:

1. Create a base flange.
2. Add a miter flange.
3. Add an edge flange.
4. Unfold and cut the edge flange.

The details of these steps are shown below.

## Step 1: Create a base flange

**Task**

A. Open a sketch on the front plane.

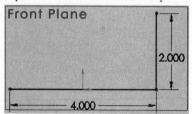

B. Select the **Base Flange/Tab** option.

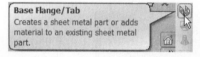

C. Fill in the information.

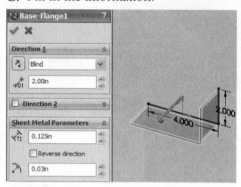

**Command Sequence to Click**

Sketch as shown to the left on the front plane of a new part.
Save the part as *tutorial 10.1.sldprt*
**Help:** The units are inches, and the horizontal line is centered on the origin.

Without exiting the sketch, select **Base Flange/Tab** (**Sheet Metal** tab) as shown to the left to create a sheet metal part from the sketch.

Input data shown to the left => Green check mark to finish.

## Step 2: Add a miter flange

**Task**

A. Select the **Miter Flange** tool.

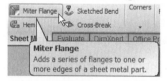

B. Create the sketch plane for the miter flange profile.

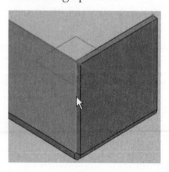

**Command Sequence to Click**

**Sheet Metal => Miter Flange** as shown to the left

Select the vertical edge as shown to the left.
**Why:** This will create a sketch plane normal to that edge to sketch the profile of the miter flange.

| Task | Command Sequence to Click |
|---|---|

C. Sketch the profile of the miter flange.

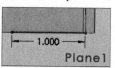

Starting from the origin of the sketch, draw a horizontal line as shown to the left, and then exit the sketch.

D. Propagate the flange.

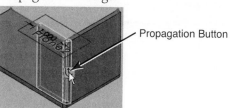

Select the propagation button shown to the left.

E. Fill in the options as shown below.

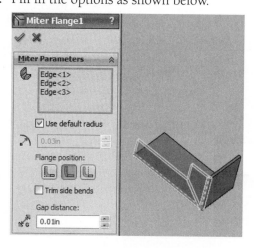

Set the **Material Outside** and the **Gap distance** as shown to the left.

## Step 3: Add an edge flange

| Task | Command Sequence to Click |
|---|---|

A. Select the **Edge Flange** tool.

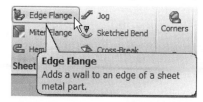

**Sheet Metal => Edge Flange** as shown to the left

B. Select the edge to use to create the flange.

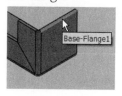 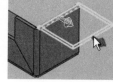

Select the edge and drag the mouse in the direction shown to the left, and then click the mouse a second time.

| Task | Command Sequence to Click |
|---|---|
| C. Fill in the options as shown below. | Set the **Flange Length** and **Flange Position** as shown to the left. |

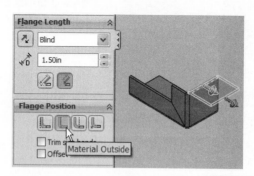

## Step 4: Unfold and cut the edge flange

| Task | Command Sequence to Click |
|---|---|
| A. Select the **Unfold** tool. | **Sheet Metal => Unfold** as shown to the left |

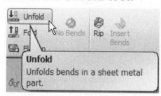

| | |
|---|---|
| B. Select a fixed face. | Select the vertical face as shown to the left for the **Fixed face.** |

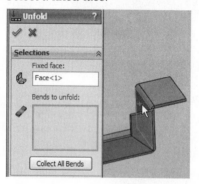

| | |
|---|---|
| C. Select the bend of the edge flange. | Select the edge as shown to the left to unfold. |

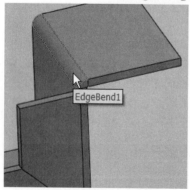

| Task | Command Sequence to Click |
|---|---|

**D.** Sketch a circle as shown below on the unfolded side.

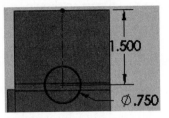

**E.** Cut extrude the circle through the part as shown below.

**F.** Fold the edge back down.

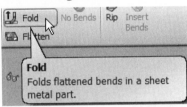

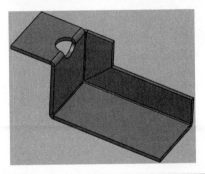

**Sheet Metal => Fold** as shown to the left => Select the same edge that was unfolded in Task A of Step 4.

**Why:** We have to unfold the model to cut the hole and then fold it back for two reasons: (1) This is how the part would be cut in real life. (2) It will be difficult to orient the hole correctly while in the folded state.

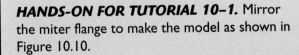

*HANDS-ON FOR TUTORIAL 10–1.* Mirror the miter flange to make the model as shown in Figure 10.10.

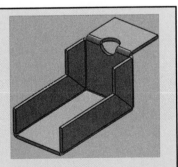

**FIGURE 10.10**
A sheet metal part with two miter flanges

# Tutorial 10–2: Create Sheet Metal Drawings

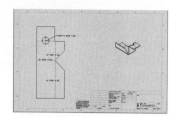

**FIGURE 10.11**
A sheet metal drawing

### Modeling task

Create a drawing of the sheet metal part as shown in Figure 10.11.

### Modeling synthesis

This tutorial covers the basic sheet metal drawing options.

### Modeling plan

Create a drawing of the model created in Tutorial 10–1.

### Design intent

Ignore for this chapter.

### CAD steps

We create the drawing in two steps:

1. Create a sheet metal drawing.
2. Change the bend callout display options.

   The details of these steps are shown below.

## Step 1: Create a sheet metal drawing

| Task | Command Sequence to Click |
|---|---|
| A. Open the part created in Tutorial 10–1 shown below.  | **File => Open** => *tutorial 10.1* => **Open** |
| B. Edit the **Sheet-Metal1** node of the features tree.  | Edit the sheet metal properties by right-clicking on **Sheet-Metal1** in the features tree and selecting **Edit Feature** as shown to the left. |
| C. Change the **Auto Relief**.  | Change the **Auto Relief** to **Tear** as shown to the left. **Why:** This will allow the part to be flattened. |
| D. Create a drawing of this part. 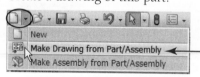 | **File => Make Drawing from Part/Assembly** (or select from the drop-down as shown to the left) |

474

| Task | Command Sequence to Click |
|---|---|
| E. Insert an isometric drawing and set the scale to 1:2. | **View Layout => Model View** as shown to the left |

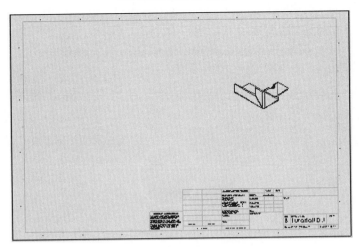

| F. Insert a second view that is a flat pattern. | **View Layout => Model View => Flat pattern** as shown to the left |

| G. Place the view as shown below. | Insert the flat pattern with a scale of 1:1. |

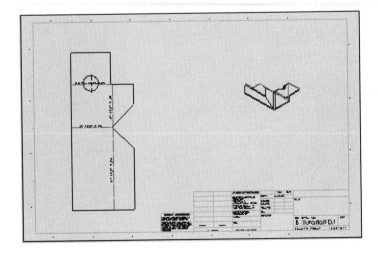

## Step 2: Change the bend callout display options

| Task | Command Sequence to Click |
|---|---|
| **A.** Box select the bend callouts. | Select the bend callouts as shown to the left. |

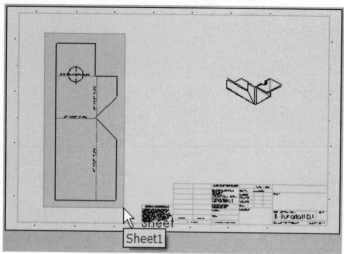

| Task | Command Sequence to Click |
|---|---|
| **B.** Change the font size. | Deselect **Use document font** and click on the **Font** button as shown to the left. Change the font size to 15 point. |

| Task | Command Sequence to Click |
|---|---|
| **C.** Add a leader to the callout. | Select the **Down 90.0 R.03** callout, and select **Leader** option as shown to the left. |

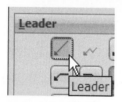

| Task | Command Sequence to Click |
|---|---|
| **D.** Move the callout. | Drag the callout as shown to the left. |

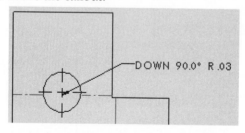

DOWN 90.0° R .03

**E.** Select the two vertical callouts.

UP 90.0° R .03

| Task | Command Sequence to Click |
|------|---------------------------|
| F. Change the display angle.  | Change the display angle to zero so that the callouts read horizontally as shown to the left. |

**HANDS-ON FOR TUTORIAL 10–2.** Add another view to the drawing such that only the miter edges are unfolded.
Help: Use the **Unfold** options discussed in Tutorial 10–1 along with the **Current Model Display** option on the drawing.

## Tutorial 10–3: Create Sheet Metal Part from Solid Body

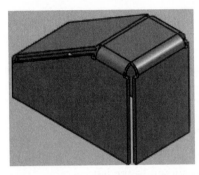

**FIGURE 10.12**
A sheet metal part converted fron a solid body

**Modeling task**

Create a sheet metal part from a solid part, as shown in Figure 10.12.

**Modeling synthesis**

This tutorial covers the ability to convert a solid part into a sheet metal part.

**Modeling plan**

Create a new part, and then convert it into a sheet metal part.

**Design intent**

Ignore for this chapter.

**CAD steps**

We create the part in two steps:

1. Create a solid part.
2. Convert the part to sheet metal.

The details of these steps are shown below.

### Step 1: Create a solid part

| Task | Command Sequence to Click |
|------|---------------------------|
| A. Create the sketch. | Sketch as shown to the left on the front plane.<br>**Help:** The units are in mm. |

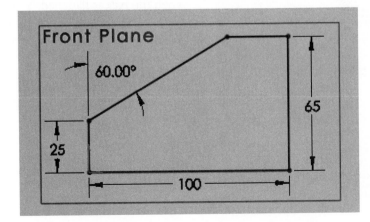

|  Task | Command Sequence to Click |
|---|---|
| **B.** Extrude as shown. | Extrude 50.0 mm as a **Mid Plane** as shown to the left. |

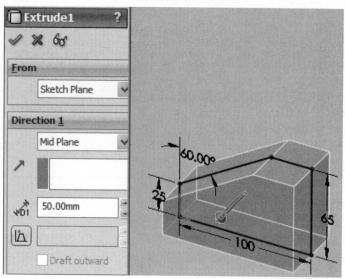

## Step 2: Convert the part to sheet metal

|  Task | Command Sequence to Click |
|---|---|
| **A.** Select the **Convert to Sheet Metal** tool. | **Sheet Metal => Convert to Sheet Metal** as shown to the left |

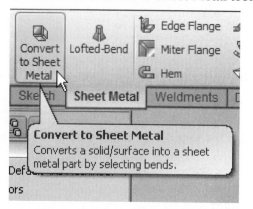

**B.** Select the fixed entity.

Select the top square face as the fixed entity as shown to the left.

**Why:** The fixed face remains in place when the part is flattened. You can select only one face. Think of the fixed face as a face you hold the part from to flatten its other faces.

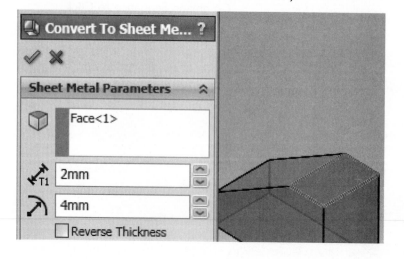

**Task**

C. Select **Bend Edges** to complete the conversion.

**Command Sequence to Click**

Select the four edges on the top face as well as the edge on the other end of the angled face for the **Bend Edges** as shown to the left => Green check mark to finish.

**Help:** The software will automatically select the edges that will be ripped.

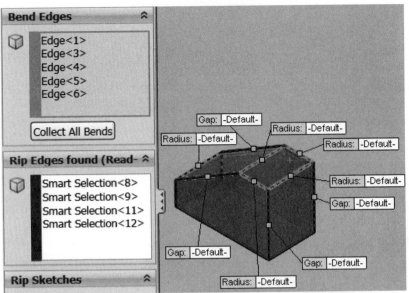

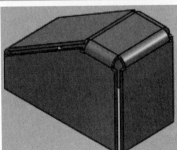

> **HANDS-ON FOR TUTORIAL 10–3.** Create a drawing for the part created in Tutorial 10–3. Insert both a folded isometric view and a flat pattern view. Choose the scale accordingly and submit a screenshot.

## Tutorial 10–4: Create Sheet Metal Part from Flattened State

Modeling task

Create a sheet metal part from a flattened state, as shown in Figure 10.13.

**FIGURE 10.13**
A sheet metal part created from a flattened state

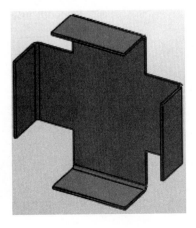

### Modeling synthesis

This tutorial covers the ability to create a sheet metal part by sketching a base flange and bending it.

### Modeling plan

The model is created by sketching a base flange, sketching bend lines, and folding the flange using the bend lines.

### Design intent

Ignore for this chapter.

### CAD steps

We create the part in three steps:

1. Create a base flange.
2. Sketch bend lines.
3. Bend the flange using the bend lines.

   The details of these steps are shown below.

## Step 1: Create a base flange

| Task | Command Sequence to Click |
|---|---|
| A. Create the base flange. 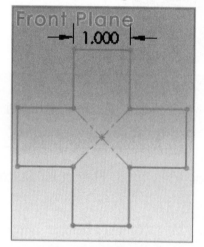 | Sketch as shown to the left on the front plane of a new part. **Help:** The units are inches, and all of the lines in the sketch are equal in length. |
| B. Select the **Base Flange/Tab**. 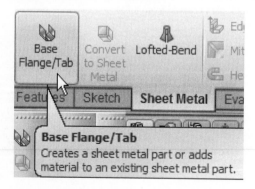 | **Sheet Metal** tab => **Base Flange/Tab** as shown to the left |

| Task | Command Sequence to Click |
|---|---|
| C. Set the options as shown. | Create a .032 in. thick base flange as shown to the left. |

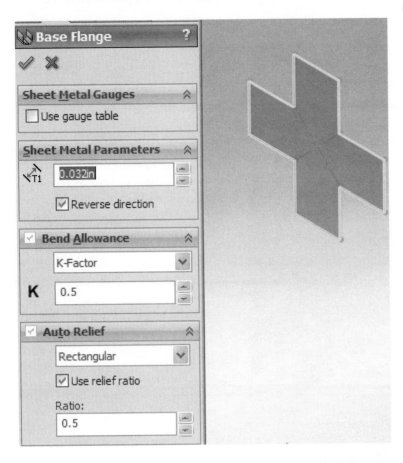

## Step 2: Sketch bend lines

| Task | Command Sequence to Click |
|---|---|
| A. Sketch the four bend lines. | Sketch as shown to the left on the front face, and exit the sketch. |
| | **Help:** Each line connects the midpoints of the edges. |

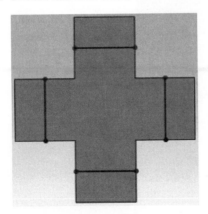

# Step 3:  Bend the flange using the bend lines

| Task | Command Sequence to Click |
|---|---|

**Task**

A. Select the **Sketched Bend** tool.

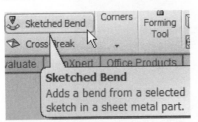

**Command Sequence to Click**

Select the sketch and open the **Sketched Bend** tool as shown to the right.

B. Set the parameters as shown below.

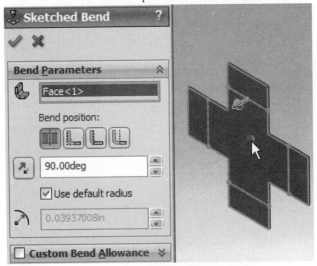

Select the **Fixed Entity** face somewhere inside of the four lines as indicated by the cursor shown to the left to create the sheet metal part as shown to the left in the second image.

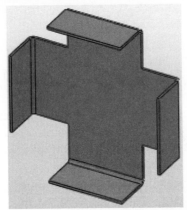

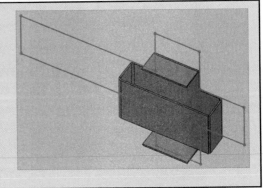

### HANDS-ON FOR TUTORIAL 10–4.
Modify the sketch shown in Task A of Step 1 to create the sheet metal part shown in Figure 10.14. Submit a copy of the model.

**FIGURE 10.14**
A sheet metal part with touching bends

# Tutorial 10–5:   Learn How to Create a Weldment

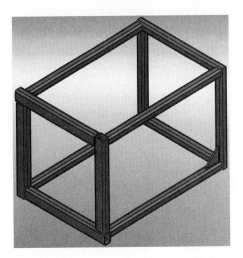

**FIGURE 10.15**
A weldment structure

### Modeling task

Use the weldment commands to create the weldment structure shown in Figure 10.15.

### Modeling synthesis

This tutorial covers the basic weldment operations.

### Modeling plan

We create the 2D sketches first and then add structural members along them.

### Design intent

Ignore for this chapter.

### CAD steps

We create the weldment structure in four steps:

1. Create the sketches.
2. Create the weldment.
3. Insert a gusset.
4. Insert a fillet bead.

The details of these steps are shown below.

## Step 1:   Create the sketches

| Task | Command Sequence to Click |
|---|---|
| **A.** Create a cross section on the front plane. | Sketch as shown on the front plane of a new part to the left. Save the part as *tutorial 10.5.sldprt*.<br>**Help:** The units are inches, and the horizontal line starts on the origin. |

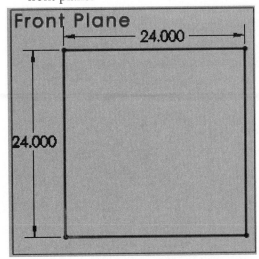

| Task | Command Sequence to Click |
|---|---|
| **B.** Create a plane to copy sketch of above task. | Create a plane 36 in. from and parallel to the front plane. |

| Task | Command Sequence to Click |
|---|---|

**C.** Copy geometry.

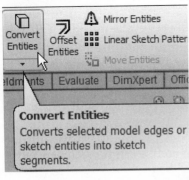

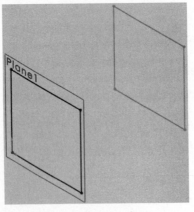

Select **Sketch1** from features tree =>
**Convert Entities** to create an identical
sketch in Plane1 as shown to the left.

**D.** Create a cross section on the
right plane.

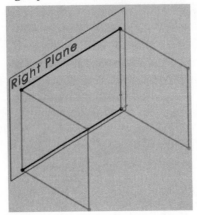

Create a sketch on the right plane as
shown to the left to bridge both of the
first two sketches.

**E.** Create a plane to copy the sketch
of Task D.

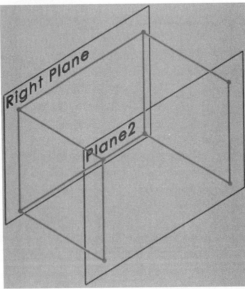

**Insert => Reference Geometry =>
Plane** => Create a plane that is 24 in.
away from and parallel to the right
plane as shown to the left.

| Task | Command Sequence to Click |
|---|---|
| F. Copy geometry. | Select **Sketch2** from features tree => **Convert Entities** to create an identical sketch in Plane2 as shown to the left. |

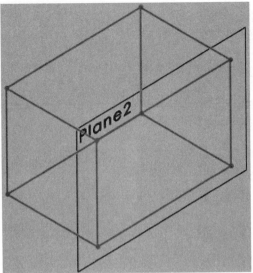

## Step 2: Create the weldment

| Task | Command Sequence to Click |
|---|---|
| A. Start the creation of structural members. | **Weldments** tab => **Structural Member** as shown to the left |

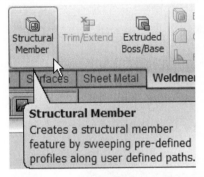

| Task | Command Sequence to Click |
|---|---|
| B. Create a group of structural members. | **Structural Member** => Select **Sketch1** from the features tree => Green check mark to finish. <br> **Help:** The following Tasks C through F use different parts of the **Structural Member** pane shown to the left. |

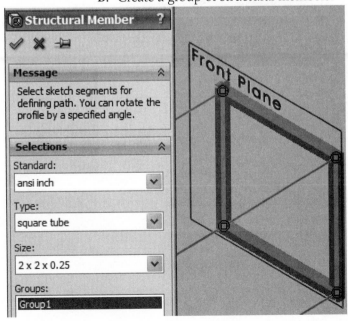

| Task | Command Sequence to Click |
|---|---|
| C. Create a miter corner. | Set the corner treatment to **End Miter** as shown to the left. |

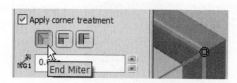

| | |
|---|---|
| D. Create a second group, **Group2**, of structural members. | Without exiting the **Structural Member** feature, select **New Group** button as shown to the left.<br>**Why:** Each line segment in a group can be joined only to one other line segment. Therefore, secondary groups within a structural member type are created when other members branch off. |

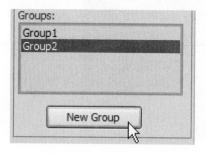

| | |
|---|---|
| E. Select **Group2** members. | Select the four longer lines contained within the right plane and Plane2 as shown to the left. |

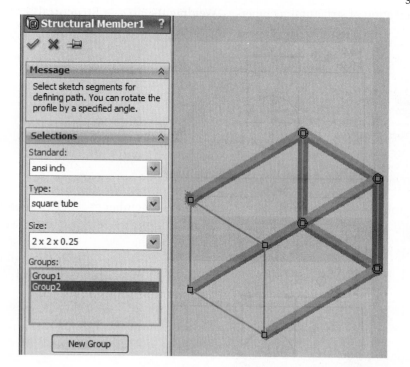

| Task | Command Sequence to Click |
|---|---|

**F.** Exit the **Structural Member** tool.

Green check mark to exit the weldment structure shown to the left.

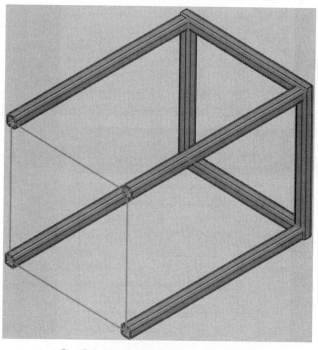

**G.** Create a new structural member.

Create a new structural member and select the four line segments in Plane1. Use a 3 × 2 × 0.25 in. rectangle tube and miter the corners as shown to the left.

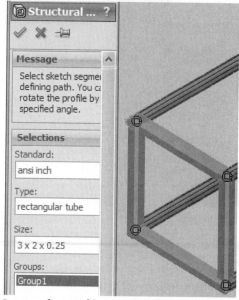

**H.** Locate the profile.

**Rotation Angle** => Set the angle at 90° => **Locate Profile** => Select the point as shown to the left.

| Task | Command Sequence to Click |
|---|---|
| **1.** Finish creating the structural member. | Accept and save the part as shown to the left. |

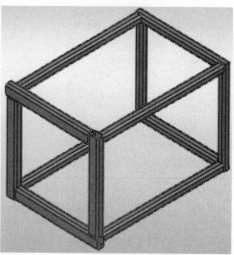

## Step 3: Insert a gusset

| Task | Command Sequence to Click |
|---|---|
| **A.** Prepare to create a gusset. | **Zoom** the graphics region into the corner where the front plane intersects Plane2 as shown to the left. |

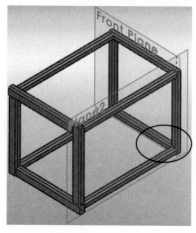 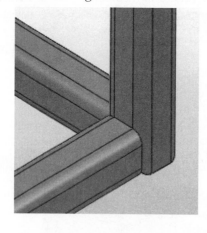

| **B.** Open the **Gusset** tool. | **Weldments => Gusset** as shown to the left |

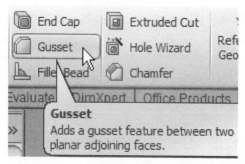

| Task | Command Sequence to Click |
|---|---|
| C. Create the gusset as shown below. | Select the two faces as shown. Create a 4 × 4 in. triangular gusset, .375 in. thick, and located in the center of the weldment members, as shown to the left. |

## Step 4: Insert a fillet bead

| Task | Command Sequence to Click |
|---|---|
| A. Open the **Fillet Bead** tool. | **Weldments => Fillet Bead** as shown to the left |

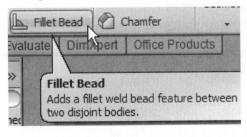

|  | Task | Command Sequence to Click |
|--|------|---------------------------|

**B.** Select the faces as shown below.

Input .125 in. for the bead thickness. Select the gusset face for **Face Set1** and the faces of the structural members as **Face Set2**, as shown to the left.

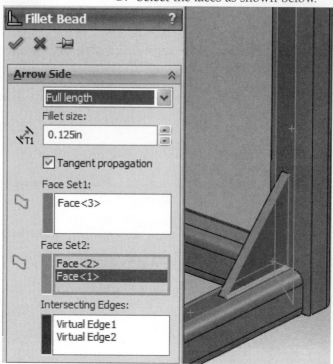

**C.** Create the fillet bead of the other side of the gusset.

Repeat Task B of Step 4 for the other side of the gusset as shown to the left.

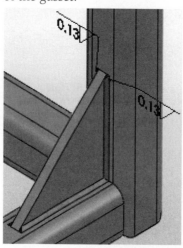

***HANDS-ON FOR TUTORIAL 10–5.*** Add a gusset and a 0.125 in. fillet bead to all of the corners of the weldment shown in Figure 10.16.

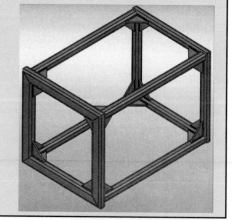

**FIGURE 10.16**
A weldment structure with gussets

# Tutorial 10–6:   Create a Weldment Drawing

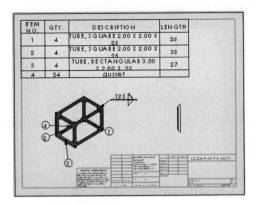

| ITEM NO. | QTY. | DESCRIPTION | LENGTH |
|---|---|---|---|
| 1 | 4 | TUBE, SQUARE 2.00 X 2.00 X 25 | 26 |
| 2 | 4 | TUBE, SQUARE 2.00 X 2.00 X 25 | 35 |
| 3 | 4 | TUBE, RECTANGULAR 3.00 X 2.00 X 25 | 27 |
| 4 | 24 | gusset | |

**FIGURE 10.17**
A weldment drawing

## Modeling task

Create the drawing shown in Figure 10.17 for the weldment created in Tutorial 10–5.

## Modeling synthesis

This tutorial covers the basic weldment drawing operations.

## Modeling plan

We create a drawing for the weldment of Tutorial 10–5.

## Design intent

Ignore for this chapter.

## CAD steps

We create the weldment drawing in five steps:

1. Insert an isometric view.
2. Insert a cut list table.
3. Add weld callouts.
4. Add balloons.
5. Add a view of a structural member.

The details of these steps are shown below.

## Step 1:   Insert an isometric view

### Task

A. Open the weldment part of Tutorial 10–5 shown below.

### Command Sequence to Click

**File => Open** => *tutorial 10.5.sldprt* => Open

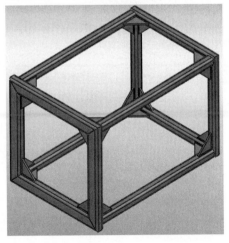

B. Create a new drawing as shown below.

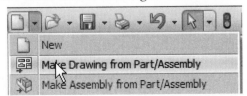

| Task | Command Sequence to Click |
|---|---|

**C.** Insert an isometric view.

*Isometric

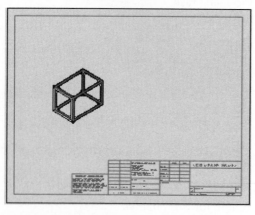

Drag the **Isometric** icon from the pane on left of display screen. Place it as shown to the left.

## Step 2: Insert a cut list table

| Task | Command Sequence to Click |
|---|---|

**A.** Return to the model.

Right-click on the isometric view created in Task C of Step 1 => Select **Open Part** from the context menu that shows up (hover over the icons until you find it).

**B.** Modify the properties of the gusset.

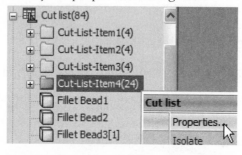

Expand the **Cut list** (Click the + symbol in the features tree) => Right-click the **Cut-List-Item4 => Properties** as shown to the left.

**C.** Modify the **Property** box.

|   | Property Name | Type | Value / Text Expression | Evaluated Value |
|---|---|---|---|---|
| 1 | DESCRIPTION | Text ▼ | gusset | ▼ gusset |
| 2 |  | ▼ |  |  |

For **Property Name**, select **Description**. For **Type**, select **Text**. Manually type the word "Gusset" in the box as shown to the left => Press **Enter** on the keyboard => **OK** => Right-click in the graphics pane => Expand the menu => Select **Open Drawing** to return to the drawing.

| Task | Command Sequence to Click |
|---|---|

**D.** Insert a **Weldment Cut List** table.

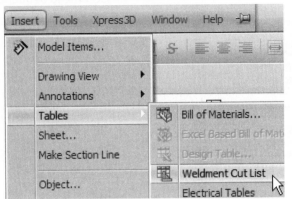

**Insert** menu => **Tables** => **Weldment Cut List** as shown to the left
**Help:** You must be in a drawing to see the items shown to the left.

**E.** Select the isometric view.

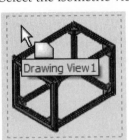

Select the isometric view when it prompts you to select the model to specify as shown to the left.

**F.** Accept the default options and place the table as shown below.

Do not change any of the options at this point.

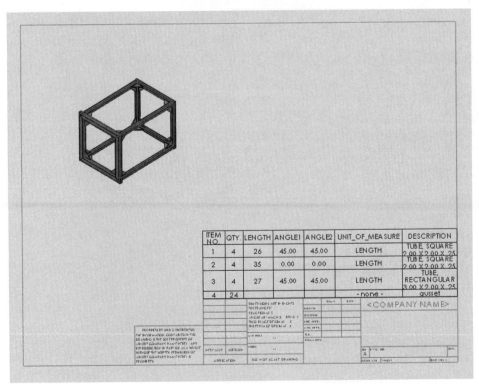

## Step 3: Add weld callouts

Task

A. Select **Model Items**.

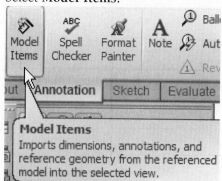

Command Sequence to Click

**Annotations** tab => **Model Items** as shown to the left

B. Insert weld annotations.

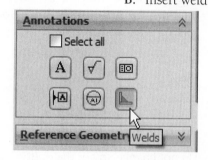

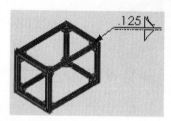

Click the **Annotations** pane to expand => Deselect all options except **Welds** as shown to the left => Green check mark to finish. The resulting drawing is shown to the left.

## Step 4: Add balloons

Task

A. Insert balloons.

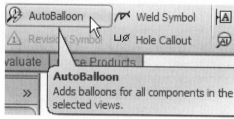

Command Sequence to Click

**Annotations** tab => **AutoBalloon** as shown to the left

B. Set the balloon layout.

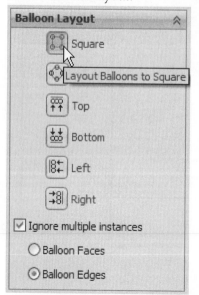

Select **Square** for the balloon layout as shown to the left.

| Task | Command Sequence to Click |
|---|---|

**C.** Review the drawing shown below.

The number inside a balloon refers to the **Item Number** in the table.

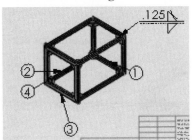

## Step 5: Add a view of a structural member

| Task | Command Sequence to Click |
|---|---|

**A.** Select the view type.

**Insert** tab => **Drawing View** => **Relative To Model** as shown to the left

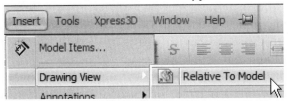

**B.** Select the model with respect to which we generate the view.

Select the ISO view of the model as shown to the left.

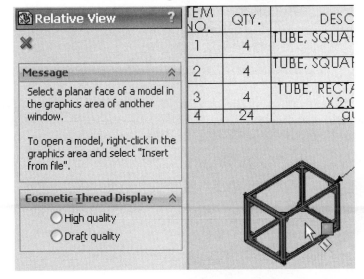

| Task | Command Sequence to Click |
|---|---|

**C.** Select the structural member.

Check **Selected Bodies** option under **Scope** as shown to the left.

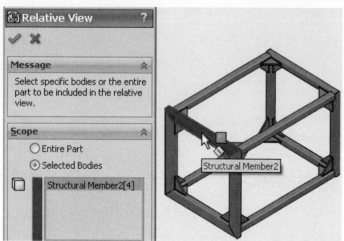

**D.** Select one orientation of the new view.

Click where Face<1> is shown to the left => Select the face as shown to the left.

**Why:** We need two orientations to fully define the new view relative to the existing model. The first face you select here defines the front (by default) of the new view.

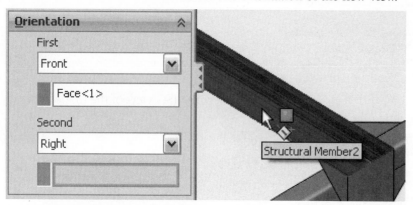

**E.** Select another orientation of the new view.

Select the face as shown to the left => Green check mark to finish.

**Why:** The face you select here defines **Right** (by default) orientation of the new view.

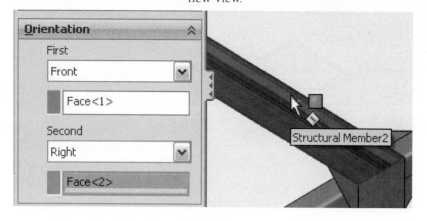

## Task

F. Place the new view.

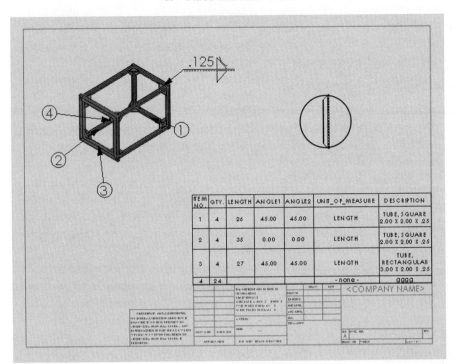

| ITEM NO. | QTY. | LENGTH | ANGLE1 | ANGLE2 | UNIT_OF_MEASURE | DESCRIPTION |
|---|---|---|---|---|---|---|
| 1 | 4 | 26 | 45.00 | 45.00 | LENGTH | TUBE, SQUARE 2.00 X 2.00 X .25 |
| 2 | 4 | 35 | 0.00 | 0.00 | LENGTH | TUBE, SQUARE 2.00 X 2.00 X .25 |
| 3 | 4 | 27 | 45.00 | 45.00 | LENGTH | TUBE, RECTANGULAR 3.00 X 2.00 X .25 |
| 4 | 24 | | | | - none - | gggg |

## Command Sequence to Click

SolidWorks will bring you back to the drawing document where you click anywhere on the drawing to place the new **Relative To Model** view as indicated by the arrow shown to the left.

---

***HANDS-ON FOR TUTORIAL 10–6.*** First, manually add the dimensions to the relative view as shown in Figure 10.18. Then change the properties of the bal-loons so that the balloons associated with the structural members display the length of each member, and the balloons associated with the gussets display the quantity of gussets.

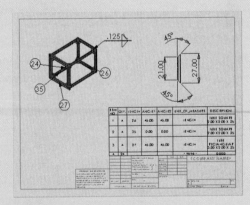

**FIGURE 10.18**
A weldment drawing with dimensions

## INDUSTRY CHAT

This section provides practical insight into how the chapter material is used in industry in the real world and practice. This section summarizes the chat with Mr. Kurt Larson (Senior Engineer) of Commercial Sheetmetal Co. Inc., the sponsor of this chapter. The structure of the chat follows the chapter sections.

**Chapter Section 10.1:**    Introduction

**ABE:**    Provide an overview of sheet metal process at Commercial Sheetmetal.

**KURT:**    We have several ways of producing product. Customers may provide us with fully detailed and dimensioned blueprints, send us E-files, raw geometry files, or convey their needs verbally with some basic overall dimensions. For example, a customer would like to cover an old steam radiator that is heating their home. They would give us basic dimensions and we would design a cosmetically pleasing cover with perforations to let heat escape, create a blueprint, and have the customer make or suggest any modifications they would like.

Because of the fact that a lot of these designs are not made by sheet metal engineers, a part may not be able to be made as to what the blueprint suggests. We may have to convert and modify as needed to fabricate it as a sheet metal part. For example, for a shelled part "raw geometry," although it may look like the end product, we would have to use the rip feature of SolidWorks in order to flatten this part into a sheet metal part before it could be manufactured.

**Chapter Section 10.2:**    Sheet Metal

**ABE:**    How do you specify and use K-Factor, bend allowance, and bend deduction?

**KURT:**    You can find your basic K-Factor formula in a machinist handbook and there are many charts and cheat sheets for K-Factor out there for sheet metal. I use a program that was written by one of our engineers. Over the years we have tested different materials by bending them and modifying our calculations to come as close as we can to what is actually happening in fabrication.

Different types of metal react differently while bending. For example: the bend deduction for stainless steel will be different than aluminum. Also the type of bending on the same type of material could alter the K-Factor. To end up with a 90 degree bend, sometimes you may have to coin a bend (apply more pressure and bend the material over 90 degrees) in order to compensate for the material spring back or memory. If the 90 degrees is not a big issue we can air bend (where the punch does not press the sheet metal up against the die; it just folds it) it and as long as it comes close to our goal, it is acceptable.

**Chapter Section 10.3:**    Sheet Metal Features

**ABE:**    Which sheet metal features do you use the most?

**KURT:**    We use them all. I like to start by using base flange and build my sides or flanges off of that. The mitered flange feature works great if you're designing an enclosure that has multiple sides and flanges that come together in the corners at 45 degrees. The hem feature we use to strengthen a raw edge of material or increase the edge's rigidity. The hem also will eliminate sharp edges. I would also like to point out that in creating anything in SolidWorks, it is more or less a personal style, and everyone has their own method.

### Chapter Section 10.4: Sheet Metal FeatureManager Design Tree

**ABE:** How do you use the sheet metal features tree effectively during design?

**KURT:** The features tree is very handy. If you want to change the K-Factor or metal thickness, edit the **Sheet-Metal1** node of the tree. I can also do other edit activities as normal. The tree also shows the default sketch planes and the origin. I usually set the origin at the middle of the part. We rename the tree nodes. For example, if I cut a hole, I can rename its node to "2.5 diameter hole," so I can easily access this hole, edit it, and make any changes.

### Chapter Section 10.5: Sheet Metal Methods

**ABE:** Which of the four methods do you use the most or the least at Commercial Sheetmetal? Why or Why not?

**KURT:** For the most part we use method 1 (use sheet metal features). The other methods have their problems or I should say I have problems with them. For example, for method 2 (converting a solid body to sheet metal), if this part has any discrepancy like a slight variance in metal thickness throughout the entire part or in how it was built or designed in SolidWorks, it will error out when converting. The same holds true for method 3 (convert a shelled solid body to sheet metal). Again keep in mind that not everyone who uses SolidWorks is a sheet metal engineer or knows how sheet metal reacts when being fabricated.

### Others

**ABE:** Any other experience you would like to share with our book readers?

**KURT:** I would like to say, "Everything looks great on paper." But when you get to the reality part, the two may not quite match up. For example: I could put a good size dent in a piece of sheet metal. Try drawing it in SolidWorks. Once you do, try using the flatten feature or the unfold. Let me know how you make out.

### Chapter Section 10.6: Weldments

**ABE:** Provide an overview of weldment process at Commercial Sheetmetal.

**KURT:** I would say the majority of the welding that we do would be corner type seam welding. The design of how the corner being welded will be made is determined by the material type. For example: on aluminum, the corner surfaces being welded in most cases will not overlap each other. Aluminum melts at a relatively low temperature (approximately 1220 degrees F) and will puddle and flow to fill this open gap. On a steel corner which melts at higher temperature (approximately 2500 degrees F) we would either fully close or partially overlap the metal in the corners because of the weld not flowing as much and to ensure weld penetration on both surfaces being welded. We also do quite a lot of spot welding where we incorporate a lap joint or spot weld flange in the corners of a part.

*(continued)*

We have several varieties of equipment to achieve different welding applications.

For the most part we arc weld (mig or tig welding) where an electrical arc melts the two surfaces while we add more material (welding wire). Also gas welding (torch type) is mainly used for cutting through thicker material.

Our welding personnel have to be certified because of our customer requirements and a lot of the enclosures we make have to be water tight. Some projects may even require an x-ray of the welds to ensure that there are no incursions, bubbles or impurities in the welds.

**Chapter Section 10.7:**   Weldment Features

ABE:   Which Weldment features do you use the most?

KURT:   We do not use weldment features of SolidWorks. Instead, we use assemblies and mate parts in such a way that they are weldable. We use this approach because it is faster for us to accomplish the same goal in less time, thus saving time and money. For example, I may generate a gusset as a separate part, and then assemble it in the assembly. Then we weld it. It is easier to create weld features as parts, create them, and create drawings. On the drawing, we can specify weld seams. In doing so, people on the shop floor will know what to do.

**Chapter Section 10.8:**   Weld Symbols

ABE:   Describe your welding engineering drawings and which weld symbols do you use?

KURT:   Most of our welding is seam type, spot-weld, fillet or stitch. We normally do not use the welding symbol feature on the drawings because as discussed in Section 10.7 we did not use the welding features. Instead we would use annotations with arrows to convey what is needed. I can make the parts look very pretty looking in SolidWorks but by the time I get it to my liking the part could already be built. "Unfortunately time is money."

**Others**

ABE:   Any other experience you would like to share with our book readers?

KURT:   In industry, time and money are important. We at Commercial Sheetmetal have our innovative, albeit different, approach to creating weldments by using an assembly instead of using weldment features as discussed in Section 10.7.

1. What is so special about sheet metal parts that they cannot be modeled using the conventional features modeling approach?

2. Why should we not use the assembly modeling approach to create welded parts as assemblies?

3. Define sheet metal. What distinguishes it from foil or plates?

4. Select one of the sheet metal processes (e.g., punching, rolling, stamping, etc.), and describe how the process works. Provide a report of the process details with sketches.

5. Find out the standard gauges of sheet metal for different materials and their corresponding thicknesses. For example, Gauge 10 for Aluminum is 3 mm.

6. Find typical values for K-Factor, bend allowance (BA), and bend deduction (BD) for sheet metal materials.

7. Calculate the flat length of the sheet metal shown in Figure 10.1. Use the following parameters: material is aluminum, $L_1 = L_2 = 100$ mm, $T = 5$ mm, $R = 10$ mm, $A = 90°$, and the K-Factor for aluminum = 0.485.

8. What is the difference between an edge flange and a miter flange?

9. List and describe the four methods to create sheet metal parts.

10. The seat belt buckle of an airplane seat is a sheet metal part. Create the sheet metal part of the buckle. Also, create an engineering drawing.

11. Look around you for a sheet metal part, and create its model and its engineering drawing.

12. Create the sheet metal part and drawing of a razor blade.

13. Figure 10.19 shows the cross sections of various channels. Create the sheet metal parts of the channels. Also, create their engineering drawings.

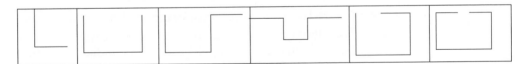

**FIGURE 10.19**
Cross sections of channels

14. Find a metal bracket or angle part around you, and create its sheet metal part and engineering drawing.

15. Find a gusset around you, and create its sheet metal part and engineering drawing.

16. Find a sump around you, and create its sheet metal part and engineering drawing.

17. Use the flattened state method, and create the sheet metal parts shown in Figure 10.20 using one flat base flange for both parts.

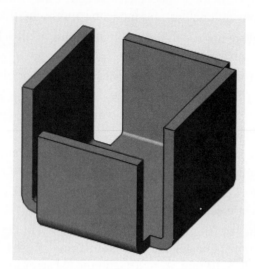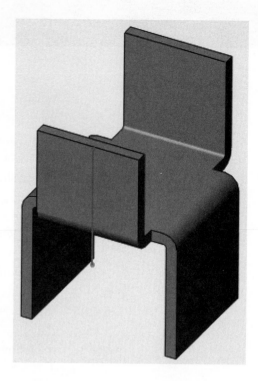

**FIGURE 10.20**
Sheet metal part

18. Select one of the welding processes (e.g., gas welding, arc welding, resistance welding, etc.), and describe how the process works. Provide a report of the process details with sketches.

19. List and describe three weld defects and why they happen.

20. Many weld joints exist. List four of them. How do you decide which weld joint to use?

21. List and describe the steps to create welded parts.

22. Why does SolidWorks use Weldment features?

23. What does a fillet weld symbol you find on a drawing show?

24. Figure 10.21 shows the weld frame (skeleton) of a building front. Follow the four steps of Section 10.7 to create the welded part. Assume all dimensions. *Hint:* You may want to model your own building metal front, so you can physically look at it when you need to.

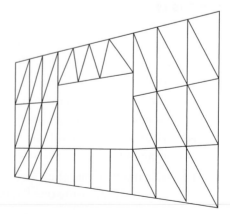

**FIGURE 10.21**
Metal frame of a building front

Part III Advanced Part Modeling

25. Figure 10.22 shows the weld frame (skeleton) of a building metal front gate. Follow the four steps of Section 10.7 to create the welded gate part. Assume all dimensions. *Hint:* You may want to model your own metal gate, so you can physically look at it when you need to.

**FIGURE 10.22**
Metal frame of a building front gate

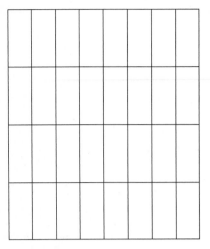

26. Figure 10.23 shows the weld frame (skeleton) of an outdoor tent. Follow the four steps of Section 10.7 to create the welded tent part. Assume all dimensions. *Hint:* You may want to model your own metal tent frame, so you can physically look at it when you need to.

**FIGURE 10.23**
Metal frame of an
outdoor tent

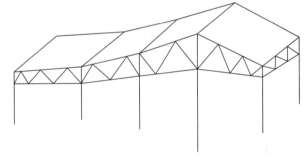

27. Figure 10.24 shows the weld frame (skeleton) of a corner guardrail for a balcony of a house. The rail has two straight perpendicular sides that are connected by a circular corner. Follow the four steps of Section 10.7 to create the welded guardrail part. Assume all dimensions. *Hint:* You may want to model your own metal guardrail frame, so you can physically look at it when you need to.

**FIGURE 10.24**
Metal frame of a
balcony guardrail

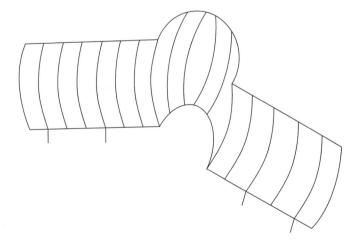

28. Figure 10.25 shows the weld frame (skeleton) of a campfire metal grill. The grill has a rectangular frame, four legs, supporting brackets at the legs, and a top uniform metal mesh. Follow the four steps of Section 10.7 to create the welded grill part. Assume all dimensions. *Hint:* You may want to model your own metal campfire grill, so you can physically look at it when you need to.

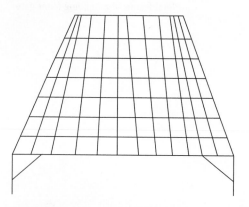

**FIGURE 10.25**
Metal frame of a campfire grill

29. Figure 10.26 shows the weld frame (skeleton) of a house gutter segment. Follow the four steps of Section 10.7 to create the welded gutter part. Assume all dimensions. *Hint:* You may want to model your own aluminum house gutter, so you can physically look at it when you need to.

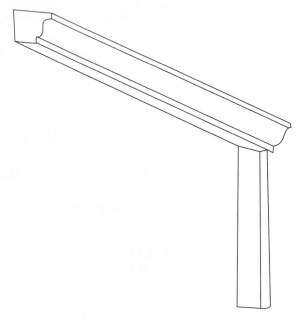

**FIGURE 10.26**
Aluminum gutter segment of a house

# Sustainable Design

## 11.1 Introduction

Not too long ago engineering design would focus on in-service requirements such as functional and strength requirements. Today, design must also consider stringent environmental requirements and the handling of products after their "death." The central question is, What do you do with products after they reach the end of their useful life? Even during their useful life, products must conform to limited natural resources and be evaluated especially in terms of energy consumption and pollution.

Sustainable design represents a paradigm shift in how we design products. It is a direct outcome of strict regulations on the environment, the use of natural resources, limited landfills for waste collection, hazardous material, health concerns, and other factors. Designers must think hard about product use and disposal including health effects and environmental impact. A good example is electronics and computer devices. Designers are trying to phase out components that represent health hazards by using new materials that are more environmentally friendly.

Sustainable design addresses two product design concerns: during life (in service) and after life (end of service). During life, a product must meet a host of environmental and energy constraints. For the environment, the product must minimize pollution and the greenhouse effect as much as possible. Some of the pollution measures include carbon dioxide emission, water pollution, and air pollution. Energy consumed by products must also be minimized by making products as efficient as possible.

Designing and producing sustainable products require sustainable design, sustainable manufacturing, and sustainable waste. We cover sustainable design in detail in this chapter. Sustainable design determines to a large extent sustainable waste (fewer emissions and less pollution of the environment). Sustainable manufacturing is controlled by materials used and the manufacturing processes themselves. In practice, the common sustainability factor is energy use in manufacturing and transporting products, as well as the energy the products use while in service.

After life, a product must equally meet a host of disposal constraints. Components of discarded products must be easy to disassemble and sort for refurbishing, recycling, and disposal. We are all familiar with the many products labeled "recycled" or with the recycle symbol. Examples include paper, printer cartridges, many plastic products, etc. Refurbished (also known as rebuilt) components are common in the automotive industry where you may buy a refurbished alternator, water pump, or brake calipers for your car. As for the disposed components, we try to minimize them in product design as much as possible.

Sustainable engineering has been used as a broader context that includes sustainable design. Other terms have been used for sustainable design such as *ecodesign*, *environmentally sustainable design*, *environmentally conscious design*, and *green design*. The latter two terms are borrowed from the manufacturing field where the terms *environmentally conscious manufacturing* and *green manufacturing* have been used to promote less polluting manufacturing methods and products that are easy to disassemble and reuse.

Minimizing energy consumption and using renewable energy (such as wind and solar energy) are important to sustainable design. The less we depend on nonrenewable energy such as fossil fuels (oil and gas), the better we preserve our natural resources. The difference between renewable and nonrenewable energy is the time required to generate the energy. Fossil fuels take million of years to form because we must wait for the decomposition of buried dead organisms. Fossil fuels contain a high percentage of carbon and hydrocarbon, two excellent sources of energy.

In order for us to learn and perform sustainable design tasks, we need to be aware of and learn the many sustainable aspects including technologies, materials, manufacturing methods, energy resources, etc. Designers can think only in terms of what they know. For example, the more materials we know (e.g., metals, plastics, ceramics, etc.), the better material we can select.

Successful and effective sustainable design tools, as many other engineering tools, are the ones that quantify the sustainability concepts. Designers would like to have design tools that allow them to compare different design alternatives to find the best one. SolidWorks **Sustainability** module fits this bill. It is a great start in the right direction.

We may ask ourselves this question before we continue: What is sustainable engineering or design? According to the WEPSD (World Engineering Partnership for Sustainable Development), **sustainable engineering** is the melting pot (integration) of three disciplines (fields): environmental, economical, and social. The use of these three fields in design defines **sustainable design**, which makes designers environmentally conscious about their designs. **Environmental sustainability** is defined as meeting the needs of the present without compromising the ability of future generations to meet their needs.

An important source when it comes to sustainability is the Brundtland Report published by the Brundtland Commission, formerly known as the World Commission on Environment and Development (WCED). The commission, created by the United Nations in 1983, began as a response to the growing concern about the deterioration of the global environment and the need for immediate action. The Brundtland Report, also known as *Our Common Future*, was published by Oxford University Press in 1987. The commission report addressed both the need for promoting sustainable development and the need for the change of policies to achieve sustainable development at the world level. The full report can be found at www.worldinbalance.net/intagreements/1987-brundtland.php.

## 11.2 Design and Society

We always practice engineering (in a broader sense) and design (in a narrower sense) within societal contexts. Engineering is inherently tied to society and human needs. Engineering design evolves over time and reflects societal needs and concerns. As society evolves, so does engineering design. Societal impact, in positive ways, is always the main drive behind engineering design.

Over time, societal needs and priorities shift and pull design along with them. Let us consider a few scenarios. When manufacturing cost became a concern in the 1980s and 1990s, there was a push for better ways to make high-quality products that are less expensive. Thus, concepts such as DFA (design for assembly), DFM (design for manu-facturing), and concurrent engineering evolved, flourished, and were embraced by the engineering profession. Similarly, the concept of six sigma was conceived and adopted to improve product quality.

When societies across the globe began to push for environmental awareness and concerns, the "green" movement made its way to design. We may use the term *DFS* (design for sustainability) for sustainable design because it extends the broader concept behind DFA, DFM, concurrent engineering, and six sigma; that is, to adapt the engineer-ing design process and its activities to address current societal concerns.

## 11.3 Guidelines and Principles

Guidelines for sustainable design have been evolving and developing. They are mostly qualitative. The following guidelines are commonly used:

A. **Minimize energy consumption:**   Design products that require less energy to oper-ate. For example, hybrid cars offer high gas mileage. Another example is the prolonging of battery life in many products, and a third example is Energy Star (energy-efficient) household appliances.

B. **Use safe materials:**   Use materials that have low impact on the environment during processing or after discarding products. For example, use nontoxic, recyclable materials that require little energy to process and manufacture. Also, use materials coming from recyclable resources as much as possible such as metal, aluminum, paper, etc.

C. **Use efficient manufacturing processes:**   Use processes that are fast to complete and for which the equipment consumes less energy. Also, these processes should have minimum pollution and other adverse environmental impacts.

D. **Minimize or reduce product carbon footprint to protect outdoor air quality:**   A **carbon footprint** of a product is defined as the total set of greenhouse gas (GHG) emissions caused by the product. It is expressed in terms of the amount of emitted carbon dioxide equivalent. The word *equivalent* means including methane, carbon monoxide, and other greenhouse gases. Carbon footprint can also be defined for a company, an organization, or a nation. Strategies to reduce carbon footprint of a product include using better process and product management, better energy consumption strategies, and alterna-tive renewable energies. The mitigation of carbon footprints is often known as carbon offsetting.

Carbon footprints exist today for many products. They have been calcu-lated by different organizations and countries. For example, the U.S. EPA (Environmental Protection Agency) has addressed paper, plastic wrappers for candy, glass, cans, computers, carpet, and tires. The U.S. Postal Service has addressed mailing letters and packages. Australia has addressed lumber and other building materials.

E. **Use life cycle assessment (LCA):**   **LCA** is defined as a method to quantitatively assess the environmental impact of a product throughout its entire life cycle, from the procurement of raw materials to production, distribution, use, disposal, and recycling of the product. Design impact measures for LCA for any product use are increasingly required and available. LCA includes many product facets including energy consumption and environmental impact.

F. **Reuse and recycling:**   Products, processes, and systems should be designed for recycling and reuse, that is, design for reuse and recycle (DFR[2]). We use many products today that are recyclable. Today, recycling is an important part of our personal daily routine and habits. Good examples are soda can and printer cartridge recycling programs.

- G. **Increase quality and durability:** The less frequently we have to replace and repair products, the more energy and resources we save.
- H. **Share resources:** We should design products for public ownership (sharing) instead of private ownership (e.g., carpooling or car rental).
- I. **Create healthy buildings:** Although not a mechanical product, buildings and houses form an important sustainable design problem. We need to design healthy buildings that are harmful neither to their occupants nor to the environment. For example, indoor air quality and energy efficient buildings are important design goals.

To promote the preceding design guidelines necessary for sustainability, the "Hannover Principles" (also known as the "Bill of Rights for the Planet") were adopted in the EXPO 2000 held in Hannover, Germany. We cast these principles in terms of engineering design as follows:

1. Humanity and nature must coexist in a healthy, sustainable way.
2. Engineering design interacts with and depends on the natural world and, as such, must consider implications on the environment.
3. Engineering design (matter and human elements) must respect and coexist with nature (spirit). As such, engineers must protect and conserve air and water quality.
4. Engineering design is responsible for the consequences of its decisions on the human well-being, the viability of natural resources, and their right to coexist.
5. Engineering design should be held accountable for future damage to the environment. Engineers should not burden future generations with potential damage and danger due to careless creation of products, processes, and standards.
6. Eliminate waste. Optimize product life cycle as much as possible to eliminate the concept of waste.
7. Use renewable energy sources as much as possible. Rely on natural energy flow such as solar and wind energies. Minimize the consumption of nonrenewable energy.
8. Engineering design should respect nature as a superpower. No matter how brilliant human design is, it is still limited and does not solve all problems. As such, we must treat nature as a role model and mentor, not as an enemy to conquer and control.
9. Promote communication and knowledge sharing. All involved in LCA and product development should communicate openly to integrate sustainable considerations and integrate natural processes with human design and activity.

In addition to this bill of rights for the planet, in 1993 the World Congress of the International Union of Architects (UIA) and the American Institute of Architects (AIA) signed a "Declaration of Interdependence for a Sustainable Future." Visit http://www.private.uia-architectes.org/texte/england/2aaf1.html. The declaration states that today's society is degrading its environment and that the UIA, AIA, and their members are committed to the following:

1. Professionals are responsible for environmental and social sustainability
2. Promote sustainable design via developing and improving practices, products, services, and standards

3. Disseminate the value of sustainable design via educating the general public
4. Help support sustainable design practices by working to change policies, regulations, and standards in government and businesses
5. Bring the existing built environment and codes to sustainable design standards

## 11.4 Life Cycle Assessment

Successful products are developed by integrating LCA directly into the engineering design process. LCA is commonly known as "cradle to grave" analysis. Although this extent of assessment is desirable to achieve, some products may be assessed based on "cradle to gate" or some other variation. Figure 11.1 shows a typical product life cycle. The main stages of the cycle are the procurement of the raw materials through production, distribution, use, disposal, and recycling. The details of these stages are described as follows:

1. **Raw material extraction:** Different procurement and extraction methods exist, depending on the type of material needed. For wood, we plant, grow, and harvest (cut) the trees. For metals, we mine raw ore. For plastics, we drill and pump oil.
2. **Material processing:** This phase converts raw materials into engineering materials ready for use in manufacturing. Wood requires cleaning and slicing the trees into wood slabs. Metals require, for example, converting ore to steel and bauxite into aluminum. Plastics require converting oil to plastics.
3. **Part manufacturing:** Manufacturing processes materials into finished goods or parts. Wood processing makes wooded products such as furniture. Metal processing machining processes convert metal to steel columns and aluminum to soda cans. Injection molding and stamping convert plastics to toys.

**FIGURE 11.1**
Product life cycle
(Courtesy of DS SolidWorks Corp.)

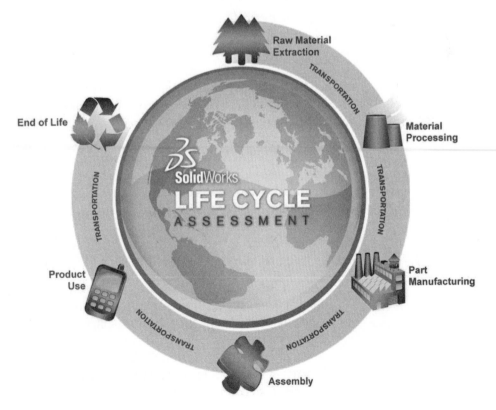

4.  **Assembly:**  Finished parts are assembled to create the final product.
5.  **Product use:**  Intended end consumers use the products for their intended life span. This use may include gasoline, electricity, etc.
6.  **End of life (EOL):**  When a product is discarded (deceased), it should be processed (buried) in an environmentally conscious way. Ideally, we should disassemble the product and decide which parts (components) of the product should be recycled, thrown in landfills for decomposition over time, or incinerated for energy recovery to minimize damage to the environment.

A product LCA evaluates the effects that a product has on the environment over its entire life period, thus increasing resource-use efficiency and decreasing environment liabilities. The LCA has an IQ (Identify and Quantify) and an impact (Evaluate and Assess). Thus, the LCA key elements are:

1.  **Identify:**  Find the environmental loads that we need to assess and evaluate. These loads could include raw materials, energy, emissions, and generated waste needed and consumed by the product throughout its life cycle.
2.  **Quantify:**  Find and use the appropriate formulas, charts, and other tools to calculate the environmental loads. For example, quantification of carbon footprint for many products already exists, as we have covered in Section 11.3.
3.  **Evaluate:**  With quantification numbers at hand, we are able to evaluate the impact of the environmental loads.
4.  **Assess:**  Repeat Steps 1 through 3 for available options, and assess these options to reduce the environmental impact.

Unlike human IQ, the lower the IQ for LCA, the more sustainable and environmentally friendly the LCA is.

## 11.5 Impact Metric

The impact on the environment of making a product comes from three categories: materials, methods, and systems. We associate materials with product design, methods with product manufacturing processes, and systems with product transportation and use during its useful life and EOL. Figure 11.1 clearly shows these three categories. We assert here that material selection is a key factor that determines the level of environmental impact of making a product and therefore determines its degree of sustainability. This is because material selection affects the product making, transportation, use, and EOL fate. For example, a material selection (metal or plastic) affects the product manufacturing process (machining or injection molding). Material selection also affects the product logistics and transportation through its different phases from transporting materials to plants to shipping product to end consumers. Some materials may be easier and faster to ship to manufacturing, thus reducing the carbon footprint. Finally, material selection controls the EOL fate of the product.

If the material selection is crucial, how can we then assess the impact of different materials on the environment? In other words, how can we measure the sustainability of a design based on material selection? We define an impact metric with the following five impact factors:

1.  **Carbon footprint:**  $CO_2$ and other gases result from burning fossil fuels. These carbon gases are trapped in the atmosphere, resulting in air pollution and in raising the earth's average temperature. Carbon footprint is measured in kilograms of $CO_2$ equivalent. Carbon footprint has very serious environmental repercussions and is responsible for the global warming effect that causes loss of glaciers, extinction of species, and extreme weather swings.

2. **Energy consumption:** This impact factor is measured by the amount of nonrenewable (bad) energy (e.g., petroleum, fossil fuel, coal, etc.) that a product consumes throughout its life cycle. This consumption is measured in MJ (megajoules). This impact factor includes all the energies that a product requires to be manufactured, transported, and used during its life cycle. The calculation of the product energy consumption takes into account the efficiencies in energy conversion.

3. **Air acidification:** In addition to releasing $CO_2$ into the air we breathe, burning of nonrenewable fuels produces other harmful gases including sulfur dioxide ($SO_2$) and nitrous oxide ($NO_X$). These and other acidic emissions to the air result in acid rain. Acid rain has serious consequences on the environment including making land and water toxic for human and animal uses as well as for aquatic life and wildlife. Acid rain also eats into and dissolves building materials such as concrete. The unit of measuring the air acidification is kilograms of sulfur dioxide equivalent ($SO_2e$) for the CML methodology. Other units of measurement exist for other impact assessment methodologies. The two most commonly used life cycle impact methodologies are CML and TRACI. CML stands for Centrum voor Milieukunde Leiden (a Dutch university). For more information about CML, visit http://cml.leiden.edu/software/data-cmlia.html. TRACI stands for Tool for the Reduction and Assessment of Chemical and Other Environmental Impacts. For more information about TRACI, visit www.epa.gov/nrmrl/std/sab/traci.

4. **Water eutrophication:** This impact factor measures water pollution that is not related to acid rain, but to dumping societal waste into the water ecosystem. For example, water waste from manufacturing plants and agricultural fertilizers contains high levels of nitrogen (N) and phosphate (also known as phosphorus) ($PO_4$). Both cause more algae to grow in water, which depletes oxygen from water, causing the death of plants and fish. The unit of measuring water eutrophication is kilograms of phosphate equivalent ($PO_4e$) for the CML methodology. Other units of measurement exist for other impact assessment methodologies such as TRACI.

5. **Water footprint:** Worldwide consumption of water has put pressure on the aquatic systems and resulted in dramatic shortage and deterioration of the global water supply, just as the nonrenewable fuels have done to the earth and the atmosphere. Water consumed by companies to make products is an important factor in both company and product sustainability. An analysis of the water footprint of a product can be calculated. The unit of measuring water footprint is cubic meters per year. You can calculate national, corporate, or individual (personal) water footprint.

Interested readers may consult these references for more details about LCA:

A. PE International, a leading company in LCA technology: www.pe-international.com
B. EPA LCA resources: www.epa.gov/nrmrl/lcaccess
C. German IFEU Research Institute: www.ifeu.de/english
D. German UBA Federal Environmental Protection Agency: www.umweltbundesamt.de
E. Water footprint calculations: www.waterfootprint.org

## 11.6 Implementation

The implementation of the LCA is guided by ISO: International Organization for Standardization (www.iso.org). ISO has multiple sustainable standards. ISO 14040/44 provides the LCA principles and framework. ISO 14062 is concerned with greenhouse assessment. ISO 14025 deals with Type III eco-label and IPCC national inventories.

The implementation of LCA provides a systematic approach for identifying, quantifying, and assessing environmental impacts through the life cycle of a product, process, or activity. This implementation considers material and energy uses and releases to the environment from "cradle to grave." The goal of LCA use is to identify "hot spots" of potential environmental impact, compare one or more aspects of a product or process, and establish a baseline for further research and comparisons.

LCA is only one of the tools used in environmental decision making. We generally use it in conjunction with other tools such as risk assessment. There are also other life cycle approaches besides LCA. LCA does not necessarily embody every approach called for.

The application and use of LCA require substantial efforts. First, we need to understand the principles and the concepts. Next, we need to quantify the LCA impact factors as we have discussed. Third, we need to collect lots of data about many materials, processes, systems, transportations, regulations in different countries, etc. Then, we need to build the LCI (life cycle inventory) database or library that houses all that data. Finally, we write software tools that designers can use during their design activities.

Although LCA can contribute to improved environmental decision making to produce better sustainable designs and products, we offer a word of caution. LCA comes with its own pitfalls. LCA users need to maximize the potential benefits of LCA. Designers and their companies need to be clear on the objectives of their LCA and the measures of success. Designers and their companies need to recognize that LCA provides only one component of a more comprehensive decision-making process, and that understanding the trade-offs between required resources and the LCA demands is important. After all, our goal as engineers and designers is to make products that are both affordable and sustainable.

## 11.7 Design Activities

Thus far, we have a set of sustainability concepts that are ready for use in our design activities. These concepts are:

A. We have identified materials, processes, and systems as key elements that affect sustainable design.
B. We have concluded that materials are the decisive and driving element in sustainable design because they directly control the choices of processes and systems.
C. We have also identified the impact factors that affect the environment significantly.
D. We have quantified the impact factors, meaning we can compute their environmental impact.

We now need to put these concepts in a systematic and logical order to provide designers with tools to enable designers to perform LCA, and create and evaluate sustainable designs. The following steps embody this order:

1. **Create part design:** Create a part as we have covered so far in the book.
2. **Select material:** Assign the part a material.
3. **Select manufacturing processes:** Based on the material selection, decide on the appropriate manufacturing processes.
4. **Select system:** This includes the part transportation and the intended region of the world where the part is used.
5. **Set baseline:** Calculate the impact factors covered in Section 11.5. This sets a baseline for sustainable design. We use this baseline to compare the selections of different materials.

6. **Repeat Steps 2 through 5:** Calculate the impact factors for the new material selection.
7. **Repeat Step 6 as many times as needed:** Do this until a satisfactory sustainable design is achieved.

## 11.8 Sustainable Design Tools

Tools for sustainable design are particularly important for both academia and industry. These tools are most useful when they are quantitative to enable designers in practice to evaluate their sustainable design alternatives and options. These tools are also useful for educating students, future engineers, of the importance of sustainability and making them aware of the environmental impact of engineering design.

Two of these tools are available in the form of software. They are offered by Solid-Works and PE International. SolidWorks offers two sustainability modules: **SustainabilityXpress** and **Sustainability**. They both evaluate the environmental impact of a design throughout the life cycle of a product. You can compare results from different designs to ensure a sustainable solution for the product and the environment. **SustainabilityXpress** analyzes parts only and is a standard option with SolidWorks core software. **Sustainability** provides more comprehensive in-depth analysis (more impact factors and expanding reports) and provides designers with more control and the ability to analyze both parts and assemblies (including configurations). These two modules are similar to SolidWorks FEM/FEA modules: **SimulationXpress** and **Simulation**.

PE International offers comprehensive sustainability solutions. Developed in-house over the course of thousands of sustainability consulting projects, PE International's comprehensive sustainability software solutions are designed to support cost-effective corporate and product sustainability projects. PE's GaBi sustainability software offers practicing engineers effective tools to aid them in their sustainable design tasks.

GaBi LCA software platform is designed to handle every stage of an LCA, from data collection to stakeholder engagement. With a modular and parameterized architecture, GaBi allows rapid modeling of even complex processes with thousands of components or dozens of different production options. GaBi automatically tracks all material, energy, and emissions flows, giving instant performance accounting in hundreds of environmental impact categories—including the option of life cycle costing and social impact categories for holistic sustainability evaluation.

The GaBi software efficiently captures different scenarios through parameterization of key variables, such as the percentages of virgin and recycled content, transportation distance and mode (shipping by train, truck, ship, or plane) and end-of-life disposition (recycling, landfilling, incinerating, or composting). Parameterization is a powerful approach to efficiently conduct several "what-if" scenarios particularly for prospective analyses that typically require refinement once preliminary results have been obtained.

GaBi supports the collection, organization, analysis, and monitoring of the environmental performance of products and processes. Additional sustainability-related criteria such as costs and social impacts can also be integrated. GaBi therefore assists life cycle assessment (LCA), life cycle engineering (LCE), design for the environment (DFE), energy efficiency/benchmarking studies, strategic risk management, and carbon footprints.

With emissions information for nearly 50,000 unit processes, GaBi is complemented by a comprehensive and high-quality LCI database available. Data include public LCI data, emissions data from reviewed publications, and proprietary models and data developed over 20 years of experience on thousands of environmental studies and projects. All data are strictly quality controlled and standardized for geographic, technology, and collection conditions, ensuring accurate and reliable results. These data, and the parameterized models for common processes developed by PE, provide out-of-the-box solutions to many data and modeling needs, cutting the costs and schedule needed for many projects.

A unique tool developed by PE to allow decision makers easy access to all the power of a full LCA model, GaBi's interactive report (i-Report) dynamically communicates the effects of changes to key model parameters in an easy-to-understand fashion. Powered by the full life cycle model developed over time, an i-Report gives internal and external stakeholders the impact information necessary for choosing the best solution now as well as improving the future environmental footprint. This interactive report tool encourages the assessment of alternative approaches, product formulations, or manufacturing processes without the need to develop full LCA models each time.

In addition to GaBi life cycle analysis tools, PE International offers SoFi corporate sustainability management software tools. The SoFi software offers a web-based solution to data collection, analysis, and presentation. Using SoFi, corporate sustainability managers can easily generate data queries for operations managers, suppliers, and other stakeholders across organizational boundaries. Able to import data from spreadsheets as well as a secure web-based data entry interface, SoFi automatically checks for data feasibility, data gaps, or overlap between entries from different users. SoFi can be used to update an existing GaBi model, allowing LCI results to be kept current without the cost of commissioning a new LCA study.

## 11.9 SolidWorks SustainabilityXpress

SolidWorks implements the concepts of sustainable design in its **SustainabilityXpress** module. It uses only the first four impact factors (carbon footprint, energy consumption, air acidification, and water eutrophication) of Section 11.5. SolidWorks generates a report for each impact factor. SolidWorks **SustainabilityXpress** measures the environmental impact based on material used, manufacturing process and region, use region, and EOL.

SolidWorks **SustainabilityXpress** is part of SolidWorks version 2010 and higher. If you have SolidWorks 2009 SP2, you need to download **SustainabilityXpress** from http://labs.solidworks.com and install it. SolidWorks **SustainabilityXpress** does not work with SolidWorks versions older than 2009 SP2. Visit http://blogs.solidworks.com/teacher/sustainability for news and updates.

SolidWorks **SustainabilityXpress** has incorporated extensive libraries of materials, manufacturing processes, and transportations from PE International (www.pe-international.com). Designers select from these libraries to investigate various sustainable scenarios. Moreover, SolidWorks has a library of manufacturing regions to select a region from. Different regions have different environmental regulations and laws. For example, designers may select a manufacturing region and/or transportation/use region.

SolidWorks **SustainabilityXpress** follows the design steps covered in Section 11.7. In addition, SolidWorks **SustainabilityXpress** provides a dashboard to display and compare results. It also enables the designer to print reports of the impact factor calculations and the sustainable design. Figure 11.2 shows SolidWorks sustainability methodology.

SolidWorks offers the **SustainabilityXpress** menu for sustainability designers to use. Click this sequence to access the menu: **Tools => SustainabilityXpress** (see Figure 11.3). Figure 11.3A shows the three key elements that affect sustainable

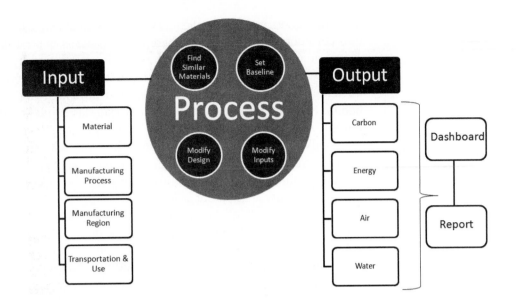

design: material, manufacturing, and transportation and use (or systems, as we call it). Figure 11.3B shows the dashboard that displays the calculation results for the four impact factors (the impact metric as we call it). Both Figures 11.3A and 11.3B are blank; yet once a designer specifies the three key elements (Figure 11.3A), the dashboard areas (Figure 11.3B) populate with the results.

FIGURE 11.3
SolidWorks
**SustainabilityXpress** user
interface

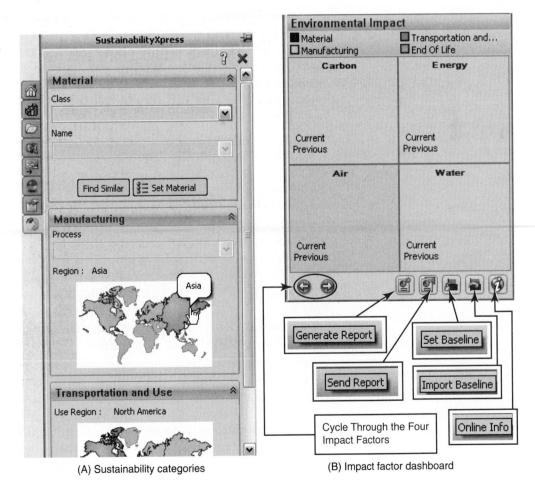

(A) Sustainability categories          (B) Impact factor dashboard

One interesting aspect of SolidWorks sustainability calculations is that they take into consideration the region where the product is made (manufacturing) and used (transportation and use). Both of these areas are affected by a host of regional issues such as cost, environmental regulations, natural resources, type of energy used (fossil, nuclear, hydroelectric, etc.), transportation infrastructure, traffic patterns, cultural habits, etc. Sample regions that SolidWorks has implemented are North America, Europe, Asia, and Japan.

SolidWorks **Sustainability** analysis begins with selecting the key elements and ends with the values of the environmental impact factors. The designer may perform parametric studies (what-if scenarios) to find the "best" sustainable design. The steps of this sustainability analysis are as follows:

1.  Create the CAD model of the part to be designed.
2.  Select the material class and name. SolidWorks supports a wide variety of material classes (e.g., steel, iron, aluminum, copper, titanium, zinc, plastics, fibers, silicon, and wood). Within each class are multiple materials. For example, the class of plastics includes ABS, PVC, nylon, and many others. Check **SustainabilityXpress** for a full list of classes and materials.
3.  Select a manufacturing process. For each material class, possible manufacturing processes that can manufacture this are supported by SolidWorks. For example, injection molding and extrusion processes exist for plastics. For the aluminum class, many processes exist including die casting, extrusion, milling, turning, forging, stamping, etc. Check **SustainabilityXpress** for a full list of available manufacturing processes.
4.  Select the manufacturing region. The region selection determines the type of energy used (how much clean renewable energy and how much nonrenewable energy) and the resources consumed by the manufacturing processes.
5.  Select the transportation and use region. A region selection here determines the environmental impact associated with transporting the product from its manufacturing location to its use location. It also affects the energy resources needed by the product while in use and its EOL destiny (landfill, incineration, or recycling).
6.  Calculate environmental impact. SolidWorks **SustainabilityXpress** uses the input from Steps 2 through 5 and calculates the four impact factors: carbon footprint, energy consumption, air acidification, and water eutrophication.
7.  Set baseline. You need to explicitly identify the results from Step 6 as baseline. SolidWorks **SustainabilityXpress** uses this baseline as a reference to compare multiple sustainable designs. If you want to use different results for baseline, you may import them as shown in Figure 11.3B.
8.  Redesign. If the environmental results in Step 6 are high, select a new material (Step 2) and repeat Steps 3 through 6. Make design changes as necessary.
9.  Evaluate the results. Use the baseline established in Step 7 to evaluate the results from Step 8.
10. Create and print a sustainable report. Once the sustainable design is finalized, print the report to document the sustainable design. Obviously, the sustainable design is above and beyond the typical CAD design that generates the engineering drawings. If the part material changes due to the sustainable calculations, we change the drawings accordingly.

SolidWorks **SustainabilityXpress** provides an online calculator that enables you to convert the environmental impact as measured by the values of the four impact factors into human measurable parameters. For example, convert carbon footprint into miles

**FIGURE 11.4**
SolidWorks Sustainability online calculator

driven by a car. Click the **Online Info** icon shown in Figure 11.3B to access the online calculator shown in Figure 11.4.

## 11.10 Tutorials Overview

The theme for the tutorial in this chapter is to practice using sustainable design concepts implemented by SolidWorks **SustainabilityXpress**. The tutorial helps you assess the impact of your design on the environment. Herman Miller Inc., with headquarters in Zeeland, Michigan, USA (www.hermanmiller.com), has sponsored this chapter. Herman Miller is an international company with manufacturing and distribution facilities in the United States as well as in China, Italy, and the United Kingdom. Herman Miller is represented through subsidiaries and corporate offices, independent dealers, and licensees in over 100 countries in North America, Asia/Pacific, Europe, Africa, the Middle East, and Latin America. Herman Miller seeks to develop and offer innovative furnishings, interior technologies, and related services that improve the human experience wherever people work, heal, learn, and live. Herman Miller has been a long-standing advocate for sustainable design. It is a leader in the area of DfE (design for the environment). We chat with Mr. Gabe Wing, Design for the Environment Manager at Herman Miller, in the Industry Chat. Figure 11.5 shows sample DfE designs.

**FIGURE 11.5**
Sample products (Courtesy
of Herman Miller Inc.)

(A) Office chair
(actual product)

(B) Office chair
(CAD model)

## Tutorial 11-1:  Redesign a Steel Washer

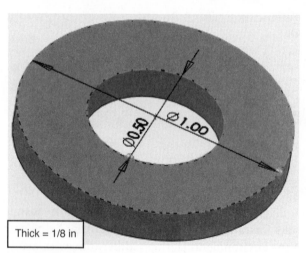

Thick = 1/8 in

**FIGURE 11.6**
A typical washer

Figure 11.6 shows the dimensions of a washer (OD, ID, and thickness in inches) made out of carbon steel. The washer must be replaced by another material such as aluminum or plastic to meet new EOL environmental constraints of recycling. Investigate which design is better for the environment. The washer is used in North America. Also, currently the steel washer is manufactured in Asia. The new washer could be manufactured in Asia, Europe, or Japan. Which of these regions is the best to produce the new washer?

### Modeling task

Redesign the washer shown in Figure 11.6 to meet environmental requirements.

### Modeling synthesis

We need to perform sustainable design evaluation on the washer to find out which new material is better (aluminum or plastic) and which manufacturing region is better. The combination of the two materials and three regions produces a total of six design scenarios to consider. We can reduce the scenarios by half as follows. First, we decide which material is better while using the current manufacturing region (Asia). Then, we use this material to compare the other two regions (Europe and Japan).

### Modeling plan

We follow Steps 1 through 10 of Section 11.9 to evaluate the design. We use the steel washer to establish the baseline for the sustainability analysis.

Design intent

Ignore for this chapter.

CAD steps

We redesign the washer in six steps:

1. Create the washer CAD model.
2. Set environmental baseline.
3. Evaluate the aluminum washer.
4. Evaluate the plastic washer.
5. Evaluate the manufacturing region.
6. Document the final sustainable design.

We hold the manufacturing region the same (Asia) in Steps 3 and 4. The details of these steps are shown below.

## Step 1: Create the washer CAD model

#### Task

A. Start SolidWorks, open a new part, create the washer as an extrusion (see below), and save it as *tutorial11.1*.

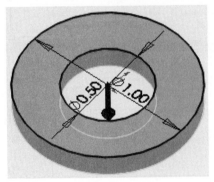

#### Command Sequence to Click

**Open => New = Part** => Create the block. Use the top plane to create the sketch => Extrude it => **Save As** => *tutorial1.1* => **Save**.

**Help:** Start with the top plane as sketch plan; create the two concentric circles at the origin as shown to the left. Then extrude the sketch down 0.125 in.

## Step 2: Set environmental baseline

#### Task

A. Select material as carbon steel.

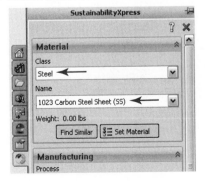

#### Command Sequence to Click

**Tools** menu => **SustainabilityXpress** => **Steel** (Class) => **1023 Carbon Steel Sheet (SS)** (Name)

**Help:** When you select **SustainabilityXpress**, the pane shown to the left opens up on the right of the screen. We select the material class and name as shown here to the left.

| Task | Command Sequence to Click |
|---|---|

**B.** Select manufacturing process.

Select **Stamped/Formed Sheetmetal** as shown to the left.
**Help:** Metal washer can be made with stamping, sheet metal, or other processes.

**C.** Select manufacturing region as Asia.

Hover over **Asia** region as shown to the left => Click it.

**D.** Select use region as North America.

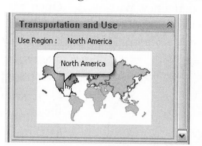

Hover over **North America** region as shown to the left => Click it.

**E.** Set baseline.

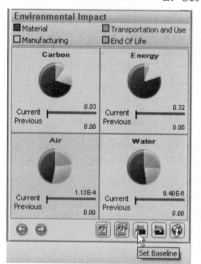

Before Baseline Set

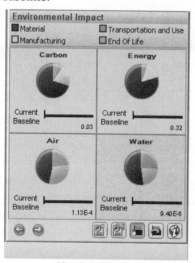

After Baseline Set

**Set Baseline** icon (as shown to the left)
**Help: SustainabilityXpress** calculates the environmental impact as shown to the left. When you click the **Set Baseline** icon, the **Current** values of the four impact factors are set to zero, and the **Current** values move to **Previous**.

## Step 3:  Evaluate the aluminum washer

### Task

A. Set all input parameters to calculate the values for the four impact factors.

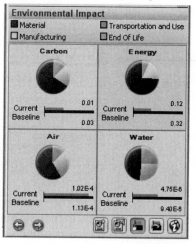

### Command Sequence to Click

**Tools** menu =>
**SustainabilityXpress** => Use
**Aluminum Alloys** (Class), **Alumina** (Name), **Stamped/Formed Sheetmetal** (Process), **Asia** (Manufacturing Region), and **North America** (Use Region)
**Why:** The material class and name we use are the closest to what we want. You may try other materials.
**Help:** The screenshot shown to the left demonstrates that the environmental impact of aluminum (**Current**) is less than steel (**Baseline**).

## Step 4:  Evaluate the plastic washer

### Task

A. Set all input parameters to calculate the values for the four impact factors.

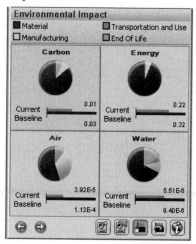

### Command Sequence to Click

**Tools** (menu) =>
**SustainabilityXpress** => Use **Plastics** (Class), **Epoxy unfilled** (Name), **Injection Molded** (Process), **Asia** (Manufacturing Region), and **North America** (Use Region). The results are shown to the left.
**Why:** The material class and name we use are the closest to what we want. You may try other materials.
**Help:** Material alone is not the only decisive factor in sustainable design. Other design considerations such as functional requirements, cost, conductivity, strength, etc. are as important.

## Step 5: Evaluate the manufacturing region

### Task

**A.** Calculate the environmental impact of the plastic washer using Japan as a manufacturing region.

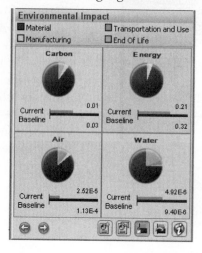

### Command Sequence to Click

Use the same input parameters as in Step 4; only replace Asia with Japan as the manufacturing region. The results are shown to the left.

**Help:** Comparing the screenshot shown to the left and the one in Step 4 shows that Japan is a slightly better manufacturing region than Asia.

**Help:** How would you compare designs if you did not have screenshots to look at? You may set the previous design as a baseline. Thus, each time you have a better design than the previous one, you set it as a baseline. Another approach is to create a report for each design and compare the reports.

**B.** Calculate the environmental impact of the plastic washer using Europe as a manufacturing region.

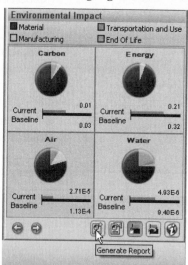

Use the same input parameters as in Step 4; only replace Asia with Europe as the manufacturing region. The results are shown to the left.

**Help:** Comparing the screenshot shown to the left and the one in Task A of Step 5 shows that Japan is a slightly better manufacturing region than Europe.

**Help:** The best washer sustainable design is a plastic washer manufactured in Japan and used in North America. Create a report for this final design.

## Step 6: Document the final sustainable design

Task

A. Generate the design report.

Command Sequence to Click

Click the **Generate Report** icon shown in the screenshot of Task B of Step 5.
**Help:** The screenshot shown to the left shows part of the report, not the full report.
**Help:** The screenshot shown to the left presents the environmental impact of the final design.
**Help:** After you generate the report for the first time, the icon shown in Task B of Step 5 reads **Update Report** instead of **Generate Report**.

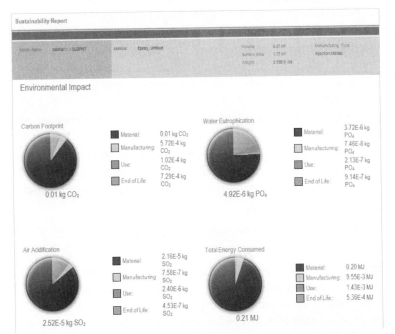

Sustainability Report

| Model Name: | tutorial11.1.SLDPRT | Material: | Epoxy, Unfilled | Volume: | 0.07 in³ | Manufacturing Type: |
| | | | | Surface Area | 1.77 in² | Injection Molded |
| | | | | Weight: | 2.59E-5 /os | |

Environmental Impact

Carbon Footprint

| Material: | 0.01 kg CO₂ |
| Manufacturing: | 5.72E-4 kg CO₂ |
| Use: | 1.02E-4 kg CO₂ |
| End of Life: | 7.29E-4 kg CO₂ |

0.01 kg CO₂

Water Eutrophication

| Material: | 3.72E-6 kg PO₄ |
| Manufacturing: | 7.46E-8 kg PO₄ |
| Use: | 2.13E-7 kg PO₄ |
| End of Life: | 9.14E-7 kg PO₄ |

4.92E-6 kg PO₄

Air Acidification

| Material: | 2.16E-5 kg SO₂ |
| Manufacturing: | 7.58E-7 kg SO₂ |
| Use: | 2.40E-6 kg SO₂ |
| End of Life: | 4.53E-7 kg SO₂ |

2.52E-5 kg SO₂

Total Energy Consumed

| Material: | 0.20 MJ |
| Manufacturing: | 9.55E-3 MJ |
| Use: | 1.43E-3 MJ |
| End of Life: | 5.36E-4 MJ |

0.21 MJ

---

**HANDS-ON FOR TUTORIAL 11–1.** Investigate the washer design with two new materials: copper and rubber. Which design is better for the environment? Is either of the new materials better than plastic?

---

**INDUSTRY CHAT**

This section provides practical insight into how the chapter material is used in industry in the real world and practice. This section summarizes the chat with Mr. Gabe Wing (Manager of the Design for the Environment group) of Herman Miller, the sponsor of this chapter. The structure of the chat follows the chapter sections.

**Chapter Section 11.1:** Introduction

ABE: Describe your company and its sustainable engineering activities.

GABE: Herman Miller has been a proponent of the environment since its inception. Our founder, D.J. De Pree, strongly advocated corporate environmental stewardship and his values helped to shape the values of Herman Miller. As an example, in 1991 we eliminated the use of rosewood, an endangered species, from our classic Eames lounge chair and helped found the Tropical Forest Foundation. In 2001, we formed our Design for the Environment (DfE) team, which I lead. My team was put in place to evaluate the sustainable attributes of our products and improve them.

In 2004, Herman Miller launched our "Perfect Vision" program. The program set the following goals for the year 2020: zero landfill, zero hazardous waste, zero air emissions, zero process water use, and 100% renewable electricity. We have also

*(continue)*

targeted that 100% of product sales must comply with our DfE protocols. It is important to point out that in achieving the "Perfect Vision" goals, we do not outsource our pollution.

As for our sustainable engineering activities, we are integrated into the stage gate development process. We begin with the exploration phase by educating our product designers on the sustainable design principles and tools we use at Herman Miller. Next comes the development phase in which our engineers work with the designers' vision and help translate it into products that we can manufacture. During this phase, our DfE team works closely with the engineers and designers. We apply life cycle thinking by looking at material chemistry (how safe each material is), design for disassembly, recyclability, and recycled content to make the product as sustainable as possible.

We use a scorecard to evaluate the conceptual designs. Based on the score, we may or may not accept a design. Our goal is that 100% of our products meet our DfE requirements. Today, just over 50% of our products meet these strict requirements.

**Chapter Section 11.2:**  Design and Society

> ABE:  Have you changed your design philosophy over time to meet societal needs?

> GABE:  We have not changed our design philosophy, but we have deliberately incorporated sustainability into our actions. In 2001, the scope of our work was limited to new products. Today, our goal is to ensure that every single product that Herman Miller sells meets our DfE scorecard requirements by 2020.

**Chapter Section 11.3:**  Guidelines and Principles

> ABE:  Which guidelines and principles of sustainable design are usable in your design?

> GABE:  We use everything covered in this section, except item H (designing products for public ownership). We have a holistic approach that is aligned with the principles in this chapter. Item B (use of safe materials) is extremely important to our company and to our customers.

For products that do not consume energy during their use phase, material selection drives the life cycle impacts. For products that consume energy, energy consumption drives the life cycle impacts. Consider a car, for example. While the material you use is important, the overall fuel consumption is more important. Similarly, the efficiency of a lightbulb dominates the life cycle impact for a lamp.

**Chapter Section 11.4:**  Life Cycle Assessment

> ABE:  How does your company use and apply LCA?

> GABE:  We use LCA as one of our tools for our DfE team. We also use the "cradle to cradle" design protocol, or C2C. C2C emphasizes safer material chemistry. LCA focuses on total life cycle impacts from raw material extraction to end of life. These two tools complement each other and give us a more complete view of the impacts associated with our products.

**Chapter Section 11.5:**  Impact Metric

> ABE:  How do you measure the environmental impact of your design?

> GABE:  We use C2C to measure and identify potential human health and environmental hazards with material selections. We use the TRACI

methodology in North America to determine our LCA impacts. The impact factors you list in Section 11.5 are the leading ones. Carbon footprint is one of the most commonly requested impacts and I believe that demand for water foot-printing will grow in the future.

## Chapter Section 11.6:  Implementation

**ABE:** Describe the implementation of LCA in your company. Do you use software tools?

**GABE:** We start with life cycle thinking and apply cradle to cradle concepts. We use GaBi software to measure product carbon footprint. More importantly, we use LCA to identify the source of the largest impacts. GaBi provides a summary report with all of the TRACI impact categories. We evaluate the data based on the following life cycle stages: raw material extraction, production, distribution, and end of life (EOL). My team is the primary user of GaBi, not the product designers or engineers. We are a service group that supports all development projects.

## Chapter Section 11.7:  Design Activities

**ABE:** What sustainable design activities do you use in your company?

**GABE:** We follow, more or less, the design steps listed in Section 11.7. One of the challenges is to keep pace with shortening product development cycles. The C2C framework we use is designed to match our product development cycle. However, LCA typically can't keep pace with every design iteration. We are using LCA to answer common design questions as a way to provide a "short-cut." An example would be, "Should I make this component out of steel or plastic?"

## Chapter Section 11.8:  Sustainable Design Tools

**ABE:** What sustainable design tools do you use in your company?

**GABE:** We use GaBi software and C2C as described in my previous answers.

## Chapter Section 11.9:  SolidWorks SustainabilityXpress

**ABE:** How do you use SolidWorks for sustainable design?

**GABE:** We do not use SolidWorks but we use GaBi for our sustainable design studies.

## Others

**ABE:** Any other experience you would like to share with our book readers?

**GABE:** Sustainability is becoming increasingly important for product manufacturers. Our customers simply expect that our products will be "green." Sustainability is becoming just another aspect of quality. LCA is just one way to measure products. It is powerful tool, but not the only tool.

Keep in mind that it is not easy to find literature on the real-world application of sustainable design. The way you are addressing sustainability in this chapter as part of a CAD course is ideal. The principles of sustainability will become mainstream once they are incorporated into the core curriculum of all higher education institutions. For example, I don't think that green chemistry should be taught as a specific class. All chemistry classes, especially labs, should be designed to promote sustainability and safer chemicals. By doing this, we can provide the next generation of students with the tools and knowledge to move us toward a more sustainable future.

1. What is the core idea behind sustainable engineering?

2. List the three possible venues for disassembled components of a product at its end of life.

3. What is the difference between renewable and nonrenewable energy? Give examples of each.

4. Explain the core concept behind each of the following design paradigms: DFA, DFM, DFS, and concurrent engineering.

5. List and describe five of the sustainable design guidelines.

6. List and describe the Hannover Principles.

7. List and describe the elements of the "Declaration of Interdependence for a Sustainable Future."

8. Define product LCA.

9. List and describe the stages of an LCA.

10. List and describe the key elements of an LCA.

11. List and describe the impact metric (factors) of an LCA. How is each factor measured?

12. List and describe the design steps (activities) that a designer needs to follow to create and evaluate sustainable designs.

13. What are the input parameters that SolidWorks requires to calculate the environmental impact factors?

14. What are the four environmental impact factors that SolidWorks uses to evaluate sustainable designs?

15. Use SolidWorks to calculate the environmental impact of the flange model shown in Figure 2.45 of Chapter 2. Use steel for material, turning to produce the flange, Asia for production region, and Asia for use. Submit the values for the four impact values and the sustainability report.

16. Redo Problem 15 but for the L bracket shown in Figure 2.50 of Chapter 2. Use aluminum for material, stamping to produce the bracket, Japan for production region, and Japan for use.

17. Redo Problem 15 but for the pattern block shown in Figure 2.51 of Chapter 2. Use steel for material, milling to produce the block, Europe for production region, and Europe for use.

18. Redo Problem 15 but for the pattern wheel shown in Figure 2.52 of Chapter 2. Use steel for material, milling to produce the hub, Asia for production region, and North America for use.

PART

# IV

# Part Development and Analysis

The primary goal of Part IV is to explore and cover the design activities that follow the completion of CAD (geometric) models. During these activities, we use various engineering analyses and simulations to ensure that designs are safe and meet strength requirements.

Chapter 12 (Tolerances) covers the details of tolerances, their types, and their impact on manufacturing. Chapter 13 (Analysis Tools) covers the most widely used analysis and simulation tools. This includes mass property calculations, animation and motion analysis, flow simulation, and finite element modeling and analysis. Chapter 13 also covers data exchange between CAD/CAM systems.

# Tolerances

## 12.1 Introduction

You have probably heard the saying "life is never perfect," and so it is with manufacturing. You can never manufacture a perfect form. An example of a perfect form is a block with $5 \times 3 \times 4$ inch dimensions. Instead, variability is an inherent characteristic of manufacturing. Sources of variability are abundant and include the skills of the machine operator (machinist), the accuracy and age of the machine, the ambient conditions, the condition and age of the cutting tool, etc. Therefore, producing parts with perfect dimensions would be impossible and prohibitively expensive. Thus, we attempt to control manufacturing variability rather than entirely eliminate it.

In addition to controlling physical attributes of manufacturing such as training operators well and maintaining the machines and cutting tools, we also specify and control the acceptable range of variability of part dimensions. We use the concept of tolerances during part design to specify the acceptable variations for part dimensions that still allow the part to perform its intended function. A **tolerance** is an amount of deviation (variability) in a part dimension from the perfect form. For example, we may specify a tolerance amount of $\pm 0.010$ inch on the $5 \times 3 \times 4$ inch dimensions of the block. This means that any of the block dimensions is allowed to change within this tolerance. For example, the 5 inch dimension may assume any values between 4.090 and 5.010 inches inclusive.

Tolerances play a crucial role in design and manufacturing. Designers use them to meet functional requirements; for example, they specify clearance between two moving parts. For manufacturing, tolerances control the manufacturing cost of parts. The smaller (tighter) the tolerances, the more expensive it is to make the part. Tolerances also have an effect on the part surface finish. The tighter the tolerances, the better the surface finish. This is because tighter tolerances require more precise and better manufacturing processes.

Tolerances are the key behind the concept of spare (replacement) parts or interchangeability. Without tolerances, we would not be sure that a spare part (e.g., a car part) would fit perfectly. We may ask the following question: When we replace a part, why may the new part feel a little tighter or looser than the old one? Also, different copies of the same new product may feel different; some are tighter than others. This is because the tolerance we specify on a part dimension generates a normally distributed population of the part. The mean of the normal distribution is the perfect form (i.e., the dimension without tolerances on it), for example, the 5 inch dimension of the block. Thus, depending on where a product copy falls in the distribution population, we get tighter or looser products when we assemble the parts.

Geometric dimensioning and tolerancing (GD&T) provide many other benefits in addition to what has been mentioned. These benefits are:

1.  Having standardized design language for communication among designers
2.  Clearly communicating the design intent to designers, customers, suppliers, manufacturing, inspection, and the entire product supply chain
3.  Calculating the worst-case assembly scenario by using tolerance limits
4.  Making production and inspection repeatable via using datum (covered later in the chapter)
5.  Assembling parts to create products is guaranteed because all the parts belong to their respective normally distributed populations

## 12.2  Types

Tolerances are divided into two types: conventional and geometric. Conventional tolerances are more widely used than geometric tolerances because they are the first to develop and they are easier to apply and understand. Conventional tolerances control the part size (dimensions). Geometric tolerances (GTOL) control the part form (i.e., its shape). Consider a rectangle. Controlling the width and height is achieved via conventional tolerances, whereas controlling the angles of the rectangle and the parallelism of its sides is achieved via geometric tolerances. Geometric tolerances are also known as geometric dimensioning and tolerancing (GD&T).

Both types of tolerances are used for part inspection after manufacturing. There exist off-the-shelf inspection gauges that are used to check whether the parts meet the tolerance requirements, that is, whether their dimensions are within the specified values (limits). A commonly used inspection gauge is the Go-NoGo gauge. If the part fails inspection, it is rejected by the inspection team and becomes scrap. A high percentage of scrap makes the part manufacturing more expensive and calls for changes to better control the manufacturing processes. Inspection is an element of the part quality control (QC) and quality assurance (QA). Other elements include visual inspection and surface finish (roughness) measurements.

## 12.3  Concepts

Both conventional and geometric tolerances introduce concepts and definitions that we must understand to use tolerances correctly in our designs and to be able to use the tolerance tools offered by CAD/CAM systems. The concepts are covered in the ASME Y14.5M-1994 publication titled "Dimensioning and Tolerancing." We cover the following concepts here:

1.  Size:   A **size** refers to a dimension of a feature, for example, length of an edge, or radius/diameter of a shaft or a hole. Three types of sizes are used in conjunction with tolerances: nominal, basic, and actual. A **nominal size** is a size (value) without decimals (e.g., 5). A **basic size** is a nominal size with decimals to indicate its accuracy (e.g., 5.0, 5.00, or 5.000). Note that these three basic sizes are not the same although their nominal size (5) is the same. They require dimensional accuracy of one, two, and three decimal places, respectively. An **actual size** is the measured length on the manufactured part of the basic size. The actual size must be a value within the specified tolerances of the basic size; otherwise, the part is rejected during inspection. Figure 12.1 shows the nominal and basic sizes.

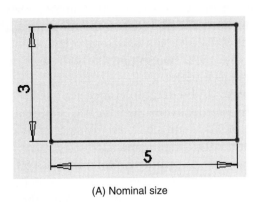

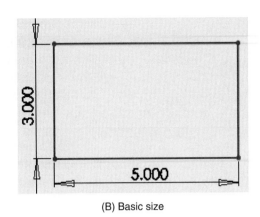

(A) Nominal size

(B) Basic size

**FIGURE 12.1**
Nominal and basic sizes

2. **Shaft and hole:** The tolerance concepts are based on a shaft fitting into a hole. Each has a basic size of $d_s$ for the shaft and $d_h$ for the hole. Although $d_s = d_h$, each has a different tolerance. Figure 12.2A shows a shaft and a hole.

3. **Tolerance zone:** The amount of change in $d_s$ and $d_h$ is known as the **tolerance zone** $s$ and $h$, respectively. This amount is related to the specified tolerance on the shaft or the hole and can be determined from that tolerance. Figure 12.2B shows the two tolerance zones.

4. **Hole and shaft systems:** Both the dimensions of a shaft or a hole are subject to variability during manufacturing. In order to specify and calculate tolerances, we need to fix one relative to the other. We may use either as a reference. If we use the hole as a reference, we have a hole-based system for specifying and calculating tolerances. A shaft-based system uses the shaft as a reference. The hole-based system is more widely used in practice over the shaft-based system because it is believed that manufacturing a hole is more difficult than manufacturing a shaft. Thus, it is beneficial to fix the hole size and change the shaft size to achieve the desired tolerance. An example application that uses the shaft-based system is the textile industry.

5. **Limit dimensions:** A **limit dimension** is the maximum or minimum value of a basic size. For example, the limit dimensions of a basic size of 3.000 and tolerance of $\pm 0.005$ are 3.005 (maximum) and 2.995 (minimum).

6. **Unilateral tolerances:** A dimension may change in one direction from the basic size or in both directions. A **unilateral tolerance** is a tolerance in which variation is permitted in only one direction from the basic size. For example, the

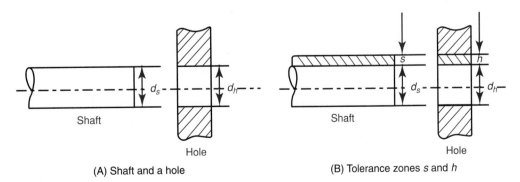

(A) Shaft and a hole

(B) Tolerance zones $s$ and $h$

**FIGURE 12.2**
Shaft and hole tolerance zones

limit dimensions of a basic size of 3.000 and a unilateral tolerance of $+0.005$ are 3.005 (maximum) and 3.000 (minimum). And, the limit dimensions of a basic size of 3.000 and a unilateral tolerance of $-0.005$ are 3.000 (maximum) and 2.995 (minimum). In both cases, we may think that the other tolerance is 0.000.

7. **Bilateral tolerance:** A **bilateral tolerance** is a tolerance in which variation is permitted in both directions from the basic size. For example, the limit dimensions of a basic size of 3.000 and a bilateral tolerance of $+0.005$ and $-0.003$ are 3.005 (maximum) and 2.997 (minimum).

8. **Symmetric tolerance:** A **symmetric tolerance** is a bilateral tolerance with equal variations in both directions from the basic size. For example, a basic size of 3.000 with a symmetric tolerance of $\pm0.005$ has the limits of 3.005 (maximum) and 2.995 (minimum).

9. **Material condition:** The **material condition** is a condition we attach to a geometric tolerance to indicate to the inspection department how the part feature should be inspected. The material condition is an important concept when designing design inspection gauges. The design ensures that a part will not pass inspection unless its dimensions meet the specified tolerances under the specified material condition. Three types of material conditions exist: maximum, least, and regardless of feature size. A maximum material condition (MMC) is designated by the symbol of the letter M inside a circle. The MMC ensures that the maximum amount of material stays in the part after manufacturing, that is, minimum hole size and maximum shaft size. A least material condition (LMC) is the opposite of MMC. It is designated by the symbol of the letter L inside a circle. The LMC ensures that the least amount of material stays in the part after manufacturing, that is, maximum hole size and minimum shaft size. A regardless of feature size material condition (RFS) is designated by the symbol of the letter S inside a circle. The RFS indicates, to the part inspector, that the tolerance applies regardless of the actual produced (manufactured) size of the feature. Applicability of MMC, LMC, and RFS is limited to features subject to variations in size. The MMC is the one most commonly used in practice because it minimizes the amount of manufacturing scrap, thus saving material and keeping the manufacturing cost down.

10. **Datum:** Datums are used in conjunction with geometric tolerances. A **datum** is a part feature (plane) that is used as a reference to specify geometric tolerances. The part inspector uses the datums during inspection to check whether the manufactured part is within the specified tolerances. The datum concept is required to be able to control the form (shape) of a part. For example, we need a datum against which we can measure the perpendicularity or parallelism of a part face. A datum is usually an actual face of the part. To use a part face as a datum requires that the machinist use a highly accurate machining process to machine the face. In addition to controlling form, the datum is also used to measure part linear dimensions from.

11. **Datum target:** Datum targets define how we define a target. As a datum is a part plane, how do define a plane? We define a datum via three noncollinear points, or via a line and a point not lying on it. Datum targets have physical significance during inspection. The inspection department uses the targets to design and produce the gauge that is used to inspect the part. When the part inspector places the part on the inspection gauge, its faces must make contact with the inspection gauge at the target points and/or lines to pass inspection; otherwise, it does not pass and becomes scrap.

## 12.4  ASME Tolerance Rules

We briefly discussed ASME tolerances in Chapter 5. Here are some ASME tolerance rules:

1. **Express tolerances correctly:** There are four methods to specify tolerance in an engineering drawing:
   A. **Limit dimensioning:** Show the minimum and maximum values of a dimension. Use the MMC to show the limits, as shown in Figure 12.3A. Show the maximum value above the minimum value for a shaft and vice versa for a hole. This minimizes the amount of scrap. Keep in mind that the machinist can only remove material, but the material cannot be added once it has been removed. Also, keep in mind that the machinist will attempt, naturally, to meet the dimension value above the dimension line first.
   B. **Plus and minus tolerancing:** Show the basic size followed by a ± tolerance value, as shown in Figure 12.3B. A plus and minus tolerance may be bilateral or symmetric. This method of tolerancing is practiced most widely because machinists prefer it. A machinist typically aims to meet the basic size (dimension) value during machining.
   C. **As a note referring to specific dimension:** Include a note in the drawing to specify tolerances on specific dimensions, as shown in Figure 12.3C.
   D. **In the title block:** Specify general tolerances in the title block of the engineering drawing, as shown in Figure 12.3D.

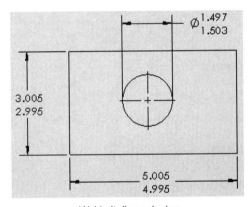

(A) Limit dimensioning

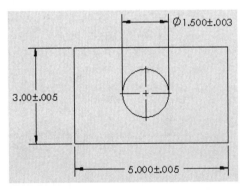

(B) Plus and minus tolerancing

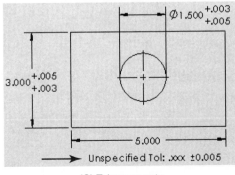

(C) Tolerance note

| UNLESS OTHERWISE SPECIFIED: | |
|---|---|
| DIMENSIONS ARE IN INCHES TOLERANCES: | DRAWN |
| FRACTIONAL± | |
| ANGULAR: MACH±   BEND ± | CHECKED |
| .XX  ± 0.01 | ENG APPR. |
| .XXX ± 0.005 | |
| UNLESS OTHERWISE SPECIFIED | MFG APPR. |
| | |
| INTERPRET GEOMETRIC TOLERANCING PER: | Q.A. |
| | COMMENTS: |

(D) Title block

**FIGURE 12.3**
Methods of specifying tolerances in an engineering drawing

2. Ensure tolerance accuracy matches the dimension decimal: The number of decimals in the basic size dictates the accuracy of the tolerance specified for that size. For example, a basic size of 3.500 should have a tolerance of ±0.005. And a basic size of 3.50 should have a tolerance of ±0.05. Also, note that the two sizes 3.500 and 3.50 are not the same.

3. Follow these rules for millimeter (metric) tolerances:
   A. For unilateral tolerancing, use a single zero without ± as shown in Figure 12.4A. Note that SolidWorks demonstrates the sign as shown in Figure Figure 12.4A.
   B. For bilateral tolerancing, you should use the same number of decimal places, using zeros when necessary, as shown in Figure 12.4B.
   C. Limit dimensions should have the same number of decimal places by adding zeros, if necessary, as shown in Figure 12.4C.
   D. Drop the zeros in a basic size if you do not specify conventional (size) tolerance on it, as shown in Figure 12.4D.

   Note that SolidWorks enforces these rules as shown in Figure 12.4 when using the MMGS (millimeter, gram, second) Units system. Also, make sure you select **ISO** drafting standard; use this sequence: **Tools** (SolidWorks menu) => **Options** => **Document Properties** tab => **Drafting Standard** => **ISO** (from drop-down list) => **OK**.

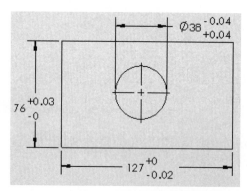

(A) Use a single zero in zero-tolerance value

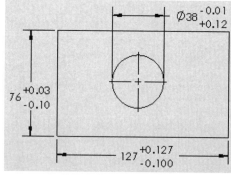

(B) Use same number of decimals for both tols

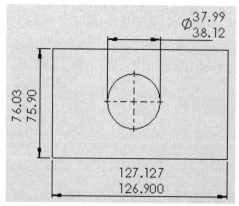

(C) Use same number of decimals for limits

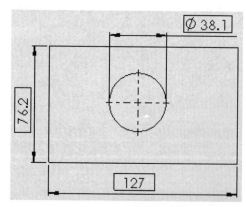

(D) Drop zeros in basic size

**FIGURE 12.4**
Rules of millimeter tolerances

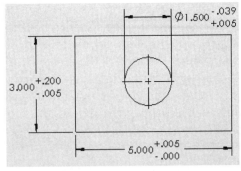

(A) Use many zeros in zero-tolerance value

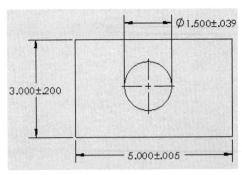

(B) Use same number of decimals as basic size

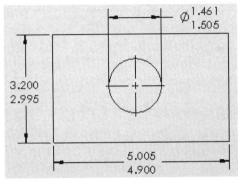

(C) Use same number of decimals for limits

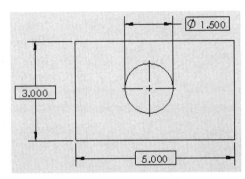

(D) Keep zeros in basic size

**FIGURE 12.5**
Rules of inch tolerances

4. Follow these rules for inch (English) tolerances:
   A. For unilateral tolerancing, use the same number of zeros for the zero value as the nonzero tolerance value with the proper sign, as shown in Figure 12.5A.
   B. For bilateral tolerancing, you should use the same number of decimal places in the tolerance values as used in the basic size, using zeros when necessary, as shown in Figure 12.4B.
   C. Limit dimensions should have the same number of decimal places by adding zeros, if necessary, as shown in Figure 12.4C.
   D. Keep the zeros in a basic size if you do not specify conventional (size) tolerance on it as shown in Figure 12.5D.

      Note that SolidWorks enforces these rules as shown in Figure 12.5 when using the IPS (inch, pound, second) Units system. Also, make sure you select **ANSI** drafting standard; use this sequence: **Tools** (SolidWorks menu) => **Options** => **Document Properties** tab => **Drafting Standard** => **ANSI** (from drop-down list) => **OK**.
5. When you use tolerances on an angle dimension, use the same number of decimals in the tolerance value as in the basic size, that is, **45.00° ± 0.10°**, or **45° ± 0° 30′** (which can also be written as **45° ± 0.5°**):  Note that a degree has 60 minutes and a minute has 60 seconds. The symbols of degree, minute, and second are, respectively, °, ′, and ″.
6. Interpret tolerances during inspection:  All limits are absolute regardless of the accuracy (number of decimal places) of the specified tolerances; that is, 5.002 means 5.0020000 . . . 0. However, the number of decimals informs the inspection

personnel what to do. They compare the measured value with the specified value, and any deviation outside the specified limiting value is ignored.

7. **Use single limit appropriately:** You may use MIN or MAX to specify a tolerance on a dimension where other elements of the design clearly determine the other unspecified limit. That is, the design intent is clear and the unspecified limit can be zero or approach infinity and will not result in design problems. Use a single limit for features such as the depth of a hole, length of a thread, corner radii, chamfers, etc. SolidWorks uses this format to specify a MIN or MAX: 5.000 MIN or 5.000 MAX.

## 12.5 Tolerancing Tapers

There exist two types of tapers: conical and flat, as shown in Figure 12.6. An example of a conical taper is a conical shaft, and example of a flat taper is a wedge. Figure 12.6 also shows how to specify (dimension) a taper. The dimensioning and tolerancing of a taper depend heavily on its functional requirements. Figure 12.6A shows the two common schemes to dimension a conical taper. Scheme 1 implies that the taper cross section at distance $L$ from the left end with a diameter $d$ is important and should be toleranced. For example, the conical taper may plug a conical hole at the specified location to prevent a leak. Thus, the location and the diameter are crucial to the taper functionality. Scheme 2 implies that the taper end diameters, $D$ and $d$, and its overall length $L$ are important and should be toleranced. For example, the taper may be a floating core of a valve that must block the block gas or fluid flow from one end of the valve to the other. The dimensioning and tolerancing of a flat taper follow similar rules.

Figure 12.6A shows how to specify the conical face of a taper. Option 3 shows the use of an angle and option 4 shows the use of a slope. Note the use of the slope symbol. SolidWorks does not have the slope symbol for the conical taper, shown in

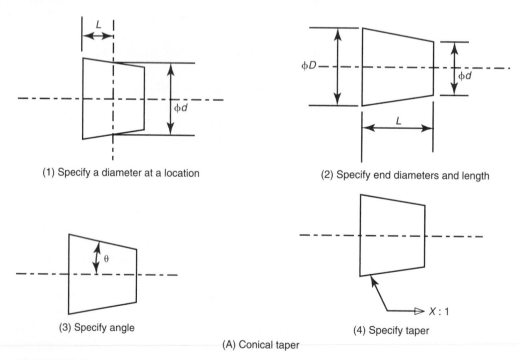

(1) Specify a diameter at a location

(2) Specify end diameters and length

(3) Specify angle

(4) Specify taper

(A) Conical taper

**FIGURE 12.6**
Types and dimensioning of tapers

Part IV Part Development and Analysis

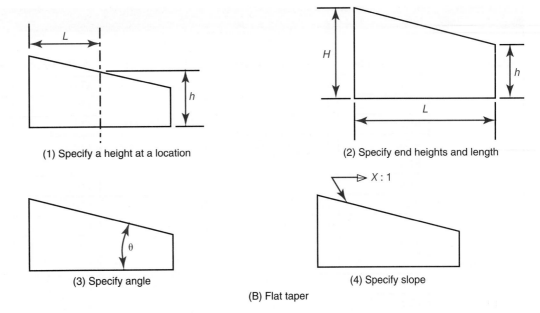

(1) Specify a height at a location

(2) Specify end heights and length

(3) Specify angle

(4) Specify slope

(B) Flat taper

**FIGURE 12.6**
(*Continued*)

Figure 12.6A4, but it does have the symbol for the flat taper shown in Figure 12.6B4. The taper of the conical taper shown in Figure 12.6A4 is defined by the following equation:

$$\text{Taper} = (D - d)/L \tag{12.1}$$

And the slope of the flat taper shown in Figure 12.6B4 is given by:

$$\text{Slope} = (H-h)/L \tag{12.2}$$

Figures 12.6A4 and 12.6B4 show the taper and slope as normalized values of $x{:}1$, where $x$ is the right-hand side of each equation. Observe that the definitions of the taper and the slope, given by Eqs. (12.1) and (12.2), are a little different from each other. These definitions are set by the ASME Y14.5M-1994 standard. The tutorials of this chapter apply the taper concepts discussed here using SolidWorks.

## 12.6 Limits of Dimensions

The bottom line of using tolerances is to calculate the limits on the hole and shaft sizes, that is, the maximum and minimum sizes of each. These are the sizes (dimensions) that the designer specifies and the ones that the machinist aims to achieve while manufacturing the part; otherwise, the part would be rejected during inspection. We show the limits on a drawing according to the MMC, as shown in Figure 12.3.

The two questions we answer in this section are: Why and how do we standardize tolerances? And how do we use them to calculate the limits of a dimension? We need to standardize tolerances to standardize part manufacturing and inspection. This in turn ensures parts interchangeability, which guarantees that replacement (spare) parts fit well into products as intended. Both ANSI and ISO standards have developed two equivalent systems of standard classes of fits that designers can use. Each fit has standard tolerances associated with it depending on the basic size that the designer wants to assign tolerances to. Table 12.1 shows the ANSI fits and their ISO equivalents. These fits are divided into three classes: clearance, transition, and interference. Clearance fit occurs when the shaft moves loosely inside the hole it fits into. Transition fit occurs when the shaft is in transition from clearance to interference; that is, the shaft is snug fit into the hole.

## TABLE 12.1 ANSI and ISO Fits

| Class | ANSI Symbol | ISO Symbol Hole | ISO Symbol Shaft | Class | ANSI Symbol | ISO Symbol Hole | ISO Symbol Shaft |
|---|---|---|---|---|---|---|---|
| Clearance fits | RC1 | H5 | g4 | Transition fits | LT1 | H7 | js6 |
| | RC2 | H6 | g5 | | LT2 | H8 | js7 |
| | RC3 | H7 | f6 | | LT3 | H7 | k6 |
| | RC4 | H8 | f7 | | LT4 | H8 | k7 |
| | RC5 | H8 | e7 | | LT5 | H7 | n6 |
| | RC6 | H9 | e8 | | LT6 | H7 | n7 |
| | RC7 | H9 | d8 | Interference fits | LN1 | H6 | n5 |
| | RC8 | H10 | c9 | | LN2 | H7 | p6 |
| | RC9 | H11 | c11 | | LN3 | H7 | r6 |
| | LC1 | H6 | h5 | | FN1 | H6 | n6 |
| | LC2 | H7 | h6 | | FN2 | H7 | s6 |
| | LC3 | H8 | h7 | | FN3 | H7 | t6 |
| | LC4 | H10 | h9 | | FN4 | H7 | u6 |
| | LC5 | H7 | g6 | | FN5 | H8 | x7 |
| | LC6 | H9 | f8 | | | | |
| | LC7 | H10 | e9 | | | | |
| | LC8 | H10 | d9 | | | | |
| | LC9 | H11 | c10 | | | | |
| | LC10 | H12 | c12 | | | | |
| | LC11 | H13 | c13 | | | | |

Interference fit occurs when the shaft is pressed into the hole and cannot move inside it. There are different grades (levels) within each tolerance class: very loose, moderate, or tight clearance or interference. Think of the fits as a sliding scale from very loose clearance to very tight interference, and anything in between.

Table 12.1 shows that each ANSI fit designation has two ISO symbols. For example, the ANSI fit designation of RC1 is equivalent to the ISO fit designation of H5/g4. H5 and g4 designate the hole and shaft, respectively. All holes use the letter H to indicate that we use a hole-based system whereas shafts use different letters. Each letter represents a fit class. The number next to each letter is the tolerance grade number or the IT grade. Our example of H5/g4 implies that the hole has a class and IT grade of H and 5, respectively, and the shaft has g and 4, respectively. The hole IT grade is always 1 higher than the shaft IT grade because manufacturing the hole is harder than manufacturing the shaft. There exist ANSI tables (not shown here) that relate the tolerance IT grades to the different manufacturing processes. Each process is capable of producing a range of IT grades.

Having answered the first question, we now show how to use the fits in Table 12.1 to calculate the limits on a dimension. These calculations require the introduction of the concept of allowance $a$. While the shaft and hole tolerance zones $s$ and $h$ shown in Figure 12.2B control the dimensions of each of the shafts and the holes individually, they do not have an effect on how loose or tight the assembly of the two is; that is, $s$ and $h$ cannot control the type of fit between the shaft and the hole. The concept of allowance $a$ gives us this control. We can produce the three classes of tolerances (clearance, transition,

Part IV Part Development and Analysis

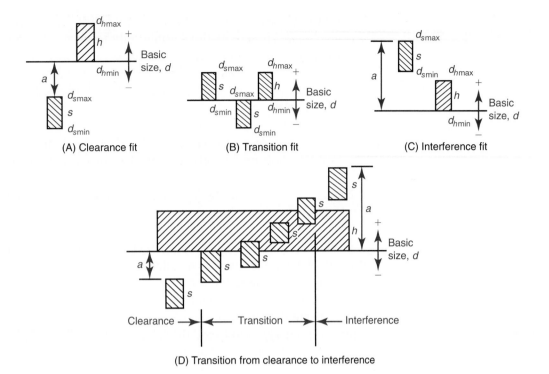

(A) Clearance fit    (B) Transition fit    (C) Interference fit

Clearance ⟶|⟵ Transition ⟶|⟵ Interference

(D) Transition from clearance to interference

**FIGURE 12.7**
Representing classes of fit using a hole-based system

and interference) by controlling the allowance $a$. There are variations within each class. For example, we have loose and tight clearances, tight and shrink-fit interferences, etc. The **allowance $a$** is an abstract algebraic value; it is positive for clearance and negative for interference.

The three values of the three parameters $s$, $h$, and $a$ determine the shaft and hole limits as well as the type of fit of their assembly. These parameters provide the designer with full control over the functional requirements of an assembly. They also ensure that manufacturing meets these requirements. Figure 12.7 shows the three classes of fit in terms of the three tolerance zones for $s$, $h$, and $a$. As Figure 12.7 shows, we use the basic size $d$ of the shaft or the hole as a reference ($X$-axis). We place the tolerance zones as shown for each fit. The allowance $a$ is defined as the difference between the maximum shaft and the minimum hole dimensions. This definition is consistent with the MMC. A transition fit is the changeover fit from clearance to interference, as shown in Figure 12.7D. Also, notice that the hole tolerance zone $h$ always butts the basic size reference line, thus ensuring that $d_{hmin}$ is always equal to the basic size $d$. This is a result of using the hole-based system. Also, notice that a transition fit may be a clearance (represented by tolerance zone $s$ below the reference line of Figure 12.7B) or interference (represented by tolerance zone $s$ above the reference line of Figure 12.7B). Finally, notice that the allowance $a$ may be zero for a transition fit (Figure 12.7B) or not (Figure 12.7D).

We use Figure 12.7 to calculate the dimension limits for both the hole and the shaft. The following equations are easily derived:

$$d_{hmin} = d \tag{12.3}$$
$$d_{hmax} = d + h \tag{12.4}$$
$$d_{smax} = d - a \tag{12.5}$$
$$d_{smin} = d - a - s \tag{12.6}$$

Equations (12.3) through (12.6) are applicable to any fit type because the allowance $a$ is algebraic. These equations apply only to clearance and interference fits. They fail for transition fits because we cannot define $a$ clearly, and because the $s$ zone is split by the basic size reference line. We use the tolerance tables listed in Appendix A to calculate the limits for all types of fits. Follow these steps to calculate the dimension limits:

1.  Select a fit class from Table 12.1 based on the desired fit type between the shaft and the hole under consideration. This type is determined by the functional requirements of the shaft/hole assembly.
2.  Use ANSI tolerance tables listed in Appendix A to calculate the limits on both the shaft and the hole.

While Step 1 is straightforward, we elaborate Step 2. The tolerance tables in Appendix A implement the fits shown in Table 12.1 for different basic sizes. They also implement Eqs. (12.3) through (12.6). This facilitates the job of the designer to calculate the dimension limits. Also, the tables in Appendix A have three columns for each fit to help you calculate the limits for each fit. Use the Hole and Shaft columns to determine the limits, respectively. Simply add the values algebraically to the basic size. SolidWorks has implemented the tables of Appendix A.

---

**Example 12.1**    Calculate the limits for the following three fits: clearance of RC3, transition of LT4, and interference of FN2. Use a basic size of 4.0000 in.

**Solution**    Using Appendix A tables and Eqs. (12.3) through (12.6), Table 12.2 shows the results.

**TABLE 12.2    Limits for Basic Size $d$ = 5.000 in.**

| Fit | $h$ | $s$ | $a$ | $d_{hmin}$ | $d_{hmax}$ | $d_{smin}$ | $d_{smax}$ |
|---|---|---|---|---|---|---|---|
| RC3 (H7/f6) | 0.0016 | 0.0010 | 0.0016 | 5.0000 | 5.0016 | 4.9974 | 4.9984 |
| LT4 (H8/k7) | 0.0025 | 0.0016 | | 5.0000 | 5.0025 | | |
| FN2 (H7/s6) | 0.0016 | 0.0010 | −0.0045 | 5.0000 | 5.0016 | 5.0035 | 5.0045 |

The limits for the transition fit are left blank because we cannot determine the allowance $a$ from Appendix A for LT4 fit. However, if we use the values in the Hole (H8) and Shaft (k7) columns and add them to the basic size, we get:

$$d_{hmin} = 5.0000 + 0 = 5.0000 \text{ in.}$$
$$d_{hmax} = 5.0000 + 0.0025 = 5.0025 \text{ in.}$$
$$d_{smin} = 5.0000 + 0.0001 = 5.0001 \text{ in.}$$
$$d_{smax} = 5.0000 + 0.0017 = 5.0017 \text{ in.}$$

These limits and the others shown in Table 12.2 agree with SolidWorks results shown in Figure 12.8.

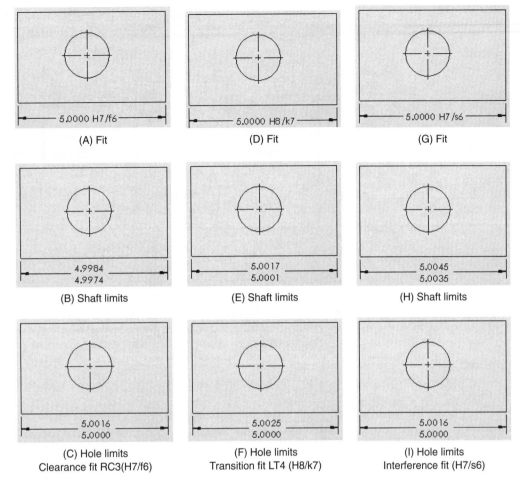

| (A) Fit | (D) Fit | (G) Fit |
| 5.0000 H7/f6 | 5.0000 H8/k7 | 5.0000 H7/s6 |

| (B) Shaft limits | (E) Shaft limits | (H) Shaft limits |
| 4.9984 / 4.9974 | 5.0017 / 5.0001 | 5.0045 / 5.0035 |

| (C) Hole limits | (F) Hole limits | (I) Hole limits |
| Clearance fit RC3(H7/f6) | Transition fit LT4 (H8/k7) | Interference fit (H7/s6) |
| 5.0016 / 5.0000 | 5.0025 / 5.0000 | 5.0016 / 5.0000 |

**FIGURE 12.8**
Limits verification using SolidWorks

---

***HANDS-ON FOR EXAMPLE 12.1.*** Find the dimension limits for RC5, LT2, and FN5. Use a basic size of 6.0000 in.

---

## 12.7 Tolerance Accumulation

**Tolerance accumulation** is the chain effect of a series of tolerances. Tolerance accumulation is controlled by the dimensioning scheme. For example, a horizontal or vertical chain of toleranced dimensions results in tolerance accumulations. You should avoid tolerance accumulation as much as possible by changing dimensioning schemes. Figure 12.9 shows a toleranced stepped shaft. Our goal is to dimension the shaft in such a way to minimize tolerance accumulation between planes A and B due to the part functional requirements. We investigate the effect of the following three dimensioning schemes on tolerance accumulation:

1.  **Chain dimensioning:** Figure 12.9A shows this dimensioning scheme, which is a horizontal dimension chain. This is the worst dimensioning scheme of the three schemes shown in Figure 12.9 because it produces the maximum tolerance accumulation. The maximum variation between planes A and B is equal to the sum of the tolerances between the two planes (i.e., ±0.15).

**FIGURE 12.9**
Tolerance accumulation

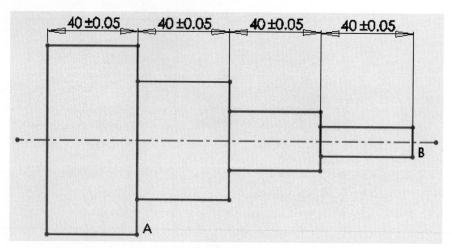

(A) Chain dimensioning

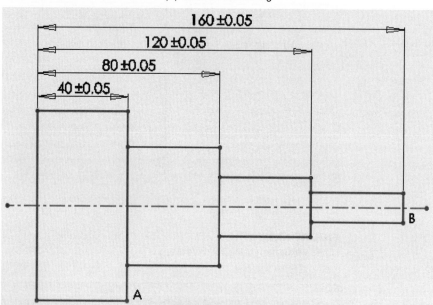

(B) Baseline dimensioning

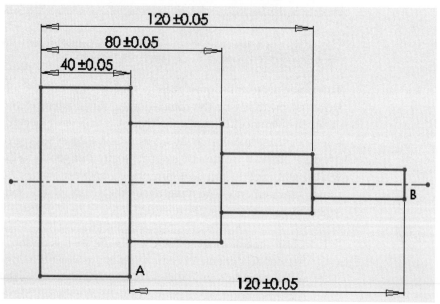

(C) Direct dimensioning

2.  **Baseline dimensioning:** Figure 12.9B shows this dimensioning scheme. The maximum variation between the two planes is equal to the sum of the two dimensions from the farmost left plane (origin) to the two planes (i.e., ±0.10). This results in a reduction of the tolerance accumulation from the preceding scheme.
3.  **Direct dimensioning:** Figure 12.9C shows this dimensioning scheme. It is the best of the three schemes shown in Figure 12.9 because it does not produce any tolerance accumulation. The maximum variation between planes A and B is equal to the tolerance of the dimension between the two planes (i.e., ±0.05).

## 12.8 Statistical Tolerancing

When we assign tolerances to parts (components), our goal is to control the assembly of these parts into a functional assembly. As we discussed in Section 12.1, specifying a tolerance on a part dimension generates a normally distributed population of the part. Figure 12.10 shows this distribution (bell curve). The horizontal axis represents the actual dimension produced, and the vertical axis represents the probability of producing a given dimension. The mean, $\mu$, of the normal distribution is the perfect form (i.e., the basic size $d$). The two extremes of the curve are the maximum and minimum sizes, $d_{max}$ and $d_{min}$, respectively, as shown in Figure 12.10, and represent the maximum and minimum material conditions. The distance between the mean and any of the two extremes is known as $3\sigma$, where $\sigma$ is the standard deviation. The area under the bell curve that is bounded by $\pm 3\sigma$ includes 99.73% of all the possible parts produced (manufactured) with the specified tolerance.

All manufacturing processes subject to common cause variation produce parts that vary in size around the basic size, $d$. If the manufacturing process is "perfectly" capable, then very few parts are produced at the extremes of the bell curve (Figure 12.10), that is, at maximum or minimum conditions. In other words, the probability of getting parts on both tails of the curve is very small as the curve shows, whereas the probability of getting parts around the basic size is very high. Thus, we can use this observation to relax tolerances on dimensions in a calculated manner. In such a case, we use the concept of statistical tolerancing. **Statistical tolerancing** is a method of tolerancing that is based on the fact that it is highly unlikely that you would get mating parts (in an assembly) at both maximum or minimum material conditions.

Unlike statistical tolerancing, arithmetic tolerancing assumes all parts are produced at the maximum or minimum material conditions. When using arithmetic tolerances is

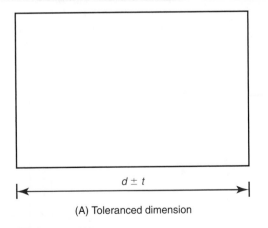

(A) Toleranced dimension

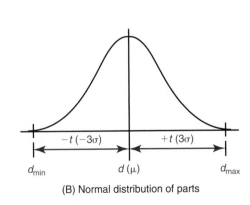

(B) Normal distribution of parts

**FIGURE 12.10**
Population of a toleranced dimension

**FIGURE 12.11**
Specifying statistical and
arithmetic tolerances

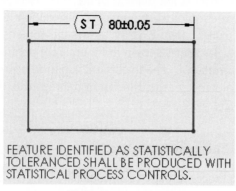

FEATURE IDENTIFIED AS STATISTICALLY
TOLERANCED SHALL BE PRODUCED WITH
STATISTICAL PROCESS CONTROLS.

(A) Statistical tolerance

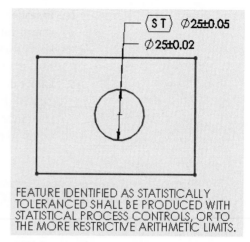

FEATURE IDENTIFIED AS STATISTICALLY
TOLERANCED SHALL BE PRODUCED WITH
STATISTICAL PROCESS CONTROLS, OR TO
THE MORE RESTRICTIVE ARITHMETIC LIMITS.

(B) Statistical tolerancing with arithmetic limits

restrictive, we may use statistical tolerancing to increase tolerances on a dimension. The increased tolerance may reduce manufacturing cost, but should be employed where the appropriate process control is used to control the manufacturing process.

Specifying statistical tolerances on dimensions is designated as shown in Figure 12.11. Designers can use SolidWorks to specify statistical tolerances as shown in the figure. To access the <ST> symbol, click the **More** button while inserting a dimension to access the Symbol library. The shown designations in Figure 12.11 follow the ASME Y14.5M-1994 standard. Figure 12.11A shows the use of the statistical tolerance symbol. The standard mandates that the statement shown be placed on the drawing. Figure 12.11B shows an interesting example where it may be necessary to designate both the statistical and arithmetic limits when the dimension has the possibility of being produced without statistical process control (SPC). In such a case, the shown note must be placed on the drawing. Note that the arithmetic tolerance is tighter than the statistical tolerance, thus making it more expensive to manufacture the part.

## 12.9  True Position

The concept of true position is part of geometric tolerancing. True position applies to locating and tolerancing a hole in a part. A hole has a size (radius or diameter) and a location (center). Tolerancing the hole size is straightforward and uses conventional tolerances. Tolerancing the hole center depends on how we locate it. We specify the center as $(x, y)$ coordinates measured from two planes. Thus, we specify a tolerance on each coordinate (dimension), that is, $\pm \Delta x$ and $\pm \Delta y$, as shown in Figure 12.12A. Although this logic seems to make sense, it is not good because it "under-tolerances" the part; that

**FIGURE 12.12**
True position of a hole

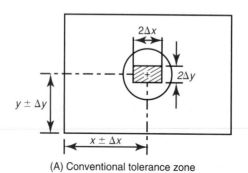

(A) Conventional tolerance zone

(B) True position of a hole

is, the hole location has more tolerance than we intend. The tolerances produce a rectangular tolerance area that is $2\Delta x \times 2\Delta y$, as shown in Figure 12.12A, thus allowing more tolerance on the hole location than specified. The length of the diagonal of the tolerance area is given by:

$$2\sqrt{(\Delta x)^2 + (\Delta y)^2}$$ (12.7)

The hole center can move along the diagonal whose length is larger than the specified $2\Delta x$ or $2\Delta y$. This allows the part to pass inspection while in realty it should not.

The preceding problem can be easily solved by decoupling the tolerance on the hole center from its $(x, y)$ coordinates. In other words, remove the $\pm\Delta x$ and $\pm\Delta y$. The concept of true position achieves that, as shown in Figure 12.12B. **True position** is defined as specifying the hole $(x, y)$ coordinates without any tolerances. The true position allows us to define a circular tolerance zone on the hole, as shown in Figure 12.12B. We customarily show the hole coordinates in boxes, as shown in Figure 12.12B. How do we specify tolerances on the hole location then? We define a position tolerance as we show when we cover geometric tolerances.

## 12.10 Geometric Tolerances

Geometric tolerances complement conventional tolerances. They control the location, shape (form), and profile of individual features. Table 12.3 shows the different geometric tolerances and their symbols as specified by ASME Y14.5M-1994 standard.

To master geometric tolerances, we need to know how to assign and interpret them. Assigning a geometric tolerance requires the following steps:

1. Specify needed datums. These datums are used to measure dimensions from.
2. Decide on the type of geometric tolerance you need to apply to a given feature. Select the desired tolerance from Table 12.3.
3. Create the geometric tolerance details.

Figure 12.13 shows an example. Figure 12.13A indicates the elements of a geometric tolerance, which you create one by one in SolidWorks. You may use this as a template. The

| TABLE 12.3 Symbols for Geometric Tolerances | | | |
|---|---|---|---|
| **Feature Type** | **Tolerance Type** | **Description** | **Symbol** |
| Individual feature | Form | Straightness | — |
| | | Flatness | ▱ |
| | | Circularity (roundness) | ○ |
| | | Cylindricity | ⌀ |
| Individual or related features | Profile | Line profile | ⌒ |
| | | Surface profile | ⌓ |
| Related features | Orientation | Angularity | ∠ |
| | | Perpendicularity | ⊥ |
| | | Parallelism | // |
| | Location | Position | ⊕ |
| | | Concentricity | ◎ |
| | Runout | Circular runout | ↗ |
| | | Total runout | ↗↗ |

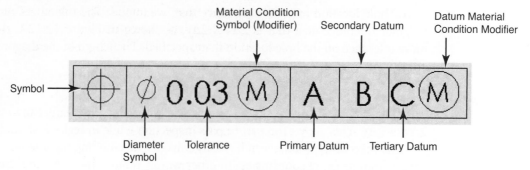

Material Condition
Symbol (Modifier)    Secondary Datum    Datum Material
                                        Condition Modifier

Symbol ──→

Diameter    Tolerance    Primary Datum    Tertiary Datum
Symbol

(A) Anatomy of a geometric tolerance specification

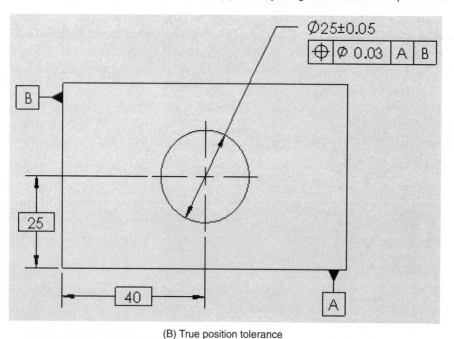

(B) True position tolerance

(C) Interpret position tolerance

**FIGURE 12.13**
Sample geometric tolerance

symbol comes from Table 12.3, depending on the tolerance you need to create (position tolerance in our example). The tolerance amount (zone) follows the symbol. The diameter symbol is optional and used when it makes sense. In this example, we need it because we specify a tolerance zone for the center of the hole. The material condition symbol (modifier) is optional. The next three letters indicate the datums. The first datum is the primary datum, followed by the secondary datum, followed by the tertiary datum. The order shown indicates to the part inspector how to inspect the part. There are three planes of the inspection gauge that correspond to these datums. The part inspector must first align the part surface A with the primary datum (A) of the gauge, followed by the others. If the part surface A does not mate with the gauge plane at the datum target points and/or lines, the part fails inspection. Last, you may optionally specify a material condition on any datum.

Figure 12.13B shows two tolerances on the hole. One is a size tolerance on the hole diameter, which is a conventional tolerance. The other is a location tolerance on the hole center. It reads as follows: "There is a tolerance zone with a diameter of 0.03 mm on the hole center measured with respect to datums A (Primary) and B (Secondary)." In other words, the hole center is free to move from its true position within a circle whose diameter is 0.03 mm and which is centered at the true position point. If the hole center is located outside this circle, the part is rejected during inspection. Why do we use two datums in Figure 12.13B? It is because the hole location is determined by the (x, y) coordinates, each requiring a datum.

Using and interpreting a material condition symbol (modifier) is the hardest to do and can be well understood only in the context of designing an inspection gauge. For a Go-NoGo gauge, the location of the gauge pin or hole is located where the condition is met, thus forcing the part to meet the specified condition as well. Typically, it takes time and experience to use material condition modifiers in geometric tolerances. The required depth of coverage needed to fully understand the use and interpretation of material conditions is beyond the scope of this book.

Interpreting geometric tolerances is important to learn because it enhances our understanding and therefore enables us to assign geometric tolerances correctly. When you interpret geometric tolerance, always look for the tolerance zone that results from the tolerance, the part feature (surface) that is affected by it, how it moves within the tolerance zone, and how the datum planes influence the interpretation. Let us apply these four observations to the hole tolerances shown in Figure 12.13B. The resulting tolerance zones are shown in Figure 12.13C. The true position tolerance on the hole location (center) produces circle I. This is a circular tolerance zone with a diameter of 0.03 mm as specified by the geometric tolerance. Thus, the hole center is free to move within this circle and still passes inspection. In other words, any part produced with a hole center within this circle is acceptable and meets the design requirements. The datums shown in the tolerance specification instruct the part inspector to measure the hole center from these two datums during inspection; that is, the inspection gauge must be set up this way.

The size tolerance on the hole indicates that the hole diameter is acceptable anywhere between circles II and III shown in Figure 12.13D. These two circles represent the maximum material condition (circle II with a diameter of 24.95 mm) and minimum material condition (circle III with diameter of 25.05 mm). The dashed circle shown in Figure 12.13C represents the basic size of the hole (Ø25 mm). When you combine the effect of both the size and location tolerances, you can think of infinite combinations for the resulting hole. All these holes fall under the bell curve shown in Figure 12.10B. Each part with a hole is a point under the curve. The correct inspection gauge is capable of checking for all these infinite combinations and passing only the ones that fit under the curve.

## 12.11  Datum Target Symbols

As discussed at the end of Section 12.3, datum targets are designated points, lines, or areas of contact on a part to define a datum (feature of reference). These designated targets are used during inspection. We use datum targets to define datums because an entire feature (planar or cylindrical feature) cannot be used to establish a datum due to the irregularity of the part feature that serves as a datum. A datum is always an actual surface of a part.

Points, lines, and areas on datum features are designated on a drawing via datum target symbols. Figure 12.14 shows different ways to define datum targets. These targets are created in SolidWorks. Figure 12.14A shows how to indicate a datum target point. In this case, we specify (define) datum A by the point located at 40 mm from the left face of the part. When we want to specify a datum (A) by a line, we specify two points, A1 and A2, on the line, as shown in Figure 12.14B. Figure 12.14C shows how to specify a datum (C) by an area. Datum C is the front plane.

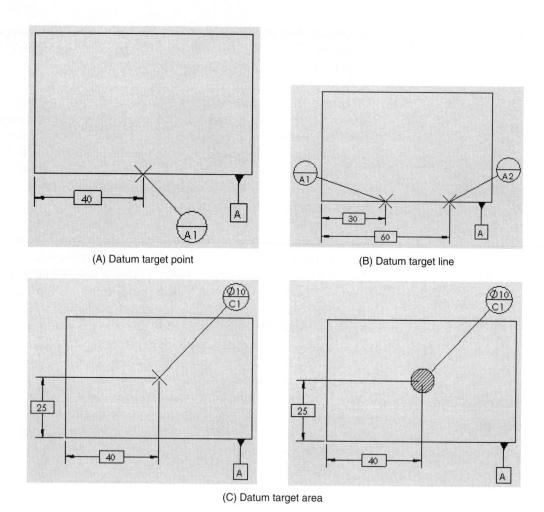

(A) Datum target point

(B) Datum target line

(C) Datum target area

**FIGURE 12.14**
Datum targets

The area is indicated by a diameter (Ø10). Figure 12.14C shows the two options to specify the datum: with or without a shaded area. The area indicates that an area of contact is necessary to establish to ensure establishment of a datum. The shape of the target area may be circular or rectangular. Consult SolidWorks menu; click **Insert => Annotations => Datum Target**.

## 12.12 Tolerance Interpretation

Interpreting tolerances is important to understanding them. Conventional tolerances are usually easier to interpret than geometric tolerances. The underlying principle is that a tolerance defines a zone within which the toleranced feature resides. The toleranced feature assumes any location and orientation within the tolerance zone. Figure 12.13C shows a tolerance zone bounded by circles II and III. The hole surface may be anywhere within this zone (band). Table 12.4 shows sample tolerances with their graphical interpretations. These tolerances (except for the size tolerance) correspond to those shown in Table 12.3.

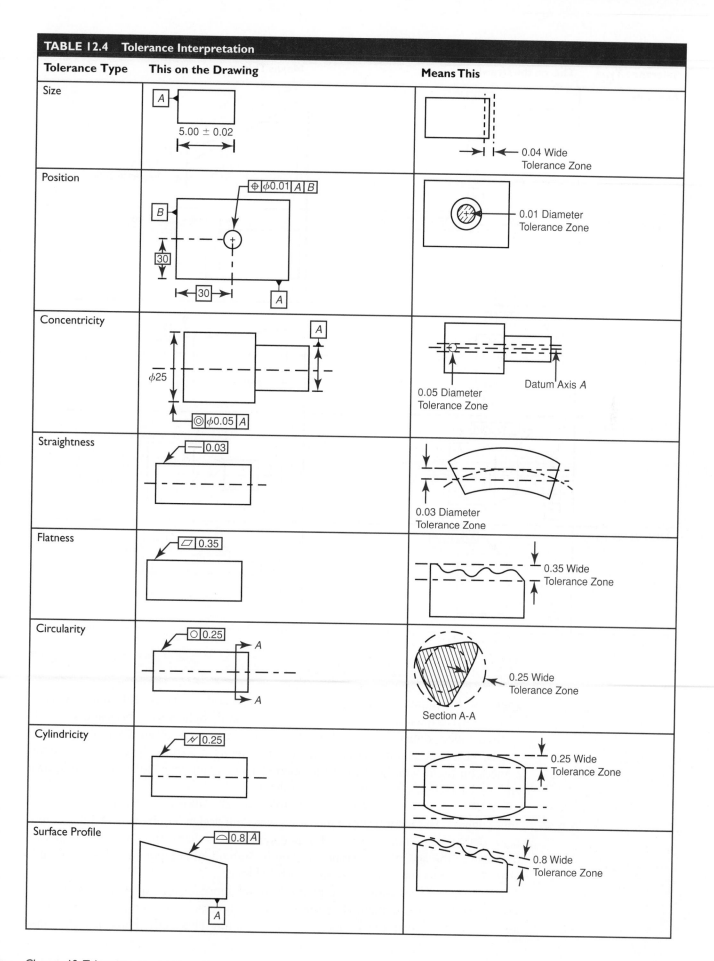

| Tolerance Type | This on the Drawing | Means This |
|---|---|---|
| Size | $A$    5.00 ± 0.02 | 0.04 Wide Tolerance Zone |
| Position | ⊕ $\phi$0.01 $A$ $B$    $B$    30    30    $A$ | 0.01 Diameter Tolerance Zone |
| Concentricity | $A$    $\phi$25    ◎ $\phi$0.05 $A$ | 0.05 Diameter Tolerance Zone    Datum Axis $A$ |
| Straightness | — 0.03 | 0.03 Diameter Tolerance Zone |
| Flatness | ⬭ 0.35 | 0.35 Wide Tolerance Zone |
| Circularity | ○ 0.25   $A$    $A$ | 0.25 Wide Tolerance Zone    Section A-A |
| Cylindricity | ⌭ 0.25 | 0.25 Wide Tolerance Zone |
| Surface Profile | ⌓ 0.8 $A$    $A$ | 0.8 Wide Tolerance Zone |

**TABLE 12.4 Tolerance Interpretation**

**TABLE 12.4**   *Continued*

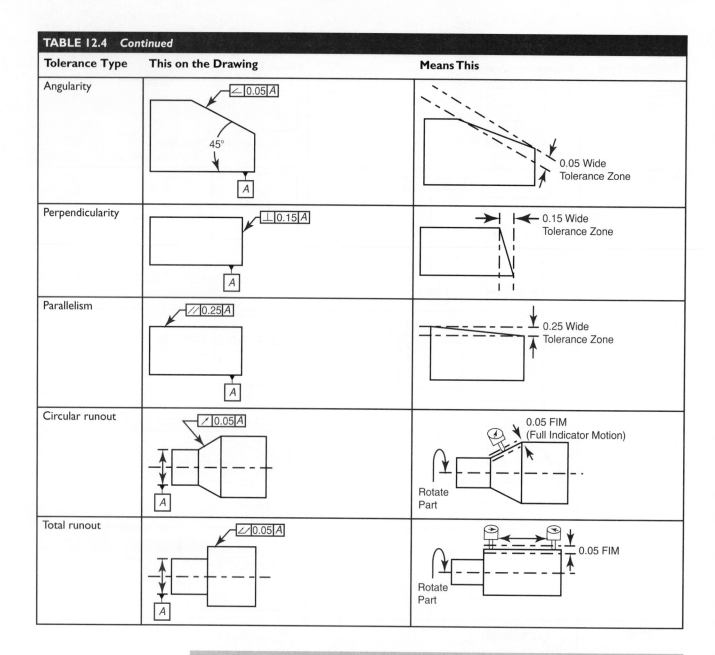

| Tolerance Type | This on the Drawing | Means This |
|---|---|---|
| Angularity | | 0.05 Wide Tolerance Zone |
| Perpendicularity | | 0.15 Wide Tolerance Zone |
| Parallelism | | 0.25 Wide Tolerance Zone |
| Circular runout | | 0.05 FIM (Full Indicator Motion) / Rotate Part |
| Total runout | | 0.05 FIM / Rotate Part |

## 12.13  Tolerance Analysis

There are two types of tolerance studies: analysis and synthesis. **Tolerance analysis** (also known as tolerance stack-up analysis) is the study of how tolerances and assembly methods affect dimensional stack-up between two features of an assembly. In other words, we assign tolerances to individual components and study the effect of these tolerances on the assembly of the components. Thus, component tolerances are known and we calculate the resulting assembly tolerance.

Tolerance synthesis is also known as tolerance allocations. It is the reverse of tolerance analysis. The assembly tolerance is known from design requirements while component tolerances are not known. **Tolerance synthesis** is the method of how we allocate (distribute) the assembly tolerance among its individual components in a reasonable way. We cover tolerance analysis only in this chapter.

The two most commonly used methods for tolerance analysis are worst case and statistical. The worst-case method assumes that the dimension of each component in the assembly is at its worst, that is, maximum or minimum. This method produces the worst possible assembly limits. In the worst-case analysis, the assembly tolerance is given by the linear summation of the component tolerances. For one-dimensional assemblies with $N$ components, the assembly tolerance is given by:

$$T = \sum_{i=1}^{i=N} T_i \qquad (12.8)$$

where $T$ and $T_i$ are, respectively, the assembly tolerance and the component tolerance. One-dimensional assembly means an assembly in which toleranced dimensions form a chain in one direction (horizontal, vertical, or any other direction).

For multidimensional assemblies, Eq. (12.8) becomes:

$$T = \sum_{i=1}^{i=N} \left| \frac{\partial f}{\partial x_i} \right| T_i \qquad (12.9)$$

where $|.|$ is the absolute value, $x_i$ is the nominal component dimensions, and $f(x_i)$ is an assembly function describing the resulting dimension of the assembly, such as clearance or interference. The partial derivatives represent the sensitivity of the assembly tolerance to variations in individual component dimensions.

Equations (12.8) and (12.9) assume that the tolerances are symmetric (i.e., the negative and the positive limits are equal). If the tolerances are bilateral (i.e., the limits are not equal), Eqs. (12.8) and (12.9) can be applied to each limit to give:

$$T_{\min} = \sum_{i=1}^{i=N} T_{i\min} \qquad (12.10)$$

for the lower tolerance limit, and

$$T_{\max} = \sum_{i=1}^{i=N} T_{i\max} \qquad (12.11)$$

for the higher tolerance limit.

The statistical method of tolerance analysis is based on the statistical concepts covered in Section 12.8. This method uses the RSS (root sum squared) to evaluate the statistical tolerance stack-up. The method assumes a normal (Gaussian) distribution for the component variations. In this case, the one-dimensional assembly tolerance is given by:

$$T = \sqrt{\sum_{i=1}^{i=N} T_i^2} \qquad (12.12)$$

For a multidimensional assembly, the assembly tolerance is given by:

$$T = \sqrt{\sum_{i=1}^{i=N} \left( \frac{\partial f}{\partial x_i} \right)^2 T_i^2} \qquad (12.13)$$

For cases of non-normal distributions, the Monte Carlo simulation method is used to evaluate the tolerance stack-up. The coverage of this method is beyond the scope of this book.

Equations (12.12) and (12.13) assume that the tolerances are symmetric (i.e., the negative and the positive limits are equal). If the tolerances are bilateral (i.e., the limits are not equal), Eqs. (12.12) and (12.13) can be applied to each limit to give:

$$T_{\min} = \sqrt{\sum_{i=1}^{i=N} T_{i\min}^2} \qquad (12.14)$$

for the lower tolerance limit, and

$$T_{\max} = \sqrt{\sum_{i=1}^{i=N} \left( \frac{\partial f}{\partial x_i} \right)^2 T_{i\max}^2} \qquad (12.15)$$

for the higher tolerance limit.

**Example 12.2**   An assembly consists of four identical boxes that are stacked on top of each other. We need to control the assembly overall height, $h$, to be between 3.9 and 4.1 in. The height of each box is $1.00 \pm 0.03$ in. Does the tolerance specification on each box height meet the assembly tolerance requirement?

**Solution**   The assembly height is $4.00 \pm 0.10$ in. (3.9, 4.1). Thus, the assembly tolerance is $\pm0.10$ in. Using the worst-case method, Eq. (12.8) gives:

$$T = 0.03 + 0.03 + 0.03 + 0.03 = 0.12 \text{ in.}$$

The tolerance stack-up (0.12 in.) is more than the assembly allowable tolerance limit of 0.10 in. Thus, the tolerance of the box height must be tightened.

Using the statistical method, Eq. (12.10) gives:

$$T = \sqrt{(0.03)^2 + (0.03)^2 + (0.03)^2 + (0.03)^2} = 0.06$$

The resulting statistical assembly tolerance is $\pm0.06$, thus meeting the assembly tolerance requirement. The tolerance calculated by the worst-case method is double that calculated by the statistical method. The two methods of tolerance analysis produce different results and can lead to opposite conclusions. Selecting which method of tolerancing to use is important. We would use the statistical method if the manufacturing method were well controlled, as covered in Section 12.8. However, the worst-case method is the safer approach. If the inputs (component tolerances) are within their respective tolerances, the output (assembly tolerance) is guaranteed to be within its worst-case tolerance. This is especially important for products like heart valves or critical components of airplanes. However, this guarantee comes at high cost. As discussed in Section 12.8, the worst-case scenario is highly unlikely, if not impossible, in most cases. In this example, all the four boxes must have a height of either 0.97 or 1.03. This could occur only if the manufacturing process producing the boxes had zero variation.

## 12.14  SolidWorks Tolerance Analysis

SolidWorks implements the tolerance analysis concepts covered here in its **TolAnalyst** module that helps you study how tolerances and assembly methods affect dimensional stack-up between two features of an assembly. In other words, **TolAnalyst** is used to perform stack-up analysis of an assembly. It uses both the worst-case and the statistical method covered in Section 12.13. The result of each method is a minimum (Eq. [12.10]) and maximum (Eq. [12.11]) tolerance stack, a minimum (Eq. [12.14]) and maximum (Eq. [12.15]) root sum squared (RSS) tolerance stack, and a list of contributing features and tolerances.

It is advisable that you know how to use SolidWorks **DimXpert** dimensioning module before using **TolAnalyst**. **DimXpert** is used with parts. It converts models for use with **TolAnalyst**. **DimXpert** works by inserting dimensions and tolerances, automatically or manually, into manufacturing features such as holes and slots. **TolAnalyst** automatically recognizes tolerances and dimensions created in **DimXpert**.

**TolAnalyst** performs a tolerance analysis called a *study*, which you create using four steps:

1. Measurement:   Establish the measurement, which is a linear distance between two **DimXpert** features.
2. Assembly sequence:   Select the ordered set of parts to establish a tolerance chain between the two measurement features. The selected parts form the "simplified assembly."

3. **Assembly constraints:** Define how each part is placed or constrained into the simplified assembly.
4. **Analysis results:** Evaluate and review the minimum and maximum worst-case tolerance stacks.

To create a **TolAnalyst** study:

1. Use **DimXpert** for parts to add tolerances and dimensions to parts of an assembly.
2. Open the assembly.
3. Perform the **TolAnalyst** study: Click **Tools => DimXpert => TolAnalyst Study**.
4. Follow the preceding four steps to perform the tolerance analysis (study).

To edit a **TolAnalyst** study:

1. Open the assembly containing the study.
2. In the **DimXpertManager** tab, right-click the study and select **Edit Feature**.

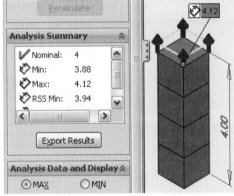

**FIGURE 12.15**
**TolAnalyst** study

**Example 12.3** Redo Example 12.2 using SolidWorks TolAnalyst. Compare the results.

**Solution** This example verifies that SolidWorks **TolAnalyst** uses the same tolerance analysis methods and equations covered in Section 12.13. Figure 12.15 shows the results of the analysis. These results are identical to those of Example 12.2. The **Min** and **Max** values shown result from the worst-case method. These values are calculated using Eqs. (12.10) and (12.11), respectively. The **RSS Min** and **RSS Max** values listed in the **Analysis Summary** result from the statistical method. These values are calculated using Eqs. (12.14) and (12.15), respectively.

The general steps to create the **TolAnalyst** study are:

1. Create the four $1 \times 1 \times 1$ boxes.
2. Create the assembly.
3. Select the assembly dimension to analyze (the assembly height in this example).
4. Define the assembly sequence. This sequence relates the dimension selected in Step 3 to the dimensions of the assembly components (parts) created in Step 1.
5. Set the assembly constraints.
6. View the analysis results.

The details of each step are shown below.

## Step 1: Create the four boxes

| Task | Command Sequence to Click |
|---|---|
| A. Start SolidWorks, and open a new part, create the first box as an extrusion, and save it as *part1*. | **Open => New = Part** => Create the box as an extrusion. Use the front plane to create the box sketch => **Save As** => *part1* => **Save**. |

| Task | Command Sequence to Click |
|---|---|
| B. Add the **DimXpert** dimension shown below.  | **Tools => DimXpert => Auto Dimension Scheme** => Select bottom face of block as **Primary Datum** => Green check mark. <br><br> **Help:** DimXpert adds the height (tolerance dimension) shown to the left automatically. Click the dimension to edit the tolerance, if needed. After done, **Save** the part. **DimXpert** dimensions are shown in pink color to distinguish them from other dimensions. <br><br> **Why:** We use the height as the desired dimension because it controls the assembly as discussed in Example 12.2. |
| C. Create the other three parts. We copy *part1* three times to create the other parts to save time. | **File** (assuming part1 is open. If it is not, open it) => **Save As** => *part2*. Repeat the **Save** twice to create *part3* and *part4*. |

## Step 2: Create the assembly

| Task | Command Sequence to Click |
|---|---|
| A. Start a new assembly and assemble (stack) the four boxes. You need two mates to assemble each box: two coincidents between edges. | **File => New => Assembly =>** Assemble the parts to stack them up as shown in Figure 12.15. |

## Step 3: Select the assembly dimension to analyze

| Task | Command Sequence to Click |
|---|---|
| A. Select the assembly height shown in Figure 12.15 to perform stack-up analysis on it. At the end of this step, SolidWorks creates a tolerance study called **Study1** and displays it in the **DimExpertManager** tab as shown below. 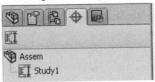 | **Tools => DimXpert => TolAnalyst Study** => Select the bottom face of the assembly => Select the top face of the assembly => Click on the screen to place the dimension => Green check mark. <br><br> **Why:** The bottom and top faces define the **Measure From** and **Measure To** features, respectively, which in turn define the assembly dimension to analyze (pink dimension 4.00 shown in Figure 12.15). <br><br> **Why:** If **TolAnalyst Study** is not active, it means that the **TolAnalyst** Add-in is not activated. Click **Tools => Add-ins => TolAnalyst** <br><br> **Help:** You may need to change the assembly model units to display the dimension using the correct units. |

## Step 4:    Define the assembly sequence

### Task

A. Select the assembly components in the sequence that you would use in real life to assemble them. Here, select *part1*, *part2*, *part3*, and *part4*, in this sequence.

### Command Sequence to Click

Right-click **Study1** node => **Edit Feature** => Select the four components (click the parts graphics or their names in the assembly tree) in the sequence mentioned to the left => Green check mark.

## Step 5:    Set the assembly constraints

### Task

A. Apply constraints between mating faces of assembly components. These constraints determine how the dimensions of the assembly components change relative to the assembly dimension to analyze.

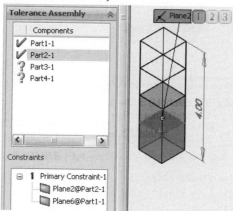

### Command Sequence to Click

Right-click **Study1** node => **Edit Feature** => Select 1 (shown to the left) from the callout that pops up to set constraint on **Part2-1** => Select **Part3-1** => Select 1 (shown to the left) from the callout that pops up to set constraint on it => Select **Part4-1** => => Select 1 (shown to the left) from the callout that pops up to set constraint on it => Green check mark.
**Help:** Each constraint relates two planes, one from each part as shown to the left for the first two components.
**Why:** These constraints are different from the mating conditions. They control how the dimensions change in the tolerance stack-up analysis.

## Step 6:    View the analysis results

### Task

A. View and analyze the tolerance analysis results.

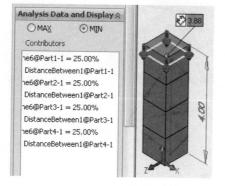

### Command Sequence to Click

Right-click **Study1** node => **Edit Feature** => View the results shown to the left => Green check mark when done analyzing.
**Help:** Figure 12.15 shows the results, which match the manual calculations done in Example 12.2. Figure 12.15 shows the **Analysis Data and Display** for the **MAX** case (default). The screenshot shown to the left shows data for the **MIN** case. Study the **Contributors** data shown to the left, which indicate the influence of each

| Task | Command Sequence to Click |
|------|---------------------------|

component dimension on the stack-up analysis.

**Help:** Toggle between **MAX** and **MIN** to view both extremes.

---

> ***HANDS-ON FOR EXAMPLE 12.3.*** Change the sizes of the boxes so that each box size is double the previous one. Assemble them and redo the stack-up analysis. How do the contributors change? Is it a linear change? Explain your answer.

---

## 12.15 Tutorials Overview

The theme for the tutorials in this chapter is to practice specifying both conventional and geometric tolerances as well as performing tolerance stack-up analysis. The tutorials show how to use the tolerances menus, **DimXpert**, and **TolAnalyst**. MDA ISI, located in Pasadena, CA, USA (www.alliancespacesystems.com), has sponsored this chapter. MDA ISI is a leading provider of mechanical systems engineering, custom design, and fabrication in composite structures, robotics and mechanisms, and mechanical analyses for systems operating in extreme environments. MDA ISI's innovative products are in use on interplanetary spacecraft, telecommunications and scientific satellites, and in many challenging terrestrial applications. We chat with Mr. Richard Fleischner, Group Supervisor for Mechanical Engineering at MDA ISI, in the Industry Chat. Figure 12.16 shows sample products of MDA ISI. Figure 12.16A shows an IDD (Instrument Deployment Device). It is an instrument-laden robotic arm. Two arms are currently operating on Mars. Each serves as a scientific appendage on the front of the rovers *Spirit* and *Opportunity* delivering its payload of instruments to examine rock and soil specimens chosen for study. Figure 12.16B shows a MahliCam (Mars Hand

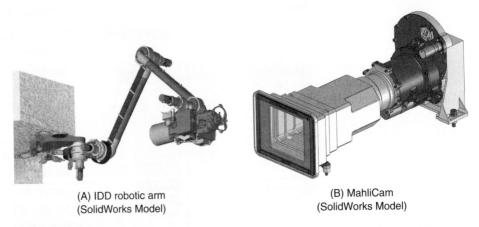

(A) IDD robotic arm
(SolidWorks Model)

(B) MahliCam
(SolidWorks Model)

**FIGURE 12.16**
Sample products (Courtesy of MDA ISI)

Part IV Part Development and Analysis

Lens Imager Camera). The cam is currently slated for operations on Mars as part of the MSL (Mars Science Laboratory) rover scheduled to launch in 2011 and arrive in 2012. Two of these cameras will serve as the stereoscopic "eyes" for the MSL rover as it traverses the Martian terrain.

# Tutorial 12–1: Use Conventional Tolerances

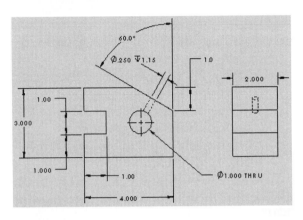

**FIGURE 12.17**
A part with conventional tolerances

### Modeling task

Add conventional tolerances, as shown in Figure 12.17 , to the drawing that was created in Tutorial 5–3 of Chapter 5.

### Modeling synthesis

This tutorial covers different ways to display tolerances on a drawing.

### Modeling plan

Conventional tolerances are added to the slider block drawing that was created in Tutorial 5–3 of Chapter 5.

### Design intent

Ignore for this tutorial.

### CAD steps

We add conventional tolerances in three steps:

1. Open the slider block drawing.
2. Change the scale of the drawing.
3. Add tolerances to the dimensions.

The details of these steps are shown below.

## Step 1: Open the slider block drawing

**Task**

A. Open the slider block drawing from *Sliderblock.slddrw.*

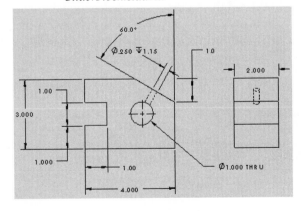

**Command Sequence to Click**

**File => Open** => *Sliderblock.slddrw* as shown to the left

## Step 2: Change the scale of the drawing

**Task**

**A.** Open the **Properties** menu.

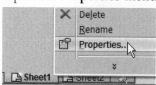

**B.** Change the drawing scale in the **Sheet Properties** window.

**Command Sequence to Click**

Right-click on **Sheet1** (the sheet name tab) in the lower left-hand corner of the sheet => Select **Properties** as shown to the left.

Change the scale to 1:2 as shown to the left.
**Why:** The change of scale is not actually necessary for the functionality of the tolerances. However, the scale is changed in order to keep the illustrations of this tutorial within the limits of the page.

## Step 3: Add tolerances to the dimensions

**Task**

**A.** Highlight the 60.0° dimension.

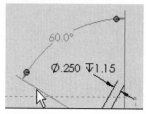

**B.** Change the number of decimals displayed.

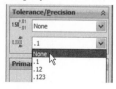

**C.** Highlight the 3.000 and the 4.000 dimensions.

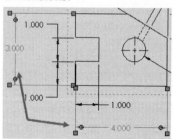

**Command Sequence to Click**

Select the 60.0° angle as shown to the left.

Select **None** from the **Unit Precision** drop-down menu in the **Tolerance/ Precision** section as shown to the left.
**Why:** The number of decimals displayed by a dimension will determine the amount of precision used when the part is machined. For example, the .1° tolerance tells the machinist that the angle must be kept within ±0.1°.
Select one dimension => Hold **CTRL** key => Select the second dimension as shown to the left.

| Task | Command Sequence to Click |
|---|---|

**D.** Select **Symmetric** for the tolerance type.

Select **Symmetric** from the **Tolerance type** drop-down menu as shown to the left.

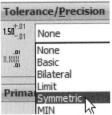

**E.** Input 0.002 for the maximum variation.

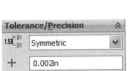

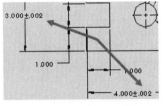

Input 0.002 in the **Maximum Variation** data box as shown to the left.
**Why:** This will inform the machinist that these two dimensions must be held within 0.002 of the nominal value.

---

**HANDS-ON FOR TUTORIAL 12–1.** Using the other types of tolerances from the drop-down menu along with various unit precision values, change the other dimensions of this same view to look as shown in Figure 12.18.

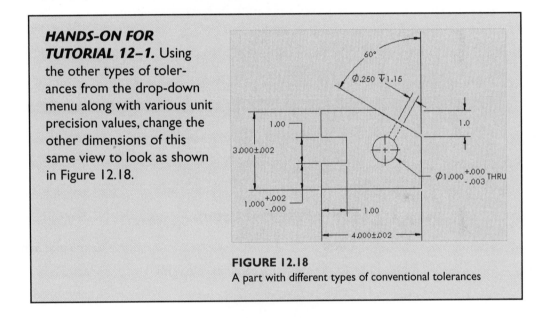

**FIGURE 12.18**
A part with different types of conventional tolerances

---

## Tutorial 12–2: Use Size and Location Geometric Tolerances

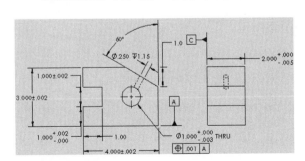

**FIGURE 12.19**
A part with geometric tolerances

### Modeling task

Add geometric tolerances to the drawing shown in Figure 12.19, which was created in Tutorial 5–3 and modified in Tutorial 12–1.

### Modeling synthesis

This tutorial covers the basic tolerance options in a drawing.

### Modeling plan

Geometric tolerances are added to the slider block drawing that was created in Tutorial 5–3 of Chapter 5.

Design intent

Ignore for this tutorial.

CAD steps

We add size and location tolerances in four steps:

1. Open the slider block drawing.
2. Set the reference datum.
3. Insert a positional tolerance.
4. Insert a size tolerance.

The details of these steps are shown below.

## Step 1: Open the slider block drawing

### Task

A. Open the slider block drawing from Tutorial 12–1.

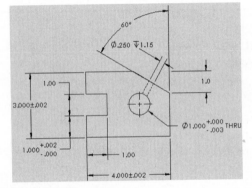

### Command Sequence to Click

**File => Open** => *Sliderblock.slddrw* as shown to the left

## Step 2: Set the reference datum

### Task

A. Choose an edge to define a datum.

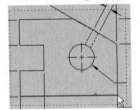

### Command Sequence to Click

Select the bottom edge of the block in the front view as shown to the left.

| Task | Command Sequence to Click |
|---|---|
| B. Select the **Datum Feature** tool. | **Annotations** tab => **Datum Feature** shown to the left |

| | |
|---|---|
| C. Set the location of the datum symbol. | Click anywhere on the sheet where you would like to set the symbol => Click again to place the symbol as shown to the left => Green check to exit the tool. |

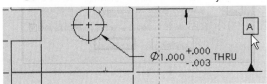

## Step 3: Insert a positional tolerance

| Task | Command Sequence to Click |
|---|---|
| A. Select the hole diameter dimension. | Click once on the hole diameter dimension to highlight it as shown to the left. |

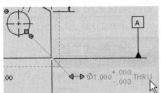

**Why:** This will allow you to add a geometric tolerance as a part of the diameter callout.

| | |
|---|---|
| B. Select the **Geometric Tolerance** tool. | **Annotations** tab => **Geometric Tolerance** shown to the left |

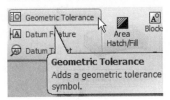

| | |
|---|---|
| C. Select a symbol. | Select the **Position** symbol from the **Symbol** drop-down list as shown to the left. |

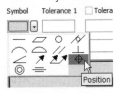

| | |
|---|---|
| D. Set Tolerance1 and reference. | Set **Tolerance 1** to .001″ and the **Primary** reference to **A** as shown to the left => **OK**. |

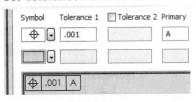

**Why:** This type of symbol informs the machinist that the hole must be located within ±.001 from the datum A.

| Task | Command Sequence to Click |
|---|---|

E. View the final dimensions shown below.

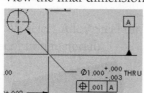

## Step 4: Insert a size tolerance

| Task | Command Sequence to Click |
|---|---|

A. Select the 1.00 in. dimension.

Click once on the dimension to highlight it as shown to the left.
**Why:** This will allow you to edit the tolerance of the dimension.

B. Change the precision of the dimension.

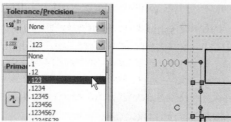

Select three decimal places from the **Unit Precision** drop-down menu as shown to the left.

C. Add a tolerance.

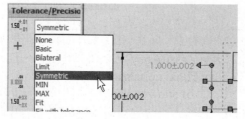

Select **Symmetric** from the **Tolerance type** drop-down menu as shown to the left.
**Why:** This is the size tolerance of the 1.000 slot in the part.

---

***HANDS-ON FOR TUTORIAL 12–2.*** Use the right view to add the tolerances as shown to the right in Figure 12.20.

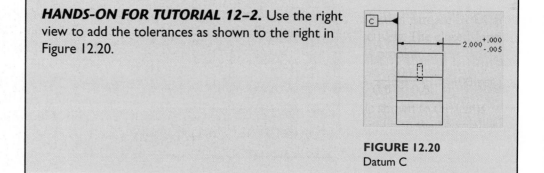

**FIGURE 12.20**
Datum C

---

## Tutorial 12–3: Use Form Tolerances

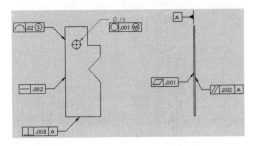

**FIGURE 12.21**
Form tolerances

### Modeling task

Add geometric tolerances to the drawing that was created in Tutorial 10–2. Figure 12.21 shows the tolerances.

### Modeling synthesis

This tutorial covers the basic tolerance options in a drawing.

### Modeling plan

Geometric tolerances are added to the sheet metal drawing that was created in Tutorial 10–2 of Chapter 10.

### Design intent

Ignore for this tutorial.

### CAD steps

We add form tolerances in four steps:

1. Open the sheet metal drawing.
2. Add a straightness tolerance to the drawing.
3. Add a datum feature to the drawing.
4. Add a flatness tolerance to the drawing.

The details of these steps are shown below.

## Step 1: Open the sheet metal drawing

**Task**

A. Open the sheet metal drawing from Tutorial 10–2.

**Command Sequence to Click**

**File => Open** => Open the drawing file that was created in Tutorial 10–2 and shown to the left.

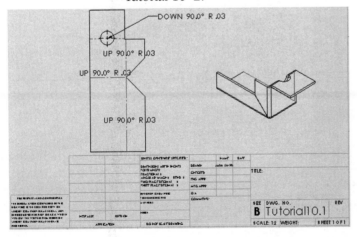

| Task | Command Sequence to Click |
|---|---|
| **B.** Change the drawing scale in the **Sheet Properties** menu. | Change the scale to 1:3 as shown to the left. |

| Task | Command Sequence to Click |
|---|---|
| **C.** Add a projected view to the flat view. | **View Layout** tab => **Projected View** as shown to the left |

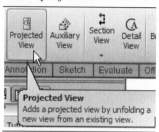

| Task | Command Sequence to Click |
|---|---|
| **D.** Set the view as shown. | Place the view as shown here to the left. |

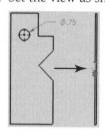

## Step 2: Add a straightness tolerance to the drawing

| Task | Command Sequence to Click |
|---|---|
| **A.** Select a vertical edge of the original view; then add a geometric tolerance. | **Annotation** tab => **Geometric Tolerance** as shown to the left |

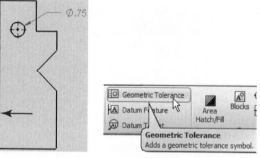

**B.** Add a straightness tolerance.

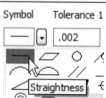

Select **Straightness** from the **Symbol** drop-down as shown to the left. Then input the values as shown to the left. **Why:** This will instruct the machinist of the part that this edge must be straight within ±.002″.

**C.** Review the drawing shown below.

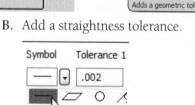

## Step 3:   Add a datum feature to the drawing

**Task**

A.  Select the vertical edge of the projected view; then add a datum reference.

**Command Sequence to Click**

**Annotation** tab => **Datum Feature** as shown to the left

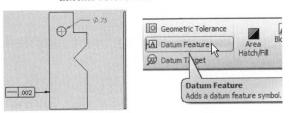

B.  Review the drawing.

Set the datum feature as shown to the left.

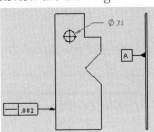

## Step 4:   Add a flatness tolerance to the drawing

**Task**

A.  Select the vertical edge of the projected view; then add a geometric tolerance as shown below.

**Command Sequence to Click**

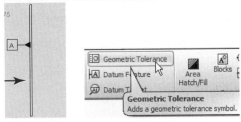

B.  Add a flatness tolerance.

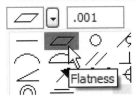

Select **Flatness** from the **Symbol** drop-down as shown to the left. Then input the values as shown to the left.
**Why:** This will instruct the machinist of the part that it must be flat within ±.001″ prior to bending.

C.  Review the drawing shown below.

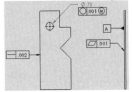

## Tutorial 12–4: Use Orientation Tolerances

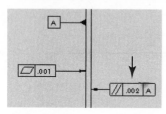

**FIGURE 12.22**
Parallelism tolerance

### Modeling task

Add a geometric tolerance to the drawing that was created in Tutorial 10–2. Figure 12.22 shows the tolerance to add.

### Modeling synthesis

This tutorial covers the basic tolerance options in a drawing.

### Modeling plan

A geometric tolerance is added to the sheet metal drawing that was created in Tutorial 10–2 of Chapter 10.

### Design intent

Ignore for this tutorial.

### CAD steps

We add the orientation tolerance in two steps:

1. Open the sheet metal drawing.
2. Add a parallelism tolerance to the drawing.

The details of these steps are shown below.

### Step 1: Open the sheet metal drawing

| Task | Command Sequence to Click |
| --- | --- |
| **A.** Open the sheet metal drawing from Tutorial 10–2. 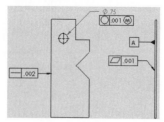 | **File => Open** => Open the drawing file that was created in Tutorial 10–2 as shown to the left. |

## Step 2: Add a parallelism tolerance to the drawing

| Task | Command Sequence to Click |
|------|---------------------------|
| **A.** Select the vertical edge from the projected view. | Click on the edge once to highlight it as shown to the left. |

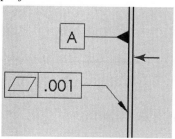

| Task | Command Sequence to Click |
|------|---------------------------|
| **B.** Open the **Geometric Tolerance** tool. | **Annotation** tab => **Geometric Tolerance** as shown to the left |

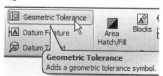

| Task | Command Sequence to Click |
|------|---------------------------|
| **C.** Create a parallel tolerance. | Insert a **Parallel** tolerance as shown to the left. |

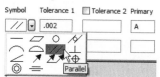

**D.** Place the geometric tolerance on the drawing as shown below.

---

**HANDS-ON FOR TUTORIAL 12–4.** Add a perpendicularity tolerance to the top view of the drawing. The tolerance must specify perpendicularity within .005 in. with respect to datum A.

---

## Tutorial 12–5: Use Profile Tolerances

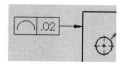

**FIGURE 12.23**
Profile tolerance

### Modeling task

Add a geometric tolerance to the drawing that was created in Tutorial 10–2. Figure 12.23 shows the tolerances.

### Modeling synthesis

This tutorial covers the basic tolerance options in a drawing.

### Modeling plan

A geometric tolerance is added to the sheet metal drawing that was created in Tutorial 10–2 of Chapter 10.

### Design intent

Ignore for this tutorial.

### CAD steps

We add the profiles tolerance in two steps:

1. Open the sheet metal drawing.
2. Add a profile tolerance to the drawing.

The details of these steps are shown below.

## Step 1: Open the sheet metal drawing

| Task | Command Sequence to Click |
|---|---|
| A. Open the sheet metal drawing from Tutorial 10–2. | **File => Open** => Open the drawing file that was created in Tutorial 10–2 as shown to the left. |

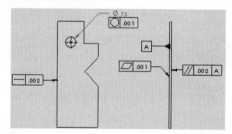

## Step 2: Add a profile tolerance to the drawing

| Task | Command Sequence to Click |
|---|---|
| A. Select the left vertical edge of the top view. | Select the edge as shown to the left. |

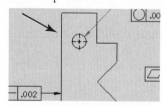

| | |
|---|---|
| B. Open the **Geometric Tolerance** tool. | **Annotation** tab => **Geometric Tolerance** as shown to the left |

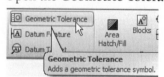

| Task | Command Sequence to Click |
|---|---|
| C. Insert a profile of line tolerance. | Add the **Profile of Line** geometric tolerance as shown to the left. |

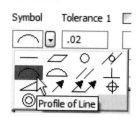

D. Place the tolerance callout on the drawing as shown below.

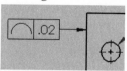

***HANDS-ON FOR TUTORIAL 12–5.*** Add a profile tolerance of .005 in. to the top edge of the top view. Submit a screenshot of the final drawing.

## Tutorial 12–6: Use Modifying Symbols

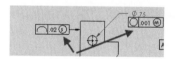

**FIGURE 12.24**
Modifying symbols

### Modeling task

Add modifying symbols to the drawing that was created in Tutorial 10–2. Figure 12.24 shows the symbols.

### Modeling synthesis

This tutorial covers the basic options in a drawing.

### Modeling plan

Modifying symbols are added to the sheet metal drawing that was created in Tutorial 10–2 of Chapter 10.

### Design intent

Ignore for this tutorial.

### CAD steps

We add modifying symbols in three steps:

1. Open the sheet metal drawing.
2. Add a modifying symbol to the diameter callout.
3. Add a modifying symbol to the line profile callout.

The details of these steps are shown below.

## Step 1: Open the sheet metal drawing

**Task**

A. Open the sheet metal drawing from Tutorial 10–2.

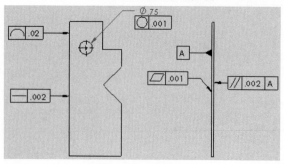

**Command Sequence to Click**

**File => Open** => Open the drawing file that was created in Tutorial 10–2 as shown to the left.

## Step 2: Add a modifying symbol to the diameter callout

**Task**

A. Double-click on the geometric tolerance that is associated with the diameter callout.

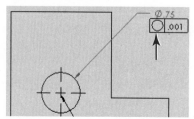

**Command Sequence to Click**

Double-click the geometric callout as shown to the left.

B. Add the **Maximum Material Condition** symbol as shown below.

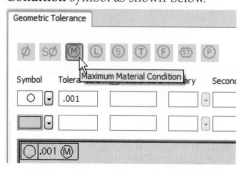

## Step 3: Add a modifying symbol to the line profile callout

**Task**

A. Double-click on the geometric tolerance that is associated with the line profile.

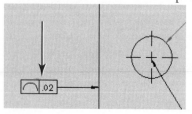

**Command Sequence to Click**

Double-click the geometric callout as shown to the left.

| Task | Command Sequence to Click |

B. Add the **Regardless of Feature Size** as shown below.

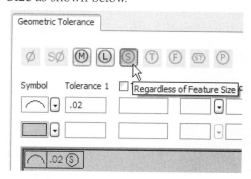

---

**HANDS-ON FOR TUTORIAL 12–6.** Replace the material condition in the tutorial with the least material condition.

---

## Tutorial 12–7:  Use Auto Dimension Scheme

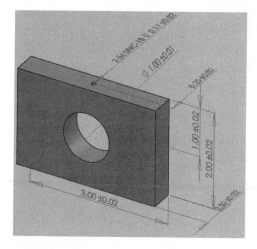

**FIGURE 12.25**
Auto Dimensions

### Modeling task

Use the **Auto Dimension Scheme** feature of the **DimXpert** tool to dimension and tolerance an existing part. Figure 12.25 shows the resulting dimensions.

### Modeling synthesis

This tutorial covers the **Auto Dimension Scheme** feature of the **DimXpert** tool.

### Modeling plan

Open *Block1.sldprt* from Tutorial 6–9. Auto Dimension the block using the **Auto Dimension Scheme** feature of the **DimXpert** tool. Show the tolerance status.

### Design intent

Ignore for this tutorial.

### CAD steps

We create the auto dimensions in three steps:

1. Open the *Block1.sldprt* part.
2. Auto Dimension the block.
3. Show the tolerance status.

   The details of these steps are shown below.

## Step 1:   Open *Block1.sldprt*

**Task**

A.  Open the part.

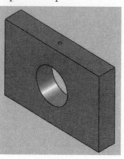

**Command Sequence to Click**

**File** => **Open** => *block1.sldprt* of Tutorial 6–9 => **Open** as shown to the left

## Step 2:   Auto Dimension the block

**Task**

A.  Dimension the part automatically.

**Command Sequence to Click**

**DimXpert** => **Auto Dimension Scheme** as shown to the left

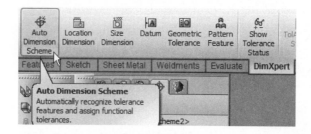

B.  Select the part and tolerance types.

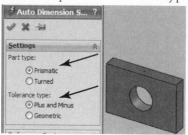

Select **Prismatic** for **Part type** and **Plus and Minus** for **Tolerance type** as shown to the left.

| Task | Command Sequence to Click |
|---|---|

C. Select the necessary datums to use in the automatic dimensioning scheme.

Select the **Primary**, **Secondary**, and **Tertiary** datums as shown from left to right.

D. Exit the **Auto Dimension Scheme** feature.

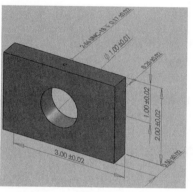

Green check mark to exit => Reposition the dimensions as shown to the left.
**Why:** The automatic dimensioning placement may not be readable; therefore, reposition the dimensions for reading clarity.

## Step 3: Show the tolerance status

| Task | Command Sequence to Click |
|---|---|

A. Check whether the part is over- or under-toleranced.

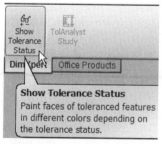

**DimXpert => Show Tolerance Status** as shown to the left

B. View the results.

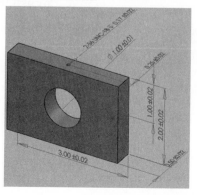

The **Show Tolerance Status** feature will display the faces and features of a part in one of three colors as shown to the left.
**Yellow => Under Constrained** (under-toleranced)
**Green => Fully Constrained** (fully toleranced)
**Red => Over Constrained** (over-toleranced)

## Tutorial 12–8: Tolerance a Taper

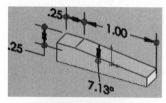

**FIGURE 12.26**
Two types of tapers

### Modeling task

Use the tolerance techniques discussed in this chapter to tolerance a flat taper and a conical taper, shown in Figure 12.26.

### Modeling synthesis

This tutorial covers how to tolerance a taper.

### Modeling plan

Create a taper. Create a drawing and tolerance the taper per ASME Y14.5M-1994 standard.

### Design intent

Instruct the machinist to keep a tolerance at a certain location of the taper.

### CAD steps

We create and tolerance the tapers in seven steps:

1. Create a ¼ in. flat tapered key.
2. Create a new drawing.
3. Tolerance the taper per ANSI standard.
4. Create a conical taper part.
5. Create a new drawing for the conical taper.
6. Use Scheme 1 to tolerance the conical taper.
7. Use Scheme 2 to tolerance the conical taper.

The details of these steps are shown below.

## Step 1: Create a ¼ in. flat tapered key

**Task**

A. Create the part.

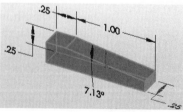

**Command Sequence to Click**

**File => New => Part =>** Create the part as shown to the left using English units.

## Step 2: Create a new drawing

| Task | Command Sequence to Click |
|---|---|
| A. Create a drawing for the key.  | **File => New => Drawing => OK => ** Select **A (ANSI) Landscape =>** OK |

## Step 3: Tolerance the taper per ANSI standard

| Task | Command Sequence to Click |
|---|---|
| A. Tolerance the drawing. | Create the tolerances shown to the left. |

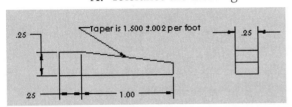

## Step 4: Create a conical tapered part

| Task | Command Sequence to Click |
|---|---|
| A. Create a new revolved part. 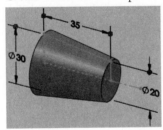 | **File => New => Part => OK => Features => Revolve =>** Create the part as shown to the left using metric units. |

## Step 5: Create a new drawing for the conical taper

| Task | Command Sequence to Click |
|---|---|
| A. Create a drawing for the key.  | **File => New => Drawing => OK =>** Select **A (ANSI) Landscape =>** OK |

## Step 6: Use Scheme I to tolerance the conical taper

| Task | Command Sequence to Click |
|---|---|
| A. Create a front view, and tolerance the part per ANSI standard. 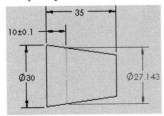 | Tolerance the part as shown. **Help:** Sketch a vertical line on the view from top to bottom. Dimension the line as shown to the left. One of the dimensions will be driven. **Why:** This method of tolerance applies a critical accuracy to a specific location of the taper. |

## Step 7: Use Scheme 2 to tolerance the conical taper

### Task

A. Create a second front view, and tolerance the part per ANSI standard.

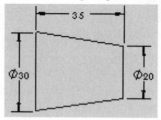

### Command Sequence to Click

Create a second front view on the same sheet. Tolerance the part as shown to the left.

**Why:** This method of tolerance applies a critical accuracy to the diameters at either end and no accuracy to the slope of the taper itself.

---

**HANDS-ON FOR TUTORIAL 12–8.** Using Figure 12.6A, find another scheme to dimension and tolerance the conical taper. Make sure you do not over dimension the conical taper. Explain your scheme.

---

## Tutorial 12–9: Use TolAnalyst

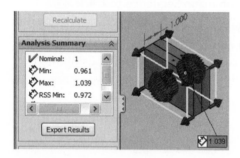

**FIGURE 12.27**
**TolAnalyst** stack-up results

### Modeling task

Use the **TolAnalyst** study to observe the tolerance stack-up of the assembly shown in Figure 12.27.

### Modeling synthesis

This tutorial covers the **TolAnalyst** feature of the **DimXpert** tool.

### Modeling plan

Create a new assembly. Add two instances of *Block1.sldprt* from Tutorial 12–7. Use the **TolAnalyst** feature of the **DimXpert** tool.

### Design intent

Ignore for this tutorial.

### CAD steps

We carry out the tolerance analysis in two steps:

1. Create a new assembly.
2. Analyze the tolerance stack-up of the assembly.

The details of these steps are shown below.

## Step 1: Create a new assembly

### Task

A. Open a new assembly and insert two instances of *Block1.sldprt*.

### Command Sequence to Click

**File => New => Assembly => Insert => Component => New**

| Task | Command Sequence to Click |
|---|---|

**Part/Assembly** => *block1.sldprt* of Tutorial 12–7 as shown to the left

B.  Mate the two blocks as shown below.

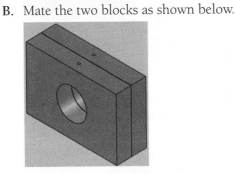

## Step 2:  Analyze the tolerance stack-up of the assembly

Task | Command Sequence to Click

A.  Add-in **TolAnalyst** tool to SolidWorks interface.

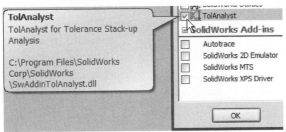

**Tools => Add-Ins => TolAnalyst** as shown to the left

B.  Open **TolAnalyst**.

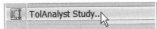

C.  Select two features to create a measurement.

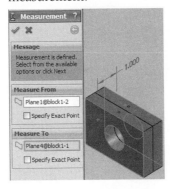

**Tools => DimXpert => TolAnalyst Study** as shown to the left

**Help: TolAnalyst** is grayed out unless the Add-in is added.

Select the front face of one block and the back face of the second => Click anywhere to place the nominal dimension as shown to the left => Click **Next** to continue as shown to the left.

**Why:** SolidWorks needs two features to study the tolerance stack-up between them.

| Task | Command Sequence to Click |
|---|---|

**D.** Select the base part.

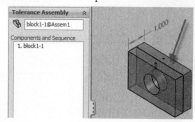

Select Instance 1 of *Block1* as shown to the left.

**Why:** We need to set up **TolAnalyst** to perform the tolerance stack-up. SolidWorks requires two parts (Steps D and E) and an alignment feature (Step F).

**E.** Select the second part.

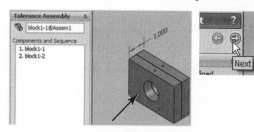

Select the remaining parts in the order in which they will be put together during assembly as shown to the left. In this case there is only one block to select => Select **Next** to continue as shown to the left.

**F.** Select the alignment feature.

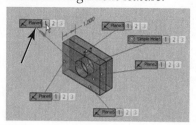

You must now select the feature that pertains to how the blocks will be aligned during assembly. Select as shown to the left.

**G.** Review results.

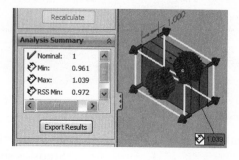

SolidWorks displays the min and max worst-case scenario as well as the RSS min and max as shown to the left. RSS the root sum squared tolerance stack that will most likely occur in real life.

## INDUSTRY CHAT

This section provides practical insight into how the chapter material is used in industry in the real world and practice. This section summarizes the chat with Mr. Richard Fleischner (Group Supervisor for Mechanical Engineering) of MDA ISI, the sponsor of this chapter. The structure of the chat follows the chapter sections.

**Chapter Section 12.1:** Introduction

ABE: How important are tolerances to your product design and manufacturing?

RICHARD: Tolerances are extremely important to us because our products are deployed in space and work autonomously. Many of our designs are precision mechanisms and gears with very close tight tolerances. We need these tight tolerances to govern the fit of bearings or some of the features of parts like optical elements to align them properly. Oftentimes, we deal with many times less than 0.001 inch tolerances.

**Chapter Section 12.2:** Types

ABE: How much conventional versus geometric tolerances do you use in your company?

RICHARD: We use both. I would say we use more geometric tolerances than conventional tolerances. In our company, we generally design and build prototypes. We do not have mass production. We do not deal with statistical tolerances. The use of conventional versus geometric tolerances depends on the type of product we design, that is, whether it is flight or test equipment. We have our own machine shop. Thus, sometimes we sketch on paper and tell machinists what to do. When we send the design outside to be machined, we use the full GD&T specifications. When we do "art to part," we use only the tolerances that govern the tight tolerances. Then there are generic tolerances specified for anything else not toleranced on the drawing.

**Chapter Section 12.3:** Concepts

ABE: Which tolerance concepts do you use the most in your company?

RICHARD: We use all the concepts. They are all equally important. Most of our work is milling and turning work, not too much contouring or complex surfaces. There are not often important surfaces that need complex tolerancing schemes. So we do not use datum targets that often. We use all the ASME Y14.5M-1994. Another very important issue to us is the following. No matter how good you are in mastering Y14.5, half of the machine shops out there in the market do not understand geometric tolerances. Sometimes we make tolerance mistakes (e.g., forget to assign a true position tolerance), and

*(continued)*

machine shops do not catch it. They simply are not very knowledgeable in geometric tolerances.

**Chapter Section 12.4:** ASME Tolerance Rules

ABE: Describe the tolerance practice in your company. Which tolerance style do you use the most on a drawing: limit dimensioning or plus/minus tolerances?

RICHARD: We mostly use basic tolerances with what is controlling the true position. We use the plus/minus (±) tolerances all the time on engineering drawings. We do not use limit dimensioning. You design a part, make it basic, and put profile tolerance on it. The next important thing is to specify tolerances on limited dimensions like drilled holes. When we do not see tolerances on dimensions on a drawing, they are governed by the company specifications specified as general tolerances in the drawing title block or somewhere on the drawing.

Here is the reason we use the plus/minus (±) all the time. For most parts, machine shops like the middle dimension (the basic size as called here in this chapter). That is what they want because this is how they set up the part for machining in the shop. In some special cases, such as drilling a hole, we model the drill size. So, the tolerances become bilateral (e.g., +0.005/−0.001 for ¼ inch hole); the bigger the hole, the bigger the tolerance range.

**Chapter Section 12.5:** Tolerancing Tapers

ABE: Do you use tapers? If you do, which type and how do you tolerance them?

RICHARD: We do not use taper tolerances. We do have some tapered shapes, but not taper tolerances. Instead we control the shape with a profile tolerance.

**Chapter Section 12.6:** Limits of Dimensions

ABE: Do you use fits in your product design? Which fits are most usable in your product design? How do you calculate the resulting tolerances?

RICHARD: No, we do not use fits. We use explicit tolerances based on our experience. Or, we specify tolerances on one part and leave the other mating part to the machine shop. We tell them to fit in real time a clearance fit or other type of fit. We do it this way because we do prototyping only, not mass production. Also, specifying a fit such as H7/g6 requires looking up and calculations. Our engineers do these details to save time in the machine shop and also try to avoid making mistakes on the shop floor.

We use clearance fit more than interference fit because the latter makes it harder to disassemble and take the parts apart. Thus, most of our fits are clearance fits. In some cases, we use interference fits. If you use interference fits, you must have a way to get the parts away (have a hole in one part and pry the parts away) or use hot/cold treatment (heat the parts, separate them, and then cool them down). We prefer not to heat/cool parts because of the residual stresses that result. If it is a simple pin in a hole, we do not perform a thermal analysis; otherwise we do it especially for space devices.

### Chapter Section 12.7: Tolerance Accumulation

**ABE:** How do you deal with the tolerance accumulation problem?

**RICHARD:** We try, as much as we can, to dimension the part in a way that does not stack up. We create designs so that most of them do not stack up. We generally do not perform stack-up analysis. In essence, we put stack up the parts, and before we put the last part, we measure and cut if needed. We usually shim the part to produce the desired mating effect. We shim the part by reducing its thickness by cutting it or increasing its thickness by adding thin shims in different shapes (donut, etc.). The other thing we do is to adjust the part thickness after machining. For example, we build the part with 0.090 inch tolerance instead of 0.060 inch. We wait until the mating part is machined. Then, we see what needs to be done. We could cut the 0.090 down to, say, 0.063 inch. A third thing we do is related to mechanisms. We take measurements and make adjustments. While our way is good for what we do (prototyping) and enables us to know what we get at the end, it does not lend itself to mass production.

### Chapter Section 12.8: Statistical Tolerancing

**ABE:** How do you use statistical tolerancing? How does it impact manufacturing and inspection?

**RICHARD:** We do not do statistical tolerance analysis very often. We have done statistical analysis in few cases. We only use it when we have very complex geometry that is hard to shim, that is, cannot shim out the "air." We had a complex example where we had so many interacting tolerances, affecting the angle of a mechanism. So, our expert (a mathematician) ran statistical analysis using Monte Carlo method to figure out the tolerances. We tend to simplify tolerances because we have so many people who need to understand and use it. It has to be simple.

### Chapter Section 12.9: True Position

**ABE:** Do you use true position in your drawings? How does it help your product design?

**RICHARD:** Yes, we use true position tolerance for holes, slots, notches, bosses, and other classic features. It helps our design. The ± stack-up makes it hard to understand, but the true position makes it easy to see how things fit together. In general, always make your design easy to understand.

### Chapter Section 12.10: Geometric Tolerances

**ABE:** Using Table 12.3, which geometric tolerances do you use the most and why?

**RICHARD:** We use almost everything in the table except straightness, line profile, and concentricity. We use flatness instead of straightness.

*(continued)*

Straightness is a subset of flatness. Line profile is a subset of surface profile. As for concentricity, it is hard to do because you need a virtual axis to measure it. But, for example, runout is easy to do because we can measure it with a gauge.

I want to add a few words on modifiers. We use MMC predominantly on actual tolerance zones. We do not use them on datums, only on part features. Putting an MMC symbol on a datum and on part features makes it hard to interpret. MMC control is used primarily for part-to-part fits using fasteners. We use MMC so the shop can take advantage of the "bonus tolerance," which allows for greater true position variance as the hole(s) gets larger. We use LMC primarily to control edge distance because the effect of LMC is to tighten up true position as the hole (or equivalent feature) gets larger. We use RFS when we are using a feature as a target that must remain located precisely despite its feature size variation. An example of this would be a counterbore to seat and position a lens cell: even if the cell is larger or smaller, its center remains on target to within the specified true position tolerance.

**Chapter Section 12.11:**   Datum Target Symbols

ABE:   What inspection gauges does your inspection department use? Are they off the shelf?

RICHARD:   We do not use datum targets a lot. We do not have gauges in the inspection department that use datum targets. We have simple gauges (go/no-go) together with CMM (Coordinate Measuring Machines). All our inspection gauges are off-the-shelf. Sometimes we make special gauges if we need them. We have our own machine shop.

**Chapter Section 12.12:**   Tolerance Interpretation

ABE:   How do you ensure that your designers understand and know how to use geometric tolerances?

RICHARD:   We have reading material such as ASME Y14.5-1994 and other material. We also have peer-to-peer discussion. Our designers make their own drawings. They are engineers with B.S. degrees. We also have a formal continuing education course that we run in house for them. We do a 3-day refresher class every year. My job, as a supervisor, is to keep an eye on my engineers' work, work with them, and help them.

**Chapter Section 12.13:**   Tolerance Analysis

ABE:   Which tolerance analysis method do you use? Why?

RICHARD:   Please see answers to Sections 12.7 and 12.8.

**Chapter Section 12.14:**   SolidWorks Tolerance Analysis

ABE:   How do you use **TolAnalyst**? How often do you use it?

RICHARD:   We do not use it because we do not need it. If we need it, we have mathematically inclined people to solve our complex problems.

**Others**

ABE:   Any other experience you would like to share with our book readers?

RICHARD:   Avoid generalizing a simple example and extending to all situations. People see common examples and get hooked to them. They never get out of that. So, always learn and pay attention to new concepts. Always have the intention to learn and expand your knowledge whether in tolerance or other engineering concepts. We do not have our own drafting department. So, our engineers do their own drawings. So, we all learn how to do it.

Another important tool in GD&T is CMM. They are time saving. However, the foundation to using these machines effectively is GD&T, all related to datums. With CMM, there are no A, B, or C datum plane surfaces that the part registers against; rather, it is the faces on the actual part itself that are probed by the CMM to derive the various datum planes. Another example is that in Y14.5 a hole that is declared a datum feature is outfitted with a "perfectly cylindrical" pin slipped into the hole from which the datum axis is generated; but with a CMM, the datum axis is measured and generated directly from the hole by probing its cylindrical surface. Since the datum representation is generated by the CMM software, if the hole is irregular, the calculated best fit cylinder is a direct function of the chosen probe points (more points are better!).

1. List the sources of variability in manufacturing.

2. Why do we need tolerances?

3. List the two types of tolerances. What does each type control?

4. Inspection gauges are used to check whether a part is within its tolerance limits. Perform an in-depth research study on inspection gauges including their types, their design, and how they are used during part inspection.

5. What is the difference between a nominal and a basic size? Give an example.

6. Three types of a dimension change exist: unilateral, bilateral, or symmetric. Describe each type and its related tolerance. Give an example for each.

7. List the three types of material conditions. Explain each type.

8. What is a datum? Why do we need them? How is a datum defined?

9. Which ASME tolerance rule should you use to show dimension limits on a drawing? Sketch an example showing a shaft and hole dimensioning.

10. The basic size of a dimension and its tolerance are specified as 3.500 in. and $\pm 0.05$, respectively. Is this specification correct? Explain your answer.

11. How do you fully define a conical or flat taper? How do you tolerance it?

12. List and describe the three types of fit.

13. The three parameters (tolerance zones) that determine a fit are $s$, $h$, and $a$. Sketch the combination of the three for clearance, transition, and interference fits.

14. Calculate the tolerance zones and limits for the following fits:
    a. Clearance fit of RC5 for a basic size of 5.0000 in.
    b. Transition fit of LT3 for a basic size of 3.0000 in.
    c. Interference fit of FN4 for a basic size of 6.0000 in.

    Sketch the tolerance zones following the style shown in Figure 12.7.

15. Figure 12.28 shows a stepped and grooved block with a depth of 2 in. Create the block in SolidWorks. Apply the three dimensioning schemes introduced in Section 12.7 to the block sketch shown in Figure 12.28. Calculate, manually, the coordinates of point $P$ for each scheme. Which scheme has the worst tolerance accumulation on the point location? Calculate the accumulation for each scheme. *Note:* All missing dimensions are either 1 in. or 0.5 in.

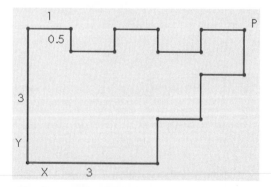

**FIGURE 12.28**
Stepped and grooved block

16. What is the difference between arithmetic and statistical tolerancing? Which one is more restrictive and why?

17. Figure 12.29 shows a toleranced hole. What is the problem with this tolerancing method? How do you solve it? All dims are in mm.

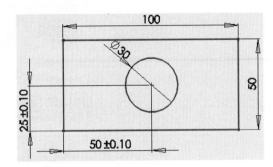

**FIGURE 12.29**
Specifying tolerances on a hole position

18. What type of geometric tolerance should you use to control the following variability in a part?
    a. The orientation of one its planes
    b. How straight a surface is
    c. How flat a surface is
    d. How parallel two surfaces are, and
    e. How perpendicular two surfaces are

    Illustrate your answer by sketching, manually, the tolerance symbol for each on a block with a rectangular cross section. Also, sketch the interpretation of each tolerance.

19. Define and sketch, manually, datum targets for the datums you use in Problem 18.

20. Figure 12.30 shows a four-bar mechanism assembly. Each bar of the assembly has the tolerance shown. The mechanism is fixed at point $A$, and its free end is $D$ and can only move horizontally. Calculate the tolerance on $D$ when the mechanism is in the horizontal position. How would you calculate the tolerance in a nonhorizontal position, for example, when rod $AB$ is at 45° from the horizontal? Use both the worst-case and statistical methods.

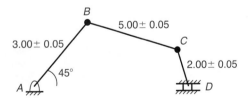

**FIGURE 12.30**
Four-bar mechanism

21. Figure 12.31 shows a Hinge assembly. The functional requirement of the hinge requires a clearance fit, that is, $D > A + B + C$ for any assembly. The dimensions of the assembly components (parts) are $2.00 \pm 0.05$, $2.00 \pm 0.05$, $30.00 \pm 0.05$, and $35.00 \pm 0.10$ for $A$, $B$, $C$, and $D$, respectively. Does the

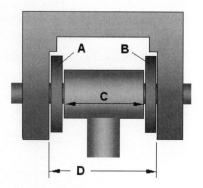

**FIGURE 12.31**
A Hinge assembly

tolerance specification on a component meet the assembly tolerance requirement? Use both the worst-case and statistical methods.

22. Solve Problem 15 using SolidWorks.

23. Solve Problem 20 using SolidWorks.

24. Solve Problem 21 using SolidWorks.

25. Use SolidWorks to create the following geometric tolerances in Figure 12.32. Assume any missing dimensions. All dims are in mm.

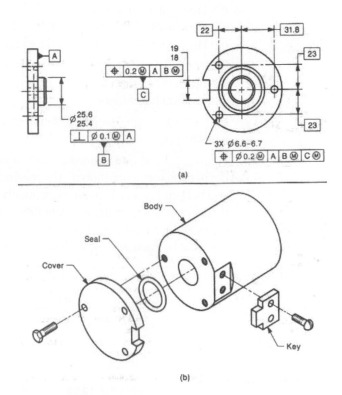

**FIGURE 12.32**
Part where angular orientation is important
(Reprinted from ASME Y14.5M-1994 [R2004], by permission of The American Society of Mechanical Engineers. All rights reserved)

Part IV Part Development and Analysis

26. Use SolidWorks to create the following geometric tolerances in Figure 12.33. Assume any missing dimensions. All dims are in mm.

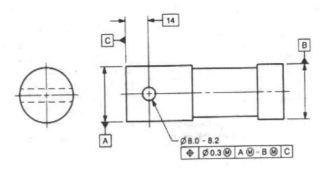

**FIGURE 12.33**
Two datum features, single datum axis

27. Use SolidWorks to create the following geometric tolerances in Figure 12.34. Assume any missing dimensions. All dims are in mm.

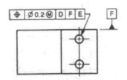

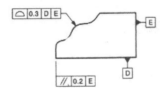

**FIGURE 12.34**
Using multiple datums

**28.** Use SolidWorks to create the following datum targets in Figure 12.35. Assume any missing dimensions. All dims are in mm.

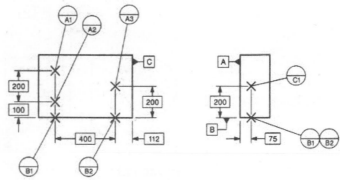

(A) Use target points

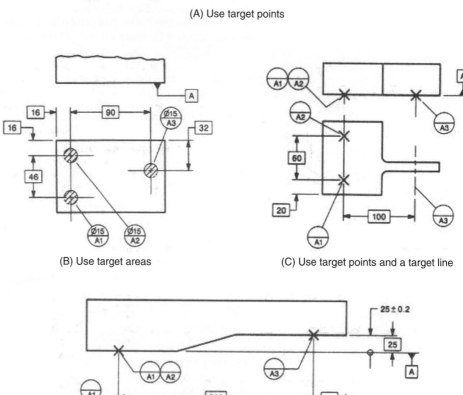

(B) Use target areas

(C) Use target points and a target line

(D) Use step datum feature

**FIGURE 12.35**
Defining datum targets
(Reprinted from ASME Y14.5M-1994 [R2004], by permission of The American Society of Mechanical Engineers. All rights reserved)

Part IV Part Development and Analysis

**29.** Use SolidWorks to create the geometric tolerances in Figure 12.36. Assume any missing dimensions. All dims are in mm.

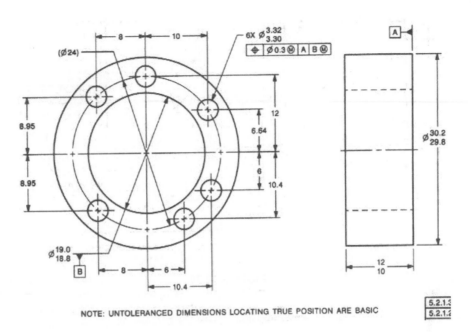

NOTE: UNTOLERANCED DIMENSIONS LOCATING TRUE POSITION ARE BASIC

**FIGURE 12.36**
Position tolerance using two datums
(Reprinted from ASME Y14.5M-1994 [R2004], by permission of The American Society of Mechanical Engineers. All rights reserved)

**30.** Use SolidWorks to create the geometric tolerances in Figure 12.37. Assume any missing dimensions. All dims are in mm.

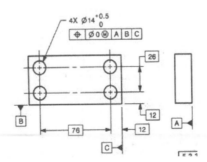

**FIGURE 12.37**
Zero position tolerance
(Reprinted from ASME Y14.5M-1994 [R2004], by permission of The American Society of Mechanical Engineers. All rights reserved)

**31.** Use SolidWorks to create the geometric tolerances in Figure 12.38. Assume any missing dimensions. All dims are in mm.

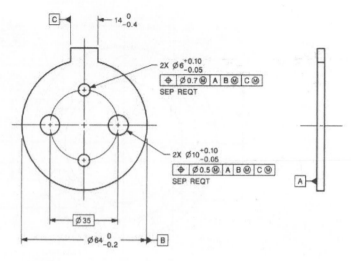

**FIGURE 12.38**
Multiple features, separate requirements
(Reprinted from ASME Y14.5M-1994 [R2004], by permission of The American
Society of Mechanical Engineers. All rights reserved)

**32.** Use SolidWorks to create the geometric tolerances in Figure 12.39. Assume any missing dimensions. All dims are in mm.

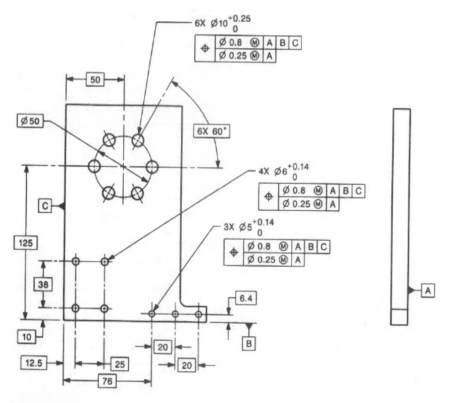

**FIGURE 12.39**
Hole patterns located by composite positional tolerances
(Reprinted from ASME Y14.5M-1994 [R2004], by permission of The American Society of Mechanical
Engineers. All rights reserved)

Part IV Part Development and Analysis

33. Use SolidWorks to create the geometric tolerances in Figure 12.40. Assume any missing dimensions. All dims are in mm.

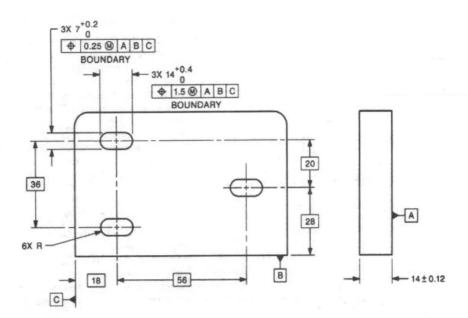

**FIGURE 12.40**
Using the BOUNDARY concept

34. Use SolidWorks to create the geometric tolerances in Figure 12.41. Assume any missing dimensions. All dims are in mm.

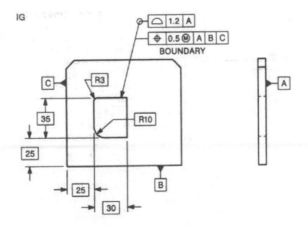

**FIGURE 12.41**
Specifying profile tolerance

**35.** Use SolidWorks to create the geometric tolerances in Figure 12.42. Assume any missing dimensions. All dims are in mm.

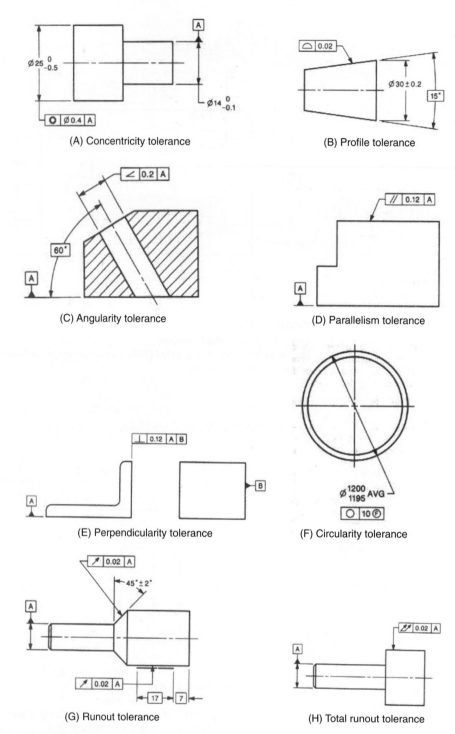

**FIGURE 12.42**
Specifying geometric tolerances
(Reprinted from ASME Y14.5M-1994 [R2004], by permission of The American Society of Mechanical Engineers. All rights reserved)

**36.** Interpret the geometric tolerances of Problem 35. Sketch the tolerance zone and the feature shape for each case of A through G.

# Analysis Tools

## 13.1 Introduction

The creation of a geometric model is not an end in itself, but rather a means to study the part or assembly design to ensure that it meets the functional requirements of the design, be it stress analysis, fatigue analysis, thermal analysis, buckling, etc. CAD/CAM systems offer a multitude of analysis tools that the designer can use to verify his or her design.

The crucial factor in using these analysis tools is understanding how to set up the problem correctly, use the right input parameters, and interpret the results. Each tool is based on and implements a mathematical model. The effective use of these tools requires that the designer be versed in the area of the analysis that the tools implement. For example, the designer must possess a sound understanding of finite element method to effectively use the stress analysis tool of a CAD/CAM system.

Analysis tools include such applications as mass property calculations, finite element method, thermal analysis, fatigue analysis, frequency analysis, mold flow analysis, buckling analysis, simulation, fluid flow analysis, etc. We cover some of these analysis tools in this chapter. Although data exchange is not exactly considered an analysis tool, we cover it here because we consider it part of model activities after the model's creation.

CAD/CAM systems offer analysis tools in three ways: built-ins, add-ins, or separate packages. Built-in tools come with the CAD/CAM system as part of the CAD/CAM software installation (e.g., mass properties is a built-in application). The user simply uses them. Add-ins also come with the CAD/CAM system, but the user needs to activate them. **Simulation** in SolidWorks is an example. Separate packages require separate installations and interface with CAD/CAM systems via file share. For example, a specialized analysis package may read a CAD/CAM file and perform its analysis on it.

## 13.2 Data Exchange

Data exchange is routinely done in practice to transfer CAD/CAM files from one system to another. For example, a company that outsources its manufacturing needs to send its CAD models to its subcontractors who may not use the same CAD/CAM system. Data exchange solves the following problem. How do you transfer CAD/CAM models from/to one CAD/CAM system to/from another? Each CAD/CAM system, like any application, has its own proprietary native file format; that is, the system saves the model (part) in its own format. Such a file is not transferrable to another system; the other system cannot open or read it.

The common solution to solving this data exchange problem is to save the files in "neutral" formats that are commonly read by all CAD/CAM systems. Some of these formats are standard whereas others are de facto standards. Examples of standard neutral file formats are STEP and IGES. Examples of de facto formats are AutoCAD DXF and ACIS. SolidWorks supports all these formats and more. Another group is image and Web formats. Image format includes saving a model as a JPEG image. Web format includes saving a model as a VRML (virtual reality markup language) model.

Data exchange occurs between two CAD/CAM systems. The user exports or imports a CAD file from one system to another. Consider a file exchanged from system A to system B. We say the user exports the file from system A when the user saves it in system A in a neutral file format. Conversely, we say the user imports the file to system B when the user reads the neutral file into system B, thus converting it to the native format of system B. In summary, we say the user exports the file from system A and imports it to system B.

Data exchange come with its potential problems. Each CAD/CAM system has two translators: one to export its native format to neutral format, and an opposite one to import neutral format to its native format. Translators for standards such as IGES and STEP are developed and written by interpreting sets of ISO and ANSI standards. Such interpretations open the door for translation errors. Thus, translating model data from their native format to neutral format, and vice versa, has the potential of data loss. Thus, the exchanged files need to be carefully inspected, including visual inspection, to ensure no data loss or no corruption occurred during the exchange process. CAD/CAM systems developers utilize multiple tests to check the accuracy of their translators.

Figure 13.1 shows all the possible file formats that SolidWorks supports. In the table on the next page, we offer a brief description of each format and when to use it.

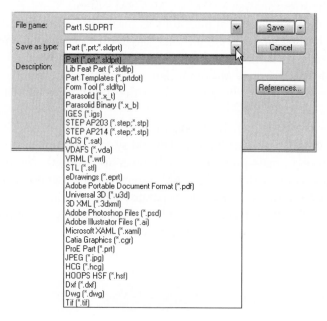

**FIGURE 13.1**
SolidWorks file formats

Out of the formats listed next, we use a handful of them. We recommend using STEP to exchange CAD models, eDrawings to read files in a Web browser, and JPEG to generate images of CAD models to include in reports. Other formats may be used on an as-needed basis. For example, use DXF/DWG formats if you deal with AutoCAD files, etc.

| File Type | Description |
|---|---|
| .sldprt | Part file. This is the most commonly used format. |
| .sldfp | Library feature for reuse. The feature becomes usable in the future. |
| .prtdot | Template or master for reuse, similar to saving a Word template. |
| .sldftp | Form tool part that is used in sheet metal work. SolidWorks saves the tool in the Design Library. Use the tool to deform a sheet metal, e.g., make complex dents, etc. |
| .x_t | Parasolid text file. Parasolid is another CAD/CAM system created by Unigraphics. |
| .x_b | Parasolid binary file. Parasolid is another CAD/CAM system created by Unigraphics. |
| .igs | IGES file. IGES is a standard neutral file format supported by all CAD/CAM systems. |
| .step | STEP file. STEP is a standard neutral file format supported by all CAD/CAM systems. STEP is more comprehensive and encompassing than IGES. |
| .sat | ACIS file. ACIS is a defacto standard. ACIS is a powerful geometric engine that is used and/or supported by multiple commercial CAD/CAM systems. |
| .vda | VDAFS file. This neutral file format is used to exchange surface geometry. STEP replaces both IGES and VDAFS. |
| .wrl | VRML file. This is a Web format that enables viewing CAD models in a Web browser. You need to download and install a VRML plug-in for the browser. |
| .stl | STL file. This is the standard prototyping format. A prototyping machine uses the STL file to build the prototype. |
| .eprt | eDrawing file. You can view the file in a Web browser. Chapter 2 has more details. |
| .pdf | PDF file. Convert the model display into a PDF file for ease of communication. |
| .u3d | Universal 3D file. You can open a .u3d file in Adobe Acrobat 3D software. Or, you can insert .u3d files into a PDF document and view it in Acrobat Reader. |
| .3dxml | 3DXML file. 3DXML is a proprietary 3D file format developed by Dassault Systemes, the parent company of SolidWorks, to enable file transfer between SolidWorks and Dassault CATIA CAD/CAM systems. |
| .psd | Photoshop file. Convert a SolidWorks file to a Photoshop file for use in media, etc. |
| .ai | Adobe Illustrator file. Use this file in company marketing material, brochures, manuals, etc. |
| .xaml | Microsoft XML file. XAML is a modified version of the standard XML format. Use an XML parser to process (parse) the file. |
| .cgr | CATIA graphics file. CGR is a proprietary file format developed by Dassault Systemes, the parent company of SolidWorks, to enable file transfer between SolidWorks and Dassault CATIA CAD/CAM systems. CGR is a triangulation form of the 3D model. |
| .prt | Pro/E file. This a direct translation between Pro/E and SolidWorks. |
| .jpg | JPEG file. Converts 3D model to an image. |
| .hcg | HCG file. HCG (highly compressed graphics) is a proprietary file format developed by Dassault Systemes, the parent company of SolidWorks, to enable file transfer between SolidWorks and Dassault CATIA CAD/CAM systems in CATWeb. |
| .hsf | HOOPS file. HOOPS is a format that allows streaming graphics files; i.e., download the file piece by piece to a Web page. It is helpful to display large files. |
| .dxf | DXF file. This format is AutoCAD defacto standard. It is a direct translation between SolidWorks and AutoCAD. |
| .dwg | DXF/DWG file. This is an AutoCAD file format. |
| .tif | TIF file. Another image format similar to JPEG. |

SolidWorks offers two versions of STEP: AP203 and AP214. AP203 is used in any mechanical CAD sector whereas AP214 is used specifically in the automotive industry. STEP is ISO 10303 standard. Both AP203 and AP214 support application protocols (AP) in the mechanical design area (other areas include building, ship, manufacturing, and life cycle). AP203 and AP214 use the same definitions for 3D part geometry (curves, surfaces, features, and topology), assembly data, and basic product information. Therefore, CAD vendors can support both versions with the same software code. AP203 supports 3D designs of mechanical parts and assemblies. AP203 has been used in the aerospace industry with considerable success. AP214 is designed for the automotive industry and supports core data for automotive mechanical design processes, specifically the car body, power train, chassis, and interior parts of a car. AP214 goes well beyond AP203, providing a far more comprehensive model for automotive applications and covering the life cycle of a design from engineering through manufacturing. It also covers design issues such as colors and layers, geometric dimensioning and tolerancing, and design intent. AP214 is considered an extension of AP203.

SolidWorks performs checks when it imports a neutral file. It asks you a series of questions to validate its translation of the file. You can perform the following simple test to experience this translation process. Create a box. Save it as AP203 format. Then read it back into SolidWorks. SolidWorks asks you whether you need to run diagnostics on the part. If you confirm, SolidWorks displays any faulty faces and/or any gaps between faces. Finally, it asks you whether you need to proceed with feature recognition. If you confirm again, it maps the features stored in the neutral files to its native format and creates a SolidWorks native features tree.

The understanding of this CAD file translation process requires knowledge of the boundary representation (B-rep) of a CAD model. A B-rep defines a CAD model by its boundary elements, that is, vertices (points), edges (curves), and faces (surfaces). Each model feature you create consists of this B-rep. A B-rep also maintains the CAD model topology. This understanding of B-rep explains SolidWorks questions to you during the translation process. The diagnostics test detects faulty faces that may have resulted from the translation from the other CAD system (exporting system; SolidWorks is the importing system in this case). It also detects any gaps between faces. Both of these problems occur due to the numerical accuracy used by each system to represent the geometry. It may also occur due to the internal representation (equations) used by each CAD system to define the geometry. After SolidWorks does not find any problems, it converts the B-rep into features and displays the model and its features tree. The model is now good and in native SolidWorks format, and so it is ready for you to use in your design and other activities.

## 13.3 Mass Properties

Mass properties calculations are the oldest application offered by CAD/CAM systems. The foundation behind this application comes from your basic engineering courses. These calculations include volume, mass, center of mass, first and second moments of inertia, and principal moments and axes of inertia. The following equations provide these properties:

Volume:

$$V = \iiint_V dx\,dy\,dz \tag{13.1}$$

Mass:

$$M = \rho V \tag{13.2}$$

Center of mass (centroid):

$$\begin{bmatrix} x_c \\ y_c \\ z_c \end{bmatrix} = \frac{1}{V} \begin{bmatrix} \iiint_V x\,dV \\ \iiint_V y\,dV \\ \iiint_V z\,dV \end{bmatrix} \tag{13.3}$$

Second moments of inertia:

$$I_{xx} = \int_M (y^2 + z^2)dm \tag{13.4}$$

$$I_{yy} = \int_M (x^2 + z^2)dm \tag{13.5}$$

$$I_{zz} = \int_M (x^2 + y^2)dm \tag{13.6}$$

First moments of inertia:

$$I_{xy} = \int_M (xy)dm \tag{13.7}$$

$$I_{xz} = \int_M (xz)dm \tag{13.8}$$

$$I_{yz} = \int_M (yz)dm \tag{13.9}$$

Inertia tensor:

$$[I] = \begin{bmatrix} I_{xx} & -I_{xy} & -I_{xz} \\ -I_{xy} & I_{yy} & -I_{yz} \\ -I_{xz} & -I_{yz} & I_{zz} \end{bmatrix} \tag{13.10}$$

Principal inertia tensor:

$$[I] = \begin{bmatrix} I_x & 0 & 0 \\ 0 & I_y & 0 \\ 0 & 0 & I_z \end{bmatrix} \tag{13.11}$$

The evaluation of the integrals shown in Eqs. (13.1) – (13.9) is done numerically because they are evaluated over the boundaries of the 3D CAD model. This makes the exact integration of these equations impossible. The most efficient and accurate numerical integration method is Gauss quadrature. (Matlab has Gauss quadrature built into it.) CAD/CAM systems use this method to calculate the mass properties. Gauss quadrature converts an integral equation into a summation that is easily calculated over the integral limits. The integral could be single or double. These integrals are functions of $u$ or $(u, v)$ parameters. These two types of integrals take the following general forms:

$$I = \int_a^b f(u)du \tag{13.12}$$

$$I = \int_c^d \int_a^b f(u,v)du\,dv \tag{13.13}$$

The single integral given by Eq. (13.12) is used to integrate functions over a curve, whereas the double integral given by Eq. (13.13) is used to integrate functions over a surface.

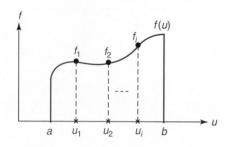

**FIGURE 13.2**

Gauss quadrature

The calculations of mass properties proceed as follows. We know that CAD/CAM systems use parametric equations to represent and store the curves and surfaces that make up the features of CAD/CAM models. Thus, we recast Eqs. (13.1) through (13.9) in terms of the parameters $u$ and $(u, v)$ and convert them to the forms given by Eqs. (13.12) and (13.13). This recast is beyond the scope of this book. Once we have Eqs. (13.12) and (13.13), we integrate them numerically using Gauss quadrature to calculate the mass properties.

Gauss quadrature is a simple, but accurate, numerical integration method. We know from calculus that the area under a bounded curve is the integral of the curve function. Figure 13.2 shows the graphical representation of Eq. (13.12). Gauss quadrature samples the function at selected sampling points (Figure 13.2 shows three sampling points), evaluates $f(u)$ at these points, and evaluates the integral. Using this procedure, Eq. (13.12) becomes:

$$I = \int_a^b f(u)du = \frac{b-a}{2} \sum_{i=1}^n W_i f_i = W_1 f_1 + W_2 f_2 + W_3 f_3 + \cdots + W_n f_n \quad (13.14)$$

where $n$ is the number of sampling points, $W_i$ are Gauss weights that are assigned to the functions $f_i$. The functions $f_i$ are calculated at the sampling points $u_i$ given by:

$$u_i = \frac{b-a}{2} C_i + \frac{b+a}{2} \quad (13.15)$$

where $C_i$ is the Gaussian location of the sampling points. Table 13.1 shows the values for $C_i$ and $W_i$ for different numbers of sampling points. How many sampling points should a CAD/CAM system use in mass property calculations? Before we answer this question, keep in mind that $f(u)$ is a polynomial in the CAD/CAM field because it comes from the parametric representation that uses only polynomials. Gauss quadrature produces exact results (equal to the results if you could evaluate the integral in exact form) for integrating polynomials according to this rule. Use $n$ sampling points for polynomials of degree $\leq 2n - 1$. Thus, three sampling points ($n - 3$) should produce exact results for a polynomial of degree of 5. This is more than adequate for CAD/CAM because the highest order polynomial we use is 3.

| TABLE 13.1 Gauss Quadrature Data | | |
|---|---|---|
| **Number of Sampling Points, $n$** | **Location, $C_i$** | **Weight, $W_i$** |
| I | 0.0000000000000000 | 2.000000000000000 |
| 2 | ±0.577350269189626 | 1.000000000000000 |
| 3 | ±0.774596669241483 | 0.555555555555556 |
| | 0.0000000000000000 | 0.888888888888889 |

The evaluation of the double integral of Eq. (13.3) using Gauss quadrature is the same as for the single integral and yields the following equation:

$$I = \int_c^d \int_a^b f(u,v)du\,dv = \frac{(b-a)}{2} \frac{(d-c)}{2} \sum_{i=1}^n \sum_{j=1}^m W_i W_j f_{ij} \quad (13.16)$$

The calculations of $W_i$, $W_j$, and $f_{ij}$ are the same as for the single integral. Think of extending the calculations from 1D to 2D. $f_{ij}$ is evaluated at the sampling point located at $(u_i, v_j)$.

**Example 13.1**   Use Gauss quadrature to evaluate this integral:

$$\int_1^3 (u^4 - u)\,du$$

**Solution**   The polynomial degree is 4. Using the rule of exact integration, we need $2n - 1 = 4$, or $n = 2.5$ sampling points for Gauss quadrature to yield the exact results. Thus, we use $n = 3$. Here are the steps to evaluate the integral:

1.  Using the integral, we identify the following parameters: $a = 1, b = 3, f(u) = u^4 - u$.
2.  Using Eq. (13.14) for 3 sampling points, we write

$$I = \frac{3 - 1}{2}(W_1 f_1 + W_2 f_2 + W_3 f_3) \qquad (13.17)$$

3.  Using Table 13.1 for $n = 3$, calculate $f_i$ at the three sampling points; we designate them by their Gauss data $(C_i, W_i)$. Let us designate $f_1, f_2$, and $f_3$, respectively, by $(0.774597, 0.555556)$, $(0.0, 0.888889)$, and $(-0.774597, 0.555556)$. Calculating these functions requires calculating the sampling coordinate value $u_i$ at each point using Eq. (13.15). This gives $u_1 = 2.774597, u_2 = 2$, and $u_3 = 1.225403$. Thus,

$$f_1 = (2.774597)^4 - 2.774597 = 56.490589$$

Similarly, $f_2 = 14$, and $f_3 = 1.0294371$.
4.  Substituting into Eq. (13.17) and reducing give $I = 44.400042$

The exact integration of the integral gives 44.4. Gauss quadrature yields the exact value. The small error (0.000042) is due to truncation errors. We used only 6 decimal places in this example. If we use the 15 decimal places shown in Table 13.1, we will get better results.

---

**HANDS-ON FOR EXAMPLE 13.1.** Use 1 and 2 sampling points. Compare the accuracy of the results with the 3-point result.

---

**Example 13.2**   Use SolidWorks to calculate the centroid and volume of a $2 \times 2 \times 2$ in. box with a spherical void (hole) at its center. The sphere diameter is 1 in. Create the box so that its MCS is at its center.

**Solution**   This part is somewhat odd with void inside it. But it illustrates the accuracy of the mass properties calculations of SolidWorks. The box sketch is a square at the front plane with a center at the origin of the front plane WCS. Extrude the sketch using the mid plane direction, so you can use the front plane to sketch a circle for the sphere (**Revolved Cut**) and centerline (axis of revolution). Trim the circle, as shown in Figure 13.3, before revolving it around the centerline; otherwise, SolidWorks produces an error (self-intersecting) and the revolve cut fails.

Run SolidWorks mass properties by clicking **Tools => Mass Properties**. The results in Figure 13.3 show that the center of mass is located at $(0, 0, 0)$, as we would expect, because the model is symmetric with respect to the origin. The volume is listed as 7.48 in.$^3$. That is easily verifiable. The box volume is given by $2^3 = 8$ in.$^3$. The sphere volume is $(4/3)\,\pi R^3 = (4/3)\,\pi 0.5^3 = 0.52$ in.$^3$. Thus, the net volume $= 8 - 0.52 = 7.48$ in.$^3$. That is identical to the SolidWorks result.

## 13.4 Animation and Motion Analysis

SolidWorks **Simulation** provides animation and motion analysis of an assembly. Motion studies can be time based or event based. Time-based motion studies describe the response to time-based changes in motion elements on the assembly motion. Event-based motion studies are defined with a set of motion actions resulting from triggering events. You can obtain the time sequence for element changes by calculating an event-based motion study.

Use event-based motion analysis to specify motion from some combination of sensors, times, or previous events. Event-based motion requires a set of tasks. The tasks can be sequential or can overlap in time. Each task is defined by a triggering event and its associated task action that controls or defines motion during the task.

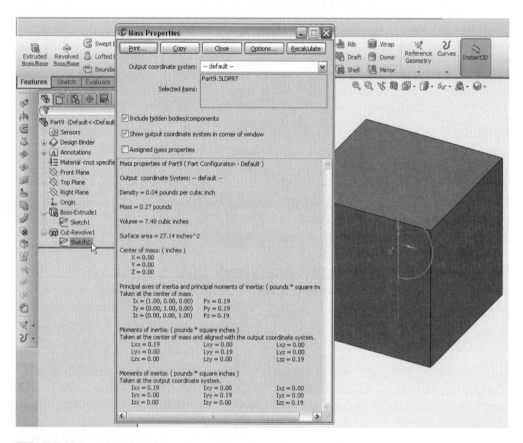

**FIGURE 13.3**
SolidWorks mass properties

## 13.5 Flow Simulation

With SolidWorks **Flow Simulation**, you are able to analyze the flow of up to 10 fluids of different types (liquids, gases/steam, real gases, non-Newtonian liquids, and compressible liquids). SolidWorks contains numerous fluids with predefined properties. In addition to preexisting fluids, SolidWorks allows you to define your own fluids. The flow analysis includes mutual dissolution of fluids. Mixing fluids must be of the same type. A simple example of flow simulation is to study the flow of water inside a ball valve and animate the streamlines to visualize the water movement.

Another example is to set up time-dependent pressure drops on cylinder inlet ports to simulate engine intake manifold valves opening and closing at each cylinder port. We can use this information to visualize the flow traversing the manifold and color it by local speed or pressure to evaluate the manifold design. We can simulate the opening at the cylinder port by dropping the lid pressure below ambient over a period of time. We assume a firing order, calculate a total period for one cycle over the rpm we want, and develop a time sequence for pulsing the pressure drop. We use Excel to store the data sets with different colors. We plot the data sets to show the pressure drops at the ports.

You need to set the fluid initial settings (boundary conditions) before you start the calculation and simulation. If you set the initial setting values closer to the anticipated final parameters, the calculation performance improves. You can set the fluid initial parameters globally at the assembly level or locally at a subassembly or an individual part level. Fluid parameters include its temperature, pressure, velocity, and compression.

## 13.6 Finite Element Method

The **finite element method** is a numerical method that is capable of solving almost any problem with any level of complexity. The method consists of finite element modeling (FEM) and analysis (FEA), or FEM/FEA. Many engineering design problems are too complex to find closed-form solutions for their governing equilibrium equations. The elegance of the finite element method is that it converts the equilibrium (differential) equation of a continuum into an integral equation. Then, instead of solving the equilibrium equation over the entire domain of the continuum, it applies the integral equation over many small regions called elements and, finally, assembles the elements' equations into a set of simultaneous algebraic equations whose solutions generate the domain solution.

Thus, the method divides a complex shape (domain) into smaller elements. Each element has designated points called nodes. The elements are adjacent to each other, with no gaps between their sides, and are connected at the nodes. Each node has a set of degrees of freedom (DOF) that depend on the problem at hand. The selection of element type, the number of nodes per element, and the DOF at each node are among the important decisions to make to create and run an accurate FEA for a problem.

The finite element method begins with modeling (FEM) and ends with analysis (FEA). The method is complex to use and requires good understanding of the problem we need to solve. CAD/CAM systems automate the method to the point that many designers use it as a black box. This is both good and bad. It is good to speed up the FEM/FEA so the designer can get answers quickly to the "what-if" design scenarios and questions. It is bad because it requires that the designer have good understanding of using FEM/FEA to be able to model the problem correctly and interpret/analyze/verify the analysis results.

FEM sets up the problem for FEA. FEM has the following steps in this order:

1. **Generate the mesh:** This includes breaking down the problem domain (the geometric model) into nodes and elements (mesh). The general rule is that the more elements and the more nodes per element we use (i.e., finer mesh), the better the accuracy of the FEA, but the more expensive it is to perform because it

requires more computational time. Keep in mind that once you create the mesh, the geometric model is only defined by the nodes of the mesh. No other points that are not nodes are recognized by the FEA. Thus, you need to make sure that points of importance are made nodes; for example, points where external load are applied. While the CAD/CAM FEM/FEA module takes care of all these details for you, you need to be aware of them.

2. **Select the element type and the number of nodes per element:** This selection depends on the type of analysis at hand and the desired accuracy of the solution. For example, we can use a quadrilateral element with minimum of four (corner) nodes and a maximum of eight nodes (four corner nodes and four mid-side nodes) and any number in between. Or, we can use a triangular element with a minimum of three (corner) nodes and a maximum of six nodes (three corner and three mid-side nodes).

3. **Assign the DOF at the nodes:** Depending on the element type and the problem to solve, assign the DOF at the nodes. For example, there is a maximum of 6 DOF per node (three translations and three rotations) for 3D problems. For a 3D stress/strain problem, we use three DOF: displacements along the three axes ($X$, $Y$, and $Z$). For a beam bending problem, we use two DOF: lateral displacement and rotation/slope.

4. **Assign boundary conditions (B.C.):** We use these conditions to reflect how the model (part) is fixed in real life. We need boundary conditions; otherwise, the model will float in space and the FEA will give wrong results (usually very large values). Example boundary conditions include fixing an end of a cantilever beam and an edge of a face or even a vertex. Boundary conditions apply to nodes by suppressing all their DOF.

5. **Apply material:** We need to assign a material to the model.

6. **Apply the external loads:** These loads cause the model to deform and create the FEA results. Loads could be forces at nodes, pressures at faces, moments, heat flux, etc. We must apply the external loads to nodes. When we apply a load, we need to specify its type (force, moment), direction (along $X$-, $Y$-, or $Z$-axis), sense (up or down), and value (amount).

The FEM/FEA modules of CAD/CAM systems automate the preceding six steps to a great extent. The designer does not see Steps 1 through 3. The CAD/CAM system generates the mesh automatically. The most commonly used type of element is tetrahedral element with 10 nodes (4 corner and 6 mid-side). The system would require the designer to supply data for Steps 4 through 6. Although all CAD/CAM systems automate the mesh generation, setting up the finite element model is very crucial to FEA in order to get both the desired and accurate results. Ideally, the designer must have a good theoretical background of FEM/FEA to be efficient in setting up the model and selecting the type of analysis (linear, nonlinear, static, dynamic, etc.). Figure 13.4 shows an overview of the preceding six steps as applied to a cantilever beam. Figure 13.5 shows the different types of elements. 2D elements (Figure 13.5B) include triangular (3 and 6 nodes) and quadrilateral (4 and 8 nodes) elements. 3D elements (Figure 13.5C) include tetrahedral (4 and 10 nodes) and hexahedral (8 and 20 nodes) elements.

Once we complete these six steps of FEM, we are ready to perform FEA. The FEA includes running the analysis to solve the finite element equations, display the results as curves and/or contours, and analyze the results. Analyzing and making sense of the results requires good understanding of the problem we are solving. After analyzing the results, the designer has two options: accept the design as is, or iterate it (change the part design, regenerate FEM, redo FEA) until satisfactory results are achieved.

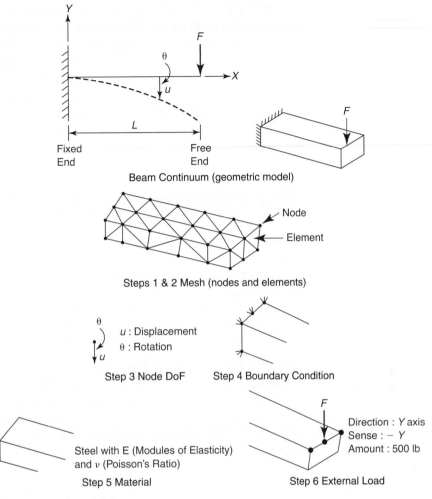

**FIGURE 13.4**
FEM steps

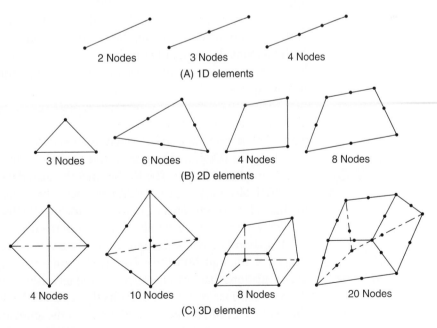

**FIGURE 13.5**
Sample finite elements

The most commonly used and simplest type of FEA is static linear analysis. FEA could be static or dynamic. Within each type, the analysis could be linear or nonlinear. Nonlinearity could be due to large deformation or nonlinear material (such as rubber or plastic). In addition, we can perform FEM/FEA at the part or assembly level. The difference comes in the modeling of the mating between the assembly parts. Parts are not rigidly connected in an assembly. Thus, we usually need clever ways to model these mating regions. Experience with modeling of mechanical systems would help greatly. Typically, we may add springs, dampers, or other mechanical elements that closely describe the behavior of the mating region.

## 13.7 Finite Element Analysis

Although it is out of the scope of this book to provide full coverage of FEA, we offer a quick overview of it to help you better understand the FEM steps and activities. Let us consider the cantilever beam shown in Figure 13.4. The beam bending equation is (also known as Euler-Bernoulli beam equation):

$$EI\frac{d^4u}{dx^4} = 0 \tag{13.18}$$

where $E$ is the modulus of elasticity of the beam material, and $I$ is the moment of inertia of the beam cross section. The B.C. are that the beam has a fixed end (does not move). The external load is the point load (force) $F$ at its free end.

Equation (13.18) is the equilibrium equation of the beam deflection under the force $F$. It is a differential equation. After processing Eq. (13.18) through the theoretical formulation of the finite element method, it becomes the following integral equation:

$$I = \frac{1}{2}\int_0^L EI\left(\frac{d^2u}{dx^2}\right)^2 dx - Fu_L \tag{13.19}$$

where $u_L$ is the beam deflection at its free end where $F$ is applied. This integral equation applies to the entire beam, that is, the continuum.

Equation (13.19) is difficult to solve (in closed form) because it still applies to the entire beam. We need to break the beam into nodes and elements, apply Eq. (13.19) to each element domain, solve it there, and then assemble the solution over the entire beam. This process results in converting the integral Eq. (13.19) into the following matrix equation:

$$[K]\boldsymbol{\delta} = \boldsymbol{P} \tag{13.20}$$

where $[K]$, $\boldsymbol{\delta}$, and $\boldsymbol{P}$ are, respectively, the beam stiffness matrix, the beam displacements or deflections (DOF) at the nodes, and the externally applied loads at the beam nodes. Both $\boldsymbol{\delta}$ and $\boldsymbol{P}$ are vectors. The $[K]$ has in it the material effect, that is, the modulus of elasticity, $E$. It also has the beam geometry and cross section ($I$) effects in it. It finally reflects the B.C. of the beam. That is, it does not include the fixed nodes at the fixed end because they do not move; they are eliminated from the $\boldsymbol{\delta}$ vector.

Equation (13.20) is the end result of FEM although the designer never sees it. FEA starts with this equation and solves it. This is a matrix equation. It consists of a set of algebraic equations that must be solved simultaneously (using Gauss elimination method) for the $\boldsymbol{\delta}$ vector. This vector is the results that CAD/CAM systems use to display the deflected shape of the beam, the stress contours, and the animation of the beam deflection.

Other types of FEA follow the same formulation. Equation (13.20) is for static linear analysis. It is linear because $[K]$ is not a function of $\boldsymbol{\delta}$ and the material is linear (such as steel or aluminum). Otherwise, we have nonlinear static analysis. The sources of nonlinearity could be large displacement or nonlinear material. Dynamic analysis occurs when the problem changes with time. If the beam force, $F$, changes with time or the beam vibrates, we have dynamic FEA. Equation (13.20) takes the following general form for dynamic FEA:

$$[M]\ddot{\delta} + [C]\dot{\delta} + [K]\delta = P \qquad (13.21)$$

where $[M]$, $[C]$, $\ddot{\delta}$, and $\dot{\delta}$ are, respectively, the mass matrix, the damping matrix, the acceleration vector, and the velocity vector. If $[C]$ and/or $[K]$ depend on $\delta$ or its derivates, we have nonlinear dynamic analysis; otherwise, we have linear dynamic analysis.

Once we solve Eq. (13.20) for the displacement, we can calculate the strain using the following equation:

$$\varepsilon = \frac{\Delta}{L} \qquad (13.22)$$

where $L$ is the length that went through displacement $\Delta$. Using the material relationship, the stress is:

$$\sigma = E\varepsilon \qquad (13.23)$$

Let us relate FEM Steps 1 through 6 to this FEA to make sense of these steps so we can use them effectively in SolidWorks **Simulation** (FEM/FEA). Steps 1 through 5 create the matrices $[M]$, $[C]$, and $[K]$. Step 6 creates the $P$ vector. This enables FEA to solve Eq. (13.20) or (13.21) and generate the results.

## 13.8 SolidWorks Simulation

SolidWorks implements the FEM/FEA concepts discussed in this chapter. It offers two FEM/FEA modules: **SimulationXpress** and **Simulation**. The former comes with standard SolidWorks licensing whereas the latter is an Add-In. SolidWorks **SimulationXpress** is a built-in first pass design analysis and verification tool for testing part designs quickly and easily. It allows you to test your design and investigate different design alternatives without having to manufacture and test the design. SolidWorks **SimulationXpress** is suitable for stress analysis of simple parts. Once you have your stress results, it can generate HTML reports and create SolidWorks eDrawings files to document and communicate the results of the analysis.

SolidWorks **SimulationXpress** provides only part analysis (geometry type); stress and displacement (analysis type); uniform pressure and forces (load type); stress, displacement, and factor of safety plots (visualization); and HTML report, eDrawings, and AVI animation files (reports). If you need additional functionality or more in-depth FEM/FEA, use SolidWorks **Simulation**. SolidWorks **Simulation** offers all that **SimulationXpress** does and more. It provides assembly (including contact and friction) analysis, more external load types (nonuniform pressure, torques, heat loading), assembly connectors (springs, elastic foundation, pins, bolts, spot welds), more visualization (ISO plots), and more reports (customization and image (bitmap, JPEG, or VRML).

SolidWorks reports the stresses as Von Mises stress. Simply stated, Von Mises stress is based on the fact that the material starts to yield when the maximum stress, $\sigma_{max}$, due to externally applied load reaches or exceeds its yield stress, $\sigma_y$; that is, when $\sigma_{max} \geq \sigma_y$. If $\sigma_{max} \geq \sigma_y$, the material fails (yields) and the part fails, causing the assembly (product) to fail and triggering failure consequences. Thus, as a designer, your FEM/FEA should ensure that the design is safe within a factor of safety (*FS*), defined as:

$$FS = \frac{\sigma_y}{\sigma_{max}} \leq 1 \qquad (13.24)$$

The factor of safety, *FS*, should always be greater than 1, for example, 1.5 or 2. Depending on how catastrophic the failure consequences of a part are, the *FS* should be determined. The worse the consequences of failure, the higher the *FS* should be. However, there is a silver lining here. Although higher *FS* seems logical, it makes the design more expensive and unnecessarily heavy because we use more material to increase the part strength. Thus, experience, heuristics, and field testing play an important role in determining a reasonable *FS* for a part design.

## 13.9 Von Mises Stress

We need to understand the stress-strain curve of a material to understand Von Mises stress. Von Mises stress is a criterion for ductile material failure. Ductile material is a material that has yield stress, $\sigma_y$, as shown in Figure 13.6. Ductile materials are also known as isotropic materials that obey Hook's law. Table 13.2 shows the strength values for some materials. The units shown in the table are gigapascal (GPa) and megapascal (MPa). Giga is 1 billion ($10^9$) and mega is 1 million ($10^6$), and a Pascal is 1 Newton per square meter ($N/m^2$). Also, 1 $N/m^2$ is equivalent to 0.0001450377 psi.

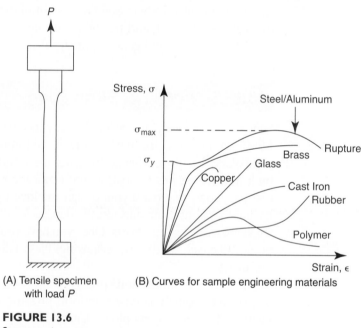

(A) Tensile specimen with load *P*

(B) Curves for sample engineering materials

**FIGURE 13.6**
Stress-strain curves

**TABLE 13.2    Material Properties for Some Materials**

| Material | Modulus of Elasticity, E (GPa) | Poisson's Ratio, $\nu$ | Yield Stress, $\sigma_y$ (MPa) | Max Stress, $\sigma_{max}$ (MPa) |
|---|---|---|---|---|
| Tungsten | 407 | 0.28 | 760 | 960 |
| Steel (1020) | 207 | 0.30 | 180 | 380 |
| Titanium | 107 | 0.34 | 450 | 520 |
| Brass (70–30) | 97 | 0.34 | 75 | 300 |
| Aluminum | 69 | 0.33 | 35 | 90 |

Steel and aluminum are sample ductile materials. The stress-strain curve is linear up to the yield stress, $\sigma_y$. The slope of the line is the material modulus of elasticity, *E*. The material is elastic in this linear zone, meaning it fully recovers when the externally applied load is removed. After the yield point, the material becomes plastic, meaning that it experiences permanent deformation. Such deformation renders the part dysfunctional in its assembly; that is, the part fails its functional requirements and must be replaced.

Figure 13.6 shows the stress-strain curves for some popular engineering materials. The figure shows that all materials have an elastic zone of their stress-strain curves. This zone ends at the material yield stress, $\sigma_y$. Materials should always operate within their elastic zone. The stress-strain curves shown in Figure 13.6 are usually derived from what is known in the materials field as a uniaxial stress test, also known as simple tension test. Scientists use a tension test machine, design and produce a tensile specimen (rod with circular cross section and square ends, as shown in Figure 13.6A), mount the specimen in the machine, and apply a progressive load, $P$, to the specimen until it breaks. While the load value is increasing, the specimen is elongating under the load. And while it is elongating, it is necking at its midpoint along its length. Scientists mount strain gages on the specimen (at the necking region) to measure its displacements. These measurements are used to plot the stress-strain curves shown in Figure 13.6B and calculate the yield stress, $\sigma_y$. There all sorts of standards and requirements the scientist must follow to create the specimen (with the required dimensions and shape) and conduct the test.

Although the simple tension test conducted in materials laboratories generates the material properties, it seldom represents loading of the material in real life. Such loading is almost always multiaxial. Multiaxial loading introduces two safety concerns for designers. First, multiaxial loading is more severe than uniaxial loading and would cause the material to fail sooner. Second, the material is loaded along all axes of loading. In such a case, which stress, along which axis, should the designer use to determine the design factor of safety?

The remedy for these two concerns is the Von Mises stress, $\sigma_y$. **Von Mises stress** is defined as an equivalent tensile stress that is used to predict yielding of materials under multiaxial loading conditions using results from the simple uniaxial stress test. In other words, the Von Mises criterion is a formula for calculating whether the stress combination at a given point will cause failure. We have at most three directions or axes ($X$, $Y$, and $Z$) along which we can apply loads. (These axes are also considered to be the principal axes of loading.) A simple example of multiaxial loading occurs when we apply a force that is not along one of the axes. For example, applying a force $F$ in the XY plane produces two force components: $F_x$ (along the $X$-axis) and $F_y$ (along the $Y$-axis), thus producing multiaxial loading.

Let us assume that loading a part produces three stresses (at a point) of $\sigma_1$, $\sigma_2$, and $\sigma_3$ along the three axes $X$, $Y$, and $Z$, respectively. Von Mises stress at this point is given by:

$$\sigma_v = \sqrt{\frac{(\sigma_1 - \sigma_2)^2 + (\sigma_2 - \sigma_3)^2 + (\sigma_1 - \sigma_3)^2}{2}} \qquad (13.25)$$

In this case, yielding occurs when the equivalent stress, $\sigma_v$, reaches the yield stress of the material in simple tension test, $\sigma_y$. In the case of uniaxial stress, $\sigma_1 \neq 0$, $\sigma_2 = \sigma_3 = 0$, and Eq. (13.25) reduces to $\sigma_v = \sigma_1$. If $\sigma_1$ reaches $\sigma_y$, the material fails.

SolidWorks **Simulation** calculates $\sigma_v$ via FEA as follows. It calculates the displacements at the nodes (points) by solving Eq. (13.20). These displacements are due to multiaxial loading that is reflected in the load vector $P$. It then uses Eqs. (13.22) and (13.23) to calculate the strains and stresses at the nodes, respectively. These equations provide three strains ($\varepsilon_1$, $\varepsilon_2$, $\varepsilon_3$) and three stresses ($\sigma_1$, $\sigma_2$, $\sigma_3$) at each node. Finally, SolidWorks substitutes these stresses into Eq. (13.25) to calculate the Von Mises stress, $\sigma_v$, at each node and displays the stress contour for the designer to evaluate and use to calculate the factor of safety, $FS$, using Eq. (12.24). The designer substitutes the maximum value of Von Mises stress for $\sigma_{max}$ into Eq. (12.25).

**Example 13.3**  Figure 13.7 shows a steel column. The column has a square cross section that is 0.5 × 0.5 in. The column has a height of 2 in. It is subjected to a tensile force of 100 lb at its top face and is fixed at its bottom face. Use FEM/FEA to calculate the stresses in the column. Verify the FEA results against the exact solution.

**Solution**  The idea behind this example is to verify the accuracy of the finite element method against the exact solution of a simple problem. The example simplifies the geometry of a tensile specimen, creates a geometric model (part) of the simplified geometry, runs the FEM/FEA, and verifies the results. We use SolidWorks **SimulationXpress** instead of **Simulation**.

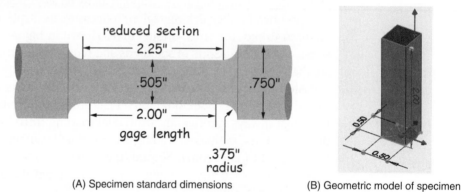

(A) Specimen standard dimensions          (B) Geometric model of specimen

**FIGURE 13.7**
Finite element modeling of a tensile specimen model

A standard tensile specimen has standard dimensions. Figure 13.7A shows a sample. Our geometric model of the specimen shown in Figure 13.7B uses the dimensions of the middle part of the specimen with simplifications. It uses a square, instead of circular, cross section. It also uses 0.5 in. instead of 0.505 in. for simplicity. We apply a force of value 100 lb at the center of the top face of the geometric model while we fix its bottom face.

The general steps to perform FEM/FEA using **SimulationXpress** are:

1.  Create the column model.
2.  Start **SimulationXpress** and set units.
3.  Apply B.C.
4.  Apply external loads.
5.  Apply material.
6.  Run FEA.
7.  Display the results.
8.  Generate the reports.

## Step 1:  Create the column model

| Task | Command Sequence to Click |
|---|---|
| A. Start SolidWorks, and open a new part; create the column as an extrusion, and save it as *example13.3*. Create the model as shown in Figure 13.7B. | **Open => New = Part** => Create the column as an extrusion. Use the top plane to create the column sketch => **Save As** => *example13.3* => **Save**. |

## Step 2: Start SimulationXpress and set units

### Task

A. Start **SimulationXpress** and set the units to English (IPS).

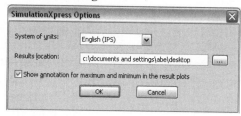

### Command Sequence to Click

**Tools => SimulationXpress => Options** (from SolidWorks SimulationXpress pane that opens up) **=> English (IPS) => OK** as shown to the left.

**Why:** The window shown to the left allows you to set the units and select the folder where the analysis reports are saved. These units are used to display the stress and displacement values on the screen.

## Step 3: Apply B.C.

### Task

A. We fix the bottom face of the model as the B.C. in this analysis. SolidWorks calls the B.C. fixtures.

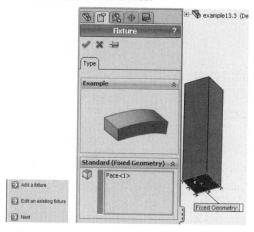

### Command Sequence to Click

**Next => Add a fixture =>** Select the bottom face of the model as shown to the left **=>** Green check mark.

**Why:** Fixing the bottom face mimics the tensile test.

**Help:** You may need to rotate the model slightly to see the bottom face to select it.

## Step 4: Apply external loads

### Task

A. We apply a tensile load of 100 lb to the top face.

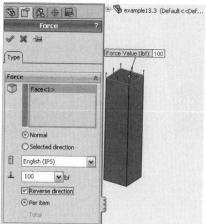

### Command Sequence to Click

**Next => Add a force =>** Select the top face of the model **=>** Type 100 for the force **=> Reverse direction =>** Green check mark as shown to the left.

**Help:** You may need to rotate the model slightly to see the top face to select it.

**Why:** SimulationXpress does not allow you to specify a point force of 100 lb at the midpoint of the top face. You can only apply the force to the top face as shown to the left.

**Why:** We turn on **Reverse direction** as shown to the left because we want the force to be tensile, not compression.

## Step 5:   Apply material

### Task

A. We select Alloy Steel for the
   column material.

### Command Sequence to Click

**Next => Choose Material =>** Select
**Alloy Steel =>** Select **Units as
English (IPS) => Apply => Close.**
**Why:** The FEM model is complete and
FEA linear static analysis is ready to run.
**Why: SimulationXpress** neither shows
you the mesh nor allows you to control
it. If you need such control and more,
you must run SolidWorks **Simulation**.
We show the mesh to the left using
**Simulation**.

## Step 6:   Run FEA

### Task

A. View and analyze the tolerance
   analysis results.

### Command Sequence to Click

**Next => Run Simulation => Stop
animation** (or **Play animation**)
**Help: Stop animation** and **Play
animation** allow you to switch these
two modes to observe the animation of
the column deformation.

## Step 7:   Display the results

### Task

A. The results consist of Von Mises stress,
   displacements, deformation, and factor
   of safety. Double-click any one to
   display and view.

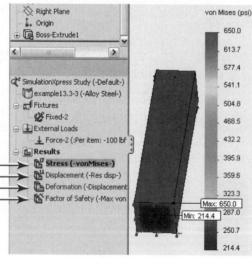

### Command Sequence to Click

**Yes, Continue =>** Double-click any
results from the list shown to the left to
display and view.
**Help:** The above **Yes** is an answer to the
question, **"Does the part deform as you
expected?"** that is displayed on the screen.
**Why:** The minimum and maximum Von
Mises stresses in this part are 214.4 and
650 psi, respectively. The closed-form
solution to this problem is:

$$\sigma = \frac{P}{A} = \frac{100}{0.5 \times 0.5} = 400 \text{ psi}$$

The stress scale shown to the left is
linear from the Min to the Max value. If
we interpolate to the midpoint of the
column (at $L = 1.0$ in.), we get a stress
value of $\sigma = 424$ psi. Thus, we have an
error of 6% (24/400). It turns out that
this is a hard problem to solve (or to
model, to be precise) using FEM/FEA
because of the point load. If we resolve
it using a uniform pressure on the top
face, we may get better results. As a

| Task | Command Sequence to Click |
|---|---|
| | matter of fact, the tensile machine does apply the load as a uniform pressure, not a point load. |

## Step 8: Generate the reports

| Task | Command Sequence to Click |
|---|---|
| A. Create Web-based reports. | **Done viewing results** => Select **Generate HTML report** (or **Generate eDrawing file**). |
| | **Help:** When you select the HTML report, SolidWorks displays a Web page in the browser. This is your report. The report is also stored in the folder specified in Task A of Step 2. |
| | **Why:** Ignore the **Optimize** step for now. |

---

**HANDS-ON FOR EXAMPLE 13.3.** Change the cross section of the column to a circular shape with a diameter = 0.5 in. Also apply a uniform pressure that is equivalent to 100 lb force to the top face. Calculate the exact stress by hand and compare with the FEM/FEA results. What is the error?

## 13.10 Tutorials Overview

The theme for the tutorials in this chapter is to practice the different analysis tools covered in this chapter including exporting CAD models, performing mass property calculations, motion analysis, flow analysis, stress FEM/FEA, and thermal FEM/FEA. Inertia Engineering + Design Inc. (IE+D), with headquarters in Toronto, Ontario, Canada (www.inertiaengineering.com), has sponsored this chapter. IE+D specializes in product design and manufacturing and serves multiple industries including automotive and consumer companies. IE+D designers and engineers use advanced engineering and design tools to deliver high-quality and accurate solutions to very complex design problems. We chat with Mr. Ray Minato, Founder and President of IE+D Inc., in the Industry Chat. Figure 13.8 shows a mobile industrial vacuum cleaner as a sample of IE+D designs.

(A) Mobile vacuum trailer (Actual product)

(B) Mobile vacuum trailer (SolidWorks model)

**FIGURE 13.8**
Sample products (Courtesy of Inertia Engineering + Design Inc.)

## Tutorial 13–1: Export Native SolidWorks Files

**FIGURE 13.9**
Block model

### Modeling task

Export a native SolidWorks file in both IGES and STEP formats.

### Modeling synthesis

Different CAD/CAM systems can output their models in different formats that other CAD/CAM systems can read. This tutorial shows how to export SolidWorks native files as other file types. We use the part shown in Figure 13.9.

### Modeling plan

Open the block that was created in Tutorial 3–4 of Chapter 3. Export the file as an IGES and as a STEP file.

### Design intent

Ignore for this chapter.

### CAD steps

We export the file in three steps:

1. Open the block from Tutorial 3–4.
2. Save the file as an IGES file.
3. Save the file as a STEP file.

The details of these steps are shown below.

## Step 1: Open the block from Tutorial 3.4

| Task | Command Sequence to Click |
|---|---|
| A. Open the block part from Tutorial 3–4 shown below. | **File => Open =>** *tutorial3.4_Block.sldprt* **=> Open** |

## Step 2: Save the file as an IGES file

| Task | Command Sequence to Click |
|---|---|
| A. Save the part as an IGES file. | **File => Save as =>** *Block.igs* **=>** Select **IGES** from the **Save as type** drop-down menu as shown to the left **=> Save.** |

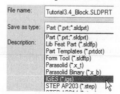

## Step 3:  Save the file as a STEP file

### Task

A.  Save the part as a STEP AP203 file.

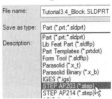

### Command Sequence to Click

**File => Save as** => *Block.igs* => Select **STEP AP203** from the **Save as type** drop-down menu as shown to the left => **Save**.

**Why:** The STEP AP203 is a general mechanical standard for STEP files, as opposed to the STEP AP214, which is primarily associated with the automotive industry.

---

**HANDS-ON FOR TUTORIAL 13–1.** Investigate the options of saving the IGES and STEP files.

---

## Tutorial 13–2:  Import IGES and STEP Files into SolidWorks

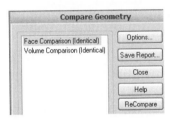

**FIGURE 13.10**
SolidWorks **Compare Geometry** tool

### Modeling task

Import the IGES file into SolidWorks, and use the **Compare Geometry** tool, shown in Figure 13.10, to verify the imported model.

### Modeling synthesis

IGES and STEP files are representations of a 3D model. This tutorial covers the operation of verifying an IGES and a STEP file versus the original solid part that they are created from.

### Modeling plan

Import the IGES file that has been created in Tutorial 13–1. Run a diagnostic on the file to verify no changes occurred due to the conversion.

### Design intent

Ignore for this chapter.

### CAD steps

We perform the import and verification in two steps:

1.  Open the IGES file created in Step 2 of Tutorial 13–1.
2.  Compare the native and imported geometry.

The details of these steps are shown below.

## Step 1:  Open the IGES file created in Step 2 of Tutorial 13–1

### Task

A.  Open the IGES block part from Tutorial 13–1.

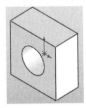

### Command Sequence to Click

**File => Open** => *Block.igs* => **Open** to create a new SolidWorks part as shown to the left.

|Task|Command Sequence to Click|
|---|---|

**B.** Run import diagnostics on the part.

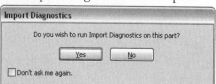

Select **Yes** to run **Import Diagnostic** as shown to the left.

**C.** Review the results of the diagnostic.

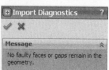

SolidWorks displays any faults found in the conversion from the IGES to SolidWorks part as shown to the left. => Green check mark to finish. Save the part as a *BLOCK_IGES.sldprt*.

## Step 2: Compare the native and imported geometry

|Task|Command Sequence to Click|
|---|---|

**A.** Open the original block from Tutorial 3–4 and the *block_iges.sldprt* created in this tutorial.

**B.** Add the **Utilities** toolbar.

**Tools** => **Add-Ins** => **SolidWorks Utilities** as shown to the left

**C.** Open the **Compare Geometry** tool.

**D.** Select the block from Tutorial 3–4 from the drop-down menu for the **Reference Document**.

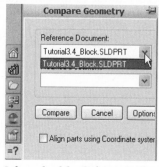

**Tools** menu => **Compare Geometry**
Select from the drop-down menu as shown to the left.

**E.** Select the block from Task A of Step 1 above from the drop-down menu for the **Modified Document**.

Select from the drop-down menu as shown to the left.

<table>
<tr><td>

**Task**

F. Review the results.

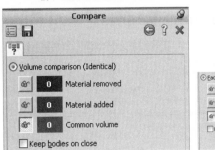

</td><td>

**Command Sequence to Click**

As shown to the left, there is no difference between the original block part and the converted IGES part.
**Help:** The two screenshots shown to the left belong to the **Compare** pane. Click the radio button for any group (**Volume** or **Face**) to view the results.

</td></tr>
</table>

---

**HANDS-ON FOR TUTORIAL 13–2.** Run the same import and compare geometry steps on the STEP AP203 part created in Step 3 of Tutorial 13–1. Report the results.

---

## Tutorial 13–3: Calculate Mass Properties of a Solid

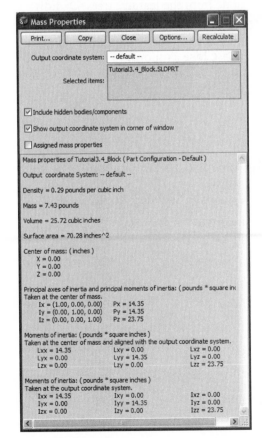

**FIGURE 13.11**
Mass properties of a solid

### Modeling task

Use the measure tools to calculate the mass properties of a part and an assembly. Figure 13.11 shows the results for a part.

### Modeling synthesis

When a part or an assembly is complicated, it is often more efficient to use SolidWorks to calculate the mass properties of that solid part or assembly. SolidWorks not only calculates the mass but also reports the location of the center of mass as well as the moment of inertia about any axis.

### Modeling plan

Open the block part that is created in Tutorial 3–4. Assign the block material properties, and then calculate the mass properties of the block.

### Design intent

Ignore for this chapter.

### CAD steps

We calculate the mass properties in three steps:

1. Open the block part file from Tutorial 3–4.
2. Assign material properties to the block.
3. Calculate the mass properties of the block.

The details of these steps are shown below.

## Step 1: Open the block part file from Tutorial 3–4

**Task**

A. Open the block part from Tutorial 3–4.

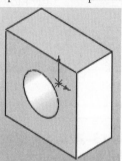

**Command Sequence to Click**

**File => Open** => Browse to find the block part from Tutorial 3–4 as shown to the left.

## Step 2: Assign material properties to the block

**Task**

A. Assign a material type to the block so SolidWorks can have a density value to work with.

**Command Sequence to Click**

Right-click **Material <not specified>** node from the features tree => **Edit Material => SolidWorks Materials => AISI 304 => Apply => Close** as shown to the left.
**Help:** The AISI 304 is a type of stainless steel.

## Step 3: Calculate the mass properties of the block

**Task**

A. Use the **Mass Properties** tool to calculate the mass properties.

**Command Sequence to Click**

**Evaluate** tab => **Mass Properties** as shown to the left

**B.** Review the result shown below.

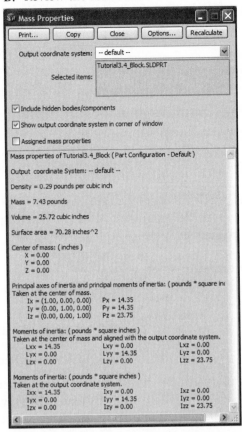

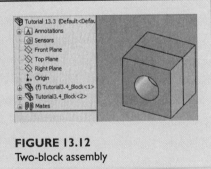

**HANDS-ON FOR TUTORIAL 13–3.**
Create the assembly shown in Figure 13.12 using two instances of the block part used in this tutorial. Manually calculate the total mass and location for the center of gravity for the assembly. Use SolidWorks to verify your answer.

**FIGURE 13.12**
Two-block assembly

## Tutorial 13–4:  Perform Motion Analysis

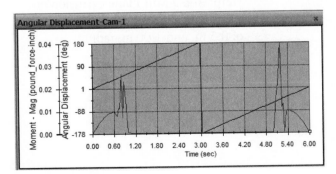

**FIGURE 13.13**
Displacement curve of a cam

### Modeling task

Create a motion analysis (see Figure 13.13) of the assembly of Tutorial 6–1.

### Modeling synthesis

SolidWorks **Motion Analysis** enables you to study the forces and reactions between components of an assembly while they are in motion. This tutorial covers the ability to graphically represent the magnitude of force between two moving components of an existing assembly.

### Modeling plan

Open the Cam assembly that was created in Tutorial 6–1. Add motors and springs to the motion study, and graph the magnitude of the forces vs. time.

### Design intent

Ignore for this chapter.

### CAD steps

We carry out the analysis in four steps:

1. Open the Cam assembly that was created in Tutorial 6–1.
2. Create a new motion study.
3. Calculate and graph the angular displacement vs. time using **Motion Analysis**.
4. Calculate and graph the magnitude of the applied torque of the motor vs. time using **Motion Analysis**.

The details of these steps are shown below.

## Step 1: Open the Cam assembly that was created in Tutorial 6–1

| Task | Command Sequence to Click |
|---|---|
| A. Open the block part from Tutorial 6–1.  | **File => Open** => Browse to find the Cam assembly from Tutorial 6–1 as shown to the left. |
| B. Suppress all previous CAM mates. 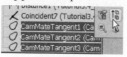 | Use **Shift** on keyboard + Click all the cam mates in the features tree => Click => **Suppress** from the context menu that pops up as shown to the left. |
| C. Add a round extrusion to the contact end of the pin.  | Modify the pin so that the contact end is round instead of flat as shown to the left. **Help:** Add a **Mid Plane** extrusion on the top plane of the pin with a thickness of 0.5 in. and 1.00 in. radius. |

| Task | Command Sequence to Click |
|---|---|
| D. Create a new cam mate between the round end of the pin and the cam surface of the cam part.<br><br>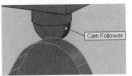 | **Assembly** tab => **Mate** => **Mechanical Mates** => **Cam** => Select the four side faces of the cam as the entities to mate => Select the side face of the round tip of the pin as the **Cam Follower** => Green check mark to finish as shown to the left. |

## Step 2: Create a new motion study

| Task | Command Sequence to Click |
|---|---|
| A. Create a new motion study.<br><br>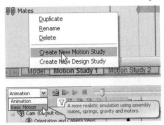 | Right-click **Motion Study1** tab on the bottom left of the screen => Select **Create New Motion Study** => Select **Basic Motion** from the drop-down list as shown to the left. |
| B. Add a rotary motor to the study.<br><br>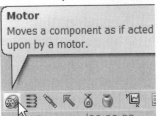 | Select the **Motor** icon as shown to the left. |
| C. Set up the motor as shown.<br><br> | Make the selection to set up the motor as shown to the right => Green check mark to exit. |
| D. Extend the timeline to 6 seconds.<br><br>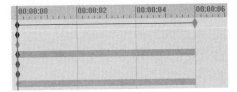 | SolidWorks automatically creates a 4-second timeline once the motor is completed. Drag the top key out to 6 seconds as shown to the left.<br>**Why:** This allows the study to complete one revolution when the motor is set at 10 rpm. |

## Step 3: Calculate and graph the angular displacement vs. time using Motion Analysis

| Task | Command Sequence to Click |
|---|---|
| **A.** Select the **Results and Plots** icon to graph the rotation versus time. | Select the icon as shown to the left. |

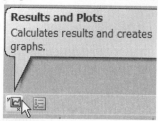

| Task | Command Sequence to Click |
|---|---|
| **B.** Create the angular displacement vs. time plot. | Set up the plot as shown to the left. |

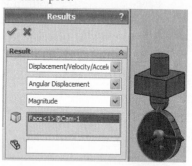

| Task | Command Sequence to Click |
|---|---|
| **C.** Calculate the motion and review the results. | Select the **Calculate** icon, and review the results on the graph as shown to the left. |

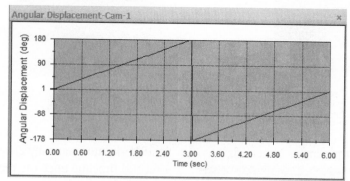

**Step 4:** Calculate and graph the magnitude of the applied torque of the motor vs. time using Motion Analysis

| Task | Command Sequence to Click |
|---|---|
| A. Select the **Results and Plots** icon. | Select the icon as shown to the left. |

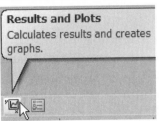

| | |
|---|---|
| B. Set up the applied torque vs. time on the same plot as Step 3. | Set up the results as shown to the left. Plot the results on the same graph as **Plot1**. |

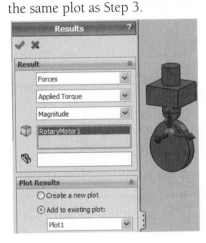

| | |
|---|---|
| C. Calculate the motion and review the results. | Select the **Calculate** icon, and review the results on the graph as shown to the left. |

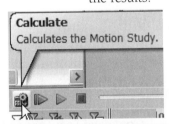

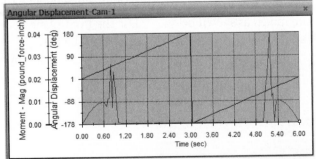

---

***HANDS-ON FOR TUTORIAL 13–4.*** Add a vertical linear spring between the pin and the block. Plot the results on the same plot. Submit a screenshot of the graph and a short paragraph explaining the results.

---

# Tutorial 13–5: Perform Static Linear Analysis on a Part

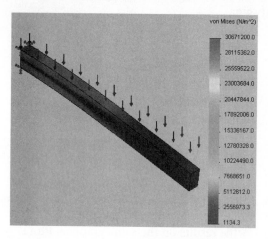

**FIGURE 13.14**
Stress contours of a cantilever beam

## Modeling task

Run a static linear analysis on a cantilever beam using Solid-Works **Simulation**. Figure 13.14 shows the stress contours (analysis results).

## Modeling synthesis

We can use different types of finite elements to model the beam. We can use a 3-node 1D beam element, a 10-node 3D tetrahedral element, or a 20-node 3D hexahedral element. SolidWorks **SimulationXpress** does not give us a choice and uses tetrahedral elements.

## Modeling plan

Create a cantilever beam model. Study the effects of an evenly distributed load along the top face of the beam.

## Design intent

Ignore for this chapter.

## CAD steps

We perform the finite element analysis in six steps:

1. Create the beam and assign it a material.
2. Start SolidWorks **Simulation**.
3. Apply the boundary conditions.
4. Apply the external loads.
5. Run the simulation.
6. Increase the part strength by 20%.

The details of these steps are shown below.

## Step 1: Create the beam and assign it a material

| Task | Command Sequence to Click |
|------|---------------------------|
| **A.** Create the beam model as shown below. | Use the front plane to create the beam as shown to the left. |
| | **Help:** Units are in mm. |

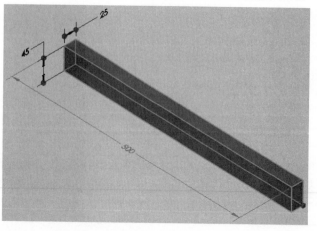

| Task | Command Sequence to Click |
|---|---|
| B. Select AISI 304 stainless steel as the beam material.<br>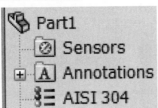 | Right-click **Material <not specified>** => **Edit Material** => **SolidWorks Materials** => **AISI 304** => **Apply** => **Close** as shown to the left. |

## Step 2: Start SolidWorks Simulation

| Task | Command Sequence to Click |
|---|---|
| A. Load SolidWorks **Simulation** Add-In.<br> | **Tools** => **Add-Ins** => **SolidWorks Simulation** as shown to the left |
| B. Open a new FEA study.<br>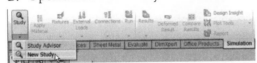 | **Simulation** tab => **Study** => **New Study** => Green check mark as shown to the left |

## Step 3: Apply the boundary conditions

| Task | Command Sequence to Click |
|---|---|
| A. Open the **Fixtures** setup menu.<br>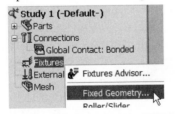 | Right-click **Fixtures** (on left pane of the screen) => **Fixed Geometry** as shown to the left. |
| B. Select the fixed face for the cantilever study.<br>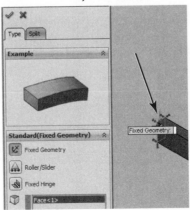 | Select the face as shown to the left => Green check mark. |

## Step 4:  Apply the external loads

Task

**A.** Apply an evenly distributed force on the top face of the cantilever beam.

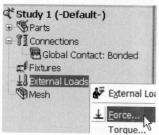

**B.** Select the loaded face for the cantilever study.

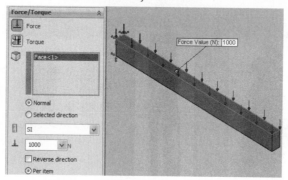

Command Sequence to Click

Right-click **External Loads => Force** as shown to the left

Select the face as shown to the left => Set the parameters as shown to the left => Green check mark.

## Step 5:  Run the simulation

Task

**A.** Run the stress analysis of the part.

**B.** Review the results.

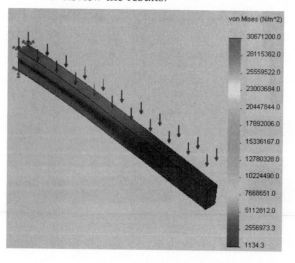

Command Sequence to Click

**Simulation** tab => **Run** as shown to the left

Review the Von Mises stresses of the beam as shown to the left.
**Help:** Double-click any of the three automatic plots such as **Stress**, **Displacement**, and **Strain** to review the results. The beam is shaped and colored according to the percent of the max value represented by the vertical scale on the right of the graphics window.

| Task | Command Sequence to Click |
|---|---|

C. Play the results.

**Simulation** tab => **Plot Tools** => **Animate** as shown to the left
**Help:** This animation can also be saved as an *.avi* file to be shared with and viewed by others.

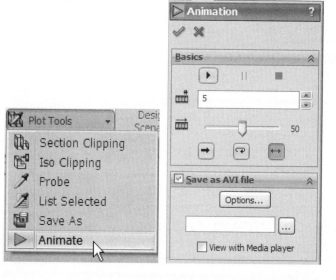

## Step 6: Increase the part strength by 20%

| Task | Command Sequence to Click |
|---|---|

A. Find the maximum stress on the beam.

**Simulation** tab => **Results Advisor** => **List Stress, Displacement and Strain** as shown to the left

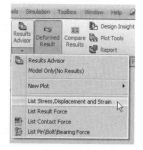

B. Select the information you want displayed.

Select the options as shown to the left.

C. Find the maximum stress value from the chart shown below.

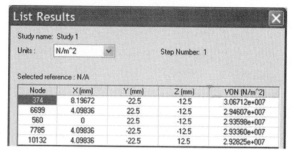

List Results

Study name: Study 1
Units: N/m^2    Step Number: 1

Selected reference : N/A

| Node | X (mm) | Y (mm) | Z (mm) | VON (N/m^2) |
|---|---|---|---|---|
| 374 | 8.19672 | -22.5 | -12.5 | 3.06712e+007 |
| 6699 | 4.09836 | 22.5 | -12.5 | 2.94607e+007 |
| 560 | 0 | 22.5 | -12.5 | 2.93598e+007 |
| 7785 | 4.09836 | -22.5 | -12.5 | 2.93360e+007 |
| 10132 | 4.09836 | -22.5 | 12.5 | 2.92825e+007 |

| Task | Command Sequence to Click |
|---|---|
| **D.** Calculate 80% of the maximum value. | 80% of Max Stress = .8*3.06712e+007 = 2.45e+007 |
| **E.** Make the part 20% stronger to achieve this calculated value.  | Change the cross section and rerun the simulation until the max stress reaches the 80% value. **Help:** The cross section shown to the left achieves the 20% increase in strength. We obviously use the trial-and-error approach (change dimensions of the cross section and rerun FEA) to find the final dimension shown to the left. |

---

**HANDS-ON FOR TUTORIAL 13–5.** Create two more beams similar to the one created in this tutorial, one with length of 250 mm and one with length of 1000 mm. Run the same **Simulation** study. Report the result of each study along with your observation of the relationship between the length and the results.

---

## Tutorial 13–6: Perform Static Linear Analysis on an Assembly

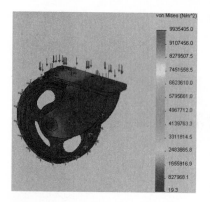

**FIGURE 13.15**
Stress contours of an assembly

### Modeling task

Run a static linear analysis on an assembly using SolidWorks **Simulation**.

### Modeling synthesis

This tutorial complements Tutorial 13–5 by running FEA on an assembly instead of a part.

### Modeling plan

Open the Caster assembly from Tutorial 2–2. Study the effect of an evenly distributed load along the top face of the flat plate as shown in Figure 13.15.

### Design intent

Ignore for this chapter.

### CAD steps

We perform the FEA in five steps:

1. Open the Caster assembly from Tutorial 2–2.
2. Apply the boundary conditions.
3. Assign materials to parts.
4. Apply the external loads.
5. Run the simulation.

The details of these steps are shown below.

## Step 1: Open the Caster assembly from Tutorial 2–2

#### Task

A. Open the Caster assembly that was created in Tutorial 2–2.

#### Command Sequence to Click

**File => Open** => *Caster.sldasm* as shown to the left

## Step 2: Apply the boundary conditions

#### Task

A. Start a new study.

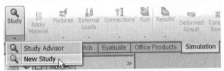

#### Command Sequence to Click

**Simulation** tab => **Study => New Study** as shown to the left

B. Open the **Fixtures** menu.

Right-click **Fixtures => Fixed Geometry** as shown to the left

C. Select the fixed entities.

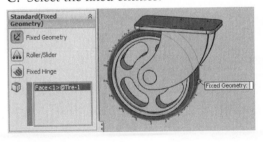

Select the tire as a fixed entity as shown to the left => Green check mark.
**Help:** We fix the tire to run FEA.
**Why:** SolidWorks does not allow you to apply the **Roller/Slider** B.C. to the tire because the FEA cannot be performed as linear analysis.

## Step 3: Assign materials to parts

#### Task

A. Select a material for each of the components.

#### Command Sequence to Click

Expand each component in the assembly tree => Right-click the **Material** node => **Edit Material => SolidWorks Materials => Steel => Plain Carbon Steel => Apply => Close** as shown to the left.
**Help:** To properly study the reaction of the applied forces, the components in the assembly must have material properties.
**Help:** Use rubber for the tire material.

## Step 4:  Apply the external loads

| Task | Command Sequence to Click |
|---|---|
| A. Open the **External Loads** menu to create a force on the assembly. | Right-click on **Fixtures => Force => Fixed Geometry** as shown to the left |

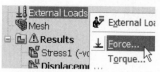

| Task | Command Sequence to Click |
|---|---|
| B. Select the top face of the top plate to apply a downward force. | Select the top face of the top plate and apply a downward force of 100 N as shown to the left. |

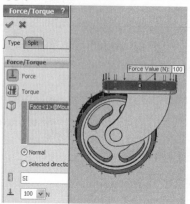

## Step 5:  Run the simulation

| Task | Command Sequence to Click |
|---|---|
| A. Perform the analysis. | **Simulation => Run** as shown to the left |

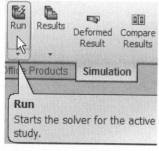

B. Review the stress results.

**Help:** SolidWorks displays the results shown to the left once the analysis is complete.

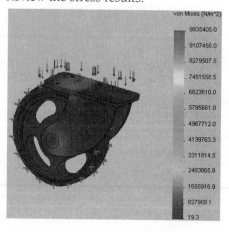

## Tutorial 13–7: Perform a Thermal Analysis

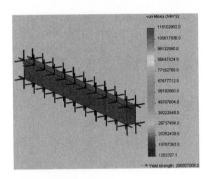

**FIGURE 13.16**
Thermal stress contours of a cantilever beam

### Modeling task

Run a thermal analysis on the beam that was created in Tutorial 13–5.

### Modeling synthesis

We perform a thermal analysis on a cantilever beam. Figure 13.16 shows the results.

### Modeling plan

Open the beam created in Tutorial 13–5. Modify the **Simulation** study to apply a thermal load instead of force load.

### Design intent

Ignore for this chapter.

### CAD steps

We perform the thermal analysis in four steps:

1. Open the beam part from Tutorial 13–5.
2. Apply the boundary conditions.
3. Apply the external loads.
4. Run the simulation.

The details of these steps are shown below.

## Step 1: Open the beam part from Tutorial 13–5

| Task | Command Sequence to Click |
|---|---|
| A. Open the beam from Tutorial 13–5. | **File => Open** => Browse to find the beam that was created and analyzed in Tutorial 13–5 of this chapter. **Help:** Use the dimensions that were used at the beginning of the tutorial as shown to the left. |

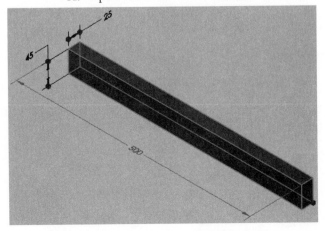

## Step 2:   Apply the boundary conditions

**Task**

A. Open a new study.

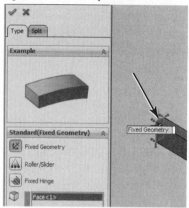

**Command Sequence to Click**

Follow Step 2 and Step 3 from Tutorial 13–5 to open a new study and select the fixed face as shown to the left.

## Step 3:   Apply the external loads

**Task**

A. Apply a temperature of 120°F to all beam faces, as if the beam were in an oven.

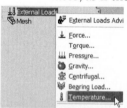

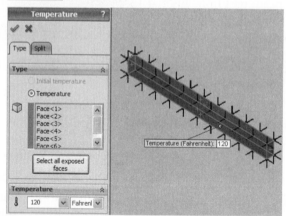

**Command Sequence to Click**

Right-click **External Loads =>
Temperature => Select all exposed
faces => Fahrenheit** => Type 120 for the temperature value as shown to the left.

## Step 4:   Run the simulation

**Task**

A. Select **Run** to calculate the thermal stresses on the part.

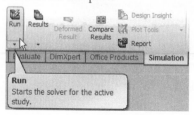

**Command Sequence to Click**

**Simulation** tab => **Run** as shown to the left

| Task | Command Sequence to Click |
|---|---|
| **B.** Review the resulting stresses. | **Help:** The Von Mises stresses shown to the left are thermal stresses because they are the result of a thermal load resulting from applying high temperature to the beam to simulate its bake in an oven. |

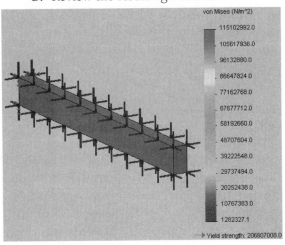

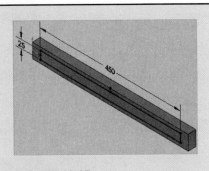

**HANDS-ON FOR TUTORIAL 13–7.**
Create a cut through the center of the part as shown in Figure 13.17. Rerun the simulation, and report the difference in the thermal stress and displacement values. Submit screenshots of the deformed model along with the stress chart.

**FIGURE 13.17**
Modified part

## Tutorial 13–8:  Perform Flow Analysis on a Pipe

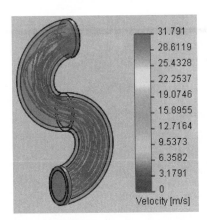

**FIGURE 13.18**
Flow simulation of a pipe

**Modeling task**

Run a flow analysis on a hose using SolidWorks **FloXpress**.

**Modeling synthesis**

The SolidWorks **FloXpress** tool can give basic insight into how water or air will flow through a part or an assembly. This tutorial studies the flow of water through a hose. Figure 13.18 shows the flow simulation.

**Modeling plan**

Create a section of a hose and then run the **FloXpress** tool to study how water will flow through.

**Design intent**

Ignore for this chapter.

### CAD steps

Perform the study in two steps:

1. Create the hose.
2. Run the **FloXpress** study.

The details of these steps are shown below.

## Step 1: Create the hose

### Task

**A.** Create a sketch on the front plane to be used as a sweep path.

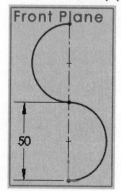

**B.** Create a second sketch on the right plane to be used as a sweep profile.

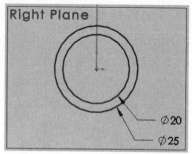

**C.** Create the section of hose by sweeping Sketch2 along Sketch1.

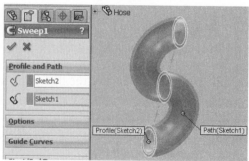

### Command Sequence to Click

**Sketch => Front Plane** => Sketch 2 half circles as shown to the left => Green check mark to exit.
**Help:** Units are in mm.

**Sketch => Right Plane** => Sketch as shown to the left => Green check mark to finish.
**Help:** Use the origin as the center of the circles to make sure that **Sketch1** is at the center of **Sketch2**.

**Features => Swept Boss/Base** => Select **Sketch2** as the sweep profile and **Sketch1** as the sweep path as shown to the left.

| Task | Command Sequence to Click |
|---|---|

**D.** Close the ends of the section of hose with two separate extrusions.

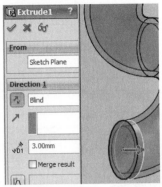

Select a flat face at one end of the hose => **Sketch** => Select the outside edge => **Convert Entities => Features => Extruded Boss/Base** => Type 3 for extrusion depth => Flip the direction of extrusion => Green check mark to finish as shown to the left. **Why: FloXpress** can only study the flow of volume within an enclosed space; therefore, we add these extrusions to contain the volume.

**E.** Close the other end of the hose.

Repeat Task D to close the other end of the hose, and then save the part as *Hose.sldprt*.

**F.** Make the hose transparent.

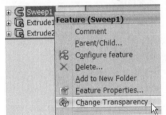

In the **FeatureManager design tree** right-click on **Sweep1** => Select **Change Transparency** as shown to the left. **Why:** The transparency will allow you to see the flow simulation inside the hose.

## Step 2:  Run FlowXpress

| Task | Command Sequence to Click |
|---|---|

**A.** Open the **FloXpress** tool.

**Tools => FloXpress** as shown to the left

**B.** Select the fluid volume you would like to view.

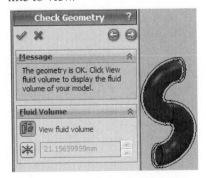

**View fluid volume => FloXpress** shows you a preview of the volume that will be studied as shown to the left => **Next**.

| Task | Command Sequence to Click |
|---|---|

C.  Choose water to flow through the hose.

Select **Water => Next** as shown to the left.

D.  Assign the model's inlet.

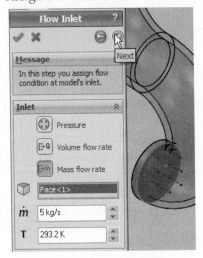

Select the inside face of **Extrusion1** as the inlet condition **=> Next** as shown to the left.

E.  Assign the model's outlet.

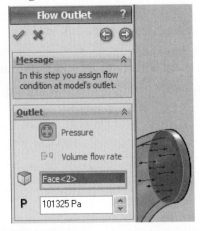

Select the inside face of **Extrusion2** as the outlet condition **=> Next** as shown to the left.

F.  Solve the fluid study by running the simulation.

**Solve** as shown to the left

| Task | Command Sequence to Click |
|---|---|

G. Review the results.

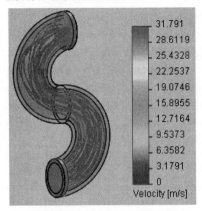

H. Generate a report.

**SolidWorks FloXpress Report**

SolidWorks FloXpress is a first pass qualitative flow analysis tool which gives insight into water or air flow inside your SolidWorks model. To get more quantitative results like pressure drop, flow rate etc you will have to use Flow Simulation. Please visit www.solidworks.com to learn more about the capabilities of Flow Simulation.

**Model**
Model Name: M:\SWModels\Chpt13Models Joe\Hose.SLDPRT

**Fluid**
Water

**Inlet Mass Flow 1**

| Type | Mass Flow Rate |
|---|---|
| Faces | <1> |
| Value | Mass Flow Rate: 5 kg/s |
| | Temperature: 293.2 K |

**Environment Pressure 1**

| Type | Environment Pressure |
|---|---|
| Faces | <1> |
| Value | Environment Pressure: 101325 Pa |
| | Temperature: 293.2 K |

**Results**

| Name | Unit | Value |
|---|---|---|
| Maximum Velocity | m/s | 32.2361 |

**FloXpress** uses colors to display the changes in a flow trajectory as shown to the left.

Select **Generate Report** as shown to the left.
**Why: FloXpress** will automatically create a text file with information about the flow study, such as the inlet, the environmental conditions used to solve the study, and the maximum velocity of flow inside the boundaries.

---

**HANDS-ON FOR TUTORIAL 13–8.** Double the diameter of the hose by modifying Sketch2. Run the same **FloXpress** study. Generate and submit a report of the second study. Was there a difference in maximum velocity? Why?

---

**INDUSTRY CHAT**

This section provides practical insight into how the chapter material is used in industry in the real world and practice. This section summarizes the chat with Mr. Ray Minato (Founder and President) of Inertia Engineering + Design Inc., the sponsor of this chapter. The structure of the chat follows the chapter sections.

**Chapter Section 13.1:** Introduction

ABE: What are the SolidWorks analysis tools you use? Which are the most important?

RAY: We use all of the tools covered in this chapter except flow simulation. We use STEP, IGES, and Parasolid all the time, and so for mass property calculations. We use animation occasionally. We use motion analysis. We use linear static FEM/FEA all the time. We also use nonlinear FEM/FEA. We do not use flow simulation.

*(continued)*

**Chapter Section 13.2:** Data Exchange

**ABE:** Do you export or import CAD/CAM data? Why? Which format do you use? Why?

**RAY:** Yes, we do it all the time, the reason being that different people use different CAD/CAM systems. Our customers, vendors, and manufacturers use different systems. We use STEP and Parasolid heavily because they are the most efficient formats for file size, especially Parasolid. We probably use more exports than imports because we deal with vendors and manufacturing shops that use different systems. Most of them use 2D, sheet metal, Mastercam, etc.

**Chapter Section 13.3:** Mass Properties

**ABE:** How important are mass properties to you? How do you verify the results, if any?

**RAY:** Very important. We use it a lot in what we do. All the designs that we do are weight and mass sensitive as well as weight-distribution sensitive, especially in vehicle and automotive design. For example, we were involved in a battery-electric delivery truck design. We performed many studies on the effect of traction battery location, versus axle loads and vehicle dynamics. Due to its large mass, the battery location has a significant effect on weight distribution. Weight distribution has a direct impact on vehicle structural requirements and the way the vehicle handles during driving.

We verify our mass property calculations that we obtain from CAD/CAM systems. We do simple hand calculations for large mass components to make sure that SolidWorks calculations are correct. Sometimes vendors send us mass properties. But, we check each component or assembly for its mass. We also calculate surface areas. We apply thickness and density to surfaces. We often do the calculations for individual components and for the entire assembly. The mass properties of an assembly are usually good if the properties of their individual components are correct.

**Chapter Section 13.4:** Animation and Motion Analysis

**ABE:** Why do you use animation? Provide some examples of using animation and motion analysis in your company.

**RAY:** We use animation lots of times to communicate to clients how mechanisms work. People understand visualization. For example, we designed a baby stroller for a client. It has a number of mechanisms. We use animation to describe how the mechanism works. We do the same for motion analysis that involves springs and cams. In such a case, we also perform force calculations.

**Chapter Section 13.5:** Flow Simulation

**ABE:** Provide some examples of using flow simulation in your company.

**RAY:** We do not use flow simulation in our company.

**Chapter Section 13.6:** Finite Element Method

**ABE:** Why do you use FEM/FEA? Provide some examples of using FEM/FEA. How do you verify the results?

**RAY:** Most of the time we use FEA to understand design and structural efficiency of our parts. We always look for and understand the load path of a part or assembly. We put more material where needed and less material where not needed. We also look at mode shapes to understand how parts deform, so we add material where needed to reduce the deformation and stresses. For example, we had to design a brake pedal for a truck. The force is applied by the driver. We calculate the stresses and deformations to make sure that they are acceptable and are within the safe limits.

We usually verify the FEA results by hand. We do some simple hand calculations. We simplify the analysis down to a cantilever beam. Lots of times, problems are more complicated than that. But, we often simplify the problem down to first principles such as a beam calculation to verify that results of the FEA are reasonable. We are also careful to make sure that the solution converges. We keep reducing the element size by controlling the finite element mesh, run the FEA, and compare the results of two consecutive runs. When the results change less than 2–3%, we can be confident that the FEA solution has converged.

**Chapter Section 13.7:**  Finite Element Analysis

   **ABE:**  What type of FEM/FEA do you use often? Why?

   **RAY:**  We use mostly linear static analysis because we design in the elastic region. We use linear static FEA to make sure that the design is good and structure is sound. Sometimes, we use nonlinear large deformation FEA, or nonlinear material (plastics) FEA. Most of the time, though, we use linear static analysis.

**Chapter Section 13.8:**  SolidWorks Simulation

   **ABE:**  Which simulation package do you use: **SimulationXpress** or **Simulation**? Why?

   **RAY:**  We use **Simulation**, not **SimulationXpress**, because it gives us full control and freedom to analyze the problem we want. Oftentimes, we analyze assemblies where we have connectors and contacts. **Simulation** package gives us control over meshing and the mesh quality. **SimlationXpress** is extremely limited for most engineering analyses.

While analyzing individual components is straightforward, analyzing assemblies is much more complicated because you have to model correctly the mating conditions between the assembly parts. For example, consider a 4-bar mechanism. You have pins between the links. You have 1 DOF joint. In these rotating links, assign frictional force to model the existence of a joint. In other cases, we may use springs and dampers to perform dynamics and motion analysis. Depending on what the assembly is connected to in real life, you want to replicate real life. Lots of times, when we perform simulation studies, we do not look for an absolute solution. Instead, we look for extremes of possibilities. We make assumptions and look for lower range and upper range of possibilities. There are two reasons for this. First, it is usually not possible to perfectly simulate a mechanical system because all the input information just doesn't exist; second, it takes a lot of time and effort to get an accurate absolute answer. It always comes down to time and money. At some point you have to use experience and engineering judgment to know how far in detail to take the analysis to obtain the appropriate level of understanding of the problem.

**Chapter Section 13.9:**  Von Mises Stress

   **ABE:**  Do engineers in your company use Von Mises stress or factor of safety to design?

   **RAY:**  We use both. We try to look at a number of ways to get a sense of the design. We try to visualize the problem. Most of the time, we use Von

*(continued)*

Mises stress. It also depends on our clients and how they demand certain solutions presented in certain ways. A client may need detailed analysis or some quick presentation.

**Others**

ABE: Any other experience you would like to share with our book readers?

RAY: Designers and engineers need to understand the basics of engineering and modeling including statics, dynamics, strength of material, elasticity, etc. Lots of times where people fail is not in the using the software; it is in the basic understanding of the problem, its modeling, the free body diagram, etc. In such a case, they get the wrong results from the software. Using software without understanding makes it impossible to judge the correctness of the software results. I have people say we have to use **SimulationXpress**, but they do not understand how to set up the problem, use proper constraints, apply proper forces and moments, and use the proper connection types. All this changes the results dramatically. This is why we try to "box" the problem. Changing boundary conditions may change the results greatly, and so we spend a lot of time evaluating the sensitivity of the results due to different boundary conditions. This is how we try to understand modeling.

1.  Why do we create CAD/CAM geometric models?
2.  How do CAD/CAM systems exchange model data among themselves?
3.  What are the potential problems that come with data exchange? How are they solved?
4.  What are the differences between STEP versions AP203 and AP214?
5.  How does a B-rep define a CAD model?
6.  List the mass properties that a CAD/CAM system can evaluate.
7.  Use Gauss quadrature to evaluate these integrals. Justify the number of sampling points you use for each problem. Compare with the exact solution:

    a.  $\int_{1}^{3} (u^5 - u^3 + 2u)du$

    b.  $\int_{1}^{3} (6u^{1/2} - u^{1/6})du$

    c.  $\int_{2}^{5} (u^3 - 2u^2 + 6u - 10)du$

    d.  $\int_{0}^{1} du$

    e.  $\int_{3}^{7} 3udu$

    f.  $\int_{0}^{1} (5u^2 - 3)du$

8.  List and describe the FEM steps.
9.  Use the finite element method to check the geometric model of the drill brace handle shown in Figure 4.20 in Chapter 4. Use a force of 200 N (~45 lb; 1 lb = 4.4482 N) at the drill bottom face. The load applies compression on the drill. Think of it as the environment is pushing on the drill. Fix the top end (face) of the drill for the B.C. Use alloy steel for material. Ignore the top handle and the middle sleeve to simplify the FEM/FEA. Use the twisted rod only. What is the factor of safety? Is the model safe? Also, submit the Von Mises stress contour.
10. Redo Problem 9, but use a torque of 100 N.m as an external load instead of the force. Apply the torque at the center of the middle part where you grip the drill. Fix both the top and the bottom faces.
11. Redo Problem 9, but for the geometric model shown in Figure 4.21 in Chapter 4. Apply a uniform pressure of 100 psi on the narrow end and fix the model (horn) at the large end.
12. Redo Problem 9, but for the geometric model shown in Figure 4.26 in Chapter 4. Apply a uniform pressure of 40 psi on the crossbar and the uprights (this simulates gusting winds pushing on them). Fix the bottom face of the post where it meets the ground.
13. Redo Problem 9, but for the geometric model shown in Figure 2.50 in Chapter 2. Apply a uniform temperature of 200°F at the vertical face.

# Part Manufacturing

The primary goal of Part V is to explore and cover part manufacturing briefly. Manufacturing is a very large field. We focus our attention here on basic manufacturing including prototyping and machining. The goal is to provide the reader with some sense of what happens to designs after they leave the design department and how they become products.

Chapter 14 (Rapid Prototyping) covers the concepts of how to produce prototypes to evaluate designs. Chapter 15 (Numerical Control Machining) covers the concepts of machine tools and basic machining processes such as turning, drilling, and milling. Chapter 16 (Injection Molding) describes injection molding as another basic manufacturing process that is different from machining. Machining applies to metals whereas injection molding applies to plastics.

# Rapid Prototyping

## 14.1 Introduction

Design prototyping has long been a common practice in engineering design. Design and manufacturing engineers always want to ensure that a product design as perceived and visualized on paper (or on a CAD/CAM screen) is what it is. The advantage of just verification is that it eliminates any hidden mistakes or surprises that may be discovered during product manufacture. These surprises are costly. Even if there are no design mistakes, holding a prototype in hand may prompt some design changes such as changes in dimensions, aspect ratio, or relocation of features for ease of access by the intended users and maintenance personnel.

Prototyping is not only found in engineering; it is also part of life. Many of us have built prototypes of amateur designs such as building a racing car for the car derby race in Boy Scouts, or building the tallest structure using balsa wood sticks. Engineering students must design and build a prototype of a device as part of their mandatory capstone design course in their senior year.

There exist multiple ways to create prototypes in industry, depending on the industry and the product. For example, the automotive industry has been using prototyping for years to model concept cars. The designers use clay (plasticine) modeling to build a full-size clay model of a concept design before, during, or after a design is completed. They typically build the car body out of clay. Once finalized, they may use the model to measure the coordinates of points on the body using a CMM (coordinate measuring machine). They feed theses coordinates to a CAD/CAM system, and use them to create free-form surfaces of the car CAD model. Alternatively, designers may create the design in a CAD/CAM system and then build a clay model. Almost all companies still produce full-size clay models toward the end of the design process. These models can produce surprises that manufacturers want to avoid before a vehicle enters tooling and production phases.

Knowing the value of prototyping and with the advances in many fields, rapid prototyping (RP) has been in existence for some time and is a common practice today. Two factors contribute to the popularity of RP. First, CAD models can easily be converted for prototyping. Second, the RP hardware prices have been falling while the RP quality has been rising, thus enabling many companies of all sizes and academic institutions to acquire RP machines. Although RP started as a method of verifying and prototyping designs, it is now used to produce parts that are included in products that are used in real life. Also, prototypes can be used as master patterns for injection molding core and cavity inserts, thermoforming, blow molding, and various metal casting processes. That is due to the advancements in prototyping material strength, the accuracy of building the process, and the ability to build prototypes of very complex parts.

Considering it as a manufacturing process, RP is distinctively different from traditional manufacturing. RP is a process that is typically referred to as additive manufacturing because the process involves adding successive layers of material to build the prototype. The process involves supplying the layers data from a CAD file as we explain later in this chapter. In contrast, traditional manufacturing processes such as milling, drilling, and turning are considered subtractive manufacturing because the process involves starting with a raw blank (stock) and removing or carving out material until we create the final shape. The primary advantage of additive manufacturing is its ability to create almost any shape or geometric feature. Another advantage is that RP is a WYSIWYG (what you see is what you get) process whereby the physical (manufactured) model and the RP virtual model are identical, unlike traditional manufacturing where the stock and the final product are very different from each other.

There are key benefits of RP, including time and cost savings as well as accuracy. A prototype can always be produced in several hours to several days, depending on the type of RP machine used and the size and complexity of the model. RP is now entering the field of rapid manufacturing and is believed to dominate this type of manufacturing. The accuracy of building a prototype is comparable to traditional manufacturing. Example tolerances are $\pm0.005$ and $0.0015$ in. Other benefits of RP are:

1. Objects of any geometric complexity or intricacy can be produced.
2. There is no need for an elaborate machine setup or final assembly.
3. The construction is manageable, straightforward, and relatively fast.
4. It reduces time to market.
5. RP helps you to better understand and communicate product designs.
6. It allows you to make rapid tooling for injection molding and investment casting.
7. RP may be less expensive than traditional manufacturing.

## 14.2 Applications

By industry sector, the automotive industry is by far the largest user of RP due to the complexity of the CAD models common to automotive designs such as engine blocks, intake manifolds, exhaust systems, etc. RP serves many purposes. It has been utilized in many applications beyond its original intent (prototyping). Here is a list of some common applications:

1. **Prototyping (visualization):** Holding a prototype in hand, turning it around, and looking at it from all sides is the best way to visualize it. And, yes, it better than visualizing a 3D CAD model on the screen. No matter how experienced a designer is at reading blueprints and CAD images of a complex object, it is still very difficult to visualize exactly the actual part. Blind holes, complex interior details, and complex free-form surfaces often lead to wrong interpretations. Analogous to the "a picture is worth a thousand words" saying, we have "a prototype is worth a thousand pictures."
2. **Verification:** Due to the speed of RP, designers have ample time to modify and re-modify the design and verify it at a reasonable cost and well within the production and release deadlines. More often than not, especially under deadline pressures, we tend to forgo minor errors although we catch them and know they are there. We tend to fix them in the next revisions. RP helps eliminate this attitude and provide timely, with reasonable cost, visual verification of designs.
3. **Testing:** A designer may need to produce a prototype to test the design before finalizing. An example is testing an airfoil shape by placing it in a wind tunnel. The designer may redesign the airfoil based on the test results.

4. **Optimization:** This can be thought of as an extension of iterating a design. Design iteration may produce multiple designs to choose from. Optimization criteria could range from size, to weight, to esthetic appearance, etc.

5. **Fabrication:** This is an important application of RP that was not intended initially. The use of prototypes as final parts for use is very beneficial because it allows us to speed up production. RP is an essential concept to rapid manufacturing. Sample RP parts that are used as end products, or as components in products, include knee and hip replacements (Figure 14.1), dentures, and ankle bracelets. A common theme among these parts is customizations. Typically, a medical imaging of the patient part (knee, hip, mouth, or ankle) is generated via imaging software. The image is then converted to a CAD model that is used to generate the RP parts. Such a process guarantees a perfect fit of the RP body part in its final placement.

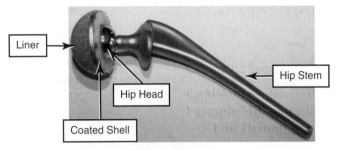

(A) Hip replacement

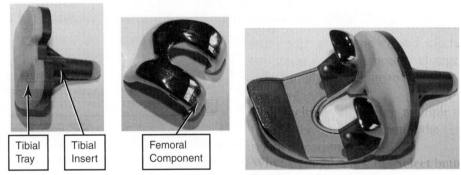

(B) Knee replacement

**FIGURE 14.1**
Hip and knee replacements

## 14.3 Overview

RP is also known as 3D printing, solid free-form fabrication, desktop manufacturing, and layered manufacturing. **Rapid prototyping** is a process that creates physical parts/products from CAD models. The underlying concept of RP is to build a prototype in layers (slices) one on top of the other, from the bottom up. The RP software slices the model into horizontal slices, and the RP hardware (machine) builds the prototype one slice at a time. Stacking the slices up builds the prototype.

Figure 14.2 shows a schematic of the RP process. This schematic is used by any RP process regardless of its details. The steps of the process are listed as follows:

1. **Create the CAD model of the part or assembly:** RP is capable of creating one single part or an assembly. Any gaps or loose parts in the assembly are built as such. An assembly created via RP is a functional one.

2. **Perform pre-processing:** The CAD/CAM software triangulates the CAD model and saves the related data in a file in STL format. This file is transferred to the RP software that reads the file, slices the CAD triangulated data, and saves the slice data in a new "build" file.

3. **Build the prototype:** The RP machine reads the slices file and builds the prototype, one slice at a time.

4. **Perform post-processing:** The prototype from Step 3 requires cleanup at minimum. In some instances, it may need further processing including baking, polishing, and finishing.

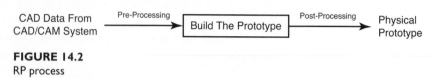

**FIGURE 14.2**
RP process

## 14.4 Concepts

An RP process uses a set of concepts regardless of the different commercial implementations. Even though different RP vendors use different RP techniques and build different machines, they all use the same concepts, which are triangulation (tessellation), build orientation, layering (slicing) thickness, and support structure.

A. **Triangulation (tessellation):** Triangulation represents the first step in the RP process. A CAD/CAM software accesses its B-rep of a CAD model and uses it to triangulate the model. Triangulating a model means converting its B-rep (all faces) to triangles (representing and preserving the model topology), as shown in Figure 14.3. The designer can control the accuracy of triangulating the model. Figure 14.3 shows three different accuracy (resolution) levels generated using SolidWorks. The accuracy directly affects the quality of the resulting physical prototype: the higher the triangulation resolution, the better the quality and accuracy of the prototype. The designer should use higher resolution if the resulting prototype is used as a final product or for experimental testing. Low or medium resolution should suffice if the model is used for visualization or verification. Just as the time to generate any triangulation resolution on a CAD/CAM system is minimal, the build time of the model on an RP machine is also unaffected by (independent of) the triangulation resolution.

Figure 14.3 shows that the resolution affects only the nonplanar faces of a CAD model. The top face shown in Figure 14.3 is triangulated into two faces regardless of the resolution we use. The left planar side of the model has a different number of triangles because it is affected by the triangulation of the cylindrical face. It is this face that is affected significantly by the resolution.

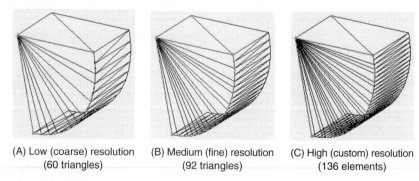

(A) Low (coarse) resolution (60 triangles)   (B) Medium (fine) resolution (92 triangles)   (C) High (custom) resolution (136 elements)

**FIGURE 14.3**
Triangulating a CAD model

B. **Build orientation:** The build orientation of a prototype affects its build time and its support structure. Figure 14.4 shows what we mean by build orientation. The figure shows a block with a hole in the center and demonstrates two build orientations: horizontal and vertical. The horizontal orientation shown in Figure 14.4A is better to use for this example because it needs less build time and no support structure. The build (RP) software usually estimates the build time. In this example, the horizontal build requires half the time (2 hours) than the vertical build requires (4 hours) for the particular RP machine we use (Stratasys Dimension modeler). The reason for the time reduction is that the horizontal orientation does not require a support structure. We have also found out that the resolution of the triangulation has an insignificant impact, if at all, on the build time. You can control the triangulated (faceted) model orientation in the RP software regardless of the model orientation in the CAD/CAM software. The RP software allows you to manipulate (rotate, translate, and/or scale up or down) the triangulated model.

 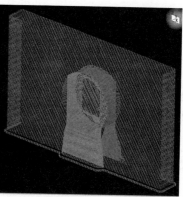

(A) Horizontal orientation    (B) Vertical orientation

**FIGURE 14.4**
Build orientation of a model

C. **Layering (slicing):** The layer (slice) thickness affects RP in two ways: model accuracy and build time. The user controls the layer thickness in the RP software during the slicing step. The larger the number of slices, the smaller the slice thickness is, and therefore the higher the build time and the more accurate the model. Figure 14.5 shows a schematic to illustrate the effect of the slice thickness.

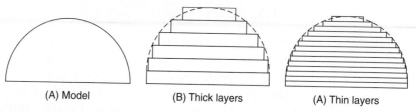

(A) Model    (B) Thick layers    (A) Thin layers

**FIGURE 14.5**
Effect of layer thickness

D. **Support structure:** Support structure is needed to build the prototype slice by slice. The structure serves as scaffolding. We need support structure any time the model boundary starts curving into nonmaterial zones. Consider building the prototype of the model shown in Figure 14.4. Building the prototype in the horizontal orientation (Figure 14.4A) does not require any support structure because each new slice is fully supported by the previously built slice. However, building the model in the vertical orientation (Figure 14.4B) requires a support structure immediately after we reach half the hole. After the half mark, the hole slices start hanging inward into the air, thus requiring support; otherwise, they fall to the hole bottom. Keep in mind that the RP build material is usually in a liquid or semiliquid state during build time. Thus, it does not have the strength to hold its own shape. Note that the support structure for the hole, shown in Figure 14.4B, extends all the way to the bottom of the RP platform to transfer the weight to the ground. RP software figures out the needed support structure automatically based on the orientation of the sliced model. The only intervention that the user does is to orient the model properly to avoid triggering the need for support structure as much as possible as Figure 14.4 shows. If a support structure cannot be avoided, the user must use the orientation that produces the least support structure. Support structures should be avoided as much as possible because they increase both the build time and the post-processing (cleanup) time, as well as consuming more material to build the prototype. Support structure is usually built from a separate material that is weaker than the build material itself. The support structure is also built as a weak structure so that it is easily broken and removed during the post-processing of the prototype. Typical shapes of support structures are honeycomb or thin stripes.

A special type of support structure is base support structure. Unlike support structure, base support structure cannot be avoided at all. It is a structure that the RP machine inserts between the prototype and its platform that holds the prototype. This structure is needed to facilitate removing the prototype from the machine platform. Figure 14.6 shows an example of a base support structure, which is built from the same material as the support structure and has the same weak structure (honeycomb or stripes). After the RP process is complete, the prototype is broken (sheared) off the platform by hand or with the help of a knife at the base support structure, and then the prototype bottom is cleaned up and smoothened out.

RP Machine Platform — Prototype — Base Support Structure

**FIGURE 14.6**
Base support structure

## 14.5 SolidWorks Triangulation

RP software uses triangulated (faceted) models saved, in files, in STL (stereolithography) format. The software slices these files and generates "build" files that the RP machine uses to build the physical prototypes. CAD/CAM systems must generate the STL files. These files are triangulated files of CAD/CAM models. Generating an STL file from a CAD model is a simple one-command activity. When we save the CAD model, we save it in STL format, thus generating a file with the *.stl* extension. Transfer the file to a RP machine via any common method (USB stick, network, e-mail, CD, DVD, etc.). Open the file using the RP software and process it there to generate the build file. Thus, we view the STL file as the interface between the CAD/CAM system and the RP machine.

SolidWorks generates STL files easily by saving a file as an *.stl* file. While a CAD part or assembly is open, click this sequence: **File** (SolidWorks menu) => **Save As** => Select **STL (*.stl)** from the **Save as type** drop-down list => **Save**. SolidWorks allows you to control the resolution of the model triangulation (see Figure 14.3) before saving the file. Click the **Options** button on the **Save As** window (not shown here) to access the **Export Options** window shown in Figure 14.7. As shown, you can generate a binary or ASCII file. We usually use the binary format because the size of the resulting file is smaller than the ASCII file.

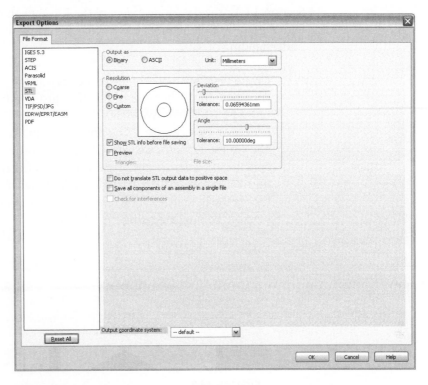

**FIGURE 14.7**
STL export options

There are three resolutions to select from, as shown in Figure 14.7. The **Custom** resolution allows you to control two tolerances that affect quality of the triangulation: **Deviation** and **Angle** shown in Figure 14.7. Triangulation replaces the CAD model with a faceted model that consists of facets (triangles). A **facet** is a small planar face that is a triangle. These facets need to be as close as possible to the model face (surface) they replace. Such closeness is a measure of the quality of the model tessellation. It is controlled via specifying the Deviation and Angle tolerances shown in Figure 14.7 and explained in Figure 14.8. The smaller these tolerances, the more accurate the STL representation of the CAD model is. Deviation tolerance controls the maximum distance allowed between the edge of a facet and the actual model face (surface), as shown in Figure 14.8A. Deviation is also known as the chord distance or the surface tolerance. Angle tolerance controls the change of orientation between two adjacent facets, as measured by the angle between their normal vectors and shown in Figure 14.8B.

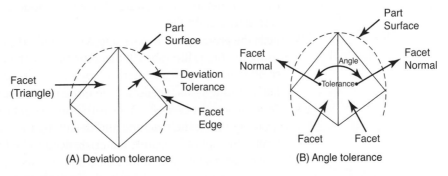

**FIGURE 14.8**
Definitions of STL tolerances

# 14.6 Steps

Section 14.3 provides an overview of the RP steps that start with a CAD model and end with a prototype of the model. We elaborate on these steps here after developing a good understanding of RP.

1.  **Create the CAD model of the part or assembly:** This step does not require any special attention because of RP. RP is just another application like mass properties, FEM/FEA, etc. We create the model as we normally do.
2.  **Perform pre-processing:** The pre-processing starts in the CAD/CAM software and ends in the RP software. The CAD/CAM software generates the STL file. The file contains the coordinates of the vertices of the triangles (facets) and the outward normal vectors of these triangles. The designer controls the accuracy of the STL file via the tolerances shown in Figure 14.8. Figure 14.9 shows SolidWorks STL message before generating the STL file.

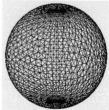

**FIGURE 14.9**
SolidWorks STL message

The STL file is read by the RP software. Several RP programs are available, and they allow the user to adjust the size, location, and orientation of the triangulated model. Model orientation used for building the part is important for several reasons. First, properties of prototypes vary from one coordinate direction to another. For example, prototypes are usually weaker and less accurate in the Z direction than in the XY plane. In addition, part orientation partially determines the amount of time required to build the model. Placing the shortest dimension in the Z direction reduces the number of layers or slices, thereby shortening the build time. The RP software slices the STL model into a number of layers from 0.01 mm to 0.7 mm thick, depending on the RP technique in use. The program may also generate a support (auxiliary) structure to support the model during the build. Supports are useful for delicate features such as overhangs, internal cavities, and thin-walled sections. Each RP machine manufacturer supplies its own proprietary RP software. The sliced model and its support structure are stored in a build file.

3.  **Build the prototype:** In this step we actually begin constructing the prototype using the build file. The RP machine builds one layer (slice) at a time using RP build material such as polymer, paper, powdered metal, etc. Most machines are fairly autonomous, needing little human intervention.
4.  **Perform post-processing:** This is the final step in RP. It involves removing the prototype from the machine and detaching the support structures that have been built. Some photosensitive materials need to be fully cured before use. Prototypes may also require minor cleaning and surface treatment. Sanding, sealing, and/or painting the model usually improve its appearance and durability, and may be done if deemed necessary.

## 14.7 Building Techniques

Stereolithography apparatus (SLA) is commonly considered to have been the first RP technique. It was developed by 3D Systems. Since then, a number of different RP techniques have become available. Each technique uses a process that forms the basis of a corresponding RP machine that reads an STL file and produces the prototype, as shown in Figure 14.2. The following RP techniques are used by commercial RP systems:

☐ Stereolithography (SLA)
☐ Laminated object manufacturing (LOM)
☐ Selective laser sintering (SLS)
☐ Fused deposition modeling (FDM)
☐ Solid ground curing (SGC)
☐ 3D printing (3DP)

Each technique uses its own build material. For example, SLA, LOM, SLS, and FDM use, respectively, photopolymer (resin), paper, thermoplastic/metal powder, and thermoplastic/eutectic metals or wax.

All these techniques use a somewhat similar process. They utilize the build file to build the prototype one layer at a time. First, a layer of the build material is deposited in the build chamber, leveled off with a sweeper (brush), and then cured to harden and adhere to the layer beneath it. After each layer is cured, the machine bed (holding the prototype in progress) is lowered by one layer thickness, a new layer of build material is applied on top and leveled off, and the curing process is repeated. This layering and curing process is repeated until the prototype is built from the bottom up.

The build material and the curing process differ from one technique to another. For example, SLA uses a laser to solidify the resin layer. LOM uses layers of adhesive-coated paper, plastic, or metal laminates. These layers are glued together and cut to shape with a knife or laser cutter. SLS is similar to SLA. It uses thermoplastic or metal powder and a high-power laser to fuse the powder particles together. FDM melts material flow coming from a nozzle that moves both horizontally and vertically via a computer control. The molten material is deposited as beads following the layer cross-section boundary. The material hardens immediately after extrusion from the nozzle. SGC uses photosensitive resin hardened in layers similar to SLA. Unlike SLA, the SGC process is considered a high throughput production process.

3D printing uses many materials, for example, powdered ceramics, powdered plastics, ABS, thermoplastics, and Ultem. 3D printing uses layering like the other techniques, but it is generally faster, more affordable, and easier to use. 3D printing has the ability to use several materials in the same build process, which is useful to prototype an assembly made of numerous materials. 3D printing is used in jewelry, footwear, dental, medical, automotive, aerospace, and other industries.

## 14.8 Bottle Prototype

This section provides a complete example from slicing an STL file to building and cleaning the prototype. We create a prototype of the bottle shown in Figure 14.10. We select this bottle because of the interesting challenges it offers. First, what is the best orientation to build it: horizontal or vertical? Second, what is the effect of its curved bottom on the base support structure? We use Stratasys Dimension modeler (RP machine) and its Catalyst software. We refrain from covering any unnecessary software- or machine-specific details here. The intent of the example is to put into

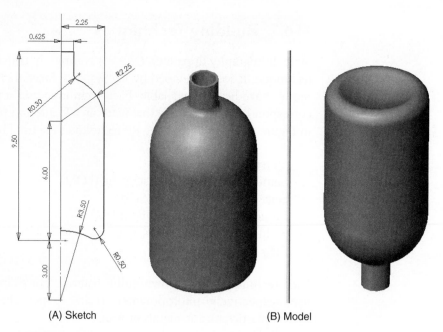

(A) Sketch                    (B) Model

**FIGURE 14.10**
Bottle CAD model

**FIGURE 14.11**
Bottle STL model

practice the many concepts covered in this chapter. We encourage the readers to build the bottle prototype using their RP machine if they have one. Here are the steps to create the prototype:

1. **Create the CAD model:** We create the CAD model of the bottle such that its overall size (enclosing box) does not exceed the limits of the RP machine. If the model size exceeds the machine limits, the RP software enables you to scale down the STL model to fit within the size of the build chamber before the building process begins. Figure 14.10 shows the bottle CAD model. All dims are in inches.

2. **Generate the STL file:** Use **Fine** resolution (Figure 14.7), and export the CAD model as an STL file. Figure 14.11 shows the STL model. The model triangulation is dense at the top and bottom zones of the bottle because of the curved faces there. The middle section of the bottle is flat in the vertical direction. The triangulation there connects the top and bottom facets.

3. **Generate the build file:** This is the pre-processing of the prototype. The software of the Stratasys Dimension modeler (RP machine) is called Catalyst. As does any RP software, it reads STL files generated by CAD/CAM systems and displays the STL models. It also provides the designer with functions to manipulate a model: pan, rotate, and scale. Most importantly, the designer can set up the RP build parameters: slicing thickness, calculating the support structures, and generating the build toolpath. The final outcome from the software is a build file that the RP machine reads to build prototype. The build file is in the machine proprietary native format.

Figure 14.12A shows the STL model in its original orientation after it is read from the STL file. Figure 14.12B shows the desired model orientation after manipulating the model in the Catalyst software. We build the prototype in the vertical, and not the horizontal, orientation because it improves the prototype quality and takes less time and support structure to build.

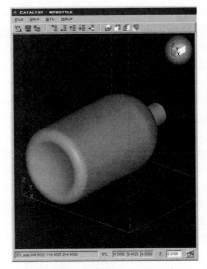

(A) Horizontal (original) orientation    (B) Vertical (desired) orientation

**FIGURE 14.12**
Orienting the STL model

After setting up the model orientation, we select the slicing thickness. This is called **Layer resolution** by Catalyst, as shown in Figure 14.13A. The RP software allows you to select from a recommended resolution list (Figure 14.13B) because the slice thickness is determined based on the RP machine build accuracy, the build material, and other factors. We also select the style of the support structure. Different styles are also shown in Figure 14.13B. Note that the RP software (Catalyst in this example) does the hard work for us by calculating the amount, location, and shape of the support structure. We can also select the style of the part interior. This is important because we can save build time, material, and cost. If the prototype is used only for visualization, we can select **Sparse** style. We select **Solid – normal** if we plan to use the prototype for testing or as a final product.

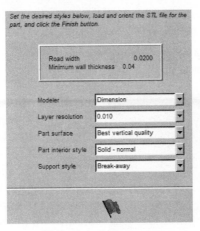

(A) Bottle build parameter    (B) General build parameters

**FIGURE 14.13**
RP build parameters

The support structure to build the bottle prototype is worth some discussion. Any support starts from the ground (the machine frame or platform) and extends up in the Z direction (build direction). The base support structure here fills the curved gap at the bottom of the bottle to support the layer build as it goes up in the Z direction. The support structure is created inside the bottle and extends from the curved bottom of the bottle all the way up to the bottom of its neck (Figure 14.12). We need support structure for only the top curved section of the bottle, as indicated by the facets shown in Figure 14.11. Thus, why do we need to start the support structure from the bottle bottom? The answer is simple; we must transfer the build weight of the curved section all the way down to the machine platform to support it. Also, notice that the bottle neck does not support because its layers (slices) are vertical. Each layer is supported by the layer beneath it.

Once we are done with setting the build parameters, Catalyst goes to work and achieves five tasks: generate the slices, generate the supports, write boundary curves, generate toolpaths, and write the build file. The slices are always generated along the Z-axis, the build axis for all RP machines. The boundary curves are used to define the shapes of the slices. The laser beam traces these boundaries and cures the build material inside them. The toolpath instructs the laser head how to move to build the prototype. All these RP data are written to the build file, ready for use. Figure 14.14 shows sample screenshots to illustrate some of these activities.

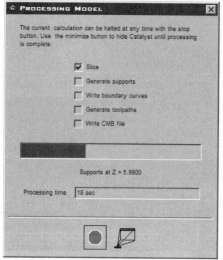
(A) Slicing STL model

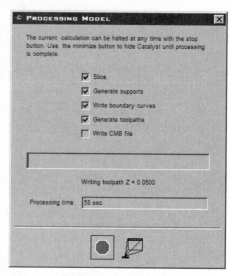
(B) Generating toolpaths

**FIGURE 14.14**
Processing build model

(A) Base support structure

(B) Full bottle

**FIGURE 14.15**
Processing simulation

During processing of the build model, Catalyst shows illustrative graphics of the progress of processing. This illustration effectively simulates the build process. It can be viewed as a last review of building the prototype. Figure 14.15 shows the simulation of the base support structure and the bottle model.

Once the processing is complete, Catalyst generates the build file and provides an estimate of the build time. The prototype model of our bottle needs 26 hours to build. It is not uncommon for prototypes to take a long time to build. RP vendors are aware of this and constantly try to reduce the build time. Many factors contribute to the build time ranging from the complexity and the size of the prototype, to the speed of the RP hardware, to the slicing resolution, etc.

RP machines are designed to build more than one prototype in one build to alleviate the long build time. If we can fit multiple models on the machine platform, the machine builds them concurrently. Figure 14.16 shows the placement of the bottle in Catalyst build envelope.

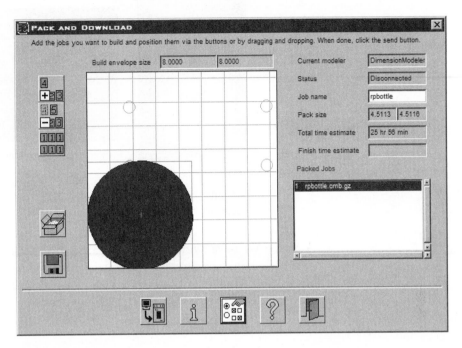

**FIGURE 14.16**
Build envelope

4. **Build the bottle prototype:** Start the machine to build. Make sure that the build file is in the machine memory ready for use. Also, make sure there are enough build and support materials. The machine builds and does not have to be attended during build time. Figure 14.17 shows the build progress.

(A) Base support structure

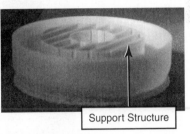

(B) Bottle progress

**FIGURE 14.17**
Build progress

5. **Remove and clean up the prototype:** This is the post-processing of the prototype. Use a putty knife to separate the prototype from the machine platform. In the case of the Stratasys machine, the platform is a foam block that is removed from the machine and thrown away after the prototype is removed. Figure 14.18 shows the foam before and after separation. Once separated, clean up the bottom of the bottle by scraping it. Other, more involved cleaning up includes oven curing or using water jets. Removing the support structure from inside the bottle prototype requires more careful handling. Keep in mind that the support structure material is always weaker than the build material.

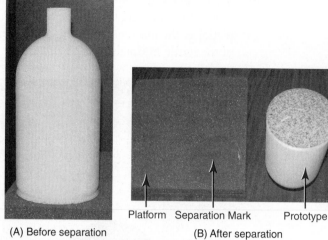

Platform   Separation Mark        Prototype

(A) Before separation              (B) After separation

**FIGURE 14.18**
Separating the prototype

While we have avoided covering any details about the machine specifics, Figure 14.19 shows the Stratasys machine to demonstrate two concepts. Figure 14.19A shows the two material trays: one for the build material and one for the support material. Figure 14.19B shows the sweeper that sweeps the material layer to flatten it before solidifying.

(A) Material bays

Head Rails   Extrusion Head   Sweeper

(B) Sweeper

**FIGURE 14.19**
Stratasys RP machine

## 14.9 Tutorials Overview

The theme for the tutorials in this chapter is to practice the triangulation concepts including parametric studies of SolidWorks faceting by investigation of the effect of the resolution. Other important concepts such as investigating orientation, slicing, and support structure are not covered because they are machine dependent. Quickparts.com, with headquarters in Atlanta, Georgia, USA (www.quickparts.com), has sponsored this chapter. Quickparts specializes in creating custom manufactured parts for its customers quickly and in a very cost-effective manner. More importantly, its prototypes are of high quality due to the in-house high-standard and rigorous quality measures used. We chat with Mr. Patrick Hunter, Vice President of Sales and Marketing at Quickparts, in the Industry Chat. Figure 14.20 shows a sample prototype of a cover of handheld rescue device. The cover houses the electronics of the device.

(A) Cover part (actual product)    (B) STL part (STL model)

**FIGURE 14.20**
Sample products (Courtesy of Quickparts)

## Tutorial 14–1:  Generate Prototype Files

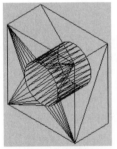

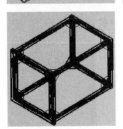

### Modeling task

Create STL prototype files for a number of parts of varying complexity as shown in Figure 14.21.

### Modeling synthesis

SolidWorks provides an easy way to generate STL files.

### Modeling plan

Save the following models from previous chapters in the STL file format to generate the prototype files.

### Design intent

Ignore for this chapter.

### CAD steps

We create each STL file in one step:

1.  Create the STL file for each model.

**FIGURE 14.21**
Prototype models

The details of this step are shown below.

## Step 1: Create an STL file for the block created in Tutorial 3–4

**Task**

A. Open the block part that was created in Step 3 of Tutorial 3–4.

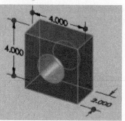

**Command Sequence to Click**

**File => Open => Part** => Open the block from the Pin Block assembly of Tutorial 3–4 as shown to the left.

B. Re-save the part as an STL file.

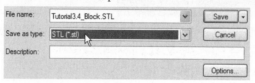

**File => Save As** => Select **STL (*.stl)** from the drop-down menu as shown to the left => **Save.**

C. Review the file STL attributes as shown below.

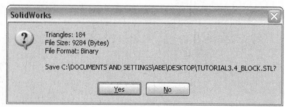

## Step 2: Repeat Step 1 for other models

**Task**

A. Create an STL file for the following model created in Tutorial 9–5.

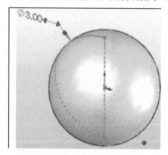

**Command Sequence to Click**

Repeat Step 1 as shown to the left.

| Task | Command Sequence to Click |
|---|---|
| **B.** Create an STL file for the following model created in Tutorial 9–1. 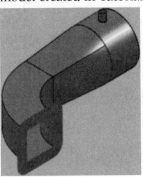 | Repeat Step 1 as shown to the left. |
| **C.** Create an STL file for the following model created in Tutorial 10–3. 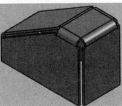 | Repeat Step 1 as shown to the left. |
| **D.** Create an STL file for the following model created in Tutorial 10–5. 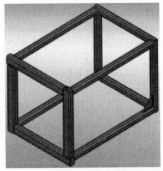 | Repeat Step 1 as shown to the left. |

---

**HANDS-ON FOR TUTORIAL 14–1.** Report the number of triangles and file size for each of the STL files created in this tutorial.

---

## Tutorial 14–2: Understand the Options of STL Files

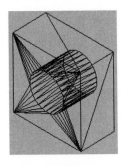

**FIGURE 14.22**
Model triangulation

**Modeling task**

Change the options when saving the model shown in Figure 14.22 as an STL file.

**Modeling synthesis**

The STL has a number of saving options.

**Modeling plan**

Save the model shown in Figure 14.22 as three different STL files. Vary the resolution of the output file.

**Design intent**

Ignore for this chapter.

### CAD steps

We create the three output formats in three steps:

1. Create the STL file for the block created in Tutorial 3–4 in coarse resolution.
2. Create the STL file for the block created in Tutorial 3–4 in fine resolution.
3. Create the STL file for the block created in Tutorial 3–4 in custom resolution.

The details of these steps are shown below.

## Step 1: Create the STL file for the block created in Tutorial 3–4 in coarse resolution

| Task | Command Sequence to Click |
|---|---|
| A. Open the block part that was created in Step 3 of Tutorial 3–4. 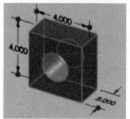 | **File => Open => Part** => Open the block from the Pin Block assembly of Tutorial 3–4 as shown to the left. |
| B. Re-save the part as a coarse STL file. 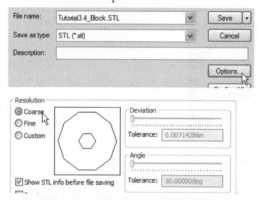 | **File => Save As => STL (*.stl) => Options** => Select **Coarse** under **Resolution** => Name the file *Tutorial3.4_Block_low* => **Save** as shown to the left. |
| C. Review the file attributes.  | Record the number of triangles and file size of the output file as shown to the left. |

## Step 2: Create the STL file for the block created in Tutorial 3–4 in fine resolution

| Task | Command Sequence to Click |
|---|---|
| A. Re-save the part as a fine STL file. 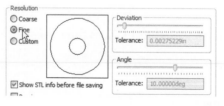 | **File => Save As => STL => Options** => Select **Fine** under the **Resolution** => Name the file *Tutorial3.4_Block_fine* => **Save** as shown to the left. |

| Task | Command Sequence to Click |
|---|---|
| B. Review the file attributes. | Record the number of triangles and file size of the output file as shown to the left. |

**Step 3:** Create the STL file for the block created in Tutorial 3–4 in custom resolution

| Task | Command Sequence to Click |
|---|---|
| A. Re-save the part as a custom STL file. | **File => Save As => STL =>** **Options** => Select **Custom** under the **Resolution** => Drag the **Deviation** and the **Angle** slider bars all the way to the right => Name the file *Tutorial3.4_Block_custom* => **Save** as shown to the left. |

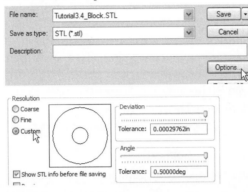

| Task | Command Sequence to Click |
|---|---|
| B. Review the file attributes. | Record the number of triangles and file size of the output file as shown to the left. |

---

***HANDS-ON FOR TUTORIAL 14–2.*** Open each of the STL files created in this tutorial back in SolidWorks. Study the files to see whether there is any visual difference between them. Submit a screenshot of each model as displayed in SolidWorks. Note that SolidWorks reconverts the STL to a solid part. Sometimes we refer to this solid as a "dummy" solid because SolidWorks cannot recognize its features or create a features tree for it. Thus, you cannot edit any of the original features of the model; for example, you cannot edit the size of the old hole feature.

---

**INDUSTRY CHAT**

This section provides practical insight into how the chapter material is used in industry in the real world and practice. This section summarizes the chat with Mr. Patrick Hunter (Vice President of Sales and Marketing) of Quickparts, the sponsor of the chapter. The structure of the chat follows the chapter sections.

*(continued)*

**Chapter Section 14.1:**   Introduction

ABE:   How important is rapid prototyping (RP) to your company? What are the benefits?

PAT:   We are a custom parts provider. So, it plays an important role in our company to provide our customers with functional models, exactly as they want them, so they can test their designs and decide. Customers require an average of three prototypes with modifications before reaching a decision. Our turnaround is quick. We build today, ship today, are in customer hands tomorrow. It all depends on the size of the part and the quantity. For example, some customers may need several prototypes if they use the part in functional products.

The benefits of rapid prototyping to our customers include the ability to receive an actual functioning part in their hands. Many people are visual and then you can also test the overall form fit and function of the part. The plastic components are just one part of the design. You can also test the fit of the PCB (printed circuit board) and any other mating components. Customers also achieve cost savings. Catching errors at the rapid prototyping phase saves them 10 to 100 times the cost of catching the errors at the production phase.

Customers like RP because it validates their design and confirms that their design will function as intended. This, in turn, saves them money. RP is like their "insurance policy." Validation of design is the most important reason our customers prototype.

**Chapter Section 14.2:**   Applications

ABE:   Provide some of your company's applications of prototyping.

PAT:   The largest user of RP is the medical industry because they are constantly developing new products. It is also a fast moving industry. The automotive industry is also a heavy user, but they have a long development cycle. Generally, fast developing companies use RP more because they are constantly developing new products.

**Chapter Section 14.3:**   Overview

ABE:   Describe your prototyping facility. What RP machine do you use?

PAT:   We have multiple facilities, depending on the process. One facility includes the RP machines and the curing and finishing area. These areas are next to each other to facilitate moving the prototypes to be cured and finished as needed. Curing and finishing are more of a cleanup after the part is made.

We have multiple RP machines. We have three types: SLA, SLS, PolyJet, and FDM (fused deposition modeling). Our SLA machines range from SLA 250 to IPRO. SLA uses resin for material. It is great for show (visualization) models. PolyJet equipment uses resin that is photo cured. PolyJet is almost like a printer. It is good for show models and patterns for vacuum casting molds. FDM uses ABS or polycarbonate plastics. FDM is great for actual parts that go to functional parts.

I also would like to say that the curing and finishing depend on the process. SLA part curing includes wet sand and bead blast to remove the support (stair stepping). PolyJet curing uses a support station to remove the gel formed during the build process. FDM uses water soluble support. So, we have a wet tank to remove the support.

I also would like to say how we package RP parts. We put each part in an individual bag, and put it in a large box with packaging peanuts and ship them to our customers.

Last, the sizes of RP parts change significantly. The smallest size fits on your fingertips. The largest part is 40 inches in size. We make the large parts in multiple sections and we connect them with the same resin they are made of.

**Chapter Section 14.4:** Concepts

ABE: Provide some examples of using the RP concepts in your company.

PAT: We do not create tessellated models. Our customers send us STL files. We review them for large facets, unshared edges, and any hollow areas. Customers decide the accuracy of the tessellations. We review them to make sure that they do not produce large facets that make the prototype suffer from staircase visual effect. We may provide customers with help to regenerate a new STL file with smaller facets.

The build orientation is important to producing a correct prototype. Typically we look for holes to build them vertically to avoid building them in an oblong shape. The other thing is to orient the part so that the important faces are not used for support surfaces. Then, the last thing is the overall height because it affects the overall time of the build. If all other factors are OK, we orient the part to minimize the height. If we run into conflicting decisions, we build in a manner that produces the best RP for the customer.

The slice resolution is another important factor. We have a lot of slice resolutions we can use, typically 0.005 to 0.006 inch thickness. We may use smaller resolutions for smaller features of the part.

Last, the support structure needs to be aligned so that it does not affect any feature when you remove it. We use honeycomb type support structure. It is the standard shape. The material of the structure is very much the same as the actual build. It is more sparse, so you can remove it easily after the build.

**Chapter Section 14.5:** SolidWorks Triangulation

ABE: Provide some examples of how you use SolidWorks export options.

PAT: Our customers provide us with STL files. So, we do not do deal with tessellation accuracy. We seldom, if any, read customer STL files back into a CAD system.

**Chapter Section 14.6:** Steps

ABE: Describe how does your company uses the RP steps.

PAT: Our customers do Steps 1 and 2. We do Steps 3 and 4.

**Chapter Section 14.7:** Building Techniques

ABE: Which technique does your company RP facility use? Why did you select it?

PAT: We do not use LOM (laminated object manufacturing) or SGM (solid ground curing). We use SLA, PolyJet, and FDM. 3D printing is much of an offshoot. You may argue that SLA and PolyJet are forms of 3D printing.

**Chapter Section 14.8:** Bottle Prototype

ABE: Provide a complete example of one of your company prototypes.

PAT: We inspect each model for important features and what the customer expectations are. We make a variety of parts. For example, we make components for NASA space vehicles, for the medical industry, e.g., in-body catheters. For the aerospace industry, we make cockpit components. For the consumer industry, we make vacuum equipments and toys.

*(continued)*

**Others**

ABE: Any other experience you would like to share with our book readers?

PAT: The most important observation is that RP technology is constantly changing. So, it is hard to master it if you do not use it constantly. So, you need to rely on people who use it every day, for the knowledge. Learn how to maximize the use of RP to speed up the design process and minimize surprises down the road during production.

1. What is the difference between rapid prototyping and traditional manufacturing?

2. List the benefits of rapid prototyping.

3. List and describe some of the applications of rapid prototyping.

4. List and describe the steps of the rapid prototyping process.

5. How many triangles does the faceted model of a block (cube with no holes) have? Why? What is the effect of the triangulation resolution?

6. Why is orienting cylindrical holes vertically better than doing it horizontally for building a rapid prototype?

7. How does the slicing (layering) thickness affect the quality of rapid prototyping?

8. Describe the two types of support structures for prototyping.

9. List and describe the concepts of rapid prototyping.

10. Explain and sketch what is meant by deviation tolerance in triangulation. How does it affect the triangulation accuracy?

11. Explain and sketch what is meant by angle tolerance in triangulation. How does it affect the triangulation accuracy?

12. List and describe the steps of the rapid prototyping process.

13. Research the stereolithography (SLA) technique. Submit a detailed report about how the technique works, the build and support structure material, the model slicing and orientation, the machine operation and how it builds the prototype, the pre-process operations, the post-process operations, and the cleanup and painting. Include a schematic of the SLA machine to show its operation mechanism including the laser operation, the vat, and the photopolymer.

14. Redo Problem 13 but for laminated object manufacturing (LOM).

15. Redo Problem 13 but for selective laser sintering (SLS).

16. Redo Problem 13 but for fused deposition modeling (FDM).

17. Redo Problem 13 but for 3D printing (3DP).

18. Use SolidWorks to generate the faceted model of the holed block shown in Figure 2.3 of Chapter 2. What is the best orientation to build the prototype? Why?

19. Redo Problem 18 but for the model shown in Figure 2.17 of Chapter 2.

20. Redo Problem 18 but for the AMP connector shown in Figure 2.43 of Chapter 2.

21. Redo Problem 18 but for the flange model shown in Figure 2.45 of Chapter 2.

22. Redo Problem 18 but for the L bracket shown in Figure 2.50 of Chapter 2.

23. Redo Problem 18 but for the pattern block shown in Figure 2.51 of Chapter 2.

24. Redo Problem 18 but for the pattern wheel shown in Figure 2.52 of Chapter 2.

25. Redo Problem 18 but for the loft feature shown in Figure 4.14 of Chapter 4.

26. Redo Problem 18 but for the helical spring shown in Figure 4.24 of Chapter 4.

27. Redo Problem 18 but for the Cam Follower assembly shown in Figure 6.9

28. Redo Problem 18 but for the Pin Block assembly created in Tutorial 3–4, Chapter 3.

29. Redo Problem 18 but for the assembly shown in Figure 6.14

30. Redo Problem 18 but for the Couch assembly of Problem 21, Chapter 6.

31. Redo Problem 18 but for the Candle Holder assembly of Problem 23, Chapter 6.

32. Redo Problem 18 but for the Ballpoint Pen assembly of Problem 25, Chapter 6.

33. Redo Problem 18 but for the Three-Hole Paper Punch assembly of Problem 26, Chapter 6.

# Numerical Control Machining

## 15.1 Introduction

Manufacturing a part is the culmination of product design. We discussed the manufacturing and CAM processes in Chapter 1. A variety of manufacturing processes exists. The manufacturing engineer (process planner) selects a suitable manufacturing process depending on the part material and design tolerances. The process planner typically has strong background in and knowledge of manufacturing processes. With this knowledge, the planner may request design changes from the design engineers to simplify part manufacturing and, as a result, reduce manufacturing cost. For example, machining a flat blind hole is harder and more expensive than machining a conical blind hole. The former requires a milling operation whereas the latter requires a drilling operation.

Different types of manufacturing also exist. Mass production is the type of manufacturing in which hundreds or millions of the same part or product are produced on a mass scale. Examples include consumer products such as cars, cell phones, and computers, to name a few. The advantage of mass production is the cost reduction realized from setting up a production operation once to produce many units. Another type of manufacturing is job shop, which is the other extreme. In job shop, we produce either one-of-a-kind pieces or a small number (tens) of units. There is also the concept of mass customization whereby companies try to combine the benefits of scale (less cost) with the benefits of meeting customer requirements.

The existing manufacturing processes (methods or operations) can be categorized based on the material they can process. The oldest traditional methods are cutting metals (steel, aluminum, etc.). These processes include turning, drilling, milling, grinding, boring (used for large holes), reaming (used for holes up to 1-inch diameter), lapping and honing, broaching, casting, forging, and EDM (electrical discharge machining). Manufacturing methods for polymers and plastics include injection molding.

A machining process directly influences the part accuracy and surface quality (roughness). For example, a turning process produces less surface quality than do honing and lapping. Milling is much better than casting and forging.

We cover only four basic machining processes in this chapter: turning, drilling, milling, and wire EDM. The goal is to provide a basic understanding of machining so we can become better designers and be abe to connect design and manufacturing. Thus, we will understand the production and cost implications of specifying tighter or looser tolerances.

Machining processes can be done manually or programmatically. Although manual machining is not used too often, it still serves as a good foundation to learn machining. Programmed machines are more common. These computer-controlled machines are known as NC (numerical control or numerically controlled) machines. Machine shops may have both manual and NC machines. We cover NC machines here and how to program them.

## 15.2 Basics of Machine Tools

Machining machines are known as machine tools. A **machine tool** is a manufacturing machine that performs one or more machining operations. For example, we can perform milling, drilling, reaming, boring, tapping, and threading using a milling machine. We need to understand both how machine tools work and what the basics of NC machining are. This section covers the basics of machine tools. Subsequent sections cover the basics of NC machining. Figure 15.1 shows sample machines. (We use the terms *machine tools* and *machines* interchangeably throughout the chapter.)

Figure 15.2 shows abstractions (schematics) of the machine tools shown in Figure 15.1. The abstract machine tool helps us understand its basics and its setup and operations. A machine tool has a solid heavy frame typically made out of cast iron. The bed, column, and head shown in Figure 15.2 are part of the machine frame. The machine also has a table that moves in two orthogonal directions controlled by two lead

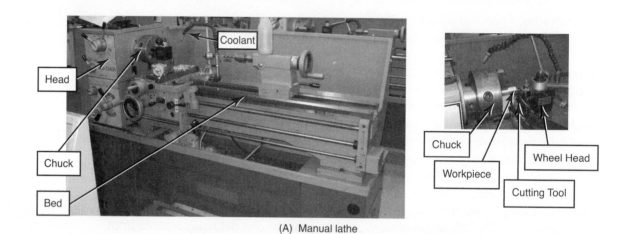

(A) Manual lathe

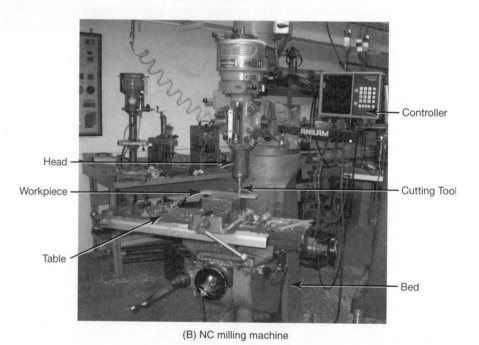

(B) NC milling machine

**FIGURE 15.1**

Machine tools

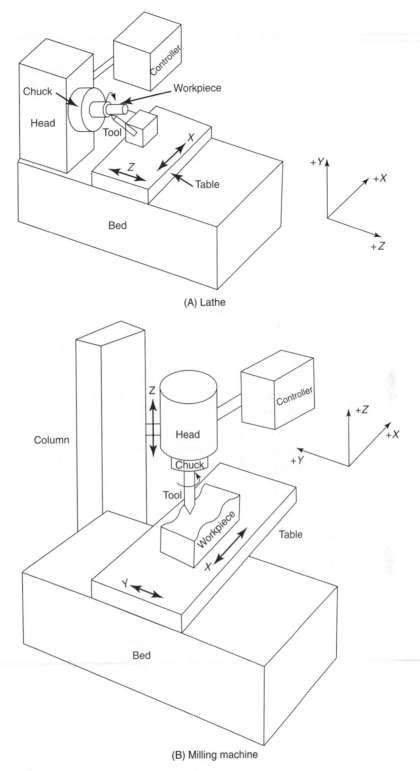

(A) Lathe

(B) Milling machine

**FIGURE 15.2**
Schematics of machine tools

screws, one for each direction. Each machine has its own Cartesian coordinate system. The table of a milling machine moves in the X and Y directions shown in Figure 15.2B, whereas the table of a lathe moves in the X and Z directions shown in Figure 15.2A. The cutting tool always moves in the Z direction as shown. The positive Z direction is always pointing away from the workpiece by convention.

The workpiece is fixed securely to the machine table via jigs and fixtures that also ensure aligning the workpiece relative to the machine table and the cutting tool for correct machining. The lathe has a chuck (instead of jigs and fixtures for a milling machine) to hold the workpiece. If the machine is numerically controlled, it has an NC controller. Manual machines do not have controllers. The machine head is where the power is transferred from the machine motor to rotate the cutting tool at high cutting speed.

We describe the operations of the two machine tools shown in Figure 15.2. A turning machine is typically used to machine axisymmetric cylindrical parts such as shafts and cylinders. A milling machine can perform many operations including drilling holes, tapping holes, and milling part surfaces of any shape.

The machining operation of a part begins by setting up the machine. The setup starts by mounting and securely fixing the workpiece (known as stock) on the machine table by the machine operator (machinist). Next, the machinist establishes the machine reference point (known as the machine zero) and the workpiece reference point (known as the workpiece zero). The machinist must align these two zeros to machine the workpiece correctly. When the machine setup is complete, the machinist turns on the machine power and begins cutting (removing material from) the workpiece. If the machine is manual, the machinist moves the machine table manually. If it is an NC machine, the machinist loads the NC program (code) to the machine controller and starts the controller to execute the program.

The machining operation could be wet or dry. Each machine tool has a coolant system that cycles cutting fluid or coolant (oil or water-miscible fluid) (see Figure 15.1A). The machinist points the coolant nozzle to pour the coolant continuously on the cutting tool and the workpiece. The coolant is caught in a tub under the machine bed, gets filtered from the machining scrap, and then is recycled again. Dry machining does not use coolant. The advantages of wet machining are twofold: it produces better surface finish than does dry machining, and it elongates the cutting tool life (does not get dull quickly). NC programming provides commands to control the coolant, that is, turn it on or off.

The skills of the machinist determine the accuracy and the quality of the finished parts. The machinist's skills become more crucial in manual machining than in NC machining. After machining is finished, the machinist removes the finished part. Further machining or processing on other machines may be required. After all machining is complete, the parts move to inspection and then are assembled into their intended products (assemblies).

## 15.3 Basics of Machining

Controlling the position and the motion of the cutting tool while it is removing (chipping) material (chips) away from a workpiece is essential and follows well-established concepts that include motion axes, cutting parameters, home position, toolpaths, and other topics that we cover here.

1. **Motion axes:** Motion axes of a machine tool determine the versatility of the machine and what type of surfaces (faces) it can cut. An **axis** defines a degree of freedom (DOF) along which a cutting tool can move. In 3D space, there is a maximum of six DOF: three translations along the $X$-, $Y$-, $Z$-axes and three rotations around these axes. However, a machine tool may have more than six DOF. There exist 2-axis, 3-axis, and multi-axis machine tools. A multi-axis machine tool has many DOF, sometimes up to 10.

   A 2-axis machine tool means that its cutting tool can move along two axes only and simultaneously. An example is a lathe in which the tool moves along the

Z-axis (length of workpiece being turned) and the X-axis (into the workpiece to re-move material), as shown in Figure 15.2A. In a 3-axis machine, the tool can move along three axes (X, Y, Z) simultaneously. A 3-axis milling machine provides an example. Most milling machines are 3-axis because you can machine any complex surface by controlling the tool motion along three axes. Additional DOF could be added either as rotations about X-, Y-, Z-axes or as translations of other parts of the machine (in addition to the tool translation). These additional DOF enable machining very complex parts as found typically in the aerospace industry. Milling machines with more than three DOF are typically referred to as machining centers. For example, a 4-axis machine has X, Y, and Z, and a fully rotating table that can rotate simultaneously while the tool is moving and cutting.

Some machine tools (specifically milling machines) are 2½-axis or 3½-axis machines. The ½ axis designation means that the motion along this axis is limited. For example, a 2½-axis milling machine means that its cutting tool can mill any shape (cross section) in a plane that is parallel to the XY plane of the machine (i.e., parallel to its table). A 3½-axis machine has X, Y, and Z as its primary axes of motion, plus an indexing table designated as an A axis. The indexing table is used for positioning; it cannot rotate simultaneously with the motion of the primary axes.

2. **Cutting tools:** Cutting tools are made of special materials and have special shapes. These materials must be harder than any material the tool is intended to cut; otherwise, the tool will not be able to cut it. The harder the cutting tool material, the more resistant it is to wear and thus the longer its life. Cutting tool materials include HSS (high speed steel), cobalt, carbide, titanium, and diamond. HSS is the softest material and diamond is the hardest material. The harder the material, the more expensive the cutting tool is, the heavier (more weight) it is, and the greater speed and feedrate it can run at.

Another important characteristic of cutting tools is the number of flutes. A **flute** is defined as a helical groove in the tool along its length (shank) to remove chips (cut material) away from the tool cutting edges (teeth) as the tool rotates. As the tool cuts into the material, the chips need a path to get out. A tool has multiple flutes depending on how many cutting edges it has. Figure 15.3 shows 2-flute, 3-flute, 4-flute, and 6-flute cutting tools. An n-flute tool has n cutting teeth; each tooth has its flute.

A third important characteristic of cutting tools is what their cutting ends look like. For example, a drill always has a conical end; this is why blind holes always have conical ends. There exist flat- or ball-end mills. Flat-end mill performs flat surface milling whereas ball-end mill performs pocket milling. Counterbore and countersink tools are shaped as shown in Figure 15.3.

Many types of cutting tools exist to support the varied cutting processes. For example, we have tools for turning, drilling, milling, threading, etc. Many tools exist for each process. Figure 15.3 shows some tools for some processes. Tools are usually designated by various parameters, depending on the tool. For example, drills and mills are designated by the tool diameter and number of flutes; for example, spot drill (use before drilling; it makes a dent to start drilling), 2-flute drill, 3-flute flat-end rough mill, or 3-flute ball-end mill. A tapping tool is used to make threads in a hole. Think of it as thread male. An example of tapping tool designation is 9/16•18NF (Figure 15.3J), referring to the thread outer diameter (9/16 inch), number of teeth per inch, or tpi (18), and the thread type (NF). Two thread types exist. One type is unified fine (UNF), which is referred to as NF (national fine) in the retail industry. The other type is unified coarse (UNC), which is known as NC (national coarse) in retail. Figure 15.3J shows this tapping tool.

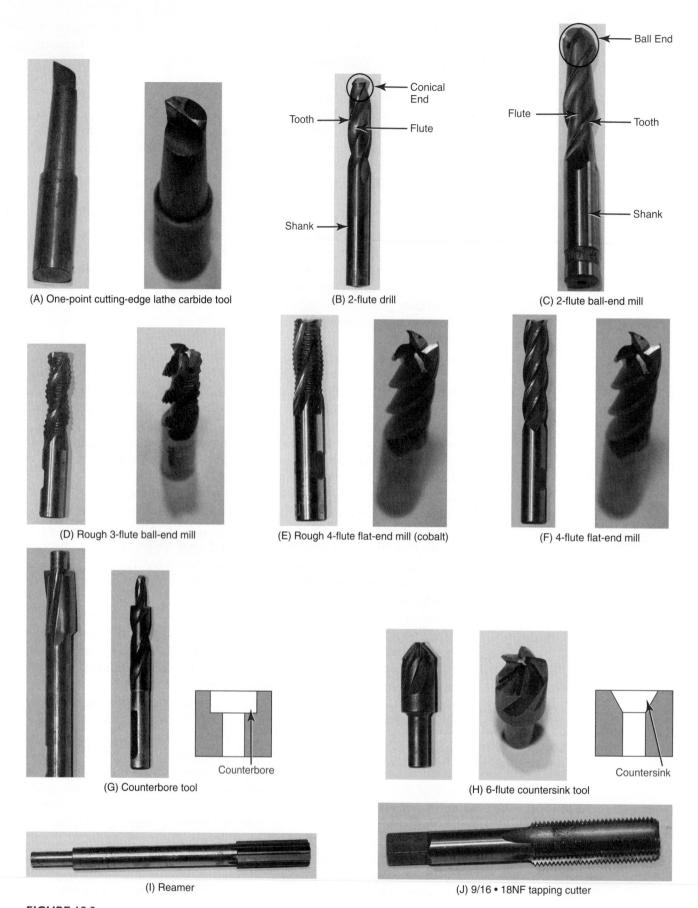

(A) One-point cutting-edge lathe carbide tool

(B) 2-flute drill

(C) 2-flute ball-end mill

(D) Rough 3-flute ball-end mill

(E) Rough 4-flute flat-end mill (cobalt)

(F) 4-flute flat-end mill

(G) Counterbore tool

(H) 6-flute countersink tool

(I) Reamer

(J) 9/16 • 18NF tapping cutter

**FIGURE 15.3**
Cutting tools

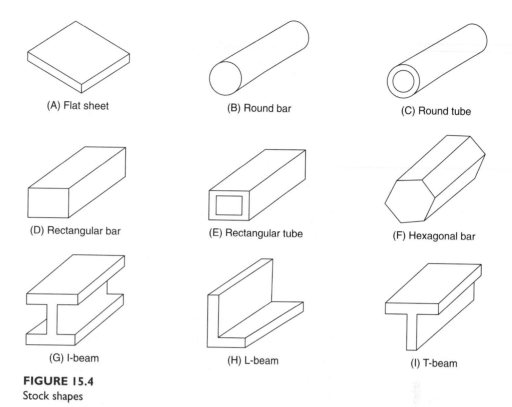

**FIGURE 15.4**
Stock shapes

3. **Stock:** A **stock** is a large material from which workpieces can be cut. The standard stock shapes are shown in Figure 15.4. Companies typically buy stocks of different materials. When needed, they cut workpieces from stocks and machine them to make parts. The terms *stock* and *workpiece* are usually used interchangeably. Workpiece dimensions are always larger than the dimensions of the finished part to allow for machining down (removing material) the stock. Stock dimensions may be ¼ inch larger than those of a finished part. The rule is that you always select a stock shape and dimensions as close as you can to the finished part to minimize material waste and avoid longer machining time.

4. **Machining parameters:** These parameters include the spindle (rotation) speed (also known as cutting speed), feedrate, and depth of cut, as shown in Figure 15.5. A turning, drilling, milling, tapping, or other similar cutting tool is connected to the machine head via a chuck. The chuck grips the tool and keeps it securely in place. A tool rotates as it penetrates the workpiece to cut it. This rotation, known as the spindle speed, is measured in rpm (revolution per minute). The tool

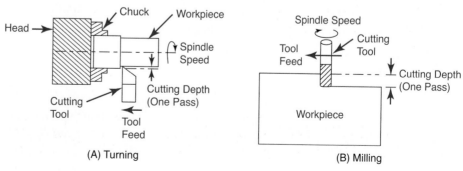

**FIGURE 15.5**
Machining parameters

chuck is connected to the machine motor spindle that transmits the rotation from the machine motor to the tool.

The feedrate is how fast the cutting tool is removing material from the workpiece; that is, it is the linear speed of the cutting tool, typically measured in feet or inches per minute. Units are typically feet per minute (fpm). Fast feedrates result in rough surface finish. The value of a feedrate depends on the materials of both the workpiece and the cutting tool. Excessive feedrate or cutting depth could result in breaking the tool.

The depth of cut (cutting depth) is the thickness of the material that the cutting tool removes from the workpiece as it travels in contact with the workpiece. This thickness represents one "pass" of the cutting tool over the workpiece. If we need to remove more material than the depth of the cut allows, we need multiple passes. Smaller depths result in a smoother surface finish. Also, an excessive depth could break the cutting tool due to the extreme force exerted on the tool from the workpiece material.

Most machining operations are conducted on machine tools that have rotating spindles. Thus, we relate the machining parameters to the spindle speed. The cutting tool rotates with the rotational speed, $N$, of the spindle and has a diameter, $D$. Thus, any point on the outer surface of the tool has a linear speed, $S$, known as the cutting speed. Figure 15.6 shows the view looking down at the

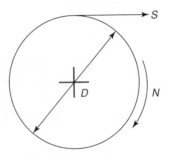

**FIGURE 15.6**
Cutter motion parameters

cutting tool along its axis. We relate the spindle rotational (angular) speed and the tool surface (linear) speed as follows:

$$N = \frac{12S}{\pi D} \tag{15.1}$$

where $N$ is in RPM (revolution per minute), $D$ is in inches, and $S$ is in feet per minute. Equation (15.1) is based on the simple equation of angular motion, $v = \omega r$. Sometimes we write $S$ as SFM (surface feet per minute). Thus, Eq. (15.1) becomes:

$$N = \frac{12SFM}{\pi D} \tag{15.2}$$

In turning, $D$ is the diameter of the workpiece being turned; in milling, drilling, reaming, and other operations that use a rotating tool, $D$ is the cutter diameter.

The calculation of the feedrate requires knowing the tooth load during cutting and the number of teeth (flutes) of the tool. The load is the force that the workpiece exerts on the tool during cutting. The feedrate is given by the following equation:

$$F = F_t TN = F_{rev}N \tag{15.3}$$

where $F$ is the feedrate (inch per minute), $F_t$ is the tooth load (feed/tooth) in inch/tooth, $T$ is the number of teeth, and $N$ is the spindle speed (RPM). $F_t$ is also known as the chip load, which is the size or amount (measured in inch per tooth, ipt) of chip that each tooth of the cutter can remove in one revolution. $F$ is the distance that the cutting tool advances per minute. $F_{rev}$ is the distance that the cutting tool advances during one revolution of the spindle measured in in./rev, and is given by:

$$F_{rev} = F_t T \tag{15.4}$$

$F_{rev}$ is sometimes known as cutting feed. The time it takes to machine a length $L$ of a workpiece is given by $L/F$ in minutes. This is the time the tool needs to travel the distance $L$.

Toolmakers publish tables of spindle speed, SFM, and feedrate. Also, machinery handbooks publish similar tables. SFM tables are typically given for a tool diameter, $D$, of 1 inch. The most common number of tool teeth is 2, 3, or 4. Here are some example values of machining parameters. Use spindle speed and feedrate of 5000 rpm and 1 in./min, respectively, if you are roughing steel workpiece with carbide cutting tool, and 2000 rpm and 1 in./min if you are finishing it. If you are cutting aluminum with a carbide tool, use 10,000 to 15,000 rpm for roughing and 5000 rpm for finishing, and 2 in./min for feedrate for both.

There are so many factors and variables that influence the selection of spindle speed and feedrate. These variables include materials and coatings of cutting tools, methods of holding the tools, different material properties of materials being cut, toolpath software, cutting technique, etc. Realizing these ever-changing values, NC machining software provides its users the ability to populate their cutting libraries and databases with new cutting values as they become available. However, NC software may provide what is called "out-of-the-box" values for machining parameters. These values are usually approximate. Interested readers should consult with their toolmakers and machine makers for the latest and most accurate values for machining parameters.

5. **Machining quality:** When we remove material away from a workpiece, we keep two goals in mind: removal speed and quality of surface finish. We need to cut away as much material as possible while producing a high-quality surface finish. To achieve this compromise, we adopt a simple but effective strategy: roughing followed by finishing. In a roughing operation, we cut away large amounts of material, leaving a poor surface finish. In a finishing operation, we remove a smaller amount of material, leaving a good surface finish. There exist cutting tools for roughing and finishing. Figure 15.3D and Figure 15.3E show two roughing end mill cutters. Figure 15.3C and Figure 15.3F show two finishing mill cutters.

6. **Squaring stock:** A machinist typically cuts a piece of stock to start a machining operation, which then becomes the workpiece. Stocks are typically produced by low-quality manufacturing processes to keep their cost down. The machinist would need to prepare the stock before machining it to make the final part. Stock preparation is what we call squaring. Squaring means just that: machine the stock so that its faces are perfectly normal to each other, within the tolerance limits. Squaring begins by milling one side and then gripping the stock correctly by the vise to square the other sides, typically by placing the milled side on the machine bed; that is, make it horizontal in a vertical milling machine. Mill the opposite horizontal side of the stock. When done, ungrip the stock, rotate it, and repeat the squaring process to square another side. Continue until you finish squaring the stock's six sides, assuming the stock is a block (see Figure 15.4).

7. **Home position:** The machinist needs to establish the machine zero before cutting. This is the home position of the cutting tool. The machine tool indexes this location and uses it to measure the tool coordinates during its movements. The home position could be a point on or near the workpiece. In an NC machine tool, the machine controller uses the home position to interpret the coordinates used in an NC program. Typically, a machinist sets the home position such that the tool is 50% out; that is, align the tool axis with an edge of the workpiece.

8. **Toolpath:** A toolpath represents a machining strategy. Once we decide on a machining operation and a cutting tool, we need to decide on the best way to perform the cutting. By "best," we mean finding the shortest and fastest path to cut the workpiece. For example, Figure 15.7 shows three strategies and their toolpaths to mill the top face of a workpiece. Which toolpath offers the best strategy? Why? The selection of a toolpath depends on machining the part correctly to avoid damaging it or requiring repair. For our example, the toolpath that creates the least burr in the part is the best. A **burr** is a raised edge or small piece of material remaining attached to the workpiece after machining. A burr must be removed via another machining process called deburring. Drilling burrs are common and happen in all materials. Deburring adds to and therefore increases the part machining cost.

Let us investigate the four toolpaths shown in Figure 15.7. The zigzag toolpath is the best and is typically used to mill a face because it produces the least burr. Also, the tool ends up at the end of the part all the time. The perimeter toolpath creates more burr all around the edges if you cut from the center of the face and out to the edges (called in-out). If the tool cuts its way in (called out-in) to reduce the burr, you create another problem because the tool leaves a spot (mark) at the center of the part because it has to spin there while not moving to mill the last area. The L and L-R-L (L Reverse L) toolpaths are a waste of time because you would waste time moving the tool to the beginning of the cut (Figure 15.7C), or you would need two moves to reverse the tool motion (Figure 15.7D). CAM software always creates the best toolpath to machine a feature.

Toolpaths come in two types depending on the machining operation: PTP (also called positioning) or continuous (also called contouring). In PTP

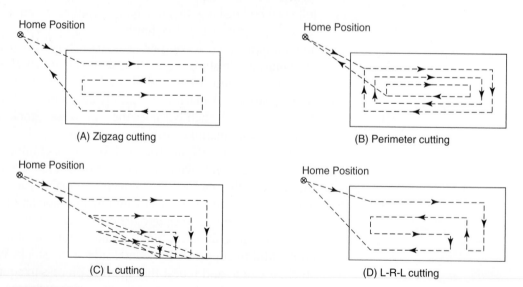

(A) Zigzag cutting     (B) Perimeter cutting

(C) L cutting     (D) L-R-L cutting

**FIGURE 15.7**
Toolpaths to mill a face

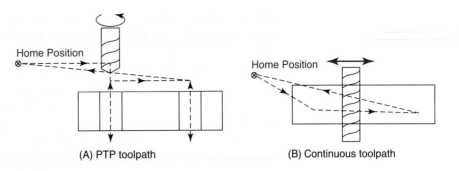

**FIGURE 15.8**
Types of toolpaths

(point-to-point) machining, the tool is not in constant contact with the workpiece during its motion. Drilling is an example of PTP machining. The cutting tool is in contact with the workpiece only momentarily to drill the hole at the desired point (location). The tool does not contact the workpiece during its travel from one point to another. Figure 15.8A shows a PTP toolpath to drill holes. In continuous path machining, the tool is in constant contact with the workpiece, as in the case of face or side (contour) milling, as shown Figure 15.8B.

While the tool is moving without being in contact with the workpiece, how high should it "fly" above the workpiece top face to clear it? In practice, machinists typically use 0.1 inch (read as 100 thousandths of an inch). Some may use half this height (i.e., 50 thousandths of an inch). We need smaller heights to save time in moving the tool toward and away from the workpiece.

The coordinates of key points on a toolpath are measured with respect to the part coordinate system, which is typically the MCS of the part CAD model. CAM software generates the toolpath using the MCS coordinates. The correct machining of the part requires the machinist to align the workpiece (part) coordinate system with that of the machine. Also, the machinist should align the zero (origin) of the workpiece (MCS) with the machine zero. Without the correct alignment between the workpiece and machine coordinate systems, the machine controller interprets the toolpath incorrectly, rendering the workpiece as scrap.

The coordinates of a point on the toolpath may be expressed in absolute or relative coordinates. In the absolute system, the coordinates are always measured with respect to the machine zero (origin of the MCS). In the relative system, the coordinates are measured with respect to the last location of the tool. For example, consider Figure 15.9. Assuming that the two holes, A and B, are centered in

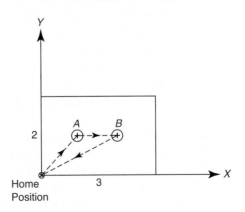

**FIGURE 15.9**
Absolute and relative coordinate measurements

the part, the absolute coordinates of their centers are (1, 1) and (2, 1), respectively. The relative coordinates of center $B$ relative to $A$ are (1, 0), and of center $A$ relative to $B$ are $(-1, 0)$. In reaching these values, we move the XY coordinate system shown and attach it to the reference point. We prefer the absolute coordinate system in practice. The major drawback of the relative coordinate system is that any toolpath point change renders all the coordinates wrong.

9. Rapid positioning:   We can move the cutting tool at two speeds: rapid and slow. When the tool is not in contact with the workpiece while moving, we use rapid motion (also known as rapid positioning) because we do not have to worry about the tool breaking or the workpiece surface finish. When the tool is touching the workpiece while moving, we move the tool carefully via specifying the feedrate. For example, we use rapid positioning to move a drill from one hole location to another, or to send a milling cutter from home position to a workpiece.

## 15.4 Turning

We next provide brief descriptions of some basic machining processes (operations): turning, drilling, milling, and wire EDM. We start with turning, which is done on a lathe. Figure 15.1A shows a lathe and Figure 15.2A shows a schematic of a lathe. Turning is used for producing cylindrical or conical parts. The workpiece is rotated while the cutting tool moves along the axis of the workpiece, as shown in Figure 15.2A. Although turning is the machining operation most widely done on a lathe, a lathe may also be used for drilling, boring, tapping, facing, threading, polishing, grooving, knurling, and trepanning. Each operation uses a different-shaped cutting tool.

Turning (boring) is a lathe operation in which the cutting tool removes metal from the outside (inside) diameter of a workpiece producing, for example, stepped shafts and other axisymmetric shapes such as candle stick holders, cylinders, cones, etc. In turning, the workpiece rotates while the tool moves parallel to the axis of rotation. A workpiece may be held in a 3-, 4-, or 6-jaw chuck, with collets, or it may also be held between centers. A single-point tool (Figure 15.3A) is used for turning.

## 15.5 Drilling

Drilling is a machining operation that creates cylindrical holes in parts. Drilled blind holes have a conical end, the same shape as the drill cutter (see Figure 15.3B). When you drill through (non-blind) holes, make sure that you feed the drill bit (tool) enough so that the drill conical end clears the bottom face of the workpiece to ensure the correct size of the hole diameter throughout the entire hole length. This would require gripping the workpiece appropriately with the jigs and fixtures to ensure that the drill end would not hit any of the holding faces.

A drilling operation could be done on a turning or milling machine, depending on the shape of the workpiece. For example, holes in a flange are drilled on a lathe whereas holes in a block are drilled on a milling machine. Sometimes, we may spot a hole before drilling it. This means that we use a "spotting drill" bit to make a dent in the workpiece first before drilling to locate (establish) the hole center. Other times, we use a "center drill" bit to make a conical starting indentation for a larger-sized drill bit used in a lathe drilling operation.

In some cases, drilling provides the base operation for other machining operations to follow. For example, we may use a reaming operation after drilling if we need a very smooth surface finish for the hole. Figure 15.3I shows a reamer. Or, we may use a tapping operation to create a threaded hole. Figure 15.3J shows a tapping cutter. Or, we may add counterbores or countersinks to holes. Figure 15.3G and Figure 15.3H show the corresponding cutting tools. Counterbores and countersinks are used to hide a bolt head or a nut. We use them either to flush the bolt head or nut with the hole top or bottom face, or to hide them a little below the face. This hiding is done for either aesthetic or safety reasons.

## 15.6 Milling

Milling is the most common and versatile machining operation. It is done on a milling machine or center, and allows us to machine almost any shape imaginable. Milling machines may be horizontal or vertical (Figure 15.1B and Figure 15.2B), although vertical milling machines are more popular than horizontal ones.

Milling machines are typically 3- or 3½-axis machines. A 3-axis milling machine provides 3 translations on the cutting tool simultaneously (see Figure 15.2B). A 3½-axis provides an indexing axis of the machine turret. A **turret** is a tool holder (changer) that holds multiple tools and changes them automatically between operations. The advantage of a turret is to eliminate changing the cutting tool manually between operations, thus saving tool-changing time. Milling centers can have more axes, providing rotational DOF and/or auxiliary translational DOF. Some vertical milling centers have flexible heads. This means that a machine head can be tilted from side to side and from front to back to allow for machining flexibility.

A variety of milling operations and tools exists. Examples include slot, face, pocket, and side milling. In slot milling, the cutter is a flat-end mill that cuts on its end face and periphery (sides). In face milling, the tool cuts on its end face. Milling a pocket is similar to milling a slot, but the tool performs multiple passes. In side milling, the tool cuts on its periphery and goes around the perimeter of the workpiece.

## 15.7 Electrical Discharge Machining

Electrical discharge machining (EDM) is a process that removes material from a workpiece via an electric spark between two conducting surfaces. (EDM removes material via spark erosion.) One surface is an electrode and the other is the workpiece itself. The workpiece material must be conductive to electricity. There are two types of EDM: sinker (plunge) and wire. Figure 15.10 shows the two types. What distinguishes the two

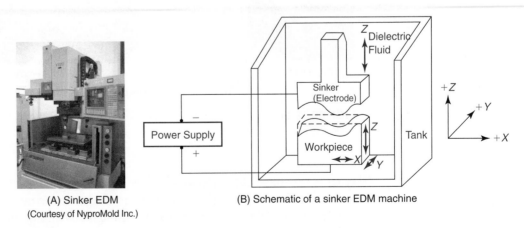

(A) Sinker EDM
(Courtesy of NyproMold Inc.)

(B) Schematic of a sinker EDM machine

**FIGURE 15.10**
EDM machines

Idle wire EDM machine

Wire EDM machine in action (creating holes)

(C) Wire EDM (Courtesy of NyproMold Inc.)

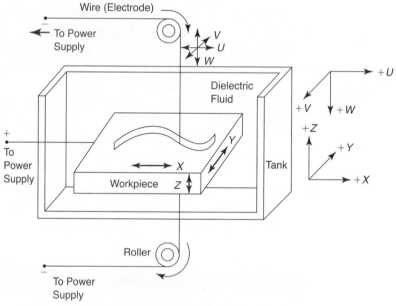

(D) Schematic of a wire EDM machine

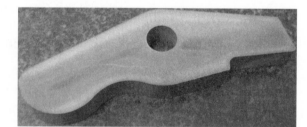

Part of a mold

A cam (a mold ejector component)

(E) Sample wire EDM parts (Courtesy of NyproMold Inc.)

**FIGURE 15.10**
(*continued*)

types is the shape of the electrode. If the electrode is a block, we have EDM. And if it is a wire, we have wire EDM. Sinker EDM is used to make mold (die) cavities and stamping dies. Wire EDM is primarily used for through hole machining; that is, to make through holes of any shape as shown in Figure 15.10D. Depending on the piece we want to keep after machining, we can have a hole or the cutout piece as the final product.

Figure 15.10B shows a schematic of an EDM sinker machine. The electrode is made from copper or graphite and is shaped as the mold or the stamp we need to create. The sinker moves up and down as a milling cutting tool. The workpiece is submerged in a tank containing dielectric (does not conduct electricity) fluid, usually oil or synthetic fluid. The sinker moves up and down only, similar to other cutting tools. The workpiece moves along the three axes as shown. When the sinker gets close to the workpiece, an electric spark is generated. The spark is strong enough to melt (erode) the workpiece to cut it to shape.

The dielectric fluid is continuously flowing in the tank. The molten particles from the spark drop in the dielectric fluid, which sweeps them away to be filtered out. The dielectric fluid is recycled after filtering. In addition to flushing the material away, the fluid serves as a coolant to minimize the heat-affected zone, thus preventing potential damage to the workpiece.

The spark is generated at a controlled frequency. Spark frequency is defined as the number of times per second that the electric current is switched on and off. Low frequency is used for roughing the workpiece and high frequency is used for finishing. The material removal is done only during the on time. The longer the on time, the more material is removed in each sparking cycle. Roughing operations use extended on time for high material removal rates. The resulting craters are broader and deeper.

Figure 15.10D shows a schematic of a wire EDM machine. The operating principles of a wire EDM are almost the same as those of the sinker EDM. The main difference is the electrode shape. The wire material could be brass, copper, tungsten, or zinc, which all have excellent electric and thermal conductivity. The wire moves over the roller like a belt and goes through the workpiece. Unlike the sinker electrode, the wire can move in three directions, as shown in Figure 15.10D. However, the wire motion in the W direction (along its length) is unidirectional. The workpiece also moves in three directions. The wire cuts the workpiece and is used only once to ensure accuracy and precise cylindrical cuts. Wire EDM machines use deionized water as the dielectric fluid.

Wire EDM is used primarily for shapes cut through a part or assembly. If a cutout needs to be created, an initial hole must be first drilled (using EDM also). Then, the wire can be fed through the hole to complete the machining. Keep in mind that the wire (negative charge) must never touch the workpiece (positive charge); otherwise, we create a short circuit. It's the spark that goes from the wire to the workpiece and cuts it.

EDM produces parts with high accuracy (tight tolerances of $\pm 5$ microns; 1 micron = 1 millionth of a meter) and quality, and it can cut any material that is conductive. EDM has many advantages over conventional machining. It is great to use to produce one or a few of a complex part (low-volume production) where traditional machining may be expensive. Wire EDM produces a burr-free, superior edge finish. It is also useful for custom parts such as jewelry or human implants. Wire EDM can cut diamonds or make orthopedic implants, aerospace and automotive parts, extrusion dies for rubber and plastics, and gears. Cutting with a wire allows you to cut any complex shapes and intricate contours. Here the wire is the tool. The wire can take any shape because it is flexible to bend and twist along its guides.

EDM can cut through a stack of workpieces (sheet materials), thus cutting several parts at the same time. EDM can also be used to create prototypes, similar to rapid prototyping (e.g., trial stamping of parts). EDM can cut parts weighing up to 10,000 pounds.

## 15.8 Manufacturing of Design

We now have a good background about manufacturing. We see how our designs are manufactured and produced. It is logical to ask this question: How can we make our designs better from a manufacturing point of view? This question addresses a broader issue. That is, designers should not only concern themselves with functional requirements and force analysis, but they should also think broader and consider their design implications on the entire product life cycle from design (product birth), to manufacturing, to assembly, to disassembly, to disposal (product death). We have covered design sustainability already in this book. Many design foci (concepts) exist to address product life cycle concerns. These include DFM (design for manufacturing), DFA (design for assembly), DFX (design for anything), concurrent engineering, PDM (product data management), and PLM (product lifecycle management).

We cannot explain each of these design foci in depth in this book, but we offer a quick overview here. Interested readers should consult other books and resources for more in-depth coverage. All these foci try to change product design during the design phase where design changes are simply a change on paper or in CAD software. Changes at the design phase are not detrimental or costly as are changes during manufacturing on the production floor.

The focus of DFM is manufacturing. DFM tries to address this question: How can we change the design to make it easier and less expensive to make? For example, do not use blind holes that have flat bottoms. The focus of DFA is assembly; change the design to make it easy to assemble. For example, reduce the number of parts of an assembly as much as possible to make it quicker to assemble. Having fewer parts per assembly also reduces its maintenance and repair cost. The "X" in DFX extends the concepts of DFM and DFA to any design concern we may have and should address.

Each of these design philosophies (DFM, DFA, DFX) has a narrow focus. As a matter of fact, these philosophies may and often do produce conflicting results. Thus, we use more encompassing approaches. Concurrent engineering approach, for example, suggests that all the teams (design, manufacturing, marketing, sales, etc.) concerned with a new product should meet and work concurrently during the product design phase to resolve any disagreements and conflicts so that the final design is acceptable to all, including customers (users of the product).

PDM and PLM are similar to concurrent engineering, but from a management and software point of view. PDM and PLM software are extensions of CAD/CAM software. PDM concerns itself with managing product design activities only. PLM goes beyond design and looks at disassembly and product end of life. SolidWorks offers **PDMWorks** for PDM and **DFMXpress** for DFM.

## 15.9 Basics of NC Machining

The basics of machining we have covered earlier in this chapter apply here. This section extends these concepts with additional ones that apply to NC machining, commonly known as NC programming. NC programming applies to NC machine tools. Each one of these machines has an NC controller, as shown in Figures 15.1B and 15.2B. The controller reads an NC program, executes it, and uses it to control the motion of both the machine table and the cutting tool. NC machining is more accurate and faster than manual machining.

Machinists use CAD models and NC software to write NC programs. NC software could be a software module in CAD/CAM software or completely separate software. For example, SmartCAM is stand-alone software and CAMWorks is an add-on to Solid-Works. Stand-alone software such as SmartCAM reads CAD models by importing their STEP or IGES files. CAMWorks reads SolidWorks native (*.sldprt*) files.

NC programs are written in different languages. We classify them into two groups: high level and low level. High-level NC programming languages use English-like syntax. APT (automatically programmed tool) is an example of high-level NC language. Low-level NC programming languages look cryptic and are written using

G-code and M-code. NC controllers read G-code and M-code instructions. NC programs written in high-level programming languages are converted to G-code and M-code before sending them to NC controllers. While G-code and M-code are ANSI/EIA standard language, some post-processing may be needed to accommodate proprietary features and different commercial interpretations of the code. The benefit of standard programming language is easy transfer of NC programs from one machine to another.

An **NC program** is a list of instructions (commands or statements) that orders an NC controller to carry out a sequence of operations on the machine tool to achieve a given machining process. After an NC program is written, it is downloaded to the machine controller. While you can write NC programs directly on NC controllers, this is not a common practice. It would be very cumbersome and difficult to program the machining of an intricate part this way. Instead, we use CAD/CAM systems to generate the NC toolpath first, verify it, edit it, and finally generate the NC program that can be downloaded to the NC controller via a network or a storage device such as a USB. **Toolpath verification** is a visual simulation of the cutting tool traversing the toolpath. The NC programmer may spot errors and correct them before real manufacturing, thus saving money and time.

We cover G-code and M-code programming here only. Before we can write NC programs, we offer the following NC programming concepts:

1. **Zero-radius programming:** The definition of the toolpath geometry requires the $(x, y, z)$ coordinates of its key points. Knowing that the cutting tool follows the toolpath, should the coordinates somehow reflect the size (diameter) of the tool? No. When we write NC programs manually or generate them using NC software, we assume the diameter of the tool to be zero. Such an NC programming approach is known as zero-radius programming, or programming the part. We specify the radius of the tool at the beginning of the program, and the NC controller compensates for the radius while executing the NC program. The advantage of this approach is that we can use the same NC program with multiple tools of different radii.

2. **Tool offset:** We can use tool offset to cut more than one part using the same program in one setup. Setup cost before machining usually increases part manufacturing cost. Consider drilling a hole in a part. Why cannot we put multiple parts in one or two rows on the machine table all at once and set them up? Then we apply an X-, Y-, or X- and Y-offset to the NC program to move the table to the right location (under the drill bit) to drill the hole. This increases machining productivity and reduces machining cost by reducing the number of setups, which in turn reduces the setup cost.

3. **Driving the tool:** During actual machining, the tool does not move (except small movements in the vertical, depth of cut, direction); the workpiece does move because it is fixed to the machine table that moves in the X, Y, and Z directions. However, in NC programming, we visualize the tool motion (tool moving around the workpiece), not the machine motion. We move the tool and hold the workpiece fixed during writing or generating NC programs. It is easier this way. The NC controller reverses the motion during executing the NC programs. Thus, the easiest way to write an NC program is to think of the cutting tool as a golf cart that we drive along the toolpath. As we look ahead, we imagine taking left and right turns along the toolpath. This approach helps us write the correct code for the toolpath.

4. **Interpolations and canned cycles:** NC controllers provide linear and circular interpolations to machine linear and circular profiles. For example, we define a line by two endpoints and a circle by a center and radius. From there, the NC controller knows how to cut these profiles in small linear increments (movements of

the machine table). The controller may also have other canned cycles such as tapping holes, etc. A **canned cycle** is a prewritten function that the NC programmer can call in an NC program.

5. **CL data:** The cutter location (CL) data define the data of the tool centerline as described by the G-code and M-code. In high-level NC programming languages, we use post-processing to generate the CL data file. CL data files are G-code and M-code files.

## 15.10 G-Code and M-Code Programming

Writing an NC program requires the context of how we perform a machining operation. First, we need to define the toolpath, and then move the tool along this path. Accordingly, an NC program defines the toolpath geometry and instructs the tool to move along it. Other machining instructions may be needed such as rapid positioning, turning coolant on and off, etc.

An NC program consists of a sequence of instructions (statements), one per line. In the G-code and M-code programming, a statement is known as a block. Each block (line) begins with a block (line) number (N) followed by a code word (e.g., G00). Each code word begins with a letter followed by numerical digits as shown. Following the code word (*code* or *word* is also used) is the required data. A block may contain more than one word. An NC controller executes one block at a time. Here is an example:

N01 G00 X1.0 Y0.0 Z0.0
N02 M13
N03 G01 X1.0 Y0.0 Z-1.0

The first block is Number 1 (N01) and uses the G00 code followed by $(1, 0, 0)$ coordinates of a point, say $P_1$. The G00 code is rapid positioning code. It instructs the NC controller to move the cutting tool from its current position rapidly to $P_1$ in preparation for the next instruction (block). The M13 code in the second block (N02) instructs the NC controller to turn on the machine spindle rotation in the clockwise direction and also turn on the coolant in preparation for drilling. Finally, the last block (N03) performs the drilling operation by moving the drill bit a $-1$ in the Z direction using the G01 code.

Prior to executing the above NC program, the machinist turns the machine power on and prepares for machining. Then, the machinist clamps the workpiece to the machine table, and lines up the machine and workpiece zeros with the zero used in this program. Finally, the machinist loads the drill bit into the NC machine chuck and runs (executes) the program. This simple program could be entered directly to the NC controller, with no need for NC software. After drilling, the machinist stops the spindle rotation, clears the workpiece from the spindle area, and unclamps and removes the workpiece, which is the finished part. The part may be inspected later to ensure that it is within the specified tolerances.

There is a finite set of codes that is available for G-code and M-code programming. The codes use all the alphabet letters, from A to Z as follows. (The bolded letters are the only ones we use in this chapter.) A to E codes define angular dimensions. **F** is the feed code. **G** is the preparatory (geometry) code. H and L are not used. I, J, and K are used for threading. **M** is the miscellaneous code. **N** is the sequence (number) code. O is the secondary sequence number. P, Q, and R are used for rapid-traverse dimensions. **S** is the spindle speed code. **T** is the tool code. U, V, and W are the codes for secondary axes of motion of the machine table. **X**, **Y**, and **Z** are the codes for the primary axes of motion of the machine table.

## TABLE 15.1 Subset of the Available G-Codes

| Code | Data | Description | Example |
|------|------|-------------|---------|
| O | Number | Program number | O0001 |
| G00 | x, y, z | Tool rapid position to the point specified by data | G00 X1.0 Y0.0 Z0.0 |
| G001 | x, y, z | Move tool linearly to point specified by data | G01 X2.0 Y0.0 Z0.0 |
| G02 | $(x_c, y_c)$, R | Circular interpolation clockwise (CW) | G02 X4.0 Y3.0 R1.5 |
| G03 | | Circular interpolation counterclockwise (CCW) | G03 X4.0 Y3.0 R1.5 |
| G04 | Number in seconds or milliseconds | Dwell is an intentional time delay where the cutting tool remains rotating and in contact with the workpiece. Use dwell to stop the NC program execution to remove chips, improve machining quality, etc. | G X2.5 in seconds, OR G P2500 in milliseconds **Help:** X or P specifies sec or millisec. P cannot take decimals. |
| G10 | x, y, z | Tool offset distance in one or all X-, Y-, Z-axes | G10 X1.0 Y2.5 Z0.0 |
| G17 | None | Select XY plane of machine tool | G17 |
| G18 | None | Select XZ plane of machine tool | G18 |
| G19 | None | Select YZ plane of machine tool | G19 |
| G20 | None | Input in inch (inch mode) | G20 |
| G21 | None | Input in mm (mm mode) | G21 |
| G28 | x, y, z | Return to reference point specified by data | G28 X3.0 Y2.0 Z0.5 |
| G90 | None | Absolute programming | G90 |
| G91 | None | Incremental programming | G91 |
| G92 | x, y, z | Set program zero to point specified by data | G92 X0.0 Y1.0 Z3.5 |
| G94 | F code | Feedrate (in./min or mm/min) | G94 F3.75 |
| G95 | F code | Feed per revolution (in./rev or mm/rev) | G95 F0.003 |

Table 15.1 shows a subset of the available G-codes. Interested readers should consult other resources for more codes. Some G-codes not listed here mean different things to different NC controllers. This is why we always need to post-process an NC program generated on a CAD/CAM to a particular NC controller to ensure its correct execution.

Table 15.2 shows a subset of the available M-codes. Interested readers should consult other resources for more codes. Some M-codes not listed here mean different things to different NC controllers.

## TABLE 15.2 Subset of the Available M-Codes

| Code | Data | Description | Example |
|------|------|-------------|---------|
| M00 | None | Unconditional automatic stop the machine. Machinist must push a button to continue with the remainder of the program | M00 |
| M01 | None | Conditional (optional) stop. Triggered only if the machinist pushes any button on the NC controller | M01 |
| M02 | None | End of program. NC machine stops | M02 |
| M03 | None | Start spindle rotation in forward (CW) direction | M03 |
| M04 | None | Start spindle rotation in reverse (CCW) direction | M04 |
| M05 | None | Stop spindle, i.e., spindle off | M05 |
| M06 | None | Tool change | M06 |
| M07 | None | Turn on coolant in mist mode | M07 |
| M08 | None | Turn on coolant in flood mode | M08 |
| M09 | None | Turn off coolant | M09 |
| M10 | None | Automatic clamping of workpiece, fixtures, spindle | M10 |
| M11 | None | Automatic unclamping of workpiece, fixtures, spindle | M11 |
| M13 | None | Start spindle rotation in forward (CW) direction and turn coolant on at the same time | M13 |
| M14 | None | Start spindle rotation in reverse (CCW) direction and turn coolant on at the same time | M14 |
| M19 | None | Oriented spindle stop. Spindle stops at predetermined angle | M19 |

**Example 15.1**  Write an NC program to turn a steel shaft. The shaft is 3 in. long and has a diameter of 1 in. We need to turn 1 in. long. The cutting parameters are spindle speed = 1500 rpm, feedrate = 1 in./min, and coolant is on in flood mode. Write the program for one pass.

**Solution**  Figure 15.11 shows the toolpath for this running operation. The cutting tool starts at the tip of the shaft of $z = 3$ and ends at $z = 2$. The Y location is $-0.5$. Here is the NC program:

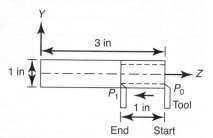

**FIGURE 15.11**
Turning a shaft toolpath

| | |
|---|---|
| N01 M03 | (start spindle) |
| N02 M08 | (turn coolant on in flood mode) |
| N03 S1500 | (set spindle speed to 1500 RPM) |
| N04 G20 | (set input mode to inch) |
| N05 G00 X0 Y-0.5 Z3.0 | (rapid to start point [home] $P_0$) |
| N06 G01 Z2.0 F1.0 | (go to $P_1$ and turn with specified feedrate) |
| N07 M05 | (turn spindle off) |
| N08 M09 | (turn coolant off) |
| N09 G00 Z3.0 | (rapid back home) |
| N10 M00 | (stop machine) |

---

**HANDS-ON FOR EXAMPLE 15.1.** Change the example code to turn a circular cut in the middle of the shaft. The cut length is ½ in.

---

**Example 15.2**  Write an NC program to drill the holes shown in Figure 15.12. The holes are 0.5 in. in diameter. The part is an aluminum plate with thickness of 0.5 in. The cutting parameters are spindle speed = 5000 rpm, feedrate = 2.5 in./min. No coolant is used.

**FIGURE 15.12**
Drilling holes toolpath

**Solution**  Figure 15.12 shows the toolpath for this drilling operation. We use a drill bit of 0.5 in. in diameter (same size as the holes). The drill bit starts at the home position, drills the holes, and goes back home. We position the drill bit 0.1 in. above the workpiece to avoid collision between the drill and the top face of the workpiece. Here is the NC program:

| | |
|---|---|
| N01 M03 | (start spindle) |
| N02 S5000 | (set spindle speed to 5000 RPM) |
| N03 G20 | (set input mode to inch) |
| N04 G00 X0 Y0 Z0.6 | (rapid to home position $P_0$; 0.6 = 0.1 + part thickness of 0.5) |
| N05 G01 X1 Y1 | (go to hole $A$ center $P_1$; NC controller uses previous $z$ value) |

| N06 G01 Z-1 F2.5 | (drill hole; use large enough $z$ value for drill bit end to clear hole) |
| N07 G01 Z1 | (bring drill bit back above the workpiece) |
| N08 G01 X2 Y1 | (go to hole $B$ center $P_2$; NC controller uses previous $z$ value) |
| N09 G01 Z-1 | (drill hole; same as first hole) |
| N10 G01 Z1 | (bring drill bit back above the workpiece; same as first hole) |
| N11 G00 X0 Y0 | (rapid to home position) |
| N12 M05 | (turn spindle off) |
| N13 M00 | (stop machine) |

---

**HANDS-ON FOR EXAMPLE 15.2.** Change the example code to drill hole $B$ first, then hole $A$.

---

**Example 15.3** Write an NC program to mill the top face of the part shown in Figure 15.11. Use a flat end mill with diameter = 0.5 inch. Use same machining parameters. Depth of cut (milling) is 0.05 in. Write the program for one pass.

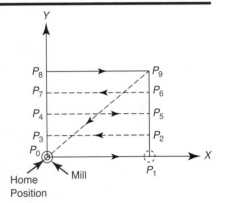

**FIGURE 15.13**
Milling top face toolpath

**Solution**  We use a zigzag toolpath as shown in Figure 15.13 for this milling operation. The cutting tool starts at the home position, mills the top face, and goes back home. We position the mill tool centerline at the home position, $P_0$.
The tool moves in both the X and Y directions. We mill the face in 5 cuts. This program is tedious to write manually although the milling operation is simple. This underscores the value of NC software. Here is the NC program:

| N01 M03 | (start spindle) |
| N02 S5000 | (set spindle speed to 5000 RPM) |
| N03 G20 | (set input mode to inch) |
| N04 G00 X0 Y0 Z0.6 | (rapid to home position $P_0$) |
| N05 G01 Z0.45 | (apply depth of cut) |
| N06 G01 X3 | (go to $P_1$ to mill the first cut) |
| N07 G01 Y0.5 | (go to $P_2$ to move the mill to the second cutline) |
| N08 G01 X0 | (go to $P_3$ to mill the second cut) |
| N09 G01 Y1 | (go to $P_4$ to move the mill to the third cutline) |
| N10 G01 X3 | (go to $P_5$ to mill the third cut) |
| N11 G01 Y1.5 | (go to $P_6$ to move the mill to the fourth cutline) |
| N12 G01 X0 | (go to $P_7$ to mill the fourth cut) |
| N13 G01 Y2 | (go to $P_8$ to move the mill to the fifth cutline) |
| N14 G01 X3 | (go to $P_9$ to mill the fifth and last cut) |
| N15 G01 Z0.55 | (lift mill by 0.1 in. from newly milled face to clear the workpiece) |
| N16 G00 X0 Y0 | (rapid to home position $P_0$) |
| N17 M05 | (turn spindle off) |
| N18 M00 | (stop machine) |

## 15.11 SolidWorks DFMXpress

SolidWorks implements the concept of DFM in **DFMXpress**. **DFMXpress** validates the manufacturability of SolidWorks parts. It identifies design areas where manufacturing may have a problem or production cost may be excessive. SolidWorks uses three DFM categories: rule description, configuration rules, and validating parts. Rule description provides rules for turning, drilling, milling, sheet metal, as well as standard hole sizes.

Turning rules discuss corner radii and reliefs as follows:

- ☐ When designing stepped shafts, have large enough diameters at the changeover edges to allow for using a tool with large nose radius.
- ☐ Provide tool relief for the bottoms of blind bored holes.

Drilling rules discuss hole diameters, holes with flat bottoms, hole entry and exit surfaces, holes intersecting cavities, partial holes, and linear and angular tolerances. Here are the drilling rules:

- ☐ Avoid holes with small diameters (< 3 mm) or large length-to-diameter ratio (> 2.75) because these holes are difficult to machine. For example, deep holes make chip removal difficult, especially if the hole is blind.
- ☐ Avoid flat-bottom holes. Use conical bottoms with angles that conform to standard drills. Flat-bottom holes have to be milled and/or reamed, two expensive operations.
- ☐ Entry and exit surfaces of holes should be perpendicular to the hole axis to minimize the shear forces on the drill bit causing it to wander or break on impact when it meets the surface.
- ☐ If a hole must intersect a cavity, the drill axis should be outside the cavity to minimize the impact of contact.
- ☐ Holes drilled on edges of features should have 75% of the hole area within the feature material.
- ☐ Tolerances should not be tighter than necessary.

Milling rules discuss deep pockets and slots, inaccessible features, sharp internal corners, and fillets on outside edges. Here are the milling rules:

- ☐ Avoid narrow slots because they are difficult to machine. Long, slender end mills required to machine them cannot meet the tolerance requirements because the tools are prone to chatter. Deep slots also make chip removal difficult.
- ☐ Avoid long corners with long radii.
- ☐ Design milled areas so that the ratio of end mill length-to-diameter ratio is ≤3.
- ☐ Avoid inaccessible features because they require special tools and machining techniques.
- ☐ Avoid sharp inside corners. For example, a pocket with sharp corners cannot be milled. We have to use EDM to cut it. A three-edge inside corner must have one of its corners with a radius equal to the radius of the end mill. If sharp corner cannot be avoided, drill a relief hole first at the corner and then mill.
- ☐ Always chamfer outside edges instead of filleting them. An outside fillet is expensive to machine because it requires a form-relieved cutter and a precise setup. Also, blending fillets into existing surfaces is expensive to manufacture, even with a ball-end mill.

Sheet metal rules discuss hole diameters, hole-to-edge distances, hole spacing, and bend radii. Here are the rules:

☐ Avoid designing parts with very small holes. Small drill bits can break easily.
☐ Have holes far enough from an edge or bend to avoid distorting the edge.
☐ Space holes well apart so the material between them does not become weak and get distorted.
☐ Do not use excessive bend; otherwise, the material might crack. A rule of thumb is to have the bend radius larger than the material thickness.

The standard hole sizes rule is simple to follow. Hole sizes should be based on the sizes of standard drill bits.

**DFMXpress** implements all these rules and helps the designer implement them. To find all these rules, click this sequence: **Tools => DFMXpress => Settings** => Select a manufacturing process to access its rules as discussed above. Also, **DFMXpress** can validate these rules for a given part design. After selecting a process from the above sequence, click **Run** and investigate the results. Figure 15.14 shows the **DFMXpress** interface. Figure 15.15 shows the standard hole sizes. To access these sizes, click the **Edit** button at the bottom of the **DFMXpress** pane.

**FIGURE 15.14**
DFMXpress rules

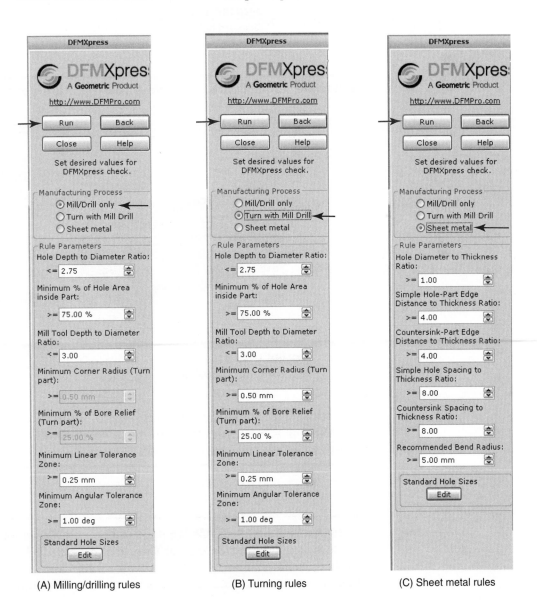

(A) Milling/drilling rules  (B) Turning rules  (C) Sheet metal rules

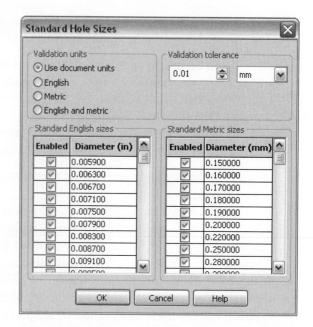

**FIGURE 15.15**
Standard hole sizes

---

**Example 15.4**   Figure 15.16 shows a part. Check the part manufacturability.

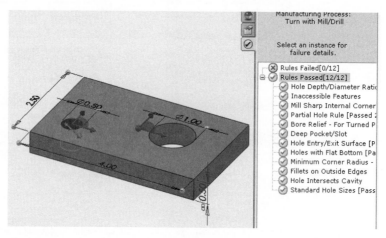

**FIGURE 15.16**
Check part manufacturability

**Solution**   While the part is open, access **DFMXpress** by clicking **Tools =>** **DFMXpress => Settings => Mill/Drill only => Run**. The results shown in Figure 15.15 indicate that the part passed DFM analysis.

---

**HANDS-ON FOR EXAMPLE 15.4.** Edit the part to move the small hole very close to the left bottom corner. Does the part pass DFM analysis? What errors do you get?

## 15.12 CAMWorks

CAMWorks is an NC software that is fully integrated into SolidWorks. CAMWorks is a separate installation from SolidWorks. However, when you install it, it becomes integrated with SolidWorks. After installation, you see CAMWorks on SolidWorks menu bar and as a separate tab, as shown in Figure 15.17. Also, CAMWorks has its own Help menu under SolidWorks Help. To access it, click SolidWorks **Help => CAMWorks 2009**.

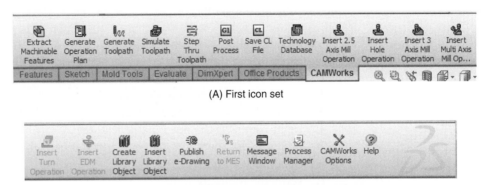

(A) First icon set

(B) Second icon set

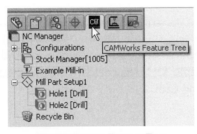

(C) CAMWorks Feature Tree

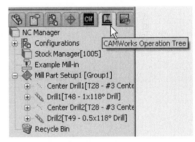

(D) CAMWorks Operation Tree

**FIGURE 15.17**
CAMWorks user interface

Figure 15.17 shows **CAMWorks** menu. CAMWorks supports turning, drilling, milling, and EDM machining operations. It also provides toolpath generation and verification, as well as post-processing by generating and saving CL data files. Figure 15.17 shows two sets of CAMWorks icons. We break up the **CAMWorks** toolbar to these two sets for visual clarity. CAMWorks implements the machining concepts covered in this chapter. It supports 2½-, 3-, and multi-axis milling. An NC programmer can generate a machining operation plan and a toolpath for a machining operation, verify (simulate) the toolpath, and post-process it. CAMWorks outputs toolpaths in G-code and M-code. It also enables the programmer to save the toolpath in a CL file.

CAMWorks has built-in intelligence and knowledge-based rules that allow the user to extract machinable features and generate operation plans, as shown in the icons of Figure 15.17A. CAMWorks also comes with a **Technology Database** that contains the data for the machining process plans. It allows the user to define machines, features, speeds, feedrates, and operations. The database is customizable by the user. CAMWorks supports knowledge reuse by allowing the user to save machining features and operations of one part, as objects, into a library (**Create Library Object** icon in Figure 15.17B) for reuse to machine other parts (**Insert Library Object**).

The last three icons shown in Figure 15.17B display information (**Message Window** and **Process Manager**) and set up machining options (**CAMWorks Options**).

Upon installing CAMWorks, it creates the two tabs shown in Figures 15.17C and 15.17D. The **CAMWorks Feature Tree** shows the machinable features identified by CAMWorks when you click the **Extract Machinable Features** icon shown in Figure 15.17A. The **CAMWorks Operation Tree** shows the machining plan (steps) when you click the **Generate Operation Plan** icon shown in Figure 15.17A. The **Recycle Bin** in both tabs behaves as you would expect. It holds the machinable features and steps that you delete from both trees. You must delete the **Recycle Bin** content to completely remove deleted items. You can use the **Recycle Bin** to store machinable features that you do not intend to machine.

The use of CAMWorks to generate toolpaths follows the same steps for its four machining operations (turning, drilling, milling, and EDM):

1. Create the part in SolidWorks.
2. Define the machine and the controller.
3. Define the stock (shape and size).
4. Define (extract) the machinable features.
5. Generate the operation plan and adjust the machining parameters if needed.
6. Generate the toolpath.
7. Verify the toolpath, if needed
8. Post-process the toolpath to generate the CL (G-code and M-code) file.

---

**Example 15.5**  Generate the CL file for turning the shaft shown in Figure 15.11. Compare the G-code and M-code with the manual code shown in Example 15.1. Figure 15.18 shows the turning toolpath and the cutting tool.

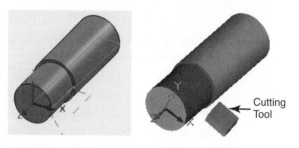

**FIGURE 15.18**
Toolpath to turn a shaft

**Solution**  We do this example to compare the manual code we wrote in Example 15.1 to the code that CAMWorks generates. We keep the machining parameters the same as in Example 15.1. The general steps to create the toolpath are:

1. Create the stepped shaft CAD model.
2. Extract the machinable features.
3. Generate the operation plan to machine the features identified in Step 3.
4. Define the machining parameters.
5. Generate the toolpath.
6. Verify the toolpath.
7. Post-process the toolpath to generate the G-code and M-code.

The details of each step are shown below.

## Step 1: Create the stepped shaft CAD model

### Task

A. Start SolidWorks, open a new part, create the shaft as two extrusions (see below), and save it as *example 15.5*.

 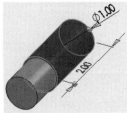

### Command Sequence to Click

**Open => New = Part** => Create the shaft. Use the front plane to create the shaft sketch => **Save As** => *example 15.5* => **Save** as shown to the left. **Help:** Start with the front plane as sketch plane, create the 1.00 in. diameter circle, and extrude 2.00 in. Then, select the shaft flat face as a sketch plane, create the 0.90 in. diameter circle (as shown to the left), and extrude 1.00 in.

## Step 2: Extract the machinable features

### Task

A. Select a turning machine.

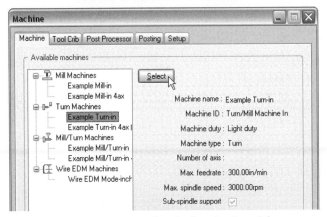

### Command Sequence to Click

**CAMWorks** tab => Right-click **Example Mill-mm** (shown to the left) => **Edit Definition** => Select **Example Turn-in machine** (shown to the left) => **Select** (button shown to the left) => **OK**.

**Help:** This sequence opens the **Machine** window shown to the left and selects a turning machine. We need to change the default milling machine to a turning machine.

The **Machine** window has multiple tabs that can be used to customize the selected machine tool.

**Why:** You must click the **Select** button (shown to the left) because selecting the machine only (highlighting it) does not set it.

B. Extract the shaft cylindrical face that is 1.00 long to turn.

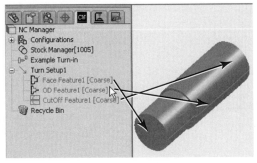

**Extract Machinable Features** (on **CAMWorks** tab)

**Help:** CAMWorks extracts the three turnable features and adds them to the **CAMWorks Feature Tree** as shown to the left. If you hover over a feature, it is highlighted in the graphics pane as shown to the left.

**Why:** We only need to turn the stepped part of the shaft for this example to

| Task | Command Sequence to Click |
|---|---|

compare the G-code and M-code with the manual approach we used in Example 15.1. As such, we delete the first and last features, and keep only the middle feature. We also modify the middle feature to keep on the stepped part of it as we show in the next step.

Right-click **Face Feature1 [Coarse]** **=> Delete => Yes**

Right-click **CutOff Feature1 [Coarse] => Delete => Yes**

**C.** Define the stepped feature we want to turn for this example.

Right-click **OD Feature1 [Coarse] => Insert Turn Feature** => Select the centerline of the shaft (shown to the left) => **Extend 2** => Select the stepped cross section (shown to the left) => Select **Extend2** => Select **Along X** **=> OK.**

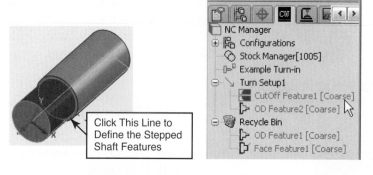

Click This Line to Define the Stepped Shaft Features

Right-click **OD Feature1 [Coarse] => Delete => Yes**

**Help:** The features you delete go to the **Recycle Bin** indicating that you do not want to machine them. You can restore them or delete them permanently. Right-click any of them and select an option.

**Why:** We delete the original **OD Feature1 [Coarse]** because we do not want to turn the entire shaft in this example. We turn only the stepped part, now defined by **OD Feature2 [Coarse]**.

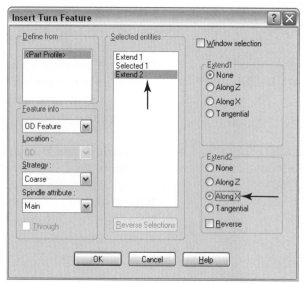

## Step 3: Generate the operation plan

| Task | Command Sequence to Click |
|---|---|

**A.** Generate the machining operation we need to turn the stepped shaft.

**Generate Operation Plan** (on **CAMWorks** tab)

Right-click **Turn Rough1[...]** shown to the left => **Delete => Yes**.

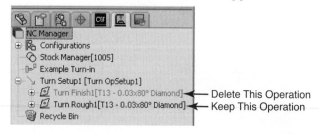

Delete This Operation
Keep This Operation

**Why:** The operation plan generates the two tree nodes in the **CAMWorks Operation Tree** as shown to the left. The two operations are roughing and finishing. We delete the finishing operation to compare with the manual code.

## Step 4: Define the machining parameters

| Task | Command Sequence to Click |
|---|---|
| **A.** Specify the spindle speed of 1500 RP and the feedrate of 1.0 in./min. | Right-click the **Turn Rough1[...]** node => **Edit Definition** => **NC** (tab in the **Operation Parameters** window that opens up and is shown to the left) => Make the changes shown to the left for the spindle data and feedrate => **OK**. **Help:** We set the **Retract type** to **None** as shown to the left to be close to the manual operation we have in Example 15.1. |

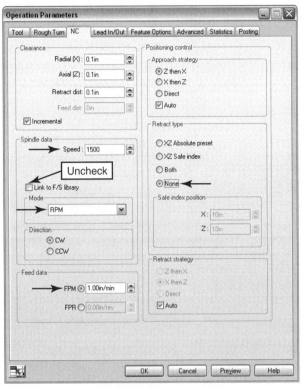

## Step 5: Generate the toolpath

| Task | Command Sequence to Click |
|---|---|
| **A.** Generate the toolpath for the one turning operation (rough turning). | **Generate Toolpath** (on **CAMWorks** tab) |

## Step 6: Verify the toolpath

| Task | Command Sequence to Click |
|---|---|
| **A.** Verify the toolpath. | **Simulate Toolpath** (on **CAMWorks** tab) **Help:** The **Simulate Toolpath** opens the **Toolpath Simulation** window shown to the left. It also shows the stock as shown to the left. When you play the simulation, the cutting tool follows the toolpath and turns the shaft. **Help:** Investigate the different icons of the **Toolpath Simulation** window shown to the left to learn more. |

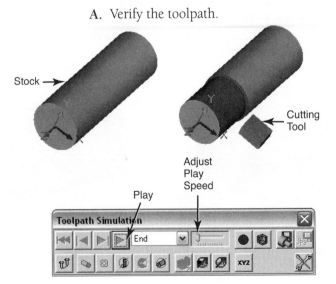

## Step 7: Post-process the toolpath

| Task | Command Sequence to Click |
|---|---|
| A. Generate the G-code and M-code shown below. | **Post Process** (on **CAMWorks** tab) => type *turnExample* as the file name (in the window that opens up) to save the code => **Save** => **Play** button shown to the left => **OK**. |

Command Sequence continued:

**Help:** When you open *turnExample.txt* file, it has the following G-code and M-code (compare with the manual code):

O0001
(Main Spindle)
(Must Customize Main Spindle Per
    Machine)
N1 G50 S3000
N2 T1300 M42
N3 G00 G97 S1500 M03
N4 G98
N5 G00 X1.2614 T1313 M08
N6 Z.2707
N7 X1.0614 Z.1707
N8 G01 X.92 Z.1 F1.
N9 Z-.99
N10 X1.1374
N11 X1.2788 Z-.9193
N12 M30

---

**HANDS-ON FOR EXAMPLE 15.5.** Change the example code to turn a circular cut in the middle of the shaft. The cut length is ½ in. *Note:* This is the same hands-on as for Example 15.1.

---

**Example 15.6** Generate the CL file for drilling the holes shown in Figure 15.11. Compare the G-code and M-code with the manual code shown in Example 15.2. Figure 15.19 shows the drilling toolpath and the cutting tool.

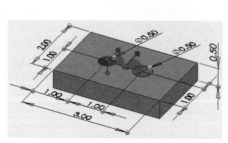

(A) CAD model

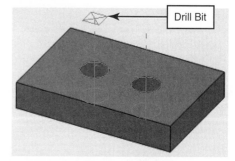

(B) Drilling toolpath

**FIGURE 15.19**
Toolpath to drill holes

**Solution**   We use this example to compare the manual code we wrote in Example 15.2 to the code that CAMWorks generates. We keep the machining parameters the same as in Example 15.2. The general steps to create the toolpath are:

1. Create the CAD model.
2. Extract the machinable features.
3. Generate the operation plan to drill the holes.
4. Define the machining parameters.
5. Generate the toolpath.
6. Verify the toolpath.
7. Post-process the toolpath to generate the G-code and M-code.

The details of each step are shown below.

## Step 1:   Create the CAD model

### Task

A. Start SolidWorks, open a new part, create the block with the two holes as an extrusion, and save it as *example 15.6*.

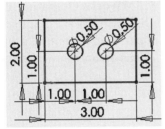

### Command Sequence to Click

**Open => New => Part** => Create the block with the holes. Use the top plane to create the block sketch => **Save As** => *example15.6* => **Save** as shown to the left.
**Help:** Block thickness is 0.5 in.

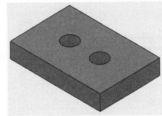

## Step 2:   Extract the machinable features

### Task

A. Select a milling machine. There is no drilling machine, per se. Drilling is done on either a milling or a turning machine.

B. Extract the two holes we need to drill.

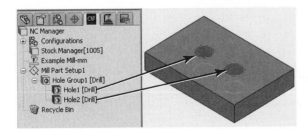

### Command Sequence to Click

**CAMWorks** (tab)
**Help: Example Mill-mm** in the **CAMWorks Feature Tree** should be the default. If not, set it up (see Example 15.5).
**Extract Machinable Features** (on **CAMWorks** tab)
**Help:** CAMWorks extracts the two drillable features and adds them to the **CAMWorks Feature Tree** as shown to the left. If you hover over a feature, it is highlighted in the graphics pane as shown to the left.

## Step 3:  Generate the operation plan

### Task

A. Generate the machining operation
we need to turn the stepped shaft.

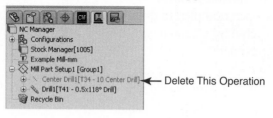

— Delete This Operation

### Command Sequence to Click

**Generate Operation Plan** (on
**CAMWorks** tab)
Right-click **Center Drill1[...]** shown to
the right => **Delete => Yes**.
**Why:** The operation plan generates the
two tree nodes in the **CAMWorks
Operation Tree** as shown to the left.
The two operations are center drilling
and drilling. We delete the center
drilling operation to compare with the
manual code. Center drill is similar to
spotting.

## Step 4:  Define the machining parameters

### Task

A. Specify the spindle speed of 5000 RPM
and the feedrate of 2.5 in./min.

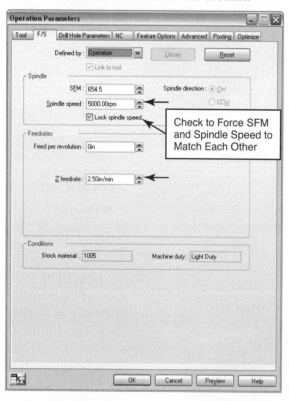

Check to Force SFM
and Spindle Speed to
Match Each Other

### Command Sequence to Click

Right-click the **Drill1[...]** node in
**CAMWorks Operation Tree => Edit
Definition => F/S** (tab in the
**Operation Parameters** window that
opens up and shown to the left) =>
Make the changes shown to the left for
the spindle data and feedrate => **OK**.

## Step 5:  Generate the toolpath

### Task

A. Generate the toolpath for the one
drilling operation.

### Command Sequence to Click

**Generate Toolpath** (on **CAMWorks**
tab)

## Step 6: Verify the toolpath

### Task

A. Verify the toolpath.

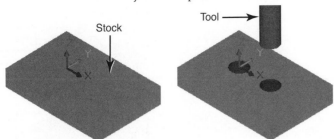

Stock

Tool →

### Command Sequence to Click

**Simulate Toolpath** (on **CAMWorks** tab)

**Help:** The **Simulate Toolpath** opens the **Toolpath Simulation** window. When you play the simulation, the drill bit follows the toolpath and drills the two holes as shown to the left.

## Step 7: Post-process the toolpath

### Task

A. Generate the G-code and M-code shown below.

### Command Sequence to Click

**Post Process** (on **CAMWorks** tab) => Type *turnExample* as the file name (in the window that opens up) to save the code => **Save** => **Play** button shown to the left => **OK**.

**Help:** When you open *turnExample.txt* file, it has the following G-code and M-code (compare with the manual code):

```
O0001
N1 G20
N2 (1/2 JOBBER DRILL)
N3 G91 G28 X0 Y0 Z0
N4 T41 M06
N5 S5000 M03
N6 G90 G54 G00 X0 Y0
N7 G43 Z.1 H41 M08
N8 G81 G99 R.1 Z-.7001 F2.5
N9 X1.
N10 G80 Z1. M09
N11 G91 G28 Z0
N12 G28 X0 Y0
N13 M30
```

---

**HANDS-ON FOR EXAMPLE 15.6.** Add counterbores to the top of both holes. The diameter of each counterbore is 0.75 in.

**Example 15.7**  Generate the CL file for milling the top face shown in Figure 15.12. Compare the G-code and M-code with the manual code shown in Example 15.3. Figure 15.20 shows the milling toolpath and the cutting tool.

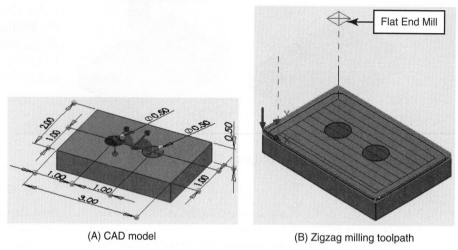

(A) CAD model                    (B) Zigzag milling toolpath

**FIGURE 15.20**
Toolpath to mill top face

**Solution**  We use this example to compare the manual code we wrote in Example 15.3 to the code that CAMWorks generates. We keep the machining parameters the same as in Example 15.3. The general steps to create the toolpath are:

1. Create the CAD model.
2. Extract the machinable features.
3. Generate the operation plan to mill the top face.
4. Define the machining parameters.
5. Generate the toolpath.
6. Verify the toolpath.
7. Post-process the toolpath to generate the G-code and M-code.

The details of each step are shown below.

## Step 1:  Create the CAD model

| Task | Command Sequence to Click |
|---|---|
| A. Start SolidWorks, open a new part, create the block with the two holes as an extrusion, and save it as *example 15.7*. 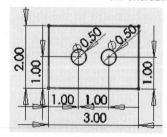 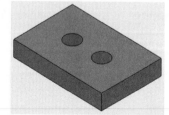 | **Open => New = Part** => Create the block with the holes. Use the top plane to create the block sketch => **Save As** => *example15.7* => **Save** as shown to the left.<br>**Help:** Block thickness is 0.5 in. |

## Step 2: Extract the machinable features

| Task | Command Sequence to Click |
|---|---|
| A. Select a milling machine. | **CAMWorks** (tab) => Right-click **Example Mill-mm** in the **CAMWorks Feature Tree** => **Edit Definition** => Select **Example Mill-in** => **Select** => **OK** (see Example 15.5). |

B. Create a milling part setup and define the top plane as the machining plane.

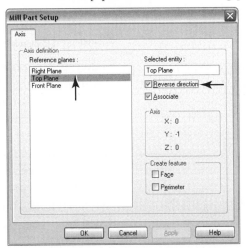

Right-click **Stock Manager[1005]** in the **CAMWorks Feature Tree** => **Insert Mill Part Setup** => Change setup as shown to the left => **OK** as shown to the left.

**Why:** We want to mill the top face using an end mill. Thus, we set up the top plane as the cutting plane and the –Y direction as the tool cutting direction as shown to the left.

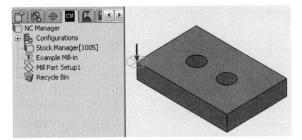

C. Define the top face as the face to mill.

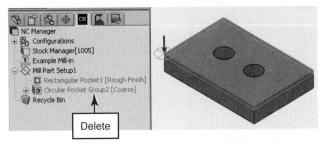

Right-click **Mill Part Setup1** (see screenshot in Task B above) => **Insert 2.5 Axis Feature** => Select **Sketch1** as shown to the left => **Next** => Change depth to 0.1 as shown to the left => **Next** => **Finish** => **Close**.

**Why:** We set the depth of cut to 0.1 to cut one pass to be consistent with Example 15.3.

**Why:** We delete the milling of the two holes from the tree shown to the left to be consistent with Example 15.3.

**Help:** When you select **Sketch 1** (see leftmost screenshot shown to the left), the **Next** button is activated. When you click it, you are able to set the cut depth (see rightmost screenshot shown to the left).

| Task | Command Sequence to Click |
|---|---|
| | **Help:** The bottom screenshot shown to the left shows the results of this step. It shows the tool orientation and two machinable features: the top face (**Rectangular Pocket1[...]**) and the two holes (**Circular Pocket Group2 [...]**). We delete the group to be consistent with Example 15.3. |

## Step 3: Generate the operation plan

| Task | Command Sequence to Click |
|---|---|
| A. Generate the machining operation that we need to mill the top face of the block. | **Generate Operation Plan** (on **CAMWorks** tab) |
| 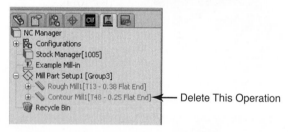 | Right-click **Contour Mil[...]** shown to the left => **Delete** => **Yes**. |
| | **Why:** The operation plan generates the two tree nodes in the **CAMWorks Operation Tree** as shown to the left. We delete the contour milling operation to be consistent with Example 15.3. |

## Step 4: Define the machining parameters

| Task | Command Sequence to Click |
|---|---|
| A. Specify the spindle speed of 5000 RPM and the feedrate of 250 in./min. | Right-click the **Rough Mill1[...]** node in **CAMWorks Operation Tree** => **Edit Definition** => **F/S** (tab in the **Operation Parameters** window that opens up and shown to the left) => Make the changes shown to the left for the spindle data and the feedrate => **OK**. |
| 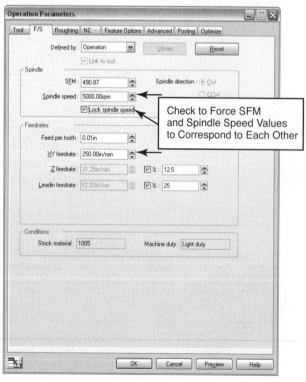 | |

## Step 5:  Generate the toolpath

### Task

A. Generate the toolpath for the milling operation.

### Command Sequence to Click

**Generate Toolpath** (on **CAMWorks** tab)

## Step 6:  Verify the toolpath

### Task

A. Verify the toolpath.

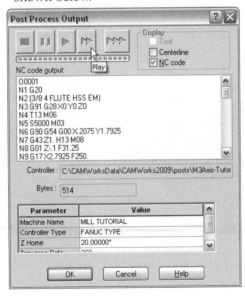

### Command Sequence to Click

**Simulate Toolpath** (on **CAMWorks** tab)

**Help:** The **Simulate Toolpath** opens the **Toolpath Simulation** window. When you play the simulation, the flat-end mill follows the toolpath and mills the top face.

## Step 7:  Post-process the toolpath

### Task

A. Generate the G-code and M-code shown below.

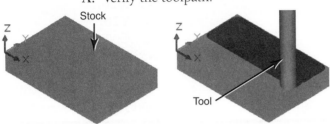

### Command Sequence to Click

**Post Process** (on **CAMWorks** tab) => Type *millExample* as the file name (in the window that opens up) to save the code => **Save** => **Play** button shown to the left => **OK**.

**Help:** When you open *millExample.txt* file, it has the following G-code and M-code (compare with the manual code):

O0001
N1 G20
N2 (3/8 4 FLUTE HSS EM)
N3 G91 G28 X0 Y0 Z0
N4 T13 M06
N5 S5000 M03
N6 G90 G54 G00 X.2075 Y1.7925
N7 G43 Z1. H13 M08
N8 G01 Z-.1 F31.25
N9 G17 X2.7925 F250.
N10 Y1.605
N11 X.2075
N12 Y1.4175
N13 X2.7925
N14 Y1.23
N15 X.2075
N16 Y1.0425
N17 X2.7925
N18 Y.855
N19 X.2075
N20 Y.6675

| Task | Command Sequence to Click |
|---|---|
| | N21 X2.7925 |
| | N22 Y.48 |
| | N23 X.2075 |
| | N24 Y.2925 |
| | N25 X2.7925 |
| | N26 Y.2075 |
| | N27 X.2075 |
| | N28 X2.7925 |
| | N29 Y1.7925 |
| | N30 X.2075 |
| | N31 Y.2075 |
| | N32 G00 Z1. |
| | N33 Z5. M09 |
| | N34 G91 G28 Z0 |
| | N35 G28 X0 Y0 |
| | N36 M30 |

**HANDS-ON FOR EXAMPLE 15.7.** Add side (contour) milling to the example toolpath; that is, side mill the four sides of the block.

**Example 15.8** Use wire EDM to machine the part shown in Figure 15.21. Figure 15.21 shows the wire EDM toolpath and the cutting tool.

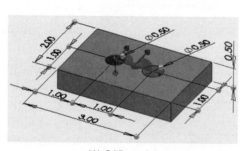

(A) CAD model

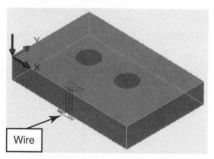

(B) Wire EDM toolpath (one contour)

**FIGURE 15.21**
Toolpath to machine a block using wire EDM

**Solution** Unlike the other examples, we machine all the part features in this example. The general steps to create the toolpath are:

1. Create the CAD model.
2. Extract the machinable features.
3. Generate the operation plan to mill the top face.
4. Define the machining parameters.
5. Generate the toolpath.
6. Verify the toolpath.
7. Post-process the toolpath to generate the G-code and M-code.

The details of each step are shown below.

# Step 1: Create the CAD model

### Task

A. Start SolidWorks, open a new part, create the block with the two holes as an extrusion, and save it as *example15.8*.

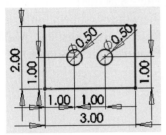 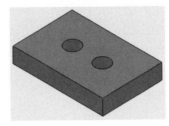

### Command Sequence to Click

**Open => New = Part** => Create the block with the holes. Use the top plane to create the block sketch => **Save As** => *example15.8* => **Save** as shown to the left.
**Help:** Block thickness is 0.5 in.

# Step 2: Extract the machinable features

### Task

A. Select a wire EDM machine.

B. Create a wire EDM part setup and define the machinable features.

### Command Sequence to Click

**CAMWorks** (tab) => Right-click **Example Mill-mm** in the **CAMWorks Feature Tree** => **Edit Definition** => Select **Wire EDM Mode-inch** => **Select** => **OK** (see Example 15.5). Right-click **Stock Manager[TOOLSTEEL]** in the **CAMWorks Feature Tree** => **Insert Part Setup** => Change setup as shown to the left => **OK.**
**Why:** We set up the cutting wire so that it is vertical, similar to mills and drills.

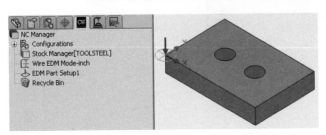

| Task | Command Sequence to Click |
|---|---|
| C. Define the features to machine. | Right-click **EDM Part Setup1** (see screenshot in Task B above) => **Insert 2.5 Axis EDM Feature** => Select **Sketch1** as shown to the left => **Insert** => **Close**. |

Help: When you select **Sketch1**, CAMWorks creates **Die - 1**, **Die - 2**, and **Die - 3** as the features. When you close the window shown to the left, the features are added to **CAMWorks Feature Tree** as shown to the left.

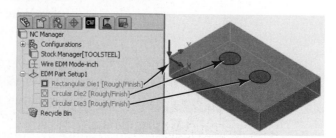

## Step 3: Generate the operation plan

| Task | Command Sequence to Click |
|---|---|
| A. Generate the wire EDM machining plan. | **Generate Operation Plan** (on **CAMWorks** tab) |

## Step 4:  Define the machining parameters

Task

A. Specify the machining parameters.

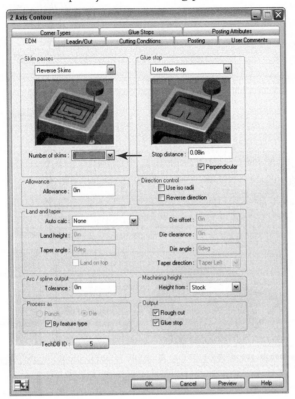

Command Sequence to Click

Right-click the **2 Axis Contour1** node in **CAMWorks Operation Tree =>
Edit Definition => EDM** (tab in the **2 Axis Contour** window that opens up and shown to the left) **=>** Select 1 for **Number of skims** as shown to the left **=> OK**.

Repeat the above sequence for the other two operations.

**Why:** We change the number of skims (passes) from 2 to 1 to keep the length of the G-code and M-code manageable, so we can inspect it manually.

## Step 5:  Generate the toolpath

Task

A. Generate the toolpath for the wire EDM operations.

Command Sequence to Click

**Generate Toolpath** (on **CAMWorks** tab)

## Step 6:  Verify the toolpath

Task

A. Verify the toolpath.

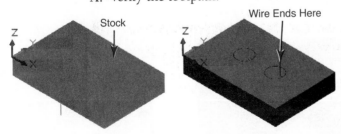

Command Sequence to Click

**Simulate Toolpath** (on **CAMWorks** tab)

**Help:** The **Simulate Toolpath** opens the **Toolpath Simulation** window. When you play the simulation, the EDM wire follows the toolpath. It starts by machining the workpiece contour (sides), then the hole on the left, followed by the hole on the right. This is the sequence specified by the operation plan shown in Step 3.

## Step 7: Post-process the toolpath

**Task**

A. Generate the G-code and M-code shown below.

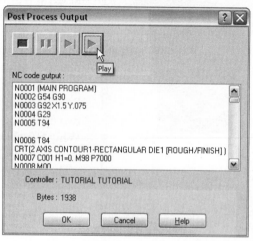

**Command Sequence to Click**

**Post Process** (on **CAMWorks** tab) => Type *wireEDMExample* as the file name (in the window that opens up) to save the code => **Save** => **Play** button shown to the left => **OK**.

**Help:** When you open *wireEDMExample.txt* file, it has the G-code and M-code (first few lines are shown here):

N0001 (MAIN PROGRAM)

N0002 G54 G90

N0003 G92 X1.5 Y.075

N0004 G29

N0005 T94

N0006 T84

CRT(2 AXIS CONTOUR1-RECTANGULAR DIE1 [ROUGH/FINISH] )

N0007 C001 H1 = 0. M98 P7000

N0008 M00

---

> **HANDS-ON FOR EXAMPLE 15.8.** Add top face machining to the example toolpath; that is, wire EDM machine the top face of the block.

---

## 15.13 Tutorials Overview

The theme for the tutorials in this chapter is to practice using the manufacturing and NC programming concepts implemented by both SolidWorks **DFMXpress** and CAMWorks. The tutorials show how to use **DFMXpress** menus and CAMWorks turning, drilling, milling, and wire EDM machining. Extol Inc., in Zeeland, MI, USA (www.extolinc.com), has sponsored this chapter. Extol Inc. is an industry leader specializing in designing and manufacturing innovative, creative, and efficient plastic-joining equipment as well as custom factory automation equipment. We chat with Mr. Marc Meeuwsen, Development Design Engineer, and Mr. Charlie Weaver, Lead CNC Engineer, of Extol Inc. in the Industry Chat. Figure 15.22 shows sample products of Extol Inc. Figure 15.22

**FIGURE 15.22**
Sample products (Courtesy of Extol Inc.)

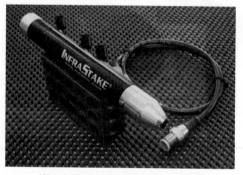

(A) InfraStake Head (Actual product)

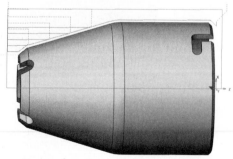

(B) InfraStake Head (CAMWorks toolpath)

shows an InfraStake® head part used in an InfraStake product. The product is used for joining two or more pieces of plastic together in the automotive, medical, and consumer electronics industries, to name a few. Figure 15.22A shows the finished head mounted on the InfraStake product. Figure 15.22B shows the lathe cutter toolpath to machine the OD (outer diameter) of the part. Other machining operations that the part requires include ID (inner diameter) turning and machining the slots at both ends.

## Tutorial 15–1:  Mill and Drill a Pattern Block

**FIGURE 15.23**
Pattern block

### Machining task

Generate milling and drilling toolpaths for the pattern block shown in Figure 15.23.

### Machining synthesis

There are multiple toolpaths that we can use to machine this block.

### Machining plan

Create mill and drill toolpaths for the pattern block shown in Figure 15.23.

### Design intent

Ignore for this chapter.

### Machining steps

We create the toolpath in seven steps:

1. Create the pattern block.
2. Create a pocket in the part.
3. Define the stock.
4. Define the machine.
5. Define the machinable features.
6. Generate the operation plan.
7. Generate the toolpath.

The details of these steps are shown below.

## Step 1:  Create the pattern block

| Task | Command Sequence to Click |
|---|---|
| A. Create the pattern block.  | **Create the pattern block** as shown to the left. **Help:** The dimensions of the pattern block are shown in Problem 36 of Chapter 2. |

## Step 2: Create a pocket in the part

**Task**

A. Create a rounded-corners square pocket in the block.

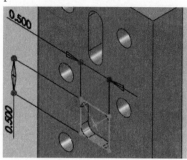

B. Suppress the slots.

**Command Sequence to Click**

**Features => Extruded Cut =>** Sketch as shown to the left => Enter .125 in. for depth => **Features => Fillets => 0.125 for radius** as shown to the left.
**Why:** We add a pocket and use it to show how to machine a pocket.

Right-click **Extrude3** and **Mirror1 => Suppress** as shown to the left.
**Why:** We suppress the slots to simplify the resulting toolpath.

## Step 3: Define the stock

**Task**

A. Switch over to the **CAMWorks Feature Tree.**

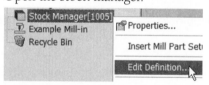

B. Open the stock manager.

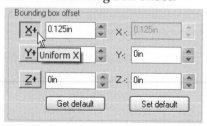

C. Edit the **Bounding box offset.**

**Command Sequence to Click**

Select the **CAMWorks** tab as shown to the left.

Right-click **Stock Manager** in **CAMWorks Feature Tree => Edit Definition**

Enter .125 in. for the X offset value => Depress the **X+** button for **Uniform X** as shown to the left.
**Why:** We create a stock piece of material that is larger than the final part by 0.125 in. on all sides. The excess material is to be removed by a milling operation later.

| Task | Command Sequence to Click |
|------|---------------------------|

**D.** Repeat Task C for the Y and Z values.

**A.** Edit the stock material.

Repeat Task C for the Y and Z values.
**Help:** Do not make the Z value uniform; i.e., do not depress it as shown to the left.
**Why:** We do not want the Z value to be uniform because we do not want to add stock at the bottom of the workpiece (−Z) to avoid flipping it to machine its bottom, for simplicity.
In the **Manage Stock** window that has been opened in Task B of Step 3, click the **Material** drop-down list shown to the left => Select **6061** => **OK**.

## Step 4: Define the machine

### Task

**A.** Define the type of machine that we use to complete all of the milling and drilling operations.

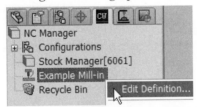

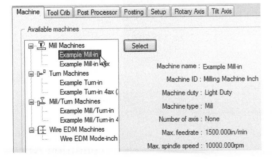

### Command Sequence to Click

Right-click **Example Mill-in** =>
**Machine** tab as shown to the left =>
A list of the machines and tools that are entered into the database is shown to the left. If this were your machine shop, you would select the appropriate machine and tool crib to complete the operations. For now we exit and use the default machine and tools.

## Step 5: Define the machinable features

### Task

**A.** Use the **Automatic Feature Recognition (AFR)** to identify all of the features that will be milled or drilled.

### Command Sequence to Click

Right-click **NC Manager** => **Extract Machinable Features** as shown to the left

| Task | Command Sequence to Click |
|---|---|

**B.** View the results of the AFR.

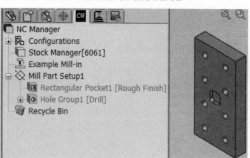

The **AFR** identifies the pocket in the center of the part as **Rectangular Pocket1** and **Hole Group1** as shown to the left.

**C.** Add a milling operation to remove the excess stock material.

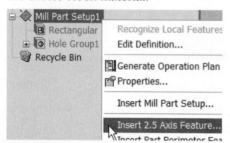

Select the front of the part => Right-click **Mill Part Setup1** => **Insert 2.5 Axis Feature** as shown to the left.

**D.** Set up the options.

Set the options shown to the left => **Next**.

**E.** Select the end condition.

Select **Upto Stock** for the **End condition** type => **Finish** => **Close** as shown to the left.

## Step 6: Generate the operation plan

| Task | Command Sequence to Click |
|---|---|

**A.** Generate the operation plan.

Right-click **Mill Part Setup1** => **Generate Operation Plan**
Why: **Generate Operations Plan** organizes the method, the tool, and in which order each feature is milled or drilled and is listed under the **CAMWorks Operation Tree**.

| Task | Command Sequence to Click |
|------|---------------------------|

B. Modify the operation for the pocket at the center of the part.

Right-click **Rough Mill2 => Edit Definition**

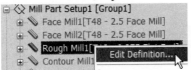

C. Change the pocketing pattern to zigzag.

**Roughing** tab => **Pattern** (drop-down list) => **Zigzag** as shown to the left

D. Set the feature options to entry hole.

**Feature Options** tab => **Method** (drop-down list) => **Entry Hole** => **OK** as shown to the left

## Step 7:  Generate the toolpath

| Task | Command Sequence to Click |
|------|---------------------------|

A. Generate the toolpaths.

**Mill Part Setup1 => Generate Toolpath** as shown to the left

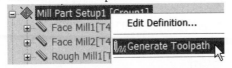

B. Review the toolpath.

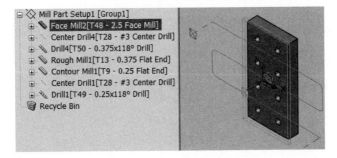

Each operation is shown in the **CAMWorks Operation Tree** as shown to the left. If you select an operation, the toolpath is highlighted in the graphics pane.

| Task | Command Sequence to Click |
|---|---|

**C.** Simulate the toolpath.

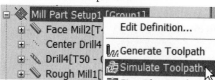

Right-click **Mill Part Setup1 =>
Simulate Toolpath** as shown to the left

**D.** Use the simulation tools to watch and verify the toolpath and operations as shown below.

**E.** Optimize the center drill toolpath.

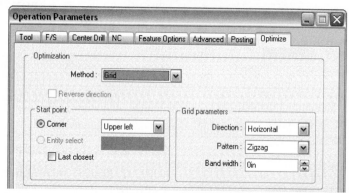

Right-click **Center Drill1 => Edit
Definition => Optimize** tab =>
**Method => Grid => OK** as shown to
the left.
**Help:** The default optimization method
is shortest path. We change it as shown
to the left to **Grid** to introduce the
concept of toolpath optimization.

**F.** Review the updated Center Drill1 toolpath.

The two screenshots shown to the left
picture the two optimization methods.
Distance wise, they are identical.

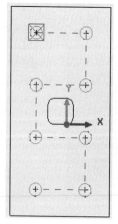

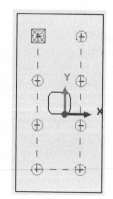

Shortest path optimization    Grid optimization

714

## Tutorial 15–2: Turn a Drain Plug

### Machining task

Generate the turning toolpath for the drain plug created in Tutorial 3–2.

### Machining synthesis

Creating turning operations in CAMWorks is very similar to creating milling operations as shown in the previous tutorial.

### Machining plan

Create the turning toolpath for the drain plug that is created in Tutorial 3–2 shown in Figure 15.24.

**FIGURE 15.24**
Drain plug

### Design intent

Ignore for this chapter.

### Machining steps

We create the toolpath in six steps:

1. Open the drain plug created in Tutorial 3–2.
2. Define the machine.
3. Define the stock.
4. Define the machinable features.
5. Generate the operation plan.
6. Generate the toolpath.

The details of these steps are shown below.

## Step 1: Open the drain plug created in Tutorial 3–2

| Task | Command Sequence to Click |
|---|---|
| A. Open the drain plug.  | **File => Open => Part** => Open the drain plug from Tutorial 3–2 as shown to the left. |

## Step 2: Define the machine

### Task

A. Define the type of machine that is used to complete all of the turning operations.

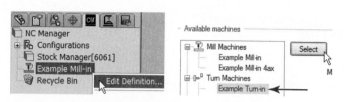

### Command Sequence to Click

Right-click **Example Mill-in** => **Edit Definition** => **Machine** tab => **Select Example Turn-in** => OK as shown to the left

## Step 3: Define the stock

### Task

A. Open the stock manager.

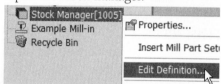

### Command Sequence to Click

Right-click **Stock Manager** => **Edit Definition** as shown to the left

B. Manage stock and edit the material.

The Default values in the **Bar stock parameters** shown to the left describe the smallest piece of material that contains all of the features of this part. Select **Material** => **6061** from **Common name** drop-down list => OK as shown to the left.

## Step 4: Define the machinable features

### Task

A. Use the **Automatic Feature Recognition (AFR)** to identify all of the features that will be turned.

### Command Sequence to Click

Right-click **NC Manager** => **Extract Machinable Features** as shown to the left

| Task | Command Sequence to Click |
|---|---|

B. View the results of the AFR.

The **AFR** identifies the features that are cut from the stock piece to create the final part as shown to the left.

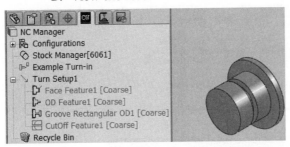

## Step 5: Generate the operation plan

| Task | Command Sequence to Click |
|---|---|

A. Generate the operation plan.

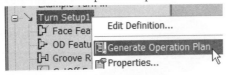

Right-click **Turn Setup1 => Generate Operation Plan** as shown to the left

B. Review the operations.

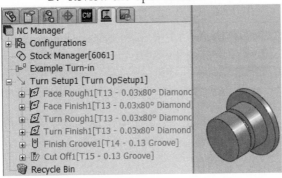

**Help:** Each of the machinable features has been associated with an operation and a tool as shown to the left.

## Step 6: Generate the toolpath

| Task | Command Sequence to Click |
|---|---|

A. Generate the toolpath.

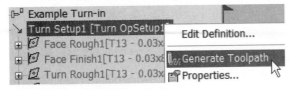

Right-click **Turn Setup1 => Generate Toolpath** as shown to the left

B. Review the toolpath.

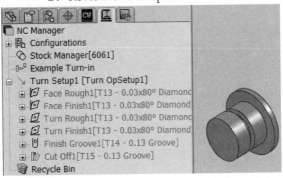

Each operation is shown in the **CAMWorks Operation Tree.** If you select an operation, the toolpath is highlighted in the graphics pane as shown to the left.

| Task | Command Sequence to Click |
|---|---|

**C.** Simulate the toolpath.

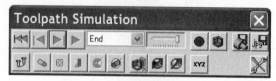

Right-click **Turn Setup1 => Simulate Toolpath** as shown to the left

**D.** Use the simulation tools to watch and verify the toolpath and operations as shown below.

---

**HANDS-ON FOR TUTORIAL 15–2.** Why does the groove not get turned? Modify the operations such that the groove is part of the toolpath. Submit a screenshot of the toolpath.

---

## Tutorial 15–3:  Wire EDM a Spline Shaft

**FIGURE 15.25**
Spline shaft

**Machining task**

Generate EDM toolpath for the spline shaft shown in Figure 15.25.

**Machining synthesis**

There is only one toolpath (shown here) to wire EDM the spline.

**Machining plan**

Create EDM toolpaths for the spline shaft shown in Figure 15.25.

**Design intent**

Ignore for this chapter.

**Machining steps**

We create the toolpath in six steps:

1. Create the spline shaft.
2. Define the machine.
3. Define the stock.
4. Insert part setup.
5. Generate the operation plan.
6. Generate the toolpath.

The details of these steps are shown below.

## Step 1:  Create the spline shaft

**Task**

A. Create the spline shaft.

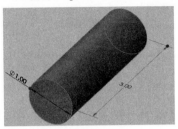

B. Sketch the spline tooth cross section.

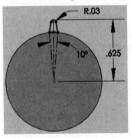

C. Pattern the spline tooth.

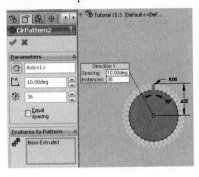

**Command Sequence to Click**

Sketch the cross section on the front plane, and extrude 3.00 in. as shown to the left.

Sketch the cross section of the spline tooth on the front plane, and extrude 3.00 in. as shown to the left.
**Help:** The tooth is symmetric about the vertical construction line as shown to the left. The tooth is constructed with two lines and two arcs.

Pattern the spline tooth as shown to the left.

## Step 2:  Define the machine

**Task**

A. Select **Wire EDM Mode-mm** from the available machines.

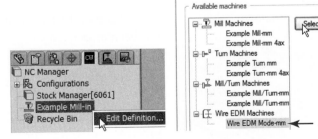

**Command Sequence to Click**

Right-click **Example Mill-mm =>** **Machine** tab => **Wire EDM Mode-mm => Select => OK** as shown to the left.

## Step 3: Define the stock

Task

A. Open the stock manager.

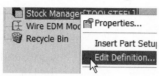

Command Sequence to Click

Right-click **Stock Manager => Edit Definition** as shown to the left.
**Help:** Do not change any of the default values for this tutorial. However, this is how you would define the stock material that the final piece would be cut from.

## Step 4: Insert part setup

Task

A. Create a part setup to define the orientation of the part to be cut.

Command Sequence to Click

Right-click **Stock Manager => Insert Part Setup** => While the **Right Plane** is highlighted in the **Reference planes** section as shown to the left, you must select the **Front Plane** from the features tree => Select **Perimeter punch =>** **OK** as shown to the left.

## Step 5: Generate the operation plan

Task

A. Generate the operation plan.

Command Sequence to Click

Right-click **EDM Part Setup1 => Generate Operation Plan** as shown to the left

B. Review the operations shown below.

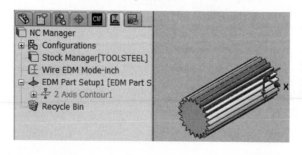

**Help:** Each of the machinable features has been associated with an operation and a tool.

## Step 6:   Generate the toolpath

Task

Command Sequence to Click

A.  Generate the toolpath.

Right click **EDM Part Setup1 =>**
**Generate Toolpath**

B.  Review the toolpath.

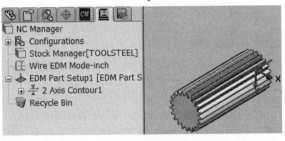

Each operation is shown in the
**CAMWorks Operation Tree** as shown
to the left.  If you select an operation,
the toolpath is highlighted in the
graphics pane.

C.  Simulate the toolpath.

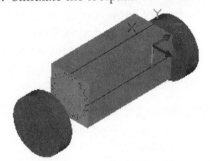

Right-click **EDM Part Setup1 =>**
**Simulate Toolpath** as shown to the left

---

***HANDS-ON FOR TUTORIAL 15–3.*** Create a hole with 0.25 in. diameter in
the spline shaft. Use wire EDM to machine it. Submit a screenshot of the toolpath.

---

**INDUSTRY CHAT**

This section provides practical insight into how the chapter material is used in
industry in the real world and practice. This section summarizes the chat with
Mr. Marc Meeuwsen (Development Design Engineer) and Mr. Charlie Weaver
(Lead CNC Engineer) of Extol, Inc., the sponsor of this chapter. The structure of the
chat follows the chapter sections.

**Chapter Section 15.1:**   Introduction

ABE:  Describe the production cycle in your company. What manufacturing processes do you use?

MARC AND CHARLIE:  We are a company that specializes in manufacturing plastics
joining equipment and custom automation equipment. Our
company has two main divisions: our standard equipment
group, that encompasses all of our plastics joining equipment,
and our custom equipment (specials) group. Having both
groups allows us to not only produce standard products but
if our customers require a custom machine for a specific

*(continued)*

application we can produce that as well. Our typical production cycle begins by receiving a P.O. (purchase order) from a customer, based on a quote that has been submitted. Once we set up our internal order for the job, we then inform our project managers and engineers that a new job has been received. Our engineers start the design process using Solid-Works and generate an initial design. After the customer reviews and approves the design, we release the design for manufacturing. The manufacturing group, Charlie leading the CNC activities, takes over to create the different parts, perform CNC machining, perform surface finish and plating, and anodizing aluminum, if needed. Once we have all the parts, we assemble them in house to create the final product. We have the customer approve the machine at runoff. Once we have the customer approval, we ship the equipment. Our jobs (projects) will range anywhere from 1 to 20 weeks and price will vary depending on the application.

As for our manufacturing processes, we incorporate a wide variety of conventional metal cutting machines including manual lathes and mills, CNC lathe and mill, brake press, saws and several different welding processes. We also rely on outside subcontractors to supply us with processes that we do not have available in house.

**Chapter Section 15.2:** Basics of Machine Tools

ABE: What are the machine tools you have? How do you train the machinists?

MARC AND CHARLIE: As stated above we have several manual and CNC lathe and milling machines. We also have saws for cutting steel, drill presses, grinding equipment, pretty much everything a shop would need to process raw materials into a finished product.

As for training machinists, some of us started as machine builders, and then worked our way to CNC. A majority of us went to apprentice or technical schools. However, we learn most of what we do on the job. Lots of training we do is on-the-job training. When we hire someone new, we teach them how to run the manual lathe and mill first. Once they learn manual machining and how to run the machines, we teach them the CNC process.

**Chapter Section 15.3:** Basics of Machining

ABE: What are the common machining concepts you use?

MARC AND CHARLIE: We use all the concepts covered in Section 15.3, depending on the details of the part we are machining. A large part of our business is custom equipment; which means we build one of a kind details and parts. When I get a stack of prints for a design from Marc, I go through them to decide on the stock shape and size. I usually write, on a print, the stock size and how much time we need to machine. I then choose the corner of the block as my home position (unless it's specified by the designer). I then do all the machining: drill holes, perform 3D coarse finish, etc. We use all the different tool-path concepts. We always machine every single part we make from scratch. We rarely make the same custom machine parts twice. Standard machine parts are a little different; we program them once and as long as we do not have a revision on the part we can reuse that program over and over.

We generally provide overall dimensions and critical tolerances on our drawings. We do not detail (dimension) every part. We rely on CAD data to program the part in CAMWorks. Working with a 3D model is very convenient.

We use carbide tools. We usually consult the charts of the cutter manufacturer to cutting parameters such as spindle speed and feedrate. It is almost impossible to provide a ball-park number for these cutting parameters because they change dramatically, depending on many factors. For example, the tool length, material type and the number of flutes change the spindle speed and feedrate. The tool length is a big determining factor when figuring our depth of cut.

**Chapter Section 15.4:** Turning

ABE: Provide some examples of the parts/features you turn. What turning operations (e.g., roughing, reaming, etc.), cutting tools, and machining parameters do you use?

MARC AND CHARLIE: We rough and finish outer and inner diameters (OD and ID). First, we face the part to get a smooth surface to start working with. Then we drill a hole (spot drill) to get the process started for an ID. We also bore, ream, and cut off parts. A cutoff feature is a process by which we cut off a part that has been turned from the stock. We catch it in a bin. It is the finished part.

Another part whose surfaces we machine tightly is called a "concentrator." This part is used to take energy from a source and concentrates it to a single point for melting plastics. Thus, its surfaces require very highly precise machining.

The machining parameters for turning are spindle speed, feedrate, chip removal load, and cutting conditions. We almost always cut wet; except for plastics, we cut dry. We use coolants, especially when we cut aluminum because it tends to heat up very quickly.

**Chapter Section 15.5:** Drilling

ABE: Provide some examples of the parts/features you drill. What drilling operations (e.g., spotting, counterbore, etc.), cutting tools, and machining parameters do you use?

MARC AND CHARLIE: We do a lot of plates for our machines. So, we do lots of drilling to create holes in these plates. We spot drill (or center drill, same thing), drill, counterbore, countersink, ream, and tap holes. Our drilling cutting tools include center drill, drill, counterbore, and countersink. The drilling machining parameters are the same as for turning.

(continued)

## Chapter Section 15.6: Milling

**ABE:** Provide some examples of the parts/features you mill. What milling operations (e.g., contouring, face/pocket miiling, etc.), cutting tools, and machining parameters do you use?

**MARC AND CHARLIE:** We mill square blocks for mounting. We mill plates. We do a lot of nesting for customer part holding. Nesting is basically the process of cutting the profile or shape of the customer's part into a block of material to secure it during the process cycle of the machine. Our milling operations include 3D contouring, rough and finish milling, facing, pocket milling, side milling, and boss cutting. We use contouring to mill a 3D surface. For side milling, we use an open profile, i.e., cutting along one surface. Boss cutting is when you go around the part sides and mill. The part can be many shapes but it is generally square.

Cutting tools include flat-end mill, ball-end mill, and hog-nose mill. A hog-nose mill tool is a tool between flat-end and ball-end mill. It has sharper radius at corner, and not much of a radius at the tip. We can screw the tip on and off, so we can replace the tip when it wears off.

## Chapter Section 15.7: Electrical Discharge Machining

**ABE:** Provide some examples of the parts/features EDM. What EDM operations (e.g., sinker, wire, etc.), cutting tools, and machining parameters do you use?

**MARC AND CHARLIE:** We do not use EDM machine in house. We outsource it if needed.

## Chapter Section 15.8: Manufacturing of Design

**ABE:** What are the manufacturing considerations you use during your part design?

**MARC AND CHARLIE:** We have developed our own Excel sheet over time with what apply to Extol, Inc. specifically. We have tailored a lot of that to our needs. So, our designers can find what they need for SolidWorks and CAMWorks. So, our designers are confident that if they create a rib or pocket, it will be feasible for machining. We talked earlier about nesting (crude injection molding). Lots of customers have tight radii that we cannot cut all the time. From a design perspective, we try to weigh our manufacturing options with our customer requirements, and at the same time we also have the assembly requirements that constrain us during design and manufacturing.

We have a list of how long a cutter should be depending on its diameter. The larger the diameter is, the longer the tool length can be. If we cannot cut it, we have to change the design. Sometimes a small design change makes manufacturing easier. For example, we split one of our big parts into two and changed the fillets to fit better into the machines. These design changes cut down the manufacturing time to 45 minutes from 4 hours. This time saving is attributed to using standard stock sizes and reducing the stock preparation machining significantly.

### Chapter Section 15.9:   Basics of NC Machining

**Abe:** What NC concepts do you use?

**Marc and Charlie:** I program in CAMWorks. I tell it which cutter and toolpaths to use. It figures all the machining parameters for me. So, I do not worry about them.

### Chapter Section 15.10:   G-Code and M-Code Programming

**Abe:** How much G-code and M-code programming do you do?

**Marc and Charlie:** We do not have to do too much with G-code and M-code. Our machines do that. We program in CAMWorks. We see the toolpath in CAMWorks. CAMWorks generates G-code and M-code automatically for us. Our programs get posted in the *.eia* file type. We can also program our CNC controller directly. We use the Mazatrol controller. However, we cannot do 3D programming using the Mazatrol controller.

### Chapter Section 15.11:   SolidWorks DFMXpress

**Abe:** Describe how you use **DFMXpress** in your company.

**Marc and Charlie:** We have not used **DFMXpress** yet, but we are investigating for future use. We use Excel sheets. We are in the process of porting our Excel knowledge base to **DFMXpress**. **DFMXpress** should save us time and effort in the long run.

### Chapter Section 15.12:   CAMWorks

**Abe:** Provide examples of using CAMWorks in your machining operations.

**Marc and Charlie:** We customize CAMWorks generic libraries to our needs. When we have figured out how a cutter works best in a certain speed and feedrate, we save it in CAMWorks. We can use it again in the future. SolidWorks and CAMWorks put out very good generic databases as a starting point. If we find something that works well for us, we save it in CAMWorks or SolidWorks hole wizard. For example, every tap has a specific size drilled hole. We tailor some of those for our needs. CAMWorks does feature recognition. So it takes a lot of the guesswork out of programming.

### Others

**Abe:** Any other experience you would like to share with our book readers?

**Marc and Charlie:** "Learn and understand what is around you." If you want to be a good designer, learn products and assemblies. Many times, we interview new grads who have high GPAs, but do not have the basic common sense to make something. Designers interface with sales and manufacturing teams. Designers need to know how to machine as well as engineer the product. The old adage of "steel is cheap" in not true anymore; understand how to manufacture a part or detail, so to not scrap out material. Know how to machine a part, and the equipment needed to move the finished part, especially if it is very large.

1. What is the difference between mass production and mass customization?
2. What types of parts can turning and milling operate on, that is, machine?
3. Describe a manual machining operation from the start to the finish.
4. What are the advantages of wet machining, that is, using a coolant during machining?
5. What does the ½ axis designation mean for a machine tool? Give an example.
6. List the materials of machining cutting tools. Which is the softest and which is the hardest material? What is the effect of material strength on the tool operating parameters?
7. Flutes (teeth) and end types characterize cutting tools. Provide examples for drilling and milling tools.
8. What does the 3/8•16UNF thread designation mean?
9. List and sketch six of the common stock shapes.
10. What are the machining parameters that we typically use in machining? Show them on sketches of turning and milling operations.
11. What is the difference between roughing and finishing machining operations?
12. Explain the concept of workpiece squaring. Why is squaring important?
13. What is machine zero? Why is it important?
14. What is a burr? Why does it occur?
15. Sketch four possible toolpaths to mill a planar face. Which is the best toolpath? Why?
16. Sketch PTP and continuous machining. What is the main difference between the two types?
17. Research the turning operations. Submit a detailed report about turning machines, turning centers, how many axes are available, turning operations (e.g., boring, reaming, threading, etc.), turning cutting tools (their materials, machining parameters, etc.), speeds, feedrates, cutting depth, jigs and fixtures used to clamp workpieces, and sample parts.
18. Redo Problem 17 but for drilling.
19. Redo Problem 17 but for milling.
20. Redo Problem 17 but for sinker EDM.
21. Redo Problem 17 but for wire EDM.
22. Explain the main difference between DFA and DFM.
23. What does zero-radius NC programming mean? What is its benefit?
24. What does tool offset in NC programming mean? What is its benefit?
25. Figure 15.26 shows a stepped shaft. Write manually the NC program using G-code and M-code to turn the shaft. The home position is shown in the figure. The shaft material is steel. Machining parameters are spindle speed = 3000 RPM, feedrate = 100 in./min, depth of cut = .1 in., coolant = on. All dims are in inches.

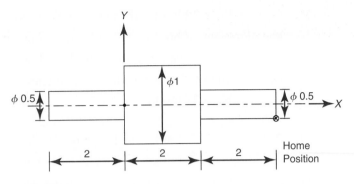

**FIGURE 15.26**
Stepped shaft

26. Figure 15.27 shows an extruded part. Part thickness is 1 in. Write manually the NC program using G-code and M-code to drill the hole. The home position is shown in the figure. The part material is aluminum. Machining parameters are spindle speed = 6000 RPM, feedrate = 50 in./min, coolant = off. All dims are in inches.

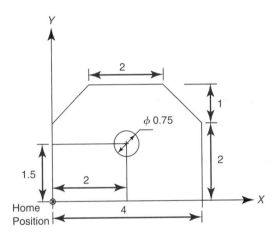

**FIGURE 15.27**
Extruded part

27. Write manually the NC program using G-code and M-code to mill the top face of the part shown in Figure 15.27. The home position is shown in the figure. The part material is aluminum. Machining parameters are spindle speed = 6000 RPM, feedrate = 50 in./min, coolant = on. All dims are in inches.

28. Use SolidWorks **DFMXpress** to check the manufacturability of the shaft shown in Figure 15.26.

29. Redo Problem 28 but for the part shown in Figure 15.27.

30. Redo Problem 28 but for the AMP connector model shown in Figure 2.43 of Chapter 2.

31. Redo Problem 28 but for the flange model shown in Figure 2.45 of Chapter 2.

32. Redo Problem 28 but for the L bracket shown in Figure 2.50 of Chapter 2.

33. Redo Problem 28 but for the pattern block shown in Figure 2.51 of Chapter 2.

34. Redo Problem 28 but for the pattern wheel shown in Figure 2.52 of Chapter 2.
35. Redo Problem 28 but for the loft feature shown in Figure 4.14 of Chapter 4.
36. Generate the CL file for turning the shaft shown in Figure 15.26.
37. Generate the CL file to machine the part shown in Figure 15.27.
38. Redo Problem 37 but for the AMP connector model shown in Figure 2.43 of Chapter 2.
39. Redo Problem 37 but for the flange model shown in Figure 2.45 of Chapter 2.
40. Redo Problem 37 but for the L bracket shown in Figure 2.50 of Chapter 2.
41. Redo Problem 37 but for the pattern block shown in Figure 2.51 of Chapter 2.
42. Redo Problem 37 but for the pattern wheel shown in Figure 2.52 of Chapter 2.
43. Redo Problem 37 but for the loft feature shown in Figure 4.14 of Chapter 4.

# CHAPTER

# 16

# Injection Molding

## 16.1 Introduction

Machining can only produce products that have surfaces that are accessible by machine tools. These are surfaces that do not have complex shapes and/or do not include geometry that is hard to reach on machine tools. Injection molding is a manufacturing process that is capable of producing any shape made of materials such as plastics or polymers. Many plastic parts such as bottles, toothbrushes, bottle caps, car parts, wires, etc. are injection molded. Injection molding is widely used in various industries including medical, consumer, automotive, health care, toys, etc. Injection molding is ideal for mass production due to the fast production cycles, and as a result the cost per item is very inexpensive.

**Injection molding** is a cyclic process whereby molten plastic is formed into a desired shape by forcing the plastic into a cavity under pressure. Sizes of molded parts vary from the smallest size components used in medical devices, to entire body panels of cars. Injection molding produces excellent dimensional tolerances. It also requires minimal or no finishing or assembly operations, making it ideal for fast delivery of finished products from the time an order is received.

Thermoplastic materials are the most commonly used for molded parts. These materials (also known as resins) include polystyrene, polyamide, polypropylene, polyethylene, polyvinyl chloride (PVC), and acrylonitrile butadiene styrene (ABS). Material selection depends on the end application and the desired strength/ductility of the resin. Another group of materials includes ceramics, metals, and hard metals. They are used in powder injection molding to produce large volumes of small complex parts. Powder injection molding combines two manufacturing processes: injection molding and sintering.

The injection molding process requires three elements: an injection molding machine, plastic material, and a mold. The plastic is melted in the machine and injected into the mold where it cools and solidifies into the final part. The process is characterized by very large forces and very small processing time. Injection pressure that presses the molten material into the mold is very high, ranging from 3000 to 40,000 psi, with a typical value of 15,000 psi. The clamping force that holds the mold together and an ejection force that ejects the part from the mold are usually very high. The processing (cycle) time to produce one molded part is very short, typically in the seconds.

Injection molding has advantages and disadvantages. Its advantages are (1) reduced material handling as the hopper holds the plastic pellets; (2) creating parts with metal inserts easily; (3) producing parts with tight tolerances; and (4) lower cost per part, resulting from highly automating the injection molding process. The disadvantages of injection molding are (1) warpage of the parts could result if the mold design and the molding process were not optimized; (2) weak parts at connection lines (known as knit lines) where they are likely to break; and (3) parts could become scrap if the mold were not designed properly. Mold design is usually an intricate and expensive task.

## 16.2 Basics of Injection Molding Machines

Injection molding requires injection molding (IM) machines, just as machining requires machine tools. With an appropriately designed mold that can be accommodated in the IM machine, it can make a variety of parts similar to a machine tool. We need to understand both how IM machines work and what the basics of IM are. This section covers the basics of IM machines. Subsequent sections cover the basics of IM. Figure 16.1 shows a sample IM machine. IM machines come in either a horizontal or vertical configuration. Horizontal configurations are common (Figure 16.1). Figure 16.1 (A and B) shows one machine. However, the machine is so long that we split it into two images as shown.

Figure 16.2 shows an abstraction (schematic) of the IM machine shown in Figure 16.1. The abstract machine helps us understand the machine operations. An IM machine has a solid frame that is usually long and skinny, as shown in Figure 16.1. The machine has a controller to operate it. The machine does not have too many externally visible moving parts, thus no moving spindles like machine tools. The IM machine operator needs a different skill than a machine tool operator. The IM machine operator needs to know about plastics viscosity, processing plastics, and IM parameters such as pressure, temperatures, etc., whereas the machine tool operator needs to know about metals, different types of cutting tools, etc.

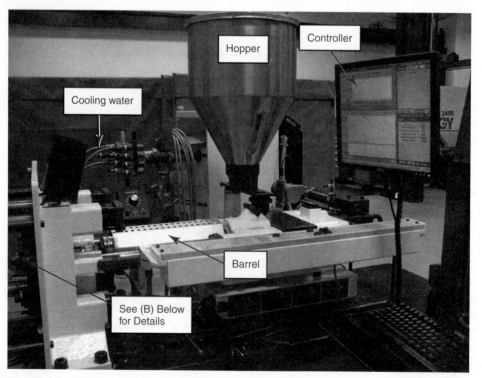

(A) Close-up view of the injection unit

**FIGURE 16.1**

An injection molding machine (Courtesy of NyproMold Inc.)

(B) Close-up view of the mold space

**FIGURE 16.1**
*(continued)*

An IM machine has three main sections as shown in Figure 16.2: injection unit, mold assembly, and clamping unit. The injection unit receives the plastic pellets from the hopper, heats up the plastic (plastic becomes plasticized, i.e., changes from a solid to a semi-viscous state), and delivers it to the mold assembly. The mold assembly section contains the mold that makes the part, which has two halves: the cavity and the core. The clamping unit holds the mold tightly closed during the injection of the plastic into the mold.

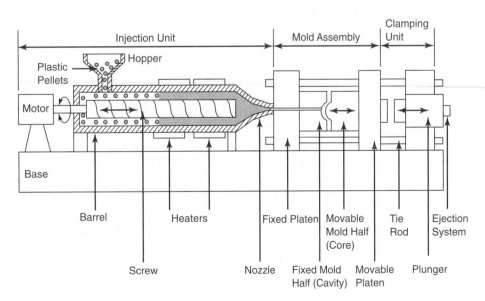

**FIGURE 16.2**
Schematic of an injection molding machine

## 16.3 Basics of Injection Molding

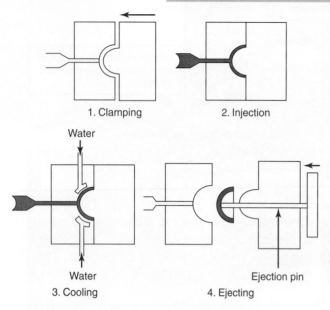

1. Clamping     2. Injection

Water

Water     Ejection pin

3. Cooling     4. Ejecting

**FIGURE 16.3**
Injection molding cycle

The IM process to make one part is called a cycle. The cycle has four stages in this order: clamping, injection, cooling, and ejecting. The cycle begins by the clamping unit securing the mold halves in place before plastic injection begins. The injection stage begins with the barrel receiving plastic pellets from the hopper (see Figure 16.2). The screw inside the barrel rotates and slides axially via the motor and pushes the pellets forward inside the barrel. When they reach the heaters area, they melt and become molten plastic. The screw continues pushing the plastic into the nozzle. The nozzle feeds into the mold cavity and fills it with plastic that takes the shape of the mold core. The clamping unit holds the mold halves tightly and presses the core into the cavity firmly to prevent any leak of the molten plastic. As soon as the plastic touches the mold, it cools down immediately. Once the cooling down is complete after a preset cooling period, the screw retracts, the clamping unit unclamps, and the ejectors eject the final part, releasing it from the core. The part is dropped to the bottom of the IM machine into a bucket or container. Figure 16.3 shows the IM cycle.

The mold halves are fixed to large plates called platens. The fixed (front) half of the mold has the cavity (also called the mold cavity) and is mounted to the stationary (fixed) platen. The movable (rear) half of the mold has the core (also called the mold core) and is mounted to the movable platen. The plunger (Figure 16.2) of the clamping unit holds the mold securely closed while the material is injected. As soon as the material hits the mold, it cools down. After the required cooling time, the mold is opened and the ejection system pushes the solidified (final) part out of the open cavity. The ejection system is usually attached to the movable (rear) half of the mold.

Each cycle produces one or more parts and is repeated at a high rate. The screw is reciprocating: pushes the plastic at the beginning of the cycle and retracts at the end of the cycle to allow more plastic to flow into the barrel for the next cycle. The cooling is typically done with water. The IM machine is connected to water pipes that circulate the water.

The plastic parts come out of the IM machine ready for use. However, some minor cleaning (post-processing) may be needed to break off extra plastic pieces. For example, if the mold is used to make multiple parts, these parts become connected by runners (branches) of plastic that must be broken off (via using a cutter) the parts. These runners represent the "chips." They can be recycled by melting and converting them into pellets for reuse. The recycling includes placing the chips in plastic grinders and grinding them into pellets (known as the regrind). Due to the change in material properties after injection, the regrind is always mixed with raw material in the proper ratio. The new mix is then used to make new molded parts (when permissible).

Defects are an expected part of manufacturing processes, and IM is no exception. Molding defects are caused by the mold itself (due to poor design) or the molding process. For example, defects may be caused by a nonuniform cooling rate due to mold nonuniform wall thickness or temperature. Possible defects are:

1. Sink marks: These marks are caused by low injection pressure and/or mold nonuniform wall thickness, causing some sections of the mold to solidify quicker than others, leading to uneven shrinkage and leaving temporary voids in the mold.

2. **Bubbles:** They are an indication that the injection temperature is too high or there is too much moisture in the plastic. These bubbles are visible on the part outer surfaces.

3. **Short shot (partial filling):** Some sections of the cavity may be unfilled because the shot size is insufficient or the plastic flow in the mold is slow, causing it to solidify before reaching the far ends of the mold, away from the gates.

4. **Ejector marks:** These are small indentations made in the part where the ejection system pushed the part out of the mold. They are an indication of too short cooling time or excessive ejection force.

5. **Warpage:** Some sections of the mold may cool faster than others, resulting in warping of the part. Warpage is an indication that cooling rate is nonuniform inside the mold.

6. **Flashing:** The molten plastic may seep out of the mold cavity between the mold halves and solidify along the parting line as a thin layer of plastic. This layer is visible after ejecting the part. It is an indication that the clamping force is too low or the injection pressure is too high.

7. **Burn marks:** These are black or brown burned areas on the part surface. They are an indication of improper venting of the tool (mold) or that the injection temperature is too high.

8. **Flow marks:** These are directional "off tone" wavy lines or patterns. They are an indication of low injection pressure.

9. **Voids:** These are hollow spots (air pockets) inside the part, indicating a lack of holding the injection pressure at the proper level during the entire injection (shot) time.

10. **Weld lines:** These are discolored lines where two flow fronts meet. They indicate low temperatures of the mold and the melt when the two fronts meet, so they do not bond well into each other.

## 16.4 Basics of Mold Design

Mold designers design molds, and tool (mold) makers make them. Mold designers use mold design software to create molds and toolmakers use precision-machining techniques to produce the molds. Mold machining combines several machining techniques including turning, milling, grinding, EDM, and polishing. We focus only on mold design here. A mold design must address all the basics covered here. Understanding mold design and successfully and efficiently using mold design software such as SolidWorks require understanding the following basic concepts of mold design:

1. **Types of molds:** There exist many types of injection molds. We can classify them in multiple ways as follows:
   A. Based on the number of cavities, we have a single- or a multi-cavity mold.
   B. Based on construction, we have 2-plate, 3-plate, side-action, or stack molds.
   C. Based on ejection, we have pin-eject or stripper-eject molds. Pin ejection occurs with pins, as shown in Figure 16.3. Stripper ejection uses a stripper that pushes the part along its perimeter (think of the rim of a cup).
   D. Based on the type of runner (feed) system, we have hot runner mold, cold runner mold, or hot to cold runner mold.

2. **Core and cavity:** These are the two halves of the mold. The cavity represents the "imprint" of the outside of the part, and the core represents the "imprint" of the inside of the part. The cavity half (mold cavity) is always attached to the fixed

(stationary) platen of the IM machine, and the core (mold core) is attached to the movable platen. We use the concept of cavity and core in mold design to be able to extract the molded (final) part easily out of the mold. Because the mold needs to be pulled apart to remove the part, the mold design should ensure this separation.

Industry uses jargon to refer to mold halves. The A (also known as fixed or cavity) half is the mold half that does not move (Figure 16.2) and the B (also known as movable or core) half is the mold half that moves before and after injection (Figure 16.2). The B half moves before injection to clamp the mold and moves after injection to allow the removal (extraction) of the molded part.

3. **Tool splitting:** Tool splitting is synonymous with core and cavity. Tool splitting is the process by which we split the mold into two halves: core and cavity. After the split, designer typically adds the gates, runner system, ejection pins, fasteners, etc.

4. **Mold components and assembly:** A mold consists of its core, cavity, and housing. The cavity and the core are the two main components. The mold **housing** is its base that houses all the mold components. These components are alignment components, feed system, cooling system, and ejection system. The housing consists of plates to affix the mold components to. The mold assembly consists of two subassemblies. The core and cavity subassembly has the core and cavity only. The housing (base) subassembly has all the other components of the mold.

5. **Shot:** A shot is defined as the amount of plastic that is injected to make one part. Each IM cycle requires one shot.

6. **Shrinkage:** Plastic expands when it is hot and shrinks when it cools down. After a shot is delivered to the mold cavity, it cools down immediately. If its size does not account for shrinkage, the molded part will be smaller than desired. Thus, the mold design should account for shrinkage. Mold analysis can help estimate the amount of shrinkage (shrink factor) and calculates the correct size of the shot accordingly. The shrink factor is based on the type of plastic and the mold conditions.

7. **Cooling time:** This is the correct amount of time needed to solidify plastic inside a mold before opening. Inaccurate calculation of cooling time results in defective parts. Mold analysis provides equations to calculate this time. Cooling channels are usually built into the mold design to allow water to flow through the mold walls near the cavity to cool down the molten plastic.

8. **Ejection:** Ejection is the last activity in the IM cycle. We use an ejection system to push the part out of the mold core when we open the mold. When the plastic cools down and solidifies at the end of the cooling time, it adheres to the mold core, in which case a force must be applied to eject the part. An ejection system is part of the mold design.

9. **Tooling:** Tooling (or custom tooling) refers to molds. A mold is typically made out of steel or aluminum. The space between the mold core and the mold cavity forms the part cavity that is filled with molten plastic to create the part. Mold may have one or multiple cavities.

10. **Parting line, surface, and axis:** A **parting line** is the line of demarcation along the part outside. It indicates where the mold halves separate. It separates the core from the cavity. The parting line can take different shapes ranging from a simple line to a piecewise line, to a curve. The parting line is a closed entity regardless of its shape.

A **parting surface** is the surface where the two mold halves contact each other. Parting surfaces may be flat, stepwise planar, angled, or curved (free-form). Molds with flat parting surfaces are less expensive to make than others.

A **parting axis** (direction) is the axis along which the two halves of a mold will separate to allow the part to be ejected.

11. **Mold base:** These are the plates that the mold cavity and core are fixed to. The cavity and the sprue are attached to the stationary (front) plate. The core and the ejection system are attached to the movable (rear) plates, as shown in Figure 16.2. The ejection system has ejector pins that are actuated to push the part off the core when the mold opens up.

12. **Gate and runner system:** This is the system that distributes the molten plastic from the nozzle shown in Figure 16.2 to the mold. The gate represents the entry point of injection of the plastic into the mold. The runners are the channels that carry the plastic from the sprue to the gates of the mold cavity. An important issue is to make sure that enough molten plastic can be pushed through the gates of the mold to avoid defective parts. Also, if the plastic flow is not fast enough, the leading edge of the plastic could solidify, preventing the plastic from reaching the entire mold cavity and causing defects as well. The design of the gates (how many, best locations, and the sizes of the orifices) and the runners (how many and how long) is important to successful injection molding.

Figure 16.4 shows a schematic of a gate and runner system. The main channel that feeds plastic to the runners from the barrel is known as the sprue. If we use only one gate, there is no need for a runner system. The sprue feeds directly to that gate, as shown in Figure 16.4A. Figure 16.4B shows a runner system where the mold has three cavities to make three parts in one injection cycle. In such a case, the sprue feeds to the runners and the runners feed to the gates. The sprue and the runners are always in perpendicular planes; the sprue is always vertical (in the middle of the mold A half) and the runners are always horizontal. In this configuration, the runners feed to the cavities from the side (horizontal). Think of Figure 16.4B as a right view of Figure 16.4A. Figure 16.4A

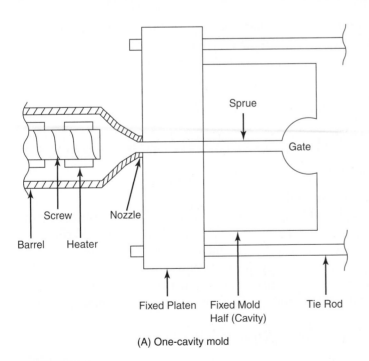

(A) One-cavity mold

(B) Multiple-cavity mold

**FIGURE 16.4**
Schematic of a gate and runner system

shows the details of the mold cavity area shown in Figure 16.2. The molten plastic inside the sprue and the runners solidifies and must be ejected along with the part.

13. **Tooling cost:** The tooling cost is the total cost of the two mold halves and the mold base. The part size determines the mold size, and the mold size, in turn, determines the size of the base. The larger the mold base, the more expensive it is. As for the mold itself, its cost depends primarily on the size and shape of its cavity or if multiple cavities are needed. The cavity machining depends on the complexity of the part's geometry. Additional machining cost could accrue from machining parting surfaces, high tolerances, and high surface finish.

14. **Draft:** **Draft** is a slight taper on selected model faces (walls) that facilitate removal (ejection) of the part from the mold without distorting or damaging it. The draft angle is specified such that the opening of the mold cavity is wider than its base. The draft taper is specified by an angle value, typically 1 to 5 degrees.

15. **Undercut:** An **undercut** is an optional feature of a molded part to help keep the part secured to the core side, that is, the moving half (where the ejection system is).

16. **Insert:** Sometimes designing a one-piece core or one-piece cavity is not feasible if the mold is too large. Thus, we split the core and cavity to pieces, each called an insert. Inserts simplify the mold cost, maintenance, and replacement.

17. **Venting:** Venting provides a path for the air to escape from the cavity as the melt displaces it. Inadequate venting of the cavity can seriously reduce the melt flow to it. Venting affects the quality of injection molded parts. A vent should always be located opposite to a gate as this will be the point of final fill. Venting prevents "burn marks" defect.

## 16.5 Basics of Part Design

Successful production of injection molded parts has two requirements: good mold design and good part design. Without both of them, molded parts may be defective. Section 16.4 covers the rules for mold design. The following rules serve as guidelines for good part design:

☐ **Part wall thickness:** Keep uniform and to a minimum to reduce the part volume and shorten the injection time.

☐ **Part edges and corners:** Avoid sharp edges and corners. Fillet the edges and round the corners.

☐ **Drafts:** Apply drafts to the part walls that are parallel to the parting axis (direction) to facilitate the part removal from the mold.

☐ **Ribs:** Add ribs to strengthen the part where needed instead of increasing the part wall thickness. Do not violate the first rule listed above. Also, always add ribs so that they are perpendicular to the axis about which bending may occur.

☐ **Bosses:** Bosses should be supported by ribs that connect to the nearest part wall.

☐ **Undercuts:** Minimize the number of undercuts as much as possible. For example, relocating the parting line and/or redesigning a part feature may eliminate some undercuts.

☐ **Threads:** Orient part features with external threads to be perpendicular to the parting axis.

## 16.6 Phases of Mold Design

According to industry practice, the three major phases of a mold design are in this sequence:

1. **Part design:** This is the part design that we are accustomed to and is covered in this book.

2. **Prepare part for mold design:** The design of parts that are to be produced by injection molding must go through thorough evaluation by mold designers before they are approved for mold design. This is because mold designers must ensure that the corresponding molds are possible to make and that they would work correctly. The evaluation process includes draft analysis, undercut analysis, and parting line analysis. The drafting analysis ensures that the final part can be ejected from the mold. The undercut analysis is needed to ensure that the part can be safely ejected. The parting line analysis allows the designer to investigate multiple pull directions and select the best one.

   Another important mold preparation activity is the flow and temperature analyses of the plastic inside the mold core and cavity. Commercial software tools such as Moldflow exist to aid designers in performing the calculations. Flow and temperature analyses inside a mold are a highly nonlinear complex problem that is solved using nonlinear FEM/FEA. Designer must have strong theoretical background to be able to model the flow problem and understand and interpret the analysis results generated by the software. Designers may display these results as contours or gradients to analyze them both visually and numerically.

3. **Mold design:** After the part design is tested, modified, and approved, a mold designer begins the mold design process. Designers follow the design concepts covered in Section 16.4 and use mold design software such as SolidWorks **Mold Tools**. They begin by scaling the model up using the plastic shrink factor to accommodate for the cooling effect of the plastic. Following that, the designer creates the parting line, shut-off surfaces, and parting surfaces. Once finished, the designer splits the tool (mold) to generate the two halves (core and cavity). The details of these activities and their explanation are covered in Sections 16.9 and 16.10 as applied to SolidWorks.

   Although the core and cavity are important components of a mold, certain other components are just as important or more important. These are the mold plates, alignment components, runner system, gates, ejection system, cooling system, and electrical systems. The mold designer designs mounting holes for screws to attach the core and cavity components to the mold plates.

## 16.7 Industry Process

Toolmakers in industry follow more or less the same process to design and build molds for their customers. In general, a tool (mold) maker receives an order for a mold from a customer. The toolmaker quotes the customer the cost of designing and making the mold. Once agreed, the toolmaker designs, manufactures, tests, and ships the mold to the customer. Table 16.1 shows the general steps of this process.

| TABLE 16.1 | Industry Process to Make a Mold |
|---|---|
| **Step** | **Activities** |
| A. Sales and administration | Toolmaker:<br><br>• Receives a request from the customer.<br>• Quotes the project based on the request details.<br>• Receives an order from the customer (verbal or written).<br>• Receives customer information, CAD part files, and other special requests. |
| B. Design | Mold designer:<br><br>• Reviews and inspects the part CAD model and verifies it against IM requirements. We call it DIM (design for injection molding), similar to DFA, DFM, etc.<br>• Performs injection molding analysis of the part design using special software such as Moldflow.<br>• Once finished with the part analysis, reviews the manufacturability of the part against a checklist to ensure that a tool is possible to make for a reasonable price.<br>• At this point, creates a preliminary mold design including deciding on the parting lines and surfaces, and creating the core and cavity.<br>• Finalizes the mold design by consulting with the customer.<br>• Releases the BOM to begin ordering mold material and other manufacturing needs.<br>• Documents the mold design by creating the engineering drawings for individual parts and the mold assembly. Some toolmakers may also create mold manuals.<br>• Releases the mold design documentation to manufacturing. |
| C. Manufacturing | Manufacturing engineers:<br><br>• Review the mold design drawings to ensure that the design is functional (by checking part movements) and manufacturable.<br>• Devise a manufacturing strategy.<br>• Select the best manufacturing methods to make the mold.<br>• Write NC programs if needed. |
| D. Shop floor production | The shop floor personnel:<br><br>• Manufacture the mold parts.<br>• Inspect the parts.<br>• Assemble the parts to create the mold assembly.<br>• Test all the mold systems: cooling, venting, electrical wiring, etc. |
| E. Trial runs | • The toolmaker uses the mold in trial runs to ensure all work as designed and manufactured.<br>• If needed, design changes may be made to some parts of the molds. |
| F. Shipping | • Once completed, the toolmaker ships the mold to the customer, along with its necessary documentation and manuals (design manual, operation manual, etc.). |
| G. Tool support | • The toolmaker provides life cycle management and maintenance for the mold. The maker also provides engineering revisions based on customer need for future changes over the mold's lifetime. |

## 16.8 Mold Analysis

Molds sustain high pressures and temperatures during operations. They are also subjected to high fatigue resulting from the many injection cycles over their lifetime. More importantly, the flow of the molten plastic and maintaining uniform pressures and temperatures are crucial to successful injection. As such, the design or the runner system and the flow analysis are important.

The proper mold design requires an in-depth analysis of the mold. Software such as Moldflow assists mold designers with many aspects of mold analysis. As with any software, the mold designer must have the proper theoretical background to use the software correctly. Table 16.2 shows typical mold analysis tasks utilized in industry.

| TABLE 16.2 Industry Mold Analysis Tasks | |
|---|---|
| **Task** | **Activities** |
| A. Import part CAD model from customer into mold analysis software | • Use proper CAD format (native or neutral file format).<br>• Check imported model visually.<br>• Review model and select the mesh type: mold analysis uses nonlinear finite element method, thus requiring a mesh. It uses tetrahedral elements to perform the nonlinear FEA. |
| B. Mesh the model in the mold analysis software | • Create the finite element mesh and inspect its quality using the software. The following screenshot shows an example mesh of an injection molded part with a sprue and runners.<br><br>(Courtesy of NyproMold Inc.) |
| C. Design the runner system | • Set the injection location.<br>• Create the runners. |
| D. Design the cooling system | • Create the cooling channels. |
| E. Prepare the flow analysis | • Select the analysis type.<br>• Assign the part and mold materials.<br>• Select the process settings, e.g., mold surface temperature, melt temperature, etc. |
| F. Run the flow analysis | • Run the analysis. |
| G. Review the analysis results | • Check the results to ensure that the mold design is correct. |
| H. Redesign if needed | • Make any necessary design changes and repeat Tasks A through G as many times as necessary to obtain a successful design. |

## 16.9 SolidWorks Mold Design

SolidWorks implements the concepts of mold design in its mold design module. In addition, it uses the following concepts:

1. **Tooling split:** This software technique is used to split the mold CAD model to create the core and cavity. Tooling split uses the parting line, parting surfaces, and shut-off surfaces (see below) to split the model.
2. **Shut-off surfaces:** These are surfaces used to split the tool into the core and cavity. We need two shut-off surfaces: one for the core and one for the cavity. Shut-off surfaces are surfaces with no holes in them, thus their name.

SolidWorks helps designers design and validate molds. SolidWorks supports the three phases of mold design covered in Section 16.6. However, SolidWorks does not provide any mold analysis tools such as Moldflow. Interested readers need to use STEP to exchange models between SolidWorks and Moldflow or other mold analysis software. SolidWorks offers integrated mold design tools that control the mold creation. These tools allow designers to analyze and correct deficiencies with CAD models of parts to be molded. These tools include:

1. **Draft analysis:** Perform it to examine whether faces have sufficient draft.
2. **Undercut analysis:** Perform it to locate model areas that become trapped to prevent model ejection from the mold. These areas require "side core" to produce the undercut relief.
3. **Parting line analysis:** This tool analyzes the transitions between positive and negative draft to optimize the parting line.
4. **Scale the model up:** This scaling is needed to account for the plastic shrinkage when it cools down. The plastic shrink factor helps in this regard.
5. **Others:** Other tools are available to repair the CAD model such as replace, move, and delete faces. We cover these tools during the tutorials.

SolidWorks offers the **Mold Tools** toolbar for mold designers to use. Click this sequence to access the toolbar: **Tools => Customize => Mold Tools => OK.** Alternatively, click this sequence: **Help** (SolidWorks menu) **=> SolidWorks Tutorials => All SolidWorks Tutorials (Set 2) => Mold Design =>** Click any **Mold Tools** icons. This second alternative is somewhat awkward, but it works for this and for any toolbar. Figure 16.5 shows the toolbar, which has four groups: surfaces, preparation, analysis, and tooling. The surfaces group provides different surfaces to help create parting surfaces and shut-off surfaces. We have covered all these surfaces in the book: what they are and when to use them. The preparation group includes all the work needed before using the tooling split. The icons of this group are split line, scale, parting lines, shut-off surfaces, and parting surfaces. The analysis group includes the draft, undercut, and parting line analyses. The tooling group includes the tooling split and core.

**FIGURE 16.5**
SolidWorks Mold Tools toolbar

The mold design process in SolidWorks begins with the CAD model and ends with the mold. SolidWorks mold design process is centered on this idea:

1. Enclose and center the CAD model inside a block (tooling block).
2. Remove (subtract or carve cut) the CAD model from inside of the block.
3. Split the block open into two halves (core and cavity).

With this idea in mind come three questions:

1. Where do you split the block?
2. How do you create the core and cavity surfaces (part imprint) in the block?
3. How do you split the block?

The answer to the first question is the parting line. The parting line defines the parting surface (plane). This surface defines where we split the tooling block. This is a geometric operation of splitting a block with a surface, but an elegant concept for mold design to create its two halves.

The answer to the second question introduces the concept of shut surfaces. Think of the cavity and core as a negative and positive. You need to imprint the part boundary (outside surfaces) into the cavity and core. These imprints (surfaces) should not have any through holes in them. Shut-off surfaces close up the through holes. Thus, you need to make changes to the part to patch the holes in its boundary. The cover of a cell phone provides an example. The molding of the cover requires a shut-off surface that is identical to the cover shape, but without holes.

The answer to the third question is the parting surface. Before we split the tooling block, we subtract the CAD model from the inside of the tooling block. This surface is planar and formed using the parting line plane. The parting surface must extend far enough beyond the size of the block to be able to split it open into two halves (core and cavity).

The steps of this mold process are as follows:

1. Create the CAD model of the part to be molded.
2. Insert mounting bosses if needed.
3. Add draft.
4. Apply shrink factor (scaling).
5. Create parting line.
6. Create shut-off surfaces, if needed.
7. Create parting surfaces.
8. Apply tooling split.
9. Separate the core and cavity.
10. Create the tooling assembly.

The draft in Step 3 ensures model ejection from the mold. The requirements of such a draft are:

☐ All faces must draft away from the parting line, which divides the core from the cavity.
☐ Design specifications must include a minimum draft angle to test against.
☐ Cavity side surfaces must display a positive draft.
☐ Core side surfaces must display a negative draft.
☐ All surfaces must display a draft angle greater than the minimum specified by the design specifications.
☐ No straddle faces must exist.

Steps 1 through 9 create a multi-body part file, which maintains the mold design in one location. (We may view this part file as a top-down assembly.) Changes to the CAD model are automatically reflected in the tooling bodies. Now, we need to create an assembly where we can add other supporting mold components such as gates, runner system, ejecting pins, etc. Step 10 creates a mold assembly file.

## 16.10 Tutorials Overview

The theme for the tutorials in this chapter is to get you to practice using mold design concepts implemented by SolidWorks **Mold Tools**. The tutorials show how to design and document molds. NyproMold, with two locations, one in Massachusetts and the other in Illinois (www.nypromold.com), has sponsored this chapter. NyproMold designs and builds injection molds for the consumer, industrial, electronics, telecommunications, and health care industries. We chat with Mr. Nishit Shah, Mold Designer and Moldflow Analyst at NyproMold, in the Industry Chat.

# Tutorial 16–1: Create a Block Mold

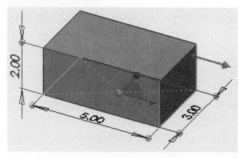

(A) Block

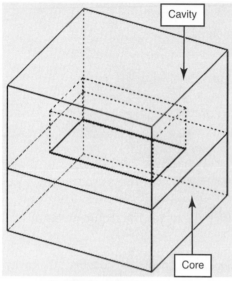

(B) Mold halves (closed position)

**FIGURE 16.6**
Core and cavity of a block mold

Create the injection mold for the plastic block shown in Figure 16.6A. All dims are in inches.

## Modeling task

Design a mold to create the block shown in Figure 16.6A.

## Modeling synthesis

There are multiple issues to consider when designing a mold. We consider the following issues for this tutorial:

☐ **Orientation of mold halves: horizontal or vertical.** We use the vertical orientation here, meaning the mold halves move up and down, not left to right, in the CAD model, as shown in Figure 16.6B. In practice, we use a horizontal injection mold machine to produce the part.

☐ **Location of parting line: top or bottom face of the block.** We use the bottom face here. The difference comes in placing the mold cavity and core in the CAD model. It is customary to place the cavity above the core in the CAD model, as shown in Figure 16.6B.

☐ **A note for the curious mind:** We could create core and cavity parts from scratch, using the part and assembly modeling concepts that have been covered in the book. As a matter of fact, as parts become complex, mold designers in practice design molds using these concepts instead of using mold software. A case in point: SolidWorks does not allow you to create a parting line in the middle of the block of this tutorial, in which case the mold's two halves become identical. To create these halves, simply create two blocks and subtract the part from each using an extrude cut operation. The difference between the halves comes in what we add to them later. The half where we add the gate becomes the cavity and the half where we add the ejection system becomes the core.

☐ **Which mold design is better:** One with a parting line in the middle, or one with a parting line on the bottom face as we do in this tutorial? Although it does not matter theoretically, the latter design is better practically. If we place the parting line in the middle, we have no control on which side the part will stick on. Consequently, you would not know where to place (on which half) the ejection system. In the case of a sphere, we have no choice but to place the parting line in the mid (symmetry) plane of the sphere.

## Modeling plan

We do not use draft, undercut, or parting line analyses in this tutorial for simplicity.

## Design intent

Ignore for this chapter.

## CAD steps

We create the mold in seven steps:

1. Create the block CAD model.
2. Apply shrink factor.
3. Create parting line.
4. Create shut-off surface.
5. Create parting surface.
6. Apply tooling split to create the mold core and cavity.
7. Create the tooling assembly.

The details of these steps are shown below.

## Step 1: Create the block CAD model

| Task | Command Sequence to Click |
|---|---|
| A. Start SolidWorks, open a new part, create the block as an extrusion (shown below), and save it as *tutorial16.1*. | **Open => New = Part** => Create the block. Use the top plane to create the sketch => **Extrude** it => **Save As** => *tutorial16.1* => **Save** as shown to the left.<br><br>**Help:** Start with the top plane as sketch plane; create the center rectangle at the origin as shown to the left. Then, extrude the sketch down 2.0 in. |

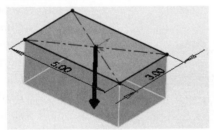

## Step 2: Apply shrink factor

| Task | Command Sequence to Click |
|---|---|
| A. Apply a shrink factor of 5%. | **Scale** (**Mold Tools** toolbar) => Enter 1.05 for the scale value as shown to the left. **Scale about** the model **Centroid**.<br><br>**Why:** We scale the model geometry up by 5% to account for the amount the plastic will shrink as it cools. The **Scale** tool scales only the geometry of the model. It does not scale dimensions, sketches, or reference geometry<br><br>**Help:** You may also use this sequence to access the scaling function: **Insert** (SolidWorks menu) => **Molds** => **Scale**. |

## Step 3: Create parting line

### Task

**A.** Define the pulling direction.

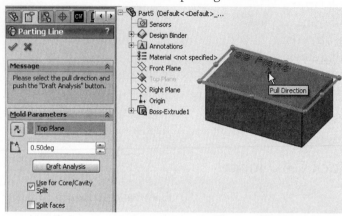

**B.** Set the draft angle and define the parting line.

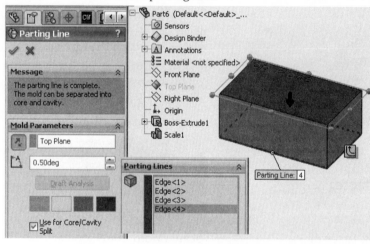

### Command Sequence to Click

**Parting Lines (Mold Tools** tab) => Select **Top Plane** from part features tree => Click the arrow direction to reverse the pull direction as shown to the left.
**Help:** The pulling direction is the direction along which we pull (eject) the part away from the cavity. This direction determines the direction of the draft of the part faces.
**Why:** We reverse the pulling direction because we place the cavity on top of the core in this tutorial.
**Help:** As a rule, the pulling direction must always pull away from the cavity.
**Draft Analysis** (button shown in the screenshot in Task A above) => Set draft angle to 0.5 degree (shown to the left) => Select the four edges on the top face and shown to the left (these edges form the parting line) => Green check mark to finish.
**Help:** The parting line must form a closed contour; otherwise, the tooling split step fails (Step 6 of this tutorial).
**Help:** Four colors are used to indicate a face draft:
**Green: positive draft**
**Yellow: no draft**
**Red: negative draft**
**Blue: straddle**

## Step 4: Create shut-off surface

### Task

**A.** Create shut-off surface.

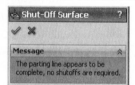

### Command Sequence to Click

**Shut-off Surfaces (Mold Tools** tab) => Red X to finish as shown to the left.
**Why:** The block mold does not need shut-off surfaces as the message shown to the left displays because the face of the parting lines does not have any holes.
**Help:** To perform tooling split, you need two complete surfaces (a core surface and a cavity surface) without any through holes. Shut-off surfaces close up the through holes. The tooling split cuts the tooling block into two pieces (halves). See Step 6 of this tutorial.

## Step 5: Create parting surface

### Task

A. Create parting surface.

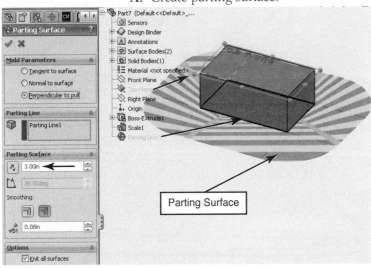

Parting Surface

### Command Sequence to Click

**Parting Surfaces** (**Mold Tools** tab) => Type 3 for parting surface thickness as shown to the left => Green check mark to finish.

**Why:** We use a value of 3.0 in. for the parting surface thickness shown on the screenshot to the left. This thickness must be large enough to extend beyond the size of the tooling split block size used in Task B of Step 6.

**Help:** The features tree shown to the left highlights the **Top Plane** (pulling direction) and **Parting Line1** (parting line) to remind the user of their existence while setting up the thickness of the parting surface.

## Step 6: Apply tooling split

### Task

A. Select the top plane, and sketch a rectangle that encloses the CAD model.

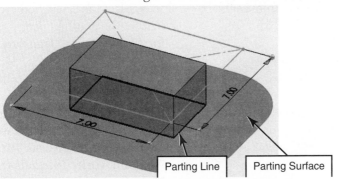

Parting Line    Parting Surface

### Command Sequence to Click

**Tooling Split** (**Mold Tools** tab) => select the **Top Plane** from the features tree => Sketch a 7 × 7 in. center rectangle as shown to the left.

**Why:** The part center rectangle is 5 × 3. Thus, the 7 × 7 encloses it.

B. Prepare the tool.

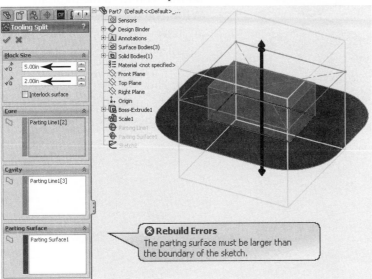

**⊗ Rebuild Errors**
The parting surface must be larger than the boundary of the sketch.

Exit the sketch => Review the tool data in the features tree as shown to the left.

**Help:** You may check off the **Interlock surface** box. The interlock surface surrounds the perimeter of the parting surfaces in a 3° taper. The interlock surface drafts away from the parting line. Interlock surfaces are used to seal the mold properly and minimize the cost of machining the mold plates across the split, because the area surrounding the interlock is planar.

**Help:** The block size of 5 and 2 in. shown to the left is arbitrary and indicates the height of the mold cavity and core, respectively.

| Task | Command Sequence to Click |
|---|---|

**Help:** The error message shown here to the left may be generated if the size of the **Parting Surface** is smaller than that of the **Block Size**. Try it.

Green check mark to finish

**Help:** The tool is created as shown to the left. What is left now is to move the two halves away to visualize the mold halves.

C. Create the tool.

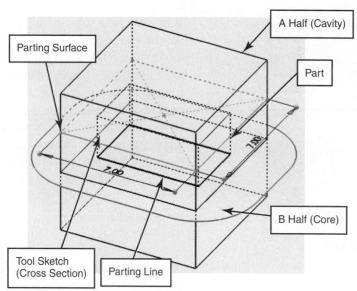

D. Separate the core from the cavity by moving them away from each other as shown below.

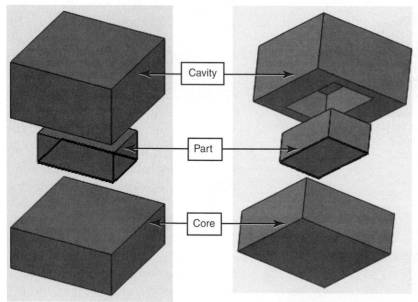

**Move/Copy Bodies** (**Data Migration** tab) => Select the cavity body (the upper half) in the graphics pane => Enter 4 for $\Delta Y$ field under **Translate** as shown to the left => Green check mark to finish. Repeat for the core (bottom half), but use $-4$ for $\Delta Y$.

**Help:** To access the **Data Migration**, click this sequence: **Help** (SolidWorks menu) => **SolidWorks Tutorials** => **All SolidWorks Tutorials (Set 2)** => **Mold Design** => Click **Move/Copy Bodies** icon from the tutorial.

**Why:** The $\Delta Y = \pm 4$ values are arbitrary, just enough to provide good visualization of the mold as shown to the left.

**Help:** Hide the parting surface and rotate the mold halves to view. Also, use transparency to view the inside.

## Step 7: Create the tooling assembly

| Task | Command Sequence to Click |
|---|---|
| **A.** While the mold file is open (from the preceding steps), save the core and cavity as parts in separate files. | **Solid Bodies** (from mold features tree) => Right-click **Body-Move/Copy1** => **Insert into New Part** (from the pop-up window) => Type *cavity* for part name => **Save** (select a folder if needed). Repeat for **Body-Move/Copy2** and save as *core* as shown to the left. **Help:** You may rename the **Body-Move/Copy1** and **Body-Move/Copy2** features in the mold part features tree to *cavity* and *core*, respectively, for convenience. **Help:** Add mold supporting components to each file, if needed. We assemble them next in Task B. |

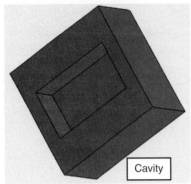

Cavity

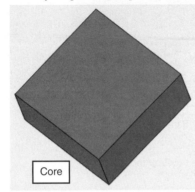

Core

| Task | Command Sequence to Click |
|---|---|
| **B.** Create a mold assembly and insert its parts. | **File** (SolidWorks menu) => **New** => **Assembly** => **OK** => Insert and assemble the core and cavity parts. Save the assembly as *moldAssembly*. **Help:** The two tooling parts are now components of the assembly, with external references to *tutorial16.1.sldprt*. You can add other mold features, create mates, etc. Changes to the block model (in *tutorial16.1* part file) are automatically reflected in the tooling parts in the assembly. |

---

> ***HANDS-ON FOR TUTORIAL 16–1.*** Add a vertical 1.0 in. diameter through hole in the block. The hole is centered in the top face of the block. Create the new mold. Submit a screenshot of the mold's two halves.

---

## Tutorial 16–2: Create a Sandbox Mold

Create the injection mold for the plastic sandbox shown in Figure 16.7A. All dims are in inches.

### Modeling task

Design a mold to create the sandbox shown in Figure 16.7A. The difference between this tutorial and Tutorial 16–1 is that the sandbox is a shell with a wall thickness.

### Modeling synthesis

Following Tutorial 16–1, we use the vertical orientation for the mold and we place the parting line at the top face of the shell. If we create the mold for the part in its present orientation, the core is placed above the cavity, which is against the customary convention. Thus, we flip the sandbox upside down to force the cavity above the core.

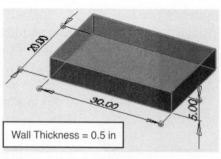

Wall Thickness = 0.5 in

(A) Sandbox

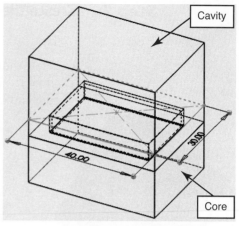

Cavity

Core

(B) Mold halves (closed position)

**FIGURE 16.7**
Core and cavity of a sandbox mold

## Modeling plan

We do not use draft, undercut, or parting line analyses in this tutorial for simplicity.

## Design intent

Ignore for this chapter.

## CAD steps

We create the mold in seven steps:

1. Create the sandbox CAD model and flip it.
2. Apply shrink factor and flip the part.
3. Create parting line.
4. Create shut-off surface.
5. Create parting surface.
6. Apply tooling split to create the mold core and cavity.
7. Create the tooling assembly.

The details of these steps are shown below.

## Step 1: Create the sandbox CAD model and flip it

### Task

A. Start SolidWorks, open a new part, create the sand as an extrusion (shown below), shell it, and save it as *tutorial16.2*.

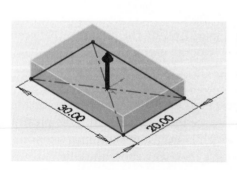

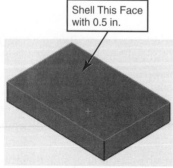

Shell This Face with 0.5 in.

### Command Sequence to Click

**Open => New => Part** => Create the sandbox. Use the top plane to create the sketch => Extrude it => Shell it => **Save As** => *tutorial16.2* => **Save.** **Help:** Start with the top plane as sketch plane; create the center rectangle at the origin as shown to the left. Then, extrude the sketch up 5.0 in. and shell it by a 0.5 in. thickness.

| Task | Command Sequence to Click |
|---|---|

**B.** Flip the sandbox upside down.

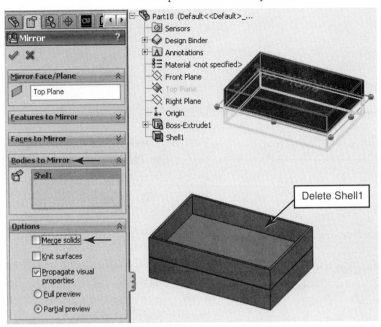

Delete Shell1

**Mirror (Features** tab) => Select the **Top Plane** as the mirror plane from the features tree => Expand the **Bodies to Mirror** pane shown to the left if it is not already expanded => Select the shell from the graphics pane => Uncheck **Merge solids** check box shown to the left => Green check mark to finish. **Why:** If we do not uncheck **Merge solids** check box, SolidWorks combines the original shell with the mirrored one. **Why:** We could have created the sandbox in an upside-down orientation to avoid this task and the next one. But that would be asking too much from the designer far ahead. While it is possible, it is not common to demand such foresight.

**C.** Delete the original shell (Shell1).

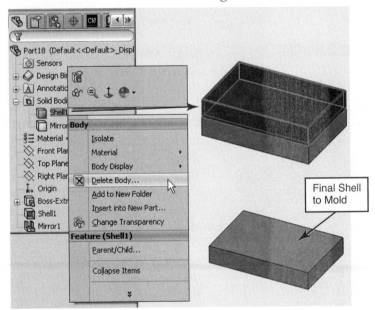

Final Shell to Mold

**Solid Bodies(2)** on the features tree (click to expand) => Right-click **Shell1 => Delete Body** => Green check mark to finish as shown to the left.

## Step 2: Apply shrink factor and flip the part

| Task | Command Sequence to Click |
|---|---|

**A.** Apply a shrink factor of 5%.

**Scale (Mold Tools** toolbar) => Enter 1.05 for the scale value as shown to the left. **Scale about** the model **Centroid.** **Why:** We scale the model geometry up by 5% to account for the amount the plastic will shrink as it cools. The **Scale** tool scales only the geometry of the model. It does not scale dimensions, sketches, or reference geometry.

| Task | Command Sequence to Click |
|---|---|
| | **Help:** You may also use this sequence to access the scaling function: **Insert** (SolidWorks menu) => **Molds** => **Scale**. |

## Step 3: Create parting line

| Task | Command sequence to click |
|---|---|
| A. Define the pulling direction. 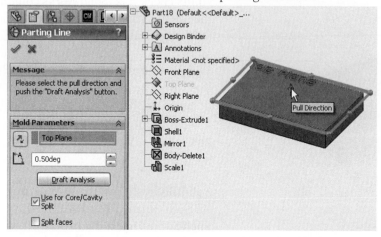 | **Parting Lines** (**Mold Tools** tab) => Select **Top Plane** from part features tree => Click the arrow direction to reverse the pull direction as shown to the left. **Help:** The pulling direction is the direction along which we pull (eject) the part away from the cavity. This direction determines the direction of the draft of the part faces. **Why:** We reverse the pulling direction because we place the cavity on top of the core in this tutorial. **Help:** As a rule, the pulling direction must always pull away from the cavity. |
| B. Set the draft angle and define the parting line. 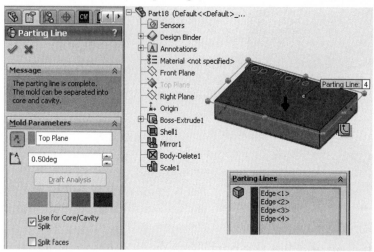 | **Draft Analysis** (button shown in the screenshot in Task A above) => Set draft angle to 0.5 degree (shown to the left) => Select the four outer edges on the top face of the shell and shown to the left (these edges form the parting line) => Green check mark to finish. **Help:** The parting line must form a closed contour; otherwise, the tooling split step fails (Step 6 of this tutorial). **Help:** Four colors are used to indicate a face draft: **Green: positive draft** **Yellow: no draft** **Red: negative draft** **Blue: straddle** |

## Step 4: Create shut-off surface

| Task | Command Sequence to Click |
|---|---|
| A. Create shut-off surface. 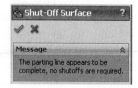 | **Shut-off Surfaces** (**Mold Tools** tab) => Green check mark to finish as shown to the left. **Why:** The sandbox mold does not need shut-off surfaces because the face of the parting lines does not have any holes. |

## Step 5: Create parting surface

### Task

A. Create parting surface.

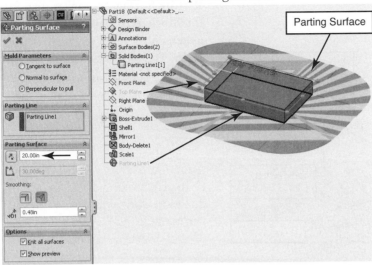

### Command Sequence to Click

**Parting Surfaces** (**Mold Tools** tab) => Type 20 for parting surface thickness as shown to the left => Green check mark to finish.

**Why:** We use an arbitrary value of 20.0 in. for the parting surface as the screenshot to the left shows. We plan to use a 40 × 30 mold because the sandbox is 30 × 20. We figure out to use 5 inch mold thickness on each side of the core or the cavity.

**Help:** The features tree shown to the left highlights the **Top Plane** (pulling direction) and **Parting Line1** (parting line) to remind the user of their existence while setting up the core thickness (parting surface).

## Step 6: Apply tooling split

### Task

A. Select the top plane and sketch a rectangle that encloses the CAD model.

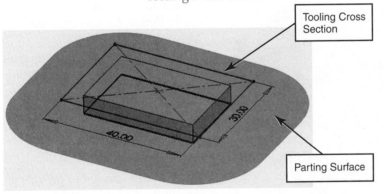

### Command Sequence to Click

**Tooling Split** (**Mold Tools** tab) => Select the **Top Plane** from the features tree => Sketch a 40 × 40 in. center rectangle as shown to the left.

**Why:** The part rectangle is 30 × 20. Thus the 40 × 30 encloses it. Make sure the 40 × 30 size is enough to enclose the part cross section, but not larger than the parting surface size of Task A of Step 5. If it is, the nest task fails.

B. Prepare the tool.

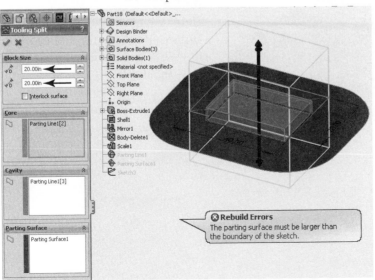

Exit the sketch => Review the tool data in the features tree.

**Help:** You may check off the **Interlock surface** box shown to the left. The interlock surface surrounds the perimeter of the parting surfaces in a 3° taper. The interlock surface drafts away from the parting line. Interlock surfaces are used to seal the mold properly and minimize the cost of machining the mold plates across the split, because the area surrounding the interlock is planar.

**Help:** The block size of 20 × 20 in. shown to the left is arbitrary and indicates the height of the mold cavity and core, respectively, as shown to the left.

| Task | Command Sequence to Click |
|---|---|

**C.** Create the tool.

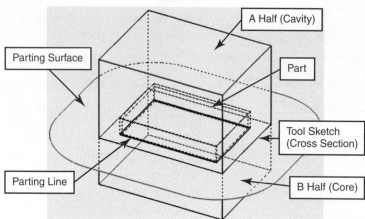

Parting Surface

A Half (Cavity)

Part

Tool Sketch (Cross Section)

Parting Line

B Half (Core)

**Help:** The error message shown to the left may be generated if the size of the **Parting Surface** is smaller than that of the **Block Size**. Try it.
Green check mark to finish
**Help:** The tool is created as shown to the left. What is left is to move the two halves away to visualize the mold halves.

**D.** Separate the core from the cavity by moving them away from each other as shown below.

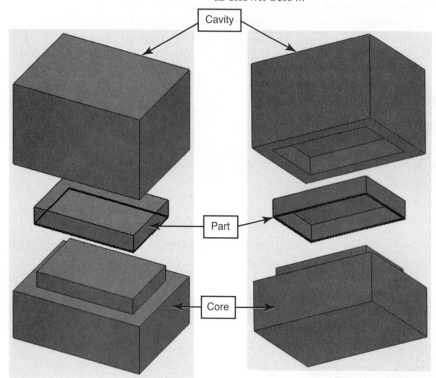

Cavity

Part

Core

**Move/Copy Bodies (Data Migration** tab) => Select the cavity body (the upper half) in the graphics pane => Enter 20 for $\Delta Y$ field under **Translate** as shown to the left => Green check mark to finish. Repeat for core, but use $-20$ for $\Delta Y$.

**Help:** To access the **Data Migration,** click this sequence: **Help** (SolidWorks menu) => **SolidWorks Tutorials** => **All SolidWorks Tutorials (Set 2)** => **Mold Design** => Click **Move/Copy Bodies** icon from the tutorial.
**Why:** The $\Delta Y = \pm 20$ values are arbitrary, just enough to provide good visualization of the mold as shown to the left.
**Help:** We hide the parting line and surface and rotate the mold components to view. We also use transparency to view the inside.

## Step 7: Create the tooling assembly

| Task | Command Sequence to Click |
|---|---|
| A. While the mold file is open (from above steps), save the core and cavity as parts in separate files. | **Solid Bodies** (from mold features tree) => Right-click **Body-Move/Copy1** => **Insert into New Part** (from the pop-up window) => Type *cavity* for part name => **Save** (select a folder if needed). Repeat for **Body-Move/Copy2** and save as *core* as shown to the left. |

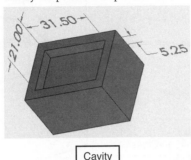

Cavity

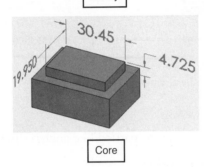

Core

**Why:** We display the core and cavity dimensions to verify that our steps are correct. Study these dimensions and make sense of them. Keep in mind that the values shown to the left reflect the 5% scaling. Note that the effect of scaling does not show in the part dimensions, only the mold halves.

**Why:** SolidWorks does not allow you to edit the mold halves in their respective parts. There are no sketches or geometry in the features tree to edit. You must edit in the CAD model.

| Task | Command Sequence to Click |
|---|---|
| B. Create a mold assembly and insert its parts. | **File** (SolidWorks menu) => **New** => **Assembly** => **OK** => Insert and assemble the core and cavity parts. Save the assembly as *moldAssembly*. |

> ***HANDS-ON FOR TUTORIAL 16–2.*** Redo the tutorial using a circular cross section for the sandbox instead of a rectangular one. The diameter of the circle is 30 in.

## Tutorial 16–3   Create a Hemisphere Mold

Create the injection mold for the plastic hemisphere shown in Figure 16.8A. All dims are in inches.

### Modeling task

Design a mold to create the hemisphere shown in Figure 16.8A.

### Modeling synthesis

We wanted to create a mold for a sphere in this example. But as we discuss in Tutorial 16–1, SolidWorks cannot create a parting line (circle) in the sphere midplane. Thus, we opt to use a hemisphere. Following Tutorial 16–1, we use the vertical orientation for the mold, and we place the parting line at the planar face of the hemisphere shown in Figure 16.8A.

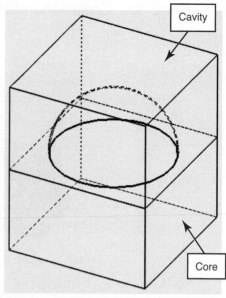

Cavity

Core

(A) Hemisphere

(B) Mold halves (closed position)

**FIGURE 16.8**
Core and cavity of a hemisphere mold

### Modeling plan

We do not use draft, undercut, or parting line analyses in this tutorial for simplicity.

### Design intent

Ignore for this chapter.

### CAD steps

We create the mold in seven steps:

1. Create the hemisphere CAD model.
2. Apply shrink factor.
3. Create parting line.
4. Create shut-off surface.
5. Create parting surface.
6. Apply tooling split to create the mold core and cavity.
7. Create the tooling assembly.

The details of these steps are shown below.

## Step 1: Create the hemisphere CAD model

| Task | Command Sequence to Click |
|---|---|
| A. Start SolidWorks, open a new part, create the hemisphere as an extrusion (see below), shell it, and save it as *tutorial16.3*. | **Open => New => Part** => Create the hemisphere. Use the top plane to create the sketch => **Revolve it** => **Save As** => *tutorial16.3* => **Save** as shown to the left.<br>**Help:** Revolve the sketch 180°. |

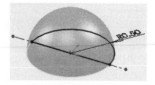

## Step 2: Apply shrink factor

### Task

A. Apply a shrink factor of 5%.

### Command Sequence to Click

**Scale** (**Mold Tools** toolbar) => Enter 1.05 for the scale value as shown to the left. **Scale about** the model **Centroid**. **Why:** We scale the model geometry up by 5% to account for the amount the plastic will shrink as it cools. The **Scale** tool scales only the geometry of the model.

## Step 3: Create parting line

### Task

A. Define the pulling direction.

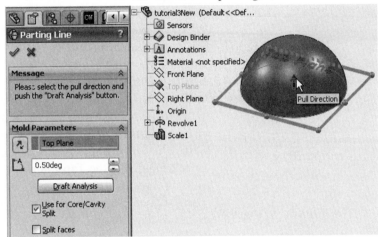

### Command Sequence to Click

**Parting Lines** (**Mold Tools** tab) => Select **Top Plane** from part features tree => Click the arrow direction to reverse the pull direction as shown to the left. **Help:** The pulling direction is the direction along which we pull (eject) the part away from the cavity. This direction determines the direction of the draft of the part faces.
**Why:** We reverse the pulling direction because we place the cavity on top of the core in this tutorial.

B. Set the draft angle and define the parting line.

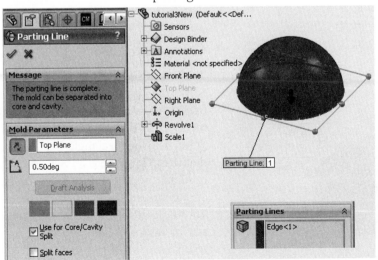

**Draft Analysis** (button shown in the screenshot in Task A above) => Set draft angle to 0.5 degree (shown to the left) => Select the edge of the top face as shown to the left => Green check mark to finish.
**Help:** The parting line must form a closed contour; otherwise, the tooling split step fails (Step 6 of this tutorial).
**Help:** Four colors are used to indicate a face draft:
**Green: positive draft**
**Yellow: no draft**
**Red: negative draft**
**Blue: straddle**

## Step 4: Create shut-off surface

Task

A. Create shut-off surface.

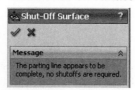

Command Sequence to Click

**Shut-off Surfaces** (**Mold Tools** tab)
=> Green check mark to finish as
shown to the left.
**Why:** The hemisphere mold does not
need shut-off surfaces because the face
of the parting lines does not have any
holes.

## Step 5: Create parting surface

Task

A. Create parting surface.

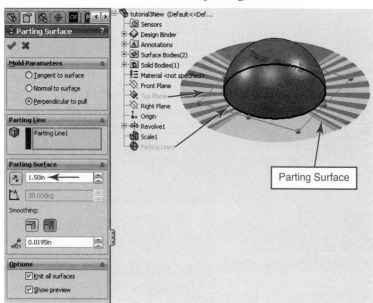

Parting Surface

Command Sequence to Click

**Parting surfaces** (**Mold Tools** tab) =>
Type 1.5 for parting surface thickness as
shown to the left => Green check mark
to finish.
**Why:** We use an arbitrary value of
1.5 in. for the parting surface as the
screenshot to the left shows. We plan to
use a 2 × 2 mold because the
hemisphere diameter is 1 in. We figure
out to use 0.5 inch mold thickness on
each side of the core or the cavity.
**Help:** The features tree shown here on
the left highlights the **Top Plane**
(pulling direction) and **Parting Line1**
(parting line) to remind the user of their
existence while setting up the core
thickness (parting surface).

## Step 6: Apply tooling split

Task

A. Select the top plane and sketch
a rectangle that encloses the
CAD model.

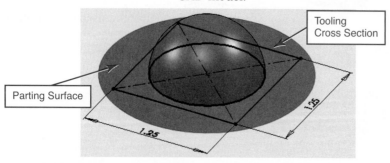

Tooling
Cross Section

Parting Surface

Command Sequence to Click

**Tooling Split** (**Mold Tools** tab) =>
Select the **Top Plane** from the features
tree => Sketch a 1.25 × 1.25 in. center
rectangle as shown to the left.
**Why:** The part rectangle is 1 in. in
diameter. Thus the 1.25 × 1.25 encloses
it. Make sure the 1.25 × 1.25 size is
enough to enclose the part cross section,
but not larger than the parting surface
size of Task A of Step 5. If it is, the nest
task fails.

| Task | Command Sequence to Click |
|---|---|

**B.** Prepare the tool.

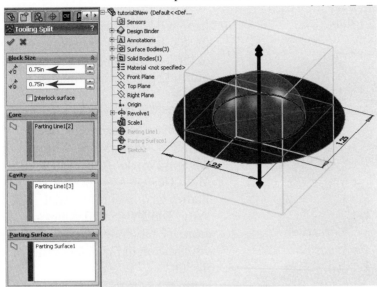

Exit the sketch => Review the tool data in the features tree as shown to the left. **Help:** You may check off the **Interlock surface** box shown here on the left. The interlock surface surrounds the perimeter of the parting surfaces in a 3° taper. The interlock surface drafts away from the parting line. Interlock surfaces are used to seal the mold properly and minimize the cost of machining the mold plates across the split, because the area surrounding the interlock is planar. **Help:** The block size of 0.75 × 0.75 in. shown to the left is arbitrary and indicates the height of the mold cavity and core, respectively.

**C.** Create the tool.

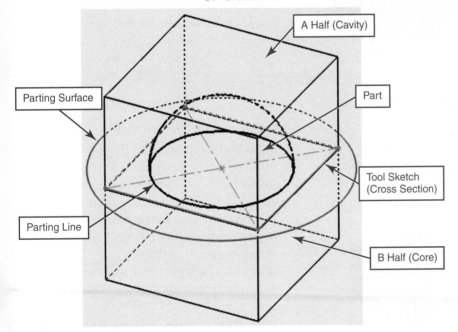

Green check mark to finish
**Help:** The tool is created as shown to the left. What is left is to move the two halves away to visualize the mold halves.

| Task | Command Sequence to Click |
|---|---|

**Task**

D. Separate the core from the cavity by moving them away from each other as shown below.

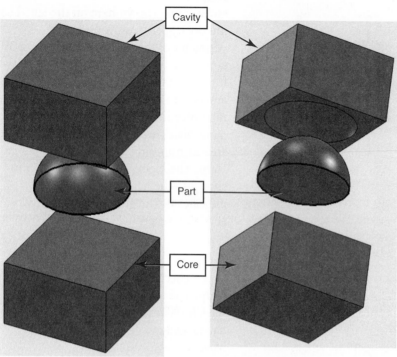

**Command Sequence to Click**

**Move/Copy Bodies** (**Data Migration** tab) => Select the cavity body (the upper half) in the graphics pane => Enter 20 for $\Delta Y$ field under **Translate** as shown to the left => Green check mark to finish. Repeat for core, but use $-20$ for $\Delta Y$.

*Help:* To access the **Data Migration**, click this sequence: **Help** (SolidWorks menu) => **SolidWorks Tutorials** => **All SolidWorks Tutorials (Set 2)** => **Mold Design** => Click **Move/Copy Bodies** icon from the tutorial.

**Why:** The $\Delta Y = \pm 20$ values are arbitrary, just enough to provide good visualization of the mold as shown to the left.

**Help:** We hide the parting line and surface, and rotate the mold components to view. We also use transparency to view the inside.

## Step 7: Create the tooling assembly

**Task**

A. While the mold file is open (from above steps), save the core and cavity as parts in separate files.

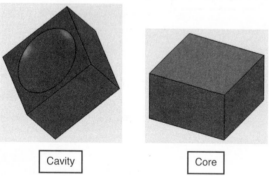

B. Create a mold assembly and insert its parts.

**Command sequence to click**

**Solid Bodies** (from mold features tree) => Right-click **Body-Move/Copy1** => **Insert into New Part** (from the pop-up window) => Type *cavity* for part name => **Save** (select a folder if needed). Repeat for **Body-Move/Copy2** and save as *core* as shown to the left.

**Why:** We display the core and cavity dimensions to verify that our steps are correct. Study these dimensions and make sense of them. Keep in mind that the values shown here on the left reflect the 5% scaling. Note that the effect of scaling does not show in the part dimensions, only the mold halves.

**Why:** SolidWorks does not allow you to edit the mold halves in their respective parts. There are no sketches or geometry in the features tree to edit. You must edit in the CAD model.

**File** (SolidWorks menu) => **New** => **Assembly** => **OK** => Insert and assemble the core and cavity parts. Save the assembly as *moldAssembly*.

> ***HANDS-ON FOR TUTORIAL 16–3.*** Add a hemisphere hole with a 0.5 in. diameter. Create the new mold. Submit a screenshot of the mold's two halves.

## Tutorial 16–4: Generate a Mold Drawing

Create the engineering drawing of the sandbox mold created in Tutorial 16–2. Follow these steps to create the drawings.

### Drawing task

Create the drawings of the mold halves.

### Drawing synthesis

We create a drawing with four views: the three typical (front, top, and right) and the ISO.

### Drawing plan

We open a drawing, insert its views, change line fonts (e.g., dashed for hidden lines), and insert dimensions. We insert a front view first, followed by inserting the other views. We will not fill the title block at this time.

### Drawing steps

We create the drawing in two steps:

1. Create the cavity drawing.
2. Create the core drawing.

The details of these steps are shown below.

## Step 1: Create the cavity drawing

| Task | Command Sequence to Click |
|---|---|
| A. Open a new drawing (SolidWorks **Drawing** mode). Also, open the cavity part file to generate the views. | Open the mold cavity part first before opening a new drawing: Click **File => Open =>** Select cavity part from the window that pops up => **Open**. Now open a new drawing: Click **File => New => Drawing => OK => OK** (to select drawing default size) => Insert the views.<br>**Help:** Make sure that the **Third Angle of projection** is selected to get the right views. |
| B. Save the drawing. | **File => Save As** => *cavity* |
| C. Insert dimensions. | **Smart Dimension** from **Annotation** tab => Select the entity to dimension => Drag the mouse to place the dimension => Repeat if needed for another dimension => Green check mark to finish.<br>**Help:** There are no model dimensions to insert using **Model items** option because there is no sketch for the cavity part. Thus, you must insert individual dimensions. |

Figure 16.9 shows the final mold cavity drawing. The dimensions shown reflect the 5% scaling (shrink) factor.

**Why:** Study and verify that these dimensions are what you would expect.

**FIGURE 16.9**
Mold cavity drawing

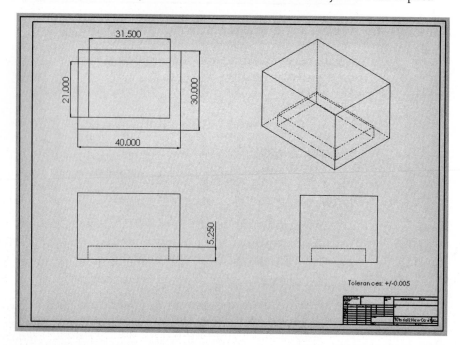

## Step 2: Create the core drawing

Repeat the above instructions of Step 1 to generate the drawing for the mold core shown in Figure 16.10.

**FIGURE 16.10**
Mold core drawing

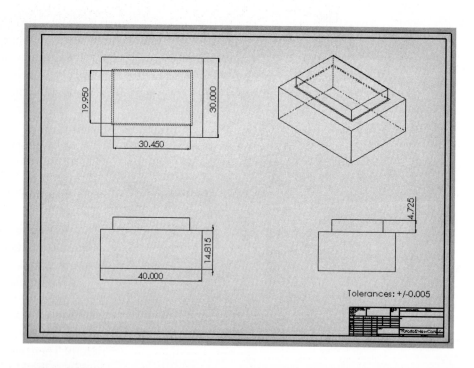

> **HANDS-ON FOR TUTORIAL 16–4.** Create an assembly drawing for the mold. Add dimensions and tolerances.

This section provides practical insight into how the chapter material is used in industry in the real world and practice. This section summarizes the chat with Mr. Nishit Shah (Mold Designer and Moldflow Analyst) of NyproMold, the sponsor of this chapter. The structure of the chat follows the chapter sections. Figure 16.11 shows a side action mold. The mold is a 16 cavity tool with side actions and stripper ejection. It is used to make a tube-like part for the health care industry. The mold is shown in the open position with the A and B halves separated. The left side is the B-half or the moving half, and the right side is the A-half or the fixed half.

Side action mold

**FIGURE 16.11**
Sample products (Courtesy of NyproMold Inc.)

**Chapter Section 16.1:**  Introduction

ABE:  Describe the injection molding activities in your company.

NISHIT:  We offer services ranging from product design to mold build and tool support. We encourage early supplier involvement (ESI) to build a partnership with the customer early on in the design process to speed up the time to market by achieving first-time quality.

**Chapter Section 16.2:**  Basics of Injection Molding Machines

ABE:  What are the injection molding machines you have? How do you train the operators?

NISHIT:  We have several injection molding machines from manufacturers such as Husky, Netstal, etc. which we use for mold qualification and production runs as per the customer's request. The operators and the process engineers undergo training through several advanced and hands-on courses in injection molding at the Nypro Institute located in Clinton, MA.

*(continued)*

### Chapter Section 16.3: Basics of Injection Molding

**ABE:** What are the mold design basics you use? Which concepts are detrimental to mold design? What is the mold rejection rate?

**NISHIT:** Designing a mold for injection molding requires thorough knowledge of various factors such as mold types, suitability of the mold type for a part, gates and runner design, cooling, ejection, venting, mold operation sequence, etc. Improper design of any of these factors could lead to a mold that produces defective parts or even a mold that does not function as intended. This could damage the mold in some cases. Such a mold can and should be reworked to resolve the issues with improper design.

### Chapter Section 16.4: Basics of Mold Design

**ABE:** Describe the important mold design rules that your company follows.

**NISHIT:** Safety is one of the most important rules and requirements at our company. This is followed by quality and productivity.

### Chapter Section 16.5: Basics of Part Design

**ABE:** What checks and balances do you perform on part designs you receive from customers to ensure their moldability?

**NISHIT:** We analyze parts using Moldflow to ensure they are moldable. If the results indicate otherwise, we recommend suitable changes that would need customer's approval. Apart from this we use draft analysis tools to identify issues with drafts and undercuts. One must know the type of mold needed for a particular part to run the necessary checks and balances.

### Chapter Section 16.6: Phases of Mold Design

**ABE:** What does the core and cavity design entail?

**NISHIT:** Core and cavity design or stack design involves the selection of an appropriate shrink factor, creating parting and shut-off surfaces, setting up the layout based on the cavitation, creating the workpiece, and splitting the workpiece to extract mold stack components and inserts. These mold components then need to be developed further by including cooling, venting, ejection, etc.

### Chapter Section 16.7: Industry Process

**ABE:** Describe the mold making process of your company with time estimates.

**NISHIT:** The mold making process at our company starts with the acquisition of the project. The next step is to evaluate the part design for moldability. After making suitable changes and getting the customer's approval we design the core and cavity stack. This is then followed by a complete mold design and a thorough design review. After all approvals the mold design is documented through detailed drawings and the design package is released to manufacturing. The time estimates for various activities in a mold design highly depend on the complexity of the part and thus the mold design. This could range from days for some molds to several weeks for others.

**Chapter Section 16.8:** Mold Analysis

ABE: Describe the mold analysis activities of your company. Which software do you use?

NISHIT: We use FEA packages such as Moldflow, Pro/Mechanica and CFDesign to evaluate part and mold designs. Moldflow allows us to analyze the plastic part for moldability and estimating process parameters, and identify issues with molding the part. Pro/Mechanica is used for structural analysis of various mold components. CFDesign is used for analyzing and optimizing cooling circuit design in various stack components to ensure efficient heat transfer rates that meet the cycle time demands.

**Chapter Section 16.9:** SolidWorks Mold Design

ABE: How do you use SolidWorks **Mold Tools** in relation to other mold design and analysis tools?

NISHIT: The primary mold design software at our company is Pro/E Wildfire. The mold splitting process, however, is quite similar across various CAD packages.

**Others**

ABE: Any other experience you would like to share with our book readers?

NISHIT: Mold design is not only an engineering feat but with increasing complexity and today's fancy shapes of plastic parts one needs to be creative in developing new design concepts that improve mold function and productivity. Since these molds run well over a million cycles producing millions of parts, the life of the mold is very important in order to ensure the cost-effectiveness.

1. What are the differences between injection molding and machining?
2. Describe the injection molding process and its phases (elements).
3. Perform research on the type of products that injection molding can produce. Submit a detailed report about products, their applications, materials, size, etc.
4. Research the injection molding materials. Submit a detailed report about the material properties, applications (type of parts it makes), melting temperature, molding pressure, etc.
5. What are the advantages and disadvantages of injection molding?
6. Describe the main sections of an injection molding machine. What does each section do? Sketch a machine.
7. Describe the phases of an injection molding cycle. Sketch these phases.
8. Sketch the core and cavity that can make these parts: solid sphere, hollow sphere (with wall thickness), half a solid sphere, half a hollow sphere, solid cylinder (rod), hollow cylinder (pipe), half solid cylinder, half a hollow cylinder, solid torus, hollow torus, half a solid torus, half a hollow torus, solid cone, hollow cone (with wall thickness), half a solid cone, half a hollow cone, and a triangle wedge.
9. Classify the mold types. Describe these types.
10. What does a shrink factor do? Why do we need it in mold design?
11. Why do we need a parting line and a parting surface in mold design?
12. What is the result of a poor design of a runner system?
13. What is the difference between a sprue and other cooling channels?
14. Describe and explain five defects of injection molding. What causes them?
15. What is the result of a poorly vented mold?
16. List and discuss some of the mold design rules.
17. What does a tooling split do?
18. What is a shut-off surface? Why do we need it?
19. Use SolidWorks to design a mold for each of the parts of Problem 8. Assume your own dimensions. Submit screenshots of the core and cavity 3D views. Also, show the critical dimensions on the 3D views to verify the correct creation of the mold. Use a 5% shrink factor.
20. Redo Problem 19 but for the flange model shown in Figure 2.45 of Chapter 2.
21. Redo Problem 19 but for the L bracket shown in Figure 2.50 of Chapter 2.
22. Redo Problem 19 but for the pattern block shown in Figure 2.51 of Chapter 2.
23. Redo Problem 19 but for the pattern wheel shown in Figure 2.52 of Chapter 2.

# ANSI and ISO Tolerance Tables

This appendix lists the ANSI and ISO tolerance tables. The tables show the ANSI fits and their equivalent ISO symbols. The tolerance values are given for ranges of the basic sizes. All numbers in the tables are in inches. The tolerance values shown in the tables must be multiplied by $10^{-3}$.

| TABLE A.1 | Clearance Fits[1] | | | | | | | | | |
|---|---|---|---|---|---|---|---|---|---|---|
| | **RC1** | | | **RC2** | | | **RC3** | | | |
| **Basic Size** | **Limits of Clearance** | **Standard Limits** | | **Limits of Clearance** | **Standard Limits** | | **Limits of Clearance** | **Standard Limits** | | |
| **Over–To** | | **Hole H5** | **Shaft g4** | | **Hole H6** | **Shaft g5** | | **Hole H7** | **Shaft f6** | |
| 0–0.12 | 0.1 | +0.2 | −0.1 | 0.1 | +0.25 | −0.1 | 0.3 | +0.4 | −0.3 | |
| | 0.45 | 0 | −0.25 | 0.55 | 0 | −0.3 | 0.95 | 0 | −0.55 | |
| 0.12–0.24 | 0.15 | +0.2 | −0.15 | 0.15 | +0.3 | −0.15 | 0.4 | +0.5 | −0.4 | |
| | 0.5 | 0 | −0.3 | 0.65 | 0 | −0.35 | 1.12 | 0 | −0.7 | |
| 0.24–0.40 | 0.2 | +0.25 | −0.2 | 0.2 | +0.4 | −0.2 | 0.5 | +0.6 | −0.5 | |
| | 0.6 | 0 | −0.35 | 0.85 | 0 | −0.45 | 1.5 | 0 | −0.9 | |
| 0.40–0.71 | 0.25 | +0.3 | −0.25 | 0.25 | +0.4 | −0.25 | 0.6 | +0.7 | −0.6 | |
| | 0.75 | 0 | −0.45 | 0.95 | 0 | −0.55 | 1.7 | 0 | −1.0 | |
| 0.71–1.19 | 0.3 | +0.4 | −0.3 | 0.3 | +0.5 | −0.3 | 0.8 | +0.8 | −0.8 | |
| | 0.95 | 0 | −0.55 | 1.2 | 0 | −0.7 | 2.1 | 0 | −1.3 | |
| 1.19–1.97 | 0.4 | +0.4 | −0.4 | 0.4 | +0.6 | −0.4 | 1.0 | +1.0 | −1.0 | |
| | 1.1 | 0 | −0.7 | 1.4 | 0 | −0.8 | 2.6 | 0 | −1.6 | |
| 1.97–3.15 | 0.4 | +0.5 | −0.4 | 0.4 | +0.7 | −0.4 | 1.2 | +1.2 | −1.2 | |
| | 1.2 | 0 | −0.7 | 1.6 | 0 | −0.9 | 3.1 | 0 | −1.9 | |
| 3.15–4.73 | 0.5 | +0.6 | −0.5 | 0.5 | +0.9 | −0.5 | 1.4 | +1.4 | −1.4 | |
| | 1.5 | 0 | −0.9 | 2.0 | 0 | −1.1 | 3.7 | 0 | −2.3 | |
| 4.73–7.09 | 0.6 | +0.7 | −0.6 | 0.6 | +1.0 | −0.6 | 1.6 | +1.6 | −1.6 | |
| | 1.8 | 0 | −1.1 | 2.3 | 0 | −1.3 | 4.2 | 0 | −2.6 | |
| 7.09–9.85 | 0.6 | +0.8 | −0.6 | 0.6 | +1.2 | −0.6 | 2.0 | +1.8 | −2.0 | |
| | 2.0 | 0 | −1.2 | 2.6 | 0 | −1.4 | 5.0 | 0 | −3.2 | |
| 9.85–12.41 | 0.8 | +0.9 | −0.8 | 0.8 | +1.2 | −0.8 | 2.5 | +2.0 | −2.5 | |
| | 2.3 | 0 | −1.4 | 2.9 | 0 | −1.7 | 5.7 | 0 | −3.7 | |

[1]Table entries are in inches. Multiply the entries in *Limits of clearance* and *Standard limits* columns by $10^{-3}$.

## TABLE A.1  Clearance Fits[2] (continued)

| Basic Size Over–To | RC4 Limits of Clearance | RC4 Standard Limits Hole H8 | RC4 Standard Limits Shaft f7 | RC5 Limits of Clearance | RC5 Standard Limits Hole H8 | RC5 Standard Limits Shaft e7 | RC6 Limits of Clearance | RC6 Standard Limits Hole H9 | RC6 Standard Limits Shaft e8 |
|---|---|---|---|---|---|---|---|---|---|
| 0–0.12 | 0.3<br>1.3 | +0.6<br>0 | −0.3<br>−0.7 | 0.6<br>1.6 | +0.6<br>0 | −0.6<br>−1.0 | 0.6<br>2.2 | +1.0<br>0 | −0.6<br>−1.2 |
| 0.12–0.24 | 0.4<br>1.6 | +0.7<br>0 | −0.4<br>−0.9 | 0.8<br>2.0 | +0.7<br>0 | −0.8<br>−1.3 | 0.8<br>2.7 | +1.2<br>0 | −0.8<br>−1.5 |
| 0.24–0.40 | 0.5<br>2.0 | +0.9<br>0 | −0.5<br>−1.1 | 1.0<br>2.5 | +0.9<br>0 | −1.0<br>−1.6 | 1.0<br>3.3 | +1.4<br>0 | −1.0<br>−1.9 |
| 0.40–0.71 | 0.6<br>2.3 | +1.0<br>0 | −0.6<br>−1.3 | 1.2<br>2.9 | +1.0<br>0 | −1.2<br>−1.9 | 1.2<br>3.8 | +1.6<br>0 | −1.2<br>−2.2 |
| 0.71–1.19 | 0.8<br>2.8 | +1.2<br>0 | −0.8<br>−1.6 | 1.6<br>3.6 | +1.2<br>0 | −1.6<br>−2.4 | 1.6<br>4.8 | +2.0<br>0 | −1.6<br>−2.8 |
| 1.19–1.97 | 1.0<br>3.6 | +1.6<br>0 | −1.0<br>−2.0 | 2.0<br>4.6 | +1.6<br>0 | −2.0<br>−3.0 | 2.0<br>6.1 | +2.5<br>0 | −2.0<br>−3.6 |
| 1.97–3.15 | 1.2<br>4.2 | +1.8<br>0 | −1.2<br>−2.4 | 2.5<br>5.5 | +1.8<br>0 | −2.5<br>−3.7 | 2.5<br>7.3 | +3.0<br>0 | −2.5<br>−4.3 |
| 3.15–4.73 | 1.4<br>5.0 | +2.2<br>0 | −1.4<br>−2.8 | 3.0<br>6.6 | +2.2<br>0 | −3.0<br>−4.4 | 3.0<br>8.7 | +3.5<br>0 | −3.0<br>−5.2 |
| 4.73–7.09 | 1.6<br>5.7 | +2.5<br>0 | −1.6<br>−3.2 | 3.5<br>7.6 | +2.5<br>0 | −2.5<br>−5.1 | 3.5<br>10.0 | +4.0<br>0 | −3.5<br>−6.0 |
| 7.09–9.85 | 2.0<br>6.6 | +2.8<br>0 | −2.0<br>−3.8 | 4.0<br>8.6 | +2.8<br>0 | −4.0<br>−5.8 | 4.0<br>11.3 | +4.5<br>0 | −4.0<br>−6.8 |
| 9.85–12.41 | 2.5<br>7.5 | +3.0<br>0 | −2.5<br>−4.5 | 5.0<br>10.0 | +3.0<br>0 | −5.0<br>−7.0 | 5.0<br>13.0 | +5.0<br>0 | −5.0<br>−8.0 |

[2]Table entries are in inches. Multiply the entries in *Limits of clearance* and *Standard limits* columns by $10^{-3}$.

| Basic Size Over–To | RC7 Limits of Clearance | RC7 Standard Limits Hole H9 | RC7 Standard Limits Shaft d8 | RC8 Limits of Clearance | RC8 Standard Limits Hole H10 | RC8 Standard Limits Shaft g9 | RC9 Limits of Clearance | RC9 Standard Limits Hole H11 | RC9 Standard Limits Shaft c11 |
|---|---|---|---|---|---|---|---|---|---|
| 0–0.12 | 1.0 2.6 | +1.0 0 | −1.0 −1.6 | 2.5 5.1 | +1.6 0 | −2.5 −3.5 | 4.0 8.1 | +2.5 0 | −4.0 −5.6 |
| 0.12–0.24 | 1.2 3.1 | +1.2 0 | −1.2 −1.9 | 2.8 5.8 | +1.8 0 | −2.8 −4.0 | 4.5 9.0 | +3.0 0 | −4.5 −6.0 |
| 0.24–0.40 | 1.6 3.9 | +1.4 0 | −1.6 −2.5 | 3.0 6.6 | +2.2 0 | −3.0 −4.4 | 5.0 10.7 | +3.5 0 | −5.0 −7.2 |
| 0.40–0.71 | 2.0 4.6 | +1.6 0 | −2.0 −3.0 | 3.5 7.9 | +2.8 0 | −3.5 −5.1 | 6.0 12.8 | +4.0 0 | −6.0 −8.8 |
| 0.71–1.19 | 2.5 5.7 | +2.0 0 | −2.5 −3.7 | 4.5 10.0 | +3.5 0 | −4.5 −6.5 | 7.0 15.5 | +5.0 0 | −7.0 −10.5 |
| 1.19–1.97 | 3.0 7.1 | +2.5 0 | −3.0 −4.6 | 5.0 11.5 | +4.0 0 | −5.0 −7.5 | 8.0 18.0 | +6.0 0 | −8.0 −12.0 |
| 1.97–3.15 | 4.0 8.8 | +3.0 0 | −4.0 −5.8 | 6.0 13.5 | +4.5 0 | −6.0 −9.0 | 9.0 20.5 | +7.0 0 | −9.0 −13.5 |
| 3.15–4.73 | 5.0 10.7 | +3.5 0 | −5.0 −7.2 | 7.0 15.5 | +5.0 0 | −7.0 −10.5 | 10.0 24.0 | +9.0 0 | −10.0 −15.0 |
| 4.73–7.09 | 6.0 12.5 | +4.0 0 | −6.0 −8.5 | 8.0 18.0 | +6.0 0 | −8.0 −12.0 | 12.0 28.0 | +10.0 0 | −12.0 −18.0 |
| 7.09–9.85 | 7.0 14.3 | +4.5 0 | −7.0 −9.8 | 10.0 21.5 | +7.0 0 | −10.0 −14.5 | 15.0 34.0 | +12.0 0 | −15.0 −22.0 |
| 9.85–12.41 | 8.0 16.0 | +5.0 0 | −8.0 −11.0 | 12.0 25.0 | +8.0 0 | −12.0 −17.0 | 18.0 38.0 | +12.0 0 | −18.0 −26.0 |

[3]Table entries are in inches. Multiply the entries in *Limits of clearance* and *Standard limits* columns by $10^{-3}$.

| TABLE A.1 | Clearance Fits[4] (continued) | | | | | | | | | |
|---|---|---|---|---|---|---|---|---|---|---|
| | **LC1** | | | **LC2** | | | **LC3** | | | |
| **Basic Size** | **Limits of Clearance** | **Standard Limits** | | **Limits of Clearance** | **Standard Limits** | | **Limits of Clearance** | **Standard Limits** | | |
| **Over–To** | | **Hole H6** | **Shaft h5** | | **Hole H7** | **Shaft h6** | | **Hole H8** | **Shaft h7** | |
| 0–0.12 | 0 0.45 | +0.25 0 | 0 −0.2 | 0 0.65 | +0.4 0 | 0 −0.25 | 0 1 | +0.6 0 | 0 −0.4 | |
| 0.12–0.24 | 0 0.5 | +0.3 0 | 0 −0.2 | 0 0.8 | +0.5 0 | 0 −0.3 | 0 1.2 | +0.7 0 | 0 −0.5 | |
| 0.24–0.40 | 0 0.65 | +0.4 0 | 0 −0.25 | 0 1.0 | +0.6 0 | 0 −0.4 | 0 1.5 | +0.9 0 | 0 −0.6 | |
| 0.40–0.71 | 0 0.7 | +0.4 0 | 0 −0.3 | 0 1.1 | +0.7 0 | 0 −0.4 | 0 1.7 | +1.0 0 | 0 −0.7 | |
| 0.71–1.19 | 0 0.9 | +0.5 0 | 0 −0.4 | 0 1.3 | +0.8 0 | 0 −0.5 | 0 2 | +1.2 0 | 0 −0.8 | |
| 1.19–1.97 | 0 1.0 | +0.6 0 | 0 −0.4 | 0 1.6 | +1.0 0 | 0 −0.6 | 0 2.6 | +1.6 0 | 0 −1 | |
| 1.97–3.15 | 0 1.2 | +0.7 0 | 0 −0.5 | 0 1.9 | +1.2 0 | 0 −0.7 | 0 3 | +1.8 0 | 0 −1.2 | |
| 3.15–4.73 | 0 1.5 | +0.9 0 | 0 −0.6 | 0 2.3 | +1.4 0 | 0 −0.9 | 0 3.6 | +2.2 0 | 0 −1.4 | |
| 4.73–7.09 | 0 1.7 | +1.0 0 | 0 −0.7 | 0 2.6 | +1.6 0 | 0 −1.0 | 0 4.1 | +2.5 0 | 0 −1.6 | |
| 7.09–9.85 | 0 2.0 | +1.2 0 | 0 −0.8 | 0 3.0 | +1.8 0 | 0 −1.2 | 0 4.6 | +2.8 0 | 0 −1.8 | |
| 9.85–12.41 | 0 2.1 | +1.2 0 | 0 −0.9 | 0 3.2 | +2.0 0 | 0 −1.2 | 0 5 | +3.0 0 | 0 −2.0 | |

[4]Table entries are in inches. Multiply the entries in *Limits of clearance* and *Standard limits* columns by $10^{-3}$.

| | LC4 | | | LC5 | | | LC6 | | |
|---|---|---|---|---|---|---|---|---|---|
| | Limits of Clearance | Standard Limits | | Limits of Clearance | Standard Limits | | Limits of Clearance | Standard Limits | |
| Basic Size | | Hole H10 | Shaft h9 | | Hole H7 | Shaft g6 | | Hole H9 | Shaft f8 |
| Over–To | | | | | | | | | |
| 0–0.12 | 0 | +1.6 | 0 | 0.1 | +0.4 | −0.1 | 0.3 | +1.0 | −0.3 |
| | 2.6 | 0 | −1.0 | 0.75 | 0 | −0.35 | 1.9 | 0 | −0.9 |
| 0.12–0.24 | 0 | +1.8 | 0 | 0.15 | +0.5 | −0.15 | 0.4 | +1.2 | −0.4 |
| | 3.0 | 0 | −1.2 | 0.95 | 0 | −0.45 | 2.3 | 0 | −1.1 |
| 0.24–0.40 | 0 | +2.2 | 0 | 0.2 | +0.6 | −0.2 | 0.5 | +1.4 | −0.5 |
| | 3.6 | 0 | −1.4 | 1.2 | 0 | −0.6 | 2.8 | 0 | −1.4 |
| 0.40–0.71 | 0 | +2.8 | 0 | 0.25 | +0.7 | −0.25 | 0.6 | +1.6 | −0.6 |
| | 4.4 | 0 | −1.6 | 1.35 | 0 | −0.65 | 3.2 | 0 | −1.6 |
| 0.71–1.19 | 0 | +3.5 | 0 | 0.3 | +0.8 | −0.3 | 0.8 | +2.0 | −0.8 |
| | 5.5 | 0 | −2.0 | 1.6 | 0 | −0.8 | 4.0 | 0 | −2.0 |
| 1.19–1.97 | 0 | +4.0 | 0 | 0.4 | +1.0 | −0.4 | 1.0 | +2.5 | −1.0 |
| | 6.5 | 0 | −2.5 | 2.0 | 0 | −1.0 | 5.1 | 0 | −2.6 |
| 1.97–3.15 | 0 | +4.5 | 0 | 0.4 | +1.2 | −0.4 | 1.2 | +3.0 | −1.2 |
| | 7.5 | −0 | −3 | 2.3 | 0 | −1.1 | 6.0 | 0 | −3.0 |
| 3.15–4.73 | 0 | +5.0 | 0 | 0.5 | +1.4 | −0.5 | 1.4 | +3.5 | −1.4 |
| | 8.5 | 0 | −3.5 | 2.8 | 0 | −1.4 | 7.1 | 0 | −3.6 |
| 4.73–7.09 | 0 | +6.0 | 0 | 0.6 | +1.6 | −0.6 | 1.6 | +4.0 | −1.6 |
| | 10 | 0 | −4 | 3.2 | 0 | −1.6 | 8.1 | 0 | −4.1 |
| 7.09–9.85 | 0 | +7.0 | 0 | 0.6 | +1.8 | −0.6 | 2.0 | +4.5 | −2.0 |
| | 11.5 | 0 | −4.5 | 3.6 | 0 | −1.8 | 9.3 | 0 | −4.8 |
| 9.85–12.41 | 0 | +8.0 | 0 | 0.7 | +2.0 | −0.7 | 2.2 | +5.0 | −2.2 |
| | 13 | 0 | −5 | 3.9 | 0 | −1.9 | 10.2 | 0 | −5.2 |

[5]Table entries are in inches. Multiply the entries in *Limits of clearance* and *Standard limits* columns by $10^{-3}$.

| Basic Size Over–To | LC7 Limits of Clearance | LC7 Standard Limits Hole H10 | LC7 Standard Limits Shaft e9 | LC8 Limits of Clearance | LC8 Standard Limits Hole H10 | LC8 Standard Limits Shaft d9 | LC9 Limits of Clearance | LC9 Standard Limits Hole H11 | LC9 Standard Limits Shaft c10 |
|---|---|---|---|---|---|---|---|---|---|
| 0–0.12 | 0.6 | +1.6 | −0.6 | 1.0 | +1.6 | −1.0 | 2.5 | +2.5 | −2.5 |
|  | 3.2 | 0 | −1.6 | 3.6 | 0 | −2.0 | 6.6 | 0 | −4.1 |
| 0.12–0.24 | 0.8 | +1.8 | −0.8 | 1.2 | +1.8 | −1.2 | 2.8 | +3.0 | −2.8 |
|  | 3.8 | 0 | −2.0 | 4.2 | 0 | −2.4 | 7.6 | 0 | −4.6 |
| 0.24–0.40 | 1.0 | +2.2 | −1.0 | 1.6 | +2.2 | −1.6 | 3.0 | +3.5 | −3.0 |
|  | 4.6 | 0 | −2.4 | 5.2 | 0 | −3.0 | 8.7 | 0 | −5.2 |
| 0.40–0.71 | 1.2 | +2.8 | −1.2 | 2.0 | +2.8 | −2.0 | 3.5 | +4.0 | −3.5 |
|  | 5.6 | 0 | −2.8 | 6.4 | 0 | −3.6 | 10.3 | 0 | −6.3 |
| 0.71–1.19 | 1.6 | +3.5 | −1.6 | 2.5 | +3.5 | −2.5 | 4.5 | +5.0 | −4.5 |
|  | 7.1 | 0 | −3.6 | 8.0 | 0 | −4.5 | 13.0 | 0 | −8.0 |
| 1.19–1.97 | 2.0 | +4.0 | −2.0 | 3.0 | +4.0 | −3.0 | 5.0 | +6.0 | −5.0 |
|  | 8.5 | 0 | −4.5 | 9.5 | 0 | −5.5 | 15.0 | 0 | −9.0 |
| 1.97–3.15 | 2.5 | +4.5 | −2.5 | 4.0 | +4.5 | −4.0 | 6.0 | +7.0 | −6.0 |
|  | 10.0 | 0 | −5.5 | 11.5 | 0 | −7.0 | 17.5 | 0 | −10.5 |
| 3.15–4.73 | 3.0 | +5.0 | −3.0 | 5.0 | +5.0 | −5.0 | 7.0 | +9.0 | −7.0 |
|  | 11.5 | 0 | −6.5 | 13.5 | 0 | −8.5 | 21.0 | 0 | −12.0 |
| 4.73–7.09 | 3.5 | +6.0 | −3.5 | 6.0 | +6.0 | −6.0 | 8.0 | +10.0 | −8.0 |
|  | 13.5 | 0 | −7.5 | 16.0 | 0 | −10.0 | 24.0 | 0 | −14.0 |
| 7.09–9.85 | 4.0 | +7.0 | −4.0 | 7.0 | +7.0 | −7.0 | 10.0 | +12.0 | −10.0 |
|  | 15.5 | 0 | −8.5 | 18.5 | 0 | −11.5 | 29.0 | 0 | −17.0 |
| 9.85–12.41 | 4.5 | +8.0 | −4.5 | 7.0 | +8.0 | −7.0 | 12.0 | +12.0 | −12.0 |
|  | 17.5 | 0 | −9.5 | 20.0 | 0 | −12.0 | 32.0 | 0 | −20.0 |

[6]Table entries are in inches. Multiply the entries in *Limits of clearance* and *Standard limits* columns by $10^{-3}$.

| Basic Size | LC10 | | | LC11 | | |
|---|---|---|---|---|---|---|
| | Limits of Clearance | Standard Limits | | Limits of Clearance | Standard Limits | |
| | | Hole H12 | Shaft c12 | | Hole H13 | Shaft c13 |
| Over–To | | | | | | |
| 0–0.12 | 4.0 | +4.0 | −4.0 | 5.0 | +6.0 | −5.0 |
| | 12.0 | 0 | −8.0 | 17.0 | 0 | −11.0 |
| 0.12–0.24 | 4.5 | +5.0 | −4.5 | 6.0 | +7.0 | −6.0 |
| | 14.5 | 0 | −9.5 | 20.0 | 0 | −13.0 |
| 0.24–0.40 | 5.0 | +6.0 | −5.0 | 7.0 | +9.0 | −7.0 |
| | 17.0 | 0 | −11.0 | 25.0 | 0 | −16.0 |
| 0.40–0.71 | 6.0 | +7.0 | −6.0 | 8.0 | +10.0 | −8.0 |
| | 20.0 | 0 | −13.0 | 28.0 | 0 | −18.0 |
| 0.71–1.19 | 7.0 | +8.0 | −7.0 | 10.0 | +12.0 | −10.0 |
| | 23.0 | 0 | −15.0 | 34.0 | 0 | −22.0 |
| 1.19–1.97 | 8.0 | +10.0 | −8.0 | 12.0 | +16.0 | −12.0 |
| | 28.0 | 0 | −18.0 | 44.0 | 0 | −28.0 |
| 1.97–3.15 | 10.0 | +12.0 | −10.0 | 14.0 | +18.0 | −14.0 |
| | 34.0 | 0 | −22.0 | 50.0 | 0 | −32.0 |
| 3.15–4.73 | 11.0 | +14.0 | −11.0 | 16.0 | +22.0 | −16.0 |
| | 39.0 | 0 | −25.0 | 60.0 | 0 | −38.0 |
| 4.73–7.09 | 12.0 | +16.0 | −12.0 | 18.0 | +25.0 | −18.0 |
| | 44.0 | 0 | −28.0 | 68.0 | 0 | −43.0 |
| 7.09–9.85 | 16.0 | +18.0 | −16.0 | 22.0 | +28.0 | −22.0 |
| | 52.0 | 0 | −34.0 | 78.0 | 0 | −50.0 |
| 9.85–12.41 | 20.0 | +20.0 | −20.0 | 28.0 | +30.0 | −28.0 |
| | 60.0 | 0 | −40.0 | 88.0 | 0 | −58.0 |

[7]Table entries are in inches. Multiply the entries in *Limits of clearance* and *Standard limits* columns by $10^{-3}$.

| | LT1 | | | LT2 | | | LT3 | | |
|---|---|---|---|---|---|---|---|---|---|
| **Basic Size**<br>**Over–To** | **Limits**<br>**of Fit** | **Standard**<br>**Limits** | | **Limits**<br>**of Fit** | **Standard**<br>**Limits** | | **Limits**<br>**of Fit** | **Standard**<br>**Limits** | |
| | | **Hole**<br>**H7** | **Shaft**<br>**js6** | | **Hole**<br>**H8** | **Shaft**<br>**js7** | | **Hole**<br>**H7** | **Shaft**<br>**k6** |
| 0–0.12 | −0.10<br>+0.50 | +0.4<br>0 | +0.10<br>−0.10 | −0.2<br>+0.8 | +0.6<br>0 | +0.2<br>−0.2 | | | |
| 0.12–0.24 | −0.15<br>+0.65 | +0.5<br>0 | +0.15<br>−0.15 | −0.25<br>+0.95 | +0.7<br>0 | +0.25<br>−0.25 | | | |
| 0.24–0.40 | −0.2<br>+0.8 | +0.6<br>0 | +0.2<br>−0.2 | −0.3<br>+1.2 | +0.9<br>0 | +0.3<br>−0.3 | −0.5<br>+0.5 | +0.6<br>0 | +0.5<br>+0.1 |
| 0.40–0.71 | −0.2<br>+0.9 | +0.7<br>0 | +0.2<br>−0.2 | −0.35<br>+1.35 | +1.0<br>0 | +0.35<br>−0.35 | −0.5<br>+0.6 | +0.7<br>0 | +0.5<br>+0.1 |
| 0.71–1.19 | −0.25<br>+1.05 | +0.8<br>0 | +0.25<br>−0.25 | −0.4<br>+1.6 | +1.2<br>0 | +0.4<br>−0.4 | −0.6<br>+0.7 | +0.8<br>0 | +0.6<br>+0.1 |
| 1.19–1.97 | −0.3<br>+1.3 | +1.0<br>0 | +0.3<br>−0.3 | −0.5<br>+2.1 | +1.6<br>0 | +0.5<br>−0.5 | −0.7<br>+0.9 | +1.0<br>0 | +0.7<br>+0.1 |
| 1.97–3.15 | −0.3<br>+1.5 | +1.2<br>0 | +0.3<br>−0.3 | −0.6<br>+2.4 | +1.8<br>0 | +0.6<br>−0.6 | −0.8<br>+1.1 | +1.2<br>0 | +0.8<br>+0.1 |
| 3.15–4.73 | −0.4<br>+1.8 | +1.4<br>0 | +0.4<br>−0.4 | −0.7<br>+2.9 | +2.2<br>0 | +0.7<br>−0.7 | −1.0<br>+1.3 | +1.4<br>0 | +1.0<br>+0.1 |
| 4.73–7.09 | −0.5<br>+2.1 | +1.6<br>0 | +0.5<br>−0.5 | −0.8<br>+3.3 | +2.5<br>0 | +0.8<br>−0.8 | −1.1<br>+1.5 | +1.6<br>0 | +1.1<br>+0.1 |
| 7.09–9.85 | −0.6<br>+2.4 | +1.8<br>0 | +0.6<br>−0.6 | −0.9<br>+3.7 | +2.8<br>0 | +0.9<br>−0.9 | −1.4<br>+1.6 | +1.8<br>0 | +1.4<br>+0.2 |
| 9.85–12.41 | −0.6<br>+2.6 | +2.0<br>0 | +0.6<br>−0.6 | −1.0<br>+4.0 | +3.0<br>0 | +1.0<br>−1.0 | −1.4<br>+1.8 | +2.0<br>0 | +1.4<br>+0.2 |
| 12.41–15.75 | −0.7<br>+2.9 | +2.2<br>0 | +0.7<br>−0.7 | −1.0<br>+4.5 | +3.5<br>0 | +1.0<br>−1.0 | −1.6<br>+2.0 | +2.2<br>0 | +1.6<br>+0.2 |
| 15.75–19.69 | −0.8<br>+3.3 | +2.5<br>0 | +0.8<br>−0.8 | −1.2<br>+5.2 | +4.0<br>0 | +1.2<br>−1.2 | −1.8<br>+2.3 | +2.5<br>0 | +1.8<br>+0.2 |

[8]Table entries are in inches. Multiply the entries in *Limits of fit* and *Standard limits* columns by $10^{-3}$.

| Basic Size | LT4 | | | LT5 | | | LT6 | | |
|---|---|---|---|---|---|---|---|---|---|
| | Limits of Fit | Standard Limits | | Limits of Fit | Standard Limits | | Limits of Fit | Standard Limits | |
| Over–To | | Hole H8 | Shaft k7 | | Hole H7 | Shaft n6 | | Hole H7 | Shaft n7 |
| 0–0.12 | | | | −0.5 +0.15 | +0.4 0 | +0.5 +0.25 | −0.65 +0.15 | +0.4 0 | +0.65 +0.25 |
| 0.12–0.24 | | | | −0.6 +0.2 | +0.5 0 | +0.6 +0.3 | −0.8 +0.2 | +0.5 0 | +0.8 +0.3 |
| 0.24–0.40 | −0.7 +0.8 | +0.9 0 | +0.7 +0.1 | −0.8 +0.2 | +0.6 0 | +0.8 +0.4 | −1.0 +0.2 | +0.6 0 | +1.0 +0.4 |
| 0.40–0.71 | −0.8 +0.9 | +1.0 0 | +0.8 +0.1 | −0.9 +0.2 | +0.7 0 | +0.9 +0.5 | −1.2 +0.2 | +0.7 0 | +1.2 +0.5 |
| 0.71–1.19 | −0.9 +1.1 | +1.2 0 | +0.9 +0.1 | −1.1 +0.2 | +0.8 0 | +1.1 +0.6 | −1.4 +0.2 | +0.8 0 | +1.4 +0.6 |
| 1.19–1.97 | −1.1 +1.5 | +1.6 0 | +1.1 +0.1 | −1.3 +0.3 | +1.0 0 | +1.3 +0.7 | −1.7 +0.3 | +1.0 0 | +1.7 +0.7 |
| 1.97–3.15 | −1.3 +1.7 | +1.8 0 | +1.3 +0.1 | −1.5 +0.4 | +1.2 0 | +1.5 +0.8 | −2.0 +0.4 | +1.2 0 | +2.0 +0.8 |
| 3.15–4.73 | −1.5 +2.1 | +2.2 0 | +1.5 +0.1 | −1.9 +0.4 | +1.4 0 | +1.9 +1.0 | −2.4 +0.4 | +1.4 0 | +2.4 +1.0 |
| 4.73–7.09 | −1.7 +2.4 | +2.5 0 | +1.7 +0.1 | −2.2 +0.4 | +1.6 0 | +2.2 +1.2 | −2.8 +0.4 | +1.6 0 | +2.8 +1.2 |
| 7.09–9.85 | −2.0 +2.6 | +2.8 0 | +2.0 +0.2 | −2.6 +0.4 | +1.8 0 | +2.6 +1.4 | −3.2 +0.4 | +1.8 0 | +3.2 +1.4 |
| 9.85–12.41 | −2.2 +2.8 | +3.0 0 | +2.2 +0.2 | −2.6 +0.6 | +2.0 0 | +2.6 +1.4 | −3.4 +0.6 | +2.0 0 | +3.4 +1.4 |
| 12.41–15.75 | −2.4 +3.3 | +3.5 0 | +2.4 +0.2 | −3.0 +0.6 | +2.2 0 | +3.0 +1.6 | −3.8 +0.6 | +2.2 0 | +3.8 +1.6 |
| 15.75–19.69 | −2.7 +3.8 | +4.0 0 | +2.7 +0.2 | −3.4 +0.6 | +2.5 0 | +3.4 +1.8 | −4.3 +0.7 | +2.5 0 | +4.3 +1.8 |

[9]Table entries are in inches. Multiply the entries in *Limits of fit* and *Standard limits* columns by $10^{-3}$.

| Basic Size Over–To | LN1 Limits of Interference | LN1 Standard Limits Hole H6 | LN1 Standard Limits Shaft n5 | LN2 Limits of Interference | LN2 Standard Limits Hole H7 | LN2 Standard Limits Shaft p6 | LN3 Limits of Interference | LN3 Standard Limits Hole H7 | LN3 Standard Limits Shaft r6 |
|---|---|---|---|---|---|---|---|---|---|
| 0–0.12 | 0 | +0.25 | +0.45 | 0 | +0.4 | +0.65 | 0.1 | +0.4 | +0.75 |
|  | 0.45 | 0 | +0.25 | 0.65 | 0 | +0.4 | 0.75 | 0 | +0.5 |
| 0.12–0.24 | 0 | +0.3 | +0.5 | 0 | +0.5 | +0.8 | 0.1 | +0.5 | +0.9 |
|  | 0.5 | 0 | +0.3 | 0.8 | 0 | +0.5 | 0.9 | 0 | +0.6 |
| 0.24–0.40 | 0 | +0.4 | +0.65 | 0 | +0.6 | +1.0 | 0.2 | +0.6 | +1.2 |
|  | 0.65 | 0 | +0.4 | 1.0 | 0 | +0.6 | 1.2 | 0 | +0.8 |
| 0.40–0.71 | 0 | +0.4 | +0.8 | 0 | +0.7 | +1.1 | 0.3 | +0.7 | +1.4 |
|  | 0.8 | 0 | +0.4 | 1.1 | 0 | +0.7 | 1.4 | 0 | +1.0 |
| 0.71–1.19 | 0 | +0.5 | +1.0 | 0 | +0.8 | +1.3 | 0.4 | +0.8 | +1.7 |
|  | 1.0 | 0 | +0.5 | 1.3 | 0 | +0.8 | 1.7 | 0 | +1.2 |
| 1.19–1.97 | 0 | +0.6 | +1.1 | 0 | +1.0 | +1.6 | 0.4 | +1.0 | +2.0 |
|  | 1.1 | 0 | +0.6 | 1.6 | 0 | +1.0 | 2.0 | 0 | +1.4 |
| 1.97–3.15 | 0.1 | +0.7 | +1.3 | 0.2 | +1.2 | +2.1 | 0.4 | +1.2 | +2.3 |
|  | 1.3 | 0 | +0.7 | 2.1 | 0 | +1.4 | 2.3 | 0 | +1.6 |
| 3.15–4.73 | 0.1 | +0.9 | +1.6 | 0.2 | +1.4 | +2.4 | 0.6 | +1.4 | +2.9 |
|  | 1.6 | 0 | +1.0 | 2.5 | 0 | +1.6 | 2.9 | 0 | +2.0 |
| 4.73–7.09 | 0.2 | +1.0 | +1.9 | 0.2 | +1.6 | +2.8 | 0.9 | +1.6 | +3.5 |
|  | 1.9 | 0 | +1.2 | 2.8 | 0 | +1.8 | 3.5 | 0 | +2.5 |
| 7.09–9.85 | 0.2 | +1.2 | +2.2 | 0.2 | +1.8 | +3.2 | 1.2 | +1.8 | +4.2 |
|  | 2.2 | 0 | +1.4 | 3.2 | 0 | +2.0 | 4.2 | 0 | +3.0 |
| 9.85–12.41 | 0.2 | +1.2 | +2.3 | 0.2 | +2.0 | +3.4 | 1.5 | +2.0 | +4.7 |
|  | 2.3 | 0 | +1.4 | 3.4 | 0 | +2.2 | 4.7 | 0 | +3.5 |

[10]Table entries are in inches. Multiply the entries in *Limits of interference* and *Standard limits* columns by $10^{-3}$.

| Basic Size | FN1 | | | FN2 | | | FN3 | | |
|---|---|---|---|---|---|---|---|---|---|
| | Limits of Interference | Standard Limits | | Limits of Interference | Standard Limits | | Limits of Interference | Standard Limits | |
| Over–To | | Hole H6 | Shaft n6 | | Hole H7 | Shaft s6 | | Hole H7 | Shaft t6 |
| 0–0.12 | 0.05 | +0.25 | +0.5 | 0.2 | +0.4 | +0.85 | | | |
| | 0.5 | 0 | +0.3 | 0.85 | 0 | +0.6 | | | |
| 0.12–0.24 | 0.1 | +0.3 | +0.6 | 0.2 | +0.5 | +1.0 | | | |
| | 0.6 | 0 | +0.4 | 1.0 | 0 | +0.7 | | | |
| 0.24–0.40 | 0.1 | +0.4 | +0.75 | 0.4 | +0.6 | +1.4 | | | |
| | 0.75 | 0 | +0.5 | 1.4 | 0 | +1.0 | | | |
| 0.40–0.56 | 0.1 | +0.4 | +0.8 | 0.5 | +0.7 | +1.6 | | | |
| | 0.8 | 0 | +0.5 | 1.6 | 0 | +1.2 | | | |
| 0.56–0.71 | 0.2 | +0.4 | +0.9 | 0.5 | +0.7 | +1.6 | | | |
| | 0.9 | 0 | +0.6 | 1.6 | 0 | +1.2 | | | |
| 0.71–0.95 | 0.2 | +0.5 | +1.1 | 0.6 | +0.8 | +1.9 | | | |
| | 1.1 | 0 | +0.7 | 1.9 | 0 | +1.4 | | | |
| 0.95–1.19 | 0.3 | +0.5 | +1.2 | 0.6 | +0.8 | +1.9 | 0.8 | +0.8 | +2.1 |
| | 1.2 | 0 | +0.8 | 1.9 | 0 | +1.4 | 2.1 | 0 | +1.6 |
| 1.19–1.58 | 0.3 | +0.6 | +1.3 | 0.8 | +1.0 | +2.4 | 1.0 | +1.0 | +2.6 |
| | 1.3 | 0 | +0.9 | 2.4 | 0 | +1.8 | 2.6 | 0 | +2.0 |
| 1.58–1.97 | 0.4 | +0.6 | +1.4 | 0.8 | +1.0 | +2.4 | 1.2 | +1.0 | +2.8 |
| | 1.4 | 0 | +1.0 | 2.4 | 0 | +1.8 | 2.8 | 0 | +2.2 |
| 1.97–2.56 | 0.6 | +0.7 | +1.8 | 0.8 | +1.2 | +2.7 | 1.3 | +1.2 | +3.2 |
| | 1.8 | 0 | +1.3 | 2.7 | 0 | +2.0 | 3.2 | 0 | +2.5 |
| 2.56–3.15 | 0.7 | +0.7 | +1.9 | 1.0 | +1.2 | +2.9 | 1.8 | +1.2 | +3.7 |
| | 1.9 | 0 | +1.4 | 2.9 | 0 | +2.2 | 3.7 | 0 | +3.8 |
| 3.15–3.94 | 0.9 | +0.9 | +2.4 | 1.4 | +1.4 | +3.7 | 2.1 | +1.4 | +4.4 |
| | 2.4 | 0 | +1.8 | 3.7 | 0 | +2.8 | 4.4 | 0 | +3.5 |
| 3.94–4.73 | 1.1 | +0.9 | +2.6 | 1.6 | +1.4 | +3.9 | 2.6 | +1.4 | +4.9 |
| | 2.6 | 0 | +2.0 | 3.9 | 0 | +3.0 | 4.9 | 0 | +4.0 |
| 4.73–5.52 | 1.2 | +1.0 | +2.9 | 1.9 | +1.6 | +4.5 | 3.4 | +1.6 | +6.0 |
| | 2.9 | 0 | +2.2 | 4.5 | 0 | +3.5 | 6.0 | 0 | +5.0 |
| 5.52–6.30 | 1.5 | +1.0 | +3.2 | 2.4 | +1.6 | +5.0 | 3.4 | +1.6 | +6.0 |
| | 3.2 | 0 | +2.5 | 5.0 | 0 | +4.0 | 6.0 | 0 | +5.0 |
| 6.30–7.09 | 1.8 | +1.0 | +3.5 | 2.9 | +1.6 | +5.5 | 4.4 | +1.6 | +7.0 |
| | 3.5 | 0 | +2.8 | 5.5 | 0 | +4.5 | 7.0 | 0 | +6.0 |
| 7.09–7.88 | 1.8 | +1.2 | +3.8 | 3.2 | +1.8 | +6.2 | 5.2 | +1.8 | +8.2 |
| | 3.8 | 0 | +3.0 | 6.2 | 0 | +5.0 | 8.2 | 0 | +7.0 |
| 7.88–8.86 | 2.3 | +1.2 | +4.3 | 3.2 | +1.8 | +6.2 | 5.2 | +1.8 | +8.2 |
| | 4.3 | 0 | +3.5 | 6.2 | 0 | +5.0 | 8.2 | 0 | +7.0 |
| 8.86–9.85 | 2.3 | +1.2 | +4.3 | 4.2 | +1.8 | +7.2 | 6.2 | +1.8 | +9.2 |
| | 4.3 | 0 | +3.5 | 7.2 | 0 | +6.0 | 9.2 | 0 | +8.0 |
| 9.85–11.03 | 2.8 | +1.2 | +4.9 | 4.0 | +2.0 | +7.2 | 7.0 | +2.0 | +10.2 |
| | 4.9 | 0 | +4.0 | 7.2 | 0 | +6.0 | 10.2 | 0 | +9.0 |
| 11.03–12.41 | 2.8 | +1.2 | +4.9 | 5.0 | +2.0 | +8.2 | 7.0 | +2.0 | +10.2 |
| | 4.9 | 0 | +4.0 | 8.2 | 0 | +7.0 | 10.2 | 0 | +9.0 |

[11]Table entries are in inches. Multiply the entries in *Limits of interference* and *Standard limits* columns by $10^{-3}$.

**TABLE A.3   Interference Fits[12] (continued)**

| Basic Size | FN4 | | | FN5 | | |
|---|---|---|---|---|---|---|
| | Limits of Interference | Standard Limits | | Limits of Interference | Standard Limits | |
| Over–To | | Hole H7 | Shaft u6 | | Hole H8 | Shaft x7 |
| 0–0.12 | 0.3 0.95 | +0.4 0 | +0.95 +0.7 | 0.3 1.3 | +0.6 0 | +1.3 +0.9 |
| 0.12–0.24 | 0.4 1.2 | +0.5 0 | +1.2 +0.9 | 0.5 1.7 | +0.7 0 | +1.7 +1.2 |
| 0.24–0.40 | 0.6 1.6 | +0.6 0 | +1.6 +1.2 | 0.5 2.0 | +0.9 0 | +2.0 +1.4 |
| 0.40–0.56 | 0.7 1.8 | +0.7 0 | +1.8 +1.4 | 0.6 2.3 | +1.0 0 | +2.3 +1.6 |
| 0.56–0.71 | 0.7 1.8 | +0.7 0 | +1.8 +1.4 | 0.8 2.5 | +1.0 0 | +2.5 +1.8 |
| 0.71–0.95 | 0.8 2.1 | +0.8 0 | +2.1 +1.6 | 1.0 3.0 | +1.2 0 | +3.0 +2.2 |
| 0.95–1.19 | 1.0 2.3 | +0.8 0 | +2.3 +1.8 | 1.3 3.3 | +1.2 0 | +3.3 +2.5 |
| 1.19–1.58 | 1.5 3.1 | +1.0 0 | +3.1 +2.5 | 1.4 4.0 | +1.6 0 | +4.0 +3.0 |
| 1.58–1.97 | 1.8 3.4 | +1.0 0 | +3.4 +2.8 | 2.4 5.0 | +1.6 0 | +5.0 +4.0 |
| 1.97–2.56 | 2.3 4.2 | +1.2 0 | +4.2 +3.5 | 3.2 6.2 | +1.8 0 | +6.2 +5.0 |
| 2.56–3.15 | 2.8 4.7 | +1.2 0 | +4.7 +4.0 | 4.2 7.2 | +1.8 0 | +7.2 +6.0 |
| 3.15–3.94 | 3.6 5.9 | +1.4 0 | +5.9 +5.0 | 4.8 8.4 | +2.2 0 | +8.4 +7.0 |
| 3.94–4.73 | 4.6 6.9 | +1.4 0 | +6.9 +6.0 | 5.8 9.4 | +2.2 0 | +9.4 +8.0 |
| 4.73–5.52 | 5.4 8.0 | +1.6 0 | +8.0 +7.0 | 7.5 11.6 | +2.5 0 | +11.6 +10.0 |
| 5.52–6.30 | 5.4 8.0 | +1.6 0 | +8.0 +7.0 | 9.5 13.6 | +2.5 0 | +13.6 +12.0 |
| 6.30–7.09 | 6.4 9.0 | +1.6 0 | +9.0 +8.0 | 9.5 13.6 | +2.5 0 | +13.6 +12.0 |
| 7.09–7.88 | 7.2 10.2 | +1.8 0 | +10.2 +9.0 | 11.2 15.8 | +2.8 0 | +15.8 +14.0 |
| 7.88–8.86 | 8.2 11.2 | +1.8 0 | +11.2 +10.0 | 13.2 17.8 | +2.8 0 | +17.8 +16.0 |
| 8.86–9.85 | 10.2 13.2 | +1.8 0 | +13.2 +12.0 | 13.2 17.8 | +2.8 0 | +17.8 +16.0 |
| 9.85–11.03 | 10.2 13.2 | +2.0 0 | +13.2 +12.0 | 15.0 20.0 | +3.0 0 | +20.0 +18.0 |
| 11.3–12.41 | 12.0 15.2 | +2.0 0 | +15.2 +14.0 | 17.0 22.0 | +3.0 0 | +22.0 +20.0 |

[12]Table entries are in inches. Multiply the entries in *Limits of interference* and *Standard limits* columns by $10^{-3}$.

## TABLE A.4  Tolerance Grades—U.S. (English) Units[13]

| Basic Size | Tolerance Grade | | | | | |
|---|---|---|---|---|---|---|
| Over–To | IT6 | IT7 | IT8 | IT9 | IT10 | IT11 |
| 0–0.12 | 0.2 | 0.4 | 0.6 | 1.0 | 1.6 | 2.4 |
| 0.12–0.24 | 0.3 | 0.5 | 0.7 | 1.2 | 1.9 | 3.0 |
| 0.24–0.40 | 0.4 | 0.6 | 0.9 | 1.4 | 2.3 | 3.5 |
| 0.40–0.72 | 0.4 | 0.7 | 1.1 | 1.7 | 2.8 | 4.3 |
| 0.72–1.20 | 0.5 | 0.8 | 1.3 | 2.0 | 3.3 | 5.1 |
| 1.20–2.00 | 0.6 | 1.0 | 1.5 | 2.4 | 3.9 | 6.3 |
| 2.00–3.20 | 0.7 | 1.2 | 1.8 | 2.9 | 4.7 | 7.5 |
| 3.20–4.80 | 0.9 | 1.4 | 2.1 | 3.4 | 5.5 | 8.7 |
| 4.80–7.20 | 1.0 | 1.6 | 2.5 | 3.9 | 6.3 | 9.8 |
| 7.20–10.00 | 1.1 | 1.8 | 2.8 | 4.5 | 7.3 | 11.4 |
| 10.00–12.60 | 1.3 | 2.0 | 3.2 | 5.1 | 8.3 | 12.6 |
| 12.60–16.00 | 1.4 | 2.2 | 3.5 | 5.5 | 9.1 | 14.2 |

[13]Table entries are in inches. Multiply the entries in *Tolerance grade* columns by $10^{-3}$.

## TABLE A.5  Fundamental Deviation—US (English) Units[14]

| Basic Size | Shaft Tolerance Symbol | | | | | | | | | |
|---|---|---|---|---|---|---|---|---|---|---|
| Over–To | c | d | f | g | h | k | n | p | s | u |
| 0–0.12 | −2.4 | −0.8 | −0.2 | −0.1 | 0 | 0 | +0.2 | +0.2 | +0.6 | +0.7 |
| 0.12–0.24 | −2.8 | −1.2 | −0.4 | −0.2 | 0 | 0 | +0.3 | +0.5 | +0.7 | +0.9 |
| 0.24–0.40 | −3.1 | −1.6 | −0.5 | −0.2 | 0 | 0 | +0.4 | +0.6 | +0.9 | +1.1 |
| 0.40–0.72 | −3.7 | −2.0 | −0.6 | −0.2 | 0 | 0 | +0.5 | +0.7 | +1.1 | +1.3 |
| 0.72–0.96 | −4.3 | −2.6 | −0.8 | −0.3 | 0 | +0.1 | +0.6 | +0.9 | +1.4 | +1.6 |
| 0.96–1.20 | −4.3 | −2.6 | −0.8 | −0.3 | 0 | +0.1 | +0.6 | +0.9 | +1.4 | +1.9 |
| 1.20–1.60 | −4.7 | −3.1 | −1.0 | −0.4 | 0 | +0.1 | +0.7 | +1.0 | +1.7 | +2.4 |
| 1.60–2.00 | −5.1 | −3.1 | −1.0 | −0.4 | 0 | +0.1 | +0.7 | +1.0 | +1.7 | +2.8 |
| 2.00–2.60 | −5.5 | −3.9 | −1.2 | −0.4 | 0 | +0.1 | +0.8 | +1.3 | +2.1 | +3.4 |
| 2.60–3.20 | −5.9 | −3.9 | −1.2 | −0.4 | 0 | +0.1 | +0.8 | +1.3 | +2.3 | +4.0 |
| 3.20–4.00 | −6.7 | −4.7 | −1.4 | −0.5 | 0 | +0.1 | +0.9 | +1.5 | +2.8 | +4.9 |
| 4.00–4.80 | −7.1 | −4.7 | −1.4 | −0.5 | 0 | +0.1 | +0.9 | +1.5 | +3.1 | +5.7 |
| 4.80–5.60 | −7.9 | −5.7 | −1.7 | −0.6 | 0 | +0.1 | +1.1 | +1.7 | +3.6 | +6.7 |
| 5.60–6.40 | −8.3 | −5.7 | −1.7 | −0.6 | 0 | +0.1 | +1.1 | +1.7 | +3.9 | +7.5 |
| 6.40–7.20 | −9.1 | −5.7 | −1.7 | −0.6 | 0 | +0.1 | +1.1 | +1.7 | +4.3 | +8.3 |
| 7.20–8.00 | −9.4 | −6.7 | −2.0 | −0.6 | 0 | +0.2 | +1.2 | +2.0 | +4.8 | +9.3 |
| 8.00–9.00 | −10.2 | −6.7 | −2.0 | −0.6 | 0 | +0.2 | +1.2 | +2.0 | +5.1 | +10.2 |
| 9.00–10.00 | −11.0 | −6.7 | −2.0 | −0.6 | 0 | +0.2 | +1.2 | +2.0 | +5.5 | +11.2 |
| 10.00–11.20 | −11.8 | −7.5 | −2.2 | −0.7 | 0 | +0.2 | +1.3 | +2.2 | +6.2 | +12.4 |
| 11.20–12.60 | −13.0 | −7.5 | −2.2 | −0.7 | 0 | +0.2 | +1.3 | +2.2 | +6.7 | +13.0 |
| 12.60–14.20 | −14.2 | −8.3 | −2.4 | −0.7 | 0 | +0.2 | +1.5 | +2.4 | +7.5 | +15.4 |
| 14.20–16.00 | −15.7 | −8.3 | −2.4 | −0.7 | 0 | +0.2 | +1.5 | +2.4 | +8.2 | +17.1 |

[14]Table entries are in inches. Multiply the entries in *Shaft tolerance symbol* columns by $10^{-3}.$

## TABLE A.6 Tolerance Grades — Metric (SI) Units[15]

| Basic Size | Tolerance Grade | | | | | |
|---|---|---|---|---|---|---|
| Over–To | IT6 | IT7 | IT8 | IT9 | IT10 | IT11 |
| 0–3 | 6 | 10 | 14 | 25 | 40 | 60 |
| 3–6 | 8 | 12 | 18 | 30 | 48 | 75 |
| 6–10 | 9 | 15 | 22 | 36 | 58 | 90 |
| 10–18 | 11 | 18 | 27 | 43 | 70 | 110 |
| 18–30 | 13 | 21 | 33 | 52 | 84 | 130 |
| 30–50 | 16 | 25 | 39 | 62 | 100 | 160 |
| 50–80 | 19 | 30 | 46 | 74 | 120 | 190 |
| 80–120 | 22 | 35 | 54 | 87 | 140 | 220 |
| 120–180 | 25 | 40 | 63 | 100 | 160 | 250 |
| 180–250 | 29 | 46 | 72 | 115 | 185 | 290 |
| 250–315 | 32 | 52 | 81 | 130 | 210 | 320 |
| 315–400 | 36 | 57 | 89 | 140 | 230 | 360 |

[15]Table entries are in millimeters. Multiply the entries in *Tolerance grade* columns by $10^{-3}$.

## TABLE A.7 Fundamental Deviation—Metric (SI) Units[16]

| Basic Size | Shaft Tolerance Symbol | | | | | | | | | |
|---|---|---|---|---|---|---|---|---|---|---|
| Over–To | c | d | f | g | h | k | n | p | s | u |
| 0–3 | −60 | −20 | −6 | −2 | 0 | 0 | +4 | +6 | +14 | +18 |
| 3–6 | −70 | −30 | −10 | −4 | 0 | +1 | +8 | +12 | +19 | +23 |
| 6–10 | −80 | −40 | −13 | −5 | 0 | +1 | +10 | +15 | +23 | +28 |
| 10–14 | −95 | −50 | −16 | −6 | 0 | +1 | +12 | +18 | +28 | +33 |
| 14–18 | −95 | −50 | −16 | −6 | 0 | +1 | +12 | +18 | +28 | +33 |
| 18–24 | −110 | −65 | −20 | −7 | 0 | +2 | +15 | +22 | +35 | +41 |
| 24–30 | −110 | −65 | −20 | −7 | 0 | +2 | +15 | +22 | +35 | +48 |
| 30–40 | −120 | −80 | −25 | −9 | 0 | +2 | +17 | +26 | +43 | +60 |
| 40–50 | −130 | −80 | −25 | −9 | 0 | +2 | +17 | +26 | +43 | +70 |
| 50–65 | −140 | −100 | −30 | −10 | 0 | +2 | +20 | +32 | +53 | +87 |
| 65–80 | −150 | −100 | −30 | −10 | 0 | +2 | +20 | +32 | +59 | +102 |
| 80–100 | −170 | −120 | −36 | −12 | 0 | +3 | +23 | +37 | +71 | +124 |
| 100–120 | −180 | −120 | −36 | −12 | 0 | +3 | +23 | +37 | +79 | +144 |
| 120–140 | −200 | −145 | −43 | −14 | 0 | +3 | +27 | +43 | +92 | +170 |
| 140–160 | −210 | −145 | −43 | −14 | 0 | +3 | +27 | +43 | +100 | +190 |
| 160–180 | −230 | −145 | −43 | −14 | 0 | +3 | +27 | +43 | +108 | +210 |
| 180–200 | −240 | −170 | −50 | −15 | 0 | +4 | +31 | +50 | +122 | +236 |
| 200–225 | −260 | −170 | −50 | −15 | 0 | +4 | +31 | +50 | +130 | +258 |
| 225–250 | −280 | −170 | −50 | −15 | 0 | +4 | +31 | +50 | +140 | +284 |
| 250–280 | −300 | −190 | −56 | −17 | 0 | +4 | +34 | +56 | +158 | +315 |
| 280–315 | −330 | −190 | −56 | −17 | 0 | +4 | +34 | +56 | +170 | +350 |
| 315–355 | −360 | −210 | −62 | −18 | 0 | +4 | +37 | +62 | +190 | +390 |
| 355–400 | −400 | −210 | −62 | −18 | 0 | +4 | +37 | +62 | +208 | +435 |

[16]Table entries are in millimeters. Multiply the entries in *Shaft tolerance symbol* columns by $10^{-3}$.

# SolidWorks Certification

SolidWorks offers certification exams to become a SolidWorks certified designer. Certification exams are common in the professional world and they exist in various professions and trades. In the software field, for example, you may become a Microsoft certified Windows programmer or a certified Oracle database programmer. In the CAD/CAM market, you may become a SolidWorks, Pro/E, or AutoCAD certified designer.

The first certification exam of SolidWorks focuses on the CAD/CAM fundamentals we have covered in this book. As a matter of fact, many of the questions are conceptual and apply to any CAD/CAM system. A typical SolidWorks certification exam consists of two or more sections. One section is a written test that asks about the fundamentals. Another section is related to modeling skills. This section requires knowing and mastering SolidWorks software, reading a drawing, and visualizing a model. The better SolidWorks user you are, the faster you can finish this part and finish it correctly. Some exams may have multiple modeling sections. For example, the professional exam has three sections: a written test, a basic skills modeling test, and an advanced skills test.

The value of a SolidWorks certificate is to increase your competitiveness in the job market and help your career plans. Some companies only hire certified Solid-Works designers. Different certification levels exist. There is a license for each Solid-Works software module that we have covered in this book. Visit www.solidworks .com/sw/mcad-certification-programs.htm for more details. All license exams are online, and you can take them in test centers around the world. The website covers the details of the online testing process. You must earn a minimum score to pass any exam and become certified in the test-related subject. The available SolidWorks exams are listed below:

## I. Certified SolidWorks Associate (CSWA)

This is the most basic certificate you can earn. The exam is 3 hours long and the minimum passing grade is 70%. It covers the basic modeling concepts. The exam has a written test and a modeling section. The following table shows a mapping of the exam topics to the book chapters to prepare and study for the certification exam:

| Exam Topic | Book Chapter and Section to Study |
|---|---|
| Sketch entities (lines, rectangles, circles, arcs, ellipses, centerlines) | Chapter 1<br>Chapter 2 |
| Sketch tools (offset, convert, trim) and sketch relations, and reference geometry (plane, axis, mate reference) | Chapter 1<br>Chapter 2 |
| Boss and cut features (extrudes, revolves, sweeps, lofts), fillets and chamfers, patterns (linear, circular, fill), and feature conditions (start and end) | Chapter 2<br>Chapter 4 (Sections 4.1 and 4.2, and Tutorials 4–1 and 4–2) |
| Drawing sheets and views, dimensions and model items, and annotations | Chapter 5 |
| Mass properties, materials | Chapter 13 (Sections 13.1 and 13.3, and Tutorial 13–3) |
| Assembly operations: insert components, standard mates (coincident, parallel, perpendicular, tangent, concentric, distance, angle) | Chapter 6 |
| Basic FEM/FEA: SimulationXpress | Chapter 13 (Sections 13.7, 13.8, 13.9, and Tutorials 13–5, 13–6, and 13–7) |

## 2. Certified SolidWorks Professional (CSWP)

This is the next level of certification above the CSWA. The exam is 3½ hours long and the minimum passing grade is 75%. It covers the design and analysis of parametric parts and assemblies with complex features. The exam has three separate segments that you can take separately. The following table shows a mapping of the exam topics to the book chapters to prepare and study for the certification exam:

| Exam Topic | Book Chapter and Section to Study |
|---|---|
| **Segment 1 Topics (90 minutes)** | |
| Create part from drawing | Chapter 5 |
| Associative dimensions and equations | Chapter 5 |
| Mass property analysis | Chapter 13 (Sections 13.1 and 13.3, and Tutorial 13–3) |
| Editing existing parts | Chapter 2<br>Chapter 3 |
| **Segment 2 Topics (40 minutes)** | |
| Configurations | Chapter 3<br>Chapter 5 |
| Mass properties | Chapter 13 (Sections 13.1 and 13.3, and Tutorial 13–3) |
| Edit part features | Chapter 2<br>Chapter 5 |
| **Segment 3 Topics (80 minutes)** | |
| Assembly operations: add parts, collision detection, create coordinate system, mass properties | Chapter 6<br>Chapter 13 (Sections 13.1 and 13.3, and Tutorial 13–3) |

## 3. CSWP – Surfacing

CSWP – Surfacing tests competency in parametric modeling in general. Other exams focus on testing competencies in specific areas. CSWP – Surfacing exam and the ones that follow here are area-specific exams. CSWP – Surfacing tests proficiency in surfaces. The exam is 90 minutes long and the minimum passing grade is 75%. The following table shows a mapping of the exam topics to the book chapters to prepare and study for the certification exam:

| Exam Topic | Book Chapter and Section to Study |
| --- | --- |
| Create splines | Chapter 8 |
| Create 3D curves | Chapter 8 |
| Create surfaces: boundary, filled, swept, planar, knit, trim, fillet, thicken | Chapter 9 |
| Edit surfaces: trim, move | Chapter 9 |

## 4. CSWP – Sheet Metal

CSWP – Sheet Metal tests proficiency in sheet metal. The exam is 2 hours long and the minimum passing grade is 75%. The following table shows a mapping of the exam topics to the book chapters to prepare and study for the certification exam:

| Exam Topic | Book Chapter and Section to Study |
| --- | --- |
| Create flanges: linear, curved, miter | Chapter 10 |
| Create closed corners and gauge tables | Chapter 10 |
| Perform bending calculations: bend allowance, bend deduction, K-Factor | Chapter 10 |
| Create sheet metal features: hem, jog, bend, | Chapter 10 |
| Perform sheet metal operations: forming tool, unfold and fold, flatten | Chapter 10 |

## 5. CSWP – Weldments

CSWP – Weldments tests proficiency in weldments. The exam is 2 hours long and the minimum passing grade is 75%. The following table shows a mapping of the exam topics to the book chapters to prepare and study for the certification exam:

| Exam Topic | Book Chapter and Section to Study |
| --- | --- |
| Create weldment profiles | Chapter 10 |
| Create and modify weldment parts | Chapter 10 |
| Create and modify weldment corners | Chapter 10 |
| Create weldment features: end caps, gussets | Chapter 10 |
| Manage cut lists in part and drawing | Chapter 10 |

## 6. CSWP – FEA

CSWP – FEA tests proficiency in FEA. The exam is 90 minutes long and the minimum passing grade is 75%. The following table shows a mapping of the exam topics to the book chapters to prepare and study for the certification exam:

| Exam Topic | Book Chapter and Section to Study |
| --- | --- |
| Static, frequency, and thermal studies | Chapter 13 (Sections 13.7, 13.8, 13.9, Tutorials 13.5, 13–6, and 13–7) |
| Working with solid and shell elements | Chapter 13 (Sections 13.7, 13.8, 13.9, Tutorials 13.5, 13–6, and 13–7) |
| Working with beams | Chapter 13 (Sections 13.7, 13.8, 13.9, Tutorials 13.5, 13–6, and 13–7) |
| Applying loads and restraints | Chapter 13 (Sections 13.7, 13.8, 13.9, Tutorials 13.5, 13–6, and 13–7) |
| Planes of symmetry | Chapter 13 (Sections 13.7, 13.8, 13.9, Tutorials 13.5, 13–6, and 13–7) |
| Nonuniform loads | Chapter 13 (Sections 13.7, 13.8, 13.9, Tutorials 13.5, 13–6, and 13–7) |
| Mesh controls | Chapter 13 (Sections 13.7, 13.8, 13.9, Tutorials 13.5, 13–6, and 13–7) |
| Use of configurations to compare designs | Chapter 13 (Sections 13.7, 13.8, 13.9, Tutorials 13.5, 13–6, and 13–7) |
| Convergence of results | Chapter 13 (Sections 13.7, 13.8, 13.9, Tutorials 13.5, 13–6, and 13–7) |
| Result forces | Chapter 13 (Sections 13.7, 13.8, 13.9, Tutorials 13.5, 13–6, and 13–7) |

## 7. CSWP – Mold Tools

CSWP – Mold Tools tests proficiency in mold design. The exam is 90 minutes long and the minimum passing grade is 80%. The following table shows a mapping of the exam topics to the book chapters to prepare and study for the certification exam:

| Exam Topic | Book Chapter and Section to Study |
| --- | --- |
| Create mold features: parting line, parting surface, shut-off surface | Chapter 16 |
| Create tooling split | Chapter 16 |
| Perform draft analysis | Chapter 16 |

Multiple academic institutions around the world use SolidWorlds certification exams to test the proficiency of their students in their CAD/CAM courses. Some instructors use these exams as supplements to their traditional measures of evaluation such as homework, projects, etc. In this case, the instructor's institution becomes a center (provider) of the exam. If you are interested, check these resources:

1. To apply to become a CSWA provider, visit www.solidworks.com/CSWAProvider.
2. For information on CSWA, visit www.solidworks.com/cswa.
3. Virtual Testing Center (where SolidWorks keeps track of test takers over their careers and employers can verify certificate), visit www.virtualtester.com/solidworks.

The remainder of the appendix shows sample test questions.

# Certified SolidWorks Associate (CSWA)

## Sample Exam Questions

The questions below represent sample CSWA Exam questions. Part modeling and assembly modeling questions that require you to build a model should be correctly answered in 45 minutes or less. Question 2 and Question 3 should be correctly answered in 5 minutes or less.

*Question 1*

Build this part in SolidWorks. Unit system: MMGS (millimeter, gram, second). Decimal places: 2. Part origin: Arbitrary A = 63 mm, B = 50 mm, C = 100 mm. All holes through all. Part material: Copper. Density = 0.0089 g/mm³

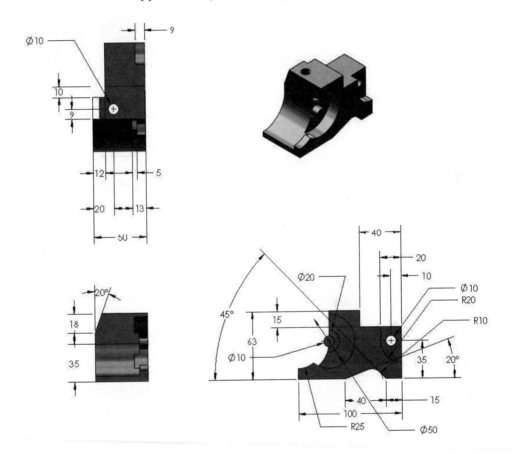

What is the overall mass of the part in grams?

a. 1205     b. 1280

c. 144      d. 1108

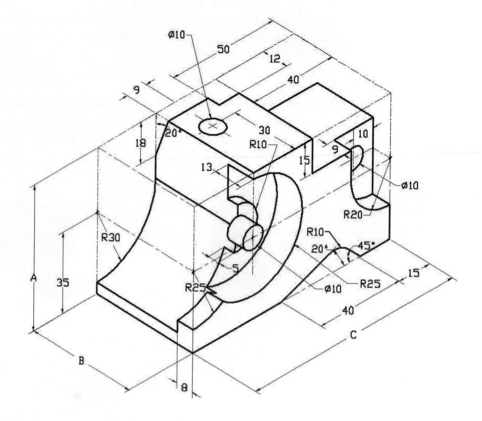

## Question 2

COSMOSXPress allows changes to mesh settings. Which of the following statements is not true?

a. A fine mesh setting produces more accurate results than a coarse mesh.

b. A coarse mesh setting produces less accurate results than a fine mesh.

c. A fine mesh setting can be applied to a specific face instead of the entire model.

d. All of the above

## Question 3

To create drawing view B, it is necessary to sketch a spline (as shown) on drawing view A and insert which SolidWorks view type?

a. Broken-out section

b. Aligned section

c. Section

d. Detail

Build this assembly in SolidWorks.

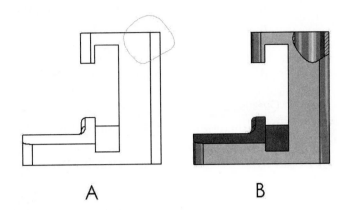

A                    B

Question 4

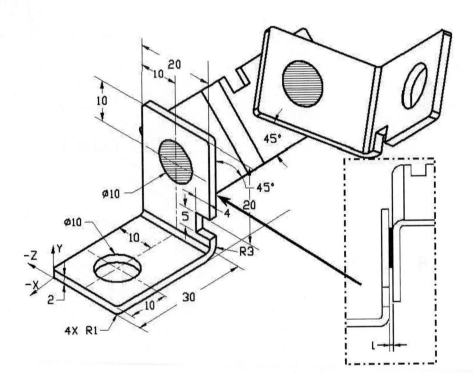

Build this assembly in SolidWorks.
It contains 3 machined brackets and 2 pins.

*Brackets:* 2 mm thickness, and equal size (holes through-all). Materials: 6061 Alloy, Density = $0.0027g/mm^3$. The top edge of the notch is located 20 mm from the top edge of the machined bracket.

*Pins:* 5 mm length and equal in diameter, Material: Titanium, Density = $0.0046g/mm^3$. Pins are mated concentric to bracket holes (no clearance). Pin end faces are coincident to bracket outer faces. There is a 1 mm gap between the brackets. Brackets are positioned with equal angle mates (45 degrees).

*Unit system:* MMGS (millimeter, gram, second). Decimal places. 2. Assembly origin: As shown. What is the center of mass of the assembly?

    **a.** X = −11.05, Y = 24.08, Z = −40.19

    **b.** X = −11.05, Y = −24.08, Z = 40.19

    **c.** X = 40.24, Y = 24.33, Z = 20.75

    **d.** X = 20.75, Y = 24.33, Z = 40.24

### Question 5

Build this assembly in SolidWorks. It contains 3 components: base, yoke, adjusting pin. Apply the MMGS unit system.

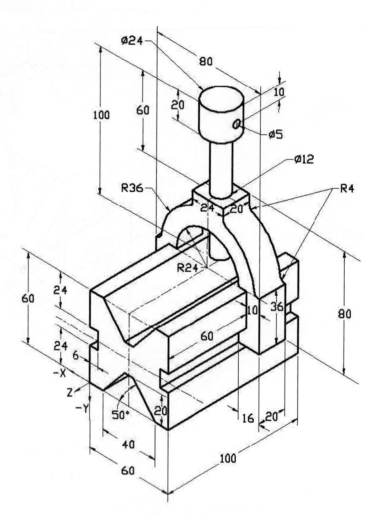

*Material:* 1060 Alloy for all components. Density = 0.0027g/mm³

*Base:* The distance between the front face of the base and the front face of the yoke = 60 mm.

*Yoke:* The yoke fits inside the left and right square channels of the base component (no clearance). The top face of the yoke contains a Ø12 mm through-all hole.

*Adjusting Pin:* The bottom face of the adjusting pin head is located 40 mm from the top face of the yoke component. The adjusting pin component contains a Ø5 mm though-all hole.

What is the center of mass of the assembly with respect to the illustrated coordinate system?

    **a.** X = −30.00, Y = −40.16, Z = −40.16

    **b.** X = 30.00, Y = 40.16, Z = −43.82

    **c.** X = −30.00, Y = −40.16, Z = 50.20

    **d.** X = 30.00, Y = 40.16, Z = −53.82

*Question 6*

Build this part in SolidWorks.

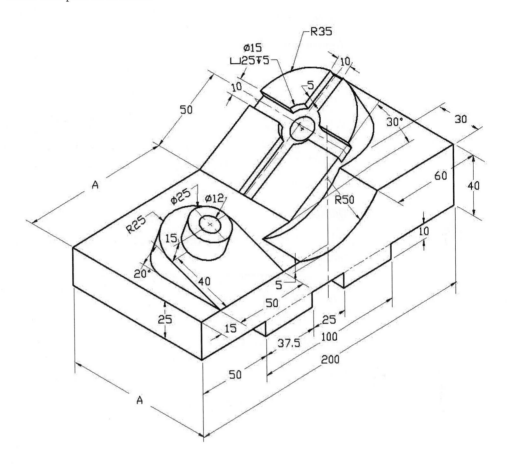

*Material:* 6061 Alloy. Density = 0.0027g/mm³

*Unit system:* MMGS (millimeter, gram, second)

*Decimal places:* 2.

*Part origin:* Arbitrary **A = 100**. All holes through

What is the overall mass of the part in grams?

    **a.** 2040.57           **b.** 2004.57

    **c.** 102.63            **d.** 1561.23

## Correct Answers:

    **1.** b        **2.** c        **3.** a

    **4.** c        **5.** d        **6.** a

# Certified SolidWorks Professional (CSWP)

## Sample Exam Questions

The questions below represent sample CSWP Exam questions.

*Question 1*

A cut-extrude assembly feature is an example of a time-dependent feature.

   **a.** True                     **b.** False

*Question 2*

You cannot reorder components within the FeatureManager design tree of an assembly.

   **a.** True                     **b.** False

*Question 3*

When creating sketches, there are two types of inferencing lines to help you work more efficiently. Blue inference lines indicate that a reference is added automatically; brown inference lines indicate that no relation is added.

   **a.** True                     **b.** False

*Question 4*

Which of the following is **not** a valid header for a column or row in an assembly design table?

   **a.** $COMMENT

   **b.** $PROPERTIES

   **c.** $PARTNUMBER

   **d.** $USER_NOTES

*Question 5*

It is necessary to have write access to a SolidWorks part file before you can mate to it in an assembly.

   **a.** True                     **b.** False

*Question 6*

If a bill of materials is too long to fit on a drawing sheet, it can be split into sections.

   **a.** True                     **b.** False

*Question 7*

What should you select when adding a <u>concentric</u> mate between two cylinders in an assembly?

   **a.** The circular edges on the ends of the cylinders

   **b.** Either the cylinder faces or circular edges

   **c.** The temporary axes that run through the centers of the cylinders

   **d.** Any of the above

## Question 8

When editing a sketch, the status bar displays the status of the sketch. Choose the answer that describes three states of a sketch:

    **a.** Under-defined, fully defined, conflicting

    **b.** Self-intersecting, open, closed

    **c.** Derived, defined in context, copied

    **d.** Dangling, not solved, open

    **e.** Under-defined, fully defined, over-defined

## Question 9

The -> symbol following a feature or a component in the FeatureManager design tree means:

    **a.** The feature or component has an external reference

    **b.** The feature or component is disjoint

    **c.** The feature or component has a rebuilt error

    **d.** The feature or component is under-defined

## Question 10

To process a part as a sheet metal part, it must have uniform thickness.

    **a.** True                **b.** False

## Question 11

The illustration to the right depicts a typical FeatureManager design tree. Look at the icons displayed alongside of FEATURE 1 through FEATURE 5. Identify the type of feature, and write the letter of its name (a–j) in the space provided below.

FEATURE 1:_____        **a.** Dome          **f.** Weld bead

FEATURE 2:_____        **b.** Tube           **g.** Loft

FEATURE 3:_____        **c.** Sweep         **h.** Rib

FEATURE 4:_____        **d.** Plane         **i.** Extrude

FEATURE 5:_____        **e.** Revolve       **j.** Shell

# Index

Pages numbers followed by t indicate table; those followed by f indicate figure.